A SHORTENED HISTORY OF ENGLAND

George Macaulay Trevelyan, O.M., C.B.E., F.B.A., born in 1876, was the third son of Sir George Otto Trevelyan and a great-nephew of Lord Macaulay. He was educated at Harrow and at Trinity College, Cambridge. In the First World War he was awarded the Silver Medal for Valour (Italy) and the Chevalier of the Order of St Maurice and St Lazarus (Italy).

He was an Hon. D.C.L., Oxford, and Hon. LL.D., St Andrews and Edinburgh, a Fellow of Trinity College, Cambridge, and an Honorary Fellow of Oriel College, Oxford. From 1927 to 1940 he was Regius Professor of Modern History at Cambridge and from 1940 to 1951 he was Master of Trinity. He was also a Trustee of the British Museum and the National Portrait Gallery. He was President of the Youth Hostels' Association from 1930 to 1950, and was Chairman of the Estates Committee of the National Trust. He died in 1962.

Among his books on British history are: *England in the Age of Wycliffe*, *England under the Stuarts*, *The English Revolution 1688*, *England under Queen Anne*, *British History in the Nineteenth Century*, *History of England*, and *Illustrated English Social History*, now available in four volumes in Pelicans. *Lord Grey of the Reform Bill*, *Lord Grey of Fallodon*, *The Life of Bright*, and the famous Garibaldi trilogy are his biographical works.

A SHORTENED HISTORY OF ENGLAND

BY

George Macaulay Trevelyan

PENGUIN BOOKS

PENGUIN BOOKS
Published by the Penguin Group
27 Wrights Lane, London W8 5TZ, England
Viking Penguin Inc., 40 West 23rd Street, New York, New York 10010, USA
Penguin Books Australia Ltd, Ringwood, Victoria, Australia
Penguin Books Canada Ltd, 2801 John Street, Markham, Ontario, Canada L3R 1B4
Penguin Books (NZ) Ltd, 182–190 Wairau Road, Auckland 10, New Zealand

Penguin Books Ltd, Registered Offices: Harmondsworth, Middlesex, England

First published in Longmans, Green & Co. Inc., New York 1942
Published in Pelican Books 1959
Reprinted in Penguin Books 1987
3 5 7 9 10 8 6 4

This book is an abridged edition of
G. M. Trevelyan's *History of England*
Published by Longmans, Green & Co. Ltd.

Made and printed in Great Britain by
Hazell Watson & Viney Limited
Member of BPCC Limited
Aylesbury, Bucks, England
Set in Monotype Times

CONTENTS

BOOK THREE

THE TUDORS

BOOK FOUR

THE STUART ERA

BOOK FIVE

FROM UTRECHT TO WATERLOO

BOOK SIX

WATERLOO TO TO-DAY

LIST OF MAPS

The maps for this edition have been drawn by Anthony Gatrell

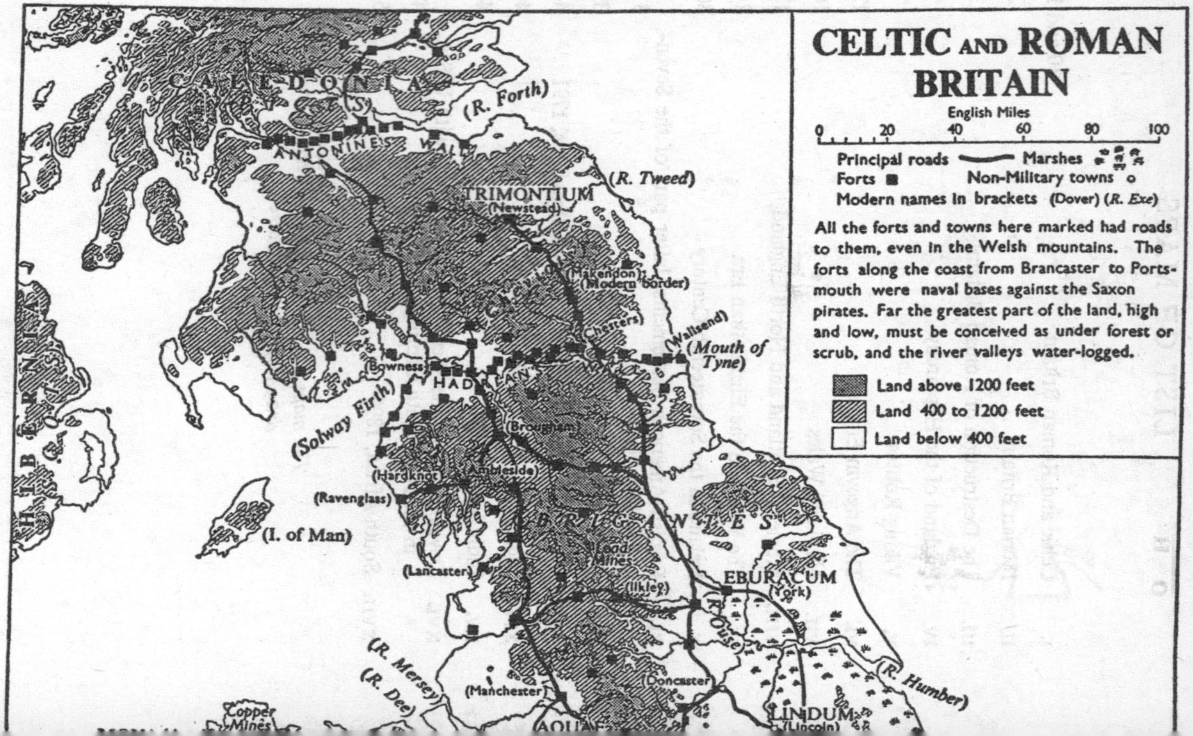
CELTIC AND ROMAN BRITAIN
English Miles
0 20 40 60 80 100
Principal roads
Marshes
Forts
Non-Military towns
Modern names in brackets (Dover) (R. Exe)
All the forts and towns here marked had roads to them, even in the Welsh mountains. The forts along the coast from Brancaster to Portsmouth were naval bases against the Saxon pirates. Far the greatest part of the land, high and low, must be conceived as under forest or scrub, and the river valleys water-logged.
Land above 1200 feet
Land 400 to 1200 feet
Land below 400 feet
CALEDONIA
(R. Forth)
ANTONINES WALL
(R. Tweed)
TRIMONTIUM
(Newstead)
(Makendon)
(Modern border)
(Chesters)
(Wallsend)
(Mouth of Tyne)
(Bowness)
HADRIAN'S WALL
(Solway Firth)
(Brougham)
(Hardknot)
(Ambleside)
(Ravenglass)
(I. of Man)
BRIGANTES
Lead Mines
(Lancaster)
(Ilkley)
EBURACUM
(York)
(R. Ouse)
(R. Mersey)
(R. Dee)
(Manchester)
(Doncaster)
(R. Humber)
LINDUM
(Lincoln)
Copper Mines
HIBERNIA

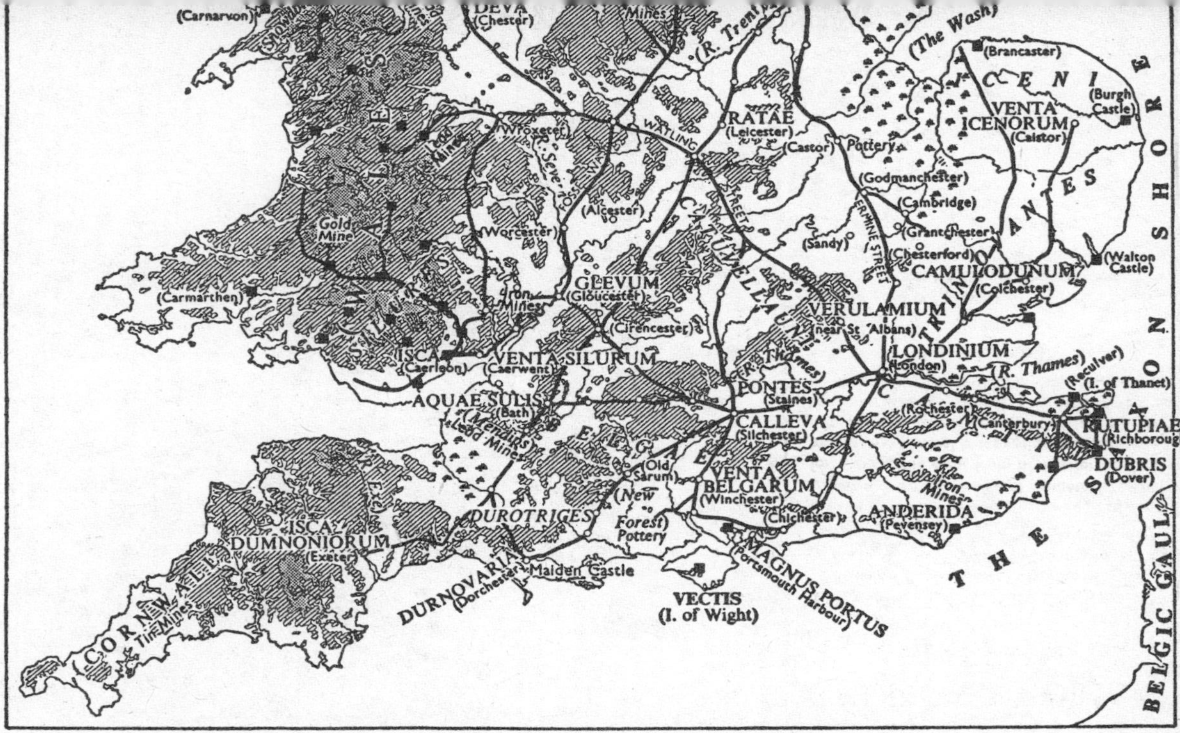

(Carnarvon)
DEVA
(Chester)
Mines
(R. Trent)
(The Wash)
(Brancaster)
ICENI
(Burgh Castle)
VENTA ICENORUM
(Caistor)
RATAE
(Leicester)
(Castor)
Pottery
WATLING
STREET
(Wroxeter)
Lead Mines
(Godmanchester)
(Cambridge)
(Grantchester)
(Chesterford)
ERMINE STREET
(Sandy)
TRINOANTES
CAMULODUNUM
(Colchester)
(Walton Castle)
SHORE
(Alcester)
(Worcester)
Gold Mine
GLEVUM
(Gloucester)
Iron Mines
(Carmarthen)
SILURES
CATUVELLAUNI
VERULAMIUM
(near St. Albans)
(Cirencester)
LONDINIUM
(London)
(R. Thames)
(Reculver)
(I. of Thanet)
ISCA
(Caerleon)
VENTA SILURUM
(Caerwent)
PONTES
(Staines)
AQUAE SULIS
(Bath)
(Mendips)
Lead Mines
CALLEVA
(Silchester)
(Rochester)
(Canterbury)
RUTUPIAE
(Richborough)
DUBRIS
(Dover)
BELGAE
(Old Sarum)
VENTA BELGARUM
(Winchester)
(New Forest)
Pottery
Iron Mines
(Chichester)
ANDERIDA
(Pevensey)
ISCA DUMNONIORUM
(Exeter)
DUROTRIGES
(Exe)
CORNWALL
Tin Mines
DURNOVARIA
(Dorchester)
Maiden Castle
VECTIS
(I. of Wight)
MAGNUS PORTUS
(Portsmouth Harbour)
THE SAXON SHORE
BELGIC GAUL

INTRODUCTION

THE history of civilized man in our country is very old; it begins long before the reign of Alfred. But the history of Britain as a leader in the world's affairs is of much shorter date; it begins with the reign of Elizabeth. The reason can be read upon the map. Map-makers, whether in ancient Alexandria or in medieval monasteries, placed our island on the north-west edge of all things. But, after the discovery of America and the ocean routes to Africa and the East, Britain lay in the centre of the new maritime movement. This change in her geographic outlook was employed to good purpose by her inhabitants, who in the era of the Stuarts made her the chief seat of the new trans-oceanic commerce and of the finance and industry that sustained it. Next, with the aid of modern science, the land of Newton applied machinery to manufacture and began the world-wide Industrial Revolution. Meanwhile, Britain was peopling and giving laws to North America; and after she had lost the Thirteen Colonies, she built up a second Empire, more widely scattered and more vast.

These latter centuries of material growth and leadership correspond with the period of greatest intellectual achievement. In spite of Bede, Roger Bacon, Chaucer, and Wycliffe, Britain's contribution to medieval science and literature is slight when compared to the world of her intellectual creation from the time of Shakespeare onward. The era when London awoke to find herself the maritime centre of the suddenly expanded globe, was also the era of the Renaissance and the Reformation – movements of intellectual growth and individual self-assertion which proved more congenial to the British than to many other races, and seemed to emancipate the island genius.

In the sphere of pure politics Britain is famous as the mother of Parliaments. In answer to the instincts and temperament of her people, she evolved in the course of centuries a system which reconciled three things that other nations have often found incompatible – executive efficiency, popular control, and personal freedom.

It is indeed in the Middle Ages that we must seek the origin of Parliament, and of the English Common Law which the ultimate victory of Parliament over the Royal power has made supreme in all English-speaking lands. The political merit of the Medieval period lay in its dislike of absolutism in the Temporal sphere, its elaborate distribution of power, its sense of corporate life, and its consultation of the various corporate interests through their representatives. But, although Parliament was a characteristic product of the Middle Ages, the development of its powers in Tudor, Stuart, and Hanoverian days, its resistance to the political theories of the Roman law received in contemporary Europe, and its transplantation to America and the Antipodes, are the great events which raised the political history of Britain into a sphere apart from the political life of the Continent. For, although France and Spain had a number of medieval Estates and Parliaments, they failed to adapt them to modern conditions. On the passing of feudalism, the Latin peoples read despotic monarchy as the political message of the new era. Against Machiavelli's princely interpretation of the new nationalism, Britain alone of the great national States successfully held out, turned back the tide of despotism, and elaborated a system by which a debating club of elected persons could successfully govern an Empire in peace and in war. During the commercial and military struggles with foreign rivals which followed between 1689 and 1815, our goods, our ships, and our armies, proved that Parliamentary freedom might be more efficient than despotism as a means of giving force to the national will. Nor, in the new era of man's life introduced by the Industrial Revolution, has this verdict yet been reversed.

In the Nineteenth Century the same Parliamentary institutions, while undergoing democratic transformation, were put to the severer test of coping with the new and bewildering conditions of social life created by the Industrial Revolution. At the same time the vast and ever-increasing Empire, of white, brown, and black communities, presented diverse and complicated problems, each one recurring in new guise every few years under the stimulus that modern economic conditions give to social and political change. Parliamentary government for the white races, and the desire to govern justly societies not yet prepared for self-government, have so far preserved this astonishing association of peoples.

Whatever, then, be our chief interest in the past – whether material progress and racial expansion, the growth of political and social institutions, or pure intellect and letters – it is the last four hundred years in British History which stand out. Yet I have not hesitated to devote a third of this work to a survey of the pre-Tudor epochs. The mingling of the armed races poured into Britain from the earliest times until 1066, and the national temper and customs which they developed in the shelter of the island guarded by the Norman and Plantagenet Kings, alone rendered it possible for five millions of people, ruled by Elizabeth, to lay hold on the splendid future offered to themselves and their descendants by the maritime discoveries and intellectual movements of that age. If the hour then came, the men, too, were ready.

Britain has always owed her fortunes to the sea, and to the havens and rivers that from the earliest times opened her inland regions to what the sea might bring. Long before she aspired to rule the waves she was herself their subject, for her destiny was continually being decided by the boat-crews which they floated to her shore. From Iberian and Celtic to Saxon and Danish settlers, from prehistoric and Phoenician traders to Roman and Norman overlords, successive tides of warlike colonists, the most energetic seamen, farmers, and merchants of Europe came by the wave-path to inhabit her, or to instil their knowledge and spirit into the older inhabitants. Her east coast lay obvious and open to Teuton and Scandinavian immigrants; her south coast to cultural influences from the Mediterranean by way of France. From Teuton and Scandinavian she acquired the more important part of her population and character and the root of her language; from the South she received the rest of her language, the chief forms of her culture, and much of her organizing power.

The Norman Conquest severed her ties with Scandinavia, which Canute had drawn very close. For several hundred years the Nordic islanders were governed by a French-speaking aristocracy and a Latin-speaking clergy. By a significant paradox it was under this foreign leadership that the English began to develop their intense national feeling and their peculiar institutions, so different in spirit from those of Italy and France. Already among the fellow-countrymen of Chaucer and Wycliffe, even when engaged in the disastrous adventure of the Hundred Years' War, we see the beginnings of a distinct English nationality, far richer than the old Saxon, composed of many different elements of race, character, and culture which the tides of ages had brought to our coasts and the island climate had tempered and mellowed into harmony. At the Reformation the English, grown to manhood, dismissed their Latin tutors, without reacting into close contact with the Scandinavian and Teuton world. Britain had become a world by itself.

It was at this crisis in England's cultural and political growth, when she was weakening her ties with Europe, that the union with Scotland came about, and at the same time the ocean offered the islanders a pathway to every corner of the newly discovered globe. The universality of the Englishman's experience and outlook – quite as marked a characteristic as his insularity – is due to his command of the ocean which has for more than three centuries past carried him as explorer, trader, and colonist to every shore in the two hemispheres.

Thus, in early times, the relation of Britain to the sea was passive and receptive; in modern times, active and acquisitive. In both it is the key to her story.

BOOK ONE
THE MINGLING OF THE RACES

From the Earliest Times to the Norman Conquest

IT is a commonplace to say that the British are a people of mixed blood. I hope, in this First Book, to indicate a little how, when, and why this mingling of races occurred.

It may be as well to say, at the outset, that the entrance into our island of the races who people it to-day was completed in main outline at the time of the Norman Conquest. With that event, which itself made less racial than social and cultural change, we come to an end of migratory invasions and of forced entry behind the point of the sword. Since Hastings there has been nothing more catastrophic than a slow, peaceful infiltration of alien craftsmen and labourers – Flemings, Huguenots, Irish, and others – with the acquiescence of the existing inhabitants of the island.

To invade Britain was singularly easy before the Norman Conquest, singularly difficult afterwards. The reason is clear. A well-organized State, with a united people on land and a naval force at sea, could make itself safe behind the Channel even against such military odds as Philip of Spain, Louis XIV, or Napoleon could assemble on the opposite shore. In recent centuries these conditions have been fulfilled, and although an invading force has sometimes been welcomed, as when Henry Tudor or William of Orange came over, no invasion hostile to the community as a whole has met with even partial success owing to the barrier of the sea. But, before the Norman Conquest, there had been long ages when neither the island State nor the island navy was formidable; even in the days of Alfred and Harold they were inadequate to their task, and in earlier times they did not exist. Except when protected by the Roman galleys and legions, ancient Britain was peculiarly liable to invasion for geographic and other reasons.

The story of the Mingling of the Races in Britain, ending with the advent of the Normans, covers a thousand years of history very dimly descried, succeeding to many thousand more of archaeological twilight. The era of Celt, Saxon, and Dane is like Macbeth's battle on the blasted heath. Prophecy hovers around. Horns are heard blowing in the mist, and a confused uproar of savage tumult and outrage. We catch glimpses of giant figures –

mostly warriors at strife. But there are ploughmen, too, it seems, breaking the primeval clod, and we hear the sound of forests crashing to the axe. Around all is the lap of waves and the cry of seamen beaching their ships.

CHAPTER I

Early Man. Iberian, and Celt

It is not my purpose to describe pre-insular Britain and the great geologic changes, the volcanoes, the rise and fall of mountains, the tropical swamps in which the coal forests grew, or the industrious building of the chalk down under the sea. Nor shall I attempt to distinguish the various races of primitive hunters, from 'Piltdown man' onwards, who may have wandered over the land during the inter-glacial periods. It was probably at the great spring-time of Northern Europe, after the glacial epoch, that the soil of the future Britain was first trodden by 'Homo Sapiens', unequivocal man. These early immigrants came over by the land-bridge from Europe as they followed northwards the last retreat of the ice; with them, or just before them, came the commonest of the wild animals, birds, flowers, and trees. These hunters of the mammoth, the horse, and the reindeer, have probably mixed their blood with some of the later races who are certainly among our ancestors. At the time of their coming overland, the chalk downs of Dover and Calais were still united in a continuous range; the majestic Thames flowed into the lower Rhine; and the Rhine itself meandered towards the Arctic Ocean through the marshy plain now submerged beneath the waves of the North Sea, where the bones of mammoth and reindeer are dredged off the Dogger Bank.

Since the flora and fauna which we call native to Britain came northward at this period to replenish a land swept bare by the snow cap of the last ice age, they are, therefore, closely identified with the flora and fauna of Northern Europe – except for the red grouse peculiar to the British Isles. Ireland was cut adrift from England before the piercing of the Dover Straits by the sea, and is, for that reason, poorer in mammals, plants, and reptiles.

For many centuries after Britain became an island the untamed forest was king. Its moist and mossy floor was hidden from heaven's eye by a close-drawn curtain woven of innumerable tree-tops, which shivered in the breezes of summer dawn and broke into wild music of millions upon millions of wakening birds; the concert was prolonged from bough to bough with scarcely a break for hundreds of miles over hill and plain and mountain, unheard by man save where, at rarest intervals, a troop of skin-clad hunters, stone-axe in hand, moved furtively over the ground beneath, ignorant that they lived upon an island, not dreaming that there could be other parts of the world besides this damp green woodland with its meres and marshes, wherein they hunted, a terror to its four-footed inhabitants and themselves afraid.

A glance at any physical map will show how Britain has always thrust out towards the continent of Europe a low coast with an undulating plain behind, easy of access through many havens and navigable rivers. It was only westward and northward, against the Atlantic, that the island presented a mountainous and iron-bound coast – though even there the mouths of Severn, Dee, Mersey, Clyde, and other lesser inlets held the makings of future history. But, from the earliest ages the flat south and east coastlines with the plains and low ridges behind them presented, so long as they were unguarded by a fleet, a standing temptation to the migratory tribes, pirates, plunderers, and traders roaming along the continental shores.

The temptation to invade the island lay not only in the pearls, the gold, and the tin for which it seems to have been noted among certain Mediterranean merchants long before the foundation of Rome; temptation lay also in its fertile soil, the rich carpet of perennial green that covered the downs and every clearing in the forest, the absence of long interludes of frost that must have seemed miraculous in a land so far to the North before men knew the secret of the Gulf Stream.

The forest of Britain swarmed with big and small game, and early man was a hunter. Whole districts, long since drained, were then shallow meres filled with fowl and fish; the greatest of these fenlands stretched from future Cambridge to future Lincoln; countless generations of early fowlers and fishermen dropped their tools and weapons of chipped flint in its waters, or on the sandy heaths round its margin, for the better instruction of archaeologists. In the age of the shepherd the open chalk downs of the South were his wealth and his delight, while the more daring swineherd followed the hunter into the dark forest below.

Flints lay about in profusion in many regions, but the best of them were buried in the chalk; shafts thirty feet deep were sunk by the earliest island miners, who laboured down at the bottom with stag-horn picks and shoulder-blades for shovels, hewing galleries through the chalk and extracting the precious flints which then made man the master of the world. The 'palaeolithic' or 'old stone' age, with its roughly chipped flints, fades by imperceptible degrees into the 'neolithic' or 'new stone' age, when men had learnt to polish their flint tools and weapons with an admirable perfection.

When, some 2000 years before Christ, the age of bronze gradually began in Britain, followed after more than a thousand years by the age of iron, the metals, too, were found in plenty, with timber at hand to smelt them. Timber grew everywhere for housing and fuel. Fresh water was widely distributed; indeed before the age of draining and well-sinking, it was found more plentifully at high levels than in the South England of to-day. And village sites, from primeval hut circles to the Saxon townships of Domesday Book, were always chosen close to fresh water.

Last, but not least, when man took to ploughing and sowing, the soil was found to yield manyfold in the eastern and southern regions, those sunniest parts of the island where wheat-growing is still generally profitable under the very different world conditions of the modern grain market. Agriculture is the greatest change of all in the early life of man, for it enables him to multiply, fixes him to the home and to the soil, draws him into larger village communities, and thereby renders other inventions and changes more easy. The plough made but a slow conquest of Britain. It reached a definable stage in the latter part of the Saxon epoch, by which time the bulk of the present-day villages had come into existence, at least in embryo, as clearings in the forest. But agriculture had been first introduced in prehistoric times, when it could only be practised in certain carefully chosen localities that were neither marshy nor encumbered by trees, nor yet mere barren heath.

Such were the attractions of this desirable land. And it stood, obvious to all, as centre to the grand semi-circle of the North European shore that stretches for two thousand miles from Norway to Ushant. From times long before the dawn of history until the Norman Conquest, all the various seafaring tribes who succeeded each other as nomads or settlers on any part of that great coastline regarded Britain as their natural prey. And Britain was the more subject to their attacks because the pressure of the folk wanderings was mainly from the East of Europe to the West. It followed, that for several thousands of years, wave after wave of seagoing adventurous races, or of races pushed behind by other adventurers, was flung upon Britain's southern and eastern shore.

Until each set of new-comers was half-way across the island, the worst natural obstacle they could meet was the widespread woodland and marsh. But where the forest was pathless or the valley too wet, the invader could either row up the river or trek round by the heaths and downs. The high-placed camps, roads, and dew-ponds of the primitive peoples, often found where only the sheep and plovers now congregate, remind us of the greater part which the bare uplands played in the life of man, before the forests were felled and the valleys drained.

The first serious geographic obstacle appeared when the invader, perhaps in the second or third generation of his advance, at length approached the north or west of the island – the mountain ranges of Wales, of North-west England, and of Scotland. Here the pursued might rally and the pursuers be forced to halt. If there had been no such mountain ranges, if England had been all one lowland, each successive invasion would have rapidly overrun the whole island. In that case no racial difference might to-day be discernible such as divides so-called Celtic Britain – Wales and the Scottish Highlands – on the one hand, from the Saxon districts on the other, for the primitive Saxons might have swept right over Wales and crossed into Ireland in the Sixth Century. But in fact the great plains of Ireland were only reached by the English of the Twelfth Century, marshalled under the feudal banner of Strongbow; the mountains of Wales and the Pennines had impeded the first rush of the Saxon immigrants. Much the same thing must have happened long before in many unrecorded Celtic and Iberian invasions. History is governed by geography. If the mountain ranges had stood along the southern and eastern shores of England instead of standing far back to west and north, the tribal invasion of the island from the continent would have been so arduous a task that Britain would not have become the early receptacle for so many different races of vigorous barbarians. The physical formation of a country is the key to the history of its early settlement, especially in days before man had the mastery of nature which he now possesses.

And so, owing to these geographic features of Britain, the same phenomena of tribal invasion were repeated again and again on the same general scheme. Again and again, how often we know not, from the early stone age till the Danish invasions, some race of warriors crossing from some part of what we now call

France, Holland, Germany, or Scandinavia, has settled on the rich lowlands of southern and eastern Britain, killed or subjected many of the older inhabitants, and driven the rest into the mountains of the north and west or into the barren and remote peninsula of Cornwall.

It is thus that we must account for the variety and the present location of the races that were mingled in Britain so long ago. Cornwall, Wales, and the Highlands of Scotland are inhabited by the oldest stocks: we call them, to-day, 'the Celtic fringe' of the island. But most of them are pre-Celtic – as also are the Irish. The Celts, late comers into western Europe, were tall men, fair or red-haired, who entered Britain and Ireland only a few hundred years before the coming of Julius Caesar. The bulk of those whom we miscall 'Celts' are for the most part dark-haired people whose ancestors had been in the island thousands of years before the red Celt was ever heard of. They were the folk whom Matthew Arnold in his poem describes as 'dark Iberians', coming down, 'shy traffickers', to chaffer with the Phoenician traders on the shore.

We may conveniently speak of these pre-Celtic peoples, collectively, as 'Iberians', though in fact they consisted of many different races, not all of them dark-haired. Some 'Iberian' blood probably flows in the veins of every modern Englishman, more in the average Scot, most in the Welsh, and Irish. The Iberians were no mere savages. They raised themselves, during the long stone and bronze ages in Britain, from savagery on to the first steps of civilized life. At first hunters and users of flint, then shepherds also, they gradually learnt the uses to which man can turn the dog, the sheep, the goat, the ox, the pig; they adopted the use of metals; they became the men of the bronze age skilled in weaving and in crafts of many kinds, including agriculture. If in earlier times the largest political unit consisted of a tribe of a few hundred souls, living in dread of wolves and bears, and of their nearest human neighbours, the Iberians acquired in some parts of the country a much higher political organization, designed gigantic earthworks like the Maiden Castle near Dorchester on a scientific military plan, and reared Stonehenge, no mean engineering feat. Although the earliest of them had come over in coracles or canoes, they learnt to build the 'long ship' or low war-galley.

Many of these improvements, especially agriculture, metal-work, and long-ship building, were probably taught to the islanders by merchants from the distant South, or by continental tribes who had learnt from those merchants. The Levant was the cradle of European civilization. The inhabitants of Mesopotamia, Egypt, and Crete, in days before Tyre, Athens, or Rome, evolved agriculture, metal-craft, shipbuilding, and many other of the arts of life. Such Promethean secrets, starting on their journey from South and East, handed on from trader to trader and from tribe to tribe ever northward and westward across the forests of barbarous Europe, or travelling more quickly by merchant galleys round the Pillars of Hercules, reached at last those half-fabulous 'tin islands' in the mists and tides of the northern seas.

The trade of Britain with the Levant, or rather of the Levant with Britain, is far older than the Celtic Conquest. English jet found in Spain is believed to date from 2500 B.C. and Egyptian beads found in England from about 1300 B.C. So early, perhaps much earlier, the Mediterranean traders had discovered the British islands with their wealth of pearls and gold, to-day long exhausted, and their metals, not yet at an end. But if these eastern merchants have the credit of bringing civilization to Britain, the Iberian tribesmen had the wit to adapt their teaching.

Either the traders, or else some conquering race, brought from overseas the first weapons of bronze that have been discovered in the island. But since copper and tin both lay near the surface in different parts of the island, particularly Cornwall, the natives were soon taught to smelt the two together and so make bronze for themselves. After that, the end of the long stone age was in sight; it was only a matter of time before bronze, and iron after it, was lord of all. Some of the islanders attained high technical skill in metal working, and indeed some of the finest enamel work on bronze that the world contains was produced by these Iberian ancestors of ours. Many of the centres of this ancient civilization – Stonehenge perhaps – were placed on sites agriculturally barren, but once famous for the best flints or for surface gold, tin, or copper, long since exhausted.

Trade routes and trade connexions grew up within the island itself between very distant tribes; and there were ports trading with Ireland for gold, and others that shipped tin to the continent. Ancient trackways, running along bare downs and ridges, linked up the various centres of civilization which were otherwise separated by wide morasses and long leagues of forest. The fortifications were placed chiefly on the high bare land on the route of the trackways. They often ran along the edge of the chalk downs below the top of the tableland but above the marshy and tangled forest of the plain, like the track along the south edge of the North Downs, long afterwards known and used as the 'Pilgrims' Way' to Canterbury, and still at places available to the pedestrian as it was four thousand and more years ago.

So too, ages before the arrival of the Celt, the Icknield Way ran along the chalk close under the ridge of the Chilterns, and was carried on westward by the line of the downs south of Thames; its object was to join up the fenland and agricultural civilization of East Anglia with the great downland civilization gathered round the circles of Avebury and Stonehenge, where man was most thickly congregated, because there he was most free from the impediment of forest and of marsh. The forest, still impenetrable save by a few daring hunters, lay deep on both sides of the Icknield Way. Ideas and arts of vast import to man have been carried along its springy turf by wayfarers listening anxiously to the noises of the forest, to distinguish the howl of wolves, the growl of bears, or the yet more dreaded voice of hostile tribesmen.

From the seventh to the third centuries before Christ, the Celtic tribes, originally occupying North-western Germany and the Netherlands, were moving across Europe in many different directions. In the first centuries after Christ the Teuton tribes, starting from homes rather further to the east, were destined to move over much the same ground in much the same manner; but between the folk-wanderings of Celt and of Teuton was to be interposed the great event of the Roman penetration north of the Alps.

The Celts, in their earlier day, showed as much vigour in migration as any race that came after them. One great body settled in France and became an important element in the racial content of the Gaulish nation. A southern wing settled in the valley of the Po, put an end to the Etruscan hegemony in Italy, and about 387 B.C. sacked Rome, when the geese were said to have saved the Capitol. Others pushed into Spain, others into the Balkans. During the same centuries a northern wing of this great world movement overran our island and imposed Celtic rule and language on its inhabitants. The Celtic invaders of Britain came in successive tribal waves, kindred indeed but mutually hostile and each with a dialect of its own. Erse, Gaelic, and Welsh are still extant variations of the tongues which they and the Iberians evolved. Wave after wave of Celts, each entering Britain by the lowlands of south and east, slaughtered, subdued,

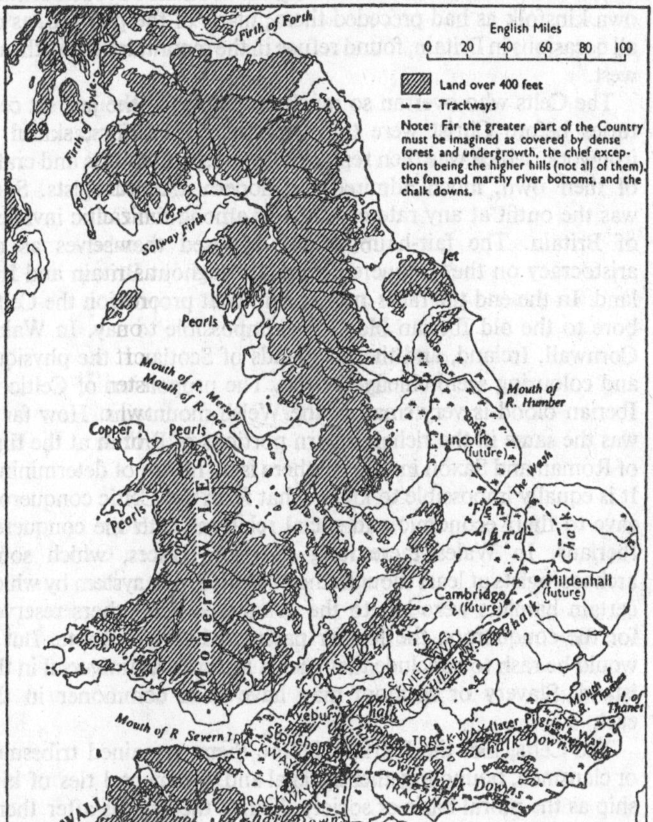

MAP II. IBERIAN BRITAIN

or chased across the island not only the Iberians but such of their own kinsfolk as had preceded them; many of the pursued, as on all occasions in Britain, found refuge in the mountains to north and west.

The Celts who overran so much of Europe in the last six centuries before Christ were tall, light-haired warriors, skilful in ironwork, which was then replacing bronze, and in arts and crafts of their own, much admired by modern archaeologists. Such was the outfit at any rate of the later among the Celtic invaders of Britain. The fair-haired Celts imposed themselves as an aristocracy on the conquered tribes throughout Britain and Ireland. In the end the races mixed, but what proportion the Celtic bore to the old Iberian blood it is impossible to say. In Wales, Cornwall, Ireland, and the Highlands of Scotland, the physique and colouring seem chiefly Iberian. The proportion of Celtic to Iberian blood is very small in the Welsh mountains. How far it was the same in the richer eastern portions of Britain at the time of Roman and Saxon invasions, there is no means of determining. It is equally impossible to know what form the Celtic conquerors gave to their economic and social relations with the conquered Iberians. In Wales there long remained traces, which some archaeologists at least thought they detected, of a system by which certain hamlets were left to the conquered and others reserved for the conquerors, the former paying a heavier tribute. But it would be rash to conclude that such a system was universal in the island. Slavery or serfdom may have been commoner in the east.

The Celts, like the Iberians before them, remained tribesmen or clansmen, bound together by legal and sentimental ties of kinship as the moral basis of society. Unlike the Saxons after them, they developed no strictly territorial, still less any feudal organization. A thousand years after England had been subjected to Saxon conquest, Wales, Ireland, and the Scottish Highlands were in different degrees still governed by the tribal rules of life. And we may be sure that in the palmy day of Celtic lordship in the British Isles, the Kings were tribal chiefs, rather than territorial or feudal monarchs. Justice was the justice of the clan, which punished and protected its members, exacting on their behalf from other clans either vengeance, or else payment in reparation for injuries done. The Celtic tribes, when the Romans came over, were perpetually at war with one another, but they formed large accretions, each tribe being spread over a considerable area, often equal to several modern counties.

Agriculture continued to progress slowly in the iron age under the Celts, as in the bronze age under the Iberians. Wheat was grown in the south, oats further north – as to-day. The Celt loved to cheer or fuddle his brain with mead – grain fermented with honey. But the acreage under plough was small, for the forests remained unfelled, and those river valleys, like Thames and Trent, where drainage was a necessary prelude to close habitation, remained marshy and sparsely peopled.

Herds of swine wandering by thousands through the virgin oak forests were a feature of Saxon and Norman times and must have been no less a feature of Celtic and pre-Celtic economy. Pig in various forms is still favourite feeding in England, and in primitive times it was the staff of life not only in Ireland but in Britain. Sheep and oxen were perhaps the chief source of accumulated wealth and the chief means of barter. Horses were bred to drag the war chariots of the Celtic chiefs to battle, but the plough was drawn by oxen.

Taking the Celtic island as a whole, agriculture was not the preoccupation it became in Saxon and medieval times. Hunting, fishing, herding, weaving, bee-keeping, metal work, carpentry, and, above all, fighting occupied most of the time and thought of a small population scattered wide over a land not yet drained and deforested. The 'trevs' or hamlets of the Celtic families consisted of light structures of timber, wattles, or mud, easily and frequently destroyed in tribal wars. In the west, at least, the population readily moved the site of its 'trevs' to get fresh pasture and hunting ground, as the Welsh continued to do until late in the Middle Ages.

The most advanced regions of the Celtic civilization in Britain lay in the south and south-east. There were the best grainlands, the open pastures of the downs, the iron mines and forges of the Sussex Weald, the Channel ports and shipping (though London as yet counted for nothing), the easiest communications with the Mediterranean traders and with the Celtic kinsmen overseas. Though there was no town-life proper in the whole island, the largest assemblies of huts were probably to be found near St Albans and Colchester. Already 150 years before Christ, south British tribes had a gold coinage of their own, imitated from the gold *stater* of the Kings of Macedon. In the last century before Christ the British Belgae and other southern tribes were in close political intercourse with their brethren of Northern Gaul; some of them had even for a few years acknowledged a King of the continental Belgae as their suzerain. When, therefore, they learnt that the Romans were marching to subdue the north Gallic tribes, the Britons sent over ships and men who fought against Caesar both by sea and land. It was one of the causes of his invasion of Britain.

CHAPTER II

Roman Britain

THE Roman occupation intervened between the coming of the Celt and the coming of the Saxon, and delayed the latter for perhaps two hundred years. Celt, Saxon, and Dane came over to slaughter or expel the inhabitants and settle in their place, but the Romans came to exploit and govern by right of superior civilization. In this they resembled the Europeans in Africa rather than the Pilgrim Fathers in America. Yet the natives of Britain were white men, capable of adopting Latin ways more fully than most Africans are capable of adopting the ways of Europe. Nor, on the other hand, had the Gauls and Britons an elaborate civilization of their own, like the inhabitants of the Greek and Oriental lands subject to the Roman sway. And, therefore, once the Roman conquerors had glutted their first rage for plunder, their main effort was to induce their Western subjects to assimilate Latin life in all its aspects. Their success with the Gauls was permanent, and became the starting point of modern European history. But in Britain, after a great initial success, they had complete ultimate failure. 'From the Romans who once ruled Britain,' wrote Haverfield, the great student of the archaeology of the occupation, 'we Britons have inherited practically nothing.'

In the end the Romans left behind them here just three things of value: the first of these would have amused or shocked Caesar, Agricola, and Hadrian, for it was Welsh Christianity; the second was the Roman roads; the third, a by-product of the second, was the traditional importance of certain new city sites, especially that of London. But the Latin life of the cities, the villas, the arts, the language, and the political organization of Rome vanished like a dream. The greatest fact in the early history of the island is a negative fact – that the Romans did not succeed in permanently Latinizing Britain as they Latinized France.

Julius Caesar won his place in the history of the world by a double achievement – the political renovation of the Roman Empire and its extension into northern Europe. He planted the power of the Mediterranean peoples broad and firm on the north side of the Alps, making Gaul a Latin country for ever. And he showed how the outworn machinery of the ancient world could be reconstructed on new principles, by converting the provincial-minded Roman Republic, tossed about between a selfish aristocracy and a debased city mob, into a disciplined and catholic-minded Empire of the Civilized World, at once popular and despotic. When his successors had rebuilt the Roman State on these lines, its life was renewed for another five hundred years in the West, and another fifteen hundred in the Near East. The Caesarean Empire became the link between the ancient and modern world. It secured that enough of the influence of Greece and Rome should survive to give some degree of common culture to the races composing the future Europe. It became the arena for the propagation of Christianity, which travelled to the four corners of civilization by the roads built and guarded by the Roman soldiers.

In order of time, Caesar's work in Gaul was the prelude to his work for the Empire as a whole. And the subjugation of Gaul was only half accomplished when he found himself one day gazing across the Dover Straits. He surveyed the white cliffs like Napoleon, but with other thoughts in his head: for there was nothing to impede a visit to the island and nothing to prevent his safe return; the only question was whether it was worth his while to make the voyage, with more important work on hand.

His decision to invade Britain was not taken in the hope of setting up a Roman administration on the spot. He had neither the time nor the men to spare for that; his military position in Gaul, his political prospects in Italy were too precarious, for the rulers of the Republic loved him as little as the Senators of Carthage had loved Hannibal. But as leader of the opposition party, playing to the gallery in Rome, he had need of showy exploits; and he had need of tribute and slaves to enrich his partisans, pay his soldiers, and fill his war-chest. An invasion of Britain might answer all these requirements. Besides, the tribes of North Gaul and South Britain were so closely allied that Gaul would be more submissive if its neighbour were constrained to pay tribute and to fear the mighty name of Rome. At least some first-hand knowledge of the politics and geography of the island was necessary for the would-be governors of Gaul.

As a military undertaking his first expedition was a failure. He took too small a force, and scarcely moved ten miles inland 55 B.C.
from the Dover Straits. In the next year's invasion on a larger

scale, he won several battles, forded the Thames in the face of the enemy, and penetrated into the Hertfordshire territories of Cassivelaunus, King of Catuvellauni. That tribe was dominant in southern Britain, and the jealousies caused by its hegemony turned some of its rivals and subjects into allies of the Roman invader, both in the time of Julius and a hundred years later during the Claudian conquest. But many of the Britons, including the men of Kent, put up a stout fight against Caesar, and though their undisciplined infantry were useless against the 'legion's ordered line', the yellow-haired, athletic aristocracy of the Celts in their scythed chariots clattered down the war-ways of the battle like heroes of Homer, in a manner disconcerting even to the veterans of the Tenth. The chariot, however, had seen its day as a method of warfare; it had already been abandoned in Celtic Gaul as well as in the Hellenized East, and the British chiefs would have been more truly formidable if they had taught themselves to fight as cavalry. But the island never had the luck to be defended by an aristocracy trained to fight from the saddle, until the Norman Conquest acclimatized the medieval knight.

The expedition of 54 B.C., though not a failure like that of the year before, was no great success. As Cicero complained to his cronies, the famous British gold was secured in very inadequate quantities; the slaves were too ignorant to fetch fancy prices in the market, and there had been neither the time nor the means to carry off rebellious clans wholesale to the auctioneer, as was Caesar's practice in Gaul. The expedition had no permanent results, except as a memory on both sides of the Channel. The tribute soon ceased to be paid. The rising of Vercingetorix, which proved the real crisis of the war in Gaul, put an end to Caesar's further plans for Britain, if he had any. Then the long Civil Wars, followed by the reorganization of the Empire under Augustus and Tiberius, gave the distant island a hundred years of respite.

The conquest of Gaul by Julius Caesar, more decidedly than his invasions of Britain, had brought the South British tribes into the orbit of Latin civilization. They were of the same race and political group as the northern Gauls, and the Gauls were now Roman subjects, many of them Roman citizens. A peaceful penetration of the island resulted from the work of Caesar, and prepared the way for the conquest under Claudius. The hundred most important years in the history of the world were not wholly a blank even in Britain. While Julius was being murdered and avenged, while the loves of Antony and Cleopatra were raising the question of the relations of East and West inside the Roman world, while Augustus was cannily constructing the Empire, while Christ was preaching and while Paul was being converted, far in the north Roman traders and colonists, working from the base of the Latinized province of Gaul, were establishing settlements in the interior of Britain and gaining influence at the courts of its tribal Kings.

To this time, perhaps, belongs the origin of London as a city. Finds have been made in the river bed which suggest that the first edition of London Bridge may have been erected in timber before the Roman Conquest but during the age of Roman influence. It was perhaps during this transitional period that London began to exist at the bridge-head on the northern shore. There was certainly a place of some kind known as London at the time of the invasion under Claudius.

In any case the city that was to play so great a part first in English and then in world history, attained its original importance under the Roman rule. The name of London is Celtic, but it was not a great centre of Iberian or of Celtic civilization: in Caesar's time and long afterwards, Middlesex was a forest and much of future London a marsh. But a bluff of hard ground afforded a good bridge-head where roads from the Kentish ports could cross the river and spread out again thence on their journeys northward and westward over the island. It was also the best landing-place for continental commerce coming up the estuary of the Thames. The bridge and port coincided in situation, and their geographic coincidence made the greatness of London.

The Romans, after they had conquered the island, made the fortune of London Bridge by concentrating upon it one half of their great roads, from both north and south. And they made the fortune of London port by creating an extensive commerce with the Continent, which found in the long-neglected Thames the best means of entry. London was the point at which goods from Europe could be unshipped well inside the land, and sent to its most distant parts by roads planned not for the local needs of tribes but for the imperial needs of the province. The principal exports of Roman Britain, with which she purchased the luxuries of the world, were tin, skins, slaves, pearls, and sometimes grain.

London became larger and richer under the Romans than she ever was again after their departure, until near the Norman Conquest. The Roman walls enclosed an area corresponding very closely to the walls of the City in medieval times, which were in fact only the Roman walls restored. In both periods London was a commercial, not a governmental centre. Officially she ranked lower in the Roman hierarchy than much smaller and less important towns.

It was under the Emperor Claudius, a century after Caesar's
A.D. 43 exploring expeditions, that the actual conquest of the island took place. For many years it had been demanded and planned, as readers of Horace remember. As soon as there was an Emperor with a forward policy and leisure to carry it out, he was sure to annex those Celtic lands that lay beyond the Channel, and so round off his Gallic territories. Traders who had settled in Britain, courtiers and soldiers greedy for a fresh supply of slaves, lands, and offices, were all agog for annexation. They were right in supposing it would not be very difficult. National resistance was out of the question among chiefs already half Romanized. It was only when the legionaries found themselves on the edge of the Welsh mountains and the northern moors that the Romans, like every other successful invader of Britain, began to meet with serious difficulties. Until some effective system of military control had been established over Wales and the North, warlike tribes would be continually descending from those reservoirs of savagery to plunder the demilitarized inhabitants of city and villa in the plains below.

The Roman armies who for so many generations addressed themselves to this problem, were very different from the warrior swarms of Celt, Saxon, and Dane, very different too from the feudal host of Norman times. A Roman army was a highly drilled, long-service force, held together under strict discipline all the year round and from year to year, accustomed, when not fighting, to fatigue duty in building roads, bridges, and forts. Unlike the other invaders of Britain, the Romans did not achieve their conquests by indiscriminate slaughter and destruction, nor by ushering in a host of farmer immigrants, nor by the erection of private castles. Their method of conquest was to make military roads, planned on system for the whole island, and to plant along them forts garrisoned by the regular troops. It was thus that the legions were able, after a first check, to do what the Saxons failed to do, and the castle-building Norman Barons only did after long centuries, namely, to subjugate and hold down the Welsh mountaineers. They could not Romanize the mountains as they Romanized the eastern and southern plains, nor plant cities at the foot of Snowdon and Plynlymmon. But by means of roads and forts they had made an effective military occupation of Wales within five-and-thirty years of their landing.

Devon and Cornwall they neglected, as an area too small and isolated to be dangerous. Roman remains are scarce beyond Exeter. But Somerset played an important part in the new Britain. Within six years of the Claudian invasion, the new Government was working the Mendip lead-mines. And the waters of Aquae Solis soon made Bath the centre of fashion, luxury, and leisure for Romano-British society, desperately resolved to reproduce under leaden skies the gay, lounging life of Imperial Rome.

But the real difficulty of the frontier problem, never wholly solved, lay in the North. Between Tyne and Humber lay the moorlands of heather and white grass that we know, varied in those days by vast forests of brushwood, birch, and dwarf oak destined to disappear before the nibbling of sheep when the wool trade developed in a later England. In those desolate regions the savage Brigantes refused to listen to the voice of the Roman charmer, or to lay aside their native habits and warlike aspirations. Beyond them, in modern Scotland, lay the Caledonians, of Pictish and other race, partly Celtic; they were no more submissive than the Brigantes, and were yet more formidable from the remoteness and the physical character of their territory.

It was not till a century and a half had passed after the Claudian conquest that the Emperor Severus marked the final limit of the northern frontier by renovating (A.D. 210) the wall that Hadrian had erected (A.D. 123) from Solway to the mouth of the Tyne. Several times the Romans had tried to conquer Scotland; once under Tacitus' father-in-law Agricola, the great Governor of Britain, with his victory at the 'Mons Graupius' somewhere on the edge of the Highlands (A.D. 84); once in the reign of Antoninus Pius (A.D. 130); and once again under Severus himself. But the Romans failed in Scotland as repeatedly as the English Plantagenet Kings. Their failure was due not only to the frontal resistance of the Picts in their water-logged straths and inaccessible mountains and forests, but to the frequent rebellions of the Brigantes in the rear. Until they abandoned Caledonia, the Romans' line of communication was too long, being exposed to the likelihood of attack all the way from the Humber northwards.

Some well-trenched camps and the ruins of Antoninus' turf wall from Forth to Clyde were all that the legions left behind them in Scotland – except indeed a greater sense of cohesion among the Pictish tribes, inspired by the common purpose of resisting and ruining the Roman Empire with all its walls and works. No attempt was made to add Ireland to the territory of the Caesars.

The area of true Roman occupation was therefore confined almost exactly to modern England and Wales. But this area was itself divided into two sharply contrasted regions, the Latinized South and East, the barbarian North and West.

North of Humber and Trent, west of Severn and Exe, Celto-Iberian tribalism survived in its more primitive form. This moorland half of Britain, where nearly all the garrison spent nearly all its time, was indeed the chief area of military occupation, but it was nothing more. It was patrolled by some 40,000 men, nearly a tenth of the total forces of the Empire. Their three bases were the great fortresses of York, Chester, and Caerleon, each the headquarters of a legion. In Wales, the Pennines, Cumberland, and Northumbria, the mail-clad infantry marched and counter-marched along the roads they had made from mountain camp to mountain camp, through a sparse and savage population, either hostile or indifferent to their passage. Devon and Cornwall were an isolated pocket of Celtic tribalism. It was in the fruitful plains of the South-East that the Latinized Britons were concentrated, in a peaceful and civilian land, where the sight of a cohort on the march was a rarity, but where Roman cities and villas were plentiful and Roman civilization powerful in its attraction.

Owing to this cultural distinction between the two geographic sections of the island, it happened that the districts destined to be overrun by the Saxon destroyer were the districts most given over to the Latin influences of city and villa life. On the other hand, Wales and Cornwall, Strathclyde and Lancashire, where alone independent Celtic life was destined to survive the coming of the Saxons, were precisely those districts wherein Celtic life had been least altered by the Roman occupation. This accident goes far to explain why Roman influence was permanent in no part of the island.

But a second and more general reason can be given for Rome's failure to Latinize Britain as she Latinized Gaul. Britain was too far from the Mediterranean. Southern France is itself a Mediterranean land. But the civilization of the Italian city, the life of the forum and piazza, shivers when transplanted too far north. The ancient world was a Mediterranean civilization. It was the medieval world that first became truly European, by losing the Levant and North Africa and by winning Germany for Christendom. In the ancient world, Britain was a distant and isolated outpost; in the Middle Ages, it was much nearer to the heart of the Christian and feudal civilization. Therefore the Norman work in the island had more permanence than the Roman. Not enough Italian or Mediterranean folk came to Celtic Britain to change the character of its civilization except superficially. But the superficial success of the Romans in the richest agricultural districts of South and East was very remarkable, all the more remarkable since it proved so transient.

The Mediterranean civilization, of which Rome had become the armed missionary, was based on city life. In that respect it differed from the Celtic civilization which it conquered and from the Saxon and feudal civilization that was destined to succeed it. The Roman Empire had grown out of a city state; it had annexed a number of other city states in the Mediterranean, and had planted new cities among the tribes of Gaul. The true life of the Empire lay in the hundreds of walled towns, linked up by military roads, that held together its otherwise unwieldy bulk. From each of these cities it strove to govern and transform the surrounding countryside. And so in south Britain the first thing the Romans did was to build cities.

Besides London and the greater municipalities there were many lesser towns like Silchester, which the Romans planned out in their rectangular fashion, and in most cases protected with stone walls. In these towns even the common workmen talked Latin and were educated enough to read and write it, as we know from the words they scribbled for their amusement on tile and potsherd as they worked, which modern archaeologists have dug up and interpreted. It was a high civilization, much more elaborate than anything seen again for many centuries in England. But it was not a native product, sprung from the soil; it was the life of the great cosmopolitan Empire oversea, of which the more progressive among the island tribes were content for a while to become a part. These cities did not thrive; they seldom grew to much above 3000 inhabitants each. And with the exception of the commercial port of London they had fallen into decay more than a century before the final downfall of Roman rule in the island.

Beyond the city walls Roman civilization petered away by degrees, through regions of Romano-British 'villadom', into regions of mere Celtic tribalism. The countryside was sprinkled with smart Roman villas, built of stone in the Italian style, adorned with mosaics, frescoes, and baths. Attached to each villa was an estate, worked by slaves, or by *coloni* who were bound to the soil and to its proprietor under rules as harsh as those which bound the medieval villein. If there was not liberty there was peace. So real was the *Pax Romana* in the demilitarized districts of the South-East that these country-houses were not fortified or even protected by a moat, like the medieval castle and manor house. The only people trained to fight were the soldiers of the regular army: this was one reason why Romanized Britain fell so easy a prey to the invader when men could no longer count on the protection of the legions.

The area of agriculture and the area of land reclaimed from forest and fen were both extended in Roman times, at least in some districts, as for instance in Cambridgeshire. But even there the work was only begun; and the Midlands from Bucks to Warwickshire were still left in the main to the forest. The valleys of Thames and Trent, still water-logged, contained no connected line of important towns and villages as in later days. The Roman did something for deforesting and draining, but the yeoman's work in these matters was left for the stalwart industry of Saxon and Danish townships, extended over a thousand years.

The government of Britain was far from being a rigid and uniform bureaucracy. For the Roman Empire, though at bottom a military despotism standing on the social basis of slavery, was in some respects very liberal. In accordance with its custom, the privileged municipalities in the island not only enjoyed selfgovernment but had jurisdiction each over a rural area about as large as a modern county. There were five such governing cities: Verulamium, Colchester, Lincoln, Gloucester, and York; mercantile London, though larger than any of these, had less official status.

The rest of civilized Britain was divided up into cantons, answering to Celtic tribal areas and bearing the tribal names. The cantonal administration was as far as possible centred on some Roman town not of municipal rank. It was characteristic of the Romans that instead of trying to stamp out native tribalism they used it as a means of government, while undermining its spirit by contact with their own more attractive civilization. Every inducement was offered to the Celtic chief to become Roman in dress, language, and heart; on these conditions he could remain a Celtic chief in relation to his tribesmen, exercising his authority over them as a toga-ed Roman official. This policy, which might appear to an iron bureaucrat to be a dangerous concession to tribalism, became in fact the means of Romanizing the Celt with his own good will. The same cantonal system was established in Gaul; but whereas the cantonal names and areas survived the Frankish conquest of Gaul, they disappeared in the more destructive Saxon invasion of Britain.

CHAPTER III

Beginning of the Nordic Invasions. Anglo-Saxon Conquest

THE settlement of the Nordic peoples in our island is the governing event of British history. The various irruptions of Anglo-Saxons and Jutes, of Danes and Norsemen form a single chapter; it has its prelude in the first plundering raids of Saxon pirates on the coast of Roman Britain well before A.D. 300, and it ends about 1020 when Canute completed the Scandinavian conquest of England by reconciling on equal terms the kindred races of Saxon and Dane. Between these dates the racial character of the inhabitants of the country was fundamentally altered. It has since undergone slight continuous modifications by the arrival of Norman, Flemish, Huguenot, Hebrew, Irish, and other immigrants. But the racial basis was fixed by the time of Canute.

The Nordic invasions are more important than the Roman interlude, more important even than the Norman Conquest. The attempt of the Romans to Latinize the Celtic civilization in Britain broke down because there were too few Romans. And the attempt of the Norman-French aristocracy and clergy to Gallicize England, though it had great and permanent consequences, was gradually abandoned in face of the facts of race, just as the attempt to Anglicize Ireland has recently been abandoned for the same cause. The Nordic conquest of England had larger permanent results than any of these conquests, because it was secured on a general displacement of Celtic by Nordic peoples in the richest agricultural districts of the island. The distinctive character of the modern English is Nordic tempered by Welsh, not Welsh tempered by Nordic. In Scotland the Celtic element is racially stronger, but in Scotland also the Nordic language and character have prevailed.

Objection may be taken to the word 'Nordic', as to all terms invented in after times for historical purposes. But to give a just conception of British history, a single word must sometimes be employed to cover the German, the Anglo-Saxon, and the Scandinavian peoples of the Fifth Century.* They had certain common features, which gave a family likeness to the innumerable and widely scattered tribes of Scandinavians, Anglo-Saxons, Franks, and Teutons, who ranged, conquering and colonizing, from Ireland to Constantinople, from Greenland to the Desert of Sahara.

*This use of 'Nordic' does not imply the ideological meaning of the word in Nazi Germany which is founded neither in history nor biology.

They had all originally come from the shores of the Baltic, though the ancestors of Franks, Goths, and Vandals had wandered off west and south long before, in the course of the last millennium before Christ. All the kinsmen had much in common: allied languages; the religion of Thor and Woden after which most of the English and some of the German days of the week are called; a body of epic poetry celebrating common racial heroes, like Sigurd or Siegfried known from Iceland to Bavaria, and Beowulf who does in Denmark and Scandinavia deeds sung in an English poem; a common art for decorating weapons, jewellery, and objects in daily use, with patterns of great beauty and richness, quite distinct from Graeco-Roman art and rather less distinct from Celtic; and lastly, common customs of war and agriculture, varying considerably according to local conditions. There was much therefore to connect German, Anglo-Saxon, and Scandinavian.

The Anglo-Saxons settled the greater part of Britain from the Forth to the borders of Cornwall, and the Jutes settled Kent and the Isle of Wight. Some modern scholars think of the Anglo-Saxons as being substantially one people, while others adhere to the distinction drawn by Bede between the Angles and the Saxons. In any case, at the time of their migration to Britain, Angles and Saxons were occupying parts of the coast of modern Denmark and Germany on both sides of the mouth of the Elbe, and the difference between them in language and customs was slight. The Jutes were a smaller tribe, kindred but distinct; they came to Britain either directly from their old home in Jutland, in northern Denmark, or, as some think, from their more recent settlements in Frisia and on the lower Rhine.

Agriculture had been practised in the north-east of Europe ever since the later stone age. Many of the Anglo-Saxon invaders of Britain were farmers seeking richer ploughlands than the sandy dunes, heaths, marshes, and forests of the north European shore. But many of them were deep-sea fishermen, seal-hunters, and whalers, trained to hardihood in conflict with the storms, the sea-monsters, and the pirates then common in the North Sea. Themselves pirates and plunderers when on the war-path by sea or land, they had a high sense of honour and much kindly good-nature in dealings with their own folk at home, as the fragments of their epic poetry testify. Fierce, courageous, and loyal, they were accustomed to follow their chosen chiefs with great fidelity on marauding expeditions along all the coasts between Norway and Frisia.

Such were the migratory habits of these amphibious, restless folk in the first centuries after Christ; but we should not call them

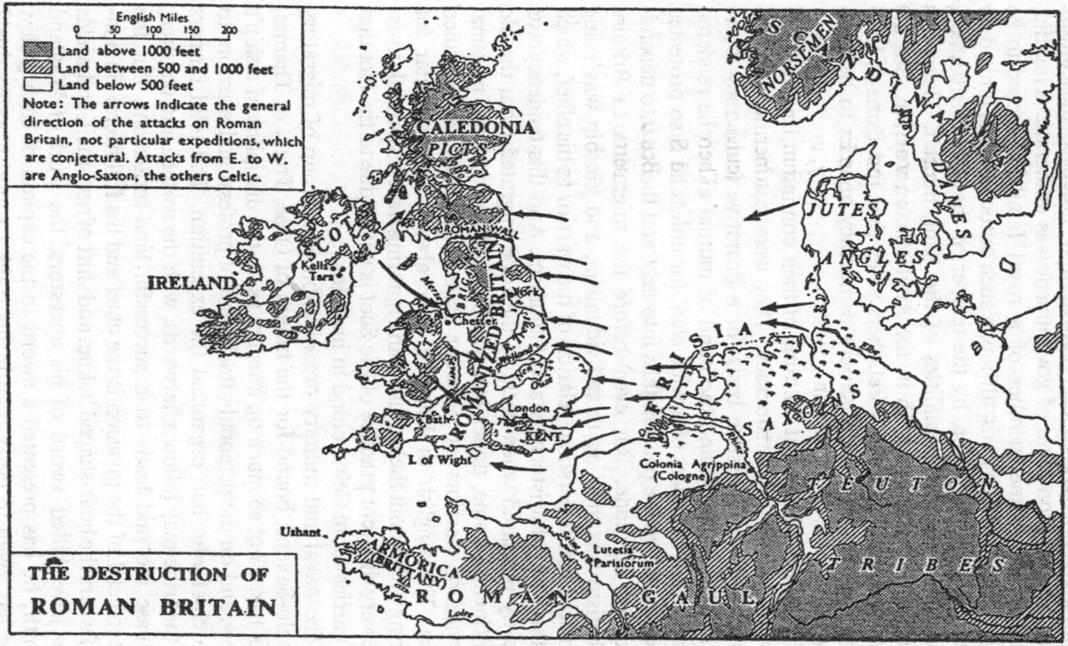
English Miles
0 50 100 150 200
Land above 1000 feet
Land between 500 and 1000 feet
Land below 500 feet
Note: The arrows indicate the general direction of the attacks on Roman Britain, not particular expeditions, which are conjectural. Attacks from E. to W. are Anglo-Saxon, the others Celtic.
THE DESTRUCTION OF
ROMAN BRITAIN
CALEDONIA
PICTS
ROMAN WALL
SCOT
Kells
Tara
IRELAND
ROMANIZED BRITAIN
BRIGA
York
Chester
Mersey
R. Trent
Welland
Severn
Ouse
London
Thames
KENT
Bath
I. of Wight
Ushant
ARMORICA
(BRITTANY)
Loire
ROMAN
GAUL
Seine
Lutetia
Parisiorum
Colonia Agrippina
(Cologne)
Rhine
FRISIA
SAXONS
Elbe
JUTES
ANGLES
DANES
SCANDINAVIA
NORSEMEN
TEUTON
TRIBES

MAP III

nomads, for wherever they settled they practised agriculture. The Anglo-Saxon form of government was autocratic Kingship, exercised by some member of a royal family supposed to be descended from the gods, although such autocracy was limited by the custom of the tribe, by the temper of the armed tribesmen, and by the personal qualities of the King himself. There was very little that was slavish in the Anglo-Saxon warrior. But the idea that our 'Teutonic' forefathers when they first came to England were in any formal sense a democracy appears to be erroneous.

The Anglo-Saxons at the time of their coming to England had both Kingship and aristocracy. They were not 'farmer republicans'. The only possible basis for a primitive democracy is the strict tie of kinship and the bond of mutual aid to be rendered between all members of a wide clan, for unless he is so protected and supported the peasant falls into debt and thence into dependence or servitude. But even before the migration to Britain, tribalism was yielding to individualism, and kinship was being replaced by the personal relation of the warrior to his chief, which is the basis of aristocracy and feudalism. And this tendency was greatly increased when parts of the tribe migrated from the old continental home, under leaders who had engaged the personal service of warriors of different clans and sometimes of alien race. The English of England have always been singular for caring little about their cousins and ignoring their distant relatives: the very different practice of the Scot is partly due to the fact that he carries more Celtic blood in his veins.

The naval and military organization of a group of migratory Anglo-Saxons, bound for the mouth of Ouse, Trent, or Thames, was based not so much on kinship, as on the discipline of a ship's crew, and on the personal attachment of professional warriors to the chief who had organized the expedition. The solid farmers of the tribe may follow afterwards, with the women and children, in case the raid leads to a successful land-settlement. But the spear-head of the invasion is the chief and his followers. He himself wears the boar-shaped helmet and shirt of ring-mail, and wields the jewel-hilted sword of his ancestors, the work of Wayland Smith; he has presented a sword to the captain of each galley, and has given to every man in his train a round wooden shield and a long spear with ashwood shaft and iron head. He has fed them bountifully all winter with flesh, bread, and strong drink at the 'ale-board' in his long timber hall, where they have praised him as their good lord, because like Beowulf he 'never slew his hearth-fellows in drunkenness'. It is he who has undertaken to lead them this summer where good plunder and better lands are to be won by the shield-wall. The bones of these nameless chiefs are dug up to-day in 'early Anglo-Saxon graveyards', lying between the rusted shield-boss and spear-head that expelled Rome from Britain and drove the Celt into the West. Some of these great unknown ones must have had what we should now call 'genius' as 'men of action'. For the true life story of a single one of them, telling why he and his men decided to cross the sea, where they landed, and in what manner they fought and wrought and thought – for that how gladly would we give whole libraries of later record!

But the past is inexorable in its silence. There are no authentic chronicles of the Saxon Conquest. The Britons in their refuge among the Welsh mountains relapsed into Celtic barbarism, and if the priest Gildas wrote for them a Book of Lamentations in Latin, it answers few of the purposes of history. The heathen Saxon invaders had indeed a Runic alphabet; it would serve for a charm on a sword or a name on a stone, but it was not used to take down annals, or to transcribe the long-lost epics sung by the gleemen in hall, of which more than one must have told the deeds of some hero who came seeking Britain over deep water.

The historian has two points of light, and even those are dim. He sees an orderly Romano-Celtic world late in the Fourth Century, beginning to fall into chaos. Two hundred years later he sees a Saxon-Celtic barbarism beginning to emerge confusedly into the renewed twilight of history, and he hears the marching chaunt of St Augustine and his monks bringing back with them the Latin alphabet and the custom of written record. Between these points stretches a great darkness. The most important page in our national annals is a blank. The chief names of this missing period of history – Hengist, Vortigern, Cerdic, Arthur – may be those of real or of imaginary men. All that archaeology and history together can do is to indicate – not the date, leaders, landings, and campaigns – but only the general character of the warfare that destroyed Roman Britain and gave the land to the English.

As early as the latter years of the Third Century, the Romans established a fleet specially charged to defend the Gallic and British shores against the plundering raids of Saxon pirates. The Empire was at the same time being disturbed from within by the wars of its own rival Emperors and armies. In this game the legions quartered in Britain often took a hand on behalf of their own chiefs. The most singular of these pretenders was Carausius, the warden against the Saxon raids, who from A.D. 286 to 293 ruled the island as a sovereign and independent section of the Empire, safe behind its own navy. Carausius has been called 'the first sea-King of Britain'. After the reform of the Empire by Diocletian and Constantine a few years later, the re-incorporated province of Roman Britain enjoyed a last golden age. An official known as 'the Count of the Saxon shore' defended the coast from the Wash to Portsmouth, by the aid of ten large fortresses, of which Richborough in Kent was the chief, and a considerable garrison withdrawn for this new purpose from the military regions of the north-west. Each of the ten fortresses commanded a port, whence a fleet could issue to fight the invaders at sea. By this provision the civilized lowlands were rendered secure from Saxon attack for another half-century. The exotic life of the cities which the Romans had planted in Britain continued to decay, but rural life prospered. More villas appear to have been built and occupied in the island from A.D. 300 to 350 than at any other period.

In the last half of the Fourth Century the downfall began. As the spade of the archaeologist gives proof, life and property then became insecure in the lowland area of Britain. Here and there villas were burnt or deserted, in the track of raiding bands of Picts and Brigantes from the North, or of the wild Irish tribesmen then known as 'Scots', who swarmed in through the unromanized districts of the West. These local catastrophes were due to the great general cause: the heart of the Empire was weakening under attack nearer home; fewer and worse soldiers and civilians were coming from the continent to serve in Britain. As a consequence, a Celtic revival began, slow at first, but visible even before the final Saxon onrush destroyed the centres of Latin influence in the island. The civil and military connexions with the Mediterranean became every year more shadowy, and the unromanized Celts from Wales, Caledonia, and Ireland poured down over the land. Before Roman Silchester was abandoned under Saxon pressure, an 'Ogam stone' with a barbarous Celtic inscription had been set up in its streets, portentous to anyone who remembered what Silchester once had been.

In the course of the first thirty or forty years of the Fifth Century, though by what exact stages it is impossible to say, the Romanized Britons found themselves left to their own devices by an Empire that confessed itself unable any longer to help. It was only then that the Saxons became the chief instrument in the destruction of Roman Britain, begun in the previous century by the Celtic barbarians of North and West. We do not know whether or with what success the Saxons had renewed their raids between 350 and 400, but it is clear that at the opening of the new century they came over with increasing numbers and boldness. The state of the island pulverized by Picts and Scots, the breakdown of the true Roman regime, the conduct of the defence by Christian missionaries of a practical turn like St Germanus in the place of regular Roman generals – such things must often have been the theme of excited debate in log-built halls of the Anglo-Saxon chiefs, after the return from each successful plundering expedition. Why, the pirate-farmers began to ask each other, as they quaffed the mead, why should we take only what we can carry away? In these favourable new conditions the idea was mooted of wholesale immigration to these warm well-watered lands, rich in grain-fields and in pasture and in oak forests swarming with deer and swine.

As all evidence is wanting, we can only guess that the Saxon conquest was achieved by two distinct types of expedition. On the one hand, in view of the amount of fighting and destruction to be done, there must surely have been bands of warriors unencumbered by women and children, moving rapidly over the island by the rivers and roads, fighting the battles, storming the earth-work camps and stone-girt cities, burning the towns and villas, slaughtering and driving away the Romanized Britons, hurling back into the West the war-bands of rival barbarians from Caledonia and Ireland. But we must also picture to ourselves the shipping over of the families of the invaders, accompanied perhaps by the less war-like of the agricultural population, to take up new homes in the ground thus roughly cleared.

For the Anglo-Saxon conquest, like the Danish settlement in Alfred's day, had two aspects, and to omit either is to misunderstand the Nordic invasions of Britain. Like the Danes after them, the Anglo-Saxons were bloody-minded pirates, rejoicing to destroy a higher civilization than their own, and at the same time Pilgrim Fathers, come to settle on the land and till it themselves, not as mere exploiters and slave masters but as honest husbandmen. If they had not been barbarians they would not have destroyed Roman civilization; if they had not been Pilgrim Fathers their race would not in the end have replaced it by something better.

The rivers, deeper and more navigable than they are to-day, were the main routes by which the English first penetrated into the interior of the country henceforth to be called by their name.

The undecked galleys of shallow draught, in which they had so daringly crossed the North Sea, could be rowed far upstream into the very heart of the country, and then left under a guard in some island among the marshes or behind a palisade of stakes hastily cut from the forest. The rest of the disembarked war-band could then march across Britain with fire and sword. Such, as we know, was the method of the Danish invaders in the time of Alfred, and such probably was the method of the Anglo-Saxon invaders before them.

When once the Roman military system had collapsed, the Roman roads only served to hasten the pace of conquest and destruction. It was indeed by the side of rivers and not by the side of roads that the new race made its first settlements, as their earliest relics show, but the roads must greatly have assisted their wholesale conquest of the island. One can see them, padding along the stone causeway, heavily laden with plunder but lightly burdened with the panoply of war. Laughing at their luck, they turn aside to sack a villa descried amid the trees. As the flames shoot up, the pampered cock pheasant, imported by the Roman to adorn his terraces, frightened now by the shouting of the barbarous seamen, scuttles off into the forest; he will there become a wild bird of the chase, destined to play a great part in the social history of the island through many changing centuries.

We can say of these Saxon warriors, as they emerge for the first time on the great stage of history, that they, like their descendants, are 'a warlike but not a military people'. A spear and wooden shield apiece, with a few swords among them, here and there a helmet, and perhaps one mail shirt to every thousand men, sufficed them to conquer the island. Yet the Latinized Britons should have been able to pit against them the disciplined infantry, the body-armour, the missile weapons and the cavalry of later Roman warfare. We do not in fact know whether the defenders fought principally in the Roman or in the revived Celtic fashion, when their half-mythical King Arthur led them to battle against the 'heathen swarming o'er the Northern sea'. But in whatever manner the Britons fought they were conquered by foot soldiers without the discipline of the barracks, without body-armour or missile weapons, but with prodigious energy and purpose. The defenders had the further advantage of formidable camps and steep earthworks crowned by stockades, very numerous all over Britain, besides the stone-walled Roman cities. But one by one all obstacles went down before the half-armed barbaric infantry landed from the long-ships.

We noticed in the last chapter, as a peculiarity of the Roman system in its best days, that no class in the peaceful South and East of the island had been trained to self-defence. The magnate of the villa, unlike the feudal lord of later times, was not a fighting man; he had no fighting train and no fortified mansion. Many of the cities indeed were defended by magnificent stone walls, but their citizens were not accustomed to war like a burgher militia in the Middle Ages. If the Roman world was more civilized than the medieval, it was proportionately more incapable of local self-help if anything happened to the central government and to the regular army. Indeed, the feudal system gradually arose out of the welter of barbarian invasions, precisely to remedy this vital defect in the social organism.

Whether the bands of invaders were small or great, whether they acted separately or in concert, the destruction which they wrought was prodigious. The tradition of the Welsh Christian remnant is summarized in the words of Gildas the priest:

> Every colony is levelled to the ground by the stroke of the battering ram. The inhabitants are slaughtered along with the guardians of their churches, priests, and people alike, while the sword gleamed on every side, and the flames crackled around. How horrible to behold in the midst of the streets the tops of towers torn from their lofty hinges, the stones of high walls, holy altars, mutilated corpses, all covered with lurid clots of coagulated blood, as if they had been crushed together in some ghastly winepress. . . Of the miserable remnant some flee to the hills, only to be captured and slain in heaps: some, constrained by famine, come in and surrender themselves to be slaves for ever to the enemy . . . Others wailing bitterly pass overseas.

The destruction of the Roman cities and villas was wholesale and almost universal. The early Anglo-Saxons were not city dwellers. They had no mercantile instincts except for selling slaves overseas, and they lost their old sea habits when they had won themselves good farm lands in the interior. The most civilized of their desires was to settle in large rural 'townships' and to till the soil on the open-field system of village agriculture. That was to be the sound basis of the new English civilization. Directed by this instinct, they began at once to build for themselves log houses grouped round the log hall of the lord. Split trunks of forest timber, set vertically side by side, composed the walls, for timber was there in plenty and they were no slovens at work. Such were the homes in which they had lived beyond the sea, and they preferred the familiar touch and smell of the walls of split oak to the nice villas and town houses, fitted with every modern convenience, which they might have occupied at their will as soon as they had buried the corpses of the late owners.

We are told on the highest authority that 'no case is known where Saxons dwelt in a Roman villa.' Time and spade may reveal some such cases, but they are scarcely likely to be numerous. And as with the villas so with the cities; the new-comers showed the same unwillingness to live or to let anyone else live within the ramparts of stone. In some cases indeed the sites had been rendered so important by natural advantages or by the convergence of imperishable Roman roads, that they could not permanently be deserted. Chester, Bath, and Canterbury were re-occupied in the course of time; it is uncertain whether London, Lincoln, and York were ever completely abandoned or not, though it appears that they ceased for some generations to be of any size or consequence. The junction of Roman roads and river passages ensured the ultimate greatness of London, Cambridge, and various other places as soon as civilization began to make any recovery at all. There at least time and barbarism could not permanently obliterate the work of Rome.

But Silchester, Wroxeter, Verulamium, and many other towns ceased for ever to be inhabited. St Albans stands half a mile from the site of Verulamium, on the other side of the river; it is as though the old site had been purposely avoided. Villas and cities are constantly being dug up out of the ground, in places given over to tillage, pasture, or moor. But for some centuries the Roman ruins must have stood, as familiar a sight as the roofless abbeys under the Stuart Kings, a useful stone quarry sometimes by day, but at night haunted in the imagination of the Saxon peasant by the angry ghosts of the races that his forefathers had destroyed. Fear lest the dead should rise shrouded in their togas, may have been one reason why so many sites were never reoccupied at all.

In the course of the Sixth Century, after the first and most savage flood of destruction had ebbed, and while the western half of England still remained in Celtic hands, however barbarously most of it may have been ravaged – a chain of separate but contiguous Anglo-Saxon kingdoms grew up, stretching from Northumbrian Bernicia to Wessex. For centuries they were shifting their frontiers like a kaleidoscope, but the names and positions of certain shires in South-East England, such as Essex, Sussex, and Kent, recall some of these very ancient States.

These early English Kingdoms were periodically at war with

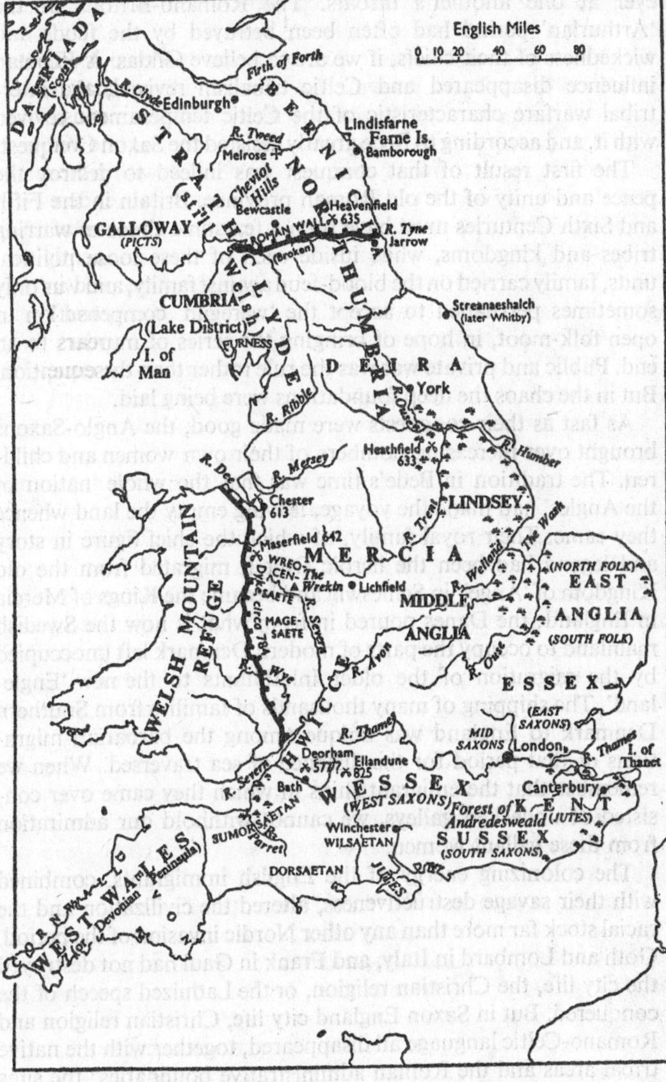

MAP IV. ENGLAND OF THE HEPTARCHY

one another, and with the wild Welsh. The Welsh too were for-ever at one another's throats. The Romano-Britons of the 'Arthurian' period had often been betrayed by the feuds and wickedness of their chiefs, if we are to believe Gildas. As Roman influence disappeared and Celtic tribalism revived, the inter-tribal warfare characteristic of the Celtic temperament revived with it, and according to Bede greatly assisted the Saxon Conquest.

The first result of that conquest was indeed to destroy the peace and unity of the old Roman province. Britain in the Fifth and Sixth Centuries must have been a fearsome chaos of warring tribes and kingdoms, while inside each of these loose political units, family carried on the blood-feud against family, and was only sometimes persuaded to accept the 'weregild' compensation in open folk-moot, in hope of bringing the series of murders to an end. Public and private war was the rule rather than the exception. But in the chaos the deep foundations were being laid.

As fast as their conquests were made good, the Anglo-Saxons brought over increasing numbers of their own women and children. The tradition in Bede's time was that the whole 'nation of the Angles' had made the voyage, leaving empty the land whence they came. Their royal family, of which the chief figure in story and legend had been the heroic Offa I, migrated from the old Kingdom of 'Angel' in Schleswig and became the Kings of Mercia in England; the Danes poured in from what is now the Swedish mainland to occupy the parts of modern Denmark left unoccupied by the migration of the older inhabitants to the new 'Engle-land'. The shipping of many thousands of families from Southern Denmark to England was unique among the barbarian migrations of that period for the distance of sea traversed. When we remember that the emigrant ships in which they came over consisted of undecked galleys, we cannot withhold our admiration from these gallant women.

The colonizing energy of the English immigrants, combined with their savage destructiveness, altered the civilization and the racial stock far more than any other Nordic invasion of the period. Goth and Lombard in Italy, and Frank in Gaul had not destroyed the city life, the Christian religion, or the Latinized speech of the conquered. But in Saxon England city life, Christian religion and Romano-Celtic language all disappeared, together with the native tribal areas and the Roman administrative boundaries; the sites of towns and villages were generally, though not universally, changed, and their names are Saxon in perhaps nine cases out of ten. These things taken together imply a great alteration in racial stock, though the completeness of the racial change has sometimes been exaggerated.

It is, on the other hand, difficult to exaggerate the injury done to Romano-British civilization. It was crushed out between two barbarisms – invading Saxondom and the Celtic revival. For the lowland districts where it had flourished were exactly the districts swept by the besom of the Saxon destroyer. In the Welsh mountains and on the Cornish moors the civilized refugees, deprived of their cities and estates and surrounded by brother-Celts far less civilized than themselves, forgot in a generation or two the arts and traditions that had once enabled them to look down on the Saxon brute. The first result of the conquest was the loss of the crafts, science, and learning of Rome; in the island as a whole there was a sharp diminution in the numbers of the population and in the acreage of cultivated land. Surviving Celt and incoming Saxon alike were rude barbarians. Yet because the Saxon now lived in the lowlands, he began to evolve a civilization of his own, which was very soon superior to that of the Welsh mountaineers. Geography inverted the course of history, making the Celt barbarous and the Saxon civilized.

The removal of the Welsh from the richest districts in the island was in part due to their own temper. They had submitted to the civilized Romans as to superior beings, but these Saxon savages could not be accepted as lords. Better to die fighting or escape across the sea to the new Brittany in Armorica of Gaul, or retire among the wild hills of Wales. The Welsh hated the Saxons so much that they would not even attempt to convert them to Christianity. For this neglect the Saxons of Bede's time afterwards reproached them, when the gospel had come from Rome and from Scotland but not from beyond Severn. The semi-nomadic habits of the dwellers in some at least of the Welsh 'trevs' made it easy for them to shift their ground and to get away from the detested Saxon conqueror. The attachment of the Welshman was less to the soil than to the clan, and the clan can move where it likes.

I have said that after the first wild onrush was checked, the border war between Welshman and Saxon went on as the normal condition of life. The chief events of this age-long war were the debouchment of the English of Wessex at the mouth of the Severn (traditionally after the victory at Deorham in Gloucestershire, A.D. 577), and the debouchment of the English of Northumbria at the mouths of Mersey and Dee, after a victory near the ruins of Chester, 'the city of the legions', in 613. The arrival of Saxondom on the Irish Channel at these two points left the Welsh of Strathclyde, Wales, and the Devonian Peninsula as three isolated pockets of Celtic tribalism, cut off from each other and from the life of the plains.

Thus in a succession of advances covering several hundred years, the Saxons, or later on the Scandinavians in their place, conquered and settled Cheshire, Lancashire, Cumberland, and Westmorland, the Severn valley, Somerset, and finally Devon, where the Saxon settlement was not completed till the Ninth or Tenth Century. But all the time the Saxons were getting more civilized and the Welsh more accustomed to them as neighbours. Long before the English advance had ended, both sides were Christian. Therefore, in these more westerly districts Celtic race and custom survived to a larger extent. But it was only in Cornwall and the unconquered Welsh mountains that language and civilization remained predominantly Celtic.

It is not possible to define accurately the proportion of Welsh to Nordic blood in any district. But it can be laid down as a general rule, good for both north and south of the island, that as we move from east to west we pass by successive stages from the Nordic to the Welsh. There are, however, exceptions to this rule: pockets of Welsh were left behind in the east, as in parts of the fen-country and of Hertfordshire; and the Norsemen afterwards made settlements on the extreme west coast, as in South Wales and North Lancashire, where the Vikings in their longships turned the rear of the Welsh from the sea.

In Wessex and Mercia, though the language was changed, there were many more Welsh left alive than in the older Saxon settlements further to the east. In Wessex, which by that time included Dorset and Somerset, we find the laws of the Saxon King Ine in 693 acknowledging the rights of a separate class called Welshmen, sometimes as holders of land and military servants of the crown. But even in Kent and East Anglia some racial elements of the former population must have been transmitted through the women. It is not possible to suppose that the Jutish and Anglo-Saxon firstcomers would at once have brought over so many women of their own that they never mingled with the captive Welshwomen, the Andromaches of the conquered race.

Unlike the German and Scandinavian, the English is a mixed race though mainly Nordic – whatever the exact proportion may be. The Celtic and pre-Celtic blood, which probably flows to some extent in the veins of everyone who to-day claims English parentage, may have influenced the English temper. On the other hand, the difference discernible between modern English and modern German or Scandinavian might also be accounted for by the long centuries of residence in the very peculiar climate of Britain, and in the social and political security of an island that was well defended against invasion after 1066. But we still like to dream that English poetry owes something to wild Celtic fancy wedded to the deep feeling and good sense of the Nordic races. Shakespeare came from a shire that was close to the old Severn valley borderland of Welsh and Saxon conflict. All such speculations are fancy, in some indeterminate relation to fact.

The Celt remained with diminished lustre, but the Roman passed away out of the story of Britain, leaving behind him three things as permanent legacies – the traditional site of London, the Roman roads, and Welsh Christianity.

It is a moot point whether or not, during the fiercest time of the Saxon Conquest, London was ever completely abandoned. If, as is possible, it was at one time quite deserted, its re-establishment as a Saxon town on a more modest scale followed very soon, for by the time of Bede (A.D. 700) it was again spoken of as an important centre of commerce, as commerce was accounted in those barbarous times. We may fairly regard the Romans as the founders of London. The concentration of their road system at that point in the navigable Thames made London's commercial revival certain, for the Romans, when they left England, did not take their roads away with them.

The importance of the Roman roads after their makers had gone, lay in this: no one made any more hard roads in the island until the turnpike movement of the Eighteenth Century. Throughout the Dark Ages and in early medieval times, these stone highways still traversed an island otherwise relapsed to disunion and barbarism. The Roman roads greatly increased the speed of the Saxon, Danish, and Norman Conquests, and aided, both in peace and in war, the slow work of Saxon and Norman Kings in uniting England as one State and making the English nation. Thanks to the Roman legacy, Britain had better national highways under the Saxon heptarchy than in Stuart times, though in the later period there were more by-roads. The imperial stone causeways, often elevated some feet above the ground, ran from sea to sea, generally keeping the higher land, but where needful marching majestically over bog and through forest. If the bridges soon fell in from neglect, the paved fords remained. For centuries wild tribes who only knew the name of Caesar as a myth, trod his gigantic highways and gave them the fantastic names of Watling Street, Ermine Street, and the Fosse Way. Gradually the stones subsided and men were too careless and ignorant to replace them. Next, the road was used as a quarry, when the medieval Englishman, having somewhat exhausted his timber, began to build for himself dwelling-houses of stone. From driving roads they declined into pack-horse tracks, finally disappearing for the most part in moor or ploughland. Stretches of them have been repaired and modernized, and the motor car now shoots along the path of the legions. But other stretches – and those the best beloved – are reserved for the Briton or Saxon who still fares on foot; they are to be traced as green lanes, starting up out of nowhere and ending in nothing, going for miles straight as a die through the magical old English countryside.

The third legacy of the Romans was Welsh Christianity. Their latest importation into Britain survived all their older and more characteristic institutions. There are but few traces of Christianity in the Romano-British world revealed by the spade of the archaeologist, and this makes all the more remarkable its survival as the only relic of that civilization among the Welsh. One reason was this: when the military and political system of the Caesars departed from Britain, it never returned; but missionaries of the Christian religion kept coming back from the Latinized continent to encourage the Welsh during the dark period after the Northumbrian wall was broken, when the Picts and Scots were attacking from north and west, and the Saxons from south and east. Deserted by the rest of the civilized world, the Welsh were not forgotten by the missionaries. Such a one was Saint Germanus, the traditional hero of the 'Hallelujah victory' that he won over an army of combined Picts and Saxons in 430. The story tells how the Saint, formerly a distinguished soldier of Rome in Gaul, having come to Britain on a mission to put down Pelagian heretics, returned to his old trade, took command of the multitude of frightened Britons and led them to victory over the dreaded heathen invader. It may indeed be an exaggerated clerical account of a transaction that is otherwise totally lost to our knowledge, but it is highly characteristic of that period – symbolic even. The Christian clergy, men of affairs and education when such qualities were becoming rare, stood in the gap whence the Roman soldier and governor were in retreat. In the day of trouble the Christian faith got a hold over the Welsh, which had not belonged to it as the official religion of later Roman rule in Britain. We shall see the same process repeated when the Saxons, newly Christianized, in their turn pass under the hammer of the heathen Danes and Norsemen. 'Give peace in our time, O Lord,' 'because there is none other that fighteth for us but only Thou, O God,' has a curious sound in the modern English liturgy; it seems to speak of the Christian God as the only ally, but not a very formidable safeguard in a world all gone wrong. But to a Welshman dispossessed by the Saxons in the Fifth Century, or a Saxon dispossessed by the Danes in the Ninth, it would have appeared a very just statement of the case.

In these circumstances, the Welsh of the Fifth and Sixth Centuries came to regard Christianity as their distinguishing mark which, together with their love of bardic music and poetry, enabled them still to feel superior to the Saxon savages who were exterminating them from the plains and confining them to the hills and moorlands of 'wild Wales'. The old Welsh bard's prophecy about the ancient races, once lords of Britain, thus describes their fate:

> Their God they shall praise,
> Their language they shall keep,
> Their land they shall lose except wild Wales.

A similar development of Celtic Christianity took place in the remote peninsula of West Wales or Cornwall. On its tin-bearing moorlands and beside its woody streams running down to coves of the rocks, a race of local saints unknown to the rest of Christendom lived their lives and left their names to the villages of Cornwall, memorials of those stirring times when British civilization perished and British Christianity found creative vigour under the ribs of death. The lost history of the romantic age of Cornwall must have been largely maritime, for it was closely connected with the history and religion of Armorica on the Gallic shore opposite. Thither the Britons of the island fled from the Saxon invader, in such numbers that Armorica of the Romanized Gauls became 'Britanny' of the Celtic revival, never to be fully absorbed in the life of Latin France, not even in the era of the French Revolution when the 'Bretons' held out so fiercely against the great changes that the rest of France had ordained.

CHAPTER IV

Mediterranean Influence Again. The Return of Christianity

PRIMITIVE societies, if they are ever to move on towards knowledge, wealth, and ordered freedom, are obliged to travel in the first instance not along the path of democratic equality, but along the path of aristocracy, kingship, and priesthood. The heathen clan or tribe may be relatively equalitarian, and poverty may be more or less equally distributed among its members, but it can never move forward in mass order towards higher civilization and the freedom of the individual. When men collectively are very poor some few must be made rich if there is to be any accumulation of wealth for civilized purposes. When men collectively are very ignorant, progress is only possible through the endowment of an educated few. In such a world, organization can only begin through personal ascendancy and can only be rendered permanent through privilege. Education and spiritual religion are, in those primitive times, inextricably bound up with superstition and the ascendancy of the priest over the layman, as Bede's History so innocently and charmingly demonstrates on every page. In our own democratic and partially scientific age these conditions of progress in the past may seem strange to some, but they are a large part of the secret of early English history. In those days kingship, feudalism, and ecclesiasticism grew together as harmonious parts of a general movement. King, thegn, and Bishop, though often rivals, in the main fostered one another's power. All three were at once the exploiters and the saviours of an otherwise helpless society. The period during and after the Danish invasions will offer the best ground for describing the growth of feudalism and Kingship, the origins of which we have already noticed in the period of the Saxon Conquest. In the present chapter, covering the years between that conquest and the coming of the Vikings, we must attempt the difficult task of appreciating the change of religion as the first great step forward of the English people on the path of civilized life.

The Christian conquest of the island was the return of Mediterranean civilization in a new form, and with a new message. At the Kentish ports, through which the legions had come and gone, landed Augustine of Rome and Theodore of Tarsus; they established here a hierarchy imitated from the officialdom of the defunct Roman Empire, and the English Kings in turn borrowed, from this new civil service of the Church, forms and policies fitted to the needs of the infant State. Christianity meant, also, the return of learning to the island, and the beginning among the barbarians of a political and legal civilization based on the arts of reading and writing in the practicable Latin alphabet.

Christianity spoke also of strange matters, totally foreign to the Nordic mind, and in great part foreign to the mind of ancient

Rome: it taught charity, humility, self-discipline, a concern about spiritual things, an active and uneasy conscience, an emphasis on the distinction between soul and body to the disparagement of the latter, a great fear and a great hope about the next life perpetually governing action in this one, the submission of the freeman to the priest – partly as being the wiser man of the two, partly from supersititous awe – great stress on dogma and consequently, as a strange corollary to the religion of brotherhood, the novel religious duty of persecuting every heathen and every heretic. Like Kingship and feudalism, medieval religion was not an unmixed blessing. But the play of these forces upon the old easy-going Nordic character produced after a thousand years the Englishmen of Tudor times, and, without disrespect to our more distant ancestry, we may confess that they thought of more things in the Mermaid Tavern than in those Saxon mead-halls where Widsith, the minstrel, 'his word-hoard unlocked'.

The worship of Odin and Thor, the religion common to primitive Anglo-Saxon and Scandinavian, was pre-eminently a layman's religion, a warrior's religion, a religion of high-hearted gentlemen not overburdened with brains or troubled about their own souls. Its grand old mythology inculcated or reflected the virtues of the race – manliness, generosity, loyalty in service and in friendship, and a certain rough honesty. The social standards of the modern English schoolboy come nearest to it, as the most elementary expression of the racial character. The Danes had a word for acts of cowardice, desertion, or dishonourableness of any kind – 'nidings vœrk' – as distinct from the ordinary breaches of the law, and more terribly punished by public opinion. It was worse to be a 'niding' than a man-slayer. The liar, too, is rather despised than honoured. The Nordic race would not have found its hero in Jacob or even in Odysseus of the many wiles – in spite of close similarities between the society described in Homer and in *Beowulf* respectively. The favourite heroes of the northern warrior world, like Njal of Iceland on the eve of the coming thither of Christianity, are praised by their neighbours because they 'never lie'.

At the time of the first contact of the Odin worshippers with Christianity, the sacrifice of slaves and captives, common to all primitive religions, had not completely died out on the continent, though there is no evidence of it in Saxon England. The sacrifice of cattle or horses was very common, accompanied by sacred feasting and drinking, which, in accordance with Pope Gregory's advice, were converted into Church feasts and 'Church ales'.

The Nordic religion was not a religion of dread, or of magic formularies to propitiate hostile powers. Instead of covering its temples with frescoes of the tortures of the damned, it taught people not to be afraid of death. Its ideal was the fellowship of the hero with the gods, not merely in feasting and victory, but in danger and defeat. For the gods, too, are in the hands of fate, and the Scandinavian vision of the twilight of the gods that was to end the world showed the heroes dying valiantly in the last hopeless fight against the forces of chaos – loyal and fearless to the last. It is an incomplete but not an ignoble religion. It contains those elements of character which it was the special mission of the Nordic peoples to add to modern civilization and to Christianity itself.

But, when all is said, the old Saxon and Danish faith was a religion of barbarism with no elements in itself of further progress, and the spontaneous conversion of its adherents to Christianity seemed a confession of this fact. The old religion was merely a traditional expression of racial character, not an outside force at work upon that character. It did little for learning or art. It did not preach humility, charity, or anything else that was difficult. It did not foster religious ardour in any form. And it was not intolerant; no missionary is recorded to have suffered martyrdom while converting the Anglo-Saxons. English heathenism had no defences, good or bad, against the Christian attack. Its scattered priesthood had no corporate consciousness, no privileged position.

The Christian missionaries had, indeed, an immense advantage in bringing a clear-cut cosmogony and definite doctrines about heaven and hell, how to attain the one and avoid the other. In contrast with these precise dogmas, the old religion only presented a vague and poetical version of popular superstitions about the next life.

Anglo-Saxon heathendom perished four hundred years before Scandinavian. From geographic causes England lay in the path of Christian influence long before it reached Denmark, Norway, or Iceland. The English Woden was overthrown in the Seventh Century by a vigorous encircling movement from North and South at once, the religion of Columba and Aidan coming from Scotland, the religion of Gregory and Augustine coming from Rome. It might, indeed, have been expected that the attack would be launched from the West, but the Welsh Christians still hated the Saxon intruder too much to try to save his soul.

Nevertheless, the Welsh had indirectly assisted in the conversion of England, for St Patrick was a Romanized Briton. Probably the lower Severn was the scene of his early home, whence raiding Scots of Ireland had carried him captive in the opening years of the Fifth Century. His subsequent conversion of Ireland (432–61) started Christianity on the long circuit by which it returned to Northern England. Columba carried it from Ireland to Western Scotland (563), and from Scotland it converted Northumbria through the mission of Aidan (635), a generation after the landing of Augustine in Kent (597).

Though the Irish Christianity of Columba and Aidan became a rival to the Roman Christianity of Gregory and Augustine, Patrick had not intended to found a Church hostile to Rome. Bearing a Roman name – Patricius – he was a citizen of the old Empire, as proud of his Roman rights as St Paul himself. He studied in Gaul, and held his commission thence from a Church which already regarded the Bishop of Rome as an important adviser on doubtful religious questions, though not as lord paramount. Patrick, though not very learned himself, brought to Ireland the inestimable gift of the Latin language of which the Celtic genius soon made such good scholarly use in profane as well as sacred letters. He did not, like Cyril, the Apostle of the Slavs, set out to found a separate Christian civilization for the race he converted. He desired to make Ireland a part of Roman Christianity and civilization, at a moment when the Roman Empire in the West had scarcely yet breathed its last and was completely identified in the minds of men with the Christian religion. The acceptance of Christianity in Ireland, as later in England, was in part due to the admiration felt by the barbarians for the Empire even in its fall, and for all things appertaining to Rome, very much as Christianity is accepted by African tribes to-day as representing Europe.

Nevertheless, the Church which Patrick caused to triumph in Ireland developed after his death in a direction away from Rome. The fall of the Empire in the West, the extirpation of Latin institutions in the neighbouring island of Britain, and the barbarian conquests in France and Italy for a while isolated Ireland from Mediterranean influence, and gave opportunity for the rise of a native Celtic Church and civilization. The fact that the barbarian inroads did not reach Ireland till the coming of the Vikings in the Ninth Century, gave time for the efflorescence of the artistic, imaginative, and literary life of early Irish Christianity.

But, though Irish Christianity flourished in the midst of Irish society, it did not transmute it as Anglo-Saxon Christianity transmuted Anglo-Saxon society. The social structure in Ireland offered no platform on which it was possible to erect a hierarchy of the Roman order, still less a parish system. Till the Vikings came there were no cities. Till Strongbow came there was no feudalism. The Irish were organized in a number of hostile and warring tribes, each tribe held together by the tie of kinship and each governed by its chief, over whom the 'High King' at Tara was suzerain rather than sovereign. Irish Christianity was perforce tribal. It was not parochial, nor in the Roman sense episcopal, though there was a plethora of insignificant Bishops, mostly without sees. Its real life was monastic. The normal Irish monastery was connected with a single tribe and acknowledged no ecclesiastical superior capable of controlling its Abbot.

Celtic monasticism did not represent the conventual ideal of St Benedict. It was a congregation of hermits planted in some remote spot, often on a rocky mountain or island. Each lived in his own beehive hut of wattle, clay, and turf; but the huts had been collected together for mutual intercourse and security in a fortified village or *kraal*, under the command of an Abbot. The monks had many-sided activities, for they were hermits, scholars, artists, warriors, and missionaries. The individual monk would sometimes go out into the world to preach, to compose tribal feuds or lead tribal wars; sometimes he would copy and illuminate manuscripts in the monastery; sometimes he would depart in search of a more complete seclusion, like St Cuthbert when he left the company of his brother monks at remote Lindisfarne for the still deeper solitude of the Farne Islands.

This Irish monasticism, both in its original home, and in its mission lands of Scotland and Northumbria, produced a rich crop of saints. The stories of their lives, many of them preserved by Bede, are singularly attractive. The freshness and the light of dawn glimmer in the legends of Aidan and of Cuthbert. To this form of monasticism we owe not only the Book of Kells but the manuscript art of Lindisfarne, wherein Celtic and Saxon native ornamentation were blended in perfect harmony with Christian traditions from southern lands. The Irish monks also revived a knowledge of classical secular literature, which had almost died out in Western Europe. While Pope Gregory the Great was reproving a Gallic Bishop for studying Latin grammar and poetry, the Irish Christians were busy saving it for the world in their remote corner where the Papal censure was unheard. Thence they carried it to the England of Benedict Biscop and Bede, where it greatly fructified; finally, in the days of Charlemagne, it was taken back across the sea by Alcuin to begin its reconquest of the illiterate continent.

Scotland, England, and Europe owe a great debt to the Irish churchmen. Yet they did little to civilize and nothing to organize the people of their own island, whose tribalism continued as before. The merits and limitations of the Celtic Church were closely connected; the breadth of freedom and individual choice implied a looseness of organization which left the Church little power when the first golden impulse had spent its force.

Such was the Christianity which invaded heathen Scotland from Ulster in 563, under the vigorous leadership of St Columba, at once warrior, statesman, hermit, and missionary – the greatest and most typical abbot of the Irish monastic ideal. On the small island of Iona off the west coast of Scotland he founded his cluster of beehive huts, whence the missionary monks swarmed over Northern Britain, and whither they returned periodically for repose, common counsel, and solitary meditation.

In Columba's day the future Scotland was already divided between Saxon and Celt. The Saxon had established himself in the south-eastern corner of the lowlands; this rich district, afterwards known as Lothian, was then the northern part of the Kingdom of Northumbria, which at its greatest extent stretched from the Humber to the Firth of Forth. King Edwin of Northumbria was fortifying his 'Edwin's Burg' on the famous rock, as the northernmost stronghold of Saxondom in the island. All the north and west, and most of the centre of the future Scotland was still Celtic; yet it was destined in the long run to adopt the Saxon tongue and civilization, perhaps without great racial change. The history of Scotland is largely the history of that process of Anglicizing the Celt. Had it not been for the early settlement of the Anglo-Saxons in the south-eastern lowlands, Scotland would have remained a Celtic and tribal country, and its future history and relations to England might have borne more resemblance to the story of Ireland or of Wales.

In the days of King Edwin, the Saxons of Northumbria were still hostile intruders in Scotland, constantly at war with the Celtic world in the upper Tweed as well as farther north. And the Celtic world was constantly at war within itself. Apart from the innumerable tribal divisions and feuds, there were three main Celtic races – the Picts of North Scotland and of Galloway, probably most of them Goidelic Celts; the Britannic Celts of Strathclyde; and the latest comers, the Scots, from Ireland, settled in Dalriada, modern Argyllshire. The Scots from oversea were destined to give their name but not their civilization to the whole land. The history of these early times, no less than the settlement of Protestant Ulster in James I's reign and the Irish immigration into Clydeside in recent times, reminds us that the connexion between West Scotland and North-east Ireland is a constant factor in history.

Columba, himself an Irish Scot, gained great influence over his fellow Scots of Dalriada, and over the Picts of the North. The Britons of Strathclyde were more gradually brought under the influence of the new religion. At the opening of the Seventh Century the Christianity of Iona had a firm hold on many at least of the Chiefs and tribes of Celtic Scotland. But the Saxons of Northumbria still vacillated, according to the chances of battle or the personal beliefs of their Kings, between the worship of Woden and the Roman form of Christianity preached to them by Paulinus, one of Augustine's men. Before describing the conversion of Northumbria by Scoto-Irish Christianity, we must turn our attention to Augustine's mission in Southern England, the other wing of the Christian invasion of the island.

Gregory the Great, the first of the great Popes, was the true founder of the medieval Papacy. In 590 he received into his charge the defenceless and impoverished Bishopric of Rome, surrounded by triumphant barbarians amid the ruins of a fallen world. In a dozen years he had raised it up in the imagination of mankind as the heir to the defunct Empire of the West.

The change of European leadership from lay to clerical hands was reflected in the personal story of Gregory's life. Having begun his career as a wealthy Roman patrician, he employed his high administrative talents as Prefect of the City for a while. Then he suddenly abandoned his social privileges and political duties to live as a humble monk on the Caelian Hill. Promoted thence to be Bishop of Rome, he exerted on behalf of the Church the genius of a Caesar and the organizing care of an Augustus. His letters of advice to the Churches of Western Europe on every religious, political, and social interest of the day, were accepted not indeed as having legal power but as having an unique moral authority. If the Papacy was, as Hobbes called it, 'no other than the ghost of the deceased Roman Empire, sitting crowned upon the grave thereof', it was a living ghost and not a phantasm. Since the governing power of the Empire had perished in the West, a ghostly authority was welcomed by distant Kings, Bishops, monks, and peoples, as giving some hope of progress, concord, and righteous impartiality in a world of chaotic violence. This new conception of old Rome was about to take a strong hold of Anglo-Saxon England.

Augustine was no more than the worthy instrument of Gregory the Great. The impulse for the conversion of the 'Angles' into 'angels' came from Gregory in person. And, when Augustine and his fellow-missioners turned in despair back from their dangerous journey, he sent them on again with admonition and encouragement.

When Augustine landed in Thanet the Kingdom of Kent was 597
evidently not unprepared to receive the gospel. It was the most civilized of the English States and had the closest connexions with Christian France. The wife of King Ethelbert of Kent was herself a Christian Frank. Owing to the absence of deep attachment to the pagan religion which we have noticed above as characteristic of the Nordic world of that day, the Kings were often persuaded by their Christian wives to adopt the religion of the more civilized part of mankind, and their subjects seldom resisted the change.

Augustine did not convert England. He converted Kent, founded the see of Canterbury, and made it the solid base for the subsequent spread of Roman Christianity over the island. Outside Kent progress was at first slow. Augustine's claim to supremacy over all Christians in Britain by virtue of his Roman commission, was rejected by the Welsh clergy at a conference near the mouth of Severn where both parties lost their temper. Nearer home, the missionaries were, after some years, expelled from London, whose citizens now reappear in the page of history in a position partially independent of the small Saxon Kingdoms on either side of the lower Thames. The continued paganism of London was a chief reason why effect was never given to Gregory's plan to make London, and not Canterbury, the Metropolitan See.

The first striking success of Roman Christianity outside Kent was Paulinus' conversion of the great King Edwin of Northumbria, again through the agency of a Christian wife. As Edwin was ruling from the Humber to the Forth, and had vassal Kings in other parts of the island, it seemed for a moment that England was already half won for Christ.

But the missionaries had as yet no deep hold on opinion outside the Royal Court, and the fortunes of religion were for a generation to come subject to the wager of battle, and to the whims or deaths of rival Princes. For thirty critical years Northumbria was fighting to preserve its supremacy in the island from the rising power of Mercia, and these political wars affected the issue between Christ and Woden. Woden was favoured by King Penda of Mercia, while the champions of the Cross were Kings Edwin and Oswald of Northumbria, who both lost their lives fighting against him. Yet the ultimate triumph of Mercia did not prevent the triumph of Christianity. The struggle was not a war of religion. Penda did not persecute Christianity and passed no such laws against its practices as the Christians subsequently passed against the cult of Woden. Penda's allies against Northumbria were the Christian Welsh under their King Cadwallon, savage mountaineers who revenged the wrongs of their race on the Northumbrian Christians with a cruelty far exceeding that of the heathens of Mercia against their brother Saxons.

The political outcome of these wars was the decline of Northumbria and the rise of Mercia. In the course of the Seventh Century Mercia not only annexed the smaller Saxon States of Hwicce, Lindsey, and Middle Anglia, but claimed lordship over East Anglia and Essex and began to thrust Wessex to the south of the Thames, struggling to wrest from her the Chiltern district. The smaller Saxon Kingdoms were being swallowed up, and the battle for their reversion lay between Wessex and Mercia. Although the independence of Northumbria as a separate Kingdom was maintained until the coming of the Vikings, she retired from the struggle for political supremacy, but retained the leadership in art, letters, and religion throughout the period of Cuthbert and Bede. Not only the Lindisfarne gospels, but the Cross at Bewcastle and the 'Franks casket' in the British Museum testify to the prolonged vigour of Northumbrian art, when the South European tradition of representing the human form had enriched the beautiful scroll and design work of Celtic and Saxon native art.

It is remarkable that until the middle of the Seventh Century, power in Saxon England had lain in the North, which never again claimed the leadership until the industrial revolution made coal and iron more valuable than cornfields. Archaeological evidence suggests that the Anglo-Saxons were slow though sure in developing the agricultural wealth of the South; and until they had done so it was always possible for the warriors of the northern moorlands to establish an ephemeral supremacy. London, too, though in a measure independent of the neighbouring kingdoms, was yet of small account. It was only after the coming of the Danes that the City of London stepped into her destined place as the leader of England, the principal seat of wealth and power though not of Royalty.

The religious consequences of the wars against Penda had been the disappearance of Paulinus' Roman Christianity from Northumbria, and its replacement by the mission of Aidan from Iona at the invitation of King Oswald in 635. Aidan founded the monastery of Melrose whence the Lothians were evangelized, and the monastery of Lindisfarne on Holy Island, a site chosen in obvious imitation of Iona. At Lindisfarne, Aidan was Abbot and Bishop in one. The ascetic yet cheerful life of these ardent, lovable, unworldly apostles of the moorland, who tramped the heather all day to preach by the burnside at evening, won the hearts of the men of the North. Indeed, Christianity had never, since its earliest years, appeared in a more attractive guise.

Until the Seventh Century was more than half spent, the monks of the Church of Iona did quite as much as the men of Canterbury to convert the English race. They re-converted relapsed Northumbria and Essex, and evangelized Mercia. Some Irish hermits established huts as far south as still heathen Sussex. But want of organization rendered the durability of their work doubtful, so soon as the zeal of their successors should decline. Already in Bede's time the historian noted how great was the falling-off in the spirit of Northumbrian religion, how lax the life of the monasteries had become, how much less the clergy were respected than in the days of Aidan and his first disciples. But by that time the organization of Rome had triumphed throughout England, and good organization can survive periodic lapses of zeal.

The success of the Iona mission on English soil revived the disputes between the Celtic and Roman Churches, which Augustine and the Welsh had defined without solving at their abortive conference on the banks of Severn. So long as the Celtic Church had remained in Celtic territory, Rome could afford to overlook its remote existence. But when rivalry began for the possession of Saxon England, the issue could no longer be evaded. The men of Iona, like the Welsh, had a date for Easter different from the Roman; and their priest-monks shaved from ear to ear across the front of the head – possibly a reminiscence of Druidism – instead of making a round tonsure on the crown. These trivialities were the ostensible subjects of dispute and anathema. But behind lay far more important differences of spirit and organization, which in that epoch were involved in the question of submission to Rome.

Again the decisive event was brought about by a woman. The

wife of Oswy King of Northumbria undermined her husband's faith in the orthodoxy of the Church of Iona, whose champion he had been ever since the death of his brother Oswald. Oswy summoned the Synod of Whitby in 664, and gave his own judgement in favour of the claims of Rome as the inheritor of Peter's commission. The men of Iona, rejected in the house of their Northumbrian friends, could no longer maintain the struggle in England. Some, like St Cuthbert, accepted the new order of things, others retired back into the Celtic wilderness. In the course of generations, Scotland, Wales, and Ireland gradually came into line with the rest of Western Europe.

It cannot be denied that the decision of Whitby contained the seeds of all the trouble with Rome, down the ages to come. But men must live in and for their own epoch. The early adhesion of all the English Kingdoms to the Roman system of religion gave a great impetus to the movement towards racial unity, kingly and feudal power, systematic administration, legislation and taxation, and territorial as against tribal politics. The English, as we have seen, were already moving away from tribalism much more rapidly than the Celts; the choice at Whitby may have been prompted in part by a desire to get away from Celtic and tribal things, and to imitate the superior organization of the Frankish Kingdom, where the Roman municipal system had not been extinguished by the barbarian invaders. The new Roman hierarchy would be a susbstitute for Roman bureaucracy and for municipal life which the Anglo-Saxons in their wilder days had destroyed, and were beginning dimly to regret.

A greater centralization and unity of system and purpose in ecclesiastical affairs throughout all the English Kingdoms led the way towards political unity under a single King. The administration of the Church became the model for the administration of the Senate. Methods and habits of mind based on discipline, system, and the work of scribes were engendered in the life of the Church and spread thence to the secular world. And since the Churchmen, being the only learned men, were the chief advisers of the Crown and its first Secretariat, the new Roman ideas passed all the more easily from the sphere of the Church into the sphere of the State. Kingship gained new allies – men as skilled to serve with brain and pen, as the thegns with muscle and sword. Kingship gained also a new sanctity and a higher claim on the loyalty of the subject, through hallowing by the Church and by clerical theories of sovereignty drawn from recollections of the Roman Law. It was only after the Norman Conquest and the days of Hildebrand, that Church and King became rivals as well as allies.

Christian leaders of the new type, by becoming statesmen and great prelates, did England yeoman's service. But the change put them in no small danger of becoming hard-faced officials, territorialists greedy above all things of lands and power for the Church. The old spirit of the Iona mission – humble, ascetic, and full of brotherly love – had one last impersonation in Cuthbert of Lindisfarne, a convert to the Whitby decisions.

The man who organized the new hierarchy and brought all monastic and episcopal England under the dominion of Canterbury, was Theodore of Tarsus, Archbishop from 669–90. The first remarkable man among the successors of Augustine, he stands out as perhaps the greatest Prince of the Church in all English history. His career is the chief example of the value to England of her close relation to the Papacy of that day, which supplied the northern island with the best that the Mediterranean civilization still had to give. At a time when France and Germany were sunk in barbarous ignorance, the Pope sent us Theodore, a Greek of Tarsus in Asia Minor, who brought with him the African Hadrian as his lieutenant. Both men were adepts in the best Greek and Latin scholarship of Italy and the Levant. With the help of the Englishman, Benedict Biscop, they brought over from the Mediterranean good store of books, the indispensable but all too rare equipment of learning. Canterbury became a school not only of Latin but of Greek. The new influences from southern lands, combining with the liberal traditions of Celtic scholarship in the north of England, produced the school of Bede at Jarrow, and the library at York where Alcuin studied. Thence religious and secular learning migrated back to the continent and taught Latin literature to the Empire of Charlemagne, when the Danish invasions for a while extinguished the lamp of learning in the monasteries and libraries of Northumbria.

The intellectual life of Bede (673–735) covered the whole of the limited range of the learning of the Dark Ages. But we moderns value him most as the 'father of English history'. The first in the long roll of medieval chroniclers of our island, he told the tale of the Church of Iona in England and its rival of Canterbury, writing at a place and time in which the memory of both was still alive. He could not be unfair to the memory of Aidan and his disciples, deeply as he deplored their unorthodoxy, for he was a Northumbrian well knowing how and by whom his own people had been converted. His feelings towards the schismatics of Wales were much less tender.

The spread of the Roman influence over the island from Canterbury carried with it Church music, till then mainly confined to Kent. The Saxons took to it kindly and it greatly strengthened the hold of Christianity on the people. The triumph of Rome meant also the growth of ecclesiastical architecture. Aidan's 'Scottish' successors had been content with timber walls and roofs of reed even for their cathedral of Lindisfarne. But after Whitby the builders of the new regime aspired to give to their churches something of the grandeur and permanence of Rome. The roofless shells of Roman cities and villas with which England was then so thickly sprinkled, afforded ready-hewn quarries of squared stone, and were not without influence as models to the church builders of the Seventh and Eighth Centuries, who had also their memories of crypts and basilicas seen on pilgrimage in Italy or in Merovingian Gaul. After the era of Charlemagne, the influence of the romanesque Rhenish and German architecture became strong in the England that recovered from the Danish invasions. Most of the Saxon churches, including all the largest, were eventually pulled down to make way for Norman or Plantagenet successors. But this should not blind us to the fact that stone churches were being multiplied in Saxon England at a time when the laity still built their halls and cottages of wood.

The organization of the English Church was begun in 669 by Theodore of Tarsus as a man of sixty-eight, and was carried on by him for twenty years of vigorous old age. There was much opposition, and he beat it down. The essence of the reform was Theodore's creation of a sufficient number of Bishoprics, not of the roving missionary type of the Celtic Church, but with definite and mutual exclusive territorial sees, all subject to Canterbury. The monasteries were also subjected to the general ecclesiastical system; they continued indeed to grow in wealth and numbers, but they were no longer independent and no longer the sole agencies of the Church, as they had almost become in Celtic Christianity.

After Theodore's day, as a result of his preparation of the ground on episcopal lines, the parish system began slowly to grow out of the soil, first in one township, then in another. Before the Norman Conquest most of the island was supplied with parish churches and parish priests, men who were not monks, and who in Saxon times were often married.

Just as in the mundane sphere the great work of Anglo-Saxon

and Dane was to multiply townships in clearings made at the expense of the forest, so in the ecclesiastical sphere the work of the same pre-Norman period was to map out England in parishes, each with an endowed priest and a place of worship. The two movements together laid the foundations of the rural England we know. The parishes were often identical in area with the townships, in districts where the township was itself a large aggregate. But in North and West England we often find a number of townships in one parish, because the townships were mere hamlets or single farms.

The chief agents in the creation of the parish system were the Bishops and the thegns. The Bishops, no longer merely monastic in their outlook, encouraged the growth of the secular, that is the non-monastic, clergy, who were more subject than the monks to episcopal authority, and were spread abroad in direct and continual contact with the laity. The thegn or local magnate gave the land or endowment. In the first instance the priest was often the private chaplain attached to the thegn's hall, but in the course of time his successor became the parson of the parish. The heirs of the original lay benefactor naturally claimed control over his nomination, but the Bishop was effectively his commanding officer.

A very large proportion of the sites of the parish churches of rural England are of Saxon origin, though not much of the Saxon building has survived the active piety of subsequent generations. The essential life of Saxon England was village life, and the parish church and the graveyard around it became the centre of the village for most purposes, mundane as well as spiritual. As the worship of Woden and Thor gradually died out, or was suppressed as devil-worship by the intolerant laws dictated by the victorious clergy, the whole population found its dearest associations in life and in death gathered round the parish church.

The growth of the power and influence of the Church, spiritual and progressive on one side, was feudal and aristocratic on the other. But it is only modern thought that speaks of the two aspects as distinct. It was one and the same movement, and contemporaries saw nothing incongruous. Ecclesiastical dues enforced by heavy penalties, the tithe or tenth of the gross produce of the soil, were necessary to build up the medieval Church, with its art, architecture, leisure, learning, and civilization. Yet these dues were a burden on the farmer, and helped to reduce many freemen to poverty and serfage.

Anglo-Saxon Kings, first of Mercia and Wessex, then of all

England, at the instigation of their favourite prelates and to save their own souls, endowed Bishoprics and monasteries with a vast proportion of the soil. It was the clergy who first taught the Kings how to alienate lands and royal jurisdiction by written charters, for the benefit of feudal magnates both lay and clerical. It was the clergy who taught Anglo-Saxon proprietors how to make written wills, and wills often enriched the Church. The Church, in elaborating the legal and learned aspects of daily life, was thereby promoting the feudal system based on territorialism, the sharp distinction of classes, and the increasingly unequal distribution of wealth and freedom. 'Richly endowed churches mean a subjected peasantry,' writes Maitland. At the time of Domesday the 'four ministers, Worcester, Evesham, Pershore, and Westminster, were lords of seven-twelfths of Worcestershire.'

In Anglo-Saxon times, both before and after the Danish invasions, it is impossible always to distinguish clearly between Church and State. Not only did Bishops and clergy compose the principal part of the King's civil service, as remained the case throughout the Middle Ages, but before the Norman Conquest there were no separate Church Courts. The Bishop sat side by side with the Ealdorman or sheriff on the bench of the Shire Court, where spiritual and secular laws were indifferently administered. Those laws of the Anglo-Saxon Kings which the clergy first reduced to writing from popular oral tradition, are an example of this state of things. Written in the Anglo-Saxon language, but in the Latin alphabet of the clerical scribes, the laws have a dual character. They are, in part, a schedule of tribal custom, particularly as regards the price to be paid for injury to life and limb in the frequent barbarous quarrels of a primitive people: 'If one man slays another, 100 shillings wergeld,' 'if a bone is laid bare, three shillings,' 'if an ear is struck off, twelve shillings.' But the laws also register the high claims and privileges of the Church and her new jurisdiction over sin. All were enforced together in the Shire Court, at once a temporal and an ecclesiastical tribunal.

The political influence of the Church was inextricably involved with the religious awe in which it was held by Kings and people. When we read in the Anglo-Saxon Chronicle of powerful rulers of Mercia and Wessex abandoning their thrones to end their days as monks or as pilgrims to Rome, we cannot wonder at the vast alienation of land to the monasteries, or at the predominance in the courts of Offa of Mercia and Egbert of Wessex of the only class who knew how to read and write, who alone understood the administrative systems of the great Frankish monarchy oversea, and who, moreover, were the only people capable of instructing the King and his thegns in the formularies necessary to avoid eternal torment and attain eternal bliss.

Yet the Anglo-Saxon world was by no means entirely given over to the cultural and ethical ideas of Mediterranean Christianity. The majority of high-hearted Nordic warriors, though generally respectful to the clergy, had not forgotten their ancestors, and were moved by much the same ideals of conduct as before. Anglo-Saxon poetry, like much medieval and modern poetry, is sincerely Christian in form when religion is specifically mentioned, but is pagan in tradition and pure human in feeling. Only a few fragments of the wonderful Saxon epics have come down to us, and there is no reason to suppose these fragments were the best. The longest of them, the poem of *Beowulf*, though the matter of the tale is as childish as the tales told by Odysseus in the hall of Alcinöus, has something of Homer's dignity of feeling and of style.

The principal virtues praised in the Saxon epics were the loyalty of the warrior to his lord, the readiness of men to meet death in battle, the courage, courtesy, and magnanimity of the lord himself. For it is the poetry of the hall, sung before Kings and thegns. The typical hero of these poems is a man unrestrained by tribal custom or religious observance, a man to whom the love of adventure is the breath of life, generous but passionate – Achilles or Hector but scarcely Odysseus. In many respects the life resembles that of Homer's day. Each was a free Heroic Age, wherein the warrior chief played his part unshackled. Even when Christianity and territorial feudalism were beginning to lay new restraints on the individual, Anglo-Saxon society had in it much that was disordered, fierce, noble, and tragic.

CHAPTER V

The Second Nordic Invasion. Viking Settlement and Influence

THUS far had the first Nordic settlers in Britain advanced on the path of civilization and national unity when the second wave of Nordic invasion broke upon them in their turn. The heathen Danes and Norsemen destroyed for a while the higher civilization of the island collected in its monasteries, and for a while increased its disunion by establishing the Danelaw over against the areas ruled by Saxon and Celt. Yet before a hundred years were out, the Scandinavian invasions were seen to have greatly strengthened the forces of progress. For the Vikings were of a stock kindred to the Saxon, but even more full of energy, hardihood, and independence of character, and with no less aptitude for poetry and learning. They brought back to the island those seafaring habits which the Saxons had lost in their sojourn on up-country farms, and it was due to them that a vigorous town life revived in England for the first time since the departure of the Romans. Had it not been for the Scandinavian blood infused into our race by the catastrophies of the Ninth Century, less would have been heard in days to come of British maritime and commercial enterprise.

The deficiencies of the Anglo-Saxons, prior to this stern process of reinvigoration, were indeed many and great. They had so much forgotten their sea-craft that when Alfred sought to make a navy he sent for Frisian mercenaries. The Saxons had never developed town life, except to a slight extent in London. Their great economic service to Britain was their work as pioneer farmers and lumbermen, living in large townships or in isolated homesteads and 'dens' in the clearings they made in the forest. But the men of the township had little concern with what went on beyond the waste surrounding their lands, and regarded with suspicion every 'foreigner' from beyond it. 'If a man from afar or a foreigner,' say the dooms of Kent and Wessex, 'fares through the wood off the highway and neither hollas nor blows a horn, he shall be counted a thief and may be slain or put to ransom.'

Kings and Bishops were striving to create a national or at least a provincial patriotism, but with very limited success. Northumbria was isolated, decadent, torn by feuds which were to leave her an easy prey to the Dane. Mercia had held the leadership in the glorious reign of Offa (757–96). But Egbert of Wessex had broken Mercia's power at Ellandune (825), and established instead the supremacy of his own Kingdom. But Egbert was no more King of all the English than Offa before him. These successive 'bretwaldas' of the pre-Danish Heptarchy – Edwin of Northumbria, Penda and Offa of Mercia, Egbert of Wessex – had only the shadow of empire in Britain. Their supremacy depended on prestige which a single stricken field could make or mar. Machinery was lacking for the permanent subjugation of distant provinces. The victors of the hour had no garrisoned forts and no standing army in the vassal States. The King's personal following of thegns, however devoted, was not large; the 'fyrd' could only be called out for a few weeks, and the Saxon farmers had no desire to colonize other Saxon Kingdoms as conquerors, though they were still busy invading and settling new lands in Welsh territory beyond Exe and Severn.

In the hour of serious foreign invasion the English Kingdoms proved able to lay aside their feuds and help one another against the Vikings, more at any rate than the tribes of Ireland in like case. Nevertheless they fell one after the other without having evolved any coherent plan of national defence. The desire to be united in one State only came into being as a later consequence of the Danish wars, after Northumbria and Mercia had been destroyed by the heathen flood. Out of the stress of the same conflict arose new feudal and civic institutions which made Egbert's descendants more truly Kings of England than the founder of their line had ever aspired to be.

The course of history would have been very different had not the royal family of Wessex provided a long succession of able warriors and statesmen, including Alfred the Great. In the absence of elaborate institutions the affairs of a primitive society depend on the personal accident of the quality of its Kings. The richest and most populous part of old agricultural England – East Anglia – had failed in the race for leadership because it had no prince of the calibre of Edwin of Northumbria, Penda of Mercia, or Alfred of Wessex. The Danes soon found how safe it was to land on the shores of helpless East Anglia and thence to overrun decadent Northumbria and declining Mercia. Wessex, the State that lay farthest removed from the landing bases of the invaders, happened at that time to have more resisting power than any other of the kingdoms, thanks to Alfred and his brothers, and it was apparently owing to this accident of historical geography that the Vikings just failed to complete their conquest of England.

Would things have been very different in the end, or very much worse, if the Scandinavians had extended their power up to the borders of Cornwall and Wales in the Ninth Century, as they did in the Eleventh under Canute? The question is not easy to answer, if we assume that once the Danes were established in England they would in any case, like the conquerors of Normandy, have soon abandoned Woden for Christ. But the might-have-beens of history are only the shadows attending on the triumphant event. The event decreed that the work of reconstructing civilization after the Danish raids, and reconciling the two branches of the Nordic race in England, should fall in the first instance to Alfred the Great and his progeny.

Although 'Viking' means 'warrior' and not 'creek-man,' the Vikings were men of the creeks. Denmark was a land of sandy flats through which crept tortuous channels of the sea. Norway was a land of fiords – precipitous gorges in the mountain plateau, carrying the tide into the heart of the hills, in some places for a hundred miles. Here and there along the winding course of these fiords, a plot of fertile ground between the precipice and the estuary left room for cornfields and a group of wooden chalets. Hard by, a steep slope bore the dark forest down to the water's edge, inviting the lumberman and the shipbuilder. Above, on ledges of the fellside, among sounding streams and waterfalls, the cattle lowed on the summer pastures. High over all, the barren mountain ranges, the breeding ground of Norse legend and poetry, rose up towards glacier and snow-field, dividing the settlements on the fiords one from another each as a puny kingdom, delaying for centuries the political union of Norway, and thrusting the hardy inhabitants out to sea to seek food and fortune there.

Fur-traders, whalers, fishermen, merchants, pirates, yet all the while assiduous tillers of the soil, the Scandinavians had always been an amphibious people. Ever since they had occupied their present homeland at some undefinable date in the stone age, the sea had been their road from settlement to settlement and their only communication with the outer world. But till the end of the Eighth Century the area of their piracy had been chiefly confined to the shores of the Baltic. They had been content to prey on one another and on their nearest neighbours. It was only in the age of Charlemagne that they began to cross the ocean and attack the Christian lands of the West.

And so in the closing years of the Eighth Century, while Offa of Mercia was still alive, occurred the first recorded Viking raid in Western Europe. Three long-ships, with perhaps a couple of hundred rascals on board, landed somewhere on the peaceful coast of Wessex, killed the King's reeve who came to demand their business, and put to sea again before they could be caught. No more Vikings were seen in those parts for long years to come, but there followed in quick succession a series of similar raids on the coasts of Northumbria, Scotland, Ireland, and Wales. The water-thieves plundered the monasteries temptingly situated, after the manner of the Celtic Church, on islands and capes peculiarly exposed to attack from the sea. Lindisfarne, Iona, and many shrines of less name were robbed of their treasures, and the monks were either massacred or carried off to be bartered as slaves on the continent. The ill-guarded wealth of the shrines would fully account for these proceedings without our being forced to attribute to the pirates a fanatical hatred of Christianity provoked by Charlemagne's Saxon crusade. Nor was the gross cruelty of these raids anything exceptional. Even while they were in process the Anglo-Saxons were dealing out the same measure to one another. 'This year,' says the Chronicle for 796, 'Kenulf, King of the Mercians, laid waste Kent as far as the marshes, and took Pren, their king, and led him to Mercia and let his eyes be picked out and his hands cut off.'

These attacks on the monasteries of the British coastline seem to have been the beginning of the Viking movement. We can imagine the next stage with likelihood enough, if we shift the scene to Norway and Denmark. The successful raiders have returned, loaded with gold and gems. Along every fiord and estuary rumours run that the churches of the west are paved with gold, that there are no warships in the western seas, and that a new way has been found to get rich quick with a little lively adventure. It is added that some of the ploughlands out west seem richer even than those of Stavanger. The needy Earls' sons talk over the tidings at the ale-board and look around for leaders and followers.

Slowly, during the fifty years or more before the movement reached its height, all Norway and Denmark awoke to the truth that there was no sea-power to protect the British Islands or the famous Carolingian Empire; that the Anglo-Saxons and Franks were land-lubbers, and that the Irish for all their missions and colonizings used mere coracles and canoes. The world lay exposed to the sea power of the Vikings, a prey for their greed and a playground for their love of joyous adventure. Soon the young man who had not been out a-Viking was chaffed at the ale-board and scorned by the maidens, some of whom accompanied their men folk oversea and fought fully armed in the shield ring. War and plunder abroad became the chief national industry, absorbing the best energies of the rising generation. The last and most important stage was reached when permanent immigration and land settlement took the place of plundering raids.

The Scandinavians had always been traders as well as pirates in their dealings with one another in home waters, and so they remained in the larger field of foreign enterprise now open to them. They combined the pride of the merchant with the very different pride of the warrior, as few people have done. In a tomb in the Hebrides a pair of scales had been found buried in a Viking chief's tomb, alongside his sword and battle-axe. Their first thought when they founded a colony in England or Ireland was to build fortified towns and to open markets. By land or sea they were prepared to trade with the new-comer or to cut his throat according to circumstances or the humour of the hour. Such indeed, for centuries to come, was the custom of sailors from every port of medieval Europe, not excluding Chaucer's Shipman and some of the Elizabethan heroes. But the Vikings put an energy all their own into the practice both of piracy and trade, adding thereto great military qualities on land, unusual with Jack ashore.

As the Ninth Century wore on, a large part of the whole Scandinavian people had been a-Viking to the most various parts of the world. They carved their runes on the stone lion of the Piraeus that now keeps guard before the Arsenal at Venice. They were known to avenge in the streets of Constantinople blood feuds begun among themselves in Dublin. Their far journeys brought them wealth, civilization, and the knowledge of cities and men. The Saxon peasant, who regarded them as outer barbarians, was ignorant and provincial compared to them. Their Eddic poetry was succeeded by no less splendid prose Sagas, historical novels recording with extraordinary realism the romance of their heroic life.

There were three routes of Scandinavian activity in the Viking era. First there was the Eastern route, followed mainly by the Swedes, who penetrated the heart of the Slav territories, to Novgorod and Kiev; at Kiev they founded the original Russian State, and sailed thence down the Dnieper and crossed the Black Sea to annoy the walls of Constantinople itself.

The other two routes lay to the West. There was the route followed mainly by the Norsemen or men of Norway, which we may call the Outer Line. It led to the most adventurous sea-voyages, to the settlement of Iceland and Greenland and the discovery of North America. It led to the Orkneys, Caithness, Ross, Galloway, and Dumfries, where large Scandinavian colonies brought the first Nordic element into the life of Highland and South-western Scotland. The Isle of Man was occupied as the Malta of the new maritime power in the Irish Sea, which had become a Scandinavian lake. By this Outer Line important colonies of Norsemen were planted in Cumberland, Westmorland, Lancashire, Cheshire, and on the coast of South Wales.

Ireland was for a while overrun, and Dublin, Cork, Limerick, Wicklow, and Waterford were founded as Danish towns, the beginning of Irish city life.

Thirdly, there was the Inner Line, mainly followed by the Danes from Denmark. By that way attacks were delivered on the

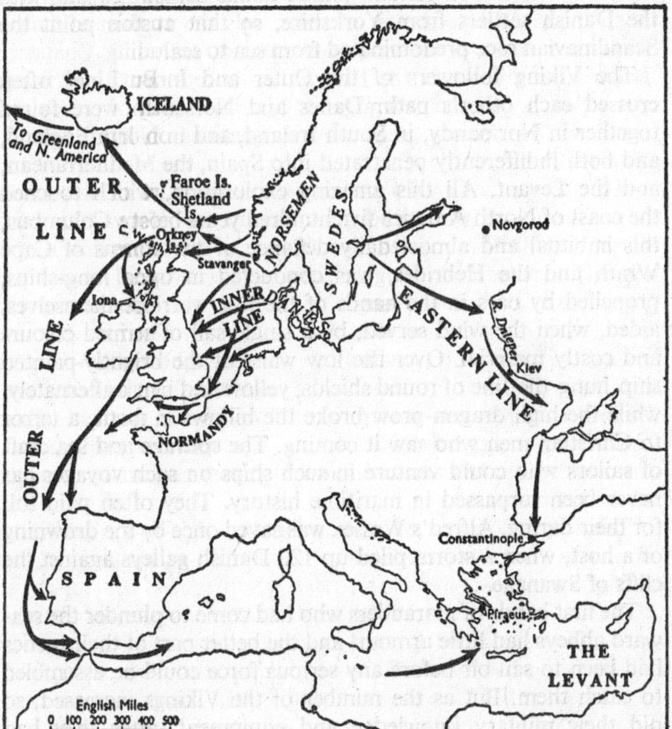

MAP V. VIKING ROUTES

north coast of Europe and the east and south coasts of England. That way went the largest hosts of Viking immigrants, in the days of Alfred of Wessex, seeking to win wide lands to plough and to rule. These great armies, composed of bands enlisted under many allied kinglets, learnt to obey a single war chief so long as the season's campaign lasted. The 'host' passed freely from France to England and back again, according as the resistance was stronger or weaker first on one side of the Channel, then on the other. Their mighty and protracted operations ended in the creation of two Danelaws, each of the first importance in history. The smaller one, which they carved out of the Frankish Kingdom, was named after them, Normandy; the larger Danelaw consisted of all eastern England between Thames and Tyne. Finally the Norse settlers in Lancashire and Cumberland joined hands across England with the Danish settlers from Yorkshire, so that at this point the Scandinavian race predominated from sea to sea.

The Viking followers of the Outer and Inner Lines often crossed each other's path. Danes and Norsemen were found together in Normandy, in South Ireland, and in North England, and both indifferently penetrated into Spain, the Mediterranean, and the Levant. All this amazing exploration, which touched the coast of North America five hundred years before Columbus, this habitual and almost daily defiance of the storms of Cape Wrath and the Hebrides, was conducted in open long-ships, propelled by oars in the hands of the free warriors themselves, aided, when the wind served, by a single sail of striped colours and costly material. Over the low waist of the brightly-painted ship hung the line of round shields, yellow and black alternately, while the high dragon-prow broke the billows in front, a terror to Christian men who saw it coming. The courage and sea craft of sailors who could venture in such ships on such voyages has never been surpassed in maritime history. They often paid toll for their daring. Alfred's Wessex was saved once by the drowning of a host, when a storm piled up 120 Danish galleys against the cliffs of Swanage.

The first bands of marauders who had come to plunder the seaward abbeys had little armour, and the better part of their tactics had been to sail off before any serious force could be assembled to catch them. But as the number of the Vikings increased, so did their military knowledge and equipment, after they had travelled and traded and fought in all the most civilized countries of Europe. Their fleets rose from three to forty, to a hundred or to three hundred and fifty ships, each ship carrying perhaps a hundred men. And in these great hosts body-armour had become the rule rather than the exception. The Vikings in their mail shirts were irresistible for the strength with which they swung the long two-handed battle-axe, the skill with which they used the bow, and the regular wedge formation in which the disciplined ships' crews were taught to fight on land. Siege craft with mangonel and mine was an art they learned to perfection. Meanwhile the Saxon peasants, called from the plough in their woollen shirts, had no weapon but shield and spear.

In mobility the odds were no less great. Until Alfred built a fleet, the Danes could move where they pleased by river and sea. And on land, when they had left the galleys behind a garrisoned stockade, they soon learned to 'horse' themselves from the breeding pastures of East Anglia. Thence, during the five terrible years that followed, the 'host' rode through the length and breadth of England, destroyed first Northumbria, then Mercia, 866–71
and finally invaded Wessex.

Until Alfred learnt to beat them at their own game, the strategy of the Danes lay in surprise attacks delivered on distant and unexpected points. It was impossible for the 'fyrd' of English farmers on their slow feet to catch up these galloping warriors, or to fight armoured men if they ever got near them. It is even doubtful how often the 'fyrd' or *levée-en-masse* of this primitive character was called out in Alfred's day. A dozen years after the first 'horsing' of the Danes, we read that Alfred with his forces 'rode' in pursuit of them. To hunt down and fight the invaders, Alfred was driven more and more to rely on his mounted and armoured thegns and their vassals, the class that specialized in war. When war becomes serious, it necessarily becomes professional, and requires changes that re-act upon the whole social system. The Danish wars meant another advance on the road to feudalism in England.

Thus both sides became mounted infantry, but not yet cavalry. Although Dane and Saxon rode to the battle-field, and fled or pursued on horseback, they had not acquired the art of fighting from the saddle. But those Vikings who had become the ruling classes in Normandy learnt the value of shock-tactics on horseback from the Frankish knights who opposed them on the banks of the Seine. In the fullness of time the Franco-Viking cavalry returned under William to the conquest of the Anglo-Danish infantry at Hastings.

Alfred the Great is naturally to be compared to Charlemagne, after whom it is possible that he modelled many of his doings. Each was the champion of Christ against the heathen, of the new feudal kingship against chaos. Each had many-sided talents as warrior, administrator, and scholar, suited to an epoch before professional men abound, when a king can himself teach, govern, and lead his subjects in peace and in war. If Alfred's lot was cast in narrower geographic limits than the Napoleonic arena of Charlemagne's activities, his work has lasted longer. He and his sons made England one for ever. The memory of Charlemagne does not suffice to unite Germany and France.

By temperament a scholar, and of ailing health, Alfred was forced into the field in early youth to lead the grimmest warfare of that terrible epoch. But harsh experience schooled without souring his gentle qualities. At the age of twenty-two he was second-in-command in the campaign of Ashdown and the eight other 'folk-fights' when Wessex was striving desperately to thrust the Danish host off the chalk ridges south of Thames; England north of the river had already submitted to the Danes. The young man at once won the confidence of the army, and when in the middle of that year of battles his elder brother died, he was chosen king by the Witan. His nephews were passed over, for minors were excluded by custom and necessity in days when a king's first business was to lead the folk to war.

878 Seven years later came the crisis of his life. The Danes, secure in the possession of North, Midlands, and East, at last overran Wessex by an unexpected raid at mid-winter. Alfred's subjects began to fly over sea. He himself with a small army of Somerset warriors held out in the island fastnesses of the Parret fenland. Fifty miles beyond lay the Cornwall of that day, where the Welsh enemies of Wessex were often in league with the Dane. On so narrow a thread hung the cause of English independence. But the Saxon thegns who had recently colonized Devon stood strongly for Alfred, and destroyed a Danish force that had been landed in his rear. Such was the confidence inspired by his leadership even in this desperate hour, that the thegns of conquered Wilts and Hampshire answered once more to his summons and rode to rejoin his banner. The battle of Ethandune reversed the whole situation, and the Danish leader, Guthrum, accepted terms, known as the Treaty of Wedmore, whereby he and his followers underwent baptism and agreed to retire into the 'Danelaw', leaving Wessex free.

Having found the resistance of South England stiffer than they had hoped, many of the 'host' transferred their operations to France. A few years later Alfred extracted from Guthrum a still more advantageous treaty defining the southern frontier of the Danelaw; it was to run along Watling Street and the Lea river from its source, leaving London to the English King.

878–900 Such was the political geography for the remainder of Alfred's reign. The Danes, on the way to becoming Christian, were settled as acknowledged masters of North-eastern England. All Saxon territory to south of them was united under Alfred. If his descendants should conquer the Danelaw, they would be the first Kings of England, for Mercia, East Anglia, and Northumbria had disappeared from the list of sovereign states.

Only the wreck of old Northumbria – Bernicia beyond Tyne – had not been conquered by the Vikings. This Saxon district between Tyne and Cheviot assumed the name of Northumberland and dragged on for many centuries a precarious existence between England and Scotland. But Saxondom between the Cheviots and the Forth, which now first began to be called Lothian, became increasingly involved in Scottish history, because the Danelaw cut it off from the main current of Saxon history to the south. At the same time the Norse invaders of the western sea cut the connexions between the Scots of Ireland and the Scots of Scotland. In these ways the Viking invasions drove Scotland in upon herself, and hammered her warring tribes into something a little more like union. It was in the Viking epoch that Kenneth MacAlpine became King of the united Picts and Scots. He moved the relics of St Columba and the centre of Scottish religion from Iona, with its backward glance over the sea at Ireland, to Dunkeld in the heart of his united kingdom.

After the Christening of Guthrum and the fixing of the limits of the Danelaw, Alfred's life entered a new and happier phase that lasted till his death. His position in southern England was relatively secure; the tide of events flowed with him now; he was regarded by all Saxons, both within and without the Danelaw, as their sole champion; even the christened Danes, constantly increasing in number, felt reverence for this English Charlemagne. There were indeed more Viking invasions from oversea, but the Danes of the Danelaw backed the newcomers half-heartedly, for they themselves were now settled men with farms and wives, fearing reprisal since they now had lands of their own to be raided. And Alfred, copying Danish methods, had rebuilt London as a walled and garrisoned town, held by English burghers, whose duty it was to defend it against attack; the chief gate of England was locked against the Danes.

In the intervals of these later and less terrible wars, Alfred enjoyed whole years of respite in which he could indulge in tasks very near to his heart. He began English prose literature by translating Bede's Latin into Anglo-Saxon, and by translating and compiling handbooks of theology, history, and geography for his subjects' use; and he initiated the keeping of the Anglo-Saxon

Chronicle, the first historical record ever composed in English. He fetched over foreign scholars, and welcomed learned refugees from Mercia and the North, in the hope of repairing, in Wessex at least, the desperate ravages of the Danish raids, which had swept away the libraries and learned men of the earlier England, and had left a clergy who no longer understood the Latin of the mass they sang. Alfred, moreover, founded the first 'public schools' for teaching letters to the sons of noblemen and thegns, extending for the first time the gifts of learning to some of the higher laity, so as to fit them for the tasks of modern administration.

The revival of letters and religion was slow and artificial, the gift of an industrious king to an ignorant clergy and people. It was no longer the glad, confident morning of Cuthbert, Bede, and Alcuin. Learning had indeed received a terrible blow in the sack of the Northumbrian and Mercian monasteries, but at least Alfred had set recovery afoot, and the new growth of city life due to the Danes would in the end do more for the higher civilization than monasticism at its best.

During the last twenty years of his reign, Alfred strengthened the institutions of Wessex both in peace and war. He created a fleet. He made an available army system, and put permanent garrisons into earthwork forts of the Danish type. He set up a sound administration worked through the shire and its officers. It was all very primitive, but better than anything there had been
900–24 before in England. Thus armed, his son, Edward the Elder, and his daughter, the lady Ethelfleda of Mercia, proceeded after his death to the reconquest of the Danelaw, which Edward's son and successor, Athelstan, completed. The Danes of the Danelaw had shown themselves deficient in political unity as soon as they settled down upon the land. A number of rival settlements, each under a ruler styled King or Earl according to fancy, had less cohesion than the English of the remodelled Kingdom of Wessex. The Vikings had been apt to unite for offensive warfare under temporary war chiefs, but the oneness of the 'host' that had trampled England under foot was not reflected in the political arrangements of the Danelaw, which therefore fell before the returning wave of Saxondom.

Edward the Elder and Athelstan are the first whom we can
959–75 justly describe as Kings of England. Edward's grandson Edgar, in a prosperous and peaceful reign, was clearly recognized as such. The Danelaw, after absorbing the other English kingdoms, had itself been absorbed by Wessex. Only Celtic Wales and Celtic Scotland were still independent, and even their kings

and princes sometimes acknowledged a vague supremacy in Athelstan and Edgar, who for their part regarded themselves as 'Emperors of Britain'.

A new unity had grown out of the cleaving and sundering of the Danish conquests. So long as the Viking battle-axe was crashing through the skulls of monks, and the English were nailing to their church-doors skins flayed off their Danish enemies, the hatred between Anglo-Saxon and Scandinavian was profound. But it was not permanent. In days before the printing-press, the memory of inter-racial wrongs and atrocities was not artificially fostered. Green earth forgets – when the school-master and the historian are not on the scene. And these two Nordic races were of kindred stock, with many instincts and customs in common. After the Danes had accepted baptism, it was easy to merge them with the English under the rule of the House of Wessex, for they had not come over to found a Scandinavian Empire, but to seek good farm lands. So far were they from enslaving their neighbours, that their Danelaw contained many freemen and no slaves, in sharp contrast to Wessex. Settled down prosperously in their new quarters, under their own Danish laws and Danish earls and lawmen, they could tolerate the light rule of English Kings.

There was now only one King, but for generations to come there was a rich variety of customs and 'laws' in the land. The Common Law – that is the law common to all England – was built up in Plantagenet times by the professional lawyers of the King's courts; but in Anglo-Saxon times there was no such body of men and no body of case law for the whole nation. Certain written laws were sometimes issued by the King with the help of his Bishops, perhaps for the guidance of all courts. But every Shire or Hundred Court and every court of private jurisdiction might also have its own customary local laws. The Danes clung strongly to their own, and the region of the 'Dane law' had its name thence.

Law, like many other good things, received a stimulus from the coming of the Danes. The very word 'law' is Danish, and has survived its rivals, the Anglo-Saxon word 'doom' and the Latin word 'lex'. The Scandinavians, when not on the Viking war-path, were a litigious people and loved to gather in the 'thing' to hear legal argument. They had no professional lawyers, but many of their farmer-warriors, like Njal the truth-teller, were learned in folk custom and its intricate judicial procedure. A Danish town in England often had, as its principal officers, twelve hereditary 'law men'. The Danes introduced the habit of making committees among the freemen in court, which perhaps made England favourable ground for the future growth of the jury system out of a Frankish custom introduced later by the Normans.

The Danelaw, during its brief period of independence as a confederation of Scandinavian communities, had been organized round the life of its towns. The Roman walls of Chester were repaired first by a Viking chief, and the commercial life of Chester and York was revived by Scandinavian enterprise. Roads were scarce but rivers were deep, and commerce was borne in barges to the wharves of inland towns. The famous 'five boroughs' of the Danes – Lincoln, Stamford, Leicester, Derby, and Nottingham – served both as military garrisons and as trading centres. Each was protected by a palisaded mound and ditch; each had its own 'law men', its own army and its own sovereign 'Jarl' or Earl. From the borough, the Earl and his army ruled a wide surrounding district. There is something analogous to Roman practice in the political importance of the Danish town, though it was purely Scandinavian in origin.

When Edward the Elder and his sister Ethelfleda of the Mercians set about conquering the Danelaw, they did it by imitating and taking over the Danish borough system. Alfred had set the example in London and elsewhere in Wessex, and his son and daughter spread the net of fortified English 'burhs' up the Severn valley and across the Midlands. They repaired the stone walls of ruined Roman cities, or piled up new earthworks round tactical points unguarded before. In each fortress they planted a permanent English garrison holding lands on burgage tenure, with the duty of defending the place. As fast as they conquered the Danelaw, they divided it into shires like those of Saxon Wessex; but each of the new shires was moulded round the administrative centre of some Danish borough, and its boundaries were probably those of the Danish military district attached thereto. Such is the origin of the shires of the east midlands – Lincoln, Derby, Nottingham, Leicester, Northampton, Huntingdon, Cambridge, Bedford. An ealdorman, with a shirereeve beside him to represent King and people, answered to the King for one or more of the old shires of Wessex, or of the new shires of recovered Mercia. But a Danish Earl answered to the English King for each shire of the annexed Danelaw.

The new English Kingdom was thus equipped with a garrison system and with organs of administration which had been wanting to the shadowy empires ruled over by Offa and Egbert. And so the familiar shape of modern England, with its famous shires and towns, comes out line by line under our eyes, as we watch the clouds drifting and lifting over the chaos of the Anglo-Danish wars. So much we can see even from far off, but if we could watch the Tenth Century map at closer quarters, we should see no less clearly one country village after another grow modestly into being along the newly drained river valleys and across the slowly diminishing area of forest.

Although the boroughs had been formed in the first instance to meet the military and administrative needs of both sides in the Danish wars, they soon took on a commercial character. The Danes were indefatigable traders, faring across the sea and claiming on their return to be 'thegn-right worthy' in their honourable character of overseas merchants, all the more if some of the goods they brought back had been won by hard knocks rather than by hard bargaining. The Saxons caught up some at least of their commercial ideas and habits. The special peace of the King protected the borough and all within it. And, when Edward the Elder published a law that all buying and selling must take place in a market-town before the town reeve, he aided the concentration of business in the new boroughs. The citizens were at once warriors, traders, and farmers of the adjoining lands. In days to come, their milder descendants might find it enough to be traders and farmers only, when the mounted Norman knight took over the fighting part of their business and retired proudly into his stone donjon overlooking the town. And when, after many centuries, specialization had been carried one step further, the citizens ceased to till the soil and confined themselves altogether to crafts and commerce.

Such, in one of its aspects, was the origin and development of the English town. But no English town has the same history as any other. And some of the larger stone-walled cities, particularly London, never completely submitted to the feudal world outside, but preserved down the ages an adequate military control of their own defence.

CHAPTER VI

Life in Later Saxon England. Feudalism Encroaching. Canute and the Nordic Maritime Empire

WAR, invasion, and bloodshed were normal conditions of life in Saxon England. Nor did the advantages of our island position begin to appear before the strong Norman Kings and their following had taken hold. So long as the sea was the highroad assistant to every invader, 'England bound in with the triumphant sea' was bound a helpless victim, and her ill-defended charms were as well known to the warrior races of Northern Europe as were Italy's to those of the South.

Nevertheless the slayers and marauders could not be everywhere in the island at once. The habitations of man were more secluded then than now, surrounded by marshland and forest; there were no maps to reveal their whereabouts and few roads to guide the spoiler to his prey. A story is told of times much more recent than the Danish raids, how Scottish moss-troopers failed for a whole day in their search for so important a place as Brinkburn Priory, amid the wooded dells of Coquet, until it was betrayed at the last moment by the sound of its own bells on the evening air. It is likely that, when the Danish 'host' was riding through a countryside, people in quiet parishes were chary of ringing their bells.

An Anglo-Saxon lived in some respects an enviable life, so long as he could avoid being 'hewed amain with swords mill-sharp' – the ending of most folk in his favourite poems. We too seldom ask ourselves what his life was like, because, while the life of the later Middle Ages and even of Roman antiquity presents itself to the eye and the imagination through the work of masonry, the Saxon period has vanished from the landscape; most pre-Conquest churches have been rebuilt, and the wooden chalets and halls where life was spent have left neither trace nor tradition, unless it be in the architecture of some of our fine old English barns. But those halls were great places in their day. Lowland Switzerland can still show us how noble and spacious a wooden structure can be, when it is the natural product of a native art tradition, with no limit to the building material on the spot, save the labour of cutting it down. The log halls of Saxon thegn and Danish jarl were decorated with carving and paint both outside and in, and hung with burnished armour, though the smoke eddying under the rafters in search of the hole in the roof diminished the sense of luxury. The thegn and his family were resplendent in cloaks of many colours. Articles of daily use were fantastically carved by native craftsmen. The art of the English jeweller was very fine, as the 'Alfred jewel' and others still remain to prove.

It was seldom that the thegn or his followers possessed any books, unless he were an assiduous courtier of King Alfred. But the bards every evening chanted their epics through the smoke drifts of the hall to an audience that loved noble and resonant language far more than their descendants of to-day. The form and colour of things seen and the sound of fine words were a greater part of the pleasures of life in that simple age than in our own more intellectual world.

Saxon and Dane each came of a thirsty race, and many an acre of barley went to fill the ale-horn. 'Yuletide' feastings, common to the earliest traditions of both races, and rehallowed as 'Christ Mass' by the Church, were as merry in the thegn's wooden hall as afterwards in the stone donjon of his Norman supplanter.

But in the main, life was an out-door affair for rich and poor, a constant hand-to-hand struggle of hardy folk with untamed nature. In the intervals of peace, when neither public war nor private blood-feud were disturbing the district, the thegn and his personal retainers laboured at spearing and netting the wolves and foxes, and keeping down the deer, hares, rabbits, and wild fowl, if the crops were to be saved and the larders well stocked with meat. Hunting was always a pleasure, but it was not then a sport. It was a duty, which, like the sterner duty of war, devolved more and more on the thegn and his attendants, as functions became more specialized. But every freeman could still hunt on his own land, and it is probable that many serfs and thralls suffered no rebuke in taking game off the limitless waste; some were employed for no other purpose. It was still a hard struggle for man collectively to make head against the forest and its denizens. The King of England did not yet 'love the tall stags as if he were their father' nor had the harsh code of the Royal Forest yet been imported from Normandy. Landlords were not yet tempted to strain their authority on behalf of game preservation, for the game could still preserve itself only too well. For ages still to come, a large proportion of the people's food consisted of wild game of all sorts, and the half-wild herds of swine in the forest. If Englishmen had been forced in the Tenth Century, as their more numerous descendants were for a while in the Nineteenth, to live chiefly on such grain as they could grow in the island, those primitive agriculturists would have been hard put to it to live at all.

What a place it must have been, that virgin woodland wilderness of all England, ever encroached on by innumerable peasant clearings, but still harbouring God's plenty of all manner of beautiful birds and beasts, and still rioting in a vast wealth of trees and flowers – treasures which modern man, careless of his best inheritance, has abolished and is still abolishing, as fast as new tools and methods of destruction can be invented, though even now the mere wrecks of old England still make a demi-paradise of the less inhabited parts of the island. We conjure up the memory of what we have lost in speaking of Robin Hood's Sherwood or Shakespeare's Arden, but it was older than Robin Hood and vaster than Arden. It was the land not merely of the outlaw and the poet but of the whole Anglo-Danish people. Had some of them at least the eyes to see the beauty in the midst of which they went about their daily tasks? When Chaucer and the late medieval ballad-makers at last found a tongue for the race, the first use to which they put it has recorded their joy in the birds and flowers, the woods and meadows. In Tudor times the popular songs of the day give the impression that the whole people has gone a-maying. Did not some such response to nature's loveliness move dimly in the hearts of the Saxon pioneers, when primrose, or bluebell, or willow-herb rushed out over the sward of the clearing they had made in the tall trees?

In certain respects the conditions of pioneer life in the shires of Saxon England and the Danelaw were not unlike those of North America and Australia in the Nineteenth Century – the lumberman with his axe, the log shanty in the clearing, the draught oxen, the horses to ride to the nearest farm five miles across the wilderness, the weapon ever laid close to hand beside the axe and the plough, the rough word and ready blow, and the good comradeship of the frontiersmen. And in Saxon England, as in later America, there were also the larger, older, and more settled townships, constantly catching up and assimilating the pioneers who had first started human life in some deep 'den' of the woodlands. Every one of the sleepy, leisurely gardenlike villages of rural England was once a pioneer settlement, an outpost of man planted and battled for in the midst of nature's primeval realm.

The work of colonization and deforestation in later Saxon England was carried on always under feudal leadership. The feudal lord was to the Anglo-Saxon pioneer what the State was to his remote descendant in America and Australia. In those early times 'the State' in the modern sense scarcely existed. A man looked to his lord for military protection, for justice or something more in court, and often for economic help as well; in return the lord restricted his freedom, became a large sharer in the profits of his labour, or claimed much of that labour for himself.

In the Anglo-Danish period the King's thegn, who is also the peasants' lord, is pre-eminently the armed warrior with helmet and chain shirt falling below the hips, the mounted infantryman in heavy armour on whom the King relies in case of invasion. The thegn devotes his life to hunting and war, and to the service of his own overlord – the King it may be, or else some Bishop or Abbot, or some greater thegn than himself. Personal loyalty rather than abstract patriotism inspires his service, and it is not always the King to whom the personal loyalty is most felt or exclusively owed. In succession to the Saxon thegn, the Norman knight, still more completely armed and trained to fight from the saddle, will stand just one step higher above his neighbours as a specialist in war, and therefore feudalism as a social system will reach its climax after the Norman Conquest. It will decline with the advent of longbow and gunpowder. For feudalism, though a system of law and land tenure, really depends for its spirit on the military superiority of an aristocracy in arms.

After the breakdown of the tribal and clan organization, and before the rise of the State, feudalism was the only method by which a helpless population could be protected, war efficiently conducted, colonization pushed forward, or agriculture carried on with increased profits. For it was a process of differentiating the functions of warrior and husbandman. The Anglo-Saxon ploughman was not only an unskilled but an unwilling soldier. He disliked being called out every few months. He wanted to be left alone in Cowstead or Nettleden to till the soil in which he had taken such strong root. He had forgotten the warlike desires of his ancestor who helped to sack the Roman villa hard by. His lord, the thegn in the high hall of the township, should protect him in local troubles; and the King and the assembled thegns should protect him in the day of national danger. The thegn, for his part, ceased to handle the plough and spent his time in war and talking about war, in hunting and talking about hunting, and in doing rough justice among his neighbours according to traditional law and custom. Already we have the embryo of the future squire and Justice of the Peace, except that the Anglo-Saxon prototype of the squire is pre-eminently a soldier.

So the ploughman ceased more and more to be a warrior, and the warrior ceased to be a ploughman. Differentiation of function led away from equality – away from liberty even. But it led to settled order, to civilization, to wealth, and finally in the course of centuries to a much fuller liberty for the individual than the freeman of a savage tribe can possibly enjoy.

During most of the Tenth Century the Viking movement was in abeyance. Emigration from the Baltic lands fell off, and the

Scandinavian colonists spent their time in building up towns, farms, and institutions in the lands which their fathers had won with the battle-axe. It was due to this ebb in the tide of invasion that Alfred's children had been able to effect a nominal reconquest of the Danelaw, on condition of leaving its Scandinavian character untouched. The era of Edgar and Dunstan followed as a brief period of peace and prosperity. And then, during the reign
978–1016 of the incompetent Ethelred the Redeless, the storm broke once more.

The Vikings were again on the war-path, and this time, under Sweyn Forkbeard, King of Denmark, they made South England the special object of their attack. Normandy and the English Danelaw, being under Scandinavian rule, they naturally spared, while their cousins in Yorkshire and East Anglia equally naturally did nothing to thwart them or to help the decadent Saxon King to save his Wessex. The unity of Saxon and Dane in the island was still incomplete, and the weakness of the new Kingdom of England stood revealed. The Danelaw has been called 'the rock on which the old English Nationality foundered'. Ethelred was indeed a weak and foolish King and his reign was one long disaster, but there were other than personal and accidental causes for the collapse of England before the renewed Danish invasions.

In the long wars that ensued before Canute won the throne, there are two features of special interest – the Danegeld and the part played by the city of London.

Danegeld had been levied and paid in Alfred's day, but in those primitive times the Danes had more often preferred to enrich themselves by direct plunder of place and person. Both sides were now rather more civilized, and the ransom in gold of the whole country became the more usual method of the latter-day Vikings. Nor does there seem to have been so much Danish demand for estates and land-settlement as in the time of Alfred. Many of the victors were content with enriching themselves out of the Danegeld, and spending the wealth so gained on houses and estates in Scandinavia. Historians are astonished at the sums paid to them in Danegeld, far exceeding what the same tax afterwards rendered to the Norman and Plantagenet exchequer, and out of all proportion to the rateable value of the land. No doubt the relative peace of the Tenth Century had enabled English thegns and churchmen to amass treasure and personal property of all kinds, especially the exquisite work of the English gold and silver smiths, which now went into the Danish melting-pot, as the plate and jewels of Renaissance England paid for the wars of Charles and Cromwell. Some of the vast ransom remained in England, being spent there by the freehanded and pleasure-loving Vikings, but much of it crossed the seas.

The sums extorted from the peasantry were ruinous, and hastened the decline of the freeholder into the serf. The Danegeld holds indeed a great place in our social, financial, and administrative history. Direct taxation began in this ignominious form. Under the weak Ethelred it was the normal way of buying off the Danes. Under the strong Canute it became a war tax for the defence of the realm. Under William the Conqueror its levy was regarded as so important a source of revenue that the first great inquisition into landed property was made with this end in view. Domesday Book was originally drawn up for the purpose of teaching the State how to levy Danegeld. The collection of this great national burden, originally entrusted to the township, passed into the hands of the lord of the manor. First Canute, and then still more definitely the Norman Kings, preferred to deal with a single man rather than with the local community, thereby subjecting each village more than ever to its lord. For the lord became the tax-farmer. And the man who answered financially for the land tended to become in the eyes of the State the owner of the land and the lord of all who lived on it.

The other remarkable feature of the renewed Danish wars is the part played by London. The city magnificently fulfilled the hopes entertained by Alfred a hundred years before, when he fortified and colonized London as the guardian of England's gate against the Danes. In Ethelred's reign her citizens were the heart of English resistance, far more than the inept and cowardly King. When at last he died, two years after his fierce Danish rival, Sweyn Forkbeard, there followed a brief struggle for the throne of England between the two young heroes, Edmund Ironside, son of Ethelred, and Canute, son of Sweyn. London was Edmund's rock of strength. But his death a few months later ended the war;
and the Saxon Witan, bowing to the necessities of the case, chose 1016
Canute as King. The proximity of the Danelaw on the flank of the contest in South England made the choice of the Danish candidate natural, and after Edmund's death inevitable. Owing to the qualities latent in the young Canute, it proved also fortunate beyond expectation.

The elective character of the English monarchy comes out more clearly at this epoch than at any other before or after. Canute, Harold, and William the Conqueror had none of them a valid legal title to the throne, save the choice of the Witan, or acknowledgement by the individual magnates of the realm. But such choice was enough to give legality to the results of conquest or the wishes of the nation. The Witan was not the origin of the later English Parliament, which grew up out of Anglo-Norman institutions. Nor was the Witan a popular or representative body. It was a haphazard assembly of Bishops, Earls, royal officials, and other magnates, who by no means always proved themselves as 'wise' as their name suggests. When once a new King was on the throne their power of controlling him depended on character and circumstance, rather than on any 'law of the constitution', for none such existed. But they had by custom the right to fill the throne vacated by death, and at the end of the Saxon period that power was being exercised with an extraordinary freedom: not merely the order of succession but the royal family itself was on more than one occasion changed. The idea of divine right of succession lodged in an individual and not capable of alteration by any human authority was, so far as English history is concerned, an invention of James I's over-busy brain.

The part played in the later Danish wars by London as an almost independent military and political power, is the more remarkable because her municipal rights were, nominally, meagre in the extreme. There was no Mayor or Alderman, and the port-reeve was a royal official. Instead of the democratic 'wards' of later London history, we find the City area divided into 'sokes' or private jurisdictions granted by the King to lay and clerical magnates. Municipal self-government was still in the future. As yet even the freedom-loving Danish towns were ruled by hereditary 'lawmen', and the other market towns and 'burhs' of England, scarcely yet distinguishable from rural villages or royal forts, were subject each to its lord, whether King or thegn, or, as often was the case, to a number of thegns.

But the real power, wealth, and independence of the port of London, alone of English cities, had far outrun her municipal status in the eye of law. The fact that Winchester rather than London was regarded as the official capital of the peripatetic monarchy gave to the great port on the Thames a measure of real political independence, and an attitude of external criticism towards the royal power; that spirit, kept in bounds by genuine loyalty and patriotism, continued to inspire London down the centuries until it culminated in the great doings of the Stuart epoch. Very different is the history of Paris, the dwelling-place of the Kings of France.

The accession of Canute, though so stoutly contested by the

Londoners, was a blessing for them in disguise. Commerce between his English and Baltic dominions grew very large, when piracy was put down on the North Sea and the ports on both sides were opened to mutual trade. The Danish merchants became the leading citizens in London, as they had long been in York and the towns of the Danelaw. In the Eleventh Century the Danish 'lithsmen' and 'butsecarles' of London took the lead in transmarine trade, in the naval defence of the island, and in disputes over the succession to the throne. Many of them at first were heathen, but St Clement Danes and dedications of City churches to St Olaf tell the tale of their conversion. 'Men of the Emperor', from Cologne and elsewhere, were also settled in London with their own trading establishments. London regained the place she had first acquired under the Romans as the chief emporium of North European commerce.

Canute, the son of Sweyn Forkbeard the old Viking, became an Emperor on the model of Charlemagne, and a King of England following in the footsteps of Alfred along the path of reconciliation and renewal. Having won Kingship over the English by force of 1016–36
arms, he put them on a real equality with the Danes, and was loved by all his subjects alike. His father had been a heathen more often and more genuinely than a Christian, and the boys had been brought up in the worship of Woden; yet Canute died in the odour of sanctity, a high favourite with monastic chroniclers. For he became a great benefactor of abbeys, and his laws enjoined the more rigorous payment of tithe and Church dues, the observance of Sunday, and the final suppression of the heathenism that lingered in parts of the Danelaw and still more among the newcomer Danes, whom he himself had led from oversea. The age of the Vikings was over at last; Canute, King of Denmark, Norway, England, and the Hebrides, had transmuted all that terrible energy into a beneficent Empire of the Nordic maritime peoples.

For the first few years after 1016 Canute was a foreign conqueror in England, holding his throne by the sword. But in 1020, after his return from a happy expedition oversea to secure his succession to the Danish throne, he adopted in England the policy of reconciling the two races on a basis of equality, and he began his famous alliance with the Church. In many vital respects his policy differed from that of the Norman who conquered England fifty years later. The Danish 'host' who had won the throne for Canute was paid off in Danegeld instead of in confiscated estates. Anglo-Saxon and Danish were in equal favour as languages in the garth of the King's House at Winchester, and Canute issued a collection of Anglo-Saxon laws. The Church in Canute's reign was governed chiefly by Anglo-Saxon churchmen, whom Canute took into high favour as civil servants at his Court; thence he promoted them to Bishoprics. Under his patronage churchmen from England went over to Norway and Denmark, and played an important part there in the prolonged struggle between Christian and pagan. There is no doubt that whereas William the Conqueror found the French clergy abler and better trained than the Saxon, Canute found the Saxon clergy less badly trained than the Scandinavian. But the whole attitude of the two Conquerors towards the leaders of the conquered English was as different as possible. Not only in the Church, but in the State and the army the Saxon thegns were trusted and used by the Danish King. The great Earldom of Wessex was governed by his favourite Saxon, Godwin, who now first rose to fame.

The supersession of Canute's work by the Norman Conquest within a generation of his death makes it very difficult to estimate either its importance or its excellence. If he had lived till sixty instead of dying at forty, he might have left a more permanent mark on the world's affairs. He was a great ruler of men, and he was on the way to found a Nordic Empire astride of the North Sea, with Scandinavia for one pillar and England for the other. Sea-power would have been its cement and its master-spirit. If he had succeeded he would have changed the history of the world. But the material difficulties of distance were too great for the rude appliances of that age. In the Eleventh Century it was as difficult to hold together an Empire astride of the North Sea, as it was difficult in the Eighteenth Century to hold together an Empire astride of the Atlantic. Indeed the connexion between Denmark, Norway, the Hebrides, and England was purely personal; they were each of them ruled by the same energetic man, but there was no Imperial machinery and no feeling of common patriotism. England herself had to be governed in four great Earldoms, and Norway was still very far from being a real political unit.

Canute's incapable Danish successors soon dissipated the
1042–66 loose confederation. Edward the Confessor, the restored Saxon monarch of independent England, looked no longer towards Scandinavia but towards French Normandy, and prepared the way for the Norman Conquest. Scandinavia and England, after being closely associated in hatred and in friendship for several centuries, drifted far apart, when England was drawn by the Normans into the orbit of France. Instead of remaining a mari-

time and Nordic State in touch with Scandinavia and only slightly connected with the main body of Europe, England became for many generations almost a part of French feudal civilization, engrossed either in her own island interests or in the continental ambitions of her French-speaking Kings. It is generally assumed that this change was quite inevitable and that on the whole more was gained than lost thereby. It may well be so. But the fact that Canute attempted a very different orientation for England is of profound interest, and though his Empire broke up, it was not without permanent effect, for it reinforced the Scandinavian and trading elements in the English nation.

CHAPTER VII

The Norman Conquest up to Hastings. 1042–1066

FROM the time of Alfred to the time of Canute, the influences that refashioned Britain had come from Scandinavia; for the next hundred years, dating from the accession of Edward the Confessor, they were to come from Normandy. The same is true in a less degree of European history as a whole.

The Norman aristocracy, Scandinavian by origin, retained all the Viking energy in colonization and in war, but had become converts to Latin culture. For that or other reasons the Normans were distinguished by a quality which the Scandinavians at home and in England lacked, the instinct for political unity and administrative consolidation. That instinct was the most valuable of the Conqueror's many gifts to England.

It was the Normans who turned back from Europe the tide of Scandinavian influence. The province which their Viking ancestors had carved out of France as another 'Danelaw' became the citadel whence the language, arms, and manners of French feudalism sallied forth to the conquest of the world, more particularly of Naples, Sicily, and the British Isles. Britain, not yet capable of becoming as in Shakespeare's day 'a world by itself', had oscillated for two hundred years between Scandinavia and continental Europe. Her position was at length rudely determined for her by the French-speaking Norman Duke. The battle of Hastings was not only a great English but a great European event. For, with Britain closed to Scandinavia and opened to France, the Vikings were locked up in their fiords, and ceased to threaten or attract Christendom. The mounted spearmen who conquered at Hastings imposed their 'chivalric' ideals and feudal relationships on the northern world, where the memory of Viking and thegn grew dim in the twilight of the past. Latin speech, literature, and religion reigned unchallenged, until many centuries later the secession of Britain upon new lines of her own again redressed the balance of North and South.

Yet we must not too closely identify Norman with Latin civilization. The culture that the Normans imported into England was indeed Franco-Italian – the culture of Taillefer, the French minstrel, and of Lanfranc and Anselm, the Italian Churchmen. But the monarchy brought over by the Normans was the monarchy of their own strong Dukes, not of the weak French Kings at Paris.

The Norman State was unique, and requires to be specially studied by searchers after the origins of things English. First founded by Danes and Norsemen, it had come to differ very widely from the districts similarly planted by the Vikings in Britain. It differed also from the rest of France. In Normandy the majority of the inhabitants were French peasants in origin and character, their backs patiently bent to the tillage of the soil. But the Scandinavian minority included the fishermen and merchants of the estuaries along the coast, and the feudal aristocracy of the land; these grandchildren of the fiord still had their faces turned seaward with unabated ancestral love of roving and adventure, although they had adopted the speech, religion, and customs of the French.

The jarl, in becoming a feudal baron, had learnt the new continental methods of war from the French enemies and allies whom he had met upon the Seine: instead of fighting on foot with the battle-axe of his fathers, he fought from the saddle with the spear and sword, and made his position in the country safe by piling up a high circular mound with a wooden fortress on the top, whence he could the more safely rule his peasants and defy his foes. Now heavily armed cavalry and private castles are the final flower of fully developed feudal society, and neither of them existed in England before the Normans brought them across the Channel.

Norman feudalism had become strictly territorial, after the French model. The barons of the province owed military service to the Duke on account of the lands they held from him, and not, as many thegns in England still owed service, on account of personal or national obligation. The barons were bound to ride under the Duke's banner in his constant wars against Anjou, Maine, or Brittany; each led his quota of five, ten, or thirty knights due from his barony, the quota being always, for purposes of military convenience, assessed in units of five knights. This system the Conqueror afterwards imposed upon England with a remarkable uniformity.

The knights in their turn held their lands from the barons by the same military tenure. The knight, if he held a 'knight's fee' of land, had to follow the banner of the baron from whom he held it, whenever the baron followed the Duke to the field or made war on his own account – such at least was the custom in Normandy.

This military service was due nominally for forty days in the year, but it was possible sometimes to exact it for rather longer in order to finish the campaign. A few weeks would serve for the private wars of baron against baron, or for the Duke's campaigns in Brittany and Anjou. But for a prolonged adventure like the conquest of England a voluntary long-service agreement had to be improvised, distinct from the feudal obligation. The period of military service due was wholly inadequate for distant enterprises; that is one of the chief reasons why feudalism broke down as communications improved. Feudalism had been originally devised for the defence of a countryside against Danish and other raids, and for the purposes of private war: it was not suited to the growth of great states or for the conduct of prolonged and extensive military operations.

From the top to the bottom of society the feudal relation of lord to man in Normandy was fixed, territorial, and heritable – passing from father to son. At the top was the Duke, under him the barons, under each of them the knights, and under all the peasants. The peasant was a serf bound to the soil and to his lord as owner of the soil. In Normandy neither peasant nor knight could transfer his vassalage at will to another lord, as many freeholders were still able to do in the less territorialized feudalism of Anglo-Danish England. Norman society was therefore less free than Scandinavian or even Anglo-Saxon, but it was more stable, and more efficienctly organized for peace and war.

Although in Normandy the social and military system was more strictly feudal than in Saxon England, the political system was less feudal, for the Duke had begun to impose on his barons an authority which the Kings of strictly feudal countries could never hope to wield. The feudal King of France claimed a vague suzerainty over the Norman Duke, but enjoyed no power in his territories, nor in any other province of France except in the small royal domain round Paris. On the other hand the Norman Duke was much more than feudal lord in his own remarkable Duchy. The traits of real monarchy in the Norman State were neither Scandinavian nor French in their character. They were peculiarly Norman. The Conqueror and his sons carried these monarchical peculiarities of their Duchy to the island soil, where they reinforced the English Kingship and developed it into that great medieval monarchy which had no parallel in France, Germany, or Spain.

In the first place there were no large baronies inside Norman territory, and no single baron was strong enough to defy the Duke with impunity. Government by great feudal Earldoms, which prevailed in the England of Edward the Confessor and in contemporary France, had no place in Normandy. The Norman Duke had real administrative officers of his own who exercised functions properly public, as distinct from the work of a bailiff of the Ducal domains. These officers were called *vicomtes*; they collected the Duke's revenues, commanded his troops, held his courts, and maintained his peace. The King of France had no such officers. The subsequent identification of the Norman *vicomte* with the old English sheriff greatly strengthened the position of the latter, and made the sheriffdom the chief pillar of the medieval English monarchy. Norman finance was the best in Europe and the Duke was proportionately powerful; he collected a revenue in hard money, while his suzerain King of France lived as best he could on rents paid in kind, moving round for his bed and board from farm to farm upon his domain. In Normandy no one besides the Duke dared to mint money. Private castles could be erected only by his licence, and were to be handed over on demand. Private war, though not yet illegal, was limited by the Ducal power.

It will therefore be seen that when England was invaded in 1066, she was being attacked not merely by a band of cosmopolitan adventurers enlisted for the nonce under a single war-chief – though that was one element in the affair; England was also being attacked by the most highly organized continental state of the day, which possessed peculiar institutions capable of rapid development in the free field of a vast and inchoate conquered territory. And even more important to England than the institutions of the Norman State were the habits of mind and action which the Norman Duke and his subjects brought over with them. William, before ever he invaded England, had fought and conquered his rebellious barons in Normandy. A bastard, called to his doubtful inheritance as a boy of eight, he had seen feudal anarchy at its worst, trampled it down, and taught men to obey.

Last but not least, the Church in Normandy was in league with the Ducal power. The later Dukes, zealous converts from Danish Woden to the French Christ, had restored and re-endowed the Abbeys and Bishoprics overthrown by their heathen ancestors. In return they appointed all the Bishops and most of the Abbots. The leaders of the Church were therefore servants of the Ducal policy. Some of them, indeed, were merely fighting barons dressed up as churchmen. The Conqueror's most powerful subject was his brutal and turbulent brother Odo, whom he had thrust into the Bishopric of Bayeux while still a boy. Odo led his own hundred and twenty knights to war, and since the Church objected to priests shedding blood with the sword, swung his mace in the thick of the mêlée at Hastings.

Other Norman prelates were of a higher type. In a land remote from the Italian centres of religion and learning, a land where barbarism might long have reigned undisturbed under heathen or Christian forms, there had grown up monasteries like that of Bec capable of attracting the greatest intellects of the day from beyond the Alps. Lanfranc of Pavia and Anselm of Aosta were successively Priors of Bec and Archbishops of Canterbury. No fact illustrates more clearly the cosmopolitan character of learning and religion in the Middle Ages, in striking contrast to the isolation in which most men had to pass their lives, bound never to leave their native village, either by their legal status as serfs or by want of means to travel. The physical and social barriers that impeded the communication of man with man were very great, but national barriers scarcely existed. Lanfranc and Anselm, from far Italy, brought the knowledge of Roman and Canon Law, and the latest theology and philosophy of the day, first to Normandy and thence to England. And few complained of them as 'foreigners'. Before the age of Universities, monasteries like Bec served as the chief centres of learning. Meanwhile architecture was already laying its massive and imperishable impress on the Norman landscape. Though the great age of stone castles was delayed till the Twelfth Century, the Norman Abbeys and Cathedrals that we know were already beginning to rise when the Conqueror sailed for England.

Yet although the Normans were ahead of barbarous Europe in certain respects which proved of the first importance in the future development of England, they were not what we should recognize as a civilized people. In spite of a few learned priests, the upper class were ignorant of the rudiments of letters; there were no lawyers and practically no professional men except the clergy; the luxury, art, commerce, and chivalry of the later Middle Ages had not yet come into existence, and nothing of that kind was to be found in the timber fortresses and occasional stone 'donjons' of this primitive baronage. The Normans were quite as inhumane as the Anglo-Saxons or Danes of contemporary England, and being more active and industrious they committed many more deeds of revolting cruelty. The lopping-off of hands and feet and the gouging out of eyes of prisoners and rebels, wholesale massacre of populations, and deliberate devastation of whole districts, were among the Norman methods of warfare, as England was soon to learn to her cost. The Norman, devoted servant of the Church as he had now become, had advanced little if at all beyond the heathen Viking in point of humane conduct. But in knowledge and organizing power he had advanced. The Church taught barbarians to organize society, and it was this better organization of society, even more than the precept and example of the Church herself, that eventually taught men to take the first halting steps in the direction of humanity and justice.

Although the Ducal power in Normandy, when transferred to England, would help to make the King's Peace supreme there, the Normandy of the Conqueror was an unquiet land, perpetually disturbed by private and public war, violence, and outrage of all kinds, like the typical feudal province of the Middle Ages. It is an error to suppose that the medieval world was safe and peaceful because its inhabitants were theoretically conscious of the unity of Christendom. It was indeed free from our modern dangers of race hatred and war organized on the national scale, for the low level of organization and transport prevented France and Germany from conceiving the idea of racial patriotism and making war on one another as nations; but they were both in a state of constant internal war between the petty feudal powers composing them, wars conducted with the utmost ferocity, although for purely personal motives. In the feudal world the hand of neighbour was perpetually raised against neighbour, and death, injustice, and outrage were the daily lot. But in the Norman Dukes' conception of their office there was that which looked distantly towards better conditions of life; if this conception could be realized in the ring fence of an island State, it might lead in the course of a few generations to a better society than the chaos of the ordinary medieval kingdom.

Meanwhile the inhabitants of England, left to themselves,

were making little or no progress towards a more united island or a stronger monarchy. The failure of Canute's sons to perpetuate his Nordic Maritime Empire or to govern England as a Danelaw, had resulted in the restoration of the House of Alfred in the person of Edward, whom after ages called the Confessor. He was the son of Ethelred the Redeless and of Emma, daughter of a former Duke of Normandy.

The return of the English line to the throne, though it put an end to the Scandinavian supremacy, failed to set the Anglo-Saxon nation again on the path of progress. If an Alfred or even a Harold had inherited the unchallenged throne at a juncture so favourable, something at least might have been done to unite and reform England without Norman interference. But the Confessor was, at heart, not an English King, but a French monk. He was entirely without political vision and almost without political ambition. What stirred his enthusiasm was the religious life as he had seen it lived among the new school of Norman clergy. He had spent among Norman monks his long years of exile, from boyhood to middle age, during the Danish rule in England. Norman by birth on his mother's side, he was at the moment of his restoration even less of an Englishman than Charles II when he landed at Dover. Edward spoke, and probably thought, in French. His role in English history was to prepare the way for the Norman Conquest, both by the little that he did and by the much that he left undone.

His only active policy was to introduce Normans into the high places of Church and State. He was prompted to show them favour not only by his personal tastes and friendships based on the experience of the best years of his life, but by the desire to find loyal and able adherents of his own to counterbalance the overpowering influence of Earl Godwin. Godwin had placed him on the throne, and like other kingmakers expected to act as Mayor of the Palace. Without his Normans, the King would have had neither the wit nor the strength of will to resist his too powerful subject.

Edward raised several Normans to be Bishops, and made one of them, Robert of Jumièges, Primate of England. A group of Sussex ports, the gateway of the continent, was placed in Norman hands. Herefordshire was entrusted to the Norman Earl Ralph; his wardship of the Welsh March, which this post implied, enabled him to introduce the Norman military system into that remote woodland shire, while some of his followers gave the inhabitants a foretaste of Norman violence and greed. Ralph and his knights built private castles, a novel portent on which the Saxon freemen looked askance, and he attempted in vain to teach the thegns to fight from the saddle in their contests with the Welsh tribesmen. The characteristic refusal of the English to learn the now indispensable art of cavalry fighting from Ralph or anyone else, sealed their doom in the Hastings campaign.

At court the Confessor's secretaries and chaplains were Normans. In the heart of London, the wine merchants of Rouen held a wharf of their own at the mouth of the Wall Brook. When therefore the Conqueror landed at Pevensey, he set foot on an island where for a quarter of a century there had been a Norman party in politics, and where Norman methods and customs were known, feared, and admired.

But what Edward left undone was even more important than what he did, in preparing the way for the Norman Conquest. In the first place he deliberately left behind him a disputed succession by his personal adherence to the monkish ideal of chastity, in spite of the fact that he went through the idle ceremony of marriage with Earl Godwin's daughter. Secondly, he never tried to unite the island administratively or to improve its laws and institutions. It would have been a hard task, impossible perhaps, for anyone but an armed conqueror to complete, but Edward never even attempted it.

The most serious bar to all national progress was the government of England in half a dozen great Earldoms, each presided over by a feudal magnate, instead of in single shires, each ruled by a royal official. It is true that the evil was no new thing in Edward's day, that England had never really been united since the departure of the Romans, and that a similar system prevailed in yet worse forms in Germany and France. But since England under the Confessor enjoyed more than twenty years of external peace, unassailed by Normandy or Scandinavia, a strong King would have used a respite so unusual to try at least to promote greater national unity, before the inevitable next onset of the foreign foe. But Edward's policy, so far as he can be said to have had any consistent plan besides the introduction of Normans, only served to encourage provincial feeling and to divide North from South. For he was fain to play off the power and the jealousy of the Northern Earls of Mercia and Northumbria against Wessex and the other Earldoms of the South presided over by the House of Godwin. The men of Wessex, of the Severn valley, and of Danelaw might each and all dislike the Normans, but they knew not one another and had no common loyalty. The appeal to unite in defence of England as a whole was never made to them in the Eleventh Century, because it would not have been understood. If it had been understood, a few thousand armoured cavalry would not have been able to conquer and share up England after Hastings.

Like the Third and Sixth Henries and other 'sore saints for the Crown', the Confessor left behind something that pleads with posterity against his political failures. Though Westminster Abbey was destined to be rebuilt once more in a greater age of architecture, it was Edward's endowments and buildings that prepared for Westminster the high place that it holds in ecclesiastical history and its supreme place in the political development of England. He moved the King's dwelling inside the walls of the City to a new Palace on the rural 'island of thorns' two miles up the river, in order to be near the great church that he was building there to St Peter, an operation on which his whole heart was set. Mighty consequences flowed from the royal flitting to Westminster. As time went on, the centre of government was inevitably drawn more and more from the old Wessex capital at Winchester to the area of London. And if the strong Norman Kings, like their Saxon predecessors, had lived actually inside London walls whenever they were in the neighbourhood, the political independence of the City would have been nipped in the bud. Yet the political independence enjoyed by the Londoners was to be the bulwark of the liberties of England in times to come, from the days of King John to the Stuart era. It was well, therefore, for British freedom that the great Plantagenet bureaucracy which grew up round the King's Palace struck root not in the City itself, but in Westminster; it was no far-seeing political philosophy that had fixed it there, but chance and Edward the Confessor's pious whim.

At the end of the Saxon period London was beginning again, for the first time since Roman days, to be a great centre of North European commerce. London was a whale among the fishes beside the other English boroughs. Within the circuit of its Roman walls, which five hundred years before had stood unrepaired and almost empty, the chief arteries of traffic and many of the narrow lanes were already laid out on the sites they occupy in 'the City' of to-day. The houses, indeed, were of wood, many of them mere market booths, and there was much open ground behind and around the buildings. But the busy, cosmopolitan character of the great port had already something about it prophetic of the future 'London'. Scandinavian, Fleming, German, and Norman all had their share in the place, but the East Anglian type prevailed among the common people. Close outside the walls spread the ploughlands and pastures of Moorfields, Smithfield, and other 'fields', growing food for the citizens, and loud with the noise of water-mills turned by streams flowing to the Thames. On the northern horizon lay wooded hills, where the lords of the London sokes and the merchant warriors of the City hawked after herons and hunted the stag, the boar, and the wild bull, in St John's Wood, in Hampstead, in Enfield Chase, and in the Hertfordshire forests beyond.

The death of the immaculate Edward left the succession to the throne in a fine confusion. The nearest heir was Edgar the Atheling, but he was a boy. If, indeed, the English State had been more highly organized, and if Englishmen had been more conscious of their nationality, they would have proclaimed the boy King and rallied round him against all comers. But as the world went then, there was great fear of anarchy if a minor should ascend the throne, especially one who had no strong connexions and no party of his own. It is small wonder that men turned rather to the tried ability and long established power of Harold, the son of the great Earl Godwin. He was, indeed, more distant from the royal line, but the blood of Scandinavian Kings was in his veins through his mother's side; and with all his experience, and his wide family estates in Southern England, he bade fair to defend and rule the land in troubled times better than the Atheling.

It may be that Harold would have done better if he had resisted the suggestions of vaulting ambition, and set himself as the guardian lion on the steps of the Atheling's throne. But his acceptance of the crown, even if ill-advised, cannot be stigmatized as a usurpation. England had never observed a strict law of hereditary succession; the passing over of minors was quite usual though not obligatory; the dying Confessor had named Harold his heir; and, above all, the Witan chose him King. But his weak title invited Scandinavia and Normandy to compete for the conquest of England – as probably they would have done even if the Atheling had been chosen in his stead, though scarcely if the Confessor had left a son. The autumn of 1066 saw England attacked by Harald Hardrada, King of Norway, and by William, Duke of Normandy, in two almost simultaneous invasions. It was the dramatic climax of the long competition between Scandinavia and Latin Europe for the prize of England. Harold might have repelled either enemy alone; he sank beneath the double attack, and the Norman, through luck and conduct, rose the only winner.

William's claims to the throne – if indeed we are willing to set aside the not altogether unimportant fact that he was a bastard – were genealogically better than Harold's, though worse than the Atheling's. But Harold had been chosen King by the Witan and William had not. William, however, won the sympathy of continental Christendom by certain arguments which appeal very little to modern minds, though they served conveniently to brand Harold for many centuries as a perjured usurper.

In that day of small feudal States, Normandy counted as a great European power, and its ruler was a statesman well versed in the intricacies of foreign politics. Like his namesake six centuries later, William prepared the way for his invasion of England by propaganda and diplomacy ably conducted in many distant countries, and by skilful settlements with his neighbours which rendered his homeland safe during his absence. Harold's case was unheard abroad and went by default. The French-speaking feudal world felt a glow of righteous enthusiasm for the bandits' league into which it entered under the great chief.

The armament that landed at Pevensey was not a feudal levy, though its members were strongly imbued with the feudal spirit and were to be rewarded by strictly feudal holdings in the conquered land. William had no power under feudal law to call out his vassals to a campaign which must last a great deal longer than forty days. But many of the barons and knights, not only of Normandy, but of Brittany, and of Flanders which owed him no allegiance, had voluntarily engaged themselves to serve under his flag. It was a joint-stock enterprise for the sharing out of the English lands. On much the same principle the conquest of Ireland in Cromwell's day – also regarded at the time as a great religious work – was carried through by military service to be paid in estates won from the conquered and by loans raised on the same speculative security. William and his confederates were at the expense of building a fleet of transports during the spring and summer of 1066, for it was essential to carry across not only the armoured men but the trained war-horses which gave them their chief hope of breaking the shield wall of Harold's famous house-carls.

It was a great armament, but its strength lay in its training and equipment rather than its size. In those days even officials were unable to count large numbers accurately, but modern historians reckon that at the highest figure the expedition did not exceed 12,000 men, of whom probably less than half were cavalry. It is certain that when England had been divided up among the conquerors, many of whom came over after Hastings, the total number of knights enfeoffed did not exceed 5000. That a country of a million and a half people should have been subdued, robbed, and permanently held down by so small a band, gives the measure of the political and military backwardness of the English system as compared to the Norman.

There was also an element of luck, decisive of the narrow margin by which William conquered at Hastings. For six weeks contrary winds had held him weatherbound in port. During that interim Harald Hardrada, King of Norway, landed with another great host to conquer England, and defeated Earls Edwin and Morcar and their local levies two miles from York. The English Harold had perforce to break up the armed watch he was keeping on the southern coast against the expected Norman armada, and hurry off to save the North. His housecarls, the finest mounted infantry in Europe, began their last admirable and tragic campaign by riding hot-spur to the gates of York, and fighting foot to foot against the great Viking host at Stamford Bridge until it was utterly destroyed. Three days later William landed at Pevensey.

Harold had removed from the Normans' path a most formidable opponent, and in doing so had reduced his own strength by many gallant warriors hewed down at Stamford Bridge. He and his housecarls rode back to London in four days, reaching it on 6 October. The battered forces of the North were following more slowly on foot; the fyrd of the South-West had not yet arrived. Rightly or wrongly Harold determined to give William battle at once in Sussex, with the thegns and fyrd of the South-Eastern counties alone, gathered round the strong nucleus of his remaining housecarls. Since infantry contending against cavalry must needs stand on the defensive, he defied William from a well-chosen position on an isolated spur of hill six miles north-west of Hastings; it stood on the southern edge of the great forest of Andredsweald from which the Saxon army had emerged. The hill, afterwards crowned by the village and Abbey of Battle, then bore no dwelling and no name, and was distinguished only by a forlorn feature on its skyline, 'the hoar apple tree'.

The storming of that hill proved a day's task almost beyond the power of the invaders, in spite of their great superiority in arms and tactics. The two hosts represented different developments of the old Nordic method ofwar, the outcome, respectively, of two different social and political systems. Norman knights and English housecarls wore indeed much the same defensive armour; the primitive shirt of ring-mail of their common ancestry had been lengthened into a garment of the same material ending in a divided skirt convenient for riders. Both sides wore the conical helmet and nose-piece then in fashion, and bore shields no longer round but in most cases of the new kite shape, long and tapering so as to protect the warrior's thigh when on horseback. Both armies contained also a number of unarmoured or half-armoured men with inferior weapons – the 'fyrd' of the neighbouring shires swelling the ranks of the Saxons in this particular. But here the similarity between the opponents ceased. The Anglo-Danes, leaving their horses in the rear, still fought on foot in the shield-ring, and still used the long Danish battle-axe, which Harold plied so manfully in his last fight. The Normans fought from the saddle, casting and thrusting with the spear and striking down with the sword. But even the shock tactics of their splendid cavalry proved unable to destroy the shield-wall on the top of the hill, without the aid of another arm. The Normans as warriors had not only learnt the new but remembered the old; they had learnt cavalry tactics from the French, but they had preserved the old Scandinavian practice of archery which the Anglo-Danes had neglected. Between the charges of horse Harold's infantry were exposed to the shafts of archers, inferior indeed to the future long-bowmen of Crécy, but superior to any who drew bow for England that day. Infantry with only striking weapons fight at desperate odds against cavalry supported by missiles. At Waterloo the English squares had missile weapons on their side against the French cuirassiers; it was otherwise at Hastings.

When night fell, Harold and all his housecarls around him were lying dead in their ranks on the hill-top, like the Scots round their King at Flodden; and the surviving warriors of the 'fyrd', battle-scarred and sick at heart, were trailing to their distant homes in every direction along the darkening tracks of the Andred-sweald.

CHAPTER VIII

The Norman Conquest Completed and Norman Institutions Established. 1066–1135

Kings: William I, 1066–87; William II, 1087–1100; Henry I, 1100–35

THE shock of the battle of Hastings would have rallied the forces of a well-organized feudal kingdom, and stirred the patriotic resistance of a nation. It had no such effect in the Anglo-

Danish realm. Earls, thegns, Bishops, sheriffs, boroughs thought only of making their private peace with the Conqueror. Even Stigand, the foremost man in Harold's party, and the special object of aversion to the Pope's Norman allies, vainly sought to retain the throne of Canterbury by an immediate submission, made while William was in the act of crossing the Thames at Wallingford. Edwin and Morcar had come south too slowly to help Harold at Hastings – whether from treachery, slackness, or unavoidable delay no one will ever know. They now slunk back to the North, leaving Southern England to make the best of the situation. Probably they reckoned that, whoever wore the crown in Wessex and on the banks of Thames, they themselves would continue to enjoy virtual independence as Earls of Mercia and Northumbria. But it was not so that William conceived of the Kingship he had won.

South England meanwhile offered little resistance. Winchester, the old Wessex capital, led the way in submission. As to London, William had not force enough to be sure of taking it by storm, and he desired to enter it in peaceful guise as Edward's acknowledged heir. He began therefore to make a wide circuit round the city to west and north, destroying as he went the villages of Buckinghamshire and Hertfordshire to hasten the surrender of the English. The policy was successful. London, after a few weeks' hesitation and a futile proclamation of Edgar Atheling as King, sent to acknowledge William and invite him to his coronation at Westminster.

There, on Christmas Day, 1066, he was crowned as lawful heir of the Confessor, while his followers, on a false alarm of treachery, were setting fire to the houses of the English outside. The noise of strife and outrage interrupted the service, and all save William and the officiating priests rushed out of the Minster to take part. Here were grim realities, in dramatic contrast to William's theory of a lawful and natural passage of the Crown. The claim to be heir to the Confessor and guardian of his 'good laws' thinly covered over the brute facts of conquest, and seemed of little avail to protect the country against French robbery and violence. Nevertheless, in the days of the Conqueror and his sons after him, the occasional alliance of the Norman King with his Saxon subjects against rebellious members of the Franco-Norman baronage, and the revival and strengthening of the fyrd and the shire-court, gave importance to the constitutional formula on which William had based his claim to the throne of England.

In the first critical months after Hastings, when the English let slip the opportunity of united resistance, many of them hoped by submission to suffer no more loss of lands and liberties than they had suffered under the foreign rule of Canute and his men from Denmark. They were soon undeceived. On the ground that everyone who had acknowledged the usurper Harold had forfeited all his possessions, the confiscation of Saxon estates for the benefit of the foreign conquerors began directly after the battle, and went on year after year as rebellions or other less good reasons gave excuse.

Nor was the yoke of Norman King or Norman baron like the easy yoke of Canute and his Earls. The new monarchy and the new feudalism were riveted on the land by the new military system. Everywhere huge circular mounds, like those still visible at Lewes and in a hundred other places throughout the land, were piled up by the forced labour of Saxon peasants, and crowned by royal or private fortresses first of timber and ultimately of stone. In front of the mound there was an outer court, called a 'bailey', protected by an earthwork enclosure. From these impregnable citadels the armoured horsemen issued forth to dominate the countryside, sometimes in the interest of order, sometimes on errands of plunder and misrule. The Londoners saw with alarm the royal masonry of the Tower donjon gradually overtopping the eastern walls of their city, and curbing though not destroying their cherished independence.

After a successful campaign in the South-west, where the power and estates of the House of Godwin had chiefly been concentrated, William by the end of 1068 was true lord of Southern England, and in the North was at least acknowledged as King. But only a portion of the landed estates of the country had as yet changed hands; in particular, Mercia and Northumbria were very much as they had been before Hastings. The *status quo* in the North would have lasted longer, had the two Earls, Edwin and Morcar, remained passively loyal. But they rebelled, were suppressed and pardoned, and then rebelled again. Their second rising 1069 was rendered formidable by the help it received from another Viking invasion, led by the sons of the King of Denmark. In Mercia the wild Welsh poured across Offa's dyke to aid the war against Norman rule.

Such was the occasion of William's great campaign in the North and of his cruel vengeance. Between York and Durham he left no house standing and no human beings alive that his horsemen could search out. As Domesday testifies, many scores of villages were still without inhabitant seventeen years later. Most of the North Riding and much of the East Riding of Yorkshire were depopulated by massacre. In County Durham the houses and cattle were destroyed, but the inhabitants had warning and escaped across the Tyne. Many sold themselves as slaves, not a few in the Lothian district of Scotland which thus obtained a strong infusion of Scandinavian blood. Devastation and massacre were let loose in more spasmodic fashion in Cheshire and the midland shires. The wooden hovels of that day could be rebuilt from the neighbouring forests more easily than houses in civilized times, but the loss in men, cattle, and farm utensils could be less easily repaired. The 'harrying of the North' was a vengeance Turkish in its atrocity, but fully in accord with the ideas and practice of the most zealously Christian warriors in medieval Europe.

This foul deed served its purpose. There could be no more rebellions after such wholesale destruction. It decided the question whether William and a few thousand armoured knights could conquer all England and coerce her inhabitants into a new manner of life. It put an end to the age-old separatism of Northern England and of the Danelaw in opposition to the kingship seated in Wessex and London. And it broke the resistance of Scandinavian society to Norman feudalism. The Durham Castle and Cathedral that we know rose as the symbol of a new Latin civilization, superimposed on these wild Nordic lands by a foreign soldiery and clergy: the splendid architecture that crowns the rock, much of it raised within one generation of the 'harrying of the North', in a region that had been poor and barbarous to a degree even before that terrible catastrophe, bears witness to the energy of the French-speaking rulers, builders, and churchmen, the handful of men whom William's Conquest sent to govern and transform those distant regions.

Not only the lands north of Humber, but Lincolnshire and East Anglia, the richest agricultural districts in England, received the new civilization, but at a heavy price in human freedom. The freemen of the Danelaw had hitherto kept at arm's length even the Anglo-Saxon forms of feudalism. Many of them could 'go with their land' to what lord they would, and some villages had no lord at all. The proportion of freemen was much greater in the Danish and Norse districts than elsewhere in England. But the Normans put an end to these old-fashioned liberties, and imposed the French system of strictly territorial feudalism on the Scandinavian North and East as well as on the Saxon South and West. The Danish freeman in most cases sank into the villein of the manor. Yet in prosperous Lincolnshire some of the villeins remained well-to-do and in certain legal aspects free men.

'The harrying of the North' diminished the number of Danes in England and especially in Yorkshire. But it appears that, as time went on, the Norsemen who had settled so thickly on the Western coast in Cumberland and Lancashire moved eastward into the depopulated regions, so that the actual acreage of Scandinavian occupation in England was perhaps not greatly reduced in the end. But Scandinavian ideals and civilization gave way to Norman. The North England of the Middle Ages, with its great families of Umfraville and Percy, its great Yorkshire Abbeys and its Palatinate of Durham, was a land very completely feudalized and Normanized in its governing class.

The same influences, by peaceful penetration across the Border in the reign of King David of Scotland, laid the impress of Norman 1124–53 ruling families on Scottish society and religion. The Bruces and Balliols, Melrose and Holyrood, were but a further extension of the Norman Conquest. South England, indeed, owing to more rapid economic progress, moved out of the feudal age in Tudor times more quickly than the northern part of the island. Yet the North, completely feudalized as it became and long remained in its social forms, retained the old Nordic temper of independent manhood all the while, underneath the feudal form of its society. The peasant of Scotland and North England, however much bound by law and attached by affection to his lord, seems to have suffered less degradation of spirit than the peasant of the Saxon South from the long centuries of feudal subjection.

The military drama of the conquest closed with the vast siege operations conducted by William against the Isle of Ely defended by Hereward. Hereward was a man of the fenland district, with a 1070–1 genius for amphibious guerrilla warfare in that difficult country. But his resistance only began after the rest of England had been conquered, and the event was therefore never in doubt. It was but the last and noblest of a series of regional revolts undertaken too late. There had been no general movement of patriotism, no Wallace or Joan of Arc. England was still a geographical expression, an aggregation of races, regions, and private jurisdictions. She still needed to be hammered into a nation, and she had now found masters who would do it.

The fact that England had been conquered piecemeal, as a result of a series of spasmodic local rebellions, gave William an excuse for depriving English landlords of their lands, and glutting his followers, lay and clerical, with feudal baronies, till every shire was divided up into knights' fees held by French-speaking knights from French-speaking Barons and Prelates, who in their turn held of the King.

The gradual character of the conquest and of the confiscation, which had moved step by step across England during a number of years, was one cause of a peculiarity in English feudalism: each individual Baron held lands in many parts of the country; his estates were not gathered in a single province as was frequently the case on the continent. Because the possessions of the typical Norman magnate in England were scattered far and wide, the royal power remained stronger than that of any single subject within the boundaries of the shire. It was therefore possible to govern it through the sheriff, a man usually of baronial rank, but removable by the King, and acting solely as his officer. The old English 'shire-reeve' was henceforth identified with the Norman *vicomte*, and the old English 'shire' was also known by the foreign title of 'County'. The sheriffdom reached its moment of greatest political power as the instrument of the Norman Kings, alike against Saxon and French-speaking malcontents.

To make way for direct royal government in each shire, William deliberately broke up the half-dozen great Earldoms into which later Saxon England had been divided for purposes of administration. First Wessex disappeared with the House of Godwin, and has never again been a unit except in Hardy's novels. Mercia and Northumbria vanished no less completely on the fall of Edwin and Morcar after their second rebellion. East Anglia was preserved for a while under a Norman Earl, but was resolved back into its component shires after the Norman Earl had himself risen in revolt against the Crown. When William Rufus died, there remained only three counties governed otherwise than by the King's officers – the hereditary Earldoms Palatine of Chester and Shrewsbury, and the County Palatine of Durham, governed by its Prince Bishop, the secular and spiritual lord of the Border. Such as they were, these exceptions were tolerated by the Norman Kings only to keep the military guard strong against Welsh and Scots.

Outside the Counties Palatine, William the Conqueror governed England by a dual system: indirectly through the feudal contract with his vassals, and directly through sheriffs and through special commissioners like those who made the Domesday survey. Those perambulating inquisitors recalled the *missi* of Charlemagne's Empire, and foreshadowed the Justices in Eyre and the Justices of Assize. There had been nothing like them in Saxon England. He would have been a bold servant of the Saxon

Crown who had set out to enquire through the sheriffs and the good men of the townships into the affairs of Godwin's Wessex or Edwin's Mercia.

The French-speaking Barons had hoped to obtain in England the privileges usually enjoyed by their caste upon the Continent. Some of these men turned with fury upon William when they realized the restrictions he was laying upon their power. In the last dozen years of his reign he was frequently called upon to suppress their turbulence, with the help not only of the loyal members of their order, but of the conquered English themselves. Racial feeling was in those days little developed, and the Saxons had been schooled to suffer the tyranny of the strong even under their native rulers. The wrongs done by the French conquest were therefore soon forgotten, enough at least to permit of the combination of the disinherited English with William himself. Yet the great King had done them wrongs such as Irishmen never forgave to England in later and more sophisticated times.

The Barons' rising of 1075 and its suppression by the King shows that the Norman Conquest proper was already complete. The robbers could afford to fall out over the spoil, and to make appeal to their victim. The subsequent rivalry in arms of William's sons for the succession, compelled Henry I to appeal to the favour of his subjects irrespective of race and rank. Charters of liberties, general and particular, were the price by which the Kingship was purchased; and the special importance of London, as a makeweight in the balance of these disputes for the succession, removed any inclination that the Norman Kings might otherwise have felt to tamper with the privileges of the City.

The Conqueror, while establishing a rigorously feudal system of land tenure, had successfully prevented England from falling into the anarchy of political feudalism prevalent on the continent. And he had cleared the ground for the gradual development of a great monarchical bureaucracy. But he did not enjoy unlimited despotic power, nor by right did anyone who ever succeeded him on the throne of England. William was doubly bound by law – by the old Saxon laws which he had ostentatiously sworn to observe, and by the feudal customs of continental Europe to which his followers from oversea were one and all devoted. It was from the marriage of these two systems that in the course of long centuries the laws and liberties of modern England were evolved. The concentration of power in a single person 'carrying the laws in his own breast' was opposed to the medieval spirit, at least in secular affairs. The omnicompetence of the modern State, the omnipotence of the monarch who says '*L'état c'est moi*,' would both have been alien to the medieval mind, which conceived of public law as a mosaic of inalienable private and corporate rights. Between the King and the baronage stood the Church, who satisfied her interest and her moral sense alike by holding the balance between the two secular forces. Again and again, from the days of Lanfranc through Langton to Grossetête, we find the Church justly maintaining the balance of the constitution; lay tyranny and lay anarchy were alike unwelcome to her, and therein she was able to speak for the dumb multitudes of the common people, in matters where her own privileges were not too directly involved to bias her judgement.

In the medieval State anarchy was a greater danger than despotism, though the opposite was the case in the medieval Church. The medieval State was a 'mixed polity' of King, Barons, and Prelates. The relation between lord and man, which was the essence of feudal politics, was based on mutual obligation. A breach of contract on either side involved penalties, and as law was ill-defined and ill-administered, resort was continually had to war to decide points of feudal right. Non-resistance to the Lord's Anointed was opposed to the central current of thought and practice of the Middle Ages. In the mutual obligations of feudalism lay the historical reality of that 'original contract between King and people' long afterwards proclaimed by the Whig philosophers in reaction against the Renaissance despots.

It was at once the privilege and the duty of a feudal King to consult his tenants-in-chief – that is the men who held land from him direct. It was at once the privilege and the duty of the tenant-in-chief to give advice to his lord the King. From this arose the royal *consilium* or *curia* common to all feudal states. Such was the 'Council' or 'Court' of William. The Witan, though not in the strict sense feudal, had been a somewhat similar body, but the strong and self-willed Norman monarchs were less governed by their vassals in Council than the Saxon Kings had been by the magnates of the Witan.

In Norman times the words *consilium* and *curia* were two words used indifferently for the general body of the advisers of the Crown, not yet divided up into administrative, judicial, and legislative organs such as Privy Council, King's Bench, and Parliament. Indeed no distinction was made in the minds of even the subtlest clerks between administrative, judicial, and legislative acts. The King consulted whatever members of his 'Court' or

'Council' happened to be with him, on the question of the moment whatever its character. He appointed Committees and sent Commissioners down to the shires for this purpose or that, according to the apparent need of the hour, without being guided by rules. As yet there were no bodies, like the House of Lords or the Court of Common Pleas, consisting of definite persons, with a right and duty to meet periodically for special purposes with a fixed procedure. This very vagueness gave an able King immense power, but he needed it all to bring any semblance of order out of the chaos of the Anglo-Norman State. But the theoretical obligation under which the King lay to consult his tenants-in-chief, however little defined by law, and however irregularly observed in practice, was never denied, and it was the seed out of which the liberties of England grew in the constitutional struggles of the Plantagenet epoch.

The greatest of the inquests carried through by the power of the King was the Domesday Survey of 1086. Its text is the surest proof we have of the obedience to which that 'stark' man, the Conqueror, had reduced Norman, Saxon, and Celt, from remote Cornish 'trevs' hidden away in woodland creeks of the sea, to the charred townships and wasted dales of Yorkshire. No such uniform set of answers to an unpopular inquest could have been wrung from any equally large district on the continent, nor again from England herself until the days of Henry II's bureaucracy. 'So narrowly did he cause the survey to be made,' moans the Saxon chronicler, 'that there was not one single hide nor rood of land, nor – it is shameful to tell but he thought it no shame to do – was there an ox, cow, or swine that was not set down in the writ.'

Domesday is primarily a 'geld book', that is a collection of facts made for a fiscal purpose, the proper collection of the Danegeld. But although all the questions asked and answered may have helped the collection of the geld, it is going too far to say that William the Conqueror could have had no further end in view. The final form in which Domesday Book itself was laboriously recast out of the original returns, points to other objects and ideas besides the Danegeld. The Book presents to the King – as lord paramount of the feudal system, from whom henceforth every acre in the realm is held – an exact account of the power and resources of his feudatories and of their vassals in every shire. The government was engaged in supplementing the Saxon scheme of local administration by a network of new feudal bodies for military, fiscal, judicial, and police purposes. Therefore – although the original evidence for Domesday was taken by the Commissioners from sworn juries consisting of the priest, the reeve, and six villeins of each township – the form in which the returns were rearranged grouped every township or section of a township in its new position as a manor in the feudal system.

Domesday Book takes full cognizance of one organ of Saxon life – the Shire. Everything is grouped under the Shire or 'County', for it is through the Shire organization that the King intends to act. But inside each Shire the unit under which all the information is rearranged is the feudal holding of the tenant-in-chief, however widely scattered his lands may be over all the Hundreds of the County. And the lesser unit in Domesday Book is not the village regarded as a township, but the village regarded as a manor belonging to a lord, be he tenant-in-chief or vassal. Thus the final form in which the Report was drawn up established the feudal maxim – *nulle terre sans seigneur* – 'no land without its lord' – with a uniformity unknown before.

In the collection of the Danegeld, the Norman King and Council laid on each Shire a round sum, which was re-allotted locally among the Hundreds. But the officers of the Shire or Hundred made their demands not from the men of each township, still less from each peasant, but from the lord of each manor, who 'answers for the manor' in the matter of taxation and must wring the geld from his tenantry as best he may. With that the Shire officers have nothing to do. In the eyes of the law the man who 'answers for the manor' becomes more and more the owner of the manor, and the old village organization slips over more into the background. It was a process begun long before in Saxon times, but it now reached its theoretic perfection and was made uniform for the whole country, including the sullen Danelaw.

In the Church the Conqueror effected a revolution hardly less important than in the State. Just as the French Barons and knights ousted the Saxon Earls and thegns, so foreign clergy replaced native Englishmen in Bishoprics and Abbacies and in the Chapters of Cathedrals. Obedience was enforced to the doctrines and standards of the reforming party on the continent in the age of Hildebrand. Some of these changes, particularly the change in the persons of the hierarchy, meant greater efficiency and a higher standard of learning and zeal. There followed four centuries of splendid ecclesiastical architecture, starting with the Norman builders, who hastened to replace the largest Saxon churches with structures yet more magnificent.

The Conqueror's great ecclesiastical reform was his division of the spiritual from the secular courts. Hitherto Bishop and Sheriff had presided together over the Shire Court, where both spiritual and secular causes came up for decision. By William's order the Bishop now retired to hold a court of his own, concerned only with spiritual affairs. The separate jurisdiction of the Church covered great tracts of human life which in modern times have been made over to the King's courts and the law of the land – such as felonies committed by persons in holy orders, and the great fields of marriage, testament, and eventually of slander. It included also many matters which are not now dealt with by any court at all, such as penance for sins and jurisdiction over heresy.

The differentiation of the functions of lay and spiritual courts was a long step towards a higher legal civilization. Without it neither Church nor State could have freely developed the law and logic of their position. The English Common Law could never have grown to its full native vigour, if its nursery had been a court shared by ecclesiastical lawyers and judges trying to measure English law by Roman rules. And the separate existence of her own courts rendered it easy for the Church to adopt the Canon Law, as fast as it was formulated on the continent in the great legal age now coming on. The Papal Canon Law was enforced in the Church Courts of England throughout the later Middle Ages. The Church as a spiritual body was subject to the Pope, but the King, representing the secular arm, dealt with the Papacy as with an honoured but a rival power. The limits to Papal power were therefore set, not by churchmen as such, but by the King acting in defence of his own authority, often with the good-will of many English priests.

It was essential to William's conception of Kingship that he should be able in practice to control the nomination of Bishops and Abbots. Without that privilege he might have reigned but could scarcely have ruled in England. He used his great power for the benefit of the reforming party in the Church, but he also used it in the secular interests of the Crown. His secretaries, his judges, and most of his civil servants were churchmen, for there were no learned laymen. Men who were learned, took orders as a matter of course. The King and his successors, right down to the Reformation, used a large part of the wealth and patronage of the Church to pay for services rendered to the State. Judges and civil servants were rewarded with benefices and even with bishoprics. Viewed ecclesiastically by modern standards, this was an abuse. But the system served the country well and rendered the enormous wealth of the medieval Church useful and tolerable to a society that might otherwise have revolted against it before the age of the Tudors. The medieval Church, served not only the purposes of piety and religion strictly defined, but all the purposes of learning and knowledge. Only when learning and knowledge spread into the lay world, a new system had to be adopted involving a limitation of the sphere of the clergy and a consequent reduction of the wealth of the Church.

William the Conqueror, a generous patron of the Church, yet a strong protector of the rights of the Crown, had ruled the country with Lanfranc as his right-hand man, in spite of
1087–1100 occasional quarrels. But William Rufus, though not without kingly qualities, was a ruffian only pious when on his sick bed. In pursuit of revenue he abused the position he had inherited from his father in relation to the Church, just as he strained his feudal rights over his lay vassals. After Lanfranc's death he refused to appoint a new Primate, and enjoyed for five years together the revenues of the See of Canterbury. At length he was taken ill, thought he was dying, and appointed the most unwilling Anselm. Then, to the surprise and grief of his subjects, he recovered, and for years led the saintly Archbishop such a life as fully explains the comic and almost cowardly reluctance that Anselm had shown to accept the post, to which the voice of the whole country had called him. The events of the reign show how the secular power, in the hands of a passionate and unscrupulous prince, could hamper the religious life of the country.

1100–35 In the reign of Henry I the inevitable clash came. Henry 'the clerk' was a very different person from his barbarian brother Rufus. But though he did not abuse he steadily maintained the rights of the Crown, while Anselm stood for the new claims of the Church. The question was that of 'investitures', then convulsing all Europe: should prelates be appointed by the Crown or by the Pope? After a fierce struggle a compromise was arranged. The King of England ceded to the Pope the right of investing the new Bishops with the spiritual staff and ring. But he retained the right of claiming their feudal homage as Barons. And the choice of the man who was to be Bishop tacitly remained with the King. The King's power of naming the Bishops whom the Cathedral Chapters were to elect, though not absolute and often subject to the approval or interference of the Pope, was the basis of the friendly relations of Church and State. During the centuries when laymen were ignorant and the States of Europe were small and weak, the medieval Church was so truly 'universal', so powerful in opinion, knowledge, and wealth, so strongly organized under the

Pope and dominant over so many sides of life that have since been left to the State or to the individual, that if she had then enjoyed all the 'liberty' of a voluntary religious denomination of modern times it would have meant the complete enslavement of society to the priesthood. That at least the medieval Kings were able to prevent.

One outcome of the Norman Conquest was the making of the English language. As a result of Hastings, the Anglo-Saxon tongue, the speech of Alfred and Bede, was exiled from hall and bower, from court and cloister, and was despised as a peasants' jargon, the talk of ignorant serfs. It ceased almost, though not quite, to be a written language. The learned and the pedantic lost all interest in its forms, for the clergy talked Latin and the gentry talked French. Now when a language is seldom written and is not an object of interest to scholars, it quickly adapts itself in the mouths of plain people to the needs and uses of life. This may be either good or evil, according to circumstances. If the grammar is clumsy and ungraceful, it can be altered much more easily when there are no grammarians to protest. And so it fell out in England. During the three centuries when our native language was a peasants' dialect, it lost its clumsy inflexions and elaborate genders, and acquired the grace, suppleness, and adaptability which are among its chief merits. At the same time it was enriched by many French words and ideas. The English vocabulary is mainly French in words relating to war, politics, justice, religion, hunting, cooking, and art. Thus improved, our native tongue re-entered polite and learned society as the English of Chaucer's Tales and Wycliffe's Bible, to be still further enriched into the English of Shakespeare and of Milton. There is no more romantic episode in the history of man than this underground growth and unconscious self-preparation of the despised island *patois*, destined ere long to 'burst forth into sudden blaze,' to be spoken in every quarter of the globe, and to produce a literature with which only that of ancient Hellas is comparable. It is symbolic of the fate of the English race itself after Hastings, fallen to rise nobler, trodden under foot only to be trodden into shape.

BOOK TWO
THE MAKING OF THE NATION

From the Conquest to the Reformation

THE medieval period, as distinct from the Dark Ages, may be said to begin about the time of the First Crusade, that start-
1095–9 ling outward thrust of the new Europe reorganized by the feudal system. Feudalism is the characteristic institution of the Middle Ages; it implies a fixed and legal subordination of certain classes of society to certain others, to obtain civilized order at the expense of barbaric anarchy. Feudal society divided up the surplus product of the labour of the rural serf among Barons and knights, Bishops and Abbots. By stereotyping and regularizing the inequality of incomes derived from the land, it enabled wealth to accumulate in the hands of Lords and Prelates, and so stimulated the rich man's demand for luxuries, whence grew the trade and the higher arts and crafts of the merchant cities. In this way the Dark Ages progressed into the Middle Ages, and barbarism grew into civilization – but decidedly not along the path of liberty and equality.

Another aspect of feudalism was that it organized military, political, and judicial power on a local basis. Not the Empire as in Roman times, or the nation as in modern times, but the barony or the manor, was the unit of power. Feudalism was a confession of the disintegration of the Empire and the extreme weakness of the State. Over against this disintegrated secular society of feudal Barons and knights, each with an outlook limited to his province or his manor, stood the pan-European Church organized from Rome, as centralized as secular society was decentralized, and, therefore, if for no other reason, its master. Furthermore, since the clergy enjoyed an almost complete monopoly of learning and clerkship, the control of Church over State in the early Middle Ages was very great.

Medieval society began as a rude arrangement, between knight, churchman, and peasant serf, for the protection of a poverty-stricken rustic village against marauders and evils, in return for its due exploitation for the benefit of knight and churchman. It was an arrangement in the making of which there were elements of force and fraud, as also of religious idealism and soldierly heroism in defence of the community. But gradually, out of these primitive arrangements of feudalism, the Middle Ages built up the Europe of Dante and Chaucer; of the Cathedrals and Universities; of the English monarchy and Parliament; of the Canon, Civil, and English Law; of the merchant communities in Italy and Flanders, and of London 'the flower of cities all'. Which of these two pictures is the true Middle Ages? The feudal village, with its ragged, frightened, superstitious, half-starved serf, leaving his chimneyless cabin to drive afield his meagre team of oxen, and fleeing to the woods at the approach of armed horsemen – or the Florence of Dante, the Flanders of Van Artevelde, the Oxford of Grossetête and of Wycliffe? Which is the true Middle Ages, the barbarism or the civilization? We may answer – 'both'. The one was developed out of the other and the two continued side by side. The Dark Ages were in four hundred eventful years transformed into the full splendour of the Renaissance, although the darkness of poverty and ignorance still lay thick in many districts of the new Europe.

The aim of the greatest minds of the Middle Ages was to provide man upon earth with a permanent resting place in unchangeable institutions and unchallengeable beliefs; but their real achievement was very different; the true merit of medieval Christendom was that as compared to Islam and Brahminism it was progressive, and that society moved constantly forward from 1100 to 1500 towards new things – out of uniformity into variety; out of feudal cosmopolitanism into national monarchy; out of a hegemony of the priesthood into lay emancipation; out of the rule of the knight into the world of the craftsman, the capitalist, and the yeoman. The spirit of medieval Europe was not static but dynamic. The best and the worst of the Middle Ages was that they were full of wolfish life and energy. Their sins were the vices not of decrepitude but of violent and wanton youth. It is useless to seek in the Middle Ages for a golden age of piety, peace, and brotherly love. It is an equal mistake to fall back into the error of the Eighteenth Century, of despising the great epoch that led man back out of the barbarism into the renewed light of civilization. We should think of the medieval era not as a fixed state but as a living process; we should not conceive it as a motionless picture in a Morris tapestry, but as a series of shifting scenes, some brilliant, some terrible, all full of life and passion.

Throughout the medieval period the British islands were still in the extreme north-west angle of all things. No one dreamt there were lands yet to be discovered beyond the Atlantic rollers – unless indeed, in remote fiords of Iceland and Norway, tales about 'Vineland' lingered among the descendants of those bold Viking crews who, a thousand years after Christ, had beached their long-ships on some point of the North American shore.

But although, when William landed at Pevensey, Britain still seemed to be poised on the world's edge no less than when Caesar first beheld the cliffs of Dover, the world itself had shifted its centre northward and drawn nearer to the British angle. Western civilization was no longer, as in Graeco-Roman times, Mediterranean, but properly European. North Africa, the Levant, and part of Spain had been lost; they had become portions of Asia and of Islam. Germany had been gained instead, and was thenceforth the trunk of the body politic of Europe, with Britain and Scandinavia its northern limbs. The cultural leadership was divided between Italy and France, but political and military power lay decisively to the north of the Alps, among the feudal knighthood of the French and German states. Flanders, Normandy, and Paris, closely connected with South England in commerce, politics, and literature, did as much for the development of medieval civilization as Italy herself. Because the centre had been shifted northwards from the Mediterranean, the Norman Conquest left more permanent traces than the Roman had done upon the life of our island.

Until the middle of the Eleventh Century, both Scandinavia and Britain had been somewhat loosely attached to the civilization of Europe. They had their own Nordic traditions and literature, perhaps the noblest product of the Dark Ages – the spirit of the Eddas and Sagas. But the Norman Conquest severed Britain from Scandinavia of the Vikings and connected her with France of the feudal knights.

The medieval Europe to which England was closely attached for four hundred years after Hastings found its unity only in its social, religious, and cultural institutions. Unlike the ancient Roman world, it was not held together as a single State. Its political structure was the legalized and regulated anarchy of the feudal system. The only name by which Europe knew itself was Christendom, and its only capital was Papal Rome. There was no political capital; the so-called 'Empire' existed in theory, but lacked administrative force. Real unity was given by the customs of feudalism, chivalry, and Roman Christianity, which were then common to all lands from the Forth to the Tagus, from the Carpathians to the Bay of Biscay. The agrarian feudal economy with its lords and villeins, the orders of clergy with their judicial powers and social privileges, feudal custom and the Canon Law, were universally accepted, as no equally important institutions could be accepted after the rise of the middle classes and of nationality had given greater variety to European life. The English knight, speaking French, and the English churchman, speaking Latin, could travel through Europe from castle to castle and from abbey to abbey, and find less that was strange to them than Englishmen touring in the same parts in Stuart or Hanoverian times.

Britain, reorganized after the Norman Conquest, became strong enough to defend herself behind the narrow seas; henceforth they served 'as a moat defensive to a house', and no longer as an open pathway to her enemies. As she gathered strength, she became the hammer instead of the anvil, the invader of France instead of the invaded. And as the French influences of the Norman Conquest became absorbed in the island atmosphere, the Norman overlords became identified with the life of their English neighbours, particularly after the loss of Normandy in the reign of John. Britain began, before any other European State, to develop a nationhood based on peculiar characteristics, laws, and institutions. Because she was an island, her life drew apart once more. Already in the reign of Henry III, the Barons of the land, the descendants, or at least the successors, of those victors of Hastings' fight who had scorned everything English, had learnt to say, '*Nolumus leges Angliae mutari*' ('We don't want the customs of old England changed').

Foreign chivalry and foreign clericalism had been the two chief methods of progress for Englishmen under the Norman and early Plantagenet Kings. High above the wooden huts and thatched roofs of the Saxon villeins towered the great stone castle and the great stone cathedral: mighty works they were, and strong the arms and subtle the minds of the men who reared them and dwelt in them. Nevertheless it was the despised English people and not their alien tutors who would prevail in the end, emerging once more, strengthened, instructed, elevated, prepared for tasks that would have astonished William and Lanfranc.

The leaders in this great work of evolution were the Anglo-French Kings. The Norman Conquest and the Angevin succession gave us, by one of those chances that guide history, a long line of Kings more vigorous than any in Europe. They used the new feudalism to enforce national unity, though elsewhere feudalism meant disruption; they built up a strong but supple administration, centralized, yet in touch with the life of the localities; their courts evolved a single system of native law for the whole realm; they stretched out their royal hands to the subjugated English, protected them against feudal oppressors, helped them to find new organs of self-expression in cities, law courts, and Parliament, and even in foreign wars won by the long-bow of the English yeoman.

Under such kingly leadership England acquired, during these centuries of foreign rule and influence, great institutions undreamt of before in the life of man; representative assemblies, Universities, juries, and much else on which our modern civilization still rests. In the Middle Ages institutional and corporate life flourished and grew, while the individual was held of little account. Some of these institutions, like the Universities, the legal profession, the city guilds and companies, and Parliament itself, had their origin or analogy elsewhere; they were characteristic products of medieval Christendom as a whole. But our Common Law was a development peculiar to England; and Parliament, in alliance with the Common Law, gave us in the end a political life of our own in strong contrast to the later developments of Latin civilization.

Yet even as late as the Fourteenth and Fifteenth Centuries, England was not yet fully conscious of her life apart, nor of the full value of her island position. Under the later Plantagenets, she abandoned her task of completing the British Empire by the assimilation of Ireland and Scotland, and tried instead to revive the Norman and Angevin Empire on the continent. The preoccupation of England with the Hundred Years' War secured Scottish freedom; left half-conquered Ireland to permanent anarchy; hastened the ruin of medieval society in France and England, and stimulated the national self-consciousness of both – leaving to the victors of Agincourt memories on which two hundred years later Shakespeare could still look back with pride as the central patriotic tradition of his native land, only in part replaced by the Armada story.

At the same time in Chaucer and Wycliffe we see a new English culture struggling to be born, not the old Saxondom of *Beowulf*, Bede, and Alfred, but something far richer and stronger – thanks to the French and Italian schoolmasters, soon to be peremptorily dismissed by full-grown Tudor England. In the Fifteenth Century we see all the conditions of medieval society silently dissolving, sure prelude to the coming revolution. The villein is achieving his emancipation under a new economic order. New middle classes in town and country are thrusting themselves in between lord and serf, the two isolated pillars of the old feudal structure. Commerce and manufacture are growing with the cloth trade, and are bursting the boundaries of medieval borough and guild. Laymen are becoming learned and are thinking for themselves. Caxton's press is replacing the monastic scribe. The long-bow of the English yeoman can stop the charge of the feudal knight, and the King's cannon can breach his donjon wall. As climax to all these profound changes, slowly at work through many passing generations, the mist is suddenly rolled back one day off the Atlantic waves, revealing new worlds beyond the ocean. England, it seems, is no longer at the extreme verge of all things, but is their maritime heart and centre. She has long been half European; she shall now become oceanic – and American as well, and yet remain English all the while.

CHAPTER I

The Anarchy and the Restoration of Royal Power. Henry II. Knights and Villeins at the Manor. The Village. The King's Courts. Common Law and the Jury.

Kings: Stephen, 1135–54; Henry II, 1154–89

THE Norman Kings had kept their Barons in order, revived the shire organization as the instrument of royal government, and established in the Exchequer an effective system of collecting the multifarious revenues of the Crown. But the peace of the land still depended on the personal activites of the King. As yet there was no automatic machinery of State that would continue to function even when the crown had been set upon a foolish head. Between the First and Second Henries, between the Norman and Angevin Kings, intervened the anarchy known as the reign of Stephen. It was, in fact, not a reign but a war of succession, waged by Stephen of Blois against Matilda, widow of the Emperor and wife of the great Plantagenet Count, Geoffrey of Anjou.

The miseries of this period prepared all men to accept the bureaucratic and judicial reforms by which Henry II afterwards extended the authority of the King's courts, and laid the basis of the Common Law, in a spirit alien to true feudalism. Of true feudalism England had enough under Stephen.

The feudal anarchy rose out of a disputed succession between a man and a woman equally unfit to fill the throne. Stephen and Matilda raised rival armies by giving a free hand to their baronial supporters, and by granting away to private persons those rights of the Crown which the Norman Kings had laboriously acquired. For two generations past, the sheriff had been a real King's officer, removable at will and subject to the inquisition of the central *Curia*. But the typical figure of the new age was Geoffrey de Mandeville, whom Matilda and Stephen in turn made hereditary sheriff and justiciary of Essex, granting to him and his heirs for ever the right of holding all the King's judicial and administrative power in the county. He was perpetually changing sides and perpetually raising the price of his allegiance. Finally he secured from Stephen these royal rights not only in Essex but in Hertfordshire, Middlesex, and London, the very heart of the Kingdom. He was a ruffian of the worst order, and the most powerful man in the East of England, not excepting the King. But, in spite of the royal charters, 'his heirs for ever' were not destined to rule those regions.

By men such as these, in local possession of sovereign power, whole districts were depopulated. The Thames valley, the South-west, and part of the Midlands suffered severely, but the worst scenes of all were enacted in the fenland, where Geoffrey de Mandeville kept an army afoot on the plunder of the countryside. In the heart of this unhappy region, in the cloisters of Peterborough, an English monk sat tracing the last sad entries of the Anglo-Saxon Chronicle, first compiled under the patronage of the great King Alfred, now shrunk to be the annals of the neglected and oppressed. In it we hear the bitter cry of the English common folk against the foreign chivalry to whom the foreign Kings had for a while abandoned them.

> They greatly oppressed the wretched people by making them work at these castles, and when the castles were finished they filled them with devils and evil men. They then took those whom they suspected to have any goods, by night and by day, seizing both men and women, and they put them in prison for their gold and silver, and tortured them with pains unspeakable, for never were any martyrs tormented as these were.

Then follows the passage so often quoted in our history books, the inventory of the tortures used, of which the mildest were starvation and imprisonment in *oubliettes* filled with adders, snakes, and toads. If we remember, that two generations later King John starved to death a highborn lady and her son, we may well believe the worst of these tales of horror wrought under the anarchy upon the friendless and the poor.

While such atrocities were things of every day in the stone castles that now covered the land, the feudal nobility who had reared them were also engaged with a peculiar zeal in founding and endowing monasteries. In Stephen's reign a hundred new foundations were made. Those who caused and exploited the anarchy were foremost in making liberal grants to the Cistercian monks, who first came over from France at this period. We need not suppose that religious motives of a very high order were always at work, any more than that they were always absent. A Baron, whose imagination was perturbed by some rude fresco in the church of a long-clawed devil flying off with an armoured knight, would reflect that a grant to a monastery was an excellent way of forestalling any such unpleasant consequences that might follow from his own habits of torturing peasants and depopulating villages.

At length, by the help of Archbishop Theobald, an accommodation was brought about between the claimants. Stephen was 1153 to wear the crown till his death, but Matilda's son should succeed as Henry II. Meanwhile unlicensed castles, reckoned at over a thousand, were to be destroyed. It was a coalition deliberately made by both parties against the too apparent evils of unchecked feudalism. But Stephen was not the man to cure the ills of the State, and it was one of England's great good fortunes that he died next year. He was a gallant warrior, a knight-errant of the new chivalric ideal, capable of giving the Lady Matilda a pass through his lines to his own great disadvantage, but careless of the public welfare and wholly unfit to be King.

Of all the monarchs who have worn the island crown, few have done such great and lasting work as Henry Plantagenet, Count of Anjou. He found England exhausted by nearly twenty years of anarchy, with every cog in the Norman machine of State either broken or rusty with disuse, the people sick indeed of feudal misrule, but liable at any moment to slip back into it for want of means to preserve order. He left England with a judicial and administrative system and a habit of obedience to government which prevented the recurrence of anarchy, in spite of the long absences of King Richard and the malignant follies of King John. After the death of the First Henry, the outcome of bad government was anarchy; after the death of the Second Henry, the outcome of bad government was constitutional reform. And the difference is a measure of the work of the great Angevin.

Henry II was as little of an Englishman as the Norman or the Dutch William. There are advantages as well as disadvantages in having a King who is a foreigner: he may see the wood more clearly for not having been born among the trees. The Angevin brought to bear on English problems not only his fierce and tireless energy and imperious will, but a clerkly mind trained in the best European learning of his day, particularly in the lore of the legal renaissance then spreading northward from the Italian Universities; he was able therefore to be the pioneer of the new jurisprudence in a land that only since his day has been famous for its native law. He was wise too in all the administrative arts of the various provinces of the empire that he ruled. For he was not merely Duke of Normandy but ruler of all western France. By marriage, diplomacy, and war, the House of Anjou had accumulated such vast possessions that the Monarchy at Paris and the Holy Roman Empire itself were for a while of less account in Europe.

Since Henry reigned from the Cheviots to the Pyrenees, he was the better able to control the English baronage, who dared not defy the lord of so many lands. The last baronial revolt of the old feudal type was in 1173, and Henry crushed it. In this way the continental power of the early English Kings was indirectly of service to the internal development of England, when the chief thing needed was a strong monarchy.

Henry's ever-moving court was filled with men of business, pleasure, and scholarship from every land in Western Europe. To the great King, who was to leave so deep an impress on English institutions, England was merely the largest of his provinces. The dominions which he administered were not divided by conscious national cleavage, but were all part of the same cultural civilization. In England the upper class still talked French, and continued to talk it till well on in the reign of Edward III. In the English village the distance between the lord and his villeins was accentuated, no longer indeed by racial feeling and the memory of Hastings, but by the ever-present barrier of a different language. The deep social gulf, characteristic of feudalism, was not in the Twelfth Century filled up by a numerous middle class of yeomen or traders. Such as they were, the bailiff, men-at-arms, and other go-betweens who linked the lord to the peasant serf must have spoken both French and English. The priest dealt in yet a third tongue – Latin, which was therefore the language of official documents. Medieval England was a polyglot community – even without taking account of the numerous provincial variations of 'old' and 'middle' English, or of the Celtic tongues spoken in Wales and Cornwall.

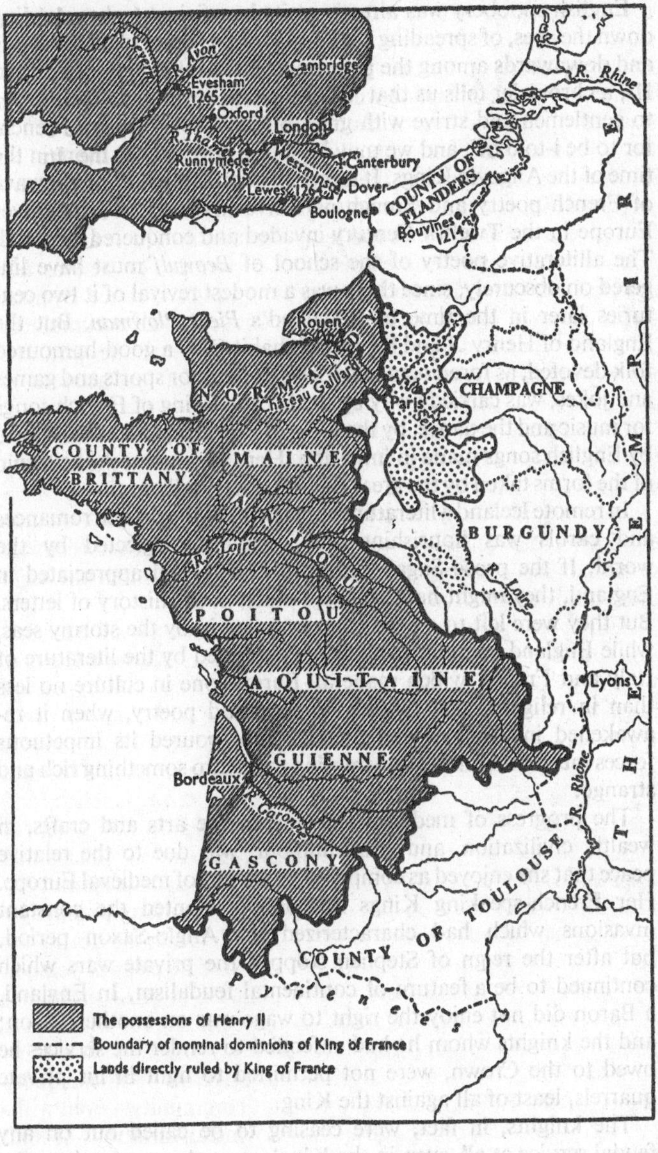

MAP VI. THE ANGEVIN EMPIRE

English snobbery was already at its beneficient task, unending down the ages, of spreading the culture of the upper class outwards and downwards among the people. As late as the reign of Edward III, a chronicler tells us that 'uplandish men will liken themselves to gentlemen and strive with great business for to speak French, for to be i-told of', and we may be sure it was so even more in the time of the Angevin Kings. It is then no wonder that the great wave of French poetry and French narrative that was sweeping over Europe in the Twelfth Century invaded and conquered England. The alliterative poetry of the school of *Beowulf* must have lingered on obscurely, since there was a modest revival of it two centuries later in the time of Langland's *Piers Plowman*. But the England of Henry II and his sons, inhabited by a good-humoured folk devoted, as foreigners remarked, to outdoor sports and games and jokes, was carried away by the lilt and swing of French songs for music and the dance, by the *verve* of French epics and tales, and by English songs made in imitation. Here we must seek the origin of the forms taken by the great English poetry of later times.

In remote Iceland a literature not inferior to the French romances and carols was flourishing and decaying, neglected by the world. If the prose Sagas had been known and appreciated in England, they might have changed much in the history of letters. But they were left to a little clan, hemmed in by the stormy seas, while England and Germany were conquered by the literature of Italy and France, which made all Europe one in culture no less than in religion. The Nordic humour and poetry, when it reawakened in Chaucer and Shakespeare, poured its impetuous forces into Latin forms, transmuting them into something rich and strange.

The progress of medieval England in the arts and crafts, in wealth, civilization, and good humour, was due to the relative peace that she enjoyed as compared to the rest of medieval Europe. Her French-speaking Kings not only prevented the constant invasions which had characterized the Anglo-Saxon period, but after the reign of Stephen stopped the private wars which continued to be a feature of continental feudalism. In England, a Baron did not enjoy the right to wage war on another Baron; and the knights whom he had enfeoffed to render the services he owed to the Crown, were not permitted to fight in his private quarrels, least of all against the King.

The knights, in fact, were ceasing to be called out on any feudal service at all, even in the King's wars. A great foreign ruler like Henry II wanted troops whom he could take to Aquitaine or beyond, and keep on foot for more than the feudal forty days. He therefore extended a system begun by Henry I, by which payments called 'scutage' or 'shield-money' were, if the King wished it, received by the Exchequer from Prelates and Barons, in lieu of the military service of their knights enfeoffed upon their lands. The cash could be used by the King to hire mercenaries either foreign or English.

And so in the reigns of Henry II and his sons, an English knight, though trained to joust and fight from the saddle, might never have seen a siege or a stricken field. His interests were growing every day more peaceful and more agricultural. He was always plotting to improve the yield of his domain lands, watching the villeins at work upon them, and going the rounds with his friend and servant the bailiff, whom he could instruct to 'sow the headland with red wheat.' He was in process of becoming that pre-eminently English figure – the country gentleman.

For these reasons the stone castle typical of Stephen's reign was gradually replaced by the stone manor-house, typical of the Plantagenet epoch. The movement was hastened by Henry II's demolition of unlicensed castles and his unwillingness to grant new licences. The stark donjon-keep was replaced by a high-roofed stone hall of the type of a college dining-hall at Oxford or Cambridge, the lineal descendant of the high timber hall of the Anglo-Danish thegn. In front of it was a walled courtyard partly surrounded by buildings. The manor-house was only to be entered through the gateway of the courtyard, and was often protected by a moat. It was built to be defensible against a mob or a troop of horse, but could not, like the castle, stand a regular siege. The men who built the Plantagenet manor-houses lived among armed neighbours easily moved to violence, but they were not preoccupied with the thought of serious war, their chief desire being to enjoy in safety the fruits of the soil and to cultivate the arts and crafts of peace.

There were indeed infinite varieties and grades of manor-house and hall, and I have here described only those of the better-to-do gentry. But some must have been very humble abodes in the Middle Ages, for even in Tudor times there were some 'halls' of the gentry that are now only used as barns, and very many that are now farm-houses.

English knights, down to the age of Chaucer and beyond, often hired themselves out to their own or other Kings to fight in Scotland, in France, or even as far afield as 'Alisandre when it was wonne'. But they were soldiers only when on campaign, and could return to their peaceful country homes. Others never left the manor except to ride to the Shire Court on county business. The more fashionable and adventurous were devoted to the sport of the tournament and to the trappings and romance of the new school of chivalry coming over from France, rather than to actual war.

Such at least was the state of the southern and midland counties, but the social landscape grew more grim as one approached the Welsh or Scottish borders. There dwelt the Marcher Lords in their high stone castles, soldiers ever on watch for the beacon fire and the raid of the racial enemy. It was these warrior nobles of the Welsh and Scottish Marches who supplied the chief fighting element in the constitutional troubles of Plantagenet times and in the pseudo-feudalism of the Wars of the Roses.

There followed, indeed, one remarkable consequence of the feudal and warlike origin of the English country gentleman. After the Norman Conquest the rule of primogeniture had gradually been adopted for land, to secure that a feoff should not be broken up among the sons of a vassal and so become unable to supply the military service due to the lord. In Saxon times an estate had normally been divided among the sons. In Plantagenet times it normally went to the eldest son alone. And therefore the younger sons, after being brought up as children of the manor-house, were sent out into the world to seek their fortunes. This had the effect of increasing the adventurous and roving spirit of the new English nation, and of mingling classes as they were not mingled in Germany or France. The English upper class never became a closed caste, like the continental nobles who married only inside their own order, and despised merchants and commerce. If English history followed a very different course, it was partly because the custom of primogeniture, though originated to meet a feudal requirement, had become part of the land-law of an England that was rapidly escaping from feudalism.

We are watching an important step towards the higher stages of civilization – the growth of a leisured class. At a time when the island held about as many people as New Zealand to-day, and when these few inhabitants were still so poor that we should not have expected any of them to be people of leisure, the feudal system had established a class of warriors living at the expense of the cultivators of the soil. And now that the Monarchy had caused war to cease in the island, this warrior class found its occupation gone. The time and endowments which it was to have spent on war and the preparation for war had become an endowment of leisure.

In the Plantagenet manor-houses, time lay heavy on the peace-bound knights, and to kill time they took to a number of different devices, each according to his tastes – to drink, sport, tournament, agricultural improvement, local administration and politics, music, letters, and art. In the primeval Saxon forest, hunting had been the duty of the thegn; it was now the pastime of the dis-occupied knight. As game and wasteland became more scarce, he struggled with the King above and with the peasantry below to preserve enough for his own diversion. Increasing wealth was supplied him by the manorial system of agriculture, by the rising population, by the increasing acreage under plough, and by the disinheritance of his younger brother under the law of primogeniture; he spent the surplus on comforts and amenities for his manor-house, on art and minstrelsy in the hall, in a thousand ways discovering for the behoof of a barbarous age what a spacious and beautiful thing man can make of life. The rich Abbot and Bishop did the like. The accumulated wealth of the feudal classes and their call for new luxuries caused the rise of the English towns, and the new middle classes engaged in manufacture, trade, and overseas commerce. The arts of civilized life were forced into being in medieval England by the unequal distribution of wealth under the feudal and manorial system, by the stability of these harsh social arrangements, and by the good peace which the King imposed on all.

It remains for us to examine the feudal system of the manor from the point of view of the peasant; to him it was a less unmixed benefit than to the privileged classes, lay and clerical, whom it was specially designed to support.

In the Twelfth Century the proportion of freeholders in an English manor was very small. The slave, who had composed nine per cent of the population recorded in Domesday, had risen into the villein class, but the free man was not markedly on the increase. The lord and his villeins shared the manor and its produce between them.

The serf or villein was by birth and inheritance bound to the soil; he and his family were sold with an estate when it changed hands. He could not marry his daughter save with the lord's consent and the payment of a heavy fine; when he died, his best beast, sometimes his only cow, was seized as 'heriot' by the lord of the manor. He could not migrate or withdraw his services at will. He could not strike. He must work on his lord's domain so many days in the year without pay, bringing his own team or half-team of oxen for the plough. It was by these services of the villein, and not by hired labour, that the lord's home farm was worked. The bailiff had to keep his eye on the unwilling workmen lest they should sit down for half an hour at a time at the end of every furrow.

But the villein, half slave as he was in these respects, held lands of his own which he tilled on those days of the year when his lord had no claim upon him or his oxen. And he had his share in the use and profit of the village meadow, the village pasture, and the village woodland and waste, where the swine and geese were turned loose.

How was his position secured? There was for him no 'equality before the law'. As late as John's reign the safeguards given by Magna Carta to the 'free man' touched him not at all. He could not sue his lord in the King's courts. But he had a double protection against ill-usage. First, the lord and bailiff found it to their interest to receive from him willing rather than unwilling work and to give him no motive to run away. For he could not be easily replaced, like an overworked slave in old Rome, or in the West Indies before Wilberforce; nor might he be driven to work with the whip. And secondly, he had the security of village tradition, legally expressed in 'the custom of the manor', and enforced in the Manor Court, which was held sometimes in the lord's hall, sometimes under the time-honoured oak tree in the middle of the village.

How much protection was the Manor Court to the villein? It was indeed his lord's court, not the King's. But at least it was an open court, in which there is reason to think that the villeins shared with the freeman the duty of acting as judges or assessors. It was at least better than the mere arbitrary word of the lord or his bailiff. Against a rapacious and wicked lord the protection seems but slender, and doubtless there was often terrible oppression, especially in Stephen's reign. But in Plantagenet times the English peasant never fell to the level of the French peasant of the *Jacquerie*.

No ancient system must be judged in the abstract, or by purely modern standards. The great merit of the manorial system in its day was this, that among men of primitive passions and violent habits it promoted stability, certainty, and law. A court that focused public opinion and tradition, and that actually kept written records from the Thirteenth Century onwards, was established as part of the normal life of the English village. When the system worked properly, a peasant knew what services he owed his lord, and he knew that the bailiff would exact those and no more. It is true that the peasant could not strike and could not legally emigrate without this lord's consent; but neither could his lord evict – in fact, whatever may have been the case in theory. Nor could the lord raise the rent or services due, once they were fairly established by custom of the Manor Court.

During the centuries when this system flourished in England, wealth slowly accumulated; more land came under plough; flocks and herds multiplied in spite of frequent murrain; and in spite of no less frequent famine and pestilence the population went up from perhaps one-and-a-quarter or one-and-a-half million when Domesday was compiled in 1086, to perhaps three-and-a-half or four millions when the Black Death of 1349 temporarily checked the increase.

But at the best of times life on the manor was hard, and the villeins were very slow in rising above the level of Anglo-Saxon rural barbarism towards the type of jolly English yeoman of later days. The serf was what poverty and submission made him – shifty, fearful, ignorant, full of superstitious Christian and pagan beliefs, trusting to charms and strange traditions of a folk-lore of immemorial antiquity; cheating and sometimes murdering the lord or his officers; incompetent and fatalistic in presence of scarcity and plague in the village and murrain among the ill-kept beasts. The soil was undrained and sodden to a degree we can now hardly conceive. The jungle kept rushing in, weeds overspreading the ploughland, as bailiffs complained. Under the open-field system with its unscientific farming, the soil after centuries of use became less fertile, and the yield per acre was reduced.

The English weather was at least as bad as it is in our day, and when the crop failed, as it often did after a wet summer, there was nothing to avert famine in the village. Animal food was less available than in Saxon times, for the vast forests of the Norman Kings and the private warrens of their vassals were guarded by cruel laws. The wild birds, the preserved pigeons and rabbits and the other animals with which the island swarmed often came marauding into the peasants' crops with the direst effects, and were taken and cooked on the sly in spite of laws and penalties. Cattle and sheep were not for the peasant to eat, though 'beef' and 'mutton' figured in the bill of fare of the French-speaking lords at the manor-house. Pig's flesh was commoner in the cottage. In fen regions fishers and fowlers supplied eels and water-fowl good and cheap.

The medieval English village, at the end of its muddy riding tracks, with its villeins bound for life not to stray from the precincts of the manor, was subject to physical and intellectual isolation that governed its life in every respect. One result of isolation was that the village had to manufacture for itself. Among the villeins were craftsmen, who might or might not be husbandmen as well. The 'wright' or carpenter could knock together the cottages, their furniture, and the wooden part of the farm machinery; the thatcher and the blacksmith could finish his work. The women and children were all 'spinsters', and village weaving of the coarser kind of cloth preceded fine weaving in England by many centuries – and indeed stretches back to prehistoric times. Much of the peasant's clothing was of hides roughly tanned. The neighbouring market town, itself an agricultural village, supplied what else had occasionally to be bought. Only the inhabitants of the manor-house were likely to go further afield in their purchases and to patronize the commerce of the towns and the traders oversea.

In Henry II's reign, the lord's dwelling, whether Abbey, castle, or manor-house, was often built of stone. But the villeins' cottages were still hovels, without chimneys or glass, and sometimes without any aperture but the door. They were built either of split logs, erected side by side in the old Saxon fashion, or, where timber became scarce, of 'half-timber' walls, with mud filling in the oaken frame-work. The art of baking bricks had died with the Romans and had not yet been revived. The roof was of turf or thatch. A small orchard, garden, or yard surrounded the villein's cottage, even when it faced the village street.

In the West and North and in districts still chiefly woodland, the cottages often stood in small hamlets of one, two, three, or half a dozen farms, and each little farm often had its own consolidated lands, sometimes surrounded by permanent enclosures. But in the best agricultural districts in East and Middle England, the prevailing system was the large village of two to five hundred souls, grouped round the parish church and manor-house, in the middle of the open field. This 'open' or 'common field', was not cut up by hedges into the chess-board appearance presented by rural England to-day. It was divided into hundreds of little strips each of an acre or half an acre, divided by 'balks' of grass or footpath. It must have looked somewhat like a group of allotments of our time, but on a gigantic scale, and all under corn.

Each of these strips was a separate holding, a unit of proprietorship as well as of agriculture. Each peasant had his property scattered about in the field in a number of separate strips, and a single freeman or villein might hold any number from one upwards; thirty formed a usual holding. The lord's domain, though part of it might be in a continuous tract separate from the village field, was in part scattered about among the peasant holdings.

Beyond the 'fields' lay the 'waste' – the marshes, heaths, and forests that had once clothed the whole acreage of the island, and still covered more than half of it. The Saxon pioneers had pierced its heart of darkness and broken it up with their 'hams' and 'dens' planted everywhere in its midst. Generation after generation, down the length of English history, the heath, fen, and woodland shrank and shrank, as new hamlets and farms sprang up, as village 'fields' were enlarged and multiplied, and as the hunter-Kings were forced to disgorge to their subjects one forest jurisdiction after another. At length, in Hanoverian times, the 'waste' dividing township from township had shrunk to a couple of village commons. Last of all, during the enclosures of the Eighteenth and Nineteenth Centuries, the remaining commons disappeared so fast that in many cases every acre of the land lying between one village and the next is to-day divided up into the chess-board of hedged fields. The townships have ended by devouring the whole 'waste' and forest, unlikely as such an event might have seemed to a bird in mid-air surveying the tree-tops of England a thousand years ago.

The greatest of many benefits that Henry II conferred upon England was legal reform. The new judicial procedure that he introduced was destined to shape the future of English society and politics, and to give distinctive habits of thought to all the English-speaking nations 'in states unborn and accents yet unknown'. For the increase of power and jurisdiction that he gave to the King's central courts and to their offshoots travelling in the shires rendered possible the rapid growth of English 'Common Law', that is to say a native system 'common' to the whole land, in place of the various provincial customs still administered in the Shire and Hundred Courts and in the countless private jurisdictions.

The organs of old Anglo-Danish life, the communal courts of Shire and Hundred, could never have become instruments for creating the supremacy of the Common Law. They were the courts of the middling class of gentry, and could not have been clothed with enough power and prestige to wrest jurisdiction from the feudal and ecclesiastical courts held by the great nobles and prelates. Moreover, the knights and freeholders who were judges in the Shire Court were themselves too much wedded to various local customs, and their intelligence was too untrained and too provincial to evolve by the light of their own wisdom a new jurisprudence for all England. Even the sheriffs who presided there were not lawyers bred in one great central school like the King's Justices. If a common law was to be created for the nation it must emanate from a single source. That source was the royal *curia*, the King's Court.

Henry II, with his foreign legal learning and his gift for choosing men, made a famous bench of royal judges. Some were in holy orders, but others, like Glanvil himself, were of the feudal warrior class. These men and their intellectual progeny in succeeding reigns evolved the Common Law from the procedure of the King's central courts. And the same men went forth to every corner of the land as Justices of Eyre or of Assize, carrying with them the Common Law as fast as it was made, teaching its new doctrines and enforcing its new procedure among 'uplandish men' in every shire.

The Common Law, the great inheritance of the English-speaking nations, has in modern times sharply divided them in their habits of thought from the world of Latin and Roman tradition. Nevertheless it was an outcome of the Norman Conquest. The men who made it between the reigns of Henry II and Edward III were lawyers who thought and pleaded in French, while making their official records in Latin. 'How shall one write a single sentence about law,' said Maitland, 'without using some such word as *debt*, *contract*, *heir*, *trespass*, *pay*, *money*, *court*, *judge*, *jury?* But all these words have come to us from the French. In all the world-wide lands where English law prevails homage is done daily to William of Normandy and Henry of Anjou.'

The Common Law owes only a little to the Anglo-Danish codes and customs with their barbarous procedure, their compurgation and their weregild, representing a bygone stage of society. It owes something to the feudal custom of all Europe, particularly as regards land tenure. But the favourite subject of study in the Twelfth Century was the 'Civil Law' of the old Roman Emperors, and the Canon Law of the Church, then in process of elaborate definition. These two Roman 'laws' served as the exemplar in legal method and science for the men who were making the very different Common Law of England. From about 1150 to 1250 the Universities of Bologna and Paris, where the 'two laws' could best be studied, drew across the sea and the Alps young English clerks, lawyers, and archdeacons by the hundred, who returned, as their countrymen complained, Italianate Englishmen full of foreign vices, but full also of strange legal learning. Oxford, almost as soon as she became a University, had flourishing schools of Civil and of Canon Law.

The question then arises – why did the law of England grow upon lines so native and so free in spite of the intellectual attraction exercised during the most critical century of its growth by these potent alien forces? No doubt the Barons of the land, already an English and a conservative body, eyed the Civil Law askance as something foreign and as favouring autocratic kingship, and they had shown in the Becket controversy that they had no love for the Church courts. These feelings on the part of the grandees of the land had to be respected by the King's lawyers, who, moreover, shared them at least in part. And so, while they used the Civil and Canon Law as lesson books in method and spirit, they rejected their positive contents, all except a few great maxims. The English 'Common Law' was not a code imitated from the Code of Justinian but was a labyrinth of precedents, cases, and decisions of the various royal courts, a labyrinth to be unravelled by the help of clues held by the legal profession.

Throughout early Plantagenet times the King's *curia* or Court began to specialize its work among various subordinate committees, each gradually acquiring a special function and a procedure of its own, as the financial Exchequer had begun to do as early as the reign of Henry I. A bench of judges, known in after times as the Court of Common Pleas, was by John's reign fixed for the convenience of the subject at Westminster, where the Exchequer also sat, thereby 'giving England a capital'. Otherwise, parties to a suit in the *curia regis* had to chase the King about on his bewildering journeys. The King's courts were as yet judicial committees of the *curia*, rather than law courts in the modern sense. But they, and the itinerant justices in the shires, had enough regularity of procedure to manufacture 'case law', the precedents which composed the Common Law of England.

By the procedure laid down in his writs, Henry II enabled the subject to bring many kinds of action in the King's courts rather than in the local and private tribunals. The Crown at this period had plenary power to issue what writs it would, and they form a great original source of English law. Only in the more constitutional times of Henry III and de Montfort, when the King's power was being limited, were the permissible forms of writ defined, and the power of issuing novel writs circumscribed. But by that time the King's courts were well on the road to becoming the ordinary courts of the land.

Partly by writs, partly by 'Assizes', which were royal decrees issued in an 'assize' or session of notables, the Kings from Henry II to Henry III enjoyed the power of creating new legal remedies, new modes of litigation, new forms of action, to the detriment of the feudal and ecclesiastical courts. Other 'legislation' in our sense of the word there was none. But Henry II, by offering the subject alternative and preferable methods of procedure in the royal courts by his 'Assizes', in effect stole from the feudal courts most of their jurisdiction as to the title and possession of land. He thereby threw the shield of the royal justice over small landowners whose estates were coveted by some great feudal neighbour.

By this Assize legislation Henry II at the same time introduced the new procedure of trial by jury.

The barbarous Anglo-Saxon method of trial by 'compurgation', when a man proved his case by bringing his friends and relations in a sufficient number to swear that they believed his oath; the superstitious 'ordeal' by hot iron, originally heathen, but latterly Christian; the Norman warriors' favourite 'trial by battle', always unpopular with the English, when the parties knocked each other about with archaic weapons of wood and horn, till one of the two was fain to cry the fatal word 'craven' – all these were methods which resulted perhaps as often as not in a wrong verdict, frequently in an unjust sentence of mutilation or death. In looking back over the martyrdom of man, we are appalled by the thought that any rational search after the truth in courts of law is a luxury of modern civilization. It was scarcely attempted by primitive peoples. In medieval England the first step in that direction was taken by Henry II, when he laid the foundation of the jury system in place of these antiquated procedures.

The jury which he established was not the jury we know to-day – persons empanelled to hear the evidence of others and decide on the facts laid before them. Henry's jurymen were themselves witnesses to the fact. Yet even this was a great advance, because hitherto courts had too seldom asked for witnesses to fact at all. Henry's Grand Assize enabled a man whose right to property in land was challenged, instead of defending himself through trial by battle, to claim trial by jury. If such were his choice, twelve neighbours who knew the facts were to testify before the King's Justices as to which party had the better right to the land. *Circa* 1179

Another kind of jury, the jury of presentment or accusation, was instituted by the Assizes of Clarendon and Northampton. 1166–76 Twelve sworn men representing each 'Hundred' were to 'present' to the court those of their neighbours who had committed crimes. Like the jurors of the Grand Assize, these jurors of presentment were not judges of fact but witnesses to fact – at least to the facts of the local reputation of the accused. Their 'presentment' sent the culprit to the ordeal, but even if the so-called judgement of God was given for him, though he escaped the gallows, he was to abjure the realm! When in 1215 the Lateran Council abolished the long-discredited ordeal, by forbidding priests any longer to conduct the mummery of the hot iron, the way was opened in England for further developments of the jury system. In the course of the later Middle Ages the jury were gradually transformed from givers of sworn evidence to judges of the evidence of others. In the Fifteenth Century the jury system, more or less as we now have it, was already the boast of Englishmen, proudly contrasted by Chief Justice Fortescue with French procedure where torture was freely used.

Henry's new justice was popular and was eagerly sought. Cruelty, violence, and oppression were things of every day in a society slowly emerging from barbarism, and the royal writ at least afforded to the defenceless occasional help and remedy. Yet there was a less attractive side to the justice of the King. His courts were a means of extortion, to fill his ever-gaping Exchequer. It was not only the disinterested desire to give his people true justice that caused Henry II to extend the profitable domain of the royal courts. Richard, John, and Henry III cared even less than he about abstract justice, and even more about money, and they all continued to foster the royal jurisdiction. The Justices were quite as busy collecting the King's revenues as enforcing the King's peace. They were two aspects of the same operation.

Henry II was an autocrat, but like his Tudor namesakes he lived in times when people wished for strong government more than anything else. And like them he was an autocrat who ruled by law, who trusted his people, and who had no standing army, but encouraged his subjects to be armed, as unpopular tyrants dare not do. The Assize of Arms of 1181 decreed in detail what weapons and armour the men of every rank to the lowest freeholders and artisans must keep ready for the King's service in time of need. It was a measure anti-feudal in tendency, looking back to the Saxon fyrd, and forward to the new England in the making.

It was owing to Henry of Anjou that anarchy was quelled in the early morning of our history, instead of the late noon, as happened in the feudal lands of the continent. And it was due to him that the King's Peace was maintained through a native Common Law, which, unlike the systems more directly drawn from the civil law of the Roman Emperors, made law itself the criterion, and not the will of the Prince.

CHAPTER II

Richard I and the Crusades. Constitutionalism grows out of Feudalism. John and Magna Carta. Simon de Montfort. Parliament. Justices of the Peace. The Friars.

Kings: Richard I, 1189–99; John, 1199–1216; Henry III, 1216–71; Edward I, 1272–1307; Edward II, 1307–27

CHRISTENDOM in the Ninth and Tenth Centuries had been ringed round by foes encroaching upon her from east, from south, and from north. Europe had been, not the attacker, but the attacked; not the explorer, but the explored. If her enemies no longer, after the days of Charlemagne, threatened her very life, they bade fair to deny her the use of the sea, the possession of her own coasts, and therewith the prospect of the commerce and the world expansion which we associate with the destiny of the European peoples. In the North, the heathen Vikings held both sea and shore. Most of Spain and Sicily were under Saracen rule. The Mediterranean was swept by Moslem and Viking craft. From the lower Danube the heathen Magyars pushed into the heart of Germany and across the Lombard plain. Both by sea and by land Western Europe was being cut off from everything outside herself, even from Constantinople, the heart of Eastern Christianity and learning.

In the course of the Eleventh and Twelfth Centuries the situation was reversed. The slow conquest of Spain from north to south began. Norman instead of Saracen reigned in Sicily. The Vikings were repelled or converted, and their splendid energies, renewed in Norman warriors and statesmen, became the spearhead of Christian chivalry. The Magyars too were baptized, and their kingdom of Hungary gave the crusading armies free access by land to the Balkan territories, the Byzantine Empire, and thence into Asia Minor and on to the Holy Land. Sea power passed into the hands of the Italian maritime Republics of Genoa and Venice, who were therefore able to convoy the soldiers of the Cross to the Levant.

This brilliant change in the prospects of Europe had been achieved in the main by feudalism. Feudal Christianity, for all its faults, had imposed its ideals on Viking and Magyar as something superior to their own social order. And it had turned back the Moslem advance. When the feudal knight charged, as he had now learnt to do, with heavy lance in rest, no one could resist his onset. Infantry were no longer of great account till the rise of the English bowmen. And during the Twelfth and Thirteenth Centuries the military power of feudalism was crowned by improvements in the science of castle-building. Richard I's famed Château Gaillard in Normandy and the fortresses of the Crusaders in the East were vastly superior to the mound-and-stockade castles with which the Normans of the Conquest had held down England. They were superior even to the square donjon-keeps whence the anarchy of Stephen's reign had emanated, for the scheme of the new military architecture was a long curtain wall, defended by towers placed at intervals along its circuit, and enclosing a single great courtyard. The type is to be seen in Conway, Carnarvon, and Harlech, with which Plantagenet England held down the Welsh, and in Bodiam Castle in Sussex.

In these altered circumstances and with these improved methods of warfare, the recovered self-confidence of feudal Christendom was bound to seek outward expansion. The Crusades satisfied at once the dictates of piety and the craving for battle, exploration, and plunder. They were the policy not of the national statesman but of the knight errant, a characteristic figure in real life during the Twelfth and Thirteenth Centuries. The Crusades were the first phase in that outward thrust of the restless and energetic races of the new Europe which was never to cease till it had overrun the globe. It was the same spirit which had inspired the Vikings, but it was directed no longer inwards against the vitals of Europe, but outwards against her Asiatic neighbours.

As yet these adventurous energies, which were one day to cross the Atlantic and Pacific Oceans, were turned to the south-east, by the reopened routes of Danube and Mediterranean. England, in the north-west corner of the world, was left in a back-water. Individual English knights long continued to go on crusade, but the movement never became a national undertaking and tradition, as it did in France. The reason is obvious. France had a Mediterranean seaboard and England had not.

England, then, had practically no share in the First and most

successful of the Crusades, when Godfrey of Bouillon liberated Jerusalem and set up the Frankish state of Syria. In the Third
1190–3 Crusade, for the recovery of these territories most of which had been lost to Saladin, King Richard Cœur de Lion won personal glory as the greatest of knight errants. He took with him other Englishmen of an adventurous disposition, but not the solid part of the baronage, who stayed at home to govern the island in his absence. As for the English common folk, the emotions of the Third Crusade touched them just enough to produce some shocking pogroms of Jews.

But indirectly the effects of the Crusades upon England were very great, because they enriched and enlarged the mentality of medieval Christendom, of which England formed part. They brought many of the ablest men of the half-developed society of the West into fruitful contact with the trade, arts, science, and knowledge of the East. Both Saracen enemy and Byzantine ally were the heirs of civilizations older and better equipped than that of contemporary Europe. Even the art of fortification was largely imitated from the castles the Crusaders found in Asia. The settlements and ports founded by the Franks in Syria gave a great impetus to commerce between the two continents. The Crusades raised Venice, as the principal carrier of that commerce, to the pinnacle of her wealth and glory, enabled her citizen Marco Polo and many Italian traders and missionaries to traverse the heart of Asia sometimes as far as the Chinese littoral, and flooded Europe and England with luxuries and crafts imported or imitated from the East; while the nascent intellectual curiosity of the West, taking shape in Universities and in heresies, was deeply affected by Eastern philosophy and science. The rich, many-coloured fabric of later medieval life, the world of Dante and of Chaucer, would never have come into existence if barbarous Europe had remained as much shut in upon herself as she had been before the Crusades.

Such were the prizes that Europe carried back from the East. Her ardour was not rewarded by the permanent liberation of the Holy Sepulchre; nor by the fraternal unity of Christendom, of which the tale of the Crusades is one long negation; nor did she permanently strengthen the Byzantine Empire, the true bulwark of our civilization against Islam, which the Crusaders of 1203 basely betrayed for their own ends. What the blood and the zeal of the Crusaders really purchased for their descendants was the increase of commerce, craftsmanship, and luxury, the lust of the eye and of the ear, the pride of intellect, the origin of science, everything that was most despised by Peter the Hermit and the zealots who first preached the movement in the simpleness of their hearts.

Richard as King of England was a negligent, popular absentee, as befitted the character of knight errant. He left the island on his long Crusade, after making provisions for the government that ensured its disturbance by his brother John. In the hands of that man, already a proved traitor and ne'er-do-weel, he placed half a dozen counties, which were to pay nothing into the Exchequer, and which no royal justices were to visit. It was a dangerous blow at the system of direct royal government built up by Henry II, but that system had taken such firm root that even a rebellion plotted by John against his absent brother failed to shake the State. Richard had just appointed Hubert Walter to be Archbishop of Canterbury and Justiciar or Chief Officer of the Crown. Hubert, backed by the official baronage and by the Mayor and Citizens of London, suppressed the treason of John, and purchased Richard's deliverance from the Austrian prison into which his fellow crusaders had thrown him on his way home. He rewarded England's loyalty by draining her of money once more, and going off again at once to defend his Angevin inheritance. He never returned to England. Five years later he received his death wound in some obscure dispute with a vassal, beneath the walls of a petty fortress. 1189–99

Hubert Walter, indeed, governed England better than Richard would have done in person. He not only enforced the King's Peace, but began a new policy of trusting the middle classes of town and country, an important preparation for the great constitutional changes of the next two reigns.

He granted charters to various towns, conveying the privilege of self-government through elected officials. The old English world 'Alderman' and the word 'Mayor', imported from France, reflect the dual origin of the liberties of the medieval English towns. Hubert, indeed, like Henry II before him, seems to have feared the peculiar power which the citizens of London derived from their wealth, numbers, and geographic position. Nevertheless, during the period of disturbance caused by John's intrigues, the Londoners had secured once for all the right of electing their own Mayor – the first officer so called in England. When John came to the throne he continued and expanded the policy of selling municipal independence to the towns.

But Hubert Walter's policy of trusting and using the middle class as instruments of government was no less observable in the affairs of the shire. The class of rural gentry, the knights who were settling down on their manors to agricultural and peaceful pursuits, were increasingly employed for county business by the wise Justiciar. It is here that we see the first sure signs of that peculiarly English system of government whereby the Crown depends largely on the amateur services of the local gentry for the enforcement of the King's Peace, instead of depending wholly on the sheriff and Judges, or on a centralized bureaucracy of the later continental type. The new policy reached its full development in the Justices of the Peace of later times. In Richard I's reign the gentry were not yet performing their tasks under that name, but already, if not earlier, they were being compelled by the government to act as Coroners to 'keep the pleas of the Crown', that is to defend the King's judicial and financial rights in the shire. Their services were not always voluntary; it was indeed a function of the medieval Kingship to force the English to acquire the habits of self-government. The Crown found in the knights of the shire a useful check upon the sheriff, who was suspected by both King and people of frequently abusing his great powers.

Nor did Hubert Walter keep the appointment of Coroners in his own or in the sheriff's hands. He ordained that the suitors of the Shire Court, in other words the local gentry, should choose four of their own number to serve as Coroners. On the same principle, he ordered that the juries, instead of being chosen as heretofore by the sheriff, should be chosen by a committee of four knights who also were to be chosen in the Shire Court.

Here we have the self-government of the shire not through its great Barons but through its gentry, and here also we have the principle of representation. Thus by the end of the Twelfth Century, two hundred years before the Franklin of Chaucer's *Prologue*, a rural middle class was arising in England, accustomed to the transaction of public business and to the idea of electing representatives. When these local activities of the smaller gentry and the idea of representation were carried up to the larger sphere of a national Parliament, mighty consequences followed to England and to the world.

1199–1216 In the reign of John the feudal resistance of the Barons to the exorbitant demands of the Crown began gradually to turn into constitutional resistance, embracing all other classes of freemen. The King by his plenary power had familiarized the country with the idea of a Common Law of the land. In the reigns of John and Henry III after him, men began to formulate more precisely the conception of law as something with a life of its own, distinct from the regal power – something above the King, by which he must rule.

John was the very man to arouse a movement of constitutional resistance. A false, selfish, and cruel nature, made to be hated, he showed pertinacity and tactical ingenuity in pursuit of his designs, but he had no broad political strategy or foresight. He strained the feudal law and misused the splendid machinery of State, to extort money from all classes of his subjects, lay and clerical, rich and poor, burgher and Baron – and then spent it in clumsy and unsuccessful attempts to defend his Angevin inheritance against the rising power of the Capet Kings of France. The loss of Normandy to Philip Augustus took place in 1204, and ten years later John's scheme to recover it through a grand European coalition against France was shipwrecked by the defeat of his German allies at Bouvines. These events, together with the long- 1214
drawn-out quarrel of John with the Pope involving the interdict on England, were the prelude to Magna Carta. John's prestige was shattered, and the strength which previous Kings of England had drawn from their foreign possessions was turned into weakness.

It was between the reigns of John and Edward III that the possessions of the English Kings abroad were reduced to reasonable dimensions. Their Angevin Empire was no more; but they still retained Gascony and the port of Bordeaux, a stimulus to overseas trade, supplying cheap and excellent wine to replace mead and ale on the tables of the English middle class, and so putting an end to the pathetic efforts of our ancestors to grow grapes under our sunless sky. But the connexion with Gascony had not the intimate character of the old connexion with Normandy, when so many Barons had lands or relations on both sides of the Channel. During the century and a quarter that intervened between the loss of Normandy and the beginning of the Hundred Years' War, the English Kings, nobles, and knights, though still talking a caricature of the French tongue, interested themselves in questions proper to England – her relations with Wales and Scotland, and the development of her law and of her Parliament. This return to a more insular outlook saved us from too close an identification with France. If the England of the Thirteenth Century had been occupied in defending the Angevin Empire against the French Kings, the energies and thoughts of our leaders would have been drawn away from national interests and internal problems. When at length, in 1337, Edward III resumed the conquest of France, the English law had already acquired, and

Parliament was fast acquiring, well-defined native forms, and the English people had become conscious of its own identity.

1215 The first great step on the constitutional road was Magna Carta. The Barons in arms who extorted it from King John at Runnymede were none of them, so far as we know, remarkable men, but their ally, the Archbishop Stephen Langton, had both moral and intellectual greatness. He was all the greater man because his support of the constitutional cause was contrary to the wishes of the great Pope Innocent III, who, in return for John's politic submission in 1213, backed him at every turn in his quarrel with his subjects and declared Magna Carta null and void. Considering that Stephen Langton owed his election to Canterbury to the Pope's support, his stoutness on political questions in England was doubly remarkable.

The Barons were acting selfishly and class-consciously to just the same degree – no more and no less – as other English classes and parties who in successive centuries have taken part in developing 'our happy constitution' by self-assertion ending in a practical compromise. Their demands were limited and practical, and for that reason they successfully initiated a movement that led in the end to yet undreamt-of liberties for all.

The Barons had come together to prevent the King from abusing feudal incidents and from raising aids and reliefs on their lands beyond what feudal custom allowed. It has been called a 'tenant-right' movement on the part of an oppressed upper class against their landlord the King, though it must be remembered that what the King unjustly extorted from the Barons had most of it to be extracted by them from the classes below. The Barons also wished to put some limit to the King's plenary power of withdrawing case after case from their courts to his own, through the procedure of writs. We may sympathize less with the latter object than with the former. But, taking the situation as a whole, it was time that the King's plenary powers were curbed or nationalized, and no one but the Barons could have made such a movement effectual.

Stephen Langton was an enlightened guide to his baronial allies, but even without him the circumstances of the age in England were forcing them into the path of true progress. For the strength of the Plantagenet State machinery precluded a return to pure feudalism, nor had the Barons any such thought in their hearts. They had no desire to destroy the work of Henry II which had become a part of their own and of the nation's life. Knowing it to be indestructible, they desired to subject it to some form of common control, to prevent it from being any longer the instrument of one man's will.

In England a hundred years before, and still in Scotland and on the continent, the policy of the Barons was each to maintain his individual independence and private 'liberties' upon his own estates to the exclusion of the King's officers. But in England after Henry II, that was no longer to be dreamt of. The new English baronial policy, enshrined in Magna Carta, is designed to obtain public 'liberties' and to control the King through the Common Law, baronial assemblies, and alliance with other classes. When the Barons extracted the famous concession that no extraordinary 'scutage or aid shall be imposed on our kingdom, unless by common council of our kingdom', 'and in like manner it shall be done concerning aids from the City of London' – although they proceeded to define the 'common council' as a strictly feudal assembly of tenants-in-chief – they were none the less taking a step towards the principle of Parliaments and of 'no taxation without representation'. It was a very short step, but it was the first, and it is the first step that counts.

Moreover the Barons of Runnymede were not strong enough to rebel against the son of Henry II without the aid of the other classes whom John had oppressed and alienated. The Londoners opened their gates to the baronial army and took the field in warlike array. The clergy gave their moral and political support. The *liberi homines* or freemen – roughly including all classes above the unregarded villeins – aided with their passive sympathy; it was useless for John to call out the fyrd of all freemen under the Assize of Arms, as Henry II would have done against baronial rebellion. The English people for the first time sided with the Barons against the Crown, because they could do so without fear of reviving feudal anarchy.

Each of the classes that aided or abetted the movement had its share of benefits in the clauses of the Great Charter. In that sense we may call it a national document, though no claim was made on behalf of 'the people' or 'the nation' as a whole, since those abstractions had not yet begun to affect the minds of men. Protection against the King's officers and the right to a fair and legal trial were assigned to all 'freemen'. The term was of limited scope in 1215, but owing to the economic and legal evolution of the next three hundred years it came to embrace the descendant of every villein in the land, when all Englishmen became in the eye of the law 'freemen'.

Several clauses in Magna Carta give expression to the spirit of individual liberty, as it has ever since been understood in England. And the constant repetition of these brave words in centuries to come, by persons who were ignorant of the technical meaning they bore to the men who first wrote them down, helped powerfully to form the national character: –

> No freeman shall be taken or imprisoned or disseised or exiled or in any way destroyed, nor will we go upon him nor will we send upon him except by the lawful judgement of his peers or (and) the law of the land.

Numerous other clauses apply sharp checks to various lawless and tyrannical habits of the King's officers, both in his forests and elsewhere, which, if patiently suffered, would have created a tradition of the worst type of continental *droit administratif*.

The Charter was regarded as important because it assigned definite and practical remedies to temporary evils. There was very little that was abstract in its terms, less even than later generations supposed. Yet it was the abstract and general character of the event at Runnymede that made it a great influence in history. A King had been brought to order, not by a posse of reactionary feudalists, but by the community of the land under baronial leadership; a tyrant had been subjected to the laws which hitherto it had been his private privilege to administer and to modify at will. A process had begun which was to end in putting the power of the Crown into the hands of the community at large.

It is for this reason that a document so technical as the Charter, so deficient in the generalizations with which the Declaration of Independence abounds, so totally ignorant of the 'rights of man', has had so profound and lasting an influence on the imagination – in every sense of the word – of succeeding ages. Throughout the Thirteenth Century the 'struggle for the Charter', with its constant reissues, revisions, infringements, and reassertions, was the battleground of parties. Until the Edwardian Parliaments were fully established, the Charter remained in the foreground of men's thoughts.

In the Fourteenth and Fifteenth Centuries it fell into the background, its task apparently accomplished. Parliament held the place in men's minds which the Charter had once occupied. The later copyists and the early printers were never called upon to issue popular English versions of the great document. In Tudor times the Charter was even more utterly out of fashion, because it emphasized the distinction between the interests of

Prince and people, which throughout the Sixteenth Century Prince and people were equally anxious to deny. Shakespeare's *King John* shows that the author knew little and cared less about the Charter; though he treated fully and freely the human tragedy of Richard II's deposition and death.

But when, under James I, Prince and people again began to take up opposing ground, Magna Carta came quickly back into more than its old splendour. The antiquarians and lawyers who asserted our Parliamentary liberties in the age of Coke and Selden, saw looming through the mists of time the gigantic figure of Magna Carta as the goddess of English freedom. Their misinterpretations of the clauses were as useful to liberty then as they are amazing to medievalists now. Under the banner of Runnymede the battle of Parliament and the Common Law was fought and won against the Stuarts.

In the Eighteenth Century, the era of unchallengeable chartered liberty and vested interest, the greatest charter of all was worshipped by Blackstone, Burke, and all England. It had become the symbol for the spirit of our whole constitution. When, therefore, with the dawn of a more strenuous era, democracy took the field against the established order, each side put the Great Charter in the ark which it carried into battle. Pittites boasted of the free and glorious constitution which had issued from the tents on Runnymede, now attacked by base Jacobins and levellers; Radicals appealed to the letter and the spirit of 'Magna Charta' against gagging acts, packed juries, and restrictions of the franchise. America revolted in its name and seeks spiritual fellowship with us in its memory. It has been left to our own disillusioned age to study it as an historical document, always remembering that its historical importance lay not only in what the men of 1215 intended by its clauses, but in the effect it has had on the imagination of their descendants.

The Barons, having no idea of Parliamentary institutions, could only devise the most clumsy means to enforce the treaty they had wrung from the momentary need of their shifty and able adversary. By one of the final clauses of the Charter, John was forced to concede to a revolutionary committee of twenty-five Barons the right, if he broke any of the terms, 'to distrain and distress us in all possible ways, namely by seizing our castles, lands, and possessions and in any other way they can'. The situation immediately after Runnymede was as black as it could well be: John was incited by the Pope and his legate to repudiate the Charter, while the Barons called in the armed intervention

of the French Prince. We were saved from having to choose between a cruel despotism and a foreign dynasty, by that fortunate
1216 surfeit of 'peaches and new cider'. John's death afforded a last chance to reunite the nation on the principles of Magna Carta.

In the hands of patriotic statesman like William Marshall and Hubert de Burgh, with Langton as mediator between parties, the cause of the infant King Henry III made successful appeal to the nation. In a few years the land was pacified. The Charter was reissued with modifications; the Frenchmen were expelled on the one hand, and on the other the growing Papal influence on our politics was kept in check. Castles which the feudal classes had built for themselves or seized from the Crown during the civil war, were pulled down or resumed into royal hands, in many cases after serious siege operations. The minority of Henry III, which began in the midst of war and bade fair to see a revival of anarchy, was turned to good account, thanks to the honesty and ability of the statesmen exercising power in the name of a King who never afterwards used it well for himself.

For a whole generation after Henry III came of age, his misgovernment continued, keeping up discontent, till it burst out in another period of civil war and constitution-making, out of which Parliament was born. This epoch of creative unrest had Simon de Montfort for its hero and Edward I for its heir. It repeated the 'struggle for the Charter' under John, but with a difference: the party of reform led by Simon was even more popular than baronial. The middle classes of town and country, the gentry and burghers, formed its rank and file, and the best religious elements among the people, led by the friars, supported it, though Pope and King were in unholy alliance. The political rhymes and writings of the hour show that the reforming party of Simon's last years had formed the great conception of Law as a thing above the King. In the final crisis, de Montfort's victory at Lewes made him England's ruler, till in the following year he was defeated and slain at Evesham (1265). But his work lived after him, for he had made a convert of his conqueror, the King's son Edward, 'one of those peoples whom revolutions teach'. Edward I, when he came to the throne on his father's death in 1272, had already learnt that the King of England must reign under and through the Law, and that the Crown opposed to the nation was less strong than the Crown in Parliament.

The name 'Parliamentum' – 'talking shop' as Carlyle translated it, 'parley' or 'discussion' as it might more fairly be rendered – was first applied in Henry III's reign to the purely feudal assemblies of tenants-in-chief sitting with the other members of the King's Curia. The name 'Parliament' as yet carried no idea of election or representation, nor did it necessarily imply a legislative or tax-voting assembly. It was simply the King's Curia or Council, when Barons and King's servants met together to 'talk', to debate high politics foreign and domestic, to discuss petitions, grievances, ways and means, and new forms of writ, and to conduct State Trials. It was not more legislative than administrative, not more financial than judicial. Having 'talked', it acted, for it was an epitome of all the powers in the State. But the method of selecting its members had not yet been defined.

In the course of Henry III's reign it became an occasional but not an invariable practice to summon to this great assembly two or more knights elected in each Shire Court to represent the county. This was not to create a new assembly, or to 'originate Parliament'; it was merely to call up some new people to the plenary session of the old *curia regis.* Neither was it a party move either of the King or of his opponents; both sides felt that it was best to know what the 'bachelors' were thinking. It was a natural evolution, so natural as scarcely to attract notice. For two generations past, knights elected in the Shire Court had transacted local business with the King's judges and officers. It seemed but a small step to summon them collectively to meet the King among his judges and officers at some central point. Moreover representatives from individual shires and boroughs had long been in the habit of attending the King's Curia to transact the business of their community. To us, with our knowledge of all that was to come, the step of summoning them collectively and officially may seem immense. But in the medieval world the representation of communities was a normal way of getting business done, and its application to the central assembly of the realm was too natural to cause remark. When the wind sows the acorn the forester takes little heed.

Then and for long afterwards the summons to Parliament was often regarded as a burden, grudgingly borne for the public good, much as the companion duty of serving on a jury is still regarded to-day. Communities, particularly boroughs, often neglected to send their representatives; and even the elected knights of the shire sometimes absconded to avoid service. Doubtless it was galling, when you looked round the Shire Court to congratulate the new member ironically on his expensive and dangerous honour, to find that he had slipped quietly on his horse and ridden for sanctuary, leaving the court to choose you in his stead! 'The elective franchise' was not yet a privilege or a 'right of man'. In Edward III's reign, the borough of distant Torrington in Devon obtained by petition the 'franchise' of not being required to send members to Parliament; for the payment of members' expenses then fell on the communities that sent them up.

Nevertheless the presence of the knights of the shire strengthened the authority and aided the counsels of the Parliament of magnates. The Government found it convenient and advantageous to enforce the presence of the 'communities' or 'commons' of the realm through their representatives. And so in the year of revolution after Lewes, Simon de Montfort summoned not only the knights of the shire, but for the first time two representatives from each of the chartered boroughs. He probably knew that the burghers would be of his faction, and he was the first of our rulers to perceive that the general position of a party government could be strengthened by calling representatives of all the communities together and talking to them. It was a form of 'propaganda', over and above any financial or judicial use that was made of the Assembly. We learn from the writs that the burghers were summoned, but we do not know how many came, or what, if anything, they did. That particular Parliament was a revolutionary assembly to which only those Barons were summoned who were of Simon's party, but it set a precedent for the summoning of burghers which was imitated in the more regular Parliaments of Edward the First.

The English Parliament had no one man for its maker, neither Simon nor even Edward. No man made it, for it grew. It was the natural outcome, through long centuries, of the common sense and the good nature of the English people, who have usually preferred committees to dictators, elections to street fighting, and 'talking-shops' to revolutionary tribunals.

Parliament was not devised on the sudden to perpetuate a revolution in which one power rose and another fell. It grew up gradually as a convenient means of smoothing out differences and adjusting common action between powers who respected one another – King, Church, Barons, and certain classes of the common people such as burgesses and knights. No one respected the villeins and they had no part in Parliament. Knowing that Parliament was hostile, 'labour', as soon as it began to be self-conscious, preferred 'direct action' like the rising of 1381. But, setting the villeins aside, Parliament represented a friendly balance of power. The English people have always been distinguished for the 'Committee sense', their desire to sit round and talk till an agreement or compromise is reached. This national peculiarity was the true origin of the English Parliament.

It was during the reigns of the first three Edwards that Parliament gradually acquired something like its present form. After his experiences in the time of de Montfort, Edward I saw in frequent national assemblies the best oil for the machinery of government. His object was not to limit the royal power or to subject it to the will of the commonalty. His object was to make the royal power more efficient by keeping it in constant touch with the life of the governed. And like Henry VIII, the only other monarch in our annals who did as much to increase the prestige of Parliament, he knew the value of the support of the middle classes in shire and town.

Edward I, therefore, decided to continue and popularize the experiment that had occasionally been made during his father's turbulent reign of summoning representatives of the counties and boroughs to attend the great conferences of the magnates of the realm. He wanted, for one thing, to collect certain taxes more easily. The difficult assessments could not be well made without the willing help and special knowledge of the local knights and burgesses. Their representatives would return from the presence of King and assembled magnates, each to his own community, awestruck yet self-important, filled with a new sense of national unity and national needs. In that mood they would help to arrange the assessments locally, and facilitate payment. And they would explain the King's policy to their neighbours, who had no other means of information.

When there were no newspapers and few letters, and when travel was difficult and dangerous, the King's rigid insistence on the perpetual coming and going of ever fresh troops of knights and burghers between Westminster and their own communities began the continuous political education of Englishmen, and perhaps did more to create the unity of the nation than Chaucer or the Hundred Years' War. Nor, without such a machinery for the easy levy of taxes, could the great Scottish and French wars of the Edwardian period have been fought. It has been said that it was not England who made her Parliament, but Parliament that made England, and there is an element of truth in the epigram.

Financial need was not the only reason why the King summoned the representatives of town and shire. Indeed Edward I sometimes called them together on occasions when he asked for no money at all. For he had another end in view, to gather together the petitions and grievances of his subjects, so as to be able to govern in accordance with real local needs, and to keep a check on the misdeeds of local officials. Thus a large part of the business of these early Parliaments consisted in receiving piles of petitions for redress, mostly from private persons or single communities, but increasingly as the Fourteenth Century went on, from the House of Commons as a whole. In the reign of Edward I these petitions were directed, not to Parliament, but to the King or Council. They were dealt with in Parliament either by the King, by his ministers, or by committees of councillors, judges, and Barons, known as 'Triers'. The redress afforded to the petitioners in these early times may now be regarded as either judicial, legislative, or administrative; the distinction was not then made. But, as time went on, while many of the private petitions were referred to judicial processes in the Chancery Court or elsewhere, the more important class emanating from the Commons' House as a whole began in the reign of Henry VI to take the form of 'bills' to be passed into law by Parliament. Such was the origin of the right of the House of Commons to initiate legislation.

But we must not speak of 'Houses' of Parliament as early as the reign of Edward I. There was then but one assembly, presided over by the King from his throne, or by his Chancellor from the woolsack; the rest of the chief officers of State were present *ex officio*, together with the Barons, lay and spiritual, summoned each by special writ; there were also present, humbly in the background, the representative knights and burghers summoned through the sheriff of each shire, not likely to speak unless they were first spoken to in such a presence. This was the 'High Court of Parliament', which is still visible to the eye in the modern House of Lords with its throne and woolsack, although the Chancellor alone of the King's Ministers can now attend *ex officio* even if he is not a peer, and although the throne is now occupied only when Parliament is opened or prorogued. Then, when the Commons flock to the bar to hear the King's words, we have the original Plantagenet Parliament reassembled.

In the reign of Edward I the representatives of the Commons were not yet a separate House. And though they often attended the sessions of the Parliament one and indivisible, their presence there was not essential for much of the important business transacted by the magnates. Their consent to legislation was not always asked. The great Statutes for which the reign was famous were some of them passed when no representatives of the Commons were in attendance. And it is probable that if knights and burgesses were present at all when high matters of foreign and domestic policy were debated by the Ministers, Barons, and Prelates, it was but as 'mutes and audience'.

The House of Commons as a separate Chamber originated in unofficial meetings of the knights and burgesses, discussing anxiously behind closed doors what collective reply they should give to some difficult question or demand with which they had been confronted by the higher powers. They were so careful to leave no reports of these proceedings that we know nothing of the internal development of the early House of Commons. We do not even know how and when the Speaker became its chairman. For the Speaker was originally the person appointed to 'speak' for the Commons in full Parliament, the other knights and burgesses being silent in presence of their betters. But until Stuart times the Speaker was a servant of the Crown much more than a servant of the House. As early as the reign of Edward III we find some of the King's household officers sitting as knights of the shire, very possibly to direct the debates and decisions of the House of Commons in the interest of the Crown, as Privy Councillors continued to do with very great effect in Tudor times. It was also in the reign of Edward III that the Chapter House of the monks of Westminster came to be regarded as the customary meeting place of the Commons.

The most important fact in the early history of our institutions is that the English Parliament, unlike analogous assemblies of the same period in Europe, divided itself, during the later Plantagenet reigns, not into three Estates of clergy, nobles, and bourgeois, but into two Houses of Lords and Commons. The greater part of our constitutional and social history is in some sense either cause or effect of that unique arrangement.

In the continental system of 'Estates', all the 'gentlemen', as we should call them, were represented in the estate of the '*noblesse*'. But the '*noblesse*', in the large sense which the word bears on the continent, was in the English Parliament divided in two. The *barones majores*, each summoned by special writ, sat in the upper house. The *barones minores*, even though tenants-in-chief, shared with knights, gentry, and 'franklins' the liability to be elected as knights of the shire. Thus the forms of English Parliamentary life abolished the distinctions of feudalism. Even a tenant-in-chief might be found sitting and working with the burghers of the towns.

This strange and significant arrangement of the Fourteenth

Century English Parliaments was rendered possible by earlier developments which we have already noticed. The active part taken by the smaller gentry in shire business had often brought them in contact with the burghers as well as with the humbler rural freeholders. The English rule of primogeniture, which sent the cadets of a noble family out into the world, had given the inhabitants of castle and manor-house a friendly interest in trade and commerce. The intermarriage of classes and the constant intercommunication of the upper and middling ranks of society were already much more marked in England than elsewhere. Ages long ago, before the battles of Bannockburn or Crécy, the House of Commons already reflected these English peculiarities. Already the knights of the shire, a semi-feudal class, were acting as elected representatives of the rural yeomen, and were sitting cheek by jowl with the citizens of the boroughs. That is why the House of Commons was able to assert its importance at a very early date, when burghers and yeomen had small political prestige unless they were acting in association with knights. That also is why the English Civil War of Stuart times was not a class war; and why the English of Burke's time could not understand what in the world the French Revolution was about.

Neither was any Estate or House of the Clergy formed as part of the English Parliament. Not only did the spirituality refrain from drawing together as a separate clerical 'Estate' in Parliament, but they voluntarily abandoned all their seats among the Commons and many of their seats among the Lords.

In the Upper House, indeed, the Bishops and certain of the greater Abbots continued to sit in their secular capacity as holders of baronies in a feudal assembly. Moreover some of the Bishops were royal ministers and civil servants. But the Prelates who were churchmen first and foremost took little stock of Parliament. The majority of the Abbots and Priors, wrapped up in local monastic interests, disliked the trouble and expense of long journeys, and feeling more bound in duty to the Pope than to the King, would not be at the pains to attend. They fell out of the national life and abandoned their places in Parliament, with results that became apparent in the Parliamentary Statute Book of Henry VIII.

So, too, the representatives of the lower clergy did not become a permanent part of the House of Commons, and gradually ceased to attend Parliament at all. The business of voting the 'fifteenths' and 'tenths' of clerical property to the King was conducted instead in the Convocations of Canterbury and York.

Those assemblies were and are ecclesiastical, not political. They were in no sense an Estate of Parliament like the French Clerical Estate which figures in the original session of the *États Généraux* of 1789. The English clergy, on the principle that the things of Caesar and the things of God were best kept apart, deliberately stepped aside from the political life and growth of the nation in the later Middle Ages. But since they also preserved their great and envied wealth and many ancient privileges, which came to be regarded as abuses in a changed world, their position was one of isolation, peculiarly exposed to attack when the Reformation began.

From humble beginnings in the reign of Edward I the House of Commons attained in the next hundred and fifty years to a great place in the constitution. The consent of its members became necessary for all making of Statutes and for all extraordinary taxation; their own petitions very frequently received the assent of the King in Parliament; and even the highest acts of State like the deposition and election of Kings took place with the Commons as parties to the deed. Their constitutional power when the Wars of the Roses broke out was indeed more apparent than real, for the strongest forces in politics were Crown, Barons, and Church, not Commons. But their recorded position in the public law of the country supplied invaluable precedents for the assumption of real power by the Lower House after the Tudor monarchs had clipped the wings of Church and baronage.

If in later Plantagenet times the Commons increased in real power much, and in nominal power more, the reason is not far to seek. They were a third party, holding the balance, and courted by the principals in the warfare of State. The constant struggle between King and Barons under the three Edwards, the equally constant struggle between the great families around the throne in the days of the House of Lancaster, put the Commons almost into the place of umpire. They were well fitted to take advantage of the position, because their interests were not wholly bound up with either Barons or King.

When Edward I died he was on the way to make himself absolute master of England and of Scotland both. He had in the last years of his life gone far to break the baronial opposition at home, and to tread out the embers of the fire that Wallace had kindled and that Bruce was trying to fan. An able successor might have destroyed constitutional liberty in England and national liberty in Scotland. Parliament might have become, not an opposition or a critic to be conciliated, but a useful cog in the 1307

machine of royal government – as no doubt Edward himself regarded it. The reign of his innocent-minded but lazy and in-
1307–27 capable son, Edward II, saved the situation. It is not good to have an unbroken succession of great rulers like Henry II, Edward I, or the Tudors. John, Edward II, and the Stuarts had their appointed place in the destiny of Britain.

The lax rule of two people of such unbusinesslike and artistic temperaments as young Edward II and his friend Piers Gaveston, presented the Barons with another chance. Gaveston was by no means the first nor the worst 'upstart', nor the most alien 'foreigner' who had risen to the head of affairs in England, but he had no prudence, for he gave nicknames to the leading Barons.
1312 In return, some of them took his life by treachery. Edward II and Gaveston were as unfit to govern England as Charles I and Buckingham. But the leaders of the baronial opposition, especially Earl Thomas of Lancaster, were stupid, selfish, and brutal men, swollen with the pride of birth. The King's next favourite, Despenser, was not an 'upstart' like Gaveston, but he developed into a tyrant. And yet the struggle between such unpromising opponents worked out to the advantage of the nation. The machinery of administration was improved, not by subjecting it to the clumsy control of the Barons, but by certain bureaucratic reforms. And the powers of Parliament were much increased, for on several great occasions it was called upon, now by Edward II, and now by the baronial opposition, to regularize their alternate victories by vote and Statute. In this new prestige of Parliament the Commons had their share.

The net result of the baronial tumults – they can scarcely be called baronial wars – during the reign of this unhappy King was not to increase the power either of Crown or of baronage. Throughout the Middle Ages the Barons were never able, in spite of repeated efforts, to dominate the King's counsels on any regular plan, though they held that on feudal principles he ought always to be guided by their noble advice, instead of by the advice of trained clerks and civil servants whose only qualification was that of understanding the King's business. The Barons failed to establish their claim to govern, because government means steady application, which a Baron could seldom give. His castles, his hunting, his estates, his retainers, his habits of life, his manors scattered over half the counties of England, very properly took up his time. He could not be the King's responsible Minister or attend to the regular sessions of the Council, because he had other duties and other pleasures.

A second reason why the Barons failed to control the government except in moments of revolution was that the King's Court and household were too large and complicated to be easily subjected to control. If an office – say the Chancery with its Great Seal – was secured by the baronial opposition, the King could dive underground and still govern the country through the Wardrobe with its Privy Seal. The King's Court was plastic and adaptable in its organization, yet highly specialized as a civil service, full of trained and able men who went on quietly governing, while far over their heads fools or scoundrels like Gaveston and Thomas of Lancaster, Despenser, and Mortimer ranted and killed each other for the benefit of posterity and the Elizabethan dramatists. Meanwhile peaceful stone manor-houses could rise in quiet corners of the land, the export of wool could increase, the population could go up, all classes could grow less poor and less ill-fed, because all the while the King's Peace was indifferently well enforced.

In the reign of Edward III an addition was made to the State machinery, significant of much. Keepers or Justices of the Peace were set up in every county to help the central power to govern. Like the Coroners before them, they were not bureaucrats but independent country gentlemen. As typical of the rising class of knights and smaller gentry, the Justices of the Peace took over more and more of the work previously done by that great man the Sheriff, or by the Judges on circuit. The 'J.P.s' seemed to strike root in the shire and grow as a native plant, equally popular with their neighbours and with the King's Council, between whom it was their task to interpret. For four hundred years their powers continued to increase, both in variety of function and in personal authority, till in the Eighteenth Century they were in a sense more powerful than the central government itself. This would not have happened if they had not responded to the needs and character of the English over a long period of time. The respect in which the English hold the law was generated not a little by this system of 'amateur justice'. For the magistrate who expounded and enforced the law for ordinary people in ordinary cases may not have known much law, but he knew his neighbours and was known of them.

In the Thirteenth Century, during the reigns of John and Henry III, two great social and intellectual changes were taking place in England, the growth of the Universities of Oxford and Cambridge, and the Coming of the Friars. Unlike our native Parliament, both were offshoots of movements begun oversea, in Italy, Spain, and France.

The earliest Franciscan friars in England, themselves converts from the class of gentry, made a great religious revival among the poor, comparable in many ways to the Puritan, Methodist, and Salvation Army movements of later days. In the spirit of their founder, St Francis of Assisi, they sought out the poorest, the most neglected, the diseased. The other secret of the friars' influence was preaching, in words which the common people would feel and understand. Parish priests were then seldom competent to preach, while the higher clergy had their heads full of worldly matters of Church and State, and the monks abode in their convents or rode about on mundane business or pleasure. Before the coming of the friars, religion relied too exclusively on the sacraments she dispensed, nor were they always at hand for those who needed them. The itinerant friars, who took all the world for their parish, not only made the sacraments more available, but erected preaching and religious instruction into a popular system. It was the destined method of Lollard, Protestant, and Puritan in later times. By enhancing the importance of the pulpit the friars prepared the way for those who were to supersede and destroy them, for they brought religion to the common people, endeavouring to make it intelligible to their minds and influential over their lives.

CHAPTER III

Celt and Saxon. Attempts to complete the Island Empire. Causes of Failure in the Middle Ages. Ireland, Wales, Scotland.

THE England of the later Middle Ages, the most highly organized of the larger States of Europe, lay alongside Wales and Ireland, each a congeries of Celtic tribes, and abutted on Scotland, a poor and thinly inhabited Kingdom, racially divided between Celt and Saxon, but already becoming Anglo-Norman in language and institutions. In such circumstances it was inevitable that attempts should be made to round off the island empire on the basis of conquest by England.

The Romans in Britain had been faced by precisely the same geographic problem. Their good genius prompted them to leave Ireland alone; they tried repeatedly and vainly to conquer Scotland; but they quickly subdued Wales by their system of military roads and forts, without, however, inducing the mountaineers to adopt the Latinized civilization of the plains. Medieval England had much the same measures of success as Roman Britain. More slowly indeed than the legions, English feudal chivalry with its network of castles made a military conquest of Wales, but the full adjustment of Welsh to Saxon civilization was left over till Tudor and Hanoverian times; the attempt to subdue Scotland was a complete failure; while beyond St George's channel, England effected not a conquest, but a lodgement in medieval Ireland, and hung on like a hound that has its fangs in the side of the stag.

A main reason why the medieval English failed in Scotland and Ireland, and never reduced even Wales to good order, is to be sought in their continental entanglements. Till the loss of Normandy in John's reign, the energies of the Norman and Angevin Kings of England had been occupied in the recovery or defence of provinces in France. The only time that the Plantagenet Kings were able to devote the best part of their thoughts and resources to purely British problems was during the century 1214–1337 that followed the final loss of Normandy and preceded the outbreak of the Hundred Years' War. During that period there was only one great King, Edward I, and in his reign, as we should expect, the power of medieval England in Wales, Ireland, and Scotland reached its high-water mark. After his death, the incapacity of Edward II, and the preoccupation of all later Kings before the Tudors with the extravagant attempt to conquer France or with resultant civil troubles at home, destroyed English rule in all Scotland and in nearly all Ireland, and weakened it even in Wales.

When we last looked towards Ireland it was in the heaviest midnight of the Dark Ages, when the light of learning sparkled in that distant corner of the world, casting back gleams on the opaque ignorance of Scotland and England, Germany and France. The saints, artists, and learned men of Irish monasticism shone by their individual merits and were free from the bondage of organization. Institutionalism was as abhorrent to the early Irish Church as to the tribal system from which it sprang. It followed that the Irish clergy never helped, as the Saxon clergy had done, to organize their race in a united Church and a single State. When the zeal and inspiration of the early saints died away, they left nothing behind but memories, and Ireland was little less dark and distracted than she had been before.

Even the suzerainty formerly exercised over the other chiefs by the 'High Kings' at Tara had become in the Eleventh Century a mere title. The career of Brian Boru, King of Cashel in Munster, the racial hero against the Viking invaders, did not permanently strengthen the 'High Kingship' or unite the Celts. But the victory of Clontarf on his death's day saved Ireland from the Norsemen and confined the Danes to the towns they had founded such as Dublin, Waterford, and Limerick. Town life and trade had no attraction for the native. Cattle-feeding and cattle-lifting, tribal war and family feud, minstrelsy and a little agriculture still occupied the time and thoughts of the Celtic tribes, as of many other tribes all the world over for many thousand years in times gone by. It is a matter of opinion whether or not these simple folk were better employed than the new restless Europe with its Crusades and Hildebrandine movements, its stone castles and cathedrals, its feudalism, its charters, its trade-routes, and all the stir of modernity. But for good or for evil the time had gone by when a European race could, with impunity, remain primitive. To eschew defensive armour, castles, and feudalism in the days of Strongbow was as dangerous as to eschew machine guns and the industrial revolution in our own.

Henry II was too busy on the continent to take up the Irish
1169–71 question himself. The conquest was, however, begun in his reign by private adventurers from Wales, led by Richard de Clare, Earl of Pembroke, nicknamed Strongbow. His partners in this last of the Norman conquests were not pure Normans, nor pure Anglo-Normans. Many of them, like the famous Fitzgeralds, were sons of Welsh mothers. They were a special border breed, these 'Marcher lords'; and their soldiers were many of them Welsh or Flemings. Perhaps the Celtic element in the blood and experience of these first 'English' conquerors of Ireland helped their descendants to mingle only too easily with the native Irish and adapt their own feudal institutions to the tribalism of the Celtic world beyond the Dublin 'Pale'. Possibly pure Normans or Anglo-Normans might have stamped more of their own character and institutions on this land, as they did on so many others.

But no Norman intruders in England, Sicily, or Scotland ever showed themselves superior in warlike efficiency to the followers of Strongbow. His chain-clad knights were supported by archers, whose skill was then the speciality not of England but of Wales. The unarmoured infantry of the Irish tribes, fighting with the Danish battle-axe and hurling stones and javelins, were helpless against the best archers and some of the best cavalry in Europe.

The only refuge of the natives was the marshes, woods, and mountains of their roadless and unreclaimed island. They knew all the arts of guerrilla war, using felled trees and earthworks to block the narrow passages through forest and bog. But the opposition to the invaders was not truly national. They found many allies both among tribesmen and churchmen. Dermot, who had invited over Strongbow, was not in his own lifetime universally execrated as the traitor that he appeared in the distant retrospect.

Castle-building was the cement of Anglo-Norman rule in Ireland, as in the sister island. Here, too, the Celt was at a great disadvantage, for the only resistance behind permanent fortifications which the invaders had to encounter was in the port-towns of the Danes. But since the battle of Clontarf, the Danes in Ireland had become peaceful traders instead of warrior Vikings, and moreover they were few in number. Their towns were easily captured, and were transformed at a stroke from Scandinavian to English. The citizens of Bristol were given the right to inhabit Dublin. Dublin Castle, first erected by the Vikings, became the centre of Saxon rule in Ireland from the Twelfth to the Twentieth Century.

The Danes were massacred or returned to Scandinavia, making way for the conquerors, who henceforward held in these port-towns the keys of entry into the island. Celtic town life did not yet exist. Even towns like Galway in the far west were of Anglo-Norman origin. Only towards the end of the Middle Ages, the English inhabitants of the towns outside the Dublin Pale gradually adopted the speech of the surrounding population with whom they bartered, and became by intermarriage and otherwise scarcely less Irish than English.

At the time of Strongbow's conquest and for long afterwards, national feeling did not exist, and foreign rule would have been accepted on its merits. All that was then necessary to put the races on a friendly understanding was strong and just government. But throughout the Middle Ages the government was neither strong nor just. Henry II, the father of rebellious sons, and the embarrassed ruler over half of western Christendom, had perforce to limit the liabilities which Strongbow had created for him, for he had neither time, money, nor men to establish his own rule in the island, in anything more than name. Yet, while he could not afford to keep up an effective royal government, he dared not let Strongbow or any of the feudal leaders obtain Viceregal authority. The adventurers therefore continued to prey on the natives, and to carve out baronies for themselves, fighting for their own hands without either proper support or proper control from the English King. For more than a century the Conquest went forward, slowly enlarging its boundaries westward, meeting no determined resistance from the natives, but divided and uncertain in its own purpose, and bringing in its train neither justice nor even a strong tyranny.

In these circumstances there grew up that three-fold division of the island which, with continual variation of boundary, held good throughout the rest of the Middle Ages. There was the Pale round Dublin, where English law was administered as in an English shire. Far in the west lay the purely Celtic chiefs and tribes, threatened but still untouched by the invasion. And between these two Irelands, and intermingled with them both, lay the areas of mixed rule, the baronies where the descendants of the great adventurers bore sway from their castles over the native population. But their Norman-Welsh feudalism was gradually transformed into something very like the Celtic tribalism which it was intended to replace. If, long afterwards, with all the differences of religion, the descendants of so many of Cromwell's soldiers were quickly absorbed into the Celtic atmosphere around them, it is no wonder that the same evolution took place in the case of the Anglo-Irish Barons. Throughout the greater part of the island English rule had been built upon the foundation of an Irish bog.

In the reign of Edward I, the greater attention paid at that period to insular affairs enabled Ireland to enjoy a brief spell of prosperity, especially in Leinster and Meath where the English interest was strongest. Villages sprang up and agriculture spread under the protecting shadow of the castles. Trading towns like Dublin, Waterford, and Cork pushed their commerce oversea.

Then came one of those rapid wrong turnings, so habitual in Irish history. Edward I's attempt to conquer Scotland led to reprisals under his feeble son. Immediately after Bannockburn the Scots under the Bruce brothers broke into Ireland through
1315–18 Ulster, where in all ages they have had strong connexions. The delicate prosperity of the new Ireland was destroyed with fire and sword, and the English influence never recovered for two centuries. The invasion of the Bruces was rather the occasion than the cause of the collapse. At bottom it was due to the character and power of the Anglo-Irish baronage, ever less distinguishable from the Celtic chiefs, and ever enlarging the boundaries of their rule at the expense of the genuinely English colony.

The Pale grew narrower both in space and in spirit. The English settlers and officials, increasingly conscious that they were a garrison in an alien land, cooped up and hard beset, drew in upon their own company and their own ideals of life. They came to regard almost everyone and everything outside the Pale ditch as belonging not to the 'English' but the 'Irish' interest. The distinction set the tone to a policy that for centuries was fruitful of mischief. The colonists drew ever more rigidly the line between the two races, and proscribed native law, language, and custom, so far as their little power extended in pre-Tudor times.

The Hundred Years' War with France distracted England's attention yet further from the overseas possession where her real duty lay. In the interval between the two parts of that long struggle, Richard II came with an army to Ireland. Then he fell, and no English King set foot in Ireland again until William of Orange. The utter neglect of Ireland by the rival Houses of Lancaster and York completed the relapse to Celtic tribalism outside the Pale, and, in spite of the efforts of one section of the colonists, Irish language and custom spread among the English of the Pale itself. The native civilization had indeed profited by the conquerors whom it had absorbed. Town life had been started; most of the towns founded by Danes and English had become, in part at least, Irish-speaking; while the Anglo-Irish nobility presided over a native world that gave in the Fifteenth Century signs of a rude social prosperity of its own.

But the bare presence of England in Ireland prevented any project of national unity from being pursued on native lines. The scant footing maintained by the English in and around Dublin, and the acknowledged claims of the English King as overlord, sufficed to prevent the union of the country under one of the Anglo-Irish Barons. It is true that in the last half of the Fifteenth Century there was a movement towards the government of the island in the name of the King by Deputies chosen from one of the great Anglo-Irish families, particularly the Fitzgeralds, Earls of Kildare. But events in the reign of Henry VII showed that this arrangement, whatever its effect upon the internal condition of Ireland, was incompatible with the safety of the King of England, whose dynastic enemies used the Fitzgeralds and the credulous Irish people as allies of Yorkist intrigues and for armed invasion of England on behalf of pretenders like Lambert Simnel. 'Aristocratic Home Rule' therefore proved a failure, since a free Ireland was employed to attack and disturb her great neighbour. 'Poynings' law' put a term to the experiment, by 1494
decreeing the complete dependence of the Irish Parliament on the English executive. The attempted solution had failed, but the

actual reconquest of Ireland was not undertaken till the following century.

England had proved too weak to conquer and govern Ireland, but strong enough to prevent her from learning to govern herself. It is significant that the island which had once been the lamp to Europe's ignorance was almost alone of European countries in having no University when the Middle Ages came to an end. It was a sorry heritage overseas which the medieval English handed on to the English of the Reformation. They had neglected Ireland for centuries when a forward and active policy might have saved the situation; when the policy of real conquest was adopted under the Tudors, it was in an age too late, an age of religious cleavage, commercial competition, and national self-consciousness all in their crudest form.

The relation of the Celt to his neighbour has proved more happy in Britain than in Ireland. And again we must look to medieval history to see why.

In the latter stages of the Anglo-Saxon conquest, the remaining territories of the Cymri or Welsh had been cut by the English advance into three separated parts – Strathclyde in the north, Wales in the centre, and the Devonian-Cornish peninsula in the south. Their collective power of racial resistance was greatly reduced by their geographic isolation from one another, which was rendered complete by their enemies' command of the sea from the Isle of Man, the Vikings' centre of operations, and from the great port-towns of Chester and Bristol. Before the Norman Conquest, Scandinavian settlers had already given a thoroughly Nordic character to the Lake District and North Lancashire, while Devon had been so far colonized by the Saxons of Wessex that it has ever since been regarded as an integral and characteristic part of the life of England. Cornwall remained as a pocket of Celtic race and language, but too small and isolated to give trouble on that score. Conquered in Anglo-Saxon times and closely annexed to the English Crown, it was subjected to Norman feudalism as Domesday Book records, and subsequently to medieval English law. But it spoke a Celtic tongue of its own until Stuart times, and it preserves a regional and Celtic character in its population to this day.

The larger problem of Wales remained. The wide extent of its mountain area had brought the Saxon Conquest to a halt behind Offa's Dyke. But the mountains which kept back the English prevented the union of the Welsh. In Edward the Confessor's reign, Harold made headway westward, and secured the alliance of some of the Celtic tribes ever at feud with one another, thus opening a road to further advance under the Normans.

From William the Conqueror till the accession of Edward I the most successful efforts to subdue Wales were made, not by the Kings of England, but by the 'Marcher Lords' and their private armies, men of the type of Strongbow and the Fitzgeralds. In blood a mixture of Norman, English, and Welsh, they represented feudal government and English economic penetration rather than the English monarchy. At one time there were reckoned to be 143 Lords Marcher, and wherever a Marcher Lord carved out for himself an estate with the sword, he built a castle and proceeded to exact feudal dues from the inhabitants, and to enforce in his own court feudal law, English law, or fragments of Welsh tribal custom. Under his protection English-speaking colonists – military, farming, and trading – settled on the land he ruled. He was in reality a petty sovereign, representing the intrusion of a new race and a more elaborate civilization.

The Anglo-Norman invasion conquered the lowlands and penetrated up the valley bottoms, because the valleys were the only gates of entry into the roadless mountains, and because they contained the arable land. But as the valleys themselves were frequently choked up with forest and marsh, the process was slow. The English had to play the part of pioneer farmers, as well as of warriors ever on the alert.

Before the coming of the Anglo-Normans, the Welsh had been a pastoral rather than an agricultural people. They did not inhabit towns, villages, or even houses, but lived in huts of boughs which they twisted together for a few months' occupation, as they followed their flocks and herds from winter to summer ground upon the mountain side. But whenever these simple tribesmen saw their valley dominated by a Norman castle of timber or stone, with a feudal court and an English-speaking agricultural village attached, one part of them fled higher into the neighbouring hills in pursuit of freedom. Others remained below as vassals of the new lord, but were often at heart faithful to the tribal chief exiled on to the neighbouring mountains, whence he was perpetually returning in destructive raids upon the vale.

To imagine such a situation in fifty different valleys is to get some idea of the chaos that Wales must have presented in the Twelfth Century. Tribalism and feudalism were struggling for the land. And mountain barriers separated district from district, increasing the tendency inherent in both tribalism and feudalism to divide political authority into fragments. In the hills tribe fought against tribe, and in the valleys Baron fought against Baron, while every baronial valley was at war with its tribal hills.

Yet civilization was advancing, however slow and however bloody the process. Time was on the side of the invaders, who were near to their own bases and were perpetually recruited by sea and land, unlike the forlorn hope of Anglo-Norman civilization, derelict among the bogs of Ireland. Ships from the great ports of Bristol and Chester commanded all the valley mouths of Wales that ran into the sea; while, inland, the upper valley of the Severn gave the invaders an easy route from Shrewsbury into the heart of the country, enabling them to overrun Powys and cut off Gwynedd in the North from Dinefawr in the South. Pembroke was planted from the sea by so many industrious English and Flemings that it lost the use of the Celtic tongue and became known as 'little England beyond Wales'. But even at the height of their power the Lords Marcher were never able to subdue the Gwynedd district centred round the impenetrable fastnesses of Snowdon.

The Lords Marcher represented a type of government more backward than that of England but more advanced than that of tribal Wales. Bohun, Mortimer, and the other Marcher families were an element of disturbance in the English polity, because they were accustomed to fighting and feudalism while the nobles and gentry of England proper were becoming accustomed to peace and centralized government. But to the tribal Celts the civilization forcibly imported by the Marcher Lords meant progress. All through the Middle Ages the native Welsh, in imitation of their English lords and neighbours, were slowly taking to agriculture, erecting permanent houses, trading in market-towns built and maintained by English-speaking folk, and learning, though slowly, to cease from the tribal blood feud and to accept the English law. Yet they preserved their own tongue, which it was their boast should answer for Wales at the Day of Judgement; and they continued to elaborate their own bardic poetry and music destined in our own day to save Welsh intellect and idealism from perishing in the swamp of modern cosmopolitan vulgarity.

The warfare that went on for so many centuries both before and after the Edwardian conquest, resembled all warfare of civilized armies against hill tribes. Giraldus, the Welshman, has described how his countrymen would rush down with terrifying shouts and blowing of long war horns, to fling themselves, with indiscriminate valour, a half-naked infantry, against ironclad horsemen. If they were not at once successful their courage ebbed, and they would fly in disgraceful panic. But they as quickly recovered, and carried on long and stern guerilla warfare, rendered doubly formidable by the character of their wooded

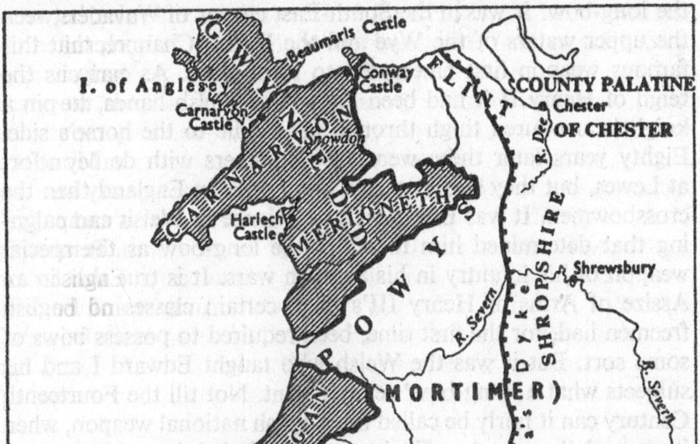

The Principality (shaded) as delimited by Edward I. is in two parts, Gwynedd, and Cardigan-Carmarthen.

All except the Principality and the English border counties may be regarded as normally Marcher Lordships.

Names of some of the chief Marcher Lords in brackets thus :- (BOHUN)

MAP VII. MEDIEVAL WALES

mountains, their own savage hardihood, and their indifference to agriculture and the arts of peace. The English had put up no such resistance to the Norman Conquest. The invaders of Wales were indeed invincible when they could charge on level ground, but there was little level ground in Wales, and much of that was swamp. Horses and armour are not easily taken up into steep hills covered by forest. The Anglo-Norman warriors had, therefore, to learn and borrow much from their despised antagonists.

Above all, the English borrowed from the Welsh the use of the long-bow. It was in the South-East corner of Wales, between the upper waters of the Wye and the Bristol Channel, that this famous weapon first emerged into local fame. As early as the reign of Henry II it had been known, in Welsh hands, to pin a knight's armoured thigh through his saddle to the horse's side. Eighty years later there were Welsh archers with de Montfort at Lewes, but they still attracted less notice in England than the crossbowmen. It was Edward I's experience in Welsh campaigning that determined him to adopt the long-bow as the special weapon of his infantry in his Scottish wars. It is true that in an Assize of Arms of Henry III's reign certain classes of English freemen had, for the first time, been required to possess bows of some sort. But it was the Welsh who taught Edward I and his subjects what a 'long-bow' really meant. Not till the Fourteenth Century can it fairly be called the English national weapon, when it crossed the seas to affright the feudal chivalry of Europe at Crécy and Poitiers.

In the early years of the Thirteenth Century a Welsh national revival took place. It was displayed not only in a fresh effervescence of bardic poetry, but in a movement to unite all the tribes under the hegemony of the Llewelyn princes, who ruled over Gwynedd, among the fastnesses of Snowdon and in the rich grain-bearing island of Anglesey, sheltered behind that lofty barrier. North Wales summoned all Wales to unite and be free.
1194– Llewelyn the Great reconquered much of Powys from the Marcher
1240 Lords. He was a prudent diplomatist as well as a great warrior, for while he called on his countrymen to rally round him as the native Prince acclaimed by the Bards, he never forgot that he was also a great feudal magnate, owing allegiance to the Crown, and could as such play a part in English faction most helpful to his other role as Welsh patriot. By the judicious policy of joining the Barons' party in England, he secured for Welsh rights three clauses of John's Magna Carta.

His grandson Llewelyn ap Griffith carried on the same double policy and allied himself with Simon de Montfort. He still further enlarged the area of his Welsh Principality at the expense of the ever divided and quarrelsome Lords Marcher, many of whom were forced to do him homage. At length he began to dream of complete separation from England. He went out of his way to defy Edward I, who was more than ready to take up the challenge. That was the beginning of the end of Welsh independence.

In the greatest of Edward's numerous Welsh campaigns he 1277
surrounded the unapproachable Snowdon fastnesses by sea and land and starved Llewelyn and his mountaineers into surrender. After another rebellion, provoked by harsh government regardless of Celtic laws and susceptibilities, another war resulted in 1282–4
another conquest and a better settlement. Royal castles such as Conway, Carnarvon, Beaumaris, and Harlech rose to make the King's authority in North Wales as secure as feudal authority in the centre and south. Edward divided up Llewelyn's 'Principality' into shires on the English model – Carnarvon, Anglesey, Merioneth, Flint, Cardigan, and Carmarthen – and soon afterwards gave to his infant son, Edward, born at Carnarvon, the title of 'Prince of Wales'. But the 'Principality' was not yet a part of England, and all the rest of Wales remained to the Lords Marcher.

Edward I would fain have abolished the feudal independence of the Marcher Lords, by subjecting their jurisdictions to a strict *quo warranto* inquiry. But he had not the power to do it, and he had need of their cooperation to keep down the spirit of the Welsh, perpetually incited by Bards recounting the glories of the House of Llewelyn. Until the Tudor reforms, Wales remained divided between the feudal territories of the Lords Marcher on the one hand, and on the other the Celtic Principality, ostensibly governed by English law, but with a large allowance for tribal custom. In both districts English and Welsh were slowly learning to mix and to cooperate. Civilization was creeping forward with the growth of towns, trade, and agriculture.

Nevertheless, by any standard of English comparison, Wales in the Fourteenth and Fifteenth Centuries was a scene of tribal feud, baronial violence, and official tyranny and extortion. In the troubled times of Henry IV, Owen Glendower, reviving the policy of Llewelyn the Great, made play with the rivalries of English factions while appealing to the hopes and grievances of 1400–15
his race. This wonderful man, an attractive and unique figure in a period of debased and selfish politics, actually revived for a few years the virtual independence of a great part of his country, at the cost of wars that proved utterly disastrous to the economic life of Wales, both in the Principality and in the Marches. The Welsh and English districts, which were then found side by side in the same county and even in the same feudal manor, were

again set by the ears, and the necessary amalgamation of the two races into the modern Welsh people was further delayed. Even after the death of Glendower and the re-establishment of English rule, the King's Peace was but poorly enforced. Between Celtic and feudal anarchy, Wales remained a paradise for the robber and the homicide, so long as the Crown was preoccupied with adventures in France and dynastic strife in England.

The disorders alike of the Principality and of the March lands preserved the military habits of the Welsh so long, that even after the Tudor pacification poets still regarded them as

> An old and haughty nation, proud in arms.

They followed the military life not only at home but in the King's armies in Scotland and France, while in every English Civil War from Henry III to Charles I it was always found easier to recruit infantry among the poor of Wales than among the settled and peaceable English. The Wars of the Roses were to a large extent a quarrel among Marcher Lords. For the great Lords Marcher were closely related to the English throne, and had estates and political interests both in England and in the Welsh March. Harry Bolingbroke of Hereford and Lancaster was a great possessor of Welsh lands, as also were his rivals, the Mortimers. The House of York, Warwick the Kingmaker, and Richard III's Buckingham were all in one way or another connected with Wales and the Marches. Such men brought a fighting element into English constitutional and dynastic faction. Because medieval England had left half done its task of conquering Wales for civilization, Welsh tribalism and feudalism revenged themselves by poisoning the Parliamentary life and disturbing the centralized government of its neglectful overlords. But when at length a Welsh army put a Welsh Tudor Prince upon the throne at Bosworth Field, Wales supplied a remedy to those ills in the English body politic which she had helped to create.

The history of Scotland presents yet another version of the contact of Saxon with Celt. Wales and Ireland were both eventually forced to submit to England's rule more completely and for a longer time than Scotland, yet they both remain to this day far more Celtic in character. The apparent paradox is explained if we remember that the wealthiest and most important districts inhabited by the Celt in Scotland had already adopted Anglo-Norman language and institutions before the struggle for national independence began in the time of Edward I. Resistance to England was not therefore identified with Celtic speech and tribal traditions, as in medieval Ireland and Wales. The wars of the Edwards against Wallace and Bruce were a struggle between two kindred nations, each organized as a feudal monarchy. The analogy to Irish or Welsh medieval history is to be found rather in England's conquest of the Highland tribes after Culloden.

It had indeed seemed likely, in the Dark Ages, that Scotland would emerge as a Celtic Kingdom with a Saxon fringe along the lowlands of her eastern coast. For the union of the Picts and 844
Scots under the Scot, Kenneth Macalpine, had enabled them to impose a name and a dynasty on the land from the Celtic capital at Scone. But history began to revolve in the other direction when Lothian, the part of Saxon Northumbria that lay to the north of Tweed and Cheviot, was detached from its southern connexions and converted into an integral part of Scotland. The change was a natural result of the dissolution of the Kingdom of Northumbria under the blows of the Viking invasions. After many generations of warfare between Celt and Saxon in the heart of Scotland, Lothian was acknowledged, in the time of Canute, to be a possession of the Scottish Crown. 1018

It was in the newly acquired territory of English-speaking Lothian, with its rich agricultural soil and its rock-fortress of Edinburgh, that the Scottish Kingship, which had been Celtic, tribal, and north-western in origin, became Anglo-Norman, feudal, and south-eastern by choice. Led or driven by the monarchy, Strathclyde and Galloway, though very largely Celtic in race, eventually adopted English speech and feudal organization. We can only notice one or two of the more obvious stages in that long, complicated, and obscure process of evolution.

First, before the period of Anglo-Norman influence, came the period of purely English influence in the last half of the Eleventh Century. Malcolm III, before he dethroned Macbeth, had spent his boyhood in exile in the England of Edward the 1057–93
Confessor. The English proclivities of his education were enhanced in later life by his second marriage with the saintly and strong-minded Margaret, sister of Edgar Atheling. As Queen of Scotland she did much to strengthen the English language and the Roman ecclesiastical system against Celtic tradition. Her pertinacious efforts, far from popular with the tribes and priests of Celtic Scotland, were helped by the catastrophe that had befallen her own race and lineage in England after the battle of Hastings. The first result of Norman conquest down south was to drive over the Border troops of Saxon and Scandinavian exiles

of all classes, from Margaret herself to the hinds of Yorkshire and Durham fleeing from the red wrath of William and his 'harrying of the North'. The Nordic element in Scotland, based on the Saxons of Lothian, was greatly strengthened by these refugees.

English influence prepared the way for Anglo-Norman pene-
1124–53 tration that followed hard on its heels. David I, a worthy son of Malcolm and Margaret, took advantage of the paralysis of England under Stephen to build Scotland anew in the form of a Norman feudal monarchy, and to appropriate as much as possible of the disputed territories in Cumberland, Northumberland, and Durham. His successes beyond Tweed and Cheviot were not permanent, and the Border between the two Kingdoms gradually took its present shape when England recovered her strength under the Plantagenets. But David's invasions of North England during the anarchy of Stephen had served to reveal how vain was the courage of the disorderly and savage clansmen of Scotland charging with their claymores, as compared to mail-clad feudal knights, whether of England or of Scotland. This had been demonstrated
1138 at the Battle of the Standard, near Northallerton. There is no wonder that the Scottish Kings embarked on a policy of change deliberately aimed at the extinction of tribalism and Celtic institutions

Warriors of Norman or English race, like the Bruces and Balliols, were invited over the Border by King David, and given by him baronies in Scotland, to be held on terms of feudal service. There was no large displacement of existing proprietors, as in conquered England after Hastings; for this was Norman penetration, not Norman conquest. Estates of the Crown and unused lands, both very extensive, enabled David to create baronies for the new-comers without resorting to wholesale confiscation. But the Celtic tribal inhabitants, or the colonists of newly occupied waste land, found themselves placed in a strictly feudal relation to their Anglo-Norman overlords, who knew how to make their new-fangled claims respected. Everywhere, as in contemporary England, rose the circular mound with the timber or stone tower on the top, whence the armoured cavalry ruled and judged the countryside.

And beside the castle rose the parish church, for the country was divided under Anglo-Norman auspices into parishes on the English system. The parish was often conterminous with the fief of the new lord. Religion as well as government was territorialized, and St Columba's Church became a ghost and a memory, like the tribes to which it had ministered. King David and his nobility vied with each other in pious bequests and endowments

MAP VIII. MEDIEVAL SCOTLAND AND NORTH ENGLAND

of the feudal type. The Twelfth and Thirteenth Centuries were the great age of ecclesiastical architecture in Scotland. Stately Cathedrals and Abbeys rose, destined to perish at the hands of English moss-troopers or Scottish reformers. From the first the people resented the tithes and other novel burdens laid on them in David's reign for the benefit of an alien clergy. And ere long the attitude of the Barons to the Church became little more than a desire to secure the ecclesiastical endowments for their own families – a desire gratified by many curious devices, such as warrior nobles masquerading as churchmen, until the Reformation introduced more direct methods.

David and his immediate successor, William the Lion, reproduced many of the features of the English State with remarkable success. The Shire system and the King's justice were brought in gradually, though much limited by the franchises of the Barons. Scottish 'burghs' received royal charters to elect their own magistrates, even more freely than the wealthier and more populous 'boroughs' of England.

The new Scotland was able to take shape and solidify, because
1124–86 she remained so long on tolerable terms with England. During the century and a half before the era of the wars of independence, the nobles of Scotland served King and country better than they ever did again. They and their vassals spread the use of the English language, nomenclature, and institutions so successfully that these were the institutions for which Scots under Wallace and Bruce were prepared to die. The world of Celtic tribalism passed away out of the Western Lowlands, making less armed resistance than we should expect, save in fierce Galloway, where things Celtic lived longest and died hardest. With his formidable following of mail-clad feudal cavalry, the King could disregard those Celtic tribal chiefs who refused to become feudal lords. The old order gradually shrank into the mountain area of the Northern Highlands, where tribal Scotland survived intact until 1746. South and east of the Highland Line men gradually adopted the names, manners, and language of the new regime.

While these great changes were in process, Crown and baronage were still necessary to each other, and both were still necessary to the best interests of the youthful nation. It was only when the war of independence against Edward I put that new-made nation to the test, that the Barons proved less responsive than the commons to the novel creed of patriotism, because feudalism is international, and their estates in England involved them in a dual allegiance. And it was only after the Scottish monarchy had established itself in the hearts and habits of the people that the baronage became its constant and most dangerous foe.

The golden age of medieval Scotland came to an end when 1286 Alexander III's horse carried him over a sea-cliff. His surviving heir was his grand-daughter Margaret, 'the maid of Norway', a girl who resided in Scandinavia during her brief reign. By the Treaty of Brigham it was arranged that she should marry the first English 'Prince of Wales', afterwards Edward II of England. The 1290 peaceable union of the whole island was close in sight. The crowns of Scotland and of England would meet on one head, but the two countries would be administered as separate realms, much as afterwards took place when James VI of Scotland became James I of England. But the course of history was not to be thus foreshortened. The Scots have seldom had luck with young Queens brought from oversea. That very autumn the Maid of Norway died in the Orkneys on her voyage home.

The chance of a peaceful solution died with the Maid. Edward I, pressing the claims of ancient English Kings to be overlords of Scotland, asserted his right to act as arbitrator between the various claimants to the vacant throne, of whom the chief were John Balliol and Robert Bruce. He decided in favour of Balliol, justly it would appear. But, not content with that, he treated Balliol as a puppet and Scotland as a subject land. Balliol, goaded to desperation, renounced his allegiance to his oppressive overlord. But he received little support from a divided and jealous baronage, and was easily deposed by Edward, who marched in triumph 1296 through the land, carried off the coronation stone from Scone to Westminster, and made himself direct King of Scotland. The Ragman Roll contains the long list of the Scots nobles who did him homage.

All seemed finished. All in fact was about to begin. Deserted by her nobles, Scotland discovered herself. The governors whom Edward I left behind him were incapable and cruel, and the foreign soldiery made the Scots feel their subjection. In the following May a guerrilla chief of genius, a tall man of iron strength, who suddenly appears on the page of history as if from nowhere, defeated at Stirling Bridge end an English army. Thence William Wallace broke ravaging into Northumberland and Cumberland.

This unknown knight, with little but his great name to identify him in history, had lit a fire which nothing since has ever put out. Here, in Scotland, contemporaneously with the very similar doings in Switzerland, a new ideal and tradition of wonderful potency was brought into the world; it had no name then, but now we should call it democratic patriotism. It was not the outcome of theory. The unconscious qualities of a people had given it reality in a sudden fit of rage. Theories of nationhood and theories of democracy would follow afterwards to justify or explain it. Meanwhile, it stood up, a fact.

Edward I had thought that he was going to yoke Scotland to England through the ordinary feudal apparatus of the time. His mistake was very natural, for by the accepted standards of the day, his proceedings were less abnormal than Wallace's amazing appeal to the Scottish democracy to save the Scottish nation. Nowadays, indeed, we expect as a matter of course to find both national feeling and democratic instincts in every part of Europe. But in medieval times things were very different. Society was divided, not perpendicularly into nations, but horizontally into feudal strata. And Edward I had the feudal magnates of Scotland mainly on his side. Anglo-Normans, owning estates in England as well as Scotland, were excusably lukewarm in their Scottish patriotism and anxious not to quarrel with England's King, from whom they held their English lands.

But the Scottish people had national feeling and democratic feeling, both hitherto unconscious and unexercised. Wallace called them into activity. The burghers and peasants, led by the lairds or small gentry of whom Wallace himself was one, defied the power of England and when necessary defied the power of their own Scottish nobles. The 'schiltrons', thick masses of plebeian spearmen, standing shoulder to shoulder, withstood on many a field the onset of the armoured English knights and their horses, who had made short work of the Celtic clan charge in Wales and Ireland. Here was a steadier spirit, and the discipline of a more settled civilization. But on other occasions the Scottish schiltrons were broken by the irresistible combination of feudal chivalry with Welsh or English long-bowmen, whose arrows
1298 prepared a passage for the horsemen through the ranks of death. Falkirk, which put an end to the effective part of Wallace's career, was but the first of many English victories won by these tactics.

But to defeat the Scottish army now and again was not to conquer Scotland. The common people were accustomed to the state of war, and every peasant was a warrior. In that at least Scotland resembled rough Wales rather than peaceful England. The Scots were ready to fire their huts and lay waste their country in front of the invader rather than give in, and again and again they were called on to put this stern virtue into practice. Two things decided the long-doubtful issue in favour of Scottish independence: the personality of Robert Bruce, and after his death the distraction of Edward III with the Hundred Years' War in France.

Robert Bruce, grandson of the claimant of 1290, had been brought up in no tradition of high-flown Scottish patriotism. Both he and his father had adopted the trimming politics common among the nobility; he had changed sides more than once in the days of Wallace. But he was betrayed into the path of duty and heroism by his own fiery temper. When once he had cut the 1306
throat of the Red Comyn in the church, he was a hunted outlaw, and had no choice but to throw himself on the patriotic section of the Scottish people, and revive the Wallace tradition. In that he found salvation for himself and his country. To the democratic traditions of Wallace were now added a much needed element of feudalism which Bruce and 'the good Sir James' Douglas could supply, and an element of true Kingship to be found in Bruce and in Bruce alone.

When the timely death of Edward I left the Scots matched 1307
with Edward II, the desperate conditions of their struggle for freedom became more equal. One by one the castles from which the English held down the land were captured and destroyed by those redoubtable men of war, Douglas and Bruce. The crowning victory of Bannockburn, in which the English failed properly 1314
to deploy their masses of cavalry or to use their archers to advantage, enabled the homely Scottish schiltrons to thrust the English baronage and knighthood at the spear's point into marsh and stream. Never before or after was there such a destruction of English chivalry. After that, the English carried off the main of their archers and men-at-arms oversea to southern lands where the peasantry had no such spirit.

The Border warfare of England and Scotland during the centuries that followed Bannockburn went best for the Scots when they fought it with guerrilla tactics. Some rude rhymes known as 'good King Robert's testament' handed on the supposed advice of Bruce to his people to avoid the open field – in spite of the great exception of Bannockburn – and to sacrifice their homes and property again and again to foil the invader. The conditions were indeed unequal for the Scots, demanding in them a marvellous patience, for while they could only raid the comparatively barren lands of Northumberland, Cumberland, and Durham, the English moss-troopers and armies again and again harried the richest parts of Scotland, lying as they did within two days' ride of the Cheviot Border.

Scottish independence was won at a heavy price, as most things worth having are won. For two centuries and a half after Bannockburn, Scotland remained a desperately poor, savage, bloodstained land of feudal anarchy, assassination, private war, and public treason, with constant Border warfare against England, with a peculiarly corrupt Church, with no flourishing cities, no Parliament worth calling such, and no other institutions that seemed to give promise of a great future. Her democratic instincts had prevented her from being annexed to England, who would have given to her wealth and civilization. But her democratic instincts had done nothing else for her politically, had not kept her feudal nobility in order, still less found expression for the national feeling in any representative system. Her alliance with France, useful militarily against England, was unnatural culturally, and could be no true substitute for the broken connexion with her nearer neighbour. What then had Scotland gained by resisting England? Nothing at all – except her soul, and whatsoever things might come in the end from preserving that.

CHAPTER IV

The Hundred Years' War. Its causes and effects.
The Birth of Nationalism. English language and patriotic feeling.
The Black Death. The Peasants' Revolt.
The Wars of the Roses.

Kings: Edward III, 1327–77; Richard II, 1377–99; Henry IV, 1399–1413; Henry V, 1413–22; Henry VI, 1422–61; Edward IV, 1461–83; Edward V, 1483; Richard III, 1483–5

It is sometimes held that the unity of medieval Christendom prevented such wars as those which have devastated Europe at intervals from the Sixteenth to the Twentieth Century. But there was, in fact, no unwillingness on men's part to wage war on one another, and the cruelty with which war was waged was even greater than in our own day. The desire to kill was under less restraint of conscience or of custom, but the means of killing were more restricted. It was not the unity of Christendom but the limit of man's control over nature, the inferior methods of locomotion, and the want of political, administrative, and financial machinery to keep and feed large bodies of men in distant campaigns, that prevented wars on the colossal scale. Europe, still very poor and with no elaborate system of credit, could not pay for the withdrawal from agriculture of a large proportion of her youth to engage in destruction as a skilled trade. The small warrior class of feudal Barons and knights were all-powerful, because they and their paid followers held a monopoly in the profession of arms. From the Eleventh to the Fifteenth Century, wars on the continent were numerous and local, instead of few and large like those of modern times. The arm of Mars was short, but it was kept in continual practice, and the peasant suffered more constantly from the soldier than he does to-day.

Perhaps the first European war that can be called national was 1337–1453 the Hundred Years' War as waged by England. The armies she sent year after year to lay waste and plunder France were indeed very small, but their efficiency was the outcome of a national organization and a national spirit. England, on account of her insular and remote position, and her strong kings, had since the Norman Conquest outstripped the rest of Europe in obtaining a certain measure of internal peace, and was passing from feudalism to nationhood. As soon as King and Parliament had endowed her with administrative machinery and national self-consciousness, she exercised these new powers at the expense of that clumsy giant, the French feudal Kingdom. She became for a while the plunderer and bully of her continental neighbours, not because she had less conscience than they, but because she had more power. In Tudor times the position was to be reversed, when united France and united Spain became each more powerful than England; but her island position saved her from reprisals, and suggested a more profitable outlet to her national energies in commerce and discovery beyond the ocean.

The Hundred Years' War was therefore a question of political dynamics. It is useless to idealize it. The fact that the plundering expeditions of four generations of Englishmen were supposed to be justified by the genealogical claims of Edward III and Henry V to the throne of France no more proves that the Middle Ages had respect for 'the idea of right', than the similar dynastic claims of Frederic the Great on Silesia can help the Eighteenth Century in like case. Froissart, much as he admired the English performance which it was his life's work to record, was under no such delusion.

'The English', he wrote, 'will never love or honour their king, unless he be victorious and a lover of arms and war against their neighbours and especially against such as are greater and richer than themselves. Their land is more fulfilled of riches and all manner of goods when they are at war than in times of peace. They take delight and solace in battles and slaughter: covetous and envious are they above measure of other men's wealth.' 'The King of England must needs obey his people and do all their will.'

Indeed no King could have constrained an unwilling people to wage war oversea for four generations. The Hundred Years' War was not, at bottom, the result of dynastic ambition, but of national, popular, and Parliamentary institutions. The new England passed through a phase of expansionist militarism, profitable at first, in the end disastrous.

It was early in the reign of Edward III that English ambitions were diverted from Scotland to France. To pick the famous lily was an enterprise of more profit, ease, and honour than to pluck the recalcitrant thistle. When English noblemen, younger sons, and yeomen returned from oversea, each brought back his share of booty, perhaps the gold vessels of an abbey, the tapestry of a merchant's house, or a brace of wealthy French knights to ransom; and each had his stock of tales for an admiring audience, in days when tales held the place in society that books and newspapers hold to-day – rich tales of adventure, battle, free quarters, and free love in the most famous cities and best vineyards of Europe. That way a man cut a finer figure in his own and his neighbour's eyes than when he returned from harrying a thrice-harried Scottish moorland, where he had burnt some empty huts and a few stooks of oats or barley, but found nothing to carry away save the skin of a cow too lame to hobble to the hiding place in the wood.

The modern mind, nursed on the theory and practice of racial nationalism, is astonished that the English should ever have thought it possible to annex France. But for many years the French resisted us less heartily and hardily than the Scots who spoke our own tongue. For Scotland was already a nation in spirit, while France was a loose collection of feudal fiefs. Moreover, when the Hundred Years' War began in 1337, Edward III and his nobles spoke French and were more at home in Gascony than in Scotland.

Because the struggle was much more than feudal or dynastic, it lasted intermittently for over a hundred years. John had failed to compel the English to fight in defence of his Norman and Angevin possessions. But from Edward III to Henry VI Parliament after Parliament voted supplies for the war, and called to account Ministers who failed to conduct it with success. Pride in the triumphs of the English archer 'for all the French boast', the joy of seeing –

Our King go forth to Normandy
With grace and might of chivalry,

and return with the proudest princes and nobles of Europe as captives in his procession through London streets intensified the patriotic sentiment that united all classes of the nation. Hatred of the French was even stronger among the common folk than in the bi-lingual upper class. Therefore we persisted so long in this disastrous enterprise, till our own well-ordered medieval society was ruined, and till we had twice goaded the French themselves, once under Du Guesclin and again fifty years later under Dunois and Joan of Arc, to become conscious of their nationality and to change the purely feudal tactics and spirit of their armies. The Hundred Years' War was the diplomatic and military aspect of the period of transition from the feudal to the national, from the Middle Ages to the Renaissance.

As so often happens in war, the armies and tactics employed by the two sides respectively represented underlying social facts, and registered changes of more than military importance.

France was a Kingdom in a very different sense from England. She was not governed in shires by the King's judges, sheriffs, and coroners sitting in the King's courts. She was governed in provinces and baronies by her feudal princes and lords, each in his own territory. The peasant serf was bitterly despised by the noble; and there was no important middle class, no substantial yeomen, and no small gentry accustomed to serve the Crown and carry on public business in close connexion with classes above and below their own. France had indeed wealthy cities, but the links were slender that connected the townsfolk with the exclusive feudal society around them; there was no cooperation between the burghers and the lesser *noblesse* as in the English shire and the English House of Commons.

These social facts were reflected in the armies that suffered defeat at Crécy, Poitiers, and Agincourt. They were feudal hosts, called out under feudal obligations, and with all the indiscipline, political and military, characteristic of feudal pride. The King of France and his generals had the same kind of difficulty with the units of their command as Montrose or Prince Charlie with the Highland chiefs. The feudal army had no idea of tactics except the unsupported cavalry charge. Its shock had decided the issue of battle for many centuries past, but the English archers put a term to its supremacy on the day of Crécy. 1346

The best missile troops the French had were Italian mercenaries – crossbowmen from Genoa. The French peasant, despised in peace, was little regarded in war. His part was to pay the ransom from the estate, when his lord had been carried off to an English manor-house, to hawk and flirt with his captor's family till the money arrived. This method of securing 'reparations' during the war itself, especially the ransoms extorted for the
1356 great haul of highborn prisoners at Poitiers, in addition to the terrible plunderings of the soldiery, goaded the starving peasants of France into the revolt of the *Jacquerie*, a gesture of mere despair.

The English social system was no less faithfully reflected in the organization and tactics of the invading armies. In the England of the Edwards, Piers Plowman was in better plight than Jacques Bonhomme across the Channel. Even the villeins were relatively wealthy and well-fed, and the proportion of freemen agriculturists above the status of villein was on the increase. Indeed the Hundred Years' War covers the greater part of the period of servile emancipation in England. Now the Plantagenet Kings had compulsorily organized all the freemen for training in military service, not on a feudal system but on the principle of the Saxon fyrd brought up to date by the Assizes of Arms. A large body of militia were kept familiar with the use of those weapons which each man was compelled by the State to possess. The fact that so many of the common folk had arms in their cottages which they knew how to use was a chief cause why the island atmosphere breathed something of political and social freedom.

In the Fourteenth Century the long-bow became more and more the prescribed weapon, and the practice at the butts behind the churchyard became the chief sport and excitement of village life. Edward III encouraged it by royal proclamations, prohibiting under pain of imprisonment –

> handball, football, or hockey (*pilam manualem, pedivam, vel bacularem*); coursing and cockfighting, or other such idle games,

which drew men away from the butts. In a later age Hugh Latimer used to tell from the pulpit the tale of his father the yeoman –

> He taught me how to draw, how to lay my body in my bow, and not to draw with strength of arms as divers other nations do, but with strength of the body. I had my bows bought me according to my age and strength; as I increased in them, so my bows were made bigger and bigger. For men shall never shoot well unless they be brought up in it.

We may be sure that Crécy and Agincourt had been vicariously won by just such careful fathers as old Latimer. For the art of the long-bow was so difficult that foreigners never learnt the knack that would send an arrow through plate-mail, and though the long-bow was for more than a century the acknowledged master-weapon in European war, it never ceased to be an English monopoly. And even in England its gradual supersession by the less efficient hand-gun of Tudor times appears to have been due to the village neglect of archery for 'football and other lewd games', or as Latimer thought, for 'bowling, drinking, and whoring' – Statues and Proclamations notwithstanding.

In Edward III's time this formidable militia was at the height of its efficiency and could on occasion be called out. When in the year of Crécy the Scots thought to make an easy prey of a land whose King and nobles were in France, the democratic levy of the shires taught the invaders, at Neville's Cross near Durham, the lesson they had learned at Northallerton and were to learn once more at Flodden, that England – though she had no national motto to remind her of it – can no more be 'provoked with impunity' than Scotland herself.

From this large body of armed and half-armed freemen, Edward III selected, by Commissions of Array addressed to each shire, a picked host to wage war oversea. For this purpose he resorted at first to conscription, eked out with volunteers. But as the French war went on, the Commissions of Array and the principle of compulsion were abandoned in favour of the system of hiring private 'companies' of professional warriors.

These 'companies' were the backbone of the long English warfare in France. They were not feudal hosts or conscript levies, but long-service professional soldiers, enlisted for pay by some noble or knight who had determined to push his fortunes in politics and in war. The King could contract with their leaders for their services at easy rates, because they counted on enriching themselves further with plunder, ransom, and free quarters. Sometimes, especially during the intervals of truce between France and England, they fought and ravaged on the continent for their own hands, like the famous Hawkwood and his English Company in Italy. When driven back to England in the reign of Henry VI, the 'companies' became a chief cause of the social and political disruption at home, which provided them with fresh occupation as 'retainers' in the Wars of the Roses.

The tactics of the English implied trust in the yeoman as a fighting man and in the long-bow as a weapon. Those lessons had been learnt in the Scottish campaigns of the first two Edwards. The feudal warriors of the continent had taken no interest in such obscure and barbarous wars, and were stricken with amazement when, on the field of Crécy, the despised islanders revealed themselves as the masters of all Europe in the art military.

The lesson learnt in the Scottish wars had been twofold. At Stirling Bridge and Bannockburn the schiltrons of Scottish spearmen had shown that under favourable circumstances a self-respecting infantry could defeat feudal knighthood hand to hand, while the English victories, such as Falkirk, had taught the value of the long-bow. From these two lessons of the Scottish war put together, the army chiefs of Edward III deduced a new method of warfare, combining the archer and the feudal knight in a single unit of battle, formidable alike for its missiles and its sword play. The English chivalry, perceiving that they had not the numbers to meet the French chivalry in the shock of horse and lance, consented to dismount and to fight in their full armour as a 'stiffening' to the line of half-armoured archer infantry, who were to win the battle by the rapidity of their penetrating volleys of cloth-yard shafts. Those of the French knights who struggled alive through the arrow-storm, came to hand grips with the English line, where the archer, drawing his sword, stood shoulder to shoulder with the armoured knights and nobles, sometimes behind a hedge or a line of portable stakes.

The French were so hopelessly defeated by these tactics at Crécy that they determined so far to imitate the victors as to fight on foot. But that by itself was not the secret, as Poitiers proved. Their other remedy against the arrows was to increase the thickness of their armour and to substitute plate for chain mail over all parts of the body. But they lost as much in mobility as they gained in protection, and the absurd helplessness of the Fifteenth Century knight, in a case too heavy for him to carry, only hastened the decline of chivalry.

The French in fact never devised a means of successfully attacking the English infantry line, once it had taken up chosen ground with flanks protected. But the English system elaborated by the Black Prince had one great defect. It was not mobile on the field of battle, like the 'thin red line' of Wellington. It could not advance to attack the mounted knights without exposing itself to be outflanked and ridden down. In short it could only win victories when the French were foolish enough to attack it in position.

The first deliverance of France was made by Du Guesclin, the man who grasped the full meaning of these facts. It was he who, in the last years of Edward III, overthrew the compromise treaty of Brétigny, which in 1360 had assigned South-western France to England. Du Guesclin hired the service of 'free companies' instead of relying on the undisciplined feudal host, and he avoided battle, except when he could surprise the English or take them in some circumstance of special disadvantage. His principal work was to besiege the castles from which the English ruled the country, and in that the French were our match, for they excelled in the early use of cannon. Gunpowder, not yet used effectively in the open field, was already revolutionizing siege operations. It helped to liberate France, but it sapped the power of feudalism, for the King, who could best afford to pay for a train of artillery, would in the end put down the feudal Baron, if he could blow a hole in his castle wall.

Yet even so feudalism died very hard in France. After Du Guesclin had freed his countrymen by finding substitutes for the feudal tactics which had failed at Crécy and Poitiers, a growth of French national monarchy at the expense of feudalism might have been expected during the generation of uneasy truce and intermittent warfare that divided the two halves of the Hundred Years' War. But no such development took place. When Henry V, on his accession, revived Edward III's pretensions to the French Crown in order 'to busy giddy minds with foreign quarrels', the English, going out to fight with the tactics of the Black Prince, found themselves opposed, not by the proved methods of Du Guesclin, but by the idiotic feudal array of Crécy and Poitiers.
Agincourt was the natural result. 1415

Indeed the similarity of the second to the first half of the Hundred Years' War is extraordinary, as regards the military methods of both sides. For a long time the French refused to learn or to remember anything. Henry V, being a great soldier – he has been called 'the first modern general' – secured the English hold on Normandy as an occupied province, and thence extended his power to the banks of the Loire. The quarrel between the great feudal Houses of Orleans and Burgundy tore France in two, and brought about the alliance of Burgundy and Flanders with England, to the delight of wool merchants on both sides of the Channel. In 1420 Henry V was acknowledged heir to the French Crown by the Treaty of Troyes. Two years later he died, leaving his ill-gotten inheritance to an infant, who was acknowledged by Northern France.

During the minority of Henry VI came the second French revival, following tactically on the lines of Du Guesclin. His

successor was Dunois, who had a harder task to face and was not his equal. But Dunois obtained a most unexpected and extra-
1429–31 ordinary ally. In one year of glory and one year of martyrdom Joan of Arc evoked a national tradition and sentiment in France which has never since looked back. Spiritually she was the Wallace of France. But more than twenty years passed after her death before the English power had been completely worn away by the Fabian tactics and siegecraft of the Dunois era.
1453 When English Talbot and his son perished in the last battle down in Gascony, the Hundred Years' War drew to a close; its aftermath in England, the Wars of the Roses, began two years later at St Albans. So little rest had England in the ill-governed Fifteenth Century.

What had we gained by the long, persistent endeavour to erect an English Empire in Europe? We had most justly earned the break-up of our own medieval society and a period of anarchy and moral prostration. We had gained the port of Calais which we kept for another hundred years, the solitary pledge of England's foretime rule in France, as Berwick-on-Tweed of her lost Scottish dominion. Calais was used as a port of vent for our raw wool abroad, where it was gathered and taxed before sale. The staple was fixed there by the King of England for that purpose. But the use of the staple gradually declined with the increase of our cloth manufacture and trading enterprise oversea. Meanwhile Calais, the bridge-head firmly held in French soil, was a standing temptation even to prudent Yorkist and Tudor Kings to revive their never abandoned claims on France. Its loss under Mary was pure gain and helped the Elizabethans to look westward for new lands.

Had the Hundred Years' War, then, done nothing but harm to England? If it brought any compensating good it was of the intangible and intellectual order – a strong national self-consciousness, more democratic than feudal; great memories and traditions; a belief in the island qualities, which helped Englishmen to carry their heads high in the coming century of eclipse behind the crescent monarchies of France and Spain. In Shakespeare we may read the inspiration given by the memory of Agincourt to the better-directed national revival under Elizabeth.

In earlier medieval times hostility was normally felt against the natives of a neighbouring town, shire, or village. This un-neighbourliness diminished as insular patriotism enlarged the mind and pointed out the Frenchman or the Spaniard as the true 'foreigner'. The habits of thought and feeling that were contracted during the Hundred Years' War with France sharply defined the new patriotic feeling in the form of racial hatred of the French. It was intensified in the era of Du Guesclin by destructive enemy raids on our South coast and not unsuccessful warfare against our shipping. The feeling against the French outlasted the war, and helped to put an end to that subordination of English to French culture which the Norman Conquest had established. From this time forward foreigners complained of the insular and surly exclusiveness of the English common people. In Henry VII's reign the Venetian envoy noted that:

> They think that there are no other men than themselves, and no other world but England; and whenever they see a handsome foreigner, they say 'he looks like an Englishman' and that 'it is a great pity that he should not be an Englishman'; and when they partake of any delicacy with a foreigner they ask him 'whether such a thing is made in his country?'

In the middle of the Tudor period a French visitor wrote:

> The people of this nation mortally hate the French as their old enemies, and always call us 'France cheneve', 'France dogue'. (French knave, French dog.)

In the reign of Elizabeth these feelings were turned for a while against the Spaniard. Yet there was often an element of good-nature in English nationalism. At the height of the Elizabethan struggle with Spain, Shakespeare's kindly caricature of Don Armado, 'a fantastical Spaniard', in *Love's Labour's Lost*, does credit to the mentality of our people at war.

The upper classes followed more slowly in the wake of the common people in the repudiation of everything from beyond the Channel. The 'English squire' was in process of evolution, but not yet evolved. Ever since the loss of Normandy and the Angevin Empire, the French-speaking upper class had been cut off from estates and connexions oversea, and their culture, severed from its roots in France, was clearly exotic. A hundred years before the days of Chaucer's Prioress, Frenchmen 'of Paris' used to laugh at the strange hybrid that passed for their tongue in the mouths of English gentlefolk. Yet, such as it was, it was their everyday speech till the reign of Edward III, and was regarded as the hall-mark of a gentlemen, till the increasingly racial character of the war compelled all men to regard French as an enemy language.

Six years after Poitiers a statute was passed through Parliament declaring that since the French tongue was 'much unknown in this Realm', all pleading and judgements in the law courts should be spoken in the English tongue and enrolled in Latin. 'Men of lawe fro that tyme shold plede in her moder tunge,' it was said. 'Their mother tongue'! Here indeed is a new and significant order of ideas! If the statute was imperfectly obeyed at first, it was obeyed before long, although lawyers, with professional conservatism, long continued to write documents in the 'law French' in which their predecessors had addressed the court.

A still more fundamental revolution was taking place in regard to the language used in the schools. English was becoming once more the tongue of the educated and of the upper class, as it had never been since Hastings. Thus humble schoolmasters prepared the road for Chaucer and Wycliffe in their own century, for Shakespeare and Milton in time to come, for the English Reformation and Renaissance, and the whole development of English national life and letters as something other than a northern offshoot of French culture. Some may regard this revolution as more important than Magna Carta or the Declaration of Independence.

During the formative period of the English language, the centuries after the Conquest when it was out of fashion with the learned and the polite, in the chrysalis stage between Saxon caterpillar and Chaucerian butterfly, it was divided into many regional dialects, of which the chief were Wessex, Northumbrian, East and West Midland. The Wessex had been the Court language in Alfred's time, but the Norman Conquest had relegated it for ever to the cottage and the plough-furrow. It was the speech of the East Midlands that became the ancestor of modern English, triumphing over the other dialects, partly because it was spoken in London, Oxford, and Cambridge; partly because it was employed by Chaucer, who enriched it with many French words, and by Wycliffe, who enriched it with many words from the Latin Vulgate. Both Chaucer and Wycliffe founded a school of imitators who used mainly the same dialect. Their writings and translations were for a while widely circulated in manuscript. Then in the later Fifteenth Century came Caxton's printing press at Westminster, under the patronage of the Yorkist Kings; it further popularized Chaucer, and spread through the land translations of various works done into English of the same type.

In this way a standard of English was being formed for all those who could read, and for all, even beyond Trent and Avon, who wished to be regarded as educated men and women. In Tudor times the Bible and the Prayer Book in the same dialect

– already regarded as 'the King's English' – obtained a diffusion and authority quite unparalleled by any works in earlier times, and firmly fixed the standard. During these two centuries from Chaucer to Elizabeth, the language in question, living on the tongues of men no less than in their books, was moving forward from strength to strength and from beauty to beauty, enriching itself with Latin words expressive of all the joy and learning of the Renaissance, until it fell into the perfecting hands of the man of Stratford. Since his day its adaptability to exact scientific statement has increased, and its poetic and literary quality has decreased, answering to the changes in the mind and life of the people who use it.

We have already considered the life of the medieval English village. We saw it, self-sufficing in its labour and its poverty; often suffering from famine but never from unemployment; little connected with the world beyond its own forest bounds, except through the personal activities and requirements of its lord; supplying nearly all its own simple needs through its own craftsmen; feeding itself by tilling, on traditional methods, the strips owned by the villeins in the open field, and by sharing the common rights over meadow and waste. We saw too that the village was a 'manor' held by some lord, resident or non-resident, lay or spiritual. We noted the relations between the lord and his villeins, who composed the great majority of the village, and by whose compulsory labour his domain was tilled under the supervision of his bailiff.

The manorial system had led England out of the Dark Ages and had enabled man to conquer the forest, subdue the soil, and colonize the land. In ages of brute force it had protected the weak behind the shield of custom, even while making them half slaves. It gave stability and peace, but checked progress and denied freedom. Its part in English history had been great, but its use was nearly exhausted, and its end was hastened by a terrible disaster.

The Black Death, on its first visitation of Europe from some mysterious fountain-head of disease in the undiscovered East, swept off perhaps a third, possibly a half, of the compatriots of Boccaccio, Froissart, and Chaucer. The most terrible feature of its first advent was its ubiquity. In the most secluded English hamlets we often read, in the list of vicars in the parish church, the names of *two* incumbents under that fatal year. Some villages and hamlets ceased to exist, the whole population having died. In the winter of 1349 the plague was stayed, but it remained in the island, and was perpetually breaking out in one insanitary township after another. Its last appearance, as Charles II's 'Plague of London', seems to have been little, if at all, worse than several plagues that had devastated the capital in Lancastrian, Tudor, and Stuart times, with no Defoe to celebrate them. Plague was a black cloud, ever hovering over the filthy streets and brief lives of our ancestors. It was a frequent sequel to the famine of a bad harvest year.

The reduction of the English subjects of Edward III in sixteen months, from perhaps four million to perhaps two and a half million souls, precipitated the class struggle, and embittered the process of emancipating the villein. In a society accustomed to very slow changes in conditions of life, the market value of labour had been doubled at a stroke. The consequence was twofold. The labourer who was already free struck for higher wages, while the villein whose labour was not free struggled against the legal demands of the bailiff for customary services which were now worth more to both parties; gradually he was led on to demand his full freedom, the right to take his labour where he would, to plead in the King's Court even against his own lord, and to be free of irksome feudal dues.

Lords and bailiffs were in a terrible dilemma. Half the domain land, half the rent-paying farms were lying untilled, turf and bushes overgrowing the strips, the ploughmen dead, the thatch falling from their deserted hovels. And the survivors were rising in open mutiny against law and custom, and sometimes also against what was economically possible. The world seemed coming to an end, yet it never occurred to the governing class to stop the French war, which was still regarded as a source of profit and plunder. Poitiers followed Crécy, as though half the world had not died in the interval.

Part of their difficulties the landlords solved well and wisely, by substituting sheep-pasture for tillage. It was not for more than a century later, when the population had nearly filled up the gaps left by the Black Death, that there was any need for landlords to evict ploughmen in order to make room for the shepherd. In 1350 death had evicted the ploughmen, and 'the deserted village' was ready to hand. In such circumstances, the multiplication of sheep-runs was pure gain to a community in distress. The export of raw wool to the Flanders looms, and the concurrent growth of cloth manufacture in England, aided by Edward III's importation of Flemish weavers to teach our people the higher skill of the craft, made demand for all the wool that English flocks could supply. In this way a national policy and distant markets were beginning to disturb and to improve the parochial economy of the old manor, and to offer alternative occupations for the emancipated or the runaway villein.

The dramatic events of June 1381 had their roots in social rather than political causes, though the revolt was precipitated by the Poll Tax, a method of taxing the poor for the French war at a moment when it was singularly unsuccessful and therefore for a while unpopular. The incompetent government of Richard II's minority was hated and despised. But what chiefly brought the men of East Anglia and the Home Counties trooping up to London were their own grievances and ambitions as peasants. It was a rising, more or less concerted and prepared by John Ball and his agents, against the gentry, the lawyers, and the wealthy churchmen. The rebels' chief demand was for the commutation of all servile dues throughout the land for a rent of fourpence an acre; many of them also demanded the disendowment of the Church, free use of forests, abolition of game laws and outlawry – a 'Robin Hood' programme suggestive of the life recently led by some of those who were taking a leading part in the revolt.

The rising took the upper class by surprise, and for some days there was little resistance, either central or local. Admitted into London by the 'prentice mob and by certain democratically minded aldermen, the rebels held the capital and the government at their mercy. The King was in the Tower, which his subjects proceeded to blockade. The situation was saved – but by very base means. Richard II was sent to a conference at Mile End with the rebels, where he made them promises of pardon and emancipation from villeinage, which his counsellors had no intention of carrying out. It was easy thus to beguile the moderate section of the rebels, who had a simple-minded belief in the King as distinct from his Council, Parliament, lawyers, Church, and knighthood. Yet in fact the Crown of England was identified with those interests.

13 June 1381

The forces of order were now beginning to rally. Another conference in the presence of the King, held in Smithfield, resulted not in further concessions, but in the slaying of a rebel leader, Wat Tyler, by the Mayor of London. After that, the insurgents soon dispersed before a mixture of force and cajolery. The revolt went on spreading over the country till it reached from South Yorkshire to the South-Western counties. But when it had lost its hold on London it was doomed.

Whether the rising of 1381 actually hastened or retarded complete emancipation it is difficult to say. The immediate result was a strong and cruel reaction, when every promise made to the peasants in the hour of need was broken, and a bloody assize made mock of the pardons granted by the King. But a class that could give its rulers such a fright could not ultimately be held down.

The suppression of the Rising by no means ended the strikes and riots against serfdom. It must have been difficult to get a good day's work on the domain out of such surly fellows. Partly for this reason, partly in obedience to the general economic tendencies of the age, landlords gradually ceased to work the domain by the forced service of villeins, and let it instead to farmers who produced for the market, and so obtained money to hire free labour.

During this period of social and intellectual unrest, began the first English movement at all resembling later Protestantism. 'Lollardry' as it was called, was of native English origin, owing its existence to John Wycliffe, the Oxford schoolman. His opinions had great influence in the University; but after his denial of the doctrine of Transubstantiation he and his were driven from Oxford in 1382 by the combined action of Church and State. Expelled by force from the schools and from the society of the learned, the Wycliffites initiated a popular movement spread by itinerant preachers, using some of the methods of their enemies the friars (see p. 160, above). Persecuted and suppressed, Lollardry never wholly died out, and survived in various counties of England in nooks and corners, till it revived and merged itself in the Lutheran movement of early Tudor times. The English translation of the Bible made by Wycliffe's followers at his instigation, was greatly used and reverenced by the Lollards; the manuscript copies were destroyed when possible by the Church authorities, who closely restricted, though they did not in all cases prohibit lay study of the Scriptures.

It is significant that the last of the English were driven out of France in 1453 and that the Wars of the Roses began only two years later in the streets of St Albans. The return of the garrisons and armies from oversea filled England with knights and archers, accustomed to war, licence, and plunder, and fit for any mischief. The unemployed and starving veteran was dangerous enough, but yet more dangerous was the 'company' of warriors in private employment, kept together by its paymaster when the

French war was over, to further his political ambitions or his designs upon his neighbours' estates.

Nor was the Hundred Years' War injurious to English society only when it came to an end. Throughout its whole course it had bred habits of lawlessness and violence at home. The Parliaments of Edward III had complained of estate-jumping, carrying off of heiresses, and breach of the peace by gentlemen and their retainers as a new and growing evil. And to the influence of the foreign campaigns must be added the older and more permanent influence of the Welsh and Scottish Borders, where the Marcher Lords in their castles, like Mortimer in Wigmore and Percy in Alnwick, lived constantly under arms, preserving the feudal customs and spirit that had disappeared from the more civilized South and East. Wales and the North between them caused the troubles under Henry IV; and the Wars of the Roses were to a large extent a quarrel between Welsh Marcher Lords, who were also great English nobles, closely related to the English throne.

A characteristic feature of this revival of anarchy in a civilized society was the combination of legal chicanery with military violence. It was an age of litigation tempered by house-breaking. In Stephen's reign the barbarous Barons had had no need to be lawyers; but under Henry VI every ambitious noble, and every country gentleman who aspired to found the fortunes of his family, was well versed in the processes of law as well as in the siegecraft of forcible entry into a moated manor-house. Such a man kept in his pay not only archers but lawyers and jurymen. The correspondence of the Paston family has made us familiar with the type in reality, and Stevenson's Sir Daniel Brackley in fiction. The law-breakers were often Justices of the Peace, and some of the worst 'ambushes' were committed by royal judges and by nobles high in office. The operations of purely private war were sometimes on a scale that matched the more regular dynastic struggle. In 1469 a dispute over Sir John Fastolf's will led to a five weeks' siege of Caister Castle by the Duke of Norfolk with 3000 men, finally ended by cannon to breach the walls – and this in East Anglia, the richest and most settled part of the island.

Juries were as regularly intimidated in Fifteenth Century England as in Nineteenth Century Ireland. 'Maintenance' was the recognized duty of the great man to protect his client in the King's courts from the consequences of illegal action, and since the English courts already insisted on the unanimity of the twelve jurymen, it was seldom possible to get verdicts against the friend of a great man. At the outbreak of the Wars of the

Roses the grievances of quiet people were summed up in these rude verses:

> In every shire with jacks and salads clean
> Misrule doth rise and maketh neighbours war.
> The weaker goeth beneath, as oft is seen,
> The mightiest his quarrell will prefer.
>
> They kill your men alway one by one,
> And who say aught he shall be beat doubtless.
> For in your realm Justice of Peace be none
> That dare aught now the contesters oppress.
>
> The law is like unto a Welshman's hose,
> To each man's legs that shapen is and meet;
> So maintainers subvert it and transpose.
> Through might it is full low laid under feet.

What are we to think of this outbreak of savage wrong-doing in the highest ranks of a society so far emerged from feudal barbarism, and artistically so much the superior of our own in the arts and crafts of daily life? But contrast is the essence of social history, and particularly of medieval history. We think of the Fifteenth Century as the era of chivalry: for did not its knights wear the plate armour in which modern artists depict Sir Galahad with his pure, schoolboy face, and was it not the century when Sir Thomas Malory produced his *Morte d'Arthur*? But the actual contemporaries of Malory would, at close quarters, have seemed to us singularly deficient in 'chivalry' according to modern notions.

Wife-beating was a recognized right of man, and was practised without shame by high as well as low. Similarly, the daughter who refused to marry the gentleman of her parents' choice was liable to be locked up, beaten, and flung about the room, without any shock being inflicted on public opinion. Marriage was not an affair of personal affection but of family avarice, particularly in the 'chivalrous' upper classes. 'For very need,' complains a member of the noble family of Scrope, 'I was fain to sell a little daughter I have, for much less than I should have done by possibility.' Betrothal often took place while one or both of the parties was in the cradle, and marriage when they were scarcely out of the nurse's charge. But side by side with the violence and materialism of medieval life, there was much also of the 'good nature and integrity of the English people' which was not a thing of yesterday.

Civilization and knowledge were all the while encroaching on the realm of ignorance. For although Oxford in the Fifteenth Century decayed in intellectual vigour prior to the blossoming of the New Learning, the end of the Middle Ages was a great period for the foundation of schools, besides William of Wykeham's Winchester and Henry VI's Eton. Guilds and private persons were constantly endowing chantries with priests to say masses for souls, and schools were often attached to them.

Reading and writing, therefore, had quite ceased, in the days of York and Lancaster, to be the monopoly of the clergy. Not only the merchants but the bailiffs of manors kept good accounts and often wrote tolerable Latin in their business documents. Members of landed families like the Pastons corresponded with one another by letters written in their own hands, usually on legal or other business or to convey political news.

For several generations after Chaucer's death in 1400, English literature remained under Chaucer's domination. The chief poets were of his school, and in the latter part of the century Caxton made haste to print him for a public that could not get enough copies of him in manuscript.

The works of Chaucer and his numerous imitators expressed to the satisfaction of the society of that age its delicate sense of the beauty of natural sights and sounds in the orchards and artificial gardens where it passed so many hours of dalliance, or in the wild wood beyond. To-day we like our gardens and parks to appear wild, because we have so terribly tamed the land outside, but from the Fifteenth to the early Eighteenth Centuries they liked artificial gardens because they had so much of wild nature elsewhere, in which their souls rejoiced no less than in the gardens. The song of birds, the run of water, the flowers in bloom, and the woods in leaf gave those country-dwellers a joy of which they were fully conscious. It is in nature that the lover seeks ease from his 'love-longing':

> And the river that I sate upon
> It made such a noise as it ron,
> Accourdaunt with the birdës' armony
> Me thought it was the best melody
> That might ben heard of any mon.

The medicine recommended for the wounds of despised love is –

> Go looke on the fresh daisie!

Or again:

A wind, so small it scarcely might be less,
Made in the leavës green a noisë soft,
Accordant to the fowlës song aloft.

The beauty of the domestic architecture of the manor-houses, then coming to perfection in stone or the new-fangled brick, the artistic merit and originality in dress, furniture, and articles of common use for farm, barn, and household, enriched life with joys that have disappeared from it, both for the craftsman who created and the owner who used his creation. Altogether a marvellous place was England at the end of the Middle Ages, so full of what we have lost, so empty of what we now have, and yet, as Chaucer and the Pastons have written and shown us, so English and so like us all the while.

When the Wars of the Roses at length broke out in form, no question of principle or even of class interest was involved in the quarrel between Lancaster and York. It was a faction fight between the families allied to the royal house, contending for power and wealth and ultimately for the possession of the Crown. On each side was ranged a group of great nobles. And each noble had his clientele of knights, gentry, led captains, lawyers, and clergy, some attached to his person, some living in distant manors, but all conscious that their fortunes were involved in the rise or fall of their 'good lord'. Changing of sides was more frequent in this civil war than in others, because there was no principle to desert. The mass of the people looked on with indifference, the towns and villages only bargaining that they should, as far as possible, be spared the horrors of war. Even London, for once, remained neutral in the civil strife convulsing England. In return, the armies were much less destructive than in France, because their chiefs knew well that if the neutrals were roused by ill treatment they could soon dispose of the few thousand partisan soldiers, who scoured the country in hot pursuit of one another from Plymouth to the foot of the Cheviots, making and unmaking the short-lived fortunes of Lancaster and York. So in spite of the wars, which were at the worst intermittent, the neutral majority suffered little, and trade followed its usual course along the rivers and riding tracks with not much more than the usual amount of disturbance from highwaymen and water-thieves.

But the actual combatants suffered severely. The fighting nobles were savage in their treatment of one another. There were many sudden turns of fortune's wheel, and each meant a fresh confiscation of great estates, and a new batch of noble heads for the block, over and above the heavy proportion of leaders killed upon the field of battle. The Crown was enriched by these confiscations and the nobles were impoverished, while their numbers, never great, were much reduced. The way was thus prepared for the Tudor policy of bridling 'overmighty subjects'. The Wars of the Roses were a bleeding operation performed by the nobility upon their own body. To the nation it was a blessing in disguise.

The hosts engaged in battles like Towton, Barnet, and Tewkesbury were partly professional mercenaries, partly friends and tenants hastily called out; they were serving under private paymasters, at whose behest they marched under the banner of York or Lancaster. The tactics were those employed by the same leaders in the recent French war. Cavalry fighting was the exception rather than the rule, the normal soldier being a mounted infantryman. Cannon and the new hand-guns were sometimes used in the field, but the long-bow was still the lord of weapons. The archer still fought on foot, in line beside the knight. But the battles had not the same character as Crécy or Agincourt, because in England there was little to choose between the archery on the two sides, and rather than stand long under the arrow-storm, men came as soon as possible to close quarters and hacked out a decision with sword and bill.

The claimants to the reversion of the throne, Yorkist and Lancastrian alike, disappeared so fast in the battles and executions of twenty-five years that, on the death of Edward V, a Welsh gentleman named Henry Tudor, Earl of Richmond, was able to put up a very respectable case for himself on the Lancastrian side. After the custom of opposition leaders in those brisk times, he had sought refuge abroad, first in the Court of Brittany, then in France. Taking advantage of the unpopularity of Richard III, he landed with a slender and untrustworthy force, at Milford Haven, on the coast of his native Wales. The racial enthusiasm of the Welsh for a descendant of their ancient British Princes – marching, as Henry was careful to march, under the red-dragon standard of Cadwallader – broke out into prophecy and song, and enabled him to raise in little more than a week a small army of zealous supporters as he traversed that ever warlike land. They, with the help of a few French and English adventurers, won Bosworth Field against a King for whom the mass of his English subjects were ashamed to fight. Here, indeed, was one of fortune's freaks: on a bare Leicestershire upland, a few thousand men in close conflict foot to foot, while a few thou- 22 Aug. 1485 sand more stood aside to watch the issue, sufficed to set upon the throne of England in the person of Henry VII the greatest of all her royal lines, that should guide her through a century of change down new and larger streams of destiny, undreamt of by any man who plied bow and bill that day in the old-world quarrel of York and Lancaster.

Shakespeare was well advised to leave the reign of Henry VII as a blank in the sequence of his historical plays. For, having once drawn Richmond, the open-hearted young champion of Bosworth Field, gambling gaily with his life and addressing his little band of brothers with the ingenuous fervour of the Prince in the fairy tale, how would he have reconciled that portrait with the character in which Henry as King impressed himself upon posterity, as the English counterpart of Louis XI, cautious and thrifty to a fault, moving silently about with keen, inscrutable glance, opening his heart to no man and to no woman? There may have been a certain truth in both pictures, each in its turn, for life is long and 'one man, in his time, plays many parts,' especially if he is an able man with an eye for the change of circumstances. After Bosworth, England wanted, not more adventures in shining armour, but peace, retrenchment and, above all, the enforcement of order. It was by putting these prosaic ideals on to a new institutiônal basis that Henry VII left England in a position to seize her great opportunities in the coming era.

The Tudor monarchy had a pedestrian beginning, and became a very far-shining affair under Queen Elizabeth, but she would have been the last to deny that her glory was founded on the spade-work of her shrewd, patient grandfather, to whose character her own bore a family likeness for double-dealing, caution, and thrift as to means, and clear, tenacious purpose as to ends. Had they not both been cruelly schooled to self-suppression by long experience of the world's treachery and danger before ever they came to the throne? And if Elizabeth's other name and nature was that of 'Gloriana' or 'the good Queen Bess', Richmond too had known how to win the people's love in showing the high courage of his race on that gallant Bosworth campaign.

BOOK THREE
THE TUDORS

Renaissance, Reformation, and Sea Power

THE Europe of to-day is divided perpendicularly into a number of separate States, each absolute sovereign in its own territories, and each purporting to represent a racial or national idea. But in the Middle Ages, Europe was divided horizontally into Estates and corporations of clergy, nobles, villeins, and burghers – governed locally by their own domestic laws, in convents, castles, manors, and walled cities. In the shelter of that framework the arts of civilization, torn up by the barbarian inroads, took root again and flourished in new forms. But the individual had little freedom in the feudal village and less in the monastery; while, even in the chartered town and guild, initiative was checked and the unprivileged stranger excluded. Expansion, progress, and individuality were hampered, until these rigid corporations had lost some of their power, and until the close control of the medieval Church over the lives and thoughts of all men had been loosened.

The only power strong enough to effect a social revolution of such extent and gravity was the power of the national State. The despotism of the State laid indeed restraints of its own upon liberty, but in England at least it cleared more elbow room for the individual than he had enjoyed in the medieval world. The era of private enterprise and expanding genius associated with Drake and Raleigh, Shakespeare and Bacon, was the outcome of two hundred years of social disruption and rebirth, of the appeal of Renaissance and Reformation to the individual mind and conscience, and the subjection of corporate power to the national will embodied in Crown and Parliament.

The medieval system passed away, not by chance or by the whim of a King impatient to be divorced, but on account of profound changes in the habits of the English people, most of which we have seen already at work in the Fourteenth and Fifteenth Centuries. The emancipation of the villeins; the growth of London; the rise of educated and active-minded middle classes; the spread of cloth manufacture and other trading activities outside the chartered towns; the unifying effect of the Common Law, the royal administration and the national Parliament; the national pride engendered by the Hundred Years' War and the democratic triumphs of the English archer over the mounted aristocrat; the adoption of the English language by the educated classes; the invention of cannon to shatter the noble's stronghold, and of the printing-press to undermine the churchman's monopoly of learning; the studies of the Renaissance, which on the one hand set religion in the light of a scholarly examination of the Scriptures, and on the other revealed in ancient Greece and Rome ideals unknown to medieval Christendom; the discovery of the ocean trade routes and of the New World, which had held no place in the intellectual outlook or commercial habits of any former age – all these changes, spiritual and material, combined to dissolve the fabric of medieval society in England.

At the same time all Western Europe was tending to group itself into national States – France, Spain, Portugal. Inside each modern State, power was increasingly concentrated in the King's hands. But whereas in France and Spain the new monarchy was allied with the old Church, in England it was allied with the old Parliament. In France and Spain medieval religion was preserved, while medieval Parliament decayed and the Roman Imperial law was received as the basis of the Prince's absolute power. In England medieval religion was changed, while we preserved medieval Parliaments, native Common Law, and the constitutional character of the Kingship. The distinction between England and continental Europe, particularly Latin Europe, which the Norman Conquest had obscured, was emphasized once more by these opposite developments on the two sides of the Channel. English and French civilization, at one time not very easily distinguishable, became not only separate but mutually repellent.

Tudor England, while effecting a great revolution in the social system, characteristically preserved the form and even the spirit of much that was old. Most of the orders, corporations, and institutions which had been the principal channels of medieval life, remained intact on condition of submitting to the sovereign authority of the State. Universities, nobles, lawyers, Bishops, secular clergy, and town corporations survived ostensibly in the old forms. Some institutions, like the cosmopolitan orders of monks and friars, could not be fitted into the new national scheme of things, and were ruthlessly destroyed by the State. Rights like those of Sanctuary and Benefit of Clergy were reduced or abolished, because they set limits to the execution of the national law. Noble and commoner, clergy and laity were made equal before the law of the land. The class of villeins excluded from these benefits disappeared, and the noblemen's coercion of the royal courts through his retainers became a thing of the past. The ecclesiastical courts exercised diminished powers over the laity, by the authority no longer of the Pope but of the King. Cosmopolitan feudalism and the cosmopolitan Church went down before the new idea of a national State with a national Church attached. The 'liberties' of the medieval clergy and aristocracy, slices of sovereignty held in private or corporate hands, were resumed in favour of the liberty of the ordinary English subject, sheltered behind the power of the State.

So, too, the regulation of trade, instead of being as formerly an affair of each chartered town or guild, became the business of the national authorities. Plantagenet Parliaments had tried to regulate wages and prices by their Statutes of Labourers, to be enforced by the King's Justices of the Peace. In Tudor times this national control of economy was carried still further. The law of apprenticeship was regulated no longer by each local guild, but by the Statute of Artificers passed by Queen Elizabeth's Parliament. The provision for the poor, formerly left to the monasteries and guilds and to private charity, was provided for as a duty incumbent on society at large, and enforced by the State. The chief agents of this statutory control of the nation's economic life – as also of its political and judicial life – were the unpaid Justices of the Peace appointed by the Crown, who formed the link between the views of the central authority and the facts of local administration. They performed as servants of the State many functions which the feudal baron had performed in his own personal right.

When the Crown in Parliament effected a series of revolutions in ecclesiastical and religious affairs, it was demonstrated beyond all question that the State had acquired unlimited sovereign authority. In the Middle Ages such radical legislation would have been regarded as altogether beyond the legal and moral competence of any power in England. But in the Tudor epoch the nation asserted its new strength, and, expelling all foreign authorities and suppressing all local immunities, claimed the right to do whatever it liked within its own frontiers. These novel claims of complete independence for the nation and omnicompetence for the State, were embodied in the person of the Prince. This is the general cause of the King-worship of the Sixteenth Century.

The plenary powers of the new State could, in that age, have been exercised only by the King. Parliament, half debating society and half court of law, had neither the strength nor the ambition for such a part. Indeed it was a main function of the Tudor Kings and their Privy Council to teach to the Parliament men at Westminster and to the Justices of the Peace in the countryside the work of real government, which had been so sadly neglected in the previous century. Parliament was ready to be the scholar and servant of royalty, like a 'prentice serving his time and fitting himself to become partner and heir.

So, too, the peculiar religious circumstances of that age of transition favoured the power of the Crown in England. By putting himself at the head of the Anti-clerical revolution that destroyed the medieval power and privilege of the Church, Henry VIII not only became the heir of much of that power, but set the new Monarchy in alliance with the strongest forces of the coming age – London, the middle classes, the seagoing population, the Protestant preachers, the squirearchy bribed and reinforced by the abbey lands; together they proved more than a match for the forces of the old world – the monks and friars, the remnant of the feudal nobility and gentry in the North, and popular Catholic piety which was strongest in districts farthest removed from London. The Bishops and secular clergy acquiesced, at first as neuters; but in the course of the long reign of Elizabeth, the parish clergy and the schoolmasters became the chief instruments of Protestant propaganda and instruction.

Roman Catholic zeal in England was at its lowest ebb when Henry struck at the medieval Church, and it failed to revive when his daughter Mary gave the old religion another chance. It only recovered vigour with the Jesuit reaction well on in the reign of Elizabeth. That revival came a generation too late for success, and it came from continental sources that infuriated the rising nationalism of the English. Catholic was identified in the vulgar mind with Jesuit, and Jesuit with Spaniard. The issue became involved in the struggle of our seamen for the free use of the ocean and the world beyond, which the Pope had divided with a stroke of the pen between Portugal and Spain. The new commercial and naval aspirations of England, embodied in the Tudor Royal Navy, in Drake and his captains, and in the trading companies of London – and Raleigh's prophetic visions of colonial Empire, were all arrayed against the old religion and sailed under the banner of the new monarchy.

In the Tudor epoch as a whole, Catholic zeal had the feebleness of age and Protestant zeal the feebleness of immaturity.

Neither dared to defy the Crown, as Catholics and Protestants then defied it in France and in Scotland, and as the Puritans afterwards defied it in England. Hence the bewildering changes of religion with every fresh Tudor monarch were accepted by laity and clergy alike much as a change of Cabinet is accepted to-day. The only successful defiance of the Tudors' claim to settle the faith of their subjects was the passive resistance of the three hundred Protestant martyrs burned in Mary's reign, and that was successful only on condition of being passive. Wyatt's Protestant rebellion failed as hopelessly as the Catholic Pilgrimage of Grace and the rising of the Earls. It was not an age of religious zeal in England, like the age of Becket or the age of Cromwell, yet the greatest of all religious questions then came up for decision. It was, therefore, the supreme moment for the Erastian Prince, who stepped into the place whence the Pope had been deposed, fully prepared, with the help of Parliament, to define the faith of all his subjects, as the great mass of them heartily desired that he should do. So long as men persisted in the medieval error that there should be only one religion tolerated, so long the only alternative to priestly rule of society was the Erastian State. Liberty of conscience slowly grew up out of the struggles between the Erastian State and the various phases and sects of religious enthusiasm.

Only towards the end of Elizabeth's reign are there indications that the House of Commons might some day acquire enough political strength and enough religious conviction to dispute the control of ecclesiastical affairs with the Crown. In that case the ensuing confusion might enable the individual conscience to come into its own. The assumption by the State of the persecuting powers of the old Church was, as we can now see, provisional in its nature; however little questioned for the moment, it was bound to break down in the end if persistently challenged by the private conscience.

The Tudors gave a new direction to the external and expansive energies of the English people. The attempt to conquer France was not seriously resumed; little England, with its four to five million inhabitants, was thrown upon the defensive in Europe by the strength of the new French and Spanish monarchies. Her rising school of diplomacy, from Wolsey to Cecil, pursued the 'Balance of Power' as England's only chance of security in face of the great continental States now being formed. Partly owing to these apprehensions, Henry VIII made, for the first time in our history, a really fine Royal Navy. Celtic Wales and the anarchic Welsh March were reduced to order and annexed on terms of equality to England – the first successful act of English Imperialism of the modern type, due to Henry VIII and his inherited understanding of things Welsh. Scotland he misunderstood, but under Elizabeth the future union of the two Kingdoms was prepared, when Scotland was detached from her old French connexions and bound in friendship to England on the basis of common Protestant interests. The future Great Britain, the heretical sea-power on the flank of the great continental despotisms, was already clearly visible in outline. At the same time the conquest of Ireland, after being neglected by England for four hundred years, was at length undertaken in earnest, in an age too late for the happiness of either party.

Last, but not least, just when social and economic change at home was setting free individuals of all classes to wander and seek fortune afar, the new paths of the ocean were opened to the adventurous, the avaricious, and the valiant, where the restless spirit of the race could find better work to do than vexing France with fresh Agincourts and England with fresh Towtons and Barnets. The descendants of the archers and retainers thronged the decks of the privateers bound for the Spanish Main, and manned the merchantmen trading to Muscovy, the Levant, and the further East. England had ceased to be at the world's extremity and was found, as the new *mappa mundi* yearly unfolded itself, to be each year nearer to the strategic centre. While the Armada was going to pieces on the rocks, England was at last entering on the wider spaces of her destiny; and the sense of adventure in untrodden regions of mind and matter inspired the rising generation, who went out in the spirit of free individual initiative to explore new worlds of land and water, knowledge and imagination. At that propitious moment the English language reached its perfection of force and beauty in the mouths of men, and at that moment Shakespeare lived to use it.

The history of the change from medieval to modern England might well be written in the form of a social history of the English cloth trade.

From prehistoric times coarse cloth had been manufactured in our island, and under the manorial system the medieval villagers not only span but wove much of their own poor clothing. But in those days little was woven fit for export, or even for the home market, so that our well-to-do classes must needs bring English wool home again in the form of Flemish cloth. The export of raw wool to the looms of Flanders and Italy gave a modest trading wealth to Plantagenet England, besides helping her to pay the Pope's agents the sums which their master extorted. But when at last the English themselves learnt to weave fine cloth for the foreign market, unexpected consequences followed in every department of life and thought.

The great change began when, under the patronage of Edward III, a large number of Flemish weavers brought their skill to this island. Many of them were refugees and allies of the English cause in the Hundred Years' War, for the French feudal nobility was constantly at war with the liberties of the burgher democracy of Ghent and the neighbouring cities led by the Van Arteveldes. The Flemish immigrants were, indeed, so little popular over here that some hundreds were massacred by the London mob in the rising of 1381, but the survivors were protected by the wise policy of the King, until their descendants became by intermarriage indistinguishable from the other English. The gift of their skill became a national treasure, destined to multiply a thousand-fold. The French and Flemish Huguenots who flocked over in Elizabethan and Stuart times found more popular favour, as being sufferers in the Protestant cause, and they were no less helpful than their medieval forerunners in developing ever new branches of the English weaving industry.

In the Fifteenth and Sixteenth Centuries, East Anglia, with Norwich for its capital, was greatly enriched by the cloth trade, as its many fine churches bear witness. Its example was followed by Taunton and the western Cotswolds, Kendal and the Yorkshire dales, and favoured spots in Hants, Berkshire, and Sussex. East and West, North and South saw weaving colonies spring up, not only inside old walled towns, but even more in rural villages like Painswick and Chipping Campden. Thence new wealth and new ideas spread among the yeomen and squires, drawing the whole countryside into a conspiracy to produce cloth. In such districts 'speed-the-shuttle' became as popular as 'speed-the-plough', and sheep had a new value in the farmer's eyes. Stone villages of the noblest Tudor architecture, encircled for miles round by Tudor farms built in the same lavish style, tell the tourist on Cotswold the tale of the ancient prosperity of the loom. And the history of the Kendal cloth trade can still be read in the stout stone walls and oak furniture of Westmorland and Cumbrian sheep-farms.

The weaving industry was conducted on 'domestic' lines, that is, the weavers and their families worked their looms in their own cottages and were supplied with material by middlemen who disposed also of the finished goods. The long trains of pack-horses, each animal with a wool-sack or a bale of cloth slung across its back, were shuttles for ever moving across the warp and woof of English life, drawing distant regions and classes together in a solid national texture. The farmer in Lincolnshire was growing fine wool for looms in Yorkshire, while the merchants and seamen of Hull and London were busy finding new markets for it in the Levant and Baltic, in the East and West Indies, and finally in Virginia and Massachusetts. The Cotswold shepherds and weavers had Gloucester and Bristol at hand in the plain below to push their wares across the sea.

All this widespread energy was taken into account by the statesmen of the Privy Council, who framed the nation's policy, foreign and economic. For all these various individual interests looked one way, when wisely guided by Cecil and Elizabeth. The town corporation and local guild could not command so wide a field of national vision as the State. Indeed the municipalities did little to control the new movement, for even when the cloth manufacture was not conducted, as it usually was, in rural surroundings, it was often set up in the 'liberties' just outside the borough jurisdiction, in order to avoid the pettifogging rules that hampered commerce within the walls. The great days of medieval corporate life in guild and borough were on the downgrade throughout Tudor times, so far as economic regulation was concerned. On the other hand, there was a great increase in the wealth and political power of London and other towns, particularly the sea ports, for the cloth trade and the discovery of the ocean routes combined to make a new era in English maritime commerce.

The influence of the cloth trade was national and individualist, not cosmopolitan or corporate. All through the Wars of the Roses, through the changes and violences of Henry's Reformation and Mary's Counter-Reformation, in the golden days of Elizabeth, on through the civil wars of King and Parliament, enterprising cloth merchants, weavers, and sheep-farmers were making and spreading wealth among many classes high and low, by their own individual initiative, subject only to State protection and control. They were at once more individualist and more nationalist than the medieval churchmen and nobles whose place they were slowly taking as leaders of the English, for they had no corporate sense of belonging to a cosmopolitan order, like the medieval Bishop, monk, noble, and burgher. They had therefore no jealousy of the Tudor national monarchy, until the

House of Commons engendered in them a new sentiment of democratic cooperation on a purely national basis.

The Protestant religion, setting up the domestic and individual forum for conscience and Bible-study, suited these men and their character well. In the Fifteenth Century great founders of chantries to save their own souls and perpetuate their own fame, with a strong tendency to anti-clericalism in early Tudor times, they became Bible-readers and Reformation men for the most part as the Sixteenth Century drew on. The richer of them, buying land and intermarrying with needy squires, founded new 'county families'. Not a few shared in the Abbey lands, having ready cash with which to join in the fierce land speculation that followed the dissolution of the monasteries. At the Universities and Inns of Courts their sons trained themselves to public service. The men of the new wealth were an indispensable mainstay first of Elizabeth and then of the Parliamentary cause in the era that followed. Through them the Tudor and Stuart navy came to rule the seas. For one chief advantage that England had over Spain in the exploitation of the New World, was that we had cloth to sell there in exchange for its goods, while the Spaniards had nothing to send out except soldiers, priests, and colonists.

CHAPTER I

The Renaissance Scholars. Wolsey and the Balance of Power. The Era of Discovery. The Cabots. Henry VIII founds the Royal Navy

THE Fifteenth Century, if we exclude its last twenty years, was intellectually barren beyond any other epoch in our history since the Norman Conquest. The violent suppression of freedom of thought at Oxford and subsequently throughout the country by the persecution of Wycliffism, was not made good by any moral or intellectual revival of a more orthodox character. There was nothing analogous to the 'coming of the friars' of two hundred years before. The triumph of mere obscurantism
reached its height in the trial and imprisonment of poor Bishop 1457
Pecock, because in arguing against the Lollards he had appealed partly to human reason instead of wholly to the authority of the Church. Among the laity, the same period was unproductive of great literature, if we except some of the popular ballads. Chaucer had readers, reproducers, and imitators, but not successors.

There was, however, the new printing-press, and an adequate supply of new schools for the middle classes; though the education given was of poor quality, the number of educated people in the island offered a wonderful field for the sower of wheat or tares. And Henry VII's reign was a season of seed.

Italy was the land of the Renaissance, and thence the new studies came to Oxford in the last two decades of the Fifteenth Century. From Italy, Grocyn, Lily, and Linacre brought home a new interest in Greek literature, Latin grammar, and scientific medicine. Slowly the long-lost world of Hellas began to take shape, as in a glass darkly, revealing to a few ardent minds a world of thought not bounded by the medieval heaven and hell, just as the material world was expanding beyond all the limits of medieval cosmography, with every new voyage of Columbus and Cabot. At the same time, studies conducted in Ciceronian Latin, replacing the useful but inelegant Latin of the Middle Ages, suggested ideals of conduct on the 'antique Roman' pattern. If these influences should once spread from Court and college into common grammar schools at Stratford and elsewhere, life even here, upon this bank and shoal of time, would become a gracious and noble adventure.

Another element formative of modern England was introduced by young Colet, a London merchant's son. On his return from
1497 Italian groves of Academe, he astonished Oxford by the announcement that he would lecture on St Paul's epistles. By sheer force of genius he compelled not only the enthusiastic undergraduates but the disapproving Abbots and doctors of divinity to listen to a young man scarcely yet ordained priest, while he set aside every landmark erected by the scholiasts, and gave straight from the Greek text a realistic and humanist exposition of the life and teaching of St Paul. He was seeking to discover what the Epistles had meant to him who wrote and to those who received them, not at all what they had meant to the dialecticians of the last three hundred years. The studies and learning of the Middle Ages crumbled like a corpse exposed to the air; Duns Scotus had once been in the van of intellectual advance, but those who were still faithful to the Subtle Doctor were now held in derision as 'dunces' by the rising generation at Oxford and Cambridge, and presently on every school bench in the land.

Dutch Erasmus was rapidly rising by the help of the printing-press to a European reputation without previous parallel. He was much in England, and both he and Sir Thomas More were

Colet's friends and allies. Between them they gave a new character to the Renaissance studies, making them moral and religious in Northern Europe, instead of artistic and pagan as in Italy. To the Italian scholars and their patron Princes and Cardinals, the Renaissance meant the ancient poets and philosophers, marble nymphs, and 'brown Greek manuscrips'. To Colet and Erasmus, and through them to the English generally, the Renaissance meant these things indeed, but it meant also the New Testament in Greek and ultimately the Old Testament in Hebrew. The difference was profound, and produced yet another rift between England and the Franco-Italian civilization which had nurtured her childhood. For the men of the Italian Renaissance lived, and their spiritual successors in France and Italy have lived ever since, in a world of art, letters, and science seldom touched by religion, in effect abandoning ecclesiastical affairs to the unaided efforts of the monks and clergy. But in England the men of the Renaissance, following the lead of Colet, used the study of Greek and Latin to reform not only the schools but the Church herself, and called on clergy and laity to act together in the task.

This movement, at once moral and intellectual, classical and Christian, did not, as is sometimes said, perish in the storms of the English Reformation. On the contrary, its spirit found expression in the educational and religious policy of the reformed schools and of the reformed Church of England that emerged under the later Tudors from the confused violence of the earlier struggle. If Colet had seen a typical Elizabethan grammar school, he would have been well pleased. If the old endowments that were confiscated under Henry and Edward are set against the new endowments that were made under Elizabeth, the quantity of educational provision was little if at all increased under the Tudors; but the quality was immensely improved.

These Oxford Reformers, as Colet and Erasmus were called, began, in the names of scholarship, religion, and morality, a series of bitter attacks on the monks and obscurantists, on the worship of images and relics, on the extortion of the ecclesiastical courts and the worldliness of the clergy. On these matters no Lollard could use stronger language, although they were no Lollards. Their influence was spreading from Oxford to London, to the Court, and ere long to Cambridge. Colet became Dean of St 1505
Paul's, and delighted the citizens and perturbed the clergy of the capital by sermons denouncing Church abuses and practices in a manner not heard from the official pulpit since the silencing of Wycliffe's priests a hundred years before. Colet also founded,

in the shadow of the Cathedral, St Paul's School with Lily as its first headmaster, to teach Greek and Ciceronian Latin, and to become the prototype of the reformed grammar school.

What would be the attitude of the new monarchy towards the New Learning? Much indeed turned upon that, for in the situation then reached by England, the nation could do nothing against the will of the Crown, and the Crown nothing against the will of the nation, but the two together could do anything they chose, even to the altering or preserving of religious doctrine and ecclesiastical privilege.

Henry VII was too busy in his great task as England's policeman to concern himself with the New Learning. The clergy to him were useful civil servants, the Pope a figure on the diplomatic chessboard. For the rest he was orthodox; he once took part in converting a Lollard at the stake, and leaving him to be burned in spite of his recantation, such being the standard of Christian charity of those times.

But what of the younger Henry? In 1509 he succeeded to the throne and to the marriage with Catherine of Aragon, since his elder brother Arthur who was to have enjoyed the lady and the realm had prematurely died. The young King of eighteen exceeded the ordinary run of his subjects in body and in brain. He was a paragon of Princes, the patron alike of all true English sportsmen and of the men of the New Learning. Succeeding with a clear title to the peace, wealth, and power that his father had painfully accumulated, and cutting off the heads of Empson and Dudley as an earnest of the great love he bare his people, he won their hearts from the first. He was as true an Englishman as 'Farmer George', but on a more brilliant pattern. He could bend a bow with the best forester in the realm, and when complimented on his archery by the French Ambassador could reply 'it was good for a Frenchman'. His colossal suit of tilting armour in the Tower reminds us that once he flashed through the lists like Launcelot, laying low his adversaries and calling for more. He was a champion at tennis and a mighty hunter. Orthodox, like his father, he continued to encourage the burning of Lollards, wrote his book
1521 against Luther, and was dubbed by the Pope *Fidei Defensor*. But he was also a friend to Colet and More, forcing the latter to take up the dangerous profession of courtier, and defending Dean Colet against the obscurantist clergy, with the declaration 'Let every man have his doctor, this is mine,' even when the fearless Dean denounced his war against France as unchristian. For 'Henry loved

a man.' And 'pastime with good company he loved,' as we read in the song which he is said to have composed and set. Among other accomplishments this Admirable Crichton was no mean musician, and played well on all known instruments. Poetry and music flourished in his Court, when the English lyrical and the English musical genius were moving forward again towards the moment of their fine flowering under Elizabeth.

It was said that Henry's Court had better store of learned men than any University. These early friends of his implanted in his mind a dislike of monks, of image worship, of relic worship, and a respect for the study of the Bible – all perfectly compatible with doctrinal orthodoxy on the Eucharist, as his subjects were to find out in the days to come when this handsome young athlete and lover of all things noble had been turned by thirty years of power and worship into a monstrous egoism moving remorselessly over the bodies of old friends and new foes towards a clearly conceived middle policy in religion, with the Royal substituted for the Papal power. All the various aspects of that later policy can be traced to opinions imbibed during his early life, and to the movement of the age in a nation which, even in his days of bloated and ferocious tyranny, Henry understood with an instinct that even Elizabeth never surpassed.

For the present those days were far ahead. As yet the Cardinal ruled – the last Cardinal and almost the last churchman ever to rule over England. While 'Harry our King was gone hunting' morning after morning, or was holding high festival at night 'with masque and antique pageantry', Wolsey was labouring over the details of home and foreign policy which in later years Henry took into his own industrious hands. But youth must be served, at least such a youth as Henry's and that was the Cardinal's day.

Wolsey, like all the greatest servants of the Tudor monarchy, was of comparatively humble birth – his father was probably an East Anglian grazier or wool merchant – but he was haughty and ostentatious to a degree that would hardly have been tolerated in a Prince of the Blood. He 'is the proudest prelate that ever breathed' reported a foreign observer, and such was the general opinion. The one blot on his splendid equipment as a diplomatist was the fury of his temper; one day he laid violent hands on the Papal Nuncio and threatened him with the Tower rack over some dealings with France. The state which Wolsey kept, in the high hall at Hampton Court or when he travelled, for a while pleased his master and dazzled his countrymen, but in the end helped to turn them all against him, and pointed for poets the moral of his fall.

In his hands the Balance of Power in Europe first became clearly defined as the object of England's foreign policy. It was dictated by the rise of the great monarchies of France and Spain, for if either of these overcame the other, it would be lord paramount of Europe, and little England's position would be ignominious and unsafe. For several years Wolsey kept the balance with consummate skill and with a minimum of expense to English blood and treasure. In 1513 the double victory over the invading Scots at Flodden and over the French at the Battle of Spurs near Guinegatte on the Netherland border, raised England to a strong position as holder of the balance. But after 1521 Wolsey's skill and foresight failed him. He backed Charles V, monarch of Spain and the Netherlands and Emperor in Germany, at a time when he should rather have supported the weakening cause of France.
1525 At the battle of Pavia the capture of Francis I and the destruction of his army laid Italy at the feet of Spain for the next 180 years, reduced France and England temporarily to impotence, and began that Hapsburg supremacy in Europe which in the days of Philip II and Elizabeth almost proved the destruction of England, and would have destroyed her but for the growth of popular, maritime, and religious forces in the island which Wolsey overlooked or opposed.

The power of Spain was not confined to the Old World. The era of ocean discovery and commerce had begun, replacing the ancient trade routes across Asia and Egypt, of which the European end had been in the hands of Genoa and Venice. From the Italian cities and the land-locked Mediterranean with its oared galleys, power and wealth were passing to the lands of Western Europe, which could send out a new type of seaman and new type of ship to sail the far ocean, to reach the markets of Asia by sea, and to discover Africa and America on the way.

It did not seem at first that England would be the chief gainer by this change. In the Fifteenth Century, Portuguese seamen, under Prince Henry the Navigator, had been beforehand along the coast of Africa and round the Cape route to India, founding a Portuguese Empire on the African littoral, destined to survive till the present day. Spain was long disunited and struggling with the Moors, but when joined into one State by the marriage of Ferdinand of Aragon with Isabella of Castile, she soon made an
1492 end of the Moors on her own side of the Straits of Gibraltar,

employed Columbus, and sent out the Conquistadores, who made her a present of the mines of Mexico and Peru and the wealth of the Spanish Main. 1519–35

The Pope had risen to the occasion. He had drawn a line down the globe from pole to pole, a hundred leagues west of the Azores, giving all lands discoverable to the west of it to Spain, 1493 and on the east to Portugal. The competition thus set on foot had incited the great voyagers in the pay of the two Iberian monarchies, had sent Magellan round by the Horn and across the Pacific, and set Amerigo Vespucci to trade the southern coastline of the continent that bears his name. As yet no one openly impeached the validity of the Pope's division. As yet Portugal and Spain had no rivals on the ocean and in the lands beyond. The Italian maritime States supplied the master mariners – Columbus, Vespucci, and Cabot – but neither Venice nor Genoa ventured upon their own account on the new ocean traffic. It was as if the heart of Italy had been broken by the decline of the old Asiatic trade-routes of which she had been mistress; neither Venice nor Genoa, as communities, had the requisite vitality to build the new type of ocean-going ship and train the new type of ocean-going sailor: it was enough for their declining powers to carry on the wrecks of the old Levant trade, and engage galley to galley with the Turkish war fleets.

Neither as yet was France or England ready to challenge the commercial and colonial monopoly of Spain and Portugal in Africa, Asia, or America. In Henry VII's reign John Cabot and his boy Sebastian, sailing in a cockle-boat with 18 gallant men 1497 of Bristol, visited certain regions in Labrador, Newfoundland, and Nova Scotia. They had sailed west to find the fabled Cathay and the Seven Cities of the East, with their spices and their gold, and found the way blocked by the foggy cod banks and dripping pine forests of North America – a better heritage for the English had they known it. But England dared not yet arouse the wrath of Spain by laying hands on this heritage; her time was not yet. Henry VII had encouraged maritime adventure, but Wolsey discouraged it. The voyages of the Cabots and the men of Bristol to North America merely staked out a claim that lay dormant for several generations as regards inland discovery or plantation, though before the middle of the new century the Newfoundland fisheries had become an important nursery of our seamen.

Such was the situation with which Henry VIII had to deal. His policy was both wise and strong. While not encouraging transoceanic adventure in the face of predominant Spanish power, he made possible the future liberation of his country's energies by the only means – the foundation of a Royal Navy. The 'narrow seas' had been held during the Hundred Years' War – so far as they had been held at all – by the pugnacious seamen of the merchant navy, fighting sometimes as individual pirates, sometimes, as at Sluys, united under the royal command. Henry V had begun to build a royal fleet, but his work had not gone far and had subsequently been neglected. Henry VII had encouraged the mercantile marine, but had not built a fleet for fighting purposes only. It was Henry VIII who built an effective fleet of royal fighting ships, with royal dockyards at Woolwich and Deptford; he also founded the corporation of Trinity House.

Henry's maritime policy had a double importance. Not only did he create ships specially manned and commissioned to fight, and to fight in the public service alone, but his architects designed many of these royal ships on an improved model. They were sailing vessels better adapted to the ocean than the rowed galleys of the Mediterranean powers, and better adapted to manoeuvring in battle than the more clumsy 'round' ships of the medieval type in which the English merchants sailed the sea, and in which the Spaniards crossed the Atlantic. The new type of English warship was three times the length of its beam or more, while the normal 'round' ship was only twice the length of its beam. Hitherto sea-battles had consisted of ramming, archery, and boarding, very much like the battles of the old Greek and Roman navies. But a new age was at hand. From the port-holes of Henry VIII's fleet protruded the iron mouths of great cannon in a row, ready to give the shattering 'broadside', the operation of war to which, more than to any other, British maritime and colonial power owe their existence. It was Henry VIII himself who had insisted that his naval architects should mount heavy cannon in the body of the ship; they had devised the expedient of piercing apertures in the very hold itself through which the great shot could be discharged.

In 1545, at the end of Henry's reign, a French armada attempted to invade England, but was foiled by the Royal Navy. England was saved from invasion, and the same year a baby called Francis Drake was born on a farm near Tavistock.

The Royal Navy was Henry's creation, and it saved both himself and his daughter after him when they adopted an island policy and defied the Catholic powers of Europe. Wolsey had no notion of the importance of sea power to England. He was a great medieval churchman, a civil servant of the old school, and a diplomatist of the Renaissance type. But of the future development of England at home and on the sea Wolsey had no vision at all. His master, with that curious instinct of oneness with the English people which was the secret of Tudor greatness, saw deeper. He could use Wolsey's consummate administrative powers during the years of his own apprenticeship in statecraft, and then pass over him along a path of his own which no Cardinal could be expected to tread.

Wolsey was a great man, but it was not he who made modern England. He had no interest in the navy and no trust in Parliament. He had indeed an active distrust of it, because the growing anti-clericalism of the country had been demonstrated in the Parliament of 1515 by an attack on Benefit of Clergy, mortuary fees, and the currency of Papal degrees in England. There had been strange talk on the judicial bench of the penalties of *praemunire* incurred by Convocation. Judges and Parliament had stood up for the royal power, as representing popular rights against clerical privilege. Neither Wolsey nor his master had been unobservant of these things. For the present indeed the Cardinal ruled and Henry watched. So Parliament was not summoned again for eight years. But if ever Henry should tire of the Cardinal and desire to rob or reform the Church and to defy the Pope, he would know to what institution he could look for support.

CHAPTER II

The Royal and Parliamentary Reformation under Henry VIII

THOSE who conceive of opinion in Tudor England as sharply divided between two mutually exclusive and clearly defined parties of Catholic and Protestant, can never understand the actual course taken by the Reformation before the latter years of Elizabeth. Opinion was in the making, not yet made. Honest men, as well as time-servers, were perpetually altering their views. Few held a consistent body of doctrine which would have satisfied the Catholic or Protestant partisans of a later day. Sir Thomas More, a scathing critic of the religious orders and the popular superstitions they fostered, became the martyr of Papal Supremacy, whereas Bishops Gardiner and Bonner, though famous as Papalists under Mary, had defended Henry's original breach with Rome. Queen Elizabeth herself would have preferred a celibate priesthood. Opinion among the mass of men was more interested in preserving the King's Peace than in raising difficulties over his religious policy.

In the north and extreme south-west, considerable zeal was shown for the defence, not indeed of the Papal jurisdiction, but of the monasteries and the old forms of religion. In London and the neighbourhood the party of change prevailed. The contrast between the citizens of Tudor London and those of Valois Paris, in their attitude towards the clergy and the doctrines of the medieval Church, goes a long way to explain the different fortunes of the Reformation in England and in France.

But the party of change, in London and elsewhere, was not wholly inspired by Protestantism or by the New Learning of Dean Colet and his friends. It was also under the influence of a passion which can best be described as anti-clerical. Anti-clericalism was in some persons a greedy desire to plunder the Church for the benefit of their own families. In others it was a rational and honourable dislike of the powers and privileges enjoyed by the priesthood. For the clergy still had the legal right to extort money in innumerable ways, and to adjudicate in their spiritual courts on points of doctrine and morals for all men, in an age when the laity had become well able to think and act for themselves. The change from medieval to modern society in the sphere of religion, consisted mainly in a reduction of the power of the priesthood, and the raising up of the laymen, first collectively through the action of the State, then individually through the freedom of private conscience. It was the first of these movements that took place under the Tudors, in the subjection of the Church to the State, and it was a movement quite as much anti-clerical as it was Protestant.

Henry VIII burnt Protestants, while hanging and beheading the Catholic opponents of an anti-clerical revolution. And this policy, which appears so strange to-day, then met with much popular approval in England. In the babel of voices heard during his reign, the strongest note is a Catholic, Nationalist anti-clericalism. It was only after Henry's death that the logic of the new situation at home and abroad drove the English Anti-clericals and Nationalists to defend themselves against Catholic reaction by alliance with the Protestants, to whose doctrines they became, in Elizabeth's reign, very fair converts.

Anti-clericalism, in fact, was not destined to become the shibboleth of a permanent party in England, as it became in France and Italy from the time of Voltaire onwards. Dislike of clerical domination and respect for religion are both more general in

England than in most parts of Europe, and both found satisfaction in our post-Reformation churches and sects. The spirit of opposition to clerical predominance sometimes supported Anglicanism against Roman or Puritan claims to govern men's lives, and sometimes joined Nonconformity against the pretensions of the State clergy. But while the power of the Pope and the medieval Church was being broken by Henry VIII, anti-clericalism appears as an independent force on the flank of both Catholicism and Protestantism, and for a few decisive years it was the strongest of the three.

The prelude to Henry's breach with the Pope was the German Reformation under Luther, which for some years almost annihilated the prestige of Rome as a centre of religious authority. In 1527 the Holy City was sacked by the armies of Charles V, Emperor in Germany and King of Spain. German heretics and Spanish Catholics rivalled each other in looting churches, raping nuns, and besieging Pope and Cardinals in the Castle of St Angelo, while a Roman Catholic wrote thus to Charles V: 1519

> Everyone considers that this has taken place by the just judgement of God, because the Court of Rome was so ill-ruled. Some are of opinion that the Holy See should not continue in Rome, lest the French King should make a patriarch in his Kingdom, and deny obedience to the said See, and the King of England and all other Princes do the same.

If ever there was a moment when European opinion made it easy for England to break with the Papacy, it was the generation that followed the revolt of Luther and the sack of Rome.

The Lutheran doctrines had no sooner been proclaimed at Wittenberg than they became a power in England, though still under the ban of Church and State. They at once absorbed the Lollard into the Protestant movement. Their effect on the men of the New Learning was twofold: some, particularly the younger men, eagerly joined the more thorough-going movement; others, particularly the older men who had brought the Renaissance to England, shrank back and reacted towards orthodoxy. Erasmus feared Protestantism; More opposed it and wrote against it. Oxford, where so much had been done for progress in the past, held back in doubt, but Cambridge stepped for the first time into the van of the national movement. From 1521 onwards, students met at the White Horse tavern in that town, to discuss Luther's propositions. The tavern was nicknamed 'Germany' and the scholars who haunted it 'Germans', but they were the makers of the new England – Tyndale and Coverdale who first gave her the Bible in Tudor English, Cranmer who gave her the Prayer Book, Latimer the soul of the popular movement, and many other future apostles and martyrs.

Latimer and Cranmer represented, each very nobly, the two aspects of the reformed English Church of the future – the moral and the reflective. Latimer was as fearless as Luther on points of religion, and was far less timorous than the German Reformer on social questions and in face of secular power. Cranmer, mild and cautious, a student scrupulously slow to choose between two sides in intellectual controversy, was a man of perpetual moral hesitations and mental revisions, but with occasional bursts of courage on behalf of his hard-won opinions, like the courage of a timid woman turning to bay in defence of her children. Both men won Henry's regard, and though Latimer's views were too uncompromising to suit the King's purposes for long, Cranmer's favour lasted through all the violent changes of royal affection and policy, to which Wolsey, More, Cromwell, and so many others of both sexes fell victims. Cranmer, indeed, remained the last personal friend that Henry cared to keep: the brutal and self-willed King was to die murmuring of his faith in God, his hand lying trustfully in that of the gentle and perplexed founder of Anglicanism. If one could rightly interpret the inner meaning of that scene one would know much of the curiosities of human nature.

But Henry had a good deal to do before he came to die. At the time of the sack of Rome he was thirty-six years old, and had reached in his slow development the prime of his intellectual power. Hunting and tournaments could no longer be a substitute for politics and government as an outlet to his immoderate energies. He was, at last, prepared to take over from Wolsey the heavy burden of administration. Moreover, like all his subjects, he was getting tired of the Cardinal, who had failed abroad and given personal offence at home, and whose fall could scarcely have been delayed much longer, even without the question of the Royal Divorce.

That question, the immediate cause of the breach with Rome that had been preparing for centuries in England, was not, strictly speaking, a question of 'divorce' at all. Technically, it was a question whether or not Henry had ever been properly married to Catherine of Aragon, since his brother Arthur had been her first husband. A former Pope had granted a dispensation for her marriage to Henry, but Clement VII was now asked to declare that the marriage had never been valid, and that Henry was yet a lusty bachelor. For he desired to marry Anne Boleyn. Like the generality of monarchs of that era and of many eras before and after, he would have been perfectly content with her as his mistress, which she soon was, had he not desired a legitimate male heir to secure for England an undisputed succession and strong rule after his death. He could expect no more children from Catherine, and the Princess Mary was their only child. There had never been a Queen Regnant in England, and the unfamiliar idea of a female succession seemed to threaten the country with civil war or the rule of a foreign Prince as Consort.

The refusal of the Pope to liberate Henry was not due to scruples: he had only recently divorced Henry's sister Margaret, Queen of Scotland, on a far less reasonable excuse, and his predecessors had released monarchs like Louis XII of France, when they desired divorce on no grounds save reasons of state. But he could not oblige Henry, because after the sack of Rome he was in the power of Charles V, who was Catherine's nephew and zealous protector. The Temporal Power of a Pope, so far from giving him freedom, made him a slave to mundane considerations, then as in other ages. Because he was an Italian Prince, Clement could not afford to displease the *de facto* lord of Italy.

To Henry it seemed intolerable that the interests of England should be subjected, through the Pope, to the will of the Emperor. In his anger at this personal grievance, he came to see what many Englishmen had seen long before, that England, if she would be a nation indeed, must repudiate a spiritual jurisdiction manipulated by her foreign rivals and enemies. The full-grown spirit of English nationalism, maturing ever since Plantagenet times, asked why we should look abroad for any part of our laws, either matrimonial or religious. Why not consult our own churchmen? Why not act through our own Parliament?

Wolsey's failure to obtain the 'divorce' from Rome sealed his doom. His death in disgrace saved him from preceding to 1530
the scaffold many high-placed victims of the Terror that now began to walk by noonday. Cranmer, learnedly arguing in favour of the 'divorce' and of England's competence to decide the question for herself, rose thereby to royal favour and became Archbishop of Canterbury. But Henry needed also a rougher and less 1532
scrupulous servant and found one in Thomas Cromwell. The revolution – anti-Papal, anti-clerical, Anglican, and Erastian all in one – was launched on the flood-tide, and was carried through with the accompaniment of violence and injustice that usually

attends all great social revolutions, whether the driving force be a man or a mob.

What was the attitude of the English people towards the question? The average Englishman retained the feeling of his ancestors against the Pope's interference in England, but held it more strongly than ever in the light of the new times, and supported Henry in his decision to settle the question once for all. The nationalism of England was fully grown; she would no longer submit to be governed by a religious authority that was seated a thousand miles beyond seas and mountains, and that judged English questions by Italian, Spanish, Imperial, and occasionally by French standards and interests, but never by English. On the other hand, even in London, the sympathies of the common people went out to the blameless and injured Catherine and her daughter Mary. Anne Boleyn was unpopular. A mistress raised to be a wife at another's expense can scarcely win respect, and Anne was a light woman with no claims of her own for a reversal of so natural a verdict.

But the political and ecclesiastical sides of the question soon swallowed up the personal, and as this change took place, Henry's position with his subjects grew stronger. In the great revolution, by which he freed the English Church and State from the bonds of Rome, suppressed the monks and friars who represented the old cosmopolitan order, and reduced the power and privilege of the clergy, he had the support of London and the South. The unpopular divorce policy involved the popular breach with Rome, and the breach with Rome involved the anti-clerical revolution at home, which enlisted in its defence the most powerful forces in the country. But neither Henry nor his subjects yet understood that these changes must lead in turn to the toleration of the Protestant religion. It was the hour of a persecuting Catholic anti-clericalism as peculiar, some would say as monstrous, as Henry himself. But for the moment it won more support than any other more logical or more merciful policy. Henry, sending the noble Sir Thomas More to the scaffold for his refusal to repudiate the Papal authority, and poor Protestants to the stake for their denial of transubstantiation, moves the angry disgust of readers accustomed to religious toleration as the basis of modern society. But these tragic scenes affected the minds of contemporaries in a different manner – with pity indeed for the victims, but with respect for a Government that was keeping order in Church and State according to the persecuting standards inherited from the past of Christian practice and never yet called in question.

King-worship under the Tudors reached its culmination in these years, in the acceptance of one man's will as the *salus publici*. It was disastrous to the character of Henry, whose egoism became a disease. But the disease affected the heart and not the brain. One result of King-worship under a strong King was that England secured the great change in her institutions without civil war, though Henry had no army with which to keep order. Brave blood was shed, but it was not shed in rivers, as in France, Holland, and Germany during the wars of religion.

The instrument chosen by Henry to effect his Royal Reformation was Parliament. The Reformation had the effect of doubling the importance of Parliament. Hitherto it had been almost as much a court of law as a legislative assembly, and under Henry VII and Wolsey its importance was on the decline. If English history had remained a branch of European history instead of going off on a course of its own, that decline would have continued until the English Parliament had followed into oblivion the medieval Estates of France and Spain. But Henry VIII chose otherwise.

The Reformation Parliament was not packed. It was not necessary to pack it. The legislation that completed the breach with Rome, destroyed the monasteries, and established the supremacy of the State over the Church in England, was prepared 1529–36 by Privy Councillors and passed after discussion by both Houses. The Reformation Parliament, unlike its predecessors, sat for seven years, and in the course of its eight sessions acquired a continuity of personal experience among its members which helped to build up the traditions of the modern House of Commons as a great instrument of government. In Henry's Parliaments debate was fairly free, at least on subjects with which the King wished the Houses to deal; he knew the value of genuine advice and criticism – provided always that he had his way in the main, and that was ensured by the nature of the times and by the character of the royal programme. Yet, in Henry's reign, several measures desired by government were rejected, and others amended by the Commons.

Louis XIV is commonly believed to have said '*L'état, c'est moi*,' and he certainly acted as if he thought so. Henry's authority was of a different kind, as he was the first to acknowledge. In 1543 he told the Commons, while confirming them in the valuable privilege of freedom from arrest:

> We be informed by our Judges that we at no time stand so high in our estate royal as in the time of Parliament, when we as head and you as members are conjoined and knit together in one body politic.

And indeed, when a series of Royal Parliamentary Statutes had revolutionized the fundamental law of Church and State, which had from time immemorial been set high above the competence of Crown or Parliament to alter, then indeed the 'Crown in Parliament' had more than doubled its power. It had become, what it had never been before, 'omnicompetent' to make any law it would within the Realm of England.

The suppression of the orders of monks and friars, and the
1536–9 secularization of their property did much to secure the Royal Parliamentary Reformátion on a basis of vested interest. Henry VIII sold great part of the confiscated Abbey lands to Peers, courtiers, public servants, and merchants, who at once resold much of it to smaller men. Syndicates of middlemen of the commercial class bought the lands to speculate in real estate. It was largely owing to these transactions that, when the Papal reaction began under Mary, it was suspect to this new element in the squirearchy. Many an Abbey had become a manor-house, or the quarry out of which a manor-house was being built, and the squire had no wish to see it an Abbey again. Such persons, though they themselves were never found at the martyr's stake, learnt the wisdom of encouraging the Protestant preachers who were more willing to serve God for nought.

In those days land meant power of a direct kind over those who lived upon it. The Reformation would never have been permitted to flourish among the tenants on monastic estates. But when land in every shire changed from the hands of corporations devoted to the Papal authority and the old religion, into the hands of laymen bound to the new order of things by the very fact of their possessing land confiscated by sacrilege, the influence exerted over a very great body of tenantry was reversed. In London, as in every other town, valuable and conspicuous sites of religious houses and much house property belonging to them passed into lay hands, removing the last check on the ever-increasing Protestantism, anti-clericalism, and commercialism of the capital. At Oxford and Cambridge the monks and friars had been very numerous and had formed the backbone of resistance to the New Learning. The first result of their disappearance was a fall in the numbers of those attending the Universities, which alarmed Latimer; but ere long the ranks of the students were swelled by an increased proportion of gentlemen's sons. This new class of lay undergraduate made the Universities a path to court favour and public service. The Cecils and Bacons fitted themselves by their academic studies to govern the country under Elizabeth, and to foster a new order of intellectual ideas which would never have taken root if Oxford and Cambridge had been left to the guidance of the monks and friars, checked only by the secular clergy.

The secular clergy had for centuries regarded the monks and friars as their rivals, who took from them tithes and fees, competed against their ministrations, and rejected the jurisdiction of their Bishops. These feelings of rivalry between the two parts of the Catholic Church in England were just as strong on the eve of the Reformation as at any former time, and this fact largely accounts for what followed. The cosmopolitan orders which stood isolated alike from the clergy and the more progressive of the laity, and looked to Rome for protection, could not possibly survive when the spirit of nationalism undertook in earnest the formation of an English Church.

In that Church the Bishops retained their place, little altered in form or in law. It was easy for them to take King instead of Pope for master, for they had long been accustomed to act as Royal rather than as Papal servants. The typical English Bishop of the Middle Ages was not Becket but William of Wykeham. Their experience as civil servants, their active part in Parliament and Privy Council, the habit of compromise between the rival claims of Church and Crown, helped the Bishops to accommodate themselves and their office to the great change. But the Abbots had, most of them, stood outside the national life, few of them attending Parliament, and hardly any of them mixing with business outside their own conventual affairs. It was natural then, that in modern England there was a great place found for the Bishop but none for the Abbot. The disappearance of those Abbots who had sat beside the Bishops in the House of Lords left the spirituality in that Chamber in a minority instead of a majority, a change of great significance.

Henry, as Supreme Head of the Church, proceeded to reform the religion of his subjects and so complete the breach with Rome. The study of the Canon Law, that intellectual link with Papal Europe, was suppressed. There were also changes of a more purely devotional character. In his morose and terrible old age, Henry put into effect the ideals which he had imbibed from the Oxford reformers in his fresh and generous youth, the more readily as he could thereby counteract the influence of monks, friars, and Papalists over the multitude. Relic-worship, image-worship, and pardon-mongering, the grosser forms of popular superstition and pious fraud which Colet and Erasmus had attacked, were put down by the heavy hand of the royal authority. All over the country relics were being destroyed, miracle-working images taken down, and their crude machinery exhibited to the people on whose credulity it had imposed. 'Dagon is everywhere falling,' said the reformers; 'Bel of Babylon is broken in pieces.' The shrine and cult of Thomas Becket, so long the chief centre of English pilgrimage, was utterly and easily suppressed, in a new age which spoke of 'the holy blissful martyr' as 'a rebel who fled the realm to France and to the Bishop of Rome to procure the abrogation of wholesome laws'.

Meanwhile, under the influence of Cranmer, an approach was being made towards a new type of appeal to the religious instincts of the masses. The Archbishop himself was drawing up forms of prayer in English which found their places in the Prayer Book of the next reign. But, meanwhile, Henry ordered priests to recite to their congregations, and fathers to teach their children the Lord's Prayer, the Commandments, and the Articles of Faith in English. Above all, at Cranmer's instigation, the Bible in English was not only permitted to circulate freely, but was ordered to be set up in every parish church. A version based on that of Tyndale, the noble scholar and martyr, and on another by his less learned successor, Miles Coverdale, became known, as Tyndale had desired, to craftsmen and to 'the boy that driveth the plough'. The English Reformation, which had begun as a Parliamentary attack on Church fees, and proceeded as a royal raid on Abbey lands, was at last to find its religious basis in the popular knowledge of the Scriptures which had been the dream of Wycliffe. In this way it acquired the strength that resisted the Marian persecution, when cobblers, clothiers, and poor women willingly offered themselves for a cause they at last understood.

Henry, having thus let in the sea, proceeded to ordain the limits of the flood. The disagreeable appearance of one of his later brides, Anne of Cleves, whom Cromwell brought over from anti-Papal Germany, helped, together with graver considerations of European policy, to remind the King that things were going too
1540 far, or at least too fast. Cromwell was beheaded. The Act of Six Articles had already been passed decreeing death against any-
1539 one who denied Transubstantiation, or the necessity of auricular confession and clerical celibacy. A man was hanged in London for eating flesh on Friday. The burning of Protestants proceeded quietly, but with no indecent haste. Latimer was permitted to retire to private life, but Cranmer remained Archbishop. It was an oscillation, not a reversal of policy. Catherine Howard, the

fifth wife, was a Catholic Anne Boleyn, who had much the same faults and suffered the same fate as her Protestant prototype. Catherine Parr, the famous survivor, was a moderating influence on religious policy, inclining cautiously to the Reformers.

Henry in fact was trying to prevent further change and to frighten people who were too prone to discuss religion, a subject on which the King's Grace had finally pronounced – at least for the present. Meanwhile men could read the Bible and think what they liked in silence. The Act of Six Articles was not unpopular, for at the moment the great majority were neither Papalists nor Protestants, and no one believed in toleration. The Act was not rigorously or regularly enforced. Henry was still in touch with the desires of the generality of his subjects, and he had their loyal support against hostile foreign powers in the last years of his reign. But times were bound to alter, and there are signs that he was meditating yet another move forward, when he was called before the only spiritual authority that was any longer competent to summon a King of England.

CHAPTER III

Interludes, Protestant and Catholic

Edward VI, 1547–53; Mary I, 1553-8

THE patient craft of Henry VII and the imperious vigour of Henry VIII had laid the foundations of modern England. Order had been restored, the nobles and their retainers had been suppressed, royal government through Council and Parliament had become a reality in every corner of England and even of Wales, the Royal Navy had been founded, the independence of the country had been established in the face of Europe, secular and spiritual, and the lay revolution in the relations of Church and State had been carried through. But all this, though accomplished, had not been secured. When Henry VIII died, the State was heavily in debt, the coinage had been debased, and the religious feuds which he seemed to have suppressed by violence were bound to break out afresh with increasing fury. The work of the Tudors might yet be ruined, unless the country could be governed on a method at once effective and cheap, and unless a form of religion was found for the new State Church sufficiently acceptable to prevent civil war leading to anarchy or counter-revolution. These problems were eventually solved by Elizabeth, a wise woman and something of a sceptic. But in the dozen years between her father's death and her own accession, government remained in the hands of fools and adventurers, foreigners and fanatics, who between them went near to wrecking the work of the Tudor monarchy, and who actually reduced England to a third-class power, torn by religious feud, a mere appanage of Spain on land and sea.

And yet this inglorious period was by no means barren of results. Religious parties and issues became more clearly defined. It was demonstrated that Henry's half-way tabernacle was not permanently habitable where he had pitched it, but that the country must choose between reunion with Rome and further advance in a Protestant direction. At the same time the national resistance to the Pope became identified in the popular mind with another issue – independence of Spain. The Prayer Book under Edward and the Protestant martyrology under Mary raised the English Reformation on to a new intellectual and moral plane, and rendered it possible for Elizabeth in 1559 to make a permanent settlement of religion, a feat no human wisdom could have achieved in the drifting chaos of opinion that still obscured the land a dozen years before.

Edward VI, son of Henry VIII and Jane Seymour, was nine years old at his accession. He was an invalid child, intellectually precocious, earnest, and severe, with more conscience than his father but scarcely more softness of heart. So far as we can judge of one who died before he was sixteen, he might, if he had lived longer, have ruined the Reformation by overdriving, much as his half-sister Mary ruined the Catholic cause. So long as he lived, two men in turn guided the State in his name. First his uncle Seymour, the Protector Somerset, a rash idealist; and after him John Dudley, Earl of Warwick, and Duke of Northumberland, a man of no principle at all except selfish ambition.

But Edward's reign was saved from futility by the two dominating figures of its religious life. The first of these was Archbishop Cranmer, whose Prayer Book, based largely on his translations from late Latin into the purer English of the Tudor age, harmonized the old and the new, and appealed successfully to the temperament and higher emotion of large sections of the population who without this rallying point might have flown off into mutually hostile factions. Henceforth the Church of England was something more than a remnant spared by the royal and anticlerical revolution: it had found what it so sorely needed – a positive religious atmosphere of its own. The final triumph of the Prayer Book was postponed till Elizabeth's reign, but it made its first voyages on the stormy seas of opinion under Edward. Cranmer, timid and time-serving at the Council Board, as soon as he took his pen in his hand in the freedom of his own study was like a man inspired.

Very different was his friend, Hugh Latimer. He did not resume the episcopal office which he had been obliged to relinquish on account of his Protestantism in Henry's reign, but remained as the free lance of the Reformation under Edward, free even to 'cry out against covetousness' in the Lords of the Council. Preaching at St Paul's Cross to the citizens and in the King's garden to the courtiers, Latimer, by his rough, homely sermons, set the standard of that English pulpit oratory which, together with the Bible and the Prayer Book, effected the conversion of the people to Protestantism in the course of the next hundred years.

Mary, through the mistakes and violence of her enemies, began her reign in an atmosphere of popular enthusiasm, which she dissipated almost as quickly as James II, when he sacrificed a like initial advantage on the same altar of fanaticism. But in character Mary was the superior of James. She showed the high Tudor courage in time of danger, and she had no personal vindictiveness; if she had been a sceptic or even a moderate in religion she might in after years have been remembered as Mary the Humane. But the narrow understanding of the daughter of Catherine of Aragon had been educated by brooding in secret, a neglected girl, over her mother's wrongs and her mother's religion, while her mother's Spanish origin drew her affections with fatal magnetism towards Southern Europe. She had no national pride on behalf of the country she ruled. She cared only for the souls of the English, and believed they would be safer in Italian and Spanish hands. From her chapel she had as little vision of the real England as her brother from his sick bed. Wrapt in doctrinal studies or religious ecstasies, neither brother nor sister had an eye for the great outlines of Tudor policy, for the broad prospect of England's ploughlands and pastures, thronged marts and manor-houses, and England's ships tossing on distant seas; no instinct told them what all those busy far-scattered subjects of theirs were thinking and needing day by day. But that vision and that instinct were the secret of all successful Tudor rule, and never deserted Elizabeth in her closest councils of State, in her devotions or her studies of theology, in her interviews with flattering foreign envoys, or even in the more dazzling presence of favourite suitors.

Identification with the Pope and Spain soon clouded the fortune that had seemed to shine upon the Catholic cause while Mary was being welcomed as Queen by the shouting 'prentices of London. On that day the Protestant cause had been associated in men's minds with violence and unrest. The robbery of the guilds and chantries, the continuous troubles of Edward's reign, above all Northumberland's headlong career ending in treason and crowned by apostasy, made the new religion for a while odious and despicable to the great body of floating opinion. It would have been safe and popular for Mary to return to the religious compromise of her father, to restore the Latin Mass, and discreetly to burn a dozen Protestants a year. If she had been content that England should rest there, at least for a while, there would have been no such revulsion to heresy as actually took place in the decisive first year of Elizabeth. But when Mary insisted on marrying Philip of Spain in flat disregard of her subjects' wishes, making England the cockboat tied to the stern of the great Spanish
1555 galleon, when she insisted further on reviving that Papal jurisdiction over the realm which even Gardiner and Bonner had helped Henry to abolish, she twice challenged the national pride in a way her father and sister would never have dared. And when,
1555–8 to crown the work, she burnt 300 Protestants in four years, she made the old religion appear to the English as a foreign creed, unpatriotic, restless, and cruel, an impression more easily made than eradicated.

In the hands of able propagandists like John Foxe, the memory of the martyrs bred a hatred of the Church of Rome, which proved the one constant element in English opinion during the coming centuries of civil religious faction. For the next two hundred years and more Foxe's *Book of Martyrs* was often placed beside the Bible in the parish churches, and was read in manor-house and cottage, by Anglican and Puritan, in an epoch when there was relatively little else to read and when interest in religion was profound and widespread.

Most of the victims were inhabitants of London or the Home Counties, and most of them were humble folk. But Latimer died as he might have desired, lighting the candle of his own clear certainty to illuminate the more complex and hesitating opinion of others. In an age of mixed measures, confused counsels, and compromise, he had held a straight course which the English of the new era could understand and imitate. Cranmer's example was of equal but different potency, for he was one of the doubters taking a line at last. He had honestly held that the Crown ought to decide on religion in England. Was he then to obey Mary or was he to stand up for his own convictions? It was a real dilemma for a convinced Erastian who had also become a convinced Protestant. Roman Catholics could only be in a like difficulty if the Pope were to turn heretic. There is no wonder that his timid nature hesitated and recanted in the presence of a terrible death. It is more wonderful that he saw his way so clearly in the end, and held the hand, which had signed the recantation, in the fire until it was consumed. Had the men of those days a less highly strung nervous system than ours, or can the power of a scholar's mind be so triumphant over physical pain? In that magnificent gesture the Church of England revived.

With Philip of Spain husband to a doting queen, England was for three years vassal of the great Spanish monarchy. So long as Mary lived and loved, all thought of a foreign policy anywhere opposed to Spain must be set aside, together with all hope of trade with America – which Philip strictly denied to his island subjects – and all dreams of colonization or sea power. The terms of the royal marriage were most injurious to England, and the Venetian envoy declared that Mary was bent on nothing but making the Spaniards masters of her kingdom. Only revolution or the Queen's death could open England's path to the freedom and greatness that awaited her upon the sea.

The capture of Calais by the French in a war fought by England Jan. 1558
to please Spain, and fought very ill, added to the heavy weight of Mary's unpopularity. Yet the loss of this cherished bridgehead on French soil, bitterly humiliating to national pride, was a blessing in disguise to an island whose future did not lie on the continent of Europe.

Childless after all, hated by her people, slighted by her husband whose favour was already turning towards the sister who must survive and succeed her, fearful that Elizabeth would quickly ruin her work for God, the most honest and ill-advised of the Tudors turned away to die. 17 Nov.
Never for centuries had England been at a lower ebb; the country was not only ill-governed and disgraced in peace and in war, without arms or leaders, unity, or spirit, but it was, to all intents and purposes, an appanage of the Spanish Empire. With a hope too like despair men turned passionately to a young woman to save them, the third and last of Henry's progeny, of whom two had failed their need; by the strangest chance in history, no elder statesman or famous captain

in all broad Europe would have served so well to lead Englishmen back to harmony and prosperity and on to fresh fields of fame.

CHAPTER IV

The Policy and Character of Elizabeth. Spain and France. The Scottish Reformation and the Future Great Britain. The 'Rising of the Earls' and the End of Feudalism in England

Elizabeth, 1558–1603

FOR centuries past many different forces had been slowly drawing the English towards a national or patriotic conception of man's duty to society, in place of that obedience to cosmopolitan orders and corporations which had been inculcated by the Catholic Church and the feudal obligation. Among the forces creative of the sense of nationhood were the English Common Law; the King's Peace and the King's Courts; the frequent intercourse of the representative of distant shires and boroughs in the national council of Parliament; the new clothing industry based on national rather than municipal organization; the new literature and the new language common to all England. Finally, the action of the Tudor monarchy had abolished or depreciated all loyalties that intervened between the individual and the State, much as Protestantism purported to eliminate all that stood between the individual and God. The Elizabethan age is at once intensely national and intensely individualistic.

Mary, indeed, had attempted to re-establish the rule of the cosmopolitan Church, which employed a foreign tongue in its services, looked across the Alps for its laws, and was itself organized on Latin and Caesarean principles of government very different from the national and Parliamentary polity which the English laity were evolving in the conduct of their secular affairs. The Marian restoration was welcomed by a large section of the clergy, and by the semi-feudal society of Northern England, but it was unpopular with the Londoners, with the sea-faring population, and with the more enterprising of the squires who were most in touch with the rising middle class; these men had no wish to have their beliefs dictated and their lives supervised by the clergy, least of all on orders from oversea.

With the help of these elements as represented in the House of Commons, Elizabeth in the first year of her reign re-established the supremacy of the national, laic State, with a national Church engaged as its servant upon honourable terms. The rest of her long life was spent in cautiously adapting the habits of the whole people to this new settlement, and defending it against internal malcontents and foreign aggressors. For many years the dangers seemed greater than the chances of success, until a new generation had grown up under the influence of the Bible, the Prayer Book, and loyalty to the Queen. The contest finally resolved itself into a maritime war against Spain as the head of the Catholic reaction in Europe and the monopolist of the ocean routes to the New World. In the heat of that struggle English civilization was fused into its modern form, at once insular and oceanic, distinct from the continental civilization of which the Norman Conquest had once made it part.

Not only was modern England created, but the future of Great Britain was mapped out. The exigencies of the struggle for island independence against the Catholic powers of the continent put an end to the long hostility between the peoples of Scotland and England, while the same causes dictated the ruthless and ill-fated conquest of Catholic Ireland.

Amongst the Elizabethan English, by land and by sea, individualism became the ally of nationalism on free and equal terms, for the national State could not afford to pay for an army and a bureaucracy to bend the individual to its will, like the France and Prussia of later days. The poverty of the Elizabethan State explains many of its worst failures and meanest shifts, and not a few also of its greatest merits and noblest attitudes. A Queen whose revenue in wartime did not reach half a million pounds a year must needs be 'niggardly'; but since her subjects would not be taxed to give her adequate supply, she was fain to appeal to their free loyalty to fight her battles and to wear themselves out in her service for love. They gave her their lives and affections more readily than their cash. For the rest, her great object, as defined in a political poem she herself wrote, was 'to teach still peace to grow', till men treasured the life of their Queen because it meant for them peace and prosperity at home while the neighbour nations were ablaze with religious war. Many who disliked her ecclesiastical compromise as being too Protestant, or not Protestant enough, accepted it as the condition of tranquil government, which in an age of rival fanaticisms seemed, and perhaps was, a miracle of statecraft.

When Elizabeth became Queen at the age of twenty-five the

country was in no condition to resist a foreign invader. Not only was it divided by fierce religious feuds such as opened contemporary France to the foreigner, but it had for several years been treated as an appanage of Spain; its financial credit, its warlike stores, and its militia, were at the lowest ebb, and if there were any men capable of leading it in peace or in war, it was left to this young woman to find them out. It was rumoured in the Spanish Embassy that the coming man was Sir William Cecil, a politician of the rising middle class of smaller gentry, a pestilent heretic at heart, the more dangerous because he was no zealot but had, like Elizabeth herself, deemed life to be well worth a Mass.

Yet Philip of Spain protected the new Queen's accession and extended his protection for years after she had fulfilled his worst fears on the score of religion. For the next heir to the English throne was Mary, Queen of Scots, a devout Catholic indeed, but married to the Dauphin of France. Throughout Elizabeth's reign it was the rivalry of the two great Catholic powers, France and Spain, that saved the heretic island from conquest, till it was too strong to be conquered. Neither rival could allow Britain to be subdued by the other. The rebellion of the Netherlands against Spain and the religious wars in France were further safeguards, and Elizabeth frequently sent men and money to keep both movements alive. But in the early years of her reign the Netherlands were not yet in open revolt and her part was still to cajole Philip. This she did by holding out hope that she would marry either him or a man of his choice, though she had no real intention of slipping any such noose over her head.

Yet anxious as she was to stand well with the Spaniards, she would not allow their ambassador to say that she in any degree owed her life, liberty, or throne to the goodwill shown her by his master in Mary's latter days. She owed all, she said, to the English people. If this was not the whole truth, it was the part of the truth that mattered most. It was one of those lightning flashes of sincerity that so often burst from the cloud of vain and deceitful words in which Elizabeth loved to hide her real thought and purpose. Sometimes, indeed, she lied for amusement rather than in hope of deceiving, as when she told the envoy of Spain 'she would like to be a nun and live in a cell and tell her beads from morning to night', on which his only comment was 'this woman is possessed by a hundred thousand devils'.

To her own people she boasted on her accession that she was 'mere English'. Her mother had been no foreign princess but an

English flirt, and her father, the founder of England's Navy and of England's religious independence, had possessed a sixth sense whereby he understood the English people, even in the highest rages of his tyranny. She inherited from both, but most from her father in whose steps it was her ambition to walk. If she was heir to her mother's vanity and coquetry, she heeded the warning of her fate; and her own bitter experiences as a girl – disgrace, imprisonment, and danger of death – had taught her, as Frederick the Great was taught by similar experiences in boyhood, that private affections and passions are not for Princes. She had learnt every lesson that adversity had to teach, and she would leave it to her rival to lose the world for love.

There was in her a certain hardness and coarseness of fibre, necessary perhaps for her terrible task in life. As a private person she would scarcely have been lovable, perhaps not even very admirable. But lonely on the throne she knew all the arts to make herself adored by her Court and her people. Without ceasing to be a woman, and while loving life in all its fullness, she made everything subservient to purposes of State. Her learning endeared her to the Universities, her courage to the soldiers and sailors. Her coquetry became a means of keeping her nobles and courtiers each in his place, and exacting from each one the last ounce of personal devotion in the public service. Leicester's neck might be tickled by the royal hand, but his rival Cecil would be trusted in matters of high policy. And Cecil too might serve her the better for a shrewd spasm of fear that she would marry the worthless and intriguing Leicester, who, though sometimes posing as patron of the Puritan party, had offered Philip to restore the Roman Church in England if Spain would secure his marriage with Elizabeth. Her love of hunting and dancing, masque, pageantry, and display, was used to strengthen the wider popularity which was her ultimate strength; her public appearances and progresses through the country, which she thoroughly enjoyed, were no dull and formal functions, but works of art by a great player whose heart was in the piece, interchanges of soul between a Princess and her loving people.

Her speeches to Parliament were very different from the official 'King's Speech' of our modern constitution. 'Though I be a woman,' she told a deputation of both Houses who had come to urge measures about the Succession, 'I have as good a courage answerable to my place as ever my father had. I am your anointed Queen. I will never be by violence constrained to do anything. I thank God I am endued with such qualities that if I were turned out of the realm in my petticoat, I were able to live in any place in Christendom.'

Men, they say, have been worn out by high office in a few years or even months; this heroic woman was her own Prime Minister in war and peace for forty-five years, most of them fraught with danger both to the State and to her own much threatened life. And all the time she was an invalid – suffering, and subject to moods, caprices, and nerve-storms that shook her but never shook her from her course. It may be true that her heart was cold, but it was a heart of oak.

'Mere English' as she was, her education had been the broadest that modern and ancient Europe could afford. She discoursed in Greek and Latin to the Universities of Oxford and Cambridge, and in fluent Italian to the natives of the land of Machiavelli. Her enemies might have called her, in the phrase of that day, '*Inglese Italianata*', though she never in her long life quitted the English shore. She had been influenced by the Italian heretics, such as Vermigli and Ochino, who were more philosophers than zealots. She was a child of the Renaissance rather than of the Reformation, so far as the two movements could any longer be distinguished. She approached religion in the modernist spirit of Colet and Erasmus; but two generations after their time, to a mind of their disposition, Rome of the Jesuits was abhorrent and transubstantiation incredible. The Church of Geneva attracted her as little, with its usurpation of the province of the State and its democratic republicanism. If it was left to her successor to say 'No Bishop, no King', she had thought it and acted on it long before.

Sceptical and tolerant in an age of growing fanaticism, all English in feeling but pan-European in education, she was born and bred to re-establish the Anglican Church, and to evade religious war by a learned compromise between Catholic and Protestant that would leave Crown and laity masters in their own island. She regarded her action as a revival of her father's policy, but changed times demanded a larger infusion of Protestantism, for the Jesuit propaganda and the spearmen and sailors of Spain were not to be conquered save with the help of men who regarded the Pope as anti-Christ and the Mass as an abomination. Cranmer's revived Prayer Book was the golden mean. It served well on board Drake's ships before and after battle with the idolaters, and in parish churches where Bernard Gilpin and other earnest Protestant clergy laboured to instil the new religion into rustic ignorance. Yet the concealed Catholic, doubtfully attending church to avoid the twelve-penny fine, was often less shocked than he feared, and could remind himself that they were still the old prayers, though in English. The book was a chameleon which could mean different things to different people – an advantage in the eyes of this wise young woman, who herself had as many different explanations of her policy as she had dresses in her wardrobe, and loved to display them all in turn.

If the year 1559 is to count as the first of modern England, it is still more decidedly the birth year of modern Scotland. The precise coincidence in time of the final breach with Rome to north and to south of the Border, though largely accidental, was of great consequence. The double event secured the unbroken permanence of the Reformation in both countries, and drew English and Scottish patriotism, which had hitherto thriven on mutual hostility, into an alliance of mutual defence. In both countries the Reformation meant release from continental dominion, secular no less than spiritual. In the autumn of 1558 England was a Roman Catholic country virtually subject to Spain, and Scotland was a Roman Catholic country virtually subject to France. Two years later each was a Protestant country cleared of foreign soldiery and rulers, and closely identifying its newly chosen religion with its national independence. The double rebellion succeeded because Spain and France remained rivals, while England and Scotland became friends for the first time since the reign of Edward I. In the stress of that twofold crisis the foundations of Great Britain were laid by William Cecil and John Knox.

England approached the Reformation through the Renaissance; Scotland approached the Renaissance through the Reformation. Catholicism as a religion had meant less to the Scots, for with them the Church was more corrupt and inefficient as a spiritual power than to the south of the Border. After the slaughter of so many leading nobles at Flodden in 1513, the secular power in Scotland was wielded more than ever by the prelates, cadets of noble families, living like laymen and fighting each other with sword and gun for the abbeys and benefices of the Church.

It is the less surprising that Protestantism obtained under the leadership of Knox the same hold on the intelligence and moral feeling of the common people in Scotland, as it obtained more gradually in England by the middle of the following century. In England the Reformation was promoted by the Crown and its satellites, while the old feudal nobility were lukewarm or hostile; in Scotland the opposite was the case. But in both countries the genuine core of the movement lay in the burghers, yeomen, and artisans and in the smaller landed gentry – the squires of England and lairds of Scotland.

It was only in the years immediately preceding 1559 that the Protestant party in Scotland had the advantage of figuring as patriots. In the forties it was the Catholic party that led the national resistance to English interference. For Henry VIII, though wisely aspiring to the union of the whole island through the marriage of his son Edward to the infant Mary Stuart, Queen of Scots, foolishly sought to force the policy on Scotland by the sword. Destructive raids in the valley of the Tweed and in the Lothians made the Scots curse the English tyrant and heretic, and frown upon his supporters in their own midst. When Henry died, the Protector Somerset carried on the same disastrous policy
1547 in the campaign of Pinkie, a dire defeat for Scotland, but a still worse blow to Somerset's prophetic daydreams of a united Great Britain, 'having the sea for wall and mutual love for its garrison'. To keep Mary Stuart out of the way of this rough and pertinacious wooing on behalf of Edward VI, the Scots sent the impressionable little girl to the court of Valois France, to learn in that most unsuitable atmosphere the art of governing their dour and stubborn selves.

But the insolence of the French army of occupation, which was the price of the French alliance, did not long suit the proud stomach of the Scots. Gallic domination became as unbearable in Scotland as Spanish domination in contemporary England. In her sixteenth year Mary, Queen of Scots was married to the Dauphin of France, and became party to a secret compact whereby her native country was to go as a free gift to the French King in case of her death without heirs. The able Regent who governed Scotland in her absence, Mary of Guise, relied on French troops, and thought of the land of Bruce as a Protectorate to be administered in the interests of France. In these circumstances the Protestants in their turn became the champions of national independence, while the Catholic party became unpopular as the catspaw of French aggression. Under Mary of Guise and Mary Tudor both North and South Britain lay beneath the 'monstrous regiment (rule) of women', which Knox bewailed all too loudly, improvident of his future relations with Elizabeth.

In these circumstances a section of the Scottish nobles, accustomed in that land of feudal anarchy to form 'bands' for the
1557 coercion of the Crown, formed a 'band' to protect the new religion. The confederates were bound together by the first of Scotland's many 'covenants' with God. This 'Congregation of the Lord', as it styled itself, was organized as an assembly of estates, in which

each Protestant notable took his place as minister of religion or as noble, laird, or burgess. It was more representative of the political forces of the country than Scotland's Parliament, which was feudal in its form and served for little more than a court of registration. The 'Congregation of the Lord' was army, Church, and political assembly in one. It formed the transition stage between Scotland's feudal warrior past with its 'bands' of rebel nobles, and her democratic religious future with its Kirk Assembly. Nobles, styled 'Lords of the Congregation', were its leaders, but the popular and religious elements were heard in its counsels, especially as they spoke through the voice of John Knox.

The Moses of Scotland was a very rare combination of genuine prophet and successful statesman. He who 'never feared the face of man' could calculate chances and consider ways and means as the utterly fearless and the 'God-intoxicated' are very seldom able to do. He had been hardened by grim servitude and meditation at the oar of a French galley, and had since been founding Church congregations all over Southern Scotland. He knew the people well and saw that the hour had come to strike.

In 1559 a democratic religious revolution, preached by Knox and accompanied by image-breaking, swept through the Scottish burghs, beginning with Perth. It was thus that Calvinist revolutions began, whether in the Netherlands or in French-speaking countries, but they were as often as not suppressed with fire and sword. In Scotland, however, the 'Congregation of the Lord' came with arms in their hands to defend the insurgent populace from the French troops and from Mary of Guise. There followed a spasmodic and ill-conducted war, in which little blood was shed; it was going ill for the Scottish Protestants when it was decided in their favour by the intervention of England. Cecil had persuaded Elizabeth to take one of the few great initiatives of her reign. The English fleet appearing in the Firth of Forth, and an English army joining the Scottish Protestants before Leith, saved the cause of the Reformation. This *coup de théâtre* being followed by the death of Mary of Guise, led to the evacuation of Scotland by the French troops in accordance with the terms of the Treaty of Edinburgh. July 1560

The Scottish Reformation was singularly bloodless, in spite of the violence of the language used on both sides. Very few Protestants had been burnt, and no Catholic was executed on account of his religion. Continental Europe, and even England in Mary Tudor's reign, presented a far bloodier spectacle of religious fanaticism.

Another Catholic force soon landed from France to take the
1561 place of the Regent and the soldiers. Mary, Queen of Scots, herself and a train of pleasure-loving ladies and favourites came over to try issues with that harsh land of old feudal power and new popular theology. An able, energetic, and attractive widow, Mary Stuart was little likely to submit her royal will to Knox and the Lords of the Congregation. They had many enemies in the land – personal, political, and religious – who would rally to the banner of the young Queen. Moreover, her eager eyes scanned horizons far beyond the borders of barren Scotland. The Catholics of Europe looked to her as their chosen champion to win back Britain to the faith. France and Rome were at her back. A great party in England hoped and intrigued to see Britain united by a counter-revolution, which should dethrone the illegitimate daughter of Henry VIII and place the English crown on the head of the rightful heir, Mary, Queen of Scots.*

The Protestant party in Scotland could not therefore afford to quarrel with Elizabeth, nor she with them. Little as she wished to abet feudal nobles and Calvinist peasants in resistance to their lawful sovereign, that sovereign was her open rival for the throne on which she sat. The situation was the more dangerous because the Catholic and feudal part of England lay precisely in the moorland counties nearest to the Scottish Border. Catholicism and feudalism were so strong to the north of the Humber that early in her reign Elizabeth was fain to employ the Catholic grandees of that region as her officials, in which capacity the Percies, Dacres,

*

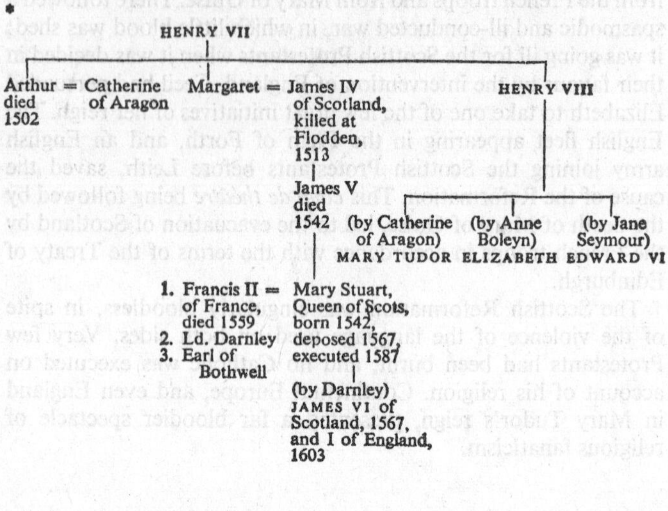

and Nevilles continued to exert their old feudal influence and to thwart the policy of the government they served. 'Throughout Northumberland,' it was reported, 'they know no other Prince but Percy.' For many years there was the greatest danger of a feudal and Catholic reaction uniting all Britain north of the Humber in a single Kingdom governed by Mary Stuart. Northern England, like Scotland, was inhabited by a race of hardy and lawless fighters, bred to Border war, not easily kept in order by a distant government that had no army. But, fortunately for Elizabeth, Northern England, like Scotland, was very thinly inhabited and very poor. Until the Industrial Revolution, wealth and population were concentrated in the South, and most of all in and near London.

Grave as were her motives for dreading any increase in the power of Mary, Elizabeth was too cautious and too short of reven- 1561–7
ue to involve herself deeply in Scottish politics. For six years of high romantic history, the struggle for power between Mary, Knox, and the nobles continued with little interference from England. There was no organ of constitutional opposition to the Catholic Queen, for the Scottish Parliament, after putting the Reformation into legal shape in 1560, had sunk back into a negligible quantity, a mere court of record once more. Mary might therefore have triumphed over the feudal aristocracy, divided as it was on the religious issue in spite of its firm adherence to the abbey lands, had not John Knox and his party created other organs of national life, and put a new spirit into the educated middle class which inspired it to compete with the old feudal power. In parish after parish arose a democracy of laymen, who elected their own minister and found a nucleus for self-expression in the Kirk Sessions of the parish. Nor was a national organization lacking for long: in the General Assembly of the Church, ministers and lairds sat side by side, representing clerical and lay forces of a very different social class from the high-born prelates and noblemen who had ruled Scotland for centuries past. The General Assembly of the Church became the centre of Scottish life almost to the extent to which Parliament was the centre of English life, and the Church became the focus of resistance to the Crown.

The Church brought Scotland freedom and bondage in one. A spirit not of sacerdotal but of democratic tyranny strove to dictate the dogma and discipline of the new religion to the government of the land, to the peasant in his cottage and to the laird in his hall. This zealous and uncompromising spirit was intolerable to many; it was a chief cause of the factions and blood-feuds of Scotland for a hundred years to come. In the end the power of the Church was subordinated to that of the State, but not before it had wrought a remarkable change. It transformed the lowland Scot from a fierce feudal vassal, ignorant of all save sword and plough, into the best educated peasant in Europe, often plunged in solitary meditation and as often roused to furious argument on points of logic and theology which few Englishmen had the mental gifts or training to understand. Times and the Church have changed, but the intellectual and moral vantage-ground won by the Scot in that hard school has not yet been lost.

But the making of modern Scotland had only begun when Mary reigned at Holyrood, and she might perchance have stopped it all at the outset by winning her battle against Knox, if she had been as ready as Elizabeth to control her private passions in deference to her public policy. But her marriage with Darnley, his murder by Bothwell at the Kirk of Field, and her too hasty marriage with the murderer, led her subjects to suppose her pre-cognizant of the deed. True, assassination was still a custom of the country. Knox had not disapproved the slaughter of Cardinal Beaton, and Darnley had conducted the tragedy of Rizzio. But people had a prejudice against the killing of husbands by their wives. Innocent or guilty, Mary had by her marriage with Bothwell delivered her reputation and her kingdom into her enemies' hands. After some confused fighting and some romantic and luck-
1568 less adventures, she was obliged to fly from Scotland. She elected, whether from rashness or from necessity, to take refuge with Elizabeth whose throne she challenged and endangered. What did she expect? If she looked for romantic generosity she had come to the wrong door. Or did she trust her own sharp wits to fool her rival?

From the moment that Mary made herself Elizabeth's captive, the politics of England, and indeed of all Europe, turned on the hinges of her prison door. Since she had thrown away her own liberty and her own power of initiative, Philip began to think that she might be used to serve the purposes of Spain instead of those of France. Urged by the Pope, Spain, and the Jesuits, the more extreme English Catholics laid plot after plot to place her on Elizabeth's throne, through assassination, rebellion, and foreign conquest. In 1570 Pope Pius V excommunicated Elizabeth and the Jesuit Mission was launched on England. In 1572 the Duke of Norfolk was executed for plotting with the agents of Philip, Alva, and the Pope to set Mary on the throne, this time as the puppet not of France but of Spain. She was to have Norfolk for her husband, the Pope undertaking to divorce her from Bothwell. The assassination of Elizabeth was henceforth a customary part of these discussions among the secular and religious chiefs of continental Europe, to whom the murder of heretics seemed a holy work.

The execution of Norfolk, the greatest nobleman in the land, following close on the fall of the Northern Earls, marked the final victory in England of the new regime over the old feudalism. It was indeed a changing world. In the same year the Massacre of 1572
St Bartholomew, which crippled but did not destroy the Huguenot cause in France, was counterbalanced by the effective rebellion of the seamen and towns of Holland against the cruelties of Philip of Spain. The Commons of England, full of rage and fear, were petitioning for the execution of Mary, Queen of Scots, as though she had not been anointed with oil. For fifteen years longer Elizabeth, obeying her pacifist and royalist instincts, stood between her people and Mary's life. She liked not the killing of Queens, and the deed would mean formal war with Spain. So long as Mary was her next heir, she might hope that Philip would bear yet a little longer with her and her seamen. But if Mary disappeared, Philip might claim England for himself and launch the invasion. Only sixty miles lay between the shores of Kent and the yet unvanquished veterans of Alva in the Netherlands. Fortunately those miles were of salt water, and turbid salt water was an element of increasing importance in this new age so disrespectful to the feudal past and to all the chiefs of chivalry.

CHAPTER V

The Origin of English Sea Power

'Which of the Kings of this land before her Majesty had their banners ever seen in the Caspian sea? Which of them hath ever dealt with the Emperor of Persia, as her Majesty hath done, and obtained for her merchants large and loving privileges? Who ever saw, before this regiment, an English Ligier (Ambassador) in the stately porch of the Grand Signor of Constantinople? Who ever found English Consuls and Agents at Tripolis in Syria, at Aleppo, at Babylon, at Balsara, and, which is more, whoever heard of Englishmen at Goa before now? What English ships did, heretofore, ever anchor in the mighty river of Plate? Pass and repass the impassable strait of Magellan, range along the coast of Chile, Peru, and all the backside of Nova Hispania further than any Christian ever passed?' – *Hakluyt.*

THROUGHOUT ancient and medieval times Britain was cramped on to the edge of the *Mappa Mundi*. Since there was nothing beyond, every impulse of private adventure and national expansion on the part of the islanders had to expend itself upon

Europe. Yet old Europe was no longer malleable stuff and could take no impress of British language and customs, even from the most vigorous efforts of young England, as the barren close of the Hundred Years' War had very clearly shown. And now the gate of return that way was bolted and barred by the rise of the great continental monarchies, so that Englishmen seemed shut in upon themselves, doomed for ever to an insular and provincial existence, sighing in old manor-houses for the departed glory chronicled by Froissart, and the spacious days of Harry the Fifth.

But it was the most unexpected that occurred. Gradually, during the Tudor reigns, the islanders became aware that their remote situation had changed into a central post of vantage dominating the modern routes of trade and colonization, and that power, wealth, and adventure lay for Englishmen at the far end of ocean voyages fabulously long, leading to the gold-bearing rivers of the African anthropophagi, to the bazaars of jewelled Asia, and to the new half-empty continent which was piecing itself together year by year under the astonished eyes of men, upsetting all known ideas of cosmogony and all customs of commerce.

In medieval, as formerly in ancient times, the great trade of the world and the centre of maritime power had lain in the Mediterranean Sea. The external trade of Europe, which in modern times traverses the ocean in European vessels, was formerly carried overland by caravans across the heart of Asia, or was taken by Oriental shipping up and down the Persian Gulf and the Red Sea. The precious goods from China and India and the Spice Islands were dumped off the backs of camels on to the wharves of Levantine ports for shipment in Italian vessels to Venice and Genoa, whence they were distributed to the rest of Christendom.

Neither the Venetian traders, nor the Romans and Phoenicians before them, had been obliged to cross the ocean at any point. Ships were only required to traverse the Mediterranean waters, and to coast along round Spain and France to the ports of England, Flanders, and Northern Germany. The navies, whether commercial or military, consisted chiefly of oared galleys. This state of things lasted from prehistoric times till the latter part of the Fifteenth Century. Then the discovery of the Cape route to India and the revelation of the American continent destroyed the trade and the maritime supremacy of the Italian cities. Thenceforward Europe went round by sea to fetch its Asiatic, African, and American goods, and on those ocean voyages the

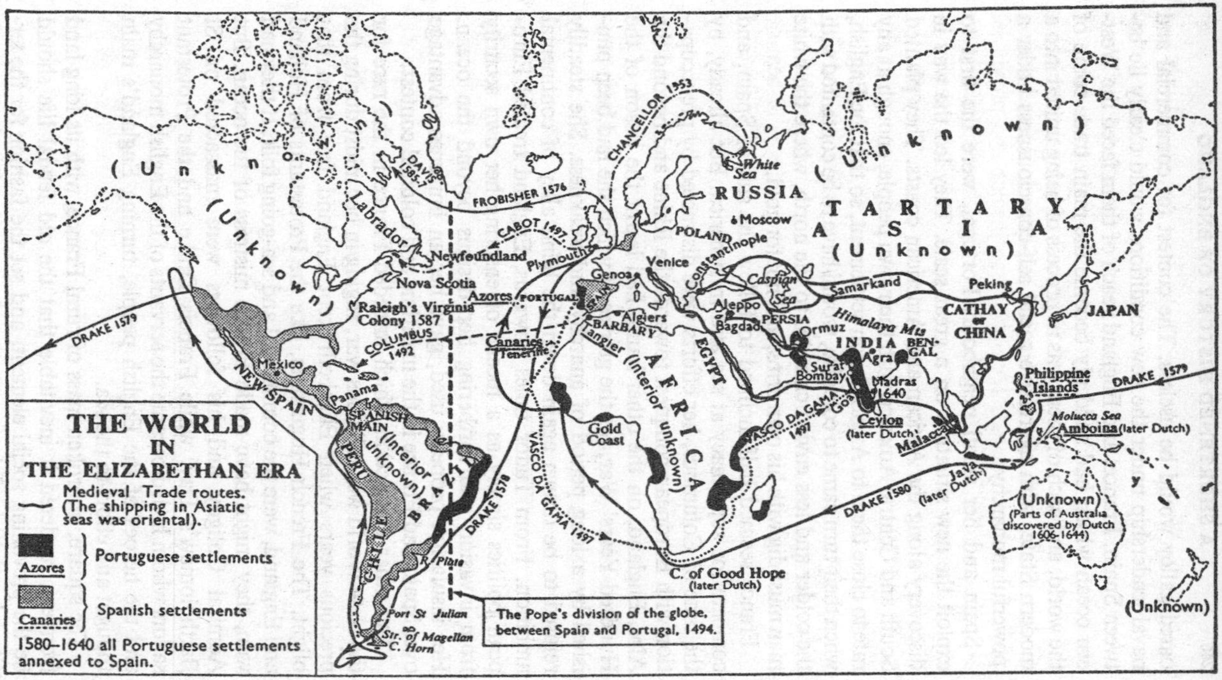
THE WORLD
IN
THE ELIZABETHAN ERA
Medieval Trade routes. (The shipping in Asiatic seas was oriental).
Azores
Portuguese settlements
Canaries
Spanish settlements
1580–1640 all Portuguese settlements annexed to Spain.
The Pope's division of the globe, between Spain and Portugal, 1494.
(Unknown)
(Unknown)
DAVIS 1585-7
Labrador
FROBISHER 1576
CABOT 1497
Newfoundland
Nova Scotia
Raleigh's Virginia Colony 1587
COLUMBUS 1492
DRAKE 1579
Mexico
NEW SPAIN
Panama
SPANISH MAIN
PERU
(Interior unknown)
BRAZIL
CHILE
R. Plate
Port St Julian
Str. of Magellan
C. Horn
DRAKE 1578
Azores
PORTUGAL
SPAIN
Plymouth
Canaries
Teneriffe
VASCO DA GAMA 1497
CHANCELLOR 1553
White Sea
RUSSIA
Moscow
POLAND
Constantinople
Venice
Genoa
Algiers
BARBARY
Tangier
EGYPT
AFRICA
(Interior unknown)
Gold Coast
C. of Good Hope
(later Dutch)
Aleppo
Bagdad
PERSIA
Caspian Sea
Ormuz
Samarkand
Himalaya Mts
INDIA
BENGAL
Agra
Surat
Bombay
Goa
Madras 1640
Ceylon
(later Dutch)
VASCO DA GAMA 1497
TARTARY
ASIA
(Unknown)
(Unknown)
Peking
CATHAY or CHINA
JAPAN
Philippine Islands
DRAKE 1579
Molucca Sea
Amboina (later Dutch)
Malacca
Java (later Dutch)
DRAKE 1580
(Unknown)
(Parts of Australia discovered by Dutch 1606-1644)
(Unknown)

MAP IX

oared galley would be useless. The contest for commercial and naval leadership under the new conditions would clearly lie between Spain, France, and England; each of them faced the Western ocean which had suddenly become the main trade route of the world, and each of them was in process of being united into a modern State, with aggressive racial self-consciousness under a powerful monarchy.

Spain and her small neighbour, Portugal, were the first to exploit the new situation on a great scale. They led the way in discovery along the African and American coasts. They planted South and Central America with their own people, enough at any rate to close them to Anglo-Saxon settlement, so that the English, when their turn came to colonize, would have to be contented with the colder and less envied climates to the north, where the white man must dig with his own arms, and not for gold.

France seemed half-inclined to follow the suit of Spain, and compete for supremacy at sea and in America. But already, by the time of Columbus, her efforts were distracted by preoccupation with European conquest towards the Rhine and beyond the Alps. England, on the other hand, had learnt the lesson of the Hundred Years' War, for the glories of which she had been punished by a long period of anarchy and weakness. She steadily refused to be drawn again down the blind alley of continental ambition. From Tudor times onwards, England treated European politics simply as a means of ensuring her own security from invasion and furthering her designs beyond the ocean. Her insularity, properly used, gave her an immense advantage over Spain and France in the maritime and colonial contest.

The other distraction which impeded France in the race for the New World was religious war, raging in her midst during the precious years when Elizabeth kept England free from that blight. The French Huguenots, like the Protestants of Holland and England, were the commercial and sea-going folk. If they had won, they might have made France mistress of the ocean. But Admiral Coligny and his followers were massacred on St Bartholomew's Day, while Francis Drake and the Protestant sailors whom he led became the servants of the English monarchy and the heroes of the English people, turning England's main thought and effort to the sea.

The square, unbroken mass of rural France, with its long land frontiers, rendered it inevitable that the old feudal life should be the prevailing social element, and set the fashion for the territorial activities of the new national monarchy. But in England, with its narrow, irregular outline, almost surrounded by a well-indented coastline, at peace at last with her only land neighbour the Scot, well supplied with harbours great and small thronged with mariners and fishermen, the State was subjected to the influences and ideas of the commercial and naval men, who formed one society with the best county families in sea-board shires like Devon. The old song expressed a feeling very general among our ancestors:

> We care not for your martial men
> That do the State disdain.
> But we care for your sailor lads
> That do the State maintain.

Indeed England's success against Spain after the defeat of the Armada was limited not so much by want of naval power as by want of military organization and tradition to seize the opportunities created by the Senior Service.

Since no point in England is more than seventy miles distant from the coast, a large proportion of her inhabitants had some contact with the sea, or at least with seafaring men. Above all, London herself was on the sea, while Paris lay inland and Madrid was as far from the coast as it was possible to be. London was Protestant, while Paris was enthusiastically Catholic. And London was so great in population and wealth as compared to the rest of the country that she gave the lead to all England. La Rochelle, the sea-port of the Huguenots, was insignificant compared to a dozen great cities of the French interior. For these and other reasons France, in the Sixteenth Century, failed to compete in earnest for maritime supremacy. The best part of her sea-force acted in religious and political alliance with the English and Dutch in preying on the Spanish ships as they passed between Cadiz and the Netherlands.

If France was more feudal than England, Spain was yet more
feudal than France. Spain, indeed, when she had annexed Port- 1580
ugal, was almost as much surrounded by the sea as England, and she had, moreover, a war fleet with a naval tradition. But it was a fleet of slave-rowed galleys and its traditions were those of the Mediterranean. The fleet that triumphed over the Turks at Lepanto, with the tactics of Salamis and Actium, would be of
little avail against Drake's broadsides; it could not cross the 1571
Atlantic and would be of limited use in the Bay of Biscay and the Channel. Spain had, indeed, her ocean-going vessels sailing up and down the Pacific coast of America, or crossing the Atlantic

between Cadiz and the Spanish Main. They served to carry out emigrants and to bring back silver and gold, but they were not warships, and therefore fell an easy prey to the English pirates. Spain, in fact, began to build ships capable of fighting England only on the very eve of the outbreak of regular war. The Armada
1588 was not the last but the first of her oceanic fighting fleets. The English, on the other hand, though their total population was small compared with French or Spaniards, had a large sea-going community, accustomed for centuries to sail the stormy tidal ocean of the North. And ever since the reign of Henry VIII they had possessed a royal fighting navy built and armed on modern principles, which gave a professional stiffening to the warlike efforts of private merchants and pirates. When Philip married Mary it had been his policy to rely on the English war navy because he could not hope to get its equal from Spain.

Naturally, the Spaniards, even when they came to build an ocean-going war-fleet in earnest, were hampered by the feudal and military ideals that permeated their social life, and by the Mediterranean traditions of their navy, adorned with the fresh laurels of Lepanto. Whether on oared galley or on wind-driven galleon, the instinct of the Spaniard at sea was to sail or row straight in, get to close quarters and either ram or board the enemy. The Spaniards, in short, like the Greeks, Romans, and Venetians before them, wanted to make sea warfare as much like land warfare as the elements would permit. They stowed their ships with soldiers, who despised the sailors and ordered them about as if they too had been galley slaves. The 'mariners', said one who knew, 'are but as slaves to the rest, to moil and toil day and night, and those but few and bad and not suffered to sleep or harbour themselves under the decks.'

It was the English who led the world in the evolution of a new kind of warfare at sea, decided by cannon fired through the portholes in the side of the ship. Drake's guns were not much smaller, though they were less numerous, than those on board Nelson's three-deckers. To serve them the seaman was more important than the soldier, because the success of the cannon-fire depended on manoeuvring the ship into favourable positions to rake the enemy, and on aiming the guns with a sailor's instinct for calculating the roll of the two vessels. To Sir Francis Drake the warship was a mobile battery; to the Duke of Medina Sidonia it was a platform to carry the swordsmen and musketeers into action. English naval history tells, indeed, of many a gallant boarding episode, from those of Drake and Hawkins themselves to Nelson at St Vincent and 'brave Broke who waved his sword'; yet it was not the boarder but the broadside that made England mistress at sea.

While the Spaniards with their feudal prejudices and Mediterranean methods of sea-warfare subordinated the sailor to the soldier even when afloat, Drake worked out the proper relation to be observed between the military and maritime elements on board ship. When he quelled the party of insubordination among the gentlemen adventurers on his voyage round the world, he laid down his golden rule to prevent 'stomaching between the gentlemen and the sailors': – '*I must have the gentlemen to hale and draw with the mariner.*' Starting from that point of new departure the 'gentlemen' gradually learnt their place on board English men-of-war, and in the course of a long evolution became 'mariners' themselves. By the time Nelson was born, each of the King's naval officers united the character of 'mariner' and 'gentleman', and the sailing and fighting service was one and indivisible.

Drake, who was first the greatest of privateers and afterwards the greatest of Royal Admirals, established as no one else could have done a complete understanding between the Royal Navy and the merchant adventurers who carried on the unofficial war against Spain. The Spaniards had slaves to row their galleys and magnificent soldiers to fight from their ships, but for the more indispensable supply of mariners they had no large and energetic class of private merchants and seamen, such as those who were the wealth and pride of England.

For indeed the technical differences between the personnel and tactics of a Spanish and an English ship represented something more profound – the difference of social character between Spain and the new England. Private enterprise, individual initiative, and a good-humoured equality of classes were on the increase in the defeudalized England of the Renaissance and Reformation, and were strongest among the commercial and maritime population. The most energetic spirits of the gentry, the middle, and the lower classes were taking to the sea together in a rough *camaraderie*, for purposes of war and of commerce. In Spain the ideas and manners of society were still feudal, though in politics the King had become absolute. Discipline, as Drake well knew, is needed on board ship, but not feudalism and class pride. The hierarchy of the sea is not the same as the hierarchy of the land.

The Spaniards at the height of their power were great soldiers and colonists, less great sailors, unenterprising merchants, execrable politicians and rulers. Catholic enthusiasm drove them to expel or kill out from their own peninsula just those classes and races which might have enabled them to seize their new commercial opportunities. No country could flourish for ever on the importation of gold and silver from the American mines, even if the English did not waylay the cargoes. Furthermore, in their zeal for religion, the Spaniards murdered the prosperity of the great cities of Flanders, which might otherwise have been England's rivals in the new age. The mariners of Holland, who inherited the commerce lost by the Flemish merchants, were compelled by Spanish cruelty to become England's allies. If ever there was a victory of the spirit of social intellectual freedom over its opposite, it was the maritime victory of England and Holland over Spain.

The success alike of maritime warfare under Elizabeth and of colonization under the Stuart Kings rested on the growth of English commerce. For lack of a native commerce to feed it, the Spanish marine power, for all Philip's political and military strength and his empire over uncounted millions scattered round half the globe, went down before the attack of a small island State and a few rebel towns among the mudflats and sand dunes of Holland. For, unlike the Spaniards, the English and Dutch learnt how to trade with the newly discovered regions of the world.

To find vent for the new cloth manufacture the Merchant Adventurers of England had from the beginning of the Fifteenth Century onwards been vigorously searching for new markets in Europe, not without constant bloodshed by sea and land in an age when piracy was so general as to be scarcely disreputable, and when commercial privileges were often refused and won at the point of the sword. Under Elizabeth they went further afield to find new markets in Africa, Asia, and America.

Hakluyt laboured to inspire the English with a consciousness of their country's destiny at sea, by patiently recording the stories that the survivors of each notable voyage had to tell. His book serves to remind us that, side by side with the more warlike enterprises of Drake in robbing the Spaniards and opening trade with their colonies at the cannon's mouth, there was much traffic of a more peaceable character in Muscovy, Africa, and the Levant. Besides Hawkins and those who dealt in the slave-trade, other English merchants preferred to develop the Guinea trade by giving the Negroes fairer treatment than they got from the Portuguese and by trying to avoid unnecessary conflict with either black or white.

Yet it is impossible to draw a clear line between the peaceful and the warlike traders, because the Portuguese attacked all who came near the African and Indian coasts. They were no less determined than the Spaniards in America to exclude all foreigners, especially heretics, from the lands and seas which the Pope had assigned to them for ever. Not seldom the African Gold Coast re-echoed to the noise of battle between English interlopers and Portuguese monopolists, and by the end of Elizabeth's reign the same sounds were already breaking the silence of the Indian seas and the Malay Archipelago. A sea fight with a pirate or a foreign rival was an unavoidable incident in the life of the most honest trader, whether in time of peace or in time of war. Companies were formed in the City to bear the expense and the risks of necessary hostilities, and were granted charters by the Queen giving them diplomatic and military authority on the other side of the world, where neither royal ships nor royal ambassadors ever came. Private English merchants, travelling on their lawful occasions, were the first men to represent their country at the Court of the Tsar at Moscow and of the Mogul at Agra.

Commerce was the motive of exploration as well as of warfare, and all three were combined in some of the greatest deeds of that generation. Romance and money-making, desperate daring and dividends, were closely associated in the minds and hearts of men. There was no line drawn between the bread-and-butter facts of life, and the life of poetry and imagination. The transactions of the money market and the war plans of sober statesmen turned on expeditions resembling those which in our own day explore Everest and the South Pole for naught save honour. Partly for that reason the Elizabethan age aroused the practical idealism of the English genius to its greatest height. Drake, Sidney, Spenser, Raleigh, and Shakespeare himself passed their lives among men to whom commerce was a soul-stirring adventure of life and death –

> As full of peril and adventurous spirit,
> As to o'erwalk a torrent, roaring loud,
> On the unsteadfast footing of a spear.

To the men of London and of Devon the unmapped world beyond the ocean seemed an archipelago of fairy islands, each hiding some strange wonder of its own, each waiting to be discovered by some adventurous knight vowed to leave his bones far away or to come back rich and tell his tale in the tavern.

To such a generation of men it seemed a light thing to find a passage through the Arctic seas by which the markets of India might be reached behind the backs of 'Portugalls' and Turks. Sebastian Cabot in his old age revived the idea in English minds in the reign of Edward VI, and in 1553 Richard Chancellor sought the North-East Passage by the White Sea, and found instead the Tsar keeping barbarous state over fur-clad tribes at Moscow; returning, he revealed to his countrymen the possibilities of a great Russian trade, and three years later perished on a second voyage. And so in Elizabeth's time the English Muscovy Company were the first Westerners to organize trade with the interior of Russia, though early in the following century they lost it for a while to the Dutch. The corresponding attempts of Frobisher and of Davis to reach India by the North-West Passage led to the Hudson Bay fur trade of Stuart times, one of the main streams of British Canadian history.

Neither did Elizabethan merchants hesitate to traverse the Mediterranean in spite of the war with Spain. The Levant Company traded with Venice and her Grecian isles and with the Mohammedan world beyond. Since the naval enemies of the Turk were the Venetians and Spaniards, the Sultan welcomed the heretic English at Constantinople. But on the way thither they had to defend themselves against Spanish galleys near the Straits of Gibraltar and 'Barbary pirates' off the Algerian shore. Such were the beginnings of English sea-power in the Mediterranean, though it was not till Stuart times that the Navy followed where the merchant service had already fought many a battle.

While the Armada was attacking England, one of these Turkey merchants named Ralph Fitch was travelling in the Far East, having started from Aleppo overland to India. After eight years of wandering he brought home reports on the Persian Gulf, Hindustan, and Malacca, which greatly encouraged the promoters of the East India Company. They obtained a Charter from Elizabeth in 1600, and proceeded to trade in the Indian seas by rounding the Cape of Good Hope in tall ships laden with goods and well armed to defend themselves against the 'Portugall'. Not lust of conquest but vent of merchandise first drew our countrymen to the great peninsula which their descendants were destined to rule. Hakluyt already had his patriot's eye on lands still further afield:

> Because (he wrote) our chiefe desire is to find out ample vent of our wollen cloth, the naturall comoditie of this our Realme, the fittest place which in all my readings and observations I find for that purpose are the manifold islands of Japan and the Northern parts of China and the regions of Tartars next adjoining.

All these trade routes and distant markets, sketched out by the daring of the Elizabethan merchants, led in Stuart times to an immense volume of commerce, particularly in the export of cloth. The Queen and her ministers understood the mercantile community and served it well. Unlike her brother and sister, Elizabeth was in close touch with London opinion, a condition of successful rule in Tudor England. She and Cecil were both personal friends of Sir Thomas Gresham, the founder of the Royal Exchange. She used him to raise State loans at home and abroad, and took his advice on financial questions. The chief of these was the difficult problem of the recoinage, which she effected at the beginning of her reign, successfully relieving her subjects of the burden laid on everyday life by her father's wanton debasement of the currency.

Elizabeth's financial difficulties were increased by the continued fall in the value of money. Prices had been rising all through Tudor times, especially after Henry tampered with the coinage. And just when his daughter had applied a remedy to that, the flow of silver and gold into Europe from the Spanish-American mines began to act as a further cause of high prices. This may not have been bad for the merchant, but it was bad for hired labour, and for the Queen in whose revenue many of the items were fixed amounts. Even in wartime barely a quarter of the royal income was derived from extra taxation put on by Parliament; the Parliamentary 'subsidy' was assessed in such a manner as to produce sums altogether incommensurate with the increasing wealth of the nation. The art of taxing the subject was not taken seriously in hand until Parliament had to find the sinews of its own warfare against Charles I.

Some historians, in their imperialist or Protestant zeal, have blamed the Queen for her parsimony, and have wondered why she did not send more men to the Netherlands, to France, to Ireland; why she lied and prevaricated so long instead of challenging Philip to open war early in her reign; and why, after the Armada, she did not seize the Spanish colonies and strike down the Spanish power. The royal accounts give a sufficient answer. The year after the Armada her total revenue was less than £400,000, of which the sum of £88,362 came by way of Parliamentary taxation. In the last five years of the war and of her reign, her average annual revenue was still well below half a million, the 'subsidies' voted by Parliament still bearing the same small proportion to the whole. If anyone is to answer at the bar of history of Elizabeth's 'parsimony', Parliament and the taxpayer must take their place there beside the Queen and her Ministers. What little money her subjects allowed her, she laid out with great wisdom for their safety and benefit. Because she refused to crusade hastily on behalf of Protestantism abroad, she was enabled to save the Reformation. Because she was a 'little Englander' and an economist in the day of small things, she laid the sea-foundations of the Empire, on which those who came after her could build.

Regular war between England and Spain was postponed until the eve of the sailing of the Armada, because Philip and Elizabeth were both of them cautious and pacific by temperament. Yet both were inflexibly set upon policies that could not fail to end in war. Philip held to the right of excluding all foreigners from approaching the newly discovered shores of Asia, Africa, and America, assigned by the Pope to Spain and Portugal. He held to the right of handing over English merchants and sailors in his dominions to the Inquisition. Nor would he tolerate an England permanently severed from Rome, though he was prepared to wait long in hopes of the death of Elizabeth, and artificially to hasten that event. Within a dozen years of her accession he was discussing plans of assassination and invasion against her, and thenceforward more and more assumed the role of executor of the Pope's decree of deposition. Yet his temperamental hesitation long restrained him from declaring open war, and compelled him to swallow many affronts and injuries at the hands of Hawkins, Drake, and the Queen herself. Probably he hoped each year that the resistance of the Dutch under William the Silent would collapse, and that then Elizabeth would become submissive or England fall an easy conquest.

The Queen saw that this delay was to her advantage, because each year made England stronger and more united. But she traded somewhat boldly on Philip's unwillingness to fight. On one occasion she laid hands on the pay for the Spanish troops
1572 in the Netherlands when the ships that carried it sought shelter in English ports; three years later she secretly connived at the capture of Brill by the Sea Beggars that founded the Dutch Republic, and she permitted English seamen to assist the rebels. In those early days the effective resistance of the Dutch was not in the
1573–4 open field, but on water and in the heroic defence of their amphibious walled towns like Haarlem and Leyden.

Above all, Elizabeth abetted the piratical attacks of Hawkins and Drake on the Spanish ships and colonies, by which the fighting power of England was trained during the years of public peace and private war. The chief scene of these irregular hostilities was Spanish America. Its ports were officially closed to foreign trade, but its inhabitants were not unwilling to purchase, under a show of compulsion, goods with which Spanish merchants were too unenterprising to provide them. Besides more innocent traffic, Hawkins dealt with them largely in Negroes whom he had kidnapped in Africa. It would have been difficult to find anyone in Europe to condemn the slave-trade from the point of view of its victims, and for two hundred years England, being the most energetic maritime community, took as much the leading part in the development of this curse of two continents as she finally took in its suppression.

Drake was less interested in the slave-trade, but he attacked and robbed Spanish ships, towns, and treasure caravans, along the American coasts. His proceedings were much in accordance with the practice of European sailors of all countries in days before the growth of international law. But they were disapproved on moral and prudential grounds by some of Elizabeth's advisers, especially by Cecil, though he himself had seized the Spanish treasure in the Channel.

In one sense England was the aggressor. But if England had not taken the aggressive she would have been forced to accept exclusion from the trade of every continent save Europe, to abandon her maritime and colonial ambitions, and to bow her neck to reconquest by Spain and Rome as soon as the resistance of Holland collapsed. A world of sheer violence, in which peaceful Englishmen were liable to be imprisoned or put to death in any Spanish possession, the world of the Inquisition and the Massacre of St Bartholomew, of Alva's appalling devilries in the Netherlands, and the Pope's deposition of Elizabeth which Catholic Europe was preparing to enforce, left no place for high standards of international conduct.

It was Sir Francis Walsingham who urged upon the Queen that her throne could be saved from the slow closing of the Spanish net only if she encouraged the lawless acts of Drake and his companions. A share in their plunder was a strong additional 1584
argument to a ruler with an insufficient revenue. Walsingham carried weight, for the system of spies he had organized repeatedly saved the Queen's life from the assassins set on by Philip and the Jesuits, who destroyed William the Silent for want of such a guard. Walsingham, inspired by a Puritan zeal against the Catholic reaction then raging on the continent, was impatient with the greater caution of the Protestant Nationalist Cecil and the 'mere English' Queen. He was ever for action, at all risks and at all

expense of treasure. If Elizabeth had taken Walsingham's advice on every occasion she would have been ruined. If she had never taken it she would have been ruined no less. On the whole she took what was best in the advice of both her great Ministers.

The situation reached its crisis over Drake's voyage round the world. Cecil was an enemy to the expedition, but Walsingham had persuaded Elizabeth secretly to take shares in the greatest piratical expedition in history. 'Drake!' she exclaimed. 'So it is that I would gladly be revenged on the King of Spain for divers injuries that I have received!' She had applied to the right man.

1520 Since Magellan had discovered a way round the southern end of America, the passage had been generally avoided as too stormy and dangerous for the tiny vessels of the day. The Spanish ships on the Pacific coast were built *in situ*, and communication with the Atlantic went overland by the isthmus of Panama.
1578–9 When therefore Drake appeared from the South upon the coast of Chile, he seemed 'like a visitation from heaven' to the secure and lightly armed Spaniards, who had learnt to think of the Pacific as an inland lake closed to the shipping of the world. Although he had less than a hundred men in the *Golden Hind*, which alone of his tempest-tost squadron had held right on past the Horn and the Straits of Magellan, it was the easiest part of his task to rob the long coast-line of its fabulous wealth, and ballast his little bark with the precious metals. Then he turned homewards across the Pacific Ocean, bound for the Cape of Good Hope.

Such was the importance attached in Spain and England to these proceedings, of which word came to Europe by Panama, and so loud was the outcry raised by the Spanish ambassador, that if Drake had failed to return home safe and rich, the victory at court might have rested with Cecil's more timid policy, and the victory in the world-contest might have fallen to Spain and Rome. Drake had told his companions that if they failed in their venture 'the like would never be attempted again'. When the *Golden Hind* grounded on a shoal in the uncharted Molucca Sea and hung for twenty hours on the edge of apparently certain destruction, to glide off safe into deep water at the last moment, vast destinies depended on the relation of a capful of wind and a tropical sandbank to a few planks of English oak.

As Drake entered Plymouth Sound after nearly three years'
1580 absence from Europe, his first question to some passing fishermen was whether the Queen were alive and well. Yes, in spite of all her enemies, she was still alive, and well enough to come next year and knight him on board his ship at Deptford. It was the

most important knighthood ever conferred by an English sovereign, for it was a direct challenge to Spain and an appeal to the people of England to look to the sea for their strength. In view of this deed, disapproved by her faithful Cecil, who shall say Elizabeth could never act boldly? Her bold decisions are few and can be numbered, but each of them began an epoch.

After the accolade at Deptford, events drifted towards open war as fast as Philip's slow spirit could move. England's final act of defiance to all comers, the execution of Mary, Queen of Scots, was the volition of the people rather than of their sovereign. 1587 Elizabeth long resisted the outcry, but her subjects forced her hand when the discovery by Walsingham of Babington's plot to murder her revealed Mary as acquainted with the design. Mary's prolonged existence raged like the fever in men's blood, for if she survived Elizabeth, either she would become Queen and the work of the Reformation be undone, or else there would be the worst of civil wars, with the national sentiment in arms against the legitimate heir backed by the whole power of Spain. The prospect was too near and too dreadful to leave men time to pity a most unhappy woman. Parliament, people, and Ministers at length prevailed on Elizabeth to authorize the execution. Her attempt to avoid responsibility for the death warrant by ruining her Secretary Davison was in her worst manner, as the knighting of Drake was in her best.

Mary's execution made it certain that Spain would at once attack England, but it united England to resist. Moderate Catholics who might have drawn sword for Mary as being by their reckoning the legitimate sovereign, stood for Elizabeth against Philip of Spain when he claimed the throne for himself. Nor had Elizabeth driven moderate Catholics to despair. Beyond fines for non-attendance at church, irregularly levied, she had not persecuted the Catholic laity for their opinions. A more ultra-Protestant Prayer-Book or a harsher persecution of 'Popish recusants', such as her Parliaments demanded, might well have led to civil war in face of the Spanish attack. As it was, a united people faced the storm of the Armada. For the Puritans, whatever they on their side suffered from Elizabeth in Church and State, would fight for her among the foremost.

The crews who manned the Invincible Armada, collected from half the sea-going populations of the Mediterranean, were many of them novices in the management of sailing ships in the open Atlantic, and acted as mere underlings of the soldiers, whom it was their privilege to carry from Spain to England. Very different was the opposing fleet. In those days the Lord High Admiral must needs be a great nobleman, but Lord Howard of Effingham, a Protestant though related to the Duke of Norfolk, was a fine sailor like his father before him, and well knew the value of the group of great seamen on whose services he could rely. Like Hawkins and Frobisher, he looked without jealousy on Drake as the master mariner of the world, who only the year before had 'singed the Spanish King's beard' destroying with his broadsides the finest war galleys afloat, in the harbour of Cadiz itself.

The numbers of the rival fleets under Howard and Sidonia were not unequal. The English, combining their Royal Navy with their armed mercantile marine, had an overwhelming mastery in weight of gun-metal, as well as in seamanship and the art of gunnery. The Spaniards were superior only in the tonnage of their secondary craft and in their soldiers, who stood ranked on deck, musketeers in front of pikemen, waiting in vain for the English to draw near according to the ancient rules of warfare at sea. But as the English preferred that it should be a duel between artillery and infantry at range chosen by the artillery, small wonder that the Spaniards, as they passed up the Channel, underwent terrible punishment. Already demoralized when they reached Calais roads, they mishandled their vessels in face of Drake's fire-ships, and failed of any attempt to embark the waiting army of Parma in the Netherlands. After another defeat in the great battle off Gravelines, they were thankful to escape total destructions on the Dutch sand-dunes owing to a change in the wind, and ran before the tempest, without stores, water, or repairs, round the iron-bound coasts of Scotland and Ireland. The winds, waves, and rocks of the remote North-west completed many wrecks begun by the cannon in the Channel. The tall ships, in batches of two and half-a-dozen at a time, were piled up on the long lee-shore, where Celtic tribesmen who knew little and cared not at all what quarrel of civilized men had flung this wreckers' harvest on their coast, murdered and stripped by thousands the finest soldiers and proudest nobles in Europe. Out of 130 great ships scarce the half reached home.

29 July 1588

Profoundly moved by a deliverance that perhaps only the seamen had confidently expected, the English took for their motto '*He blew and they were scattered*,' ascribing to the watchful providence of God and His viewless couriers a result that might without undue arrogance have been in part attributed to their own skill and courage at sea.

The first serious attempt of Spain to conquer England was also her last. The colossal effort put forth to build and equip the Armada, the child of such ardent prayers and expectations, could not, it was found, be effectively repeated, although henceforth Spain kept up a more formidable fighting fleet in the Atlantic than in the days when Drake first sailed to the Spanish Main. But the issue of the war had been decided at its outset by a single event which all Europe at once recognized as a turning point in history. The mighty power that seemed on the eve of universal lordship over the white man and all his new dominions had put out its full strength and failed. One able observer, Cardinal Allen, was quick to recognize in the Armada campaign the ruin of his life's work, to which he had sacrificed the ordinary feelings of patriotism by urging on the invasion of England. When, some years later, the traveller Fynes Moryson entered Rome in disguise to view its antiquities, he found that the Cardinal had ceased to persecute his Protestant fellow countrymen who visited the city, having changed his conduct in this respect 'since the English had overthrowne the Spanish Navy in the yeere 1588, and there was now small hope of reducing England to papistry'.

The defeat of the Armada ensured the survival of the Dutch Republic and the emancipation of France under Henri IV from Spanish arms and policies. Less directly it saved Protestant Germany, whose Lutheran Princes, at this crisis of the onslaught made by the organized and enthusiastic forces of the Counter-Reformation, had shown themselves more interested in persecuting their Calvinist subjects than in helping the common cause.

The fate of the Armada demonstrated to all the world that the rule of the seas had passed from the Mediterranean peoples to the Northern folk. This meant not only the survival of the Reformation in Northern Europe to a degree not fully determined, but the world-leadership of the Northeners in the new oceanic era.

The regular war between England and Spain continued till the death of Elizabeth in 1603. She regarded it as a first charge on her slender war-budget to see that French and Dutch independence were maintained against Philip. This was secured, partly by English help and by the holding of the seas, and partly by domestic alliance of the Calvinists with Catholic '*politiques*' averse to Spanish domination; it followed that an element of liberality and toleration very rare in the Europe of that day made itself felt in France and in Holland in a manner agreeable to Elizabeth's eclectic spirit.

The fine English regiments in Dutch pay, led by 'the fighting
1597 Veres', helped to defeat, in the battles of Turnhout and Nieuport,
1600 the infantry of Spain, till then unconquerable in the open field. Under Prince Maurice of Nassau, the son of William the Silent, the Dutch army was becoming a school of scientific warfare for all Europe, and these Englishmen in that foreign service have some claim to be regarded as founders of the modern military traditions of their native land.

What martial force Elizabeth herself could afford to pay, was for the most part sunk in the Serbonian bog of the Irish tragedy. Partly for this reason it was impossible, in spite of our naval supremacy, to dismember the Spanish empire or even to release Portugal from Philip's grasp. There were fine episodes, like the last fight of the *Revenge* off the Azores, which poetry has not greatly exaggerated, and the plunder of Cadiz, the maritime base of Spain. But England made no permanent conquests, such as were won for her by the United Services in the wars of Marlborough, Chatham, and Napoleon. The war party led by Drake had saved England and much else besides, but in the day of their apparent triumph they found themselves in eclipse. The regular war, for which they had waited and wrought so long, brought them, when it came, grave disillusionments.

England had yet to evolve a financial and a military system adequate to support her new-born naval power. Nor at the end of Elizabeth's reign, with scarce five million inhabitants, was she wealthy and populous enough to seize Spanish possessions or to found a colonial empire of her own. Even Raleigh's plantation at Virginia was premature in 1587. When in the Stuart epoch England's accumulated wealth and superfluous population enabled her to resume the work of colonization in time of peace with Spain, the path of the Puritan and other emigrants led necessarily to the Northern shores of America where no Spaniards were to be found. That way a greater future lay before Anglo-Saxon colonization than if the Elizabethans had risen to the opportunity offered by the war to annex the tropical settlements of Spain and Portugal, and had thereby directed the stream of English emigration into those deeply demoralizing climates. Here too Elizabeth's 'little Englandism' served the future of the Empire well. The limitations imposed on the scope of the war, against which Drake and Raleigh fretted, may be counted among the blessings of a reign on which Englishmen have reason to look back as the most fortunate as well as the most wonderful in their history.

CHAPTER VI

The great Elizabethan Era. Wales. Ireland. Religion. The Boundaries of Elizabethan Freedom. The Bible, Poetry, and Music

FORWARD from the time of Elizabeth, warfare against some great military empire is a recurrent *motif* of British history, but because such warfare was conducted from behind the shield of the sea and the Royal Navy, the island has never become the scene of foreign invasion, nor until the novel circumstances of 1914–18 was it ever found necessary to sacrifice a large part of the manhood of the country abroad, or to interrupt the usual course of business and pleasure at home. Such continuous security, a privilege usually confined to the countries either very humble or very remote, but enjoyed in this case by a Great Power on the very highway of the world's affairs, is the secret of much in British character and institutions. It enabled us to evolve Parliamentary government and the freedom of the subject before any other great country, and even to pride ourselves on a diversity of eccentric opinions and habits of life in our midst. Its first good gift was the rich harvest of the Elizabethan Renaissance.

The advantage of the 'moat defensive to the house' was fully understood by Shakespeare's contemporaries. During fifteen years of open war with Philip, his veteran infantry were unable 1587–
to cross from Antwerp to London, and England enjoyed greater 1603
security from 'foreign levy' and 'malice domestic' than during the three decades of troubled and dangerous peace with which Elizabeth's reign had begun. Nor did the state of war involve anything serious in the way of increased taxation or economic disturbance. A comparison may be made with the situation during the struggle with Napoleon: that later period was indeed a golden age in England for landscape-painting, poetry, novel-writing, boxing, hunting, and shooting, but it was a dark time for the mass of people owing to the economic reactions of the war, and during it the seeds were sown of future social cleavage. But during the Elizabethan war the social and economic problems of the Tudor period continued to grow less acute. Since employment increased side by side with population, it was possible for Parliament, Privy Council, and Justices of the Peace to cope with the problem of public provision for the poor. In the last year of the war a foreign traveller observed with surprise the absence of the plague

of beggars which infested continental countries, and which had so gravely disturbed England in the earlier Tudor reigns.

One cause of Elizabethan security and well-being was the fact that the outline of a united Great Britain had at length been drawn. There was lasting peace on the Scottish Border and a friendly State beyond it, as there had never been since the days of Edward I. And the Tudors had solved the problem of Wales, by which the medieval English had been baffled only less completely than by the Irish question itself.

In dealing with Wales, Henry VII had begun with two great advantages. First, he was a more powerful Marcher Lord than any of his predecessors, uniting in his own person the Marcher Lordships of the Houses of York and Lancaster to the number of some fifty. In the second place, he was a Welshman educated in Wales and retaining all his life a love of Welsh poetry and tradition. His fellow-countrymen considered that they had recovered their independence by placing one of their own Princes on the throne of England at Bosworth Field, and they flocked to his court as the Scots a century later to the court of James Sixth and First. With these advantages the prudent Tudor King was able to introduce a little order into the bloodstained anarchy of Wales, and his son completed the work.

Henry VIII, who mishandled Scotland and Ireland, understood Wales and solved its problems by a policy which combined repression of disorder with justice to the Celtic population. Rowland Lee, Bishop of Lichfield, the energetic President of the Council of the Marches, hanged thieves and murderers without mercy, and made the King's authority feared by great and small, Saxon and Celt. His methods would shock us to-day, but he gave peace to a land that had never known it before. Like many great administrators he had little faith in the future of the rude
1535 people he kept in awe, and it was contrary to his advice that Henry VIII incorporated Wales in England on equal terms. This bold measure was the first and not the least successful Act of Union in British history. Henry abolished both Principality and Marcher Lordships, dividing the whole land into twelve counties, to be governed like English counties through the Justices of the Peace, subject to the orders of the King's Council and the laws made in Parliament. The Welsh shires and boroughs were henceforth represented in the English House of Commons. The authority of the King's Council, very necessary in those disturbed districts, was brought to bear through its local offshoot

the Council of Wales and the Marches, a body corresponding to the Council of the North.

Thus supported by the strong arm of the central government, the Justices of the Peace were able to rule in the wild hill region where tribalism and feudalism had run riot for centuries. These magistrates, under the system inaugurated by Henry VIII, were not Englishmen imported to hold down the natives, but Welsh gentlemen who were the natural leaders of the people. In Wales the English government made friends with the native upper class, instead of destroying it as in Ireland.

The sight of the House of Tudor occupying the English throne enabled Celtic pride to accept union on these terms, and kept Wales loyal throughout the dangerous storms of the Tudor period. When Shakespeare represents Captain Fluellen boasting of the Welsh birth of the hero King Henry V, we suspect that the poet had overheard some honest Welshman boasting in similar terms of the racial origin of Queen Elizabeth. It was well that the Celtic population had this personal feeling for the House of Tudor, for a great strain was put on their loyalty by the English Reformation. It is true that, after the Methodist revival, Wales became the most Protestant part of Britain, but in the Sixteenth Century this was far from being the case. Protestantism under the Tudors first came to Wales in an official Anglican dress, with a Prayer Book and Bible in a tongue as little known to many Welshmen as the Latin of the Mass. And the new religion was preached at first by an alien official clergy, many of whom were absentees and sinecurists. It was a great opportunity for Rome to capture the Celtic nationality and temperament in Wales, as she was doing so successfully in Ireland under very similar religious conditions. But the Jesuit missions in Elizabeth's reign neglected Wales, partly owing to a fierce domestic quarrel between the Welsh and English in the continental seminaries.

Thus left to themselves, the Welsh people regarded the Reformation changes with apathy. While their educated and landlord classes were becoming English in speech and habits of life, while their native language was discouraged in Church and State, intellectual torpor settled down for a while on the quick-witted mountain peasantry. But though the Celtic language was neglected as an instrument of education, it survived among them more than among the Irish. At length in the Eighteenth and Nineteenth Centuries there was a great revival of national feeling and culture in connexion with Puritan religion, education, music, and Celtic poetry. In the history of the Welsh people the tribe has died, but the bard still reigns. Fortunately this later Celtic renaissance did not, like the contemporary movement in Ireland, take a form hostile to England. Henry VIII's Act of Union had been justified by leading to a union of hearts.

Very different was the outcome of Tudor policy in Ireland, inspired by an ignorance of local conditions comparable to that of Philip in his dealings with the Netherlands. In the Fifteenth Century, Ireland had been governed on the principle of 'aristocratic Home Rule' through the great Anglo-Irish families, particularly the Fitzgeralds of Kildare. But the system had begun to break down in the reign of Henry VII, and it came to a violent
1537 end when Henry VIII hanged the Earl of Kildare and his five uncles at Tyburn. No other system of government was immediately substituted. Although the Earl of Surrey reported to Henry that English conquest and colonization had become indispensable, that dread alternative was not seriously applied before the later years of Queen Elizabeth.

Henry VIII, however, contributed something to the development of the Irish tragedy besides the hanging of the Fitzgeralds. He subjected Ireland, as a matter of course, to the religious revolution that he had devised to suit conditions in England. At first, indeed, the abolition of Papal Supremacy meant little to the Celts, to whom Rome had always remained a somewhat alien power, more closely allied to the Anglo-Irish nobles than to the people at large. The simultaneous abolition of the monasteries destroyed centres of culture more valuable to Tudor Ireland than to Tudor England. For though many of the Irish monks were as worldly and useless as the Bishops and parochial clergy, they were certainly no worse, and what little education there was in the island owed much to monastic centres. Popular religion was maintained chiefly by the itinerant friars, who also fell under Henry's ban. The English brought nothing that could effectively replace that which they destroyed. They founded no University and no schools to replace the monasteries. Henry's English Bible and Edward's English Prayer Book were in a tongue then unknown to the Celt, who had moreover stood outside the current of the European Renaissance and the New Learning. But the old religion too was decadent, and there was little active resistance made to the official acts of the Reformation, until the Jesuits from abroad came to the aid of the wandering friars, whom government might proscribe but could not suppress.

Largely owing to the activity of the Jesuits, who turned to full account the English 'lack of governance' secular and spiritual

in Ireland, the situation became full of danger to Elizabeth. 'Ireland hath very good timber and convenient havens,' it was observed, 'and if the Spaniard might be master of them, he would in a short space be master of the seas, which is our chiefest force.' The Pope himself sent armed invaders to Ireland bearing his commission, six hundred of whom were captured and massacred by the English at Smerwick. Ireland was the danger point in 1580
Elizabeth's dominions, and when her enemies attacked her there she was compelled most reluctantly to undertake its conquest. Because her military and financial resources were inadequate to the task, her lieutenants used great cruelty in destroying the people by sword and famine, and in making a desert of districts which they had not the power to hold.

At the same time the policy of English colonization was favoured by government as the only means of permanently holding down the natives, who were growing more hostile every year. This opened the door to a legion of 'gentlemen-adventurers' and 'younger sons' from the towns and manor-houses of England. It has been said that the Elizabethan eagles flew to the Spanish Main while the vultures swooped down on Ireland; but they were in many cases one and the same bird. Among the conquerors and exploiters of Ireland were Humphrey Gilbert, Walter Raleigh, Grenville of the *Revenge*, and the high-souled author of the *Faerie Queene*. They saw in America and Ireland two new fields, of equal importance and attraction, where private fortunes could be made, public service rendered to their royal mistress, and the cause of true religion upheld against Pope and Spaniard. When Raleigh and Spenser were stone-blind to the realities of the Irish racial and religious problem under their eyes, it was not likely that the ordinary Englishman at home would comprehend it for several centuries to come.

And so, in the last thirty years of Elizabeth's reign, Irish history, till then fluid, ran into the mould where it hardened for three hundred years. The native population conceived a novel enthusiasm for the Roman religion, which they identified with a passionate hatred of the English. On the other hand the new colonists, as distinguished from the old Anglo-Irish nobility, identified Protestantism with their own racial ascendancy, to maintain which they regarded as a solemn duty to England and to God. Ireland has ever since remained the most religious part of the British Isles.

In such circumstances the Irish tribes finally became welded into the submerged Irish nation. The union of hatred against

England, and the union of religious observance and enthusiasm became strong enough to break down at last the clan divisions of dateless antiquity, which the English also were busy destroying from outside. The abolition of the native upper class to make room for English landlords, begun under the Tudors and completed by Cromwell, left this peasant nation with no leaders but the priests and no sympathizers but the enemies of England.

The conversion of England to Protestantism, which can be traced to origins in the time of Wycliffe, was substantially effected during the long reign of Elizabeth. When she came to the throne, the bulk of the people halted between a number of opinions, and the anti-Catholic party still consisted of anti-clericals as much as of Protestants. When she died, the majority of the English regarded themselves as ardent Protestants, and a great number of them were living religious lives based on Bible and Prayer Book.

There were two stages in the home policy of Elizabeth's reign. During the first dozen years, although the Prayer Book was the only ritual sanctioned by law, Roman Catholics were not persecuted except by moderate fines irregularly exacted. No one in that period was put to death on account of religion, and a great deal of private Roman Catholic worship was winked at by the authorities, even among persons in high State employ. But when in 1570 the Pope excommunicated the Queen, and absolved her subjects from their allegiance, the second period begins, and soon we breathe a harsher air. Jesuits from abroad travel through the island, passed on in disguise from hall to hall, hiding in 'priest-holes' behind the wainscot, infusing into the quiescent body of old English Catholicism the new zeal of the European Counter-Reformation. They checked the peaceful process by which the Catholic squires were gradually becoming habituated to the English ritual. The Jesuits' mission was religious, but, if it should succeed, its political consequences must be the deposition of the Queen and the end of everything on which the new England had set its heart, at home or beyond the seas. The Jesuits preached spiritual obedience to the Pope-King who was at war with Elizabeth, and who invaded Ireland with his own armed forces. Crown and nation struck back savagely at his missionaries, who were hanged as traitors to the English State, but were regarded by their
1581 co-religionists as martyrs to the Catholic Church. Of the two most noted leaders of the Jesuit mission in England, Campion, who cared more for religion than politics, was unfortunately caught

and hanged, while the indubitable traitor Parsons escaped abroad to work for a Spanish invasion.

On the average, four Catholics suffered for every year of Elizabeth's reign, as against 56 Protestants for every year of Mary, and the charge was no longer heresy but treason. It was a tragic business, and no doubt many English Catholics who would fain have been patriotic and loyal, but who craved for the offices of their own religion, were ground small between the upper millstone of their spiritual lord, the Pope, and the lower millstone of their temporal lord, the Queen. Both sides had declared the two loyalties to be incompatible one with the other. There were many innocent victims of this tremendous conflict, wherein for the moment no compromise was possible. In the middle of Elizabeth's reign England was in a state of siege, and adopted something of the discipline of a besieged town. Until the Roman Church throughout the world ceased to use the methods of the Inquisition, the Massacre of St Bartholomew, the deposition and assassination of Princes, the States which she had placed under her formidable ban did not dare to grant toleration to her missionaries. To do so would have been to invite defeat by pitting a naked man against a fully armed and ruthless warrior.

Under these conditions the propaganda of the Protestant religion in England went forward apace. It was favoured by the alarmed authorities; and it was identified in the minds of Englishmen with patriotism, with defiance of Spain, with sea power and Drake's American adventures, with the protection of the life of the Queen from assassins. The remodelled Grammar Schools familiarized the young with the Classics taught in the spirit of Erasmus and Colet, and with the Bible and Catechism, and so produced the men of the new English Renaissance in literature, and the champions of Protestant Anglicanism in religion. During the death-struggle with Rome, Anglo-Catholicism could not flourish, and the new generation of clergy and scholars were ardent Protestants.

The Crown in Parliament, the modern State omnicompetent within its own borders, did indeed wield terrific powers after the Tudor monarchy had subdued the Church to its will. Such powers were perhaps needful to save the country from Spanish conquest, but they set a limit to the otherwise steady growth of individual liberty. Economic and intellectual freedom had enlarged their borders by the disappearance of the medieval system. But in religion and politics the new State for a while imposed fetters scarcely less galling than those which had been broken.

The right of Catholic and Puritan to worship God each according to his own conscience was not conceded. And in politics no opposition was allowed; no one might criticize the government. Even loyal John Stubbs, for writing a pamphlet advising the Queen not to marry the French Prince, Alençon, had his right hand cut off by the hangman. Waving the bloody stump he cried from the scaffold 'Long live the Queen!' Such was the relation of that strange, subtle woman to her simple-hearted subjects. She had never had the remotest intention of marrying Alençon, but no Puritan squire was to be allowed to interfere with the mystifications of high female diplomacy.

As yet there was neither political nor religious liberty for the individual, but a split between Crown and Parliament might produce both. For England was not a despotism. The power of the Crown rested not on force but on popular support. The people still wished the Crown to exercise these coercive powers in the public interest. But it was significant that the Parliament men, while not denying the Queen's ecclesiastical authority which they themselves had restored in 1559, criticized the use she made of it against the Puritans. The English State had won control of religion from the medieval Church only by an alliance with the rights of private judgement and the forces of free speculation; it could not permanently deny the moral origin of its new-gotten authority. Puritan and Catholic might for a while be a danger and might for long be an embarrassment to statesmen. But their claim, in the name of the higher law of conscience, to challenge the religious decrees alike of the Crown and of Parliament must carry weight in the end. Since the appeal to private judgement had triumphed in England over the vast organization and immemorial prestige of the European Church of the Middle Ages, how much more certainly would it prove stronger in matters of religion than the secular authorities of the island State. And so, after another century of faction, persecution, and bloodshed, the attempt to force all Englishmen inside the doors of a State Church would be abandoned, and a larger liberty would be evolved than any dreamt of by Penry or Parsons, Whitgift or Cecil.

But outside the politico-religious sphere, intellectual and poetic freedom had already reached their fullest expansion by the end of Elizabeth's reign. The Renaissance, with its spirit of inquiry and its vision of the ancient freedom of Greek and Roman thought, had been transplanted from Italy, where it was fast withering away under the hands of Spaniards and Jesuits. It bloomed afresh in England, tended by poets who grafted it on

English trees in the Forest of Arden. There the imagination was free indeed – freer than in our own day, when it is burdened by too great a weight of knowledge, and hemmed in by the harsh realism of an age of machinery. Shakespeare and his friends, standing as they did outside the dangerous world of religious and political controversy, enjoyed in their own spacious domains a freedom of spirit perhaps irrecoverable.

But though Shakespeare may be in retrospect the greatest glory of his age, he was not in his own day its greatest influence. By the end of Elizabeth's reign, the book of books for Englishmen was already the Bible, although the Authorized Version that is still in use was only drawn up by James I's Bishops in the years immediately following her death. For every Englishman who had read Sidney or Spenser, or had seen Shakespeare acted at the Globe, there were hundreds who had read or heard the Bible with close attention as the word of God. The effect of the continual domestic study of the book upon the national character, imagination, and intelligence for nearly three centuries to come, was greater than that of any literary movement in our annals, or any religious movement since the coming of St Augustine. New worlds of history and poetry were opened in its pages to a people that had little else to read. Indeed it created the habit of reading and reflection in whole classes of the community, and turned a tinker into one of the great masters of the English tongue. Through the Bible, the deeds and thoughts of men who had lived thousands of years before in the eastern Mediterranean, translated into English during the period when our language reached its brief perfection, coloured the daily thought and speech of Britons, to the same degree as they are coloured in our own day by the commonplaces of the newspaper press. The Bible in English history may be regarded as a 'Renaissance' of Hebrew literature far more widespread and more potent than even the Classical Renaissance which, thanks to the reformed Grammar Schools, provided the mental background of the better educated. The Bible and the Classics together stimulated and enlarged the culture of the British, as their ocean voyages stimulated and enlarged their practical outlook on life.

Another source of popular inspiration and refinement in the great age that lies between the Armada and the Civil War, was music and lyrical poetry. They flourished together: many of the best poems, like the songs in Shakespeare's plays, were written to be sung. Europe recognized Elizabethan England as the country of music *par excellence*. German travellers noted with admiration how they 'heard beautiful music of violas and pandoras, for in all England it is the custom that even in small villages the musicians wait on you for a small fee.' Throughout Tudor times, fine Church music was written in England, indifferently for the Roman Mass or the Anglican service, while the Renaissance inspired non-ecclesiastical music with a fresh spirit, so that it reached its zenith under Elizabeth. The genius of Byrd adorned impartially the religious and the profane sphere, and whole troops of able composers flourished in that great age of the madrigal. The arena of Tudor and Stuart music was not the concert-hall but the domestic hearth. In days when there were no newspapers, and when books were few and ponderous, the rising middle class, not excluding Puritan families, practised vocal and instrumental music assiduously at home. The publication of music by the printing-press helped to diffuse the habit, and Elizabeth set the example to her subjects by her skill upon the virginals.

Music and song were the creation and inheritance of the whole people. The craftsman sang over his task, the pedlar sang on the footpath way, and the milkmaid could be heard 'singing blithe' behind the hedgerow, or in the North Country crooning the tragic ballads that told of Border fight and foray. The common drama was a poetical drama, and in that age was popular because it appealed to the imaginative faculties. Poetry was not an affair solely of intellectual circles, nor was music yet associated mainly with foreign composers. It was no mere accident that Shakespeare and Milton came when they did. Among a whole people living in the constant presence of nature, with eyes and ears trained to rejoice in the best pleasures of the mind, the perfect expansion of Shakespeare's poetic gifts was as much a part of the general order of society as the development of a great novelist out of a journalist would be to-day. And in the life of John Milton, born five years after Elizabeth died, we read clearly how the three chief elements in the English culture of that day – music, the Classics, and the Bible – combined to inspire the 'God-gifted organ-voice of England'.

BOOK FOUR
THE STUART ERA

Parliamentary Liberty and Overseas Expansion

THE Tudor period made, it is probable, more difference to the Englishman's outlook and habits of life than the Stuart period that followed. But the Renaissance, the Reformation, and the development of oceanic adventure, which changed so much for the Tudor English, had been world movements in which other countries took an equally active part. In the Stuart era the English developed for themselves, without foreign participation or example, a system of Parliamentary government, local administration and freedom of speech and person, clean contrary to the prevailing tendencies on the continent, which was moving fast towards regal absolution, centralized bureaucracy, and the subjection of the individual to the State. While the Estates General of France and the Cortes of Aragon and of Castile were ceasing to exercise even their medieval functions, while the political life of Germany was atrophied in the mosaic of petty Princedoms that constituted the Empire, the House of Commons, under the leadership of the squires and in alliance with the merchants and the Common Lawyers, made itself the governing organ of a modern nation. This it achieved by developing inside itself an elaborate system of committee procedure, and by striking down the royal power in a series of quarrels of which the chief motive was religious and the chief result political.

English freedom, being rooted in insular peculiarities, required, if it was ever to reach its full growth, a period of isolation from European influences and dangers. Elizabeth and Drake had rendered that isolation possible. Circumstances abroad, of which the Thirty Years' War was the chief, enabled England, behind the shield of her Navy, to work out her domestic problems undisturbed by any dread of interference by her neighbours.

It was only when the period of internal evolution had resulted in the settlement of 1688–9, that the new Parliamentary England, based on freedom in religion and politics, was matched under William III and Marlborough against the new type of continental autocracy personified in the all-worshipped Louis XIV, Grand Monarch of France. That struggle freed Europe from French domination, and left the English fleet for the first time unrivalled mistress of all the seas of the world. The wars against Louis may be regarded as the ordeal by battle which demonstrated the greater efficiency of the free community over the despotic state.

This result greatly astonished and impressed a world that had up till that time held a diametrically opposite theory of power. Despotism, it had been thought, was the secret of efficiency; freedom was a luxury to be enjoyed by small communities like the Cantons of Switzerland and the Seven Provinces of Holland – and Holland's power after a short period of glory was waning fast before the rising might of the French King. The victory of parliamentary England over despotic France was a new fact of the first order; it was the prime cause of the intellectual movement abroad against despotism in Church and State which marked the Eighteenth Century, from the time of Montesquieu onwards. The British Navy and Marlborough, the battles of La Hogue and Blenheim, gave to Locke and the other English philosophers a vogue on the continent seldom enjoyed by English philosophy in its own right. English institutions for the first time became an example to the world, though they remained somewhat of a mystery and were very imperfectly understood.

Britain's successes in the reigns of William and Anne surprised men all the more, because, prior to the Revolution of 1688, the rivalry of Parliament with the regal executive had been a cause not of efficiency but of weakness to England as a member of the European polity. Under James and Charles the First, and again under Charles and James the Second, the balance between King and Parliament made England of little account abroad.

The exception that proved the rule was the period of national efficiency under the Puritan Commonwealth. Then indeed the Parliamentary, or at least the Roundhead party, was supreme. Legislature and executive were united; and so, both before and during the period of Cromwell's personal rule, the Commonwealth Government wielded powers of taxation and of military and naval preparation which no Stuart King enjoyed. Then indeed the voice of England was heard and feared abroad. But the concentration of power in the hands of the Roundhead party was a temporary phenomenon, because it was based not on agreement but on force.

In 1660 the nation restored the balance of power between King and Parliament, between executive and legislative, in which Clarendon rejoiced as the perfection of our mixed constitution. And with this perfect balance returned financial inability to meet our engagements, national disarmament, and divided counsels, making us the mock of our enemies and the despair of our friends. This balance of the constitution, more than the wickedness or carelessness of Charles II, lay at the root of the disasters of his reign. No country can remain half monarchial and half parliamentary without paying the penalty in want of power.

It was the Revolution of 1688 that gave to Great Britain freedom and efficiency together, because it tipped the balance of power permanently on to the side of Parliament, not as forty years before by the victory in arms of one party in the State over another, but by an agreement of Whigs and Tories, thrown into each other's arms by the fortunate folly of James II.

Thenceforward there was agreement in general policy between executive and legislative, between King and Parliament, as formerly under the Tudors; but this time it was Parliament that led and the King who had to follow. Then and then only was it possible to reorganize the taxation and the credit of the country on a modern basis, to keep a small standing army on foot as well as a large fleet permanently afloat, to develop the organization necessary for a great empire, without giving rise to the jealousies which had frustrated similar attempts by Strafford and by Cromwell. Then and then only was it possible to induce the Scots to accept freely a legislative union with England, such as Cromwell had presented to them at the sword's point. At the same time, the attempt to force all Englishmen through the doors of a single State Church, the cause for so many generations past of faction and bloodshed, was at length abandoned as impracticable by the Toleration Act of 1689. The new era of latitudinarianism and religious peace greatly strengthened Britain's commercial, military, and colonizing power as against that of France, then engaged in casting out the pick of her industrial population, the Huguenots, to aid the rising manufactures of England, Holland, and Prussia.

It is during the Stuart period that we emerge from the arena of English history into the ampler spaces of British history in its largest sense. The modern relations of England to Scotland and to Ireland respectively had been outlined under Elizabeth. Under the Stuarts they were deeply engraved on the imagination of posterity by a series of dramatic events. After many vicissitudes, we reached, in the reigns of William III and Anne, a defined and permanent relation of England to Scotland which still gives satisfaction to-day, and a relation of Britain to Ireland that fixed the lines along which all subsequent misfortunes developed.

In the same Stuart period, England planted populous and self-governing communities in North America. Englishmen began to live on the other side of the world, but under the English flag and under free English institutions. Before the Seventeenth Century closed they were learning so to adjust these institutions in New York and elsewhere, that Dutch and other foreigners were happy to live under the English flag. Already we see the germ of a free Empire, of a widespread Commonwealth of many races and religions, the ideal which both the United States and the British Empire of to-day realize in two different ways but in a kindred spirit. At the close of the Seventeenth Century, the colonies of other European countries were developing on very different lines. Neither religious nor political freedom existed in French Canada or Spanish America; the Dutch colonies in Africa had no political freedom, and in America relatively little. It was England who first planted the flag of liberty beyond the ocean.

The toleration of varieties in religion, though not admitted within England herself until 1689, was part of the very liberal practice both of the Stuart Kings and of their Parliamentary enemies in colonial affairs throughout this period. Anglican, Puritan, or Roman Catholic, if discontented with his lot in the old country, could go to America with the good will of government and pray there according to his own fancy, but still under the old flag. Those who were regarded as troublesome at home, would be a strength and glory to England – on the other side of the ocean. This relatively liberal principle gave England a great advantage in the race for colonial supremacy.

Another reason why the governments of the Stuart epoch favoured the planting of colonies even by their political enemies, was the increasingly commercial and industrial character of the English polity at home. Massachusetts, New York, Virginia, and the West Indian Islands were valued as important markets for English manufactures, at a time when the Parliamentary regime was bringing commerce more and more to the front as a prime consideration in domestic and foreign policy.

The Revolution of 1688 established the supremacy of the House of Commons, but left it handicapped with the system of 'rotten boroughs' which were bound to grow more unrepresentative as years rolled by. The idea of redistributing Parliamentary seats in accordance with the movement of population was buried in the grave of Cromwell. It followed that the House of Commons and the government which it controlled became increasingly identified with the landlord class who were able to control the 'rotten boroughs'. If the Roundhead party had been able to come to terms with the rest of the nation, a considerable element of democracy might have been introduced into the English State. But after 1660 the democratic spirit disappeared until the industrial changes of the following century gave it a new form of life. The Revolution of 1688, though Parliamentary and liberal, was not democratic. Partly for that reason the nascent democracies beyond the Atlantic became increasingly out of touch with the aristocratic Parliament at home, a difference accentuated by differences in the prevalent form of religious observance in old and New England.

The downfall first of King Charles, then of the Puritan Commonwealth, and finally of James II in consequence of attempts to override the squirearchy and the chartered corporations, left the State weaker than it had been under Elizabeth in its relation to the local government of the countryside. The kind of control that Cecil and Walsingham had exercised over the doings, economic and other, of the Justices of the Peace, was on the decline throughout the Stuart era, and was conspicuously absent under the early Hanoverians. The struggle of Parliament against Crown had, indeed, from the first been rooted in a stuggle for local independence against the centre, a rebellion of the squires against the Court and the Privy Council. In that contest the yeomen and townsfolk had supported the squires, especially that section of squires that was most opposed to the Crown. The victory of Parliament, though it made England more united and efficient for action abroad, meant the subordination of the central authority to the will of the localities as regards their domestic affairs. And owing to the failure of the Puritan Revolution, the will of the localities from 1660 onwards meant the will of the squires.

The political victory over the House of Stuart finally rested with the Whigs – the section of the squires who were in alliance with London and the merchant community in matters of national policy. But the social power remained with the Justices of the Peace and the whole body of the squires who as a mass were less Whig than Tory.

The political and religious tyranny of the monarch had been effectively curbed. The State Church no longer pretended to be co-extensive with the nation. The individual was protected in freedom of speech and person by Parliament victorious over the Crown, and by the Common Lawyers victorious over the Prerogative Courts. Henceforth, so far as the government was concerned, 'a man might speak his mind' as nowhere else in Europe and as never before in England. To abolish social tyranny was more difficult. But until the advent of the Industrial Revolution the need of social emancipation from the squirearchy was not seriously felt. Under the first two Georges Englishmen regarded human freedom as a science which they had perfected. That view, partly inspired by national pride in contemplation of a continent still domineered over by Kings, priests, and nobles, was indeed erroneous. And yet it may fairly be doubted whether any set of men, since the victors of Marathon and Salamis, had done as much to establish human freedom on a practical basis as the Roundheads and Cavaliers, the Whigs and Tories of the Stuart Parliaments.

CHAPTER I

James I. Parliaments and Recusants. Decline of English Sea-power. The Spanish match. Buckingham and the Thirty Years' War. Charles I. The King, Parliament, and the Common Law. Coke and Eliot. Laud and Strafford

Kings: James I, 1603–25 (James VI of Scotland, 1567); Charles I, 1625–49

THE keynote of Tudor government had been King-worship, not despotism. Monarchs without an army at the centre of a paid bureaucracy in the countryside were not despots, for they could not compel their subjects by force. The beefeaters of the Palace could guard the barge in which a rebellious nobleman or a fallen Minister was rowed from Whitehall steps to Traitors' Gate in the Tower, because the London 'prentices never attempted a rescue on the way. But they could not coerce a population of five millions, many of whom had sword, bow, or bill hanging from the cottage rafters.

The power of the Tudors, in short, was not material but metaphysical. They appealed sometimes to the love and always to the loyalty and 'free awe' of their subjects. In the century that begins with Sir Thomas More and ends with Shakespeare, 'the deputy elected by the Lord' walks girt with a sunlike majesty. In his presence rank, genius, and religion vail their pride, or lay their heads resignedly upon the block if the wrath of the Prince demands a sacrifice. In the following century genius and religion were to show a less obliging temper.

English King-worship was the secret of a family and the spirit of an age. It owed much to the political talents of the two Henries and Elizabeth, and yet more to the need for national leadership in the period of transition from the medieval to the modern world. When, after the death of the last Tudor, James I in his pedantry tried to materialize English King-worship into the political dogma of divine hereditary right, he spilt its essence in the dust.

England had found in the Tudor monarchs adequate representatives of her own spirit and policy; but the Stuarts, while claiming yet greater powers from a higher source than English law and custom, adopted policies at home and abroad which were in some of their main lines opposed to the wishes of the strongest elements in English society. The situation thus created forced to the front claims on behalf of the House of Commons which were as new to the constitution as the claims of divine hereditary right and autocratic power on behalf of the Crown.

Whether the conflict would have come to blows without the complication and inspiration of the religious question in a religious age, may perhaps be doubted. And certainly the novel claims on behalf of the Lower House would never have been advanced, still less made good, without the preparatory work of great constitutional lawyers like Coke and Selden, and great Parliamentarians – a new profession – like Eliot, Hampden, and Pym. In the reigns of James and Charles the First the manor-houses of England produced a famous breed of men to sit in Parliament. Antiquarians in learning, and devotees of law, custom, and precedent, they persuaded themselves and their countrymen that they were only claiming ancient privileges, and carrying out the spirit and even the letter of Magna Carta. Historical science was yet in its infancy, for in fact they were innovators, unconsciously groping after a form of government new to England and new to the world. These men were not adventurers or self-seekers, and had more to lose than to gain by quitting their broad acres and private gardens; for Parliament was then the road not to power but to prison. The earnest personal character of their Protestant religion was combined with the cultured habit of mind and manner of gentlemen who were the ripe products of the English Renaissance. Only with the breach in the Parliamentary party in the second session of the Long Parliament did these two elements begin to divide, and to form the Roundhead party on the one hand and the Constitutional Royalists on the other.

When James VI of Scotland, the comic offspring of the tragic union of Mary, Queen of Scots, with Darnley, succeeded to Elizabeth's throne as James I, the English rode in from far and near to catch a glimpse of their new sovereign on his slow progress from Edinburgh to London. Those whose rank gave them access through the throng in the Midland market towns, found themselves in the presence of the good-natured, conceited, garrulous King, wise in book-learning but a poor judge of men, and so ignorant of England and her laws that at Newark he ordered a cut-purse caught in the act to be hanged without trial at a word from his royal mouth. Scotland indeed he knew and in part understood, but that knowledge would be of less than no use to him in deciphering the political map of his southern kingdom.

His new subjects, however, were in no mood to be critical. For forty years and more they had lived in the black shadow of the question 'What will beafall us when the Queen dies?' That anxiety had been aggravated and prolonged by Elizabeth's half-politic, half-coquettish dislike of the topic, and her irritation at the demand for an acknowledged heir, who might, she feared, divide the loyalty of her servants before she herself had finished with them. But Robert Cecil, wise son of a great father, had negotiated with James and smoothed the way for his undisputed accession. The relief felt by the English people at the peaceful continuity of things after Elizabeth's death is enshrined in the hyperbolical language of the Preface to the Authorized Version of the Bible.

The new sovereign brought with him one good gift that was personal to himself – the union with Scotland. Now that both crowns were set on one head, the long, romantic story of the Border came to an end. The moss-trooper's occupation was gone; he yielded place, on the moors that had known him, to the shepherd, who could now drive the flocks in security to the very ridge of the Cheviots and to the heart of the Debateable Land. But there was no union of the Parliaments, Churches, or laws of the two Kingdoms, and the Scots were disliked by their fellow-subjects as proud, beggarly rivals for the royal favour. Not till the Eighteenth Century did the Empire began to draw its full increase of strength from the union. But the close reactions of English upon Scottish and of Scottish upon English affairs make up a great part of the tangled and sanguinary skein of politics and religion under the Stuarts.

Scotland, in losing the presence of her King, who now became a mighty potentate at four hundred miles' distance from Edinburgh, was thereby subordinated to royal power as she had neve.

been before. From Whitehall the sixth James could keep the Scots nobles in awe, and at the same time prevent the Kirk from domineering over the State. To achieve the latter end, he successfully aroused the jealousy of the nobles against the small lairds and ministers who were laying hands on power through the medium of the ecclesiastical organization. He had established some humble and ill-paid Bishops, whose functions he gradually increased at the expense of the democratic Assemblies and Synods. In so doing he was protecting moderate and liberal elements in the religious life of Scotland, and preventing clerical tyranny, but he was also thwarting the only form of self-expression that was then open to the Scottish people. He did not, however, attempt to destroy the Presbyterian organization in the parishes, or to impose the English service book on the Scottish congregations. He would never have become the dupe of the strange delusion which betrayed Laud to his undoing, that there was 'no religion' in Scotland! There was a great deal more of it than James liked, and his only desire was to keep it in its place. He knew Scotland as he never knew England, and as his son Charles never knew either the one land or the other.

Not only did England remain *terra incognita* to James, but he never became aware of his ignorance. His mind was already formed when first he came to reign in Whitehall, and the flattery he received there confirmed his good opinion of his own penetration. Was not politics a science he had mastered? He was perpetually unbuttoning the stores of his royal wisdom for the benefit of his subjects, and as there was none who could venture to answer him to his face, he supposed them all out-argued. In Scotland he had had no experience of anything analogous to the English House of Commons. The Scottish 'Parliament' was in effect a court record, and he could not appreciate the much higher position of the body bearing the same name in England. In Scotland the only opposition came from feudal Barons on their estates and Presbyterian preachers in their pulpits. Who then were these squires and lawyers in the House of Commons, with their talk about 'privilege' and 'precedents', and 'fundamental laws of the realm', refusing to let him raise money from his subjects except on their conditions, and striving to dictate to him on the weightiest affairs of ecclesiastical and foreign policy? He condescendingly pointed out to them their folly, and, when they disregarded his lectures, fumed over in angry words and deeds.

James mismanaged the always difficult Roman Catholic question. Most of the English Roman Catholics were politically

'moderate', and remained loyal in spite of their grievances: but the party led by the Jesuits was always working for a counter-revolution. Partly for this reason, the royal policy wavered between concession and severity. After a promise of relief, James reinforced the fines for 'recusancy'. This so incensed a group of Catholic gentlemen of the Jesuit party that they formed the Gunpowder Plot, for the destruction of the King and the two Houses of Parliament together. In early Tudor times government could have been paralysed or overturned by murdering the King; it was now felt to be necessary to murder Parliament too. The material preparations, made by men who had served as officers in the Spanish army in the Netherlands, were all complete when the conspiracy was revealed by a man of tender conscience, though very possibly Government agents had known of the plot
1605 before.

'The attempt but not the deed confounds us': it was the heaviest moral blow suffered by the Roman Catholics between the reigns of Mary Tudor and James II. Everything that had been said about the result of the Jesuit teaching seemed to plain Englishmen to be more than confirmed, and the Protestant feast of Guy Fawkes and the Fifth of November, decorously celebrated in the Church service, had democratic rites at the street corner in which the least mystical could heartily participate. Henceforth the anti-Roman passion in England remained a constant and often a determining factor in all the mazes of the long history of the House of Stuart.

James disliked 'men of war' whether by land or sea. Until in his declining years he let the initiative pass to the volatile and ambitious Buckingham, he was the most thorough-going pacifist who ever bore rule in England. He wielded the sceptre and the pen, and held them both to be mightier than the sword. Of naked steel he had a physical horror, perhaps because he was born three months after the terrible day when armed men had burst in upon his mother's supper party and stabbed Rizzio under her eyes. And not only was James most unwarlike in his own particular: but being a Scot of that period he had no conception of the importance of sea-power. He was the only Stuart King of England who utterly neglected the Navy.

Neglect of the Navy deprived his peace with Spain of some at
1604 least of its good effects. The terms of the treaty that ended Elizabeth's war obtained for English merchants open trade with Spain and her possessions in Europe, and set some limit to the power of the Inquisition over them in Spanish ports. But the

claims of the Elizabethan seamen to trade with Spanish America and the regions monopolized by Portugal in Africa and Asia were not mentioned in the treaty, and the enforcement of these claims no longer received countenance from the English government, which let the Royal Navy decay, while it suppressed privateering to the best of its ability.

In these circumstances, private war against Spanish and Portuguese was continued without the countenance of the State. In the American Indies, the 'buccaneers' found friends and bases in the West Indian Islands and in the New English colonies on the Northern mainland, so long as they maintained, however illegally, the interests and prestige of England against the Spaniard. But their high-seas robbery was not always directed against Spaniards alone, and before the end of the Stuart era the buccaneers had degenerated far from the traditions of Drake and Raleigh towards the melodramatic villanies of Teach and the black-flag pirates. Meanwhile the trade of South America remained, by law at least, closed to all save Spaniards; but as a result of Drake's victories, North America was in practice open to English, French, and Dutch settlement.

On the coasts of Africa and the East Indies the Portuguese, then subjects of the King of Spain, endeavoured to prevent the subjects of James I from trading with the natives even in time of peace. But the English East India Company armed its ships for battle, and Captains Thomas Best and Nicholas Downton blew the Portuguese out of the water in decisive actions off Surat, and 1614–15 so established more regular trade with the native peoples of Asia than was as yet possible with the inhabitants of the guarded shores of the Spanish American colonies.

In their hostilities against the Portuguese in the East, the English merchants had the Dutch as allies. But for the rest there was enmity between the trading communities of the two Protestant nations, which increased when the Portuguese power became of no account in the Indian seas. In the reigns of James and Charles I the merchant of the Dutch East India Company had greater resources behind him than his English rival. It was the day of the amazing wealth and power of little Holland, safe at last from Spain and not yet threatened by France. She led the world in the arts and sciences, and was mistress of the sea. The Dutch became the carriers for mankind, largely to the detriment of English shipping. They ousted the English from the Russian trade, which the Elizabethans had been the first to open. They fished where they liked, and often drove English fishermen from their own grounds.

They expelled the Portuguese from Ceylon and the Spice Islands of the Molucca Sea, and in 1623 massacred the English there at Amboina; James was helpless, and it was left to Cromwell, a generation later, to exact compensation for the long-remembered outrage.

But the English East India Company, when driven from the Spice Islands, pushed its trade on the Indian mainland. In James I's reign it founded a successful trading station at Surat, and in Charles I's reign built its Fort St George, Madras, and set up other trading stations in Bengal. Such were the humble mercantile origins of British rule in India. But from the first these East India merchants were not mere 'quill-drivers'; they had destroyed the Portuguese monopoly by diplomacy at the courts of native potentates, and by the broadsides of their ships at sea.

Meanwhile James abandoned one by one the claims of the Royal Navy. The salute to the flag by other nations in the English seas was no longer demanded. The pirates from the 'Barbary' coast of North Africa raided in the Channel with impunity. The diplomatic protests of James about the treatment of his subjects by
1618 Dutch and Spaniards were laughed to scorn. Raleigh was beheaded to appease the Spanish Ambassador. We were still a maritime community, but for thirty years we almost ceased to be a naval power.

One consequence was the deep and lasting resentment of the mariners and merchants against the House of Stuart, increased by the strong Protestant feeling of those who went down to the sea in ships. The new monarchy had abandoned the Elizabethan tradition at sea and in its dealings with Spain; the indignation produced by this change of attitude was not removed even when
1634–40 Charles I honestly appropriated the illegal Ship Money to the reconstruction of the Royal Navy which his father had allowed to decay. In the hour of his need, the ships which Charles had built revolted to his enemies, and the seaports of England followed the lead of London and the House of Commons in the first Civil War with decisive effects on its fortunes. The ghost of Raleigh pursued the House of Stuart to the scaffold.

James' peaceful policy was put to a cruel test by the outbreak of
1618–48 the Thirty Years' War. At that crisis his neglect of the fighting fleet foredoomed his well-meant pacific diplomacy to failure, for why should Spain or Austria, France or Holland, listen to the man who had let England's national weapon rust, and could never prevent Spanish troops from sailing up the Channel to the Netherlands?

In its origin the Thirty Years' War was a resumption of the forward march of the great Catholic reaction to which England and Holland had set a limit in the days of Philip II. Its new protagonist was Austria, with Spain assistant. Bohemia and the Rhenish Palatinate were overrun, the first by Austrian arms, the second by Spaniards from the Netherlands, and cruel persecution put down Protestantism in both the conquered lands. The Prince who had been driven from these two dominions was none other than James I's son-in-law. His wife Elizabeth, and their infant children, Prince Rupert and Prince Maurice, began thus early their long life of disinherited wandering, which never undermined the great abilities and virtues of either mother or children. James vainly thought to effect their restoration by ingratiating himself yet more with their enemies, by subjecting English policy more than ever to Gondomar the Spanish Ambassador, and finally by proposing to marry his surviving son Charles to the Spanish Infanta.

The Spanish match, as the English people clearly saw, would lead to Spanish heirs and Catholic Kings who would endeavour to undo the work of Elizabeth. But James in his old age and Charles in his youth were alike infatuated with George Villiers, whom they made Duke of Buckingham; and Buckingham's volatile imagination was for a time dazzled by the idea of giving peace to Europe through the Spanish match. When that dangerous project broke down after the escapade of the visit of young Charles and the favourite to Madrid, a marriage only one degree less fatal was carried through, Charles being mated to the zealous Romanist Henrietta Maria of France, destined to be the mother of many troubles to England and of more to the House of Stuart.

James I died in 1625, but his death made little difference, for Buckingham's influence was no less strong over King Charles. 1625–8
The fiasco of the Spanish match was followed by a period of warlike expeditions, rashly undertaken by Buckingham, who now cast himself for the part of Protestant hero abroad. But armies and navies cannot be improvised, and the result was a series of disasters disgraceful to our arms. Some of these idle expeditions were directed to aid the Huguenots of La Rochelle against the France of Cardinal Richelieu. A wiser policy would have taken the Cardinal by the hand to resist the progress of the Catholic reaction conducted by the Hapsburg enemies of France beyond the Rhine. Other English expeditions directed against Spain were equally unsuccessful.

This tale of folly and disaster lowered the prestige of monarchy in England, and brought the Crown into fierce conflict with the House of Commons. The wars, such as they were, had led to unparliamentary taxation, billeting, arbitrary imprisonment, and martial law over civilians, all of which were defined as illegal in
1628 the famous Petition of Right conceded by Charles to his Parliament in return for a vote of five subsidies. Yet the Petition of Right, like Magna Carta, was the beginning, not the end, of a struggle for the principles it enunciated.

The House of Commons was not yet strong enough to dictate the foreign policy of the Crown, but it was strong enough to be a clog on the effective conduct of war. For it could not but be jealous of the taxing power and fearful of an army over which it had no control. If once the Crown established the right to tax the subject at will like the Kings of France and Spain, there might perhaps be a beginning of success abroad, but there would certainly be an end of Parliaments at home.

The squires who composed the Lower House, no longer as in Elizabeth's reign guided by tactful Privy Councillors sitting in their midst, were becoming an opposition rather than an organ of government. Their homespun wit enabled them to understand the interests of their own country better than the courtiers, but they knew nothing of the continent, and showed little wisdom in their advice as to how the Protestant cause was to be maintained abroad. With a royal executive and a tax-granting Parliament at loggerheads and both of them grossly ignorant of foreign affairs, with no army and a diminutive Royal Navy, England was a cypher in European politics at this crisis.

Buckingham, while still preparing warlike expeditions to re-
1628 lieve Rochelle, was murdered by a Puritan fanatic, to the shameless joy of the common folk. Charles, alienated from his people by the blood of his friend, soon abandoned warlike schemes that were clearly foredoomed to failure, and strove instead by rigid economy to govern without the Parliaments that he hated. In this design he was confirmed by a violent quarrel with the House of Commons of 1629; members held the Speaker down in the Chair while they passed the famous resolutions against 'Popery and Arminianism' and illegal Tonnage and Poundage, which the circumstances of the time associated together in the minds of men. No Parliament was held again for eleven years.

Contrary to the privileges of Parliament as respected by Queen Elizabeth, Sir John Eliot and his friends Valentine and Strode were kept in prison on account of what they had done in the House of Commons. Eliot died in the Tower, refusing to obtain release by signifying his submission to these illegal proceedings, a martyr to English law and freedom; his two friends did not regain their liberty for eleven years. The hardness of Charles in his dealings with Eliot, whom he would not even suffer to be taken for burial to his Cornish home, can most charitably be regarded as a measure of his silent grief over the murdered Buckingham, for the Commons' leader had been inveterate and even furious in his eloquent attacks upon the favourite. But such a temper in Charles towards his subjects, even if humanly excusable, was very dangerous in a king who for a dozen years to come was to rule the land at his own mere will and pleasure.

By dispensing with Parliaments and by dismissing all Judges who dared to interpret the laws impartially, Charles removed every constitutional check upon his actions. None the less, the genius of the English Common Law was still the enemy of absolute regal power, and thanks to the work of Sir Edward Coke it had become the great ally of Parliament. If Parliament ever revived and conquered royal despotism, the spirit of the Common Law would revive with it and conquer the Prerogative Courts of Star Chamber, High Commission, Requests, and Councils of Wales and the North. The professional jealousy felt by the lawyers in the courts where English Common Law was administered, against these Prerogative Courts dealing out a different law by different rules of procedure, had been deeply stirred by the leadership of the fierce and arrogant Coke, and had by him been closely connected with the Parliamentary party in the House of Commons. The Petition of Right, which was largely his work and expressed his doctrine, represented the spirit of the Common Law and the vigilance of Parliament combining to protect the subject of the land against arbitrary power.

The two men who had worked together to lay the foundations of Parliamentary resistance to the Crown were strangely different specimens of humanity. Eliot was the best type of well-to-do country gentleman, seeking nothing for himself, ardent and eloquent only in the public interest. Coke was an ambitious, pushing lawyer, a bully, and in his early days a sycophant. As Attorney-General to King James in 1603 he had attacked the prisoner Raleigh in a spirit worthy of Jeffreys, crying out to the lifelong foe of Spain, 'Thou hast a Spanish heart and thyself art a viper of hell!' Only one thing was dearer to Coke than promotion and power, and that was the Common Law. For it he sacrificed place and royal favour, stepping down off the Bench to 1616–28 make on the floor of the Lower House his alliance with the Puritan squires, a union whence sprang the liberties of England.

In essence the quarrel was this: James and Charles held, with the students of Roman Law, that the will of the Prince was the source of law, and that the Judges were 'lions under the throne', bound to speak as he directed them. Coke, on the other hand, in the spirit of the English Common Law, conceived of law as having an independent existence of its own, set above the King as well as above his subjects, and bound to judge impartially between them. Laws were alterable only by the High Court of Parliament. The Prerogative Courts, with their reception of Roman Law and their arbitrary procedure, belonged, he thought, to an alien civilization.

The battle between these two systems of law had to be fought out, for England could no longer, as under the Tudors, be governed by both at once. The first blood was drawn by Charles, who by packing the Bench seemed to have subjected the Common Law courts themselves to prerogative ideas. But the last word was to lie with the Long Parliament.

The English Common Law was a survival from the Middle Ages, while the Prerogative Courts and the increased deference for Roman Law had been a Renaissance product of Tudor times. Coke and the Parliament men whom he schooled in his doctrines, stood therefore on conservative and national ground, against innovation of the type prevalent on the continent. Their appeal was made to the past – to the past of England, not of the Roman Empire. Hence the antiquarian and historical character of their arguments, not always good history in detail, but consonant generally with a real English tradition down the ages. 'Coke on Littleton' and Coke's other Institutes were less universal and less forward-looking in their appeal than theories of the Rights of Man by Paine or Rousseau, but they have served to underprop a vast structure of progress and freedom in two hemispheres.

The legal issue between the King and his opponents was no less important than the financial or the religious, and in that litigious age it was well understood by the English people. The
1637–8 case arising from John Hampden's refusal to pay Ship Money, argued fully before the Exchequer Court, was followed in its details with intense excitement by a people better versed in legal matters than the King or his advisers were aware. The ruling made by the majority of the Judges against Hampden and in favour of the levy of Ship Money without Parliamentary sanction stood condemned by public opinion. But for a short while longer

the ruling enabled the King to exact a tax and to reconstruct the fighting Navy. The object was worthy, but it was not by such expedients that English maritime supremacy could be restored and maintained by a King who had lost the loyalty of his subjects. It was a necessary part of the new royal policy to abstain from all foreign entanglements, and allow the Thirty Years' War to pass from crisis to crisis with England as a spectator, even on occasions when a mere naval demonstration would have had important results. The adherence of the sea-going population and of the Royal Navy itself to the Parliamentary side of the quarrel bore witness to the patriotic character of Hampden's refusal to pay an illegal tax.

Laud and Wentworth, the two men with whom Charles' period of autocratic rule is associated, were of a very different order of character and intellect from Buckingham.

Archbishop Laud was a great churchman, who unfortunately was called upon by the then relations of Church and State to play also the part of statesman, for which he was unsuited alike by temper and understanding. His memory is cherished as the founder of the High Church party in the religious life of the Church of England. But the historian is principally concerned with the political consequences of his ecclesiastical policy, which in a Church that was then by law co-extensive with the nation could not fail to be of the utmost peril and importance. It was indeed the chief cause of the Civil War, because it provoked the furious reaction of armed Puritanism in which Laud himself perished.

If James I suffered as King of England from having been bred a Scot, Laud as Archbishop suffered from having been bred a don. He treated broad England as he had been permitted to treat Oxford, but it is easier to trim a University to pattern than a nation of grown men. The ritual side of worship in the parish churches was increased by episcopal command and visitation, while evangelical practice, preaching, and lecturing were effectively prohibited within the Church. At the same time nonconformist worship outside the Church was persecuted with increasing rigour. The emigration of the Puritans to America in these years was a measure of the degree to which Laud made life intolerable to them in England. Owing to his activities it became impossible for a Puritan to live in his native country and worship God freely, at a time when English Puritanism was producing men of the calibre of Cromwell and Milton, Hampden, and Pym. High Anglicanism had already its men of learning and its poets, but as yet it had not won the heart of any large section of the squires, still less of the people at large. Even men like Sir Edmund Verney, Falkland, and Hyde, who in time of need showed themselves ready to fight to save the Prayer Book, were hostile to Laud and his over-busy Bishops.

The zeal of the Primate roused against himself and against the King, not only the strongest religious sentiments of that generation, but the feeling, always very strong in England, that resents the interference of the religious in their neighbours' affairs. Laud, who could never be either wary or prudent in well-doing, revived the activity of the spiritual courts, and summoned influential laymen to answer for their sins before the priesthood. The Church Courts, with a truly catholic indifference, incurred the odium of the Puritan precisian, the loose-liver, and the ordinary laymen who had hoped that the Reformation had delivered him from clerical control. Meanwhile Bishops were beginning to replace nobles and commoners as the favourite councillors of the Crown. And in many parishes the new school of Laudian clergy enraged the squires by setting themselves up as rival sources of authority. The censorship of the press, which was then in episcopal hands, was busily employed by Laud to silence voices opposed to his own ideas. In everything Englishmen were to toe the line drawn by a particular school of clergy. There seemed, in short, to be an attempt on foot to restore the medieval relation of the clergy to the laity, and such a movement gave bitter offence alike to future Cavaliers and future Roundheads. The anti-clerical feeling which in 1661 swelled the popularity of the restored Anglican Church as the alternative to 'the rule of the Saints', in 1640 added force to the Puritan uprising against Laud's domination.

While the Archbishop persecuted the Puritans with meticulous rigour, the growing influence of Charles' French Queen stopped the persecution of Roman Catholics. The consequence was that they everywhere raised their heads: there were conversions, especially in the upper ranks of society, and Henrietta Maria's religion became fashionable at Court. Meanwhile the most determined enemies of the Church of Rome were pouring out of the country to America by thousands every year. An indefinite continuance of such a state of things must, men thought, lead to the return of England to the Papal fold. Laud did not desire that, but he applied no remedy and suffered accordingly in men's estimation.

In these circumstances the fortunes of the High Church party,

a minority attempting to coerce the principal forces in the nation, became identified with the cause of personal despotism and with the royal attempt to be rid of Parliament. The Laudian clergy preached up the doctrine of divine right and prerogative power. To crush Laud's opponents, recourse was often had to the reserves of royal authority in the Star Chamber and the Ecclesiastical High Commission: the Star Chamber, once popular under the Tudors, incurred the furious hatred of the Londoners for its cruel 1637
punishment of Prynne and Lilburne. The Puritans, on the other hand, became more than ever Parliament men, looking forward to the time when circumstances would compel Charles to summon the two Houses: all their hopes lay in the thought that –

> That two-handed engine at the door
> Stands ready to smite once and smite no more.

The political connexion of the two religious parties with King and Parliament respectively, though dictated in each case by the pressure of circumstances, was in each case a natural alliance. The authoritarian element in religion to which Laud gave renewed prominence had affinities to regal absolutism, and Parliamentary power in the State answered to the popular control of the Church, whether Presbyterian or Congregational. Between these two parties in Church and State floated indefinite masses of moderate opinion, which were frequently to decide the balance of power in the great years now coming on.

Thomas Wentworth, afterwards Earl of Strafford, had been an active member of the House of Commons in opposition to Buckingham, whose weak and mischievous rule he abhorred. But while he felt acutely the evils of royal favouritism, he did not in his heart believe that an assembly of 500 elected persons could govern a great kingdom. Besides, he was ambitious, and thought himself more fit to rule than either Parliament or Buckingham. He who had supported the Petition of Right spent the rest of his life in trying to subvert its principles. He planned to give Britain such a royal administration as Richelieu was then giving to France and as Bismarck long afterwards gave to Germany. If this great man had been Charles' chief Minister during the years when Laud was his chief ecclesiastical adviser, he might have found means to build up an army and a bureaucracy dependent on the Crown, for lack of which the autocratic system collapsed at the first touch of determined resistance. Fortunately for the liberties of Great Britain, Wentworth only became Charles' right-

1639 hand man when it was too late, after the Scots had risen with success and Englishmen had begun to realize how unanimous was their own discontent.

During the previous decade Wentworth had been employed by the King first as President of the Council of the North and then as ruler of Ireland. In these proconsular capacities he had shown a fine administrative vigour and a ruthless contempt for opinion and intolerance of all opposition; to this method he gave the name of 'Thorough', while others called it tyranny. In Ireland such fearless disrespect of persons might have been useful as the instrument of an enlightened policy. But his policy was enlightened only on its economic side. Otherwise his injustice alienated Catholics and Protestants alike.

1632 The native Irish, when he first came to rule the island, were already deeply embittered by the proscription of their religion and by the land policy of successive governments, who had handed over more and more of their soil to British landlords. The great plantation of Ulster in James' reign – the only part of the English garrison system that survives to our own day – had fixed a colony of Londoners in the good town of Derry, and some thousands of hard-working Presbyterian Scots on lands whence the Irish had been cleared. The Scots from across the narrow seas – some of whose ancestors had been in North Ireland long ago – formed the most stable part of British colonization there, because they were prepared to till the soil themselves, and not merely to exploit and rack-rent the tillers.

Wentworth harried the Protestants of Ulster for their sympathy with the Puritans of Britain, but he had not set out to propitiate the Irish Catholics. On the contrary, he planned new plantations in Connaught to deprive the natives of the lands which previous governments had left them. The fact that he ended by raising an Irish Catholic army to subdue Great Britain, certainly did not mean that he came a step nearer to solving the Irish problem than any other statesman of that century. The native Catholic rising of 1641, a terrible event in itself and yet more terrible in its consequences and its memory, was a measure of Wentworth's failure in Ireland.

Laud and Wentworth were close friends and allies, and laboured together to set up the Prerogative and its courts above Parliament and the Common Law. Laud, on his translation to Canterbury, had written to Wentworth that the Church was overmuch 'bound up in the forms of Common Law', and his friend had replied:

'No such narrow considerations shall fall in my counsels as my own preservation, till I see my master's power and greatness set out of wardship and above the exposition of Sir Edward Coke and his Year-Books, and I am most assured the same resolution governs in your lordship. Let us then in the name of God go cheerfully and boldly. . . . And thus you have my Thorough and Thorough.'

CHAPTER II

England and Scotland. The Scottish Revolt. The Long Parliament. The Great Civil War. Oliver Cromwell. Revival of Sea-power.

THE divergent courses which the Reformation had followed in England and in Scotland respectively, did much to complicate the politics of the succeeding era, when the rule of a single King over both countries constantly pointed towards ecclesiastical union that was, in fact, always impossible.

At the Reformation the laity on both sides of the Border had asserted their will against the medieval clergy, but in two very different ways. In England the Church had kept the outline of its ancient organization, remaining purely clerical in its internal structure; it followed that the control of the laity over its liturgy and doctrine had to be exercised not from within but from without, through Crown and through Parliament. In Scotland, on the other hand, the laity took an active part in Church organization and government. Only so could there be any control of religion by the laity, because they had no real Parliament to speak for them, and in the days of Mary Stuart they could not trust the Crown as contemporary Englishmen trusted Elizabeth. The Scottish nobles had indeed helped to overthrow the old religion; but the new religion had been fashioned, not from outside by the Crown or nobles, but from inside the Church by a democracy of ministers and laymen.

It was natural, therefore, that the English, whether Royalists or Parliamentarians, Anglicans or Puritans, should be Erastian in the sense that they wished the State to control the Church. It was equally natural that the Scottish Presbyterian party wished the Church to control the State. In these circumstances neither the Stuart Kings nor their enemies ever succeeded in imposing a uniform religious settlement on the whole island.

In those days, when the idea and practice of representation

were still at an early stage of development, the English were most nearly represented by their ancient Parliament, and the Scots by their novel Church. But this difference of the position at the two ends of the island was not understood by the rulers of Britain. James I, having been brought up in Scotland, had supposed that the English Parliament, like the Scottish, existed to obey the Privy Council. His son Charles, having been brought up in England, made the corresponding error of supposing that the Scottish Church could, like the English, be moulded by royal command. Confident in the power he had recently assumed as autocratic ruler of England, and knowing that the Parliament of Edinburgh was of no account, he deceived himself into supposing that he could act as absolute monarch in Scotland, even in matters of religion. His attempt to impose Laud's English Prayer Book on the Scottish Church at the very moment when he was trying to get rid of the English Parliament, outraged both nations at once, each at the point where it was strongest and most susceptible, and broke his power in both Kingdoms.

The revolt against Charles and Laud north of the Tweed took the form of a religious Covenant, and of action by the Church Assembly; the nation had to be organized on an ecclesiastical basis, because organs of political life were lacking in Scotland. This state of things naturally tempted the Church, after she had liberated the country from a foreign yoke, to claim practical control of the State and to show a most ugly temper of interference and intolerance. This in turn enabled Charles I and Charles II after him to rally the Scottish Cavalier party, in the days of Montrose and of Claverhouse, to resist the tyranny of religion. Against it the Cavaliers of the Restoration erected the tyranny of the Privy Council. The terrible feuds of the Scottish factions went on with many vicissitudes, till the Revolution settlement of 1689 established Presbyterianism as the national religion, but made it the subordinate partner of the State.

In Stuart England, where the Church never aspired to independence of the State, the religious quarrel lay between Crown and Parliament. One part of the English people demanded, through Parliament, to have the Church made purely Protestant in its services, and more representative of the laity in its internal structure. The Crown resisted this demand, backed by another part of the nation zealous for the Prayer Book, though by no means for the whole of Laud's politico-ecclesiastical system. This situation forced to the front a question that men had begun to ask themselves under Elizabeth: if Crown and Parliament disagreed, which had the right to remodel the Church of England? That was one issue fought out in the English Civil War. The other was the purely political question – is Crown or Parliament to nominate the executive and control the armed force? In practice the two issues were inseparable; to take a side on one involved taking the corresponding side on the other.

The Scottish revolt of 1638–40 began the British Revolution. Until the Scots had successfully defied Charles, in arms upon their own Border, there had been no signs of resistance in England, though many of discontent. For Stuart England had no centres of opposition except Parliament, which was in abeyance. English feudalism was dead and buried. Harry Percy's spur was cold. The squires as a class were the most peaceful and law-abiding of men – agriculturists, sportsmen, sometimes lawyers, but very seldom soldiers. The King, it is true, had no army to enforce his will, but the habit of obedience to the Crown was the great inheritance from the Tudor age. It had been the custom in medieval England for districts or persons with a grievance against government to rise in arms, but that tradition had not survived the reign of Elizabeth. If, therefore, the modern English were deprived of Parliament, they would be slaves to absolute power as their ancestors had never been before.

Scotland supplied what England no longer possessed, a rough and hardy population, accustomed to take up arms in their own defence. The two nations were the complement one of the other. The Scots could boast of no independent political institutions, no habit of obedience to good laws; the English had so long enjoyed peace under Parliament and the Common Law that they were slow to defend their privileges with the sword. England was neither feudal nor democratic; the fighting spirit of Scotland was composed of both those elements, formidably interfused.

Until very recent times every burgher and peasant in Scotland had possessed weapons which he was accustomed to employ in racial war or private broil, and along the Highland Line these habits still prevailed. Everywhere the nobles and leading gentry of Scotland, like those of England in the Wars of the Roses, still had retainers and tenants accustomed to follow them to war. In 1638 these feudal chiefs stood for the Kirk against the Crown. They had been alienated by Laud, under whose influence nobles had been superseded by Bishops on the Scottish Privy Council, and lay possessors of former Church lands had been threatened with resumption. Moreover, the nobles were true Scots, and the young Montrose himself took a leading part in armed resistance to the English-hearted King and his Prayer Book.

When Parliament was not sitting, the English were like sheep without a shepherd, but in Scotland the Church supplied a ready-made organization for political activity in every parish. It was the people themselves who had made the original Reformation by the strong hand, and it was all in the national tradition to defend it now by the same means. The Covenant with God was renewed in 1638 and embraced all ranks from highest to lowest. In every parish men signed it, weeping and lifting their right hands to heaven. When the Scots display emotion, something real is astir within them. Indeed the country had not been so moved since the days of Wallace and Bruce.

The Church Assembly at Glasgow, to which the lay members came up armed and attended, defied the King as the Long Parliament in England defied him four years later. When he dissolved the Assembly, it sat on, declared Episcopacy abolished and restored the full Presbyterian government of the Church. The action of the Glasgow Assembly was supported by the Earl of Argyle, the head of the Campbells, the most powerful fighting clan in the Highlands. That day he began the connexion of his House with the Presbyterian and popular cause in the Lowlands, an alliance which for more than a century to come remained a constant and often a determining factor in Scottish history. Thenceforth till the time of Culloden the clans hostile to the Campbells gravitated for that reason towards the party of the Stuart Kings.

Not the least of the causes that wrought Charles' downfall was this: Scotland, still as poor as a thin soil and medieval methods of agriculture could make her, and still without any considerable trade either with England or across the sea, sent forth in those days her most adventurous sons to serve abroad, not then as cashiers and foremen throughout a far-flung British Empire, but as captains and ancients in the armies of Gustavus Adolphus and other Protestant champions on the continent. These men came swarming home, eager to employ their professional skill in saving their native land from English outrage. Their leader was 'that old, little, crooked soldier', Alexander Leslie. He and they speedily put a face of disciplined war on the enthusiasm of the Scots, and camped them advantageously on
1639 Dunse Law, ready to dispute against Charles the passage of the Tweed.

The England of the pacific James and his son had bred few

'men of war': Englishmen lived at home on the fat of the land, or traded oversea, or emigrated to America. There was no nucleus of a standing army, and failure attended the belated efforts of Charles and Strafford to provide, without money and from a disaffected and unwarlike people, a force to match the army of the Covenant.

Wentworth, who was at length made Earl of Strafford, had been called over to England to be his master's right-hand man at this crisis. But he did not cease to act as ruler of Ireland, where he continued to harry the Scots of Ulster with persecution to enforce on them the 'Black Oath' of passive obedience unknown to the law. At the same time he raised regiments of Celtic Irish to coerce the King's disobedient subjects in either island, the first of a series of Roman Catholic armies whose threatening shadow from oversea so often prejudiced the cause of the House of Stuart, without ever striking a formidable blow for it in Britain.

As yet the general temper of England had found no means of expression. Strafford guessed it wrongly. He advised Charles to summon Parliament, in the hope that it would tamely provide the money to subdue Scotland. The 'Short Parliament', however, revealed the unanimity of English discontent, and was peremptorily dismissed, but not before Pym had spoken on the floor of the House the memorable words: 'The powers of Parliament are to the body politic as the rational faculties of the soul to man.' 13 Apl–5 May 1640

The Short Parliament had been summoned to vote taxes to fight the Scots; the Long Parliament was called to buy them out of the country. But redress of grievances would certainly have to precede supply, and in the autumn of 1640 redress of grievances meant a revolution of undefined scope in Church and State. Nov. 1640

The Long Parliament was not destined to prove, as half its members hoped, a turning-point in English religion comparable to the Tudor Reformation, though it did clear the way for the great incident in English religious history – the Puritan Revolution, the parent of the Free Churches of later times. On the other hand, the Long Parliament is the true turning-point in the political history of the English-speaking races. It not only prevented the English monarchy from hardening into an absolutism of the type then becoming general in Europe, but it made a great experiment in direct rule of the country and of the Empire by the House of Commons. In the course of that experiment the Long Parliament successfully organized the largest military operations ever till then conducted by Englishmen, in a four years' war against the King. After the victory it failed to make a permanent settlement at home, but it made England feared and honoured abroad. After all those memorable years, the House of Stuart might be restored, but it would never again be possible to govern the country without the participation of the House of Commons.

In all the actions of the Long Parliament it was the Commons who led, and the Lords who followed with ever-growing reluctance. We have then to ask, how did a debating assembly, which under the Tudors had passed the Bills drawn up by Privy Councillors of the Crown, and since Elizabeth's death had acted only as an opposition – how did an assembly so numerous, so plebeian, and so inexperienced succeed in taking hold of the helm of State and riding the most terrible storm in English history?

One reason why the House of Commons was able to assume the government of the country has, until recently, attracted less attention than its importance deserves. The late Tudor and early Stuart Parliaments had made great progress in forms of procedure, especially by developing the Committee system. In 1640 the Lower House was no mere debating society, but an elaborately organized business body of the modern type, capable of conducting affairs as no medieval House of Commons could possibly have done. For forty years past, Parliaments had no longer been content to have their work prepared for them by Privy Councillors, but had thrashed out subjects for themselves in committee, and so learnt to produce practical Bills and policies of their own.

In the second place the Long Parliament had at its doors an enthusiastic ally, London, already the first city in the world, surpassing any other English town many times over in wealth, population, and mental activity. It was in the London of these eventful years that Milton, the greatest of Londoners born, had his vision of England as 'an eagle mewing her mighty youth', as 'a noble and puissant nation rousing herself like a strong man after sleep and shaking her invincible locks'. London was the nursery of almost every movement of that time, in whatever part of the country it had first seen light; and 'correspondency with London' was alleged as the reason why the Roundhead party dominated most of the boroughs of England during the Civil War. Some may think that the effervescence of London's wit and passion drew Parliament down strange and questionable courses, but none can deny that the protection which it gave to the Houses was faithful and effective.

And, lastly, there were upon the benches in 1640 members of

old experience, who had sat with Eliot and Coke in committee and debate, some of whom chanced to be men of high ability, character, and courage. Pym, perhaps the strongest Parliamentary leader in history, and Hampden, the best-beloved in that choice assembly of England's best, backed by members of the type and temper of Strode and Cromwell, were not afraid to seize and wield the power of the State. The time for mere criticism had passed, and the insufficiency of Charles' signature to Statutes had been proved. Since the struggle now was for power, these men did not shrink from evoking mob passion and armed force to protect what they did from the royal reaction which had destroyed the work of every previous Stuart Parliament.

During the first session of the Long Parliament, Pym and Nov.
Hampden worked in alliance with Hyde and Falkland, a couple 1640–Aug.
not unlike to themselves in ability, character, and destiny. It is 1641
hard to say which pair of friends had in the end the most influence on the evolution of modern Britain. The 'constitutional Cavaliers' of 1642 were in 1640 as determined as the future Roundheads to bring about the fall of Strafford, and to abolish the Star Chamber, the High Commission, and the whole Prerogative system. All were opposed to Laud, who was committed to the Tower after impeachment by the unanimous vote of the Lower House, but members were early made aware of differences among themselves on religion, and were glad to postpone the settlement of the Church till the State had first been made safe.

The work of this session, so far as it extended, was built upon the rock. It was never undone, for it was work of Puritans and moderate Episcopalians, of Roundheads, and constitutional Cavaliers acting in union. It registered the great irreversible victory of 'Sir Edward Coke and his Year-Books' over Strafford and the Prerogative Courts. The Star Chamber, the High Commission, the prerogative jurisdiction of the Councils of Wales and of the North were abolished by State, and the illegality of Ship Money and Tonnage and Poundage without Parliamentary sanction was declared beyond all cavil. Thus was the Crown put back, to use Strafford's phrase, into 'wardship' to the Common Law, and made dependent on, though not necessarily subordinate to, Parliament. The first session struck an exact balance of the constitution, the same which was restored in 1660 by Hyde, the great Common Lawyer, who believed in a precise counterpoise of Crown and Parliament. Pym, on the other hand, believed that the essential power must pass on to Parliament, or mere confusion would prevail.

The other work of the first session was the trial, attainder, and execution of Strafford. In that high tragedy, unsurpassed for historical and human interest in the political annals of any time or land, Falkland and many of the future Cavaliers acted in union with Hampden and Pym. They held it necessary that the man should die who might yet, by his vigour and genius, restore the despotic powers of the Crown. Already the King was engaged in the Army Plot to rescue Strafford and dissolve Parliament. The first thing to be expected, if Strafford lived, was that as soon as Parliament was up, Charles would let him out of prison and restore him to office. So argued the Earl of Essex, typical of many members of the Upper House who feared a restoration of Strafford's insolent personal hegemony over the nobles of the land; the Earl's conclusion was that 'stone dead hath no fellow'. It was not a policy of mean revenge, like that which four years later sent Laud to the scaffold. Strafford's enemies were in deadly earnest, because while he lived they and all they strove for were in jeopardy. They did not scruple at the last to allow mob violence to extort Charles' signature to the Act of Attainder by which his great servant perished.

May 1641

With the Act of Attainder against Strafford, the King passed another Bill which forbade the dissolution of the existing Parliament without its own consent. These two measures, the first of them the bitterest humiliation of Charles' life, seemed to make the position of Parliament secure. And so it would have been, but for the religious difference which in the second session split into two hostile parties the hitherto solid phalanx of the constitutionalists. In the Commons the Puritans won, by small majorities, divisions in favour of the Root and Branch Bill abolishing episcopacy, and the Grand Remonstrance. The Grand Remonstrance demanded that the King's Councillors should be persons trusted by Parliament, and that there should be a Parliamentary reformation of the Church, on what may be described as Erastian-Presbyterian principles. It is easy now to see that the times required a compromise on religion, and that England had outgrown any orthodox strait-waistcoat which could be devised by either party. Unfortunately, it was not clear then, and no serious effort was made by Puritan or Anglican either for comprehension within, or for toleration without, the borders of the Church. Moderate Episcopalians devoted to the Prayer Book, like Falkland and Hyde, saw no way of defending their religion but to go into complete opposition to Hampden and Pym.

Nov. 1641

The religious question decided the attitude of many towards

the command of the armed forces of the Kingdom – the other great problem of the second session. Was King or Parliament to control the militia of the towns and shires, and the regular army which must forthwith be raised to suppress the rebellion in Ireland? For the Catholics there had risen to recover their lands; the Ulster plantation and the whole English interest were in the direst jeopardy, and some thousands of Protestants had perished. Law and custom assigned the command of the armed forces to the King. But if Charles had the power of the sword and Parliament had not, how much longer would he respect the concessions he had recently made? He himself answered the question by his rash and illegal attempt to arrest Pym, Hampden, Hazlerigg, Holles, and Strode on the floor of the House of Commons, which might well have been stained with blood that day by the bravoes Charles had brought with him to 'pull them out by the ears', had not the Five Members received warning and been carried by boat from Parliament stairs to the safe shelter of the City and its trainbands.

Oct. 1641

4 Jan. 1642

Charles fled to the North, leaving London and Westminster to be the focus of his enemies' power and authority. Civil war was certain, and men began to choose their side, some with enthusiasm, many with dubious sighs and searchings of heart, while the majority manifested a strong desire to remain neutral if they possibly could.

Was it then impossible for Parliamentary power to take root in England at a less cost than this national schism and appeal to force, which, in spite of many magnificent incidents, left England humanly so much the poorer and less noble in twenty years' time? It is a question which no depth of research or speculation can resolve. Men were what they were, uninfluenced by the belated wisdom of posterity, and thus they acted. Whether or not any better way could have led to the same end, it was by the sword that Parliament actually won the right to survive as the dominant force in the English constitution.

In the end the King lost the war for lack of money. The parts of England that owned his authority were on the average less wealthy than those which defied him. His headquarters were in Oxford, a small city more famous for learning than for wealth, a poor substitute for London left in the hands of his enemies. The rustic gentlemen who offered him their lives, their swords, their horses, and their plate, could not easily realize their land until it came under the hammer within the Roundhead lines as sequestrated property. And if Charles got freewill offerings, so did

Parliament. For Puritan squires and shopkeepers also had silver plate in abundance, and

> Into pikes and musqueteers
> Stampt beakers, cups, and porringers.

Parliament, no less than the King, could call on gentlemen to raise private regiments, like Hampden's Green Coats. In these appeals to individual generosity the two sides were on equal terms, and that was how the war was begun. But the Roundheads had more staying power because they could do what the King could not – negotiate loans in the City, and place regular taxes on the trade of England and on its richest districts. To pay for the Civil War, the Long Parliament introduced excise duties on goods, and an improved assessment for taxes on land and property, far more profitable to the public and far less unjust as between individuals than the happy-go-lucky assessment for the old 'subsidy'. In the ordinances of the Long Parliament we find the germ of our modern fiscal system. The resources of England, which had been grudgingly doled out to Elizabeth and denied to James and Charles, were first exploited by Parliament in the war fought upon its own behalf.

The sea was held by the King's enemies. The Royal Navy revolted to 'King Pym'. The seaports made a present to Parliament of the mercantile marine. The overseas trade of England was carried on to increase the wealth of rebels, while Charles had difficulty even in importing arms from abroad. The excise levied by Parliament was largely paid for by the higher prices which upland Cavaliers had to find for articles that had been taxed in Roundhead manufacturing centres and seaports.

If Parliament could at once have translated these financial advantages into military terms, the war would not have lasted long, and would have been won by the original Parliamentary party under Pym, Hampden, and Essex, without any need on their part to purchase the embarrassing help either of Covenanted Scots or of East Anglian Sectaries. In that case the history of England would have taken some totally different course. But it was not to be.

The Cavaliers, though starting at a great disadvantage, rapidly improved their position, largely through the adaptability of the hard-riding squires to cavalry warfare, and the military talent of the King's young nephew, Prince Rupert, trained in continental campaigns. But a still better cavalry leader, who had also the instincts of a great general, arose on the Parliament side. Oliver Cromwell, though with no previous military experience, became the leader of the English Sectaries, whom he drilled into the famous Ironsides, combining discipline with religious enthusiasm in a formidable manner. These individualists objected as much to the imposition of Presbyterian as of Anglican orthodoxy. In Milton's words – 'New Presbyter is but old Priest writ large.'

Marston Moor (1644), the battle that destroyed the Cavalier power in the North, was won by a combination of Scottish Presbyterians with Cromwell's East Anglian Sectaries. In the following winter Parliament made a New Model Army, regularly paid and organized for long-time service as no large force on either side had yet been. The money power of Parliament was at length coming fully into play, while the King's unpaid supporters took more and more to plunder. The Scots, kept busy at home by Montrose's gallant campaign, faded out of the English scene for a while. At Naseby (June 1645) the New Model Army, under Fairfax and Cromwell, broke the last of the King's field armies. And in the next twelve months the towns, castles, and manor houses that still held out for him, were reduced by the cannon and siege trains of the well-equipped 'New Model'.

The victory was completed in 1646, and the victors at once began to fall out among themselves. Parliament, no longer controlled by men of the calibre of Pym and Hampden, both of whom were dead, proceeded to act with consummate folly. The House of Commons refused to promise religious toleration to the armed Sectaries who had won the war, and would not even give them their due arrears of pay. The consequent quarrel of Parliament and Army encouraged Charles and his adherents to foment a second Civil War (1648) with the aid of the Presbyterian Scots. The attempt, though it was speedily crushed at Preston by the military genius of Cromwell, had enraged the men of prayer and iron at whose feet Parliament and country now lay prostrate. After coercing and 'purging' the 'Rump' at the House of Commons, they brought the King to trial before an illegal tribunal, and cut off his head before the Banqueting House at Whitehall on 30 January 1649.

The revulsion of feeling in favour of the King, which began during his trial and execution, and swelled to such vast proportions as years went by, was largely due to the fact that he suffered as the champion of the laws which his enemies were breaking and of the ancient institutions which they were destroying. Apart from the personal aspect of the scene, with its overmastering appeal in favour of 'the royal actor' who played his part with sincere and simple dignity, the conservative instincts of the English nation were rudely outraged. They felt that they were being carried beyond the historic current of English life into uncharted seas. It was an adventure they had not bargained for. This Republicanism, what was it? The rule of preaching colonels apparently. And yet for many years to come, the men, and in particular the man, who had seized power through means of the Army but in the name of an unconscious and bewildered 'people of England', had the courage and genius to govern, making out of an utterly impossible situation something not ignoble, and in some important respects very profitable for the future growth of Great Britain and its Empire.

The decisive factor in the triangular contest between King, Parliament, and Army had been Oliver Cromwell. As early as 1647, while he was still a back-bench Member of Parliament, and not yet in name the supreme commander of the Army, his force of character made him in effect 'our chief of men'.

King, Parliament, and Army each had an *idée fixe* and consequently they could not agree. Cromwell, who was pre-eminently an opportunist – 'none goes so far', he once said, 'as he who knows not whither he is going' – could easily have supplied them with a dozen possible solutions if they had been ready to listen to reason. Far the best solution propounded by anyone was Sept. 1647 the 'Heads of the Proposals', made by Cromwell and Ireton to Charles, based on wide toleration, the use of the Prayer Book in Church by those who wished, Bishops without coercive power, and a stop to the sequestration of Cavalier estates. But the King was only playing at negotiation, and neither Army nor Parliament had any thought of so liberal a treatment of the conquered. Cromwell and Ireton were speaking for themselves and common sense alone. They found that they must either march with the Army or perish. Cromwell underwent one of those sharp revulsions, accompanied by repentance, and prayer so timely that his enemies miscalled them hypocrisy.

The riddle of Oliver must be read not in his mutable opinions but in his constant character. His moderation and his dislike of force were often counteracted by his instinct at every cost to find a practical solution for the problem of the moment; if agreement failed, as it often does in revolutionary times, then, however reluctantly, he would cut the Gordian knot, for the nation's government must be carried on. Moreover, although common sense was the dominating quality of his intellect, it worked in an atmosphere of temperamental enthusiasm which left him no doubts or fears when once he had reached a conclusion after weeks of brooding hesitation. For his final resolve, when at last it emerged, always seemed to him the inspiration of God. God spoke in the victories of each successive war, pointing – whither-soever Cromwell's latest thoughts were leading him. When, therefore, he learnt at last that all his efforts to find an accommodation with the King had been wasted time, the fanatical mood of the Army about 'the man Charles Stuart' took possession of him. When he found also that England must be ruled for a while through the soldiers or slide into anarchy, he felt the glow of the Republican faith in which so many of his men returned from the victory at Preston, although it was not so much his settled conviction as the apparent necessity of the moment. Ten years later he was veering round again to constitutional kingship – in his own person this time – in order to get rid of military rule and put himself in line with the strongest current of thought of that day, ebbing back towards conservative and civil legality. For always this strong swimmer must ride on the crest of the wave. How many more successive waves would he have ridden, if death had not put an end to his titanic strife with circumstance?

Cromwell was not the only able and public-spirited man who had pushed his way to the front of the Roundhead side, under the double impulse of the emotional turmoil of the time and the number of careers opened to talent by civil war and revolution. The era of Vane, Blake, Ireton, Monk, and of Milton as pamphleteer and secretary, was an era of great public servants, worthy to be dignified by the name of 'Commonwealth'. The Regicide government, consisting partly of army officers and partly of members of the 'Rump' or minority which 'Pride's purge' had made supreme in Parliament, were neither poltroons nor blind fanatics. The position in which they found themselves on the last day of January 1649 was one which must have speedily led to their own ruin and the dissolution of the British Empire, had they not been men above the common in cool-headed courage. The state of public opinion, strongly alienated from them but divided against itself, rendered impossible the appeal to a free election, which their democratic theories demanded but their sense of responsibility and self-preservation forbade. Wherever they looked, the prospect was dark in the extreme. Their authority was denied, not only by Cavaliers and Presbyterians, but by radical democrats like John Lilburne, who at that time had a great popular following. The Navy was paralysed by mutiny; the Royalist privateers under Prince Rupert held the seas; Scotland and Ireland were in arms for the younger Charles; Virginia and Barbados repudiated the authority of the usurpers; Massachusetts, though not unfriendly, had since the beginning of the troubles in England acted as if it were an independent State. Holland, France, Spain, and all the continental powers regarded the regicides as pariahs and England as a cypher. Yet in four years the Council of State had overcome these dangers with the help of Cromwell's sword and Blake's broadsides, before resort was had to the final stage of the revolutionary government, the Protectorate of Oliver.

The first step in the reconstitution of the British Empire by the Republican Government was the subjugation of Ireland. It was rendered easier for Cromwell and his army because the Protestants over there, whatever their political allegiance, tended to rally round him as the champion of their race and creed, while

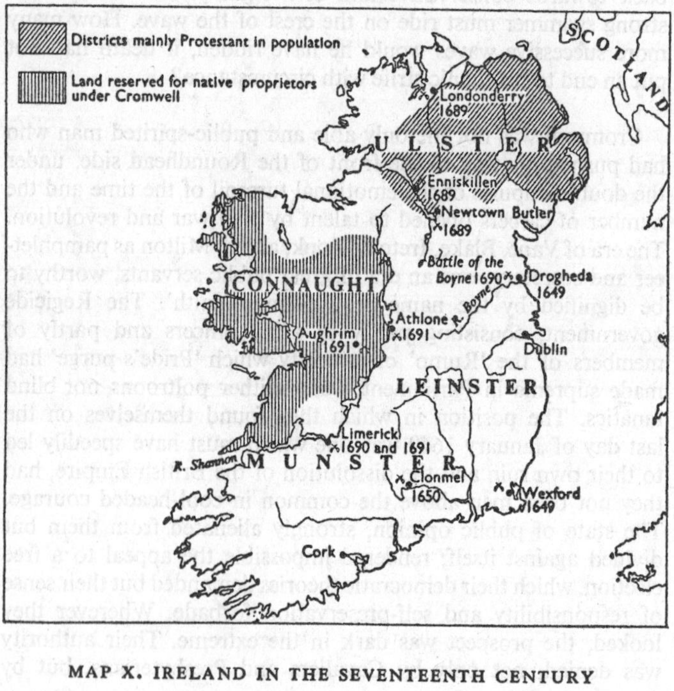

MAP X. IRELAND IN THE SEVENTEENTH CENTURY

the Irish resistance became racial and Catholic instead of Royalist. After the fall of Drogheda, Wexford, and Clonmel had broken 1649–50 the back of resistance in the East, Cromwell went home, leaving Ireton to carry on the guerrilla war of Celt and Saxon in the West to its bitter end.

The land settlement in Ireland, by far the worst part of Cromwell's constructive work within the British islands, was the part that outlived him substantially in the form he gave it. It completed the transference of the soil from Irish to British proprietors, which had been begun under the Tudors and pushed forward under the Stuart Kings. The object was threefold: to pay off in Irish land the soldiers who had fought and the capitalists who had provided the money for the conquest, in the manner in which the veterans of Caesar and of William the Conqueror had been rewarded; secondly, to render the English hold upon Ireland secure against another rebellion like that of 1641, even after the army should be disbanded; and lastly, to extirpate Catholicism. The first two objects were attained.

Ireland west of Shannon was reserved for native proprietors. The rest of the island passed to Protestant landlords. The idea of driving the whole Celtic population beyond the Shannon was entertained but not executed. The natives remained for the most part on their farms as hewers of wood and drawers of water to the new alien landowners, who rack-rented them, according to Irish custom, without being obliged to make the improvements and repairs customary in English tenancies.

In Ulster alone had the tenant some protection, and in Ulster alone the population was largely British and Protestant, on account of the immigration of hard-working Scots from the neighbouring coast beginning from the time of James I's plantation. Elsewhere in Ireland, those of Cromwell's private soldiers who were planted out as yeomen failed to preserve their religion and nationality, because they were too widely scattered and were cut off by social barriers from the Protestant gentry. Some of the yeomen threw up their farms, while others intermarried with the natives, with the result that their descendants brought Saxon and Ironside qualities to stiffen the Celtic and Catholic resistance. The landlords were left isolated in their power and privilege, until the end began with Gladstone's Land Bills and Parnell's Land League.

In Ireland as Oliver left it and as it long remained, the persecuted priests were the only leaders of the people because the English had destroyed the class of native gentry. The

Cromwellian settlement rendered the Irish for centuries the most priest-led population in Europe.

Cromwell's next task was to reduce Scotland to the obedience of the Commonwealth. North of the Tweed there was no Sectarian or Republican party and, properly speaking, no Parliamentary party. The land was divided between a rigid ecclesiastical Presbyterianism, very different from the political Presbyterianism of England, and the Cavalier interest, which in Scotland was not Laudian but represented the rebellion of the nobility and others against the rule of the State by the Church. Presbyterian and Cavalier hated each other bitterly, for the blood shed in Montrose's wars flowed between them. But they patched up a hollow alliance
1650 round the person of Charles II, whom they proposed to restore
1651 by force of arms to his throne in England. Their plans were ruined at Dunbar and Worcester, the last and, militarily, the greatest victories of Cromwell's army on British soil –

> When up the armed mountains of Dunbar
> He marched, and through deep Severn, ending war.

The only sanction of Oliver's rule beyond the Tweed was the presence of the English army and, therefore, the arrangements he made could not be permanent. But the rule of the sword, so long as it lasted, enabled Oliver to carry through without compromise his own enlightened policy for the benefit of Scotland, whose internal feuds had at length subjected her to the great neighbour she had so often defied. He united the whole island in a single Commonwealth, and Scottish members sat in the British Parliaments held under the Protectorate. For the first time Scotland enjoyed the immense advantage of free trade with England and her markets beyond sea. Order was kept and justice administered without favour, as never before in her history. Even the Highlands were garrisoned and the clans kept in awe. The government was good, but, as in England, it was costly, and the taxes were burdensome and deeply resented.

The dignity and efficiency of the Scottish Presbyterian Church were preserved, while it was no longer permitted to persecute others or to domineer over the State. 'I verily believe,' a Scottish Presbyterian wrote of the Protectorate, 'there were more souls converted to Christ in that short time, than in any season since the Reformation though of triple its duration.' The English soldiers behaved irreproachably as an army of occupation, save when they endeavoured to found Baptist Churches in an uncongenial soil, or derided the discipline of the Kirk by seating themselves on the 'stools of repentance' during divine worship, to the displeasure of 'grave livers', and the untimely mirth of the youthful part of the congregation.

The Scots hailed the Restoration of Charles II in 1660 as the return of their own national independence. It was indeed the end of formal union with England and therewith of free trade, but national independence was not, in fact, recovered till the Revolution of 1688. Till then the feuds of the Scots among themselves made their country an easy prey to the schemes of one English government after another; and of these foreign governments, Oliver's was the first and very much the least bad.

Oliver as Protector realized his vision of the united British islands. Scotland and Ireland were joined to England in legislative and economic union, their members sitting in Parliament at Westminster, their traders selling and buying freely in the English market. So long as Oliver lived, the Protestant interest in Ireland was fostered and encouraged as a part of England herself. The Restoration broke up the union of the British Isles and saw the Protestant Irish sacrificed to English trade jealousy, and to Anglican revenge on the Presbyterian religion. Not all the woes of Ireland can be laid at Oliver's door.

To the Regicide Government belongs the credit of the revival of English sea-power, and the establishment of the Navy on a basis of permanent efficiency, which every subsequent government, whatever its political complexion, honestly endeavoured to maintain. The Council of State now consisted of the men who had won two civil wars; strong men selected from every class of the community by the test of deeds, men with soldierly and practical ways of regarding each situation as it arose, and in a position never enjoyed by the Stuart Kings of raising as much money as was needed by taxation. The revolt of a third of the navy, and its organization in foreign ports by Prince Rupert to avenge his uncle on the high seas, menaced the trade of London and of all England in the Channel as it had never been menaced during the Great Civil War. The men of the new government, aware that they must subdue this peril or perish, threw their energies and resources into naval organization. Their warlike training led them to infuse into the discipline and tactics of the fleet just that military element which was needed to complete the tradition of the English fighting navy. 'Their measures,' wrote Julian Corbett, 'transformed the Navy to its modern scope and established England as the great naval power of the world.' But they would not have succeeded in so doing had they not, in a fortunate hour for England, called Robert Blake to command the fleets of the Commonwealth.

Blake, in the eyes of modern naval historians, stands as a third with Drake and Nelson. The record of his eight years of admiralty afloat, his innumerable and successful actions with all kinds of enemies – with Rupert, with the Barbary pirates of Tunis, with the greatest fleets and admirals the Dutch ever sent to sea, with the French and with the Spaniards who had so long despised us – gave to the British Navy the place which it aspired to attain under Elizabeth, lost under the early Stuarts, and never after Blake's day more than momentarily relinquished. The acceptance of the Blake tradition at sea by the Cavalier and Tory party after the Restoration, while Cromwell's militarism on land was violently rejected on account of its political associations, is one of the governing facts of modern British history.

Blake himself was bred a sailor less than either Drake or
1649–57 Nelson. As the son of a wealthy trader of Bridgwater, he was well acquainted with the merchant shipping of the Parret estuary and the Bristol Channel; but he had tried to become an Oxford don, and had succeeded in becoming a fine Puritan soldier. The defence against overwhelming odds, first of Lyme Regis and afterwards of Taunton, which Blake organized when the Cavaliers swept over the south-west in the Great Civil War, stood out among the finest deeds of the Puritan spirit in arms. But he himself was more of a public servant than a zealot. When called, a few days after the execution of the King, to take command of the fleet and recover for the English marine the lost freedom of the sea, he obeyed marvelling. Doubtless he had been chosen because his knowledge of ships and seamen was at least greater than that of other soldiers. From that moment forward, his genius blazed out his path of victory upon the waters.

Rupert, fine soldier, and fine sailor as he was, had the ill-fortune to meet Cromwell on land and Blake at sea. Blake blockaded him in the Irish ports, chased him to Portugal and out of it, and thence to the Mediterranean, where the bulk of the Cavalier fleet was destroyed. In these operations of civil war, English naval power was, for the first time, successfully introduced into the Mediterranean, to the astonishment and dismay of France, Spain, and the Italian Princes. Taught by Blake's successes there in pursuit of Rupert, Oliver a few years later sent him again to the inland sea, not only to defend our merchants there, but to add weight to the elaborate diplomacy of the Protectorate. Thenceforward, British sea-power in the Mediterranean has remained an important factor in world history.

The revival of the fighting navy under Blake, and the government of the State by a class of men closely in touch with the mercantile community and especially with London, inevitably led to renewed rivalry with the Dutch. For a generation past, the mariners of Holland had lorded it, often insolently enough, in the seas of Northern Europe and America, and in the African and Indian oceans, and had poached the fisheries and almost monopolized the carrying trade of England and her American colonies. The serious revival of English competition was marked by the Navigation Act of 1651, and the Dutch War of 1652–4. But the struggle against Dutch maritime supremacy was not decided till the early Eighteenth Century. It was not an act, but a process, of which the first conscious beginnings are visible under the Commonwealth.

Navigation Acts, to set a limit to foreign shipping in English ports, had been passed by English Parliaments as long ago as the reign of Richard II, but owing to the scarcity of English shipping it had not been possible to enforce them. There was, therefore, nothing new in the principle of the Act of 1651, and there was equally nothing new in the failure to enforce it strictly. Nevertheless, it expressed a new spirit of revolt against Dutch supremacy, and henceforth there was at least a continuous effort of enforcement, because there were many more English ships than in former times. When the Restoration Government took New York from Holland, it removed a base of Dutch maritime activity in America and so helped to put the principle into practice in the ports of New England.

The naval war of the Commonwealth against Holland arose 1652–4
out of a number of incidents in the rivalry of the two maritime communities. It cannot be attributed to one cause alone, except indeed to mutual jealousy. It was a battle of Titans, Blake against Van Tromp, commanding the two greatest fleets in the world, already little inferior to the fleets of the Nile and Trafalgar in their ship construction and the technical skill of their crews. Holland suffered more than England, because she had fewer resources on land and now, for the first time since she had become a nation, found a hostile power blocking the Channel against the merchant fleets that brought her life and wealth from afar. The greater staying power of England was clearly indicated in this first round.

The war against Holland was more popular in the City than

in the army, and Cromwell desired Protestant cooperation throughout the world. One of his first acts as Protector was to make peace with the Dutch on good terms for England.

But Oliver's direct rule failed to bring the immunity from foreign war which alone could have given his domestic system any chance of financial stability and ultimate popularity. His Protestantism and his desire to help English traders and colonists all the world over, led him into a quarrel with Spain. He revived the claim of Elizabethan Englishmen to trade with the Spanish colonies and to be entirely free from the power of the Inquisition. The Spanish Ambassador replied that this was to ask 'his master's two eyes'. Perpetual hostilities were taking place between the Spanish forces and the English colonists, traders, and buccaneers of the West Indian Archipelago, which Spain regarded as her own in spite of English settlements in so many of the islands. Oliver lent to the English of the West Indies the powerful aid of the mother country. He sent out an expedition which, though it
1655 failed at Hispaniola, captured Jamaica. This proved the most important single step in the enlargement of that West Indian island Empire which, for a century and a half to come, held so prominent a place in British trade, diplomacy, and war.

As a factor in European politics Cromwellian England was feared and respected, but achieved nothing great. The protection of the Vaudois was a noble gesture, worthy of the finest sonnet ever written by a political secretary, and was very well managed as a diplomatic feat; but it was not very important.
1655–58 The war with Spain, which was really a trans-Atlantic quarrel, did little good in Europe either to England or to Protestantism. There was glory, no doubt, in Blake's destruction of the Spanish fleet under the forts of Tenerife, where Nelson afterwards lost an arm, and there was pride in the storming of the slippery sand-dunes near Dunkirk by the red-coated infantry with the army of our French allies looking on in admiration. But the perennial British interest in the Balance of Power in Europe demanded no such vigorous interference, for the balance then stood adjusted without Cromwell's heavy weight in the scale. Spain had already decayed and France had not yet grown to any dangerous height. The Thirty Years' War was finished and, for the time, no opportunities existed for a new Gustavus Adolphus. If Oliver had been on the scene with his army and his fleet in 1618 or in 1630 or again from 1670 onwards, something notable might have been achieved. In 1654 the man was there, but the hour had passed, or not yet come. History is made up of coincidences or their absence.

On the top of the expenses of the Dutch war, the Spanish war increased the burden of taxation on the country and gravely injured its prosperity and trade. Oliver's militarism and imperialism became increasingly unpopular, not only for political reasons, but because they cost too much. That one should be forced to give a large part of one's property yearly to the tax-gatherer, though accepted as a normal condition of life to-day, seemed then an intolerable outrage. Yet, in spite of the heavy taxes, the sale of Crown and episcopal lands, the fines on 'malignants', and the confiscation of half the soil of Ireland, Oliver died in debt. From the point of view of finance alone a change of system was necessary, which would enable the army to be disbanded. But the army could not be disbanded unless some way could be found leading back to government by consent. Oliver spent his last years in the search for that way, but he had lost it, and was doomed to bear his load through the wilderness to the end.

The same arts that did gain
A power must it maintain,

wrote Andrew Marvell, the lesser but not the less shrewd of the Protector's two poet secretaries.

Oliver, unlike Strafford and others who have 'broken Parliaments', believed to the last in the necessity for Parliamentary rule. And unlike others who have founded Republics, he began and he ended his career as a believer in the uses of constitutional Kingship. Yet it was his fate to ruin the Puritan cause by dissociating it from both Kingship and Parliament, and to clear the way only by his own death for the restoration of the civil legality which he himself desired. It was his fate – was it also his fault? On that point historians who know the most are the least willing to venture a clear opinion.

His dismissal of the Rump of the Long Parliament when it 1653
endeavoured to perpetuate its power, was perhaps a necessity. It pleased the nation well for a month, during which the ballad-makers chanted:

Brave Oliver came to the House like a sprite,
His fiery face struck the Speaker dumb;
'Begone,' said he, 'you have sate long enough,
Do you think to sit here till Doomsday come?'

But the all too dramatic march of his red-coats up the floor of the House, and his guard-room jest about the mace, left in longer retrospect an indelibly bad impression. If the mace was a bauble and the crown to boot, what counted but the sword?

After he had become Protector, his later Parliaments, though elected under such restrictions as the times demanded, were not able to agree with him. Whether he should have risked more to bring about an agreement so indispensable, is a question too detailed for discussion here, although it is the heart of the problem. The alternative was government by Major-Generals, the naked rule of the sword, which outraged the country and his own instincts. His last two years were spent in the delicate operation of beginning to free himself from dependence on the army by making terms with the legalists and constitutionalists. They demanded of him that he should revive the Kingship in his own person. He began to fall in with their view of the matter, but some of the army chiefs on whom he most depended remained stubbornly Republican. The desire of many moderate and practical men, particularly of the lawyers, was that Oliver should wear the crown – the same men who two years later took the lead in recalling Charles for much the same reasons. Monarchy was seen to be essential to the restoration of Parliament and the rule of law.

3 Sept. 1658 It was in an early stage of this new evolution that death overtook the Protector. But already he had made some headway in weeding the army of its fanatical and extremist element, and for this reason Monk, the practical man, was able to represent the strongest party among his fellow soldiers, and to possess himself of power at the end of the prolonged crisis of eighteen months that followed Oliver's death. Consequently, the desired disbandment of the army, the Restoration of Monarchy, Parliament, and the rule of law took place without bloodshed, in the name of the old dynasty. Whether, if Oliver had lived, it could have taken place in his name may be doubted, but it remains an open question.

Oliver would perhaps have regarded the Restoration settlement with more equanimity than we suppose, for he was a good patriot, a great opportunist, and at heart an ardent Parliamentarian. His bitterest disappointment would have been the religious side of the new regime. Yet on English religion also he had left an indelible mark. His victory in the First Civil War made Parliament instead of King the ultimate authority on ecclesiastical questions, a decision upon which James II alone attempted to go back and in vain. His victory in the Second Civil War prevented the establishment of persecuting Presbyterian orthodoxy. His long rule had nursed the Sects into such vigorous life that they and not the Presbyterians gave English Puritanism its form and its character in the coming period of nonconformity. The variety of English religious thought and practice, not without its influence inside the borders of the Church itself, and tending always to freedom of opinion, springs no doubt from something fundamental in the English character, but historically it dates from the Cromwellian epoch.

The Protector's policy had combined comprehension within the Church and toleration without it. While he preserved tithe and endowments, he put down persecution. The benefices of the Church were held by Presbyterians, Independents, or Baptists indifferently, while free congregations of a more fanciful kind multiplied outside. Oliver thus obtained in the field of religion a reconciliation of all the various Puritan forces which he had signally failed to obtain in politics. He even tolerated the Prayer Book surreptitiously, and would have tolerated it openly but for the political situation which more and more identified Anglicanism with the cause of the exiled Stuarts. The fatal flaw in his ecclesiastical policy was that he had not been able to give to Anglicanism that share in the life of the Church which he had offered to grant it in the Heads of the Proposals. The Roman Catholics were less molested under the Protectorate than under Presbyterian or Anglican Parliaments, and though the Mass was not legally tolerated the Recusancy laws were repealed.

The great fault of the Puritans as governors of the land was that they tended to exclude all who were not Puritan from power and influence in the State; by making profession of religious zeal a shibboleth, they bred notorious hypocrites. Their tyrannical and disastrous suppression of the theatre and other clumsy attempts to make people good by force were part of the same general error. When the Restoration occurred, the non-religious part of the community had come to loathe the Puritans as, twenty years before, they had loathed the Laudian clergy. In particular the squires, the strongest class in the social order of that day, had been outraged by the military rule of Major-Generals and by the overturn of the ancient institutions of the country. Whichever side they or their fathers had taken in the Great Civil War, the squires had come to associate the political and social changes which they disapproved with Puritan religion; therefore, by a strange inversion since the days of Eliot and Pym, the anti-Puritan legislation of the Clarendon Code was the work not of the King and the courtiers but of the Parliament and the squires. Yet under a Parliamentary system the Puritan sects could hope some day to obtain a measure of toleration which they would never have obtained if the Stuart despotism had been prolonged after the pattern of Laud and Strafford.

CHAPTER III

English Village and Town Life and its Expansion Overseas. Character of Colonization and Colonial Policy in the Seventeenth Century. New England, Virginia, and the Absorption of the Dutch Middle Colonies. England, France, and Holland

EVERYDAY life in Stuart times, though full of hardship, ignorance, and cruelty as compared with our own, had great compensating advantages. It was neither ugly nor unnatural. It was lived in the country, and whatever man himself added to nature did not detract from the beauty of things. The crafts were conducted by men armed with tools to do their will, not as now by men doing the will of the machines they serve; and it is not man himself but the machine that is the enemy of grace and beauty of line. Before the mechanical age, common craftsmen were in a sense artists, doing nobler and more individual work than the modern employee engaged on mass production. They were therefore more contented with their lot in life, though many of its conditions were such as would not be tolerated in our more humane generation.

These crafts were not carried on in immense urban areas from which nature had been elaborately expelled. London, which numbered half a million inhabitants by the end of the century, was the only place in England that could answer to that description. And even there a man could take his pleasure on the Thames, then the most glorious of city highways, or, if he could not afford a boat, could convey himself on foot in half an hour out of roaring Cheapside to meadows where sportsmen set springes for snipe and partridge, close under hills haunted by nightingales. Nature could be found and wooed even by the Londoner without the intervention of mechanical transport.

The other towns of England, all much smaller in proportion to the capital than some are to-day, answered to the description that Thomas Hardy has given of the Dorchester of his own boyhood:

> Casterbridge [Dorchester] lived by agriculture at one remove further from the fountain-head than the adjoining villages – no more. The townsfolk understood every fluctuation in the rustic's condition, for it affected their receipts as much as the labourer's; they entered into the troubles and joys which moved the aristocratic families ten miles round – for the same reason. . . Casterbridge was the complement of the rural life around; not its urban opposite. Bees and butterflies in the cornfields at the top of the town, who desired to get to the meads at the bottom, took no circuitous course, but flew straight down High Street without any apparent consciousness that they were traversing strange latitudes.

Such were the towns of England from Elizabeth to George III. And, such as they were, they housed only a small part of the population, for under the Tudors and Stuarts the crafts and manufactures were increasingly carried on, not in the corporate towns but in the country. Many villages and hamlets manufactured for the national and international market. The medieval isolation of the peasant was broken down, and he came in contact in his own village with men of various occupations dealing much with distant shires. Community of trade drew the whole nation together, sharpening the wits and broadening the outlook of the villager. When the first Stuart ascended the throne, men were saying to each other:

> By the Lord, Horatio, these three years I have taken note of it . . . the toe of the peasant comes so near the heel of the courtier he galls his kibe.

While the contemporary French and German peasants were still depressed by the survivals of an outworn feudalism, the English villager was ready to play an independent part in any new development, religious or political, industrial or colonial. The Pilgrim Fathers were most of them English villagers in origin. The medieval serf would never have planted the free and self-sufficient townships of New England. French Canada, founded in this same Seventeenth Century, was the transplantation of the medieval peasant under the leadership of his feudal noble and his priest; while the English Colonial movement was the migration of a modern society, self-governing, half-industrial, awake to economic and intellectual change.

The new agriculture and the enclosures had upon the whole increased the number and importance of the well-to-do tenant-farmers and freehold yeomen. Thomas Fuller, writing at the outbreak of the Civil War, thus describes the yeoman:

> The yeomanry is an estate of people almost peculiar to England. France and Italy are like a die which hath no points between sink and ace, nobility and peasantry . . . The yeoman wears russet clothes, but makes golden payment, having tin in his buttons and silver in his pockets . . . In his own country he is a main man in juries. He seldom goes abroad and his credit stretches further than his travel. He goes not to London, but *se-defendendo*, to save himself a fine, being returned of a Jury, where seeing the King once, he prays for him ever afterwards.

The forty-shilling freeholder, who included many of this sturdy class, enjoyed the parliamentary franchise in the shire elections. The independent part played by the yeomen for King Charles' cause in the West, and for the Parliament in Hampden's Buckinghamshire and Cromwell's East Anglia, showed how far the better class of English peasant had progressed out of the ignorance and dependence of the serfs over whom the Norman Barons had ridden roughshod.

The small squires, freehold yeomen, leasehold farmers, and craftsmen formed together a large part of the rural population. But there existed also an agricultural proletariat. Towards the close of the Stuart period the publicist Gregory King surmised that the 'cottagers and paupers' considerably outnumbered the yeomen freeholders and well-to-do tenant farmers, and slightly outnumbered the 'labouring people and out-servants'. All is extremely uncertain, local variations were infinite, and there are no figures available except such guesswork as Gregory King's. But it is probable that there was a large class of poor folk in every village, part of it landless and working for hire, part of it living from hand to mouth on a few strips in the common field, or on pasture rights or squattings on the common waste. Then, too, there was the nomad population of the roads and lanes – the campers in the dingle, the tinker, and wandering craftsman, the gipsy from far lands, the highwayman, and footpad, the ballad-monger, the quack, and the showman – a world of infinite variety, entertainment, and romance, which Shakespeare loved in its prime, and George Borrow portrayed on the eve of its fading away before the remorseless regimentation of modern 'improvement'.

Every class of the rural community found an additional means of livelihood and enjoyment in the snaring of hares, wild-fowl, and rabbits in places where no one then cared to preserve them, besides more adventurous poaching in warrens and parks. During the Civil War, the 'poor foot', recruited on both sides from the rural proletariat, had the gratification of breaking up innumerable deer-parks of 'rebel' or 'malignant' gentlemen, with the result that the stock of deer never fully recovered, and fox-hunting began after the Restoration to rival stag-hunting as the usual form of the chase. Before that, foxes had been massacred for necessity, not preserved for sport. At the same time the improvement of shot-guns presented an alternative to hawking or snaring as the sportsman's favourite method of taking game. These early gunmen usually stalked the bird for a sitting shot: pheasants were shot roosting, and partridges were shot or netted on the ground. By the end of Charles II's reign, however, many gentlemen practised the most refined form of sport, and actually 'shot flying'.

England under the Stuarts was not sharply divided between an urban and a rural way of life. Since the feudal life of the manor had disappeared and municipal life had become decadent, village and town were both governed by Parliamentary Statutes rather than by local legislation, and were harmoniously related in a single economic system of national dimensions.

Yet in spite of the political and economic unity of England, means of locomotion were still so primitive, and the ill-tended roads so execrable, that provincial differences in speech, custom, and character still gave picturesqueness and piquancy to life. The absence of a newspaper press and of a standardized and universal system of education enabled local traditions to survive. Shire differed from shire, town from town, and hamlet from hamlet. There was more individuality then than now, at least in the external expression of character.

Men and women were widely scattered through the island, thrown back upon themselves during frequent hours of solitude and isolation; each had space to grow, like the spreading oak tree alone in the field, without troubling too much to conform to any conventional pattern. It was 'every man in his humour'. The typical economic life of the time, as conducted by yeoman, farmer, and small craftsman, left the individual more unfettered and self-dependent than he had been in the corporate life of medieval burgher and serf, or has become in our own day under great capitalist and labour combinations.

But such individualism, greater than is possible in the crowded world of to-day, was qualified by the greater subjection of women to men. It was still the exception for women of the upper and middle class to choose their own husbands, and when the husband had been assigned he was lord and master, so far at least as law and custom could make him. Yet even so, neither Shakespeare's women nor those of authentic Seventeenth Century memoirs, like the Verneys and Hutchinsons, seem wanting in personality and character.

This new English world, so full of vigour, freedom, and initiative, laid the foundations of the British Empire and of the United States. The migration of early Stuart times was a world-movement akin in its importance to the Anglo-Saxon and Norse settlement of England a thousand years before. The Elizabethans had prepared the sea-way for the host of emigrants who used it in the following reigns.

The great majority of the first Anglo-Americans came from the south-east of England. They were accustomed not to the hamlets and isolated farms of the West and North, but to the large villages of the South-East and Midlands; it was therefore natural for them, when they reached the other side of the Atlantic, to create the New England township, an institution which spread far, and did much to mould the destiny of all North America. They were indeed the very men to found solid institutions in the wilderness, because in their old homes they had combined self-help and economic individualism with residence in large village groups, where agriculture, crafts, and trade had flourished together. The Pilgrim Father did not go out expecting to find a job awaiting him in some specialized employment, but was prepared to turn his hand to anything that circumstances imposed, asking only for land, of which there was abundance.

A great part of the emigration under James and Charles I ran, indeed, not to New England but to the Bermudas, the West India islands, and to Raleigh's Virginia, the first of English Colonies, refounded in 1607. In these latitudes the climate was in some respects alluring; in Virginia tobacco-culture and in the islands sugar offered a way to rapid wealth for a few. The abundant slave-labour of African Negroes was only gradually introduced, but from the first there was a tendency to seek 'indentured servants', whether convict or other, to work the 'plantations' for an aristocracy. Some of the West Indian settlers were Puritan, some Anglicans inclining towards Royalist sympathies, and some were failures of the Old World sent to make a fresh start oversea, not

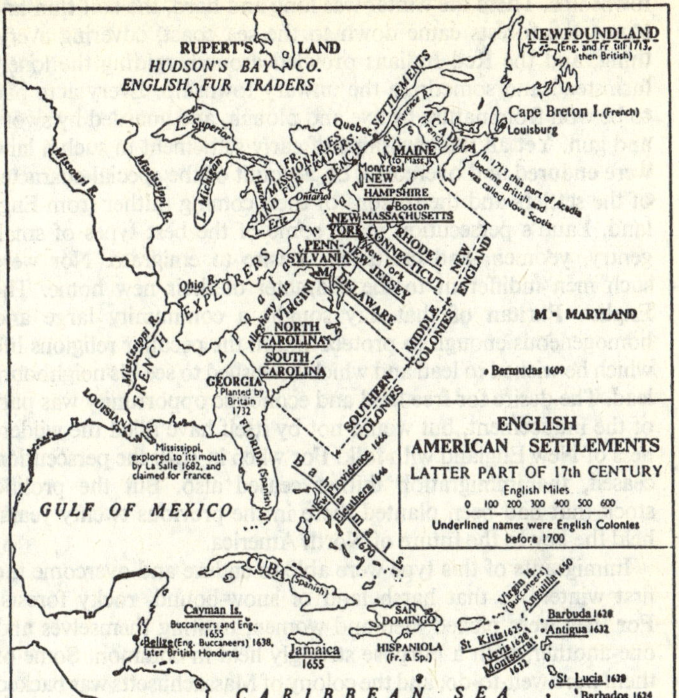

MAP XI

always with happy results for the colony. Local self-government at once became a feature of English settlements in Virginia and the islands, distinguishing them from the colonies of other nations.

But these semi-tropical colonies, important as they became, could not have imposed the English law and language on North America as a whole. The tree whose branches were destined to cover the continent from sea to sea, had its deepest roots in the close-settled, democratic, Puritan land of the New England townships. There the winter was long and hard, the soil thin and stony, the forests came down to the sea coast, covering everything, and the Red Indians prowled around, raiding the lonely farmstead and sometimes the unwary township. Every acre had to be won from nature by axe and plough, and guarded by sword and gun. Yet all the hardships of early settlement in such a land were endured and overcome, on account of the special character of the settlers and the reasons of their coming thither from England. Laud's persecution made some of the best types of small gentry, yeomen, and craftsmen, desire to emigrate. Nor were such men indifferent to the character of their new home. The English Puritan of that day sought a community large and homogeneous enough to protect him in the peculiar religious life which he wished to lead and which he wished to see his neighbours lead. The desire for free land and economic opportunity was part of the inducement, but would not by itself have filled the wilderness of New England with folk. For when in 1640 the persecution ceased, the immigration thither ceased also. But the prolific stock that had been planted there in the previous twenty years, held the key to the future of North America.

Immigrants of this type were able to endure and overcome the first winters in that harsh land of snow-bound, rocky forests. For they were picked men and women, trusting themselves and one another, with a purpose strongly held in common. Some of them were well-to-do, and the colony of Massachusetts was backed by money, supplies, and good organizers in England – wealthy Puritan Lords, squires, and London merchants, who stayed at home themselves, but supported these ventures, partly from motives of religion, partly as an investment of their capital.

Charles I set no bar to these proceedings, for he was glad to see such dangerous spirits go into voluntary exile. Indeed their departure goes far to account for the non-resistance of his English subjects during his dozen years of autocratic rule. From the time of Elizabeth onwards, Anglican persecution has always been more than half political in its motive. The Roman Church persecuted to save souls, and was therefore less compromising. Rome could not endure the thought of heresy in any part of the world; so Louis XIV would allow no Huguenots in Canada; and Spain would have no Protestants in South America. But Charles I, and, in later years, Clarendon, tolerated Puritan and Roman Catholic colonists on the other side of the ocean, provided Anglican conformity was observed at home, as the basis of the corresponding system in the political sphere.

New England was democratic in spirit from first to last. The Saxon township was brought across from East Anglia, but squirearchy was left behind. Abundant land, divided up into freeholds among all who were ready to clear it of trees and till it with their own hands, was the firm basis of the original North American democracy. Squirearchy continued to flourish in an island where land was limited and at a premium, and population at a discount, whereas the opposite conditions prevailed in New England. Feudalism had arisen in the Dark Ages to organize society for self-defence under warrior landlords; but in New England the community acted as a whole, the township and the colony undertaking the organization necessary for fighting the redskins, and the mother country helping to defeat the Dutch and the French.

Above all, the Church was democratic, and religion was the motive of the foundation of the colony; the State in early Massachusetts was ruled by a democratic Church even more than in contemporary Scotland. Full political rights were confined to 'Church members', who composed a considerable proportion of the whole population. Inside the colony there was no pretence at religious toleration. Dissidents seeking religious freedom from the particular brand of Puritanism represented in Massachusetts, moved away and founded neighbouring Rhode Island, the colony of Puritan toleration, under the leadership of Roger Williams. New England included both kinds of Puritanism, the rigid and the free.

New England was an amphibious community. The seaboard with its fine harbours and inlets, and the neighbouring fishing grounds, held the people to the coast and made them hardy mariners. Their capital was Boston, a merchant city on the sea. The forests on the water's edge of the Atlantic rendered shipbuilding easy for them, until the age of iron ships. Their houses were built of wood as universally as those of the early Saxons in the old English forest.

The inhabitants of New England and of all the English colonies on the American seaboard, not only found attraction on the coast, but were hindered from penetrating far inland by formidable geographic barriers. The Appalachian and Allegheny mountains and their continuation northwards in wooded wildernesses up to the Gulf of St Lawrence, effectually cut off the early English colonists from knowledge of the prairies of the interior and the Ohio valley, where in fact much richer soil awaited them. But no great rivers offered them an easy way into the interior, like the

St Lawrence, the highway of the French colonials. This geographic restriction favoured close settlement and the growth of a number of coastwise colonies, each of great political solidity and numerical strength. When therefore in the Eighteenth Century the English-speaking populations of the seaboard at length burst over the Appalachian barrier into the Ohio valley and the prairies of the Middle West, they were powerful enough to sweep away their French foreunners in those regions and then to advance across the empty continent with astonishing speed, planting over immense areas the New England idea, modernized and mingled with the spirit of the ever-moving frontier.

The settlement of the shores of the St Lawrence river by the French, though contemporaneous with the settlement of New England, was its opposite in every respect. The one was the plantation of a seaboard, the other of a great river highway leading far into the interior of the continent. While the early English settlers multiplied their numbers and concentrated their strength in the agricultural townships of a large but limited area, the French went up the St Lawrence as missionaries and fur traders, discovered the Great Lakes and sailed down the Mississippi. The fur trade was their economic object, and they pursued it by keeping on good terms with the Red Indian trappers from whom they purchased the furs. The New Englanders, on the other hand, wanted the Indian's hunting-grounds to plough, and regarded him as an enemy, only half human. The colour-feeling of the English race is stronger than that of the French.

French Canada was as feudal and Roman Catholic as New England was democratic and Puritan. The Breton peasant, the most religious and obedient in old France, went out under the leadership of his priest and his lord, and reconstituted on the banks of the St Lawrence the clerical and feudal society which alone he understood. There was no element of democracy or of self-government in the French North American settlements until those ideas were intruded late in the Eighteenth Century as a result of English conquest. The French royal government, which had organized and subsidized the planting of the colony, kept it under close control and subjected every male inhabitant to compulsory military service. No one could enter the colony without the permission of King Louis, and that permission was not granted to Huguenots.

The American colonies of England, the offspring of Dissent by Self-help, were much less submissive to their home government than the colonies of France, Spain, or even Holland. The English colonies had originated not in acts of State but in the venture of joint-stock companies or of individual proprietors. As they were gradually brought under the control of the Crown, the habit of self-government within the colony had perpetually to be adjusted, not without friction, to the authority of the Royal Governor. It was a 'dyarchy' that caused many quarrels, but was necessitated by the circumstances of the time.

In practice, in spite of the Governor, the colonies were self-governing as regards their own internal affairs. Laud had contemplated an attack on the religious autonomy of New England, and it cannot be doubted that if Charles I's despotism had become securely established in the old country a crisis would ere long have arisen out of an attempt to extend the system of arbitrary government across the ocean. But the civil troubles at home gave the colonies twenty years in which to nurse their independent spirit: Massachusetts made war and founded or annexed new colonies without reference to the home government. It is true that the victorious Parliament of 1649, in reasserting the unity of the Empire on a regicide basis, had proclaimed the novel doctrine that the English Parliament could legislate for and govern the colonies; but Oliver as Protector had more carefully respected the sensitive independence of New England, and the Restoration put the colonies back in direct relation with the Crown rather than with Parliament.

Massachusetts had, in fact, early adopted an attitude almost amounting to a claim to independent sovereignty. This led to a long and bitter dispute, occupying the reigns of Charles and James II. It came to a climax in 1683, when the Charter of Massachusetts was cancelled at the height of the Tory reaction in England, when so many English towns were similarly deprived of their ancient liberties. In the case of Massachusetts the provocation had been considerable, but it did not justify the attempt to subject the colony to despotic government. The Revolution of 1689 gave the opportunity to settle this, like so many other outstanding questions. A new Charter was granted and self-government restored on the condition that political rights should be extended not merely to 'Church members' but to the whole colonial community. 'Thanks to England,' writes Mr Truslow Adams, 'the final death-blow had legally been dealt to the theocracy, and the foundation laid for genuine self-government and religious toleration.'

The probability that New England would some day break off from the home government was present from the first. It was made yet more probable when on the Restoration of Charles II the social and religious differences between old and New England were stereotyped. In the homeland puritanism and democracy were once more subjugated by Anglicanism and aristocracy, an arrangement which the Revolution of 1689 modified but did not overset. Cromwell had found it easy to remain on good terms with Massachusetts, though Virginia and Barbados had to be compelled by force of arms to obey the regicide Republic. If a system of religion and society consonant with the ideas of the Protectorate had become permanent in the mother country, the social and intellectual misunderstanding between old and New England would not have become so sharp as it did in the middle of the Eighteenth Century.

Cromwell was the first ruler of England who was consciously an Imperialist. Before him, the attitude of government towards colonization had been permissive only. The Protector annexed Jamaica by force of arms, thereby greatly increasing the importance of the English possessions in the West Indian archipelago. He also annexed Acadia from France, but it was given back after the Restoration.

In spite of their surrender of Acadia, the governments of Charles II's reign, under the influence of Clarendon and of Shaftesbury, were imbued with the spirit of Cromwell's colonial policy. They took intelligent interest in the affairs of America, largely with a view to promoting English trade and finding markets for English goods. Prince Rupert and the Court supported the enterprise of the English fur-traders to Hudson Bay, turning the northern flank of the French Canadian trappers. Above all,
1664 England captured and annexed from the Dutch the group of Middle Colonies between New England and Virginia, turning New Amsterdam into New York, and so forming an unbroken coastline under the British flag from Maine to the new colony of Carolina. Behind that line of coast colonies was founded the most strange settlement of all: Charles II's government, at the moment of the strongest Tory reaction in England, permitted William
1681 Penn, the Quaker courtier and organizer, to found Pennsylvania as a refuge for persecuted Friends in the wilderness, where they practised with success the unwonted principle of just dealing with the redskins.

The annexation and further planting of these Middle Colonies brought to the front two new principles of the utmost importance in the British Empire – the union of a number of different races with equal rights under the British flag, and religious toleration for all.

Those principles had not been the contribution of New England. They were first developed on a large scale in the Middle Colonies seized from Holland, where the Dutch were quickly reconciled by the respect paid to their customs and by the enjoyment of rights of self-government such as they had not known under their own flag. In New York Colony, in Pennsylvania, in Maryland, and in New Jersey, there were welded together on equal terms of freedom, English, Dutch, Swedes, Germans, French, and Ulster Scots – that is to say, Anglicans and Puritans, Calvinists and Lutherans, Roman Catholics, Quakers, and Presbyterians. Thither, as to a most congenial atmosphere, came the Huguenot victims of renewed Roman Catholic persecution in the Europe of Louis XIV, and the Romanist and Puritan sufferers from Anglican intolerance, which operated only in the British islands.

The North America of the Eighteenth Century that ultimately revolted from Great Britain, was made up of the combination of three types of colony, New England, the Middle Colonies, and the Southern slave-owning aristocrats. The characteristic spirit of modern America, which eventually spread from Atlantic to Pacific, was a blend of the ideas and habits of the democratic township and self-dependent Puritanism of New England with the absence of religious and racial prejudice fostered among the races and religions that were first mingled in the Middle Colonies.

A third element, common to all the colonies from Maine to Carolina, was the frontier spirit. The frontier in American history does not mean, as in Europe, a fixed boundary paraded by sentries, but is the term used for that part of the wilderness into which the white man has most recently penetrated. The frontier was always moving, but the frontiersman was always the same. At whatever distance, small or great, from the Atlantic seaboard, whether in the Seventeenth or the two following Centuries, certain characteristics were always found among the pioneers of the advance into the West. Hardihood, resource, and courage; poverty and the hope of present betterment; democratic equality and dislike of all forms of training and authority, whether political or intellectual; careless generosity and shrewd self-help; lynch-law and good comradeship; complete ignorance of distant Europe – combined to make up a well-known type of character, often in sharp contrast to the settled and conservative habits of the comfortable folk nearer the coast, in districts which had themselves constituted the frontier a generation or two before.

If ever aristocratic Britain were to come into serious conflict with her colonies, she would find some sympathizers at least among the settled and well-to-do folk of the coast towns, who grew richer and somewhat more amenable as the generations went by; but she would find implacable rebels not only in the Puritan farmers of New England, but in the democratic frontiersmen at the back of every colony, an element frequently despised or forgotten by the highly civilized part of society until it was too late.

In the last half of the Seventeenth Century England's statesmen and merchants put a high value on her American colonies. They did not indeed foresee their enormous future expansion; no one dreamed for an instant that the quarter of a million inhabitants of the coast colonies in 1700 would ever be enlarged into a State of a hundred millions. The Appalachian Mountains bounded the vision not only of British statesmen but of the Anglo-Americans themselves. England prized about equally the sugar islands and the colonies of the continental seaboard.

The overseas possessions were valued as fulfilling a twofold purpose. First as supplying an appropriate outlet for the energetic, the dissident, the oppressed, the debtors, the criminals, and the failures of old England – a sphere where the energies of men who were too good or too bad not to be troublesome at home, might be turned loose to the general advantage; as yet there was no pressing question of a purely economic excess of population in England. Secondly, the colonies were valued as markets where raw materials could be bought, and manufactured articles sold, to the advantage of England's industry and commerce. 'I state to you', said Chatham, 'the importance of America; it is a double market: a market of consumption and a market of supply.' Cromwell and Clarendon, Shaftesbury and Somers, would all have said the same.

The external policy of England was falling more and more under the influence of mercantile considerations. Even the restoration of the influence of the old social order in 1660 did not go far enough to check this movement. The direction of the course of external trade by government regulation from Whitehall or Westminster, a scheme of which the Navigation Laws formed part, was worked in some respects to the advantage of the mainland colonies; in other respects it sacrificed their interest to that of the home country or the sugar islands – whereupon the New Englanders took to smuggling like ducks to water.

At the end of the Stuart period England was the greatest manufacturing and trading country in the world, and London outstripped Amsterdam as the world's greatest emporium. There was a thriving trade with the Orient, the Mediterranean, and the American colonies; its basis was the sale of English textile goods, which could be carried to the other side of the world in the large ocean-going ships of the new era. England's commerce, in America and everywhere else, largely consisted of the sale of English manufactures. In that lay her strength as compared to her forerunners in maritime power. Venice had been the carrier, at the European terminus, of the trade between all Europe and the Asiatic markets. Spain had lived on spoil, tribute, and mining for precious metals. Even Holland had lacked a sufficient hinterland of manufactures and population in her small territory.

When finally the attacks of Louis XIV drove Holland to devote her wealth and energy to self-defence on land, she gradually 1668–1714 fell behind England in the race for commercial leadership. In spite of maritime rivalry, it was in England's interest to save Dutch independence and to preserve the Spanish Netherlands from falling into French hands. For if the Delta of the Rhine had become French, the maritime power and the independence of England could not have long survived. In that respect English and Dutch interests were identical, as Charles and James II failed to see, but as the English people saw. But it was none the less to the selfish advantage of England that her two chief rivals for naval and commercial supremacy became engaged during this critical period in great military expenditure, France from deliberate choice and ambition, Holland from the necessities of self-defence.

Meanwhile in the England of the Restoration and of the Revolution Settlement, the governing classes were determined to spend as much on the Navy as was necessary, and as little on the Army as they could possibly help.

CHAPTER IV

The Restoration and the Reign of Charles II (1660–85). The Formation of the Whig and Tory Parties

THE principles of government associated with the names of Caesar and Napoleon have never been popular in England. Cromwell, like all great English soldiers, disliked the idea of ruling his countrymen by the sword, and they disliked him for doing it. In his last years he was seeking a path back to the rule of law, custom, and Parliament. But law, custom, and Parliament were in this island so inextricably interwoven with the Kingly office by centuries of continuous growth and by the inherited association of ideas, that a restoration of the monarchy was needed if the nation were to enjoy its ancient rights again.

Had Oliver himself lived, it seems likely that he would have attempted the most difficult task of his life, to restore constitutional rule by reviving the monarchy in his own person. In the person of his feeble son Richard it was frankly impossible. The
1659 rule of the sword became more undisguised and more intolerable when there was no strong hand to wield it, when regiment began to fight with regiment, and General to rise up against General as in the worst periods of the Roman Empire. To prevent anarchy from becoming chronic at home, and to stay the dissolution of the Empire oversea, there was no way but to recall the Stuart heir. The sooner and the more willingly that was done by Parliament and by the old Roundhead party, the greater would be the freedom of the subject under the restored Kingship.

The lead given by General Monk to the sane and patriotic elements in the army, enabled the Convention Parliament to
1660 be freely elected. It consisted of moderate Roundheads of the old Presbyterian party, with a strong admixture of Cavaliers. It called back Charles II from his exile in Holland. At this important crisis of the constitution, it was not the King who summoned Parliament, but Parliament that summoned the King. Though the principle of the Divine Right of Kings might be preached as the favourite dogma of the restored Anglican Church, though the lawyers might pretend after their fashion that Charles the Exile had been Charles II from the moment his father's head fell upon the scaffold, the fact was notorious that monarchy had after a long interval been renewed in his person by the vote of the two Houses, as the result of a general election.

The authority of the King and the authority of Parliament were once more regarded as inseparable. Rivals they might long remain, enemies they might on occasion become, but they would never again be two mutually exclusive methods of government as Strafford and the Regicides had made them. Absolutism and Republicanism both were dead; nor except by James II has any serious attempt since been made to revive either the one or the other in England.

So 'the King enjoyed his own again.' The second Charles could indeed be trusted to 'enjoy' whatever came his way, but 'his own' was no longer the full heritage of power which had descended to his ancestors. The crown had been stripped of many of its jewels in the first session of the Long Parliament twenty years before, and that work was not undone at the Restoration. The great Prerogative Courts, with their rival system of jurisprudence based on the laws of ancient Rome, were not revived as an eyesore to the Common Lawyers and a weapon of the Prince against the Subject: Star Chamber and High Commission remained abolished and illegal. Taxation could no longer be imposed save by vote of Parliament. Strafford's old enemies, 'Sir Edward Coke and his Year-Books', Hampden and his scruples on Ship-money, triumphed at the Restoration no less than Laud and his surplices.

Of all that generation of the illustrious dead one survivor remained to become the architect of the Restoration settlement – Edward Hyde, now Earl of Clarendon and Lord Chancellor, the faithful servant of the royal family in its long exile. To him the Stuarts owed it that they ever returned from foreign lands, because even there he had kept young Charles in some degree of connexion with the Anglican Church and the constitutional royalists, in spite of the Queen Mother and the swordsmen. And now, in the critical first months of the reign, Clarendon's wisdom and moderation, in harmony with the King's shrewdness and loose good-nature, gave peace to the land, stayed the furies of revenge, and made it to the interest of all parties to live as loyal subjects of the restored monarchy.

Clarendon, who had been the bosom friend of Falkland and the ally of Hampden against Strafford, was still the man of 1640. To that year he undertook to bring back the body politic, as though the two most crowded decades in English History had not intervened. Nor was he wholly unsuccessful. The balance of power between King and Commons was fixed in 1660 at the point where it had been set in the first session of the Long Parliament. The restored equilibrium of the Constitution served as nothing else could have done to give a breathing space for recovery and regrowth after the storms of the revolutionary era. But mere equilibrium would not provide a permanent form of government for a vigorous and growing State, as Strafford and Pym had both foreseen. State action, especially oversea, was paralysed by the division of executive and legislative into two rival bodies, neither the acknowledged master of the other in case of dispute. Until Parliament controlled foreign policy as well as finance, until the King's Ministers were also the servants of the House of Commons, the King's government would remain suspected, impoverished, and hampered; and the struggle between Crown and Houses would proceed once more, whether the Parliament were called 'Cavalier' or 'Whig'.

The greatest work of Clarendon and Charles, for which both deserve high credit, was their steady refusal to permit a general revenge upon the Roundhead party. Only so could the King fulfil the promises made in Holland that had brought him home in peace, only so could the throne be re-established as a national institution accepted by all parties. The Act of Indemnity and Oblivion was stigmatized by the Cavaliers as 'Indemnity for the King's enemies and Oblivion for the King's friends'. The royalists had looked to glut their revenge in the blood and the estates of the rival faction; but in the main they were disappointed, and they never forgave Clarendon.

A dozen regicides, and Vane the noblest survivor of the Commonwealth statesmen, were offered up as scapegoats, and their deaths appeased the cry for blood, never prolonged in England. But the cry for land was louder and more lasting. Land was still the chief goal of ambition, the chief source of wealth, power, and social consequence. On the land-question a compromise was effected by Clarendon which secured the acceptance of the new regime by the great body of former Roundheads. Church and Crown lands, and private estates of Cavalier magnates that had been confiscated and sold by the rebel governments were resumed, without compensation to those who had purchased them. But the lands which Cavaliers had themselves sold to pay the fines imposed on them as 'malignants' were left in the hands of the purchasers. A large body of new men thereby made good their footing in the English squirearchy, at the easy price of attending the restored Anglican worship. Many of these prosperous ex-Roundheads became local leaders of the Whig party in the coming era.

Under this arrangement many Cavaliers failed to recover lands which they had been forced to sell as a price of their loyalty in evil days; they were bitterly aggrieved against the government, and continued to hate the former Roundheads of every shade with a personal as well as a political hatred. This temper dictated the policy of the Cavalier Parliament that was elected at the height of the reaction in 1661. The majority of the new members formed a party – afterwards known as 'Tory' – that was more Anglican and squirearchical than royalist: it kept the Crown on a short allowance of taxes, scouted the advice of Charles and Clarendon, remodelled the Corporations in the interest of their own Church and party rather than of the Court, and set on foot by Parliamentary statute a persecution of Puritan nonconformists more cruel than any desired by the King or even by that stout Anglican the Lord Chancellor.

Indeed the so-called 'Clarendon Code' of laws against Dissenters was not the work of Clarendon, still less of Charles, but of Parliament and the squires. The 'Clarendon Code' was the 1661–5
Cavaliers' revenge for their long sufferings and their lost lands. Balked by the Act of Indemnity, they found this other outlet for their feelings. They were prompted less by religious bigotry than by political passion and the memory of personal wrongs and losses, many of them still unredressed.

The root of what the Dissenters were now to suffer may be traced to the Parliamentary fines on 'malignants' and to the executions of Laud and Charles I. It was not merely vengeance: the 'Clarendon Code' was also a measure of policy against the revival of the Roundhead party. The Act of Uniformity of 1662 restored the Prayer Book and turned adrift without compensation 2000 clergy who could not assert their 'unfeigned consent and assent' to everything the book contained. The Conventicle Act of two years later made prison and transportation the lot of those caught in acts of dissenting worship. These Statutes were the policy of Parliament, not of the King. Laud's religion triumphed, but not through the royal power nor through the clerical jurisdiction and authority which he had striven to restore, but through the action of the Parliament of squires whose right to pronounce upon religion he and Charles I had died rather than acknowledge.

The religious settlement of the Restoration was not conceived in the spirit of compromise which marked the political and social settlement. Yet it may at least be questioned whether it has not led to more religious, intellectual, and political liberty than would have resulted from a wider extension of the boundaries of the Established Church. The arrangement actually made, under which the Church of England and the various Puritan Churches followed each its own lines of development, rendered toleration inevitable ere long, and led to the variety and competition of religious bodies characteristic of modern England, utterly at variance with medieval, Tudor, or Stuart notions of Church and State.

In the second decade of the Restoration regime the Protestant Dissenters began to spy a hope of relief in a quarter that suited them much better than the royal prerogative. A minority in the two Houses of Parliament, that was steadily increased by the process of by-elections as the old members died off, held out the hope of statutory relief to 'tender consciences', and opposed both the Cavaliers and the Court.

This 'Whig' party, as it was eventually called, had religious affinities in its rank and file with Puritanism, and in its higher grades with the latitudinarianism and rationalism of the new age. Puritan and Rationalist were drawn together into common opposition to the dominant High Churchmen. The Baptist preacher, dogged by spies from conventicle to conventicle and haled from prison to prison by infuriated Justices of the Peace, when he heard that the Whig chiefs had taken up the cause of Parliamentary toleration for all Protestants, was too greatly rejoiced to enquire whether Algernon Sidney was in a state of grace, or what Shaftesbury meant by 'the religion of all wise men'.

The Royal Society and the great scientific movement that reached its full intellectual splendour in Sir Isaac Newton at Trinity College, Cambridge, was nursed in its infancy by the patronage of Charles II and the sceptical courtiers, who had at least the virtue of curiosity. The scientific and latitudinarian movement slowly created an atmosphere favourable to the doctrine of religious toleration as propounded by the Whig philosopher, John Locke, while outside the realm of politics it is noticeable that the hunt after witches, that had raged horridly in the first half of the Stuart era, began to abate, as first the Judges and then the juries began to feel the prickings of philosophic doubt.

Within the national Church, latitudinarianism had a party, respectable for its learning and eloquence rather than for its numbers, and more powerful in London than in the countryside. This was the 'Low Church' party, a name that then denoted not evangelicalism but what we should now call 'broad' or 'liberal' views. Politically the Low Churchmen, like Stillingfleet, Tillotson, and Burnet, were the advocates of Toleration and the friends of the Protestant Dissenters. Similarly the name 'High Church', given to the great majority of the clergy and their more ardent lay supporters, did not then mean ritualist; it betokened strong antipathy to Dissenters as well as to Romanists, belief in the doctrine of non-resistance to Kings and their divine hereditary right, a great reverence for King Charles the Martyr and – at least among the clergy – a high view of the authority of the Church in politics and society. Dr Johnson, though he lived a hundred years later, is an excellent example of the 'High Church' mentality any time between the Restoration and the French Revolution.

It is, indeed, remarkable how much of Puritan, or at least of strongly Protestant thought and practice survived the political and ecclesiastical fall of the Puritan sects. Family prayer and Bible reading had become national custom among the great majority of religious laymen, whether they were Churchmen or Dissenters. The English character had received an impression from Puritanism which it bore for the next two centuries, though it had rejected Puritan coercion and had driven Dissenters out of polite society. Even the Puritan Sunday survived. The anxiety of James I and Laud that the English people should continue as of old to play games on Sunday afternoon, was, one would have supposed, calculated to meet with the approval of the most athletic and 'sporting' of all nations. Yet even at the Restoration, when the very name of Puritan was a hissing and a reproach, when the gaols were crowded with harmless Quakers and Baptists, the Puritan idea of Sunday, as a day strictly set aside for rest and religious meditation, continued to hold the allegiance of the English people. The good and evil effects of this self-imposed discipline of a whole nation, in abstaining from organized amusement as well as from work on every seventh day, still awaits the dispassionate study of the social historian.

A reduction in public expenditure was one of the most popular consequences of the fall of the Cromwellian system. The King was indeed put by the Cavalier Parliament on an absurdly short allowance, which hampered all branches of the administration and ere long tempted him to sell the control of his foreign policy to Louis XIV of France. But the shortage was a natural result of the return to 'the just balance of the constitution', which Clarendon believed to be the last word of political wisdom. Till Parliament could control policy and expenditure, it would not consent to open wide the public purse. When the Commons insisted on searching the royal account books to trace the actual use made of money voted for the maritime war with Holland, Clarendon and the courtiers were scandalized at such an invasion of the province of the executive by the legislative. Yet this was a first step on the road to that Parliamentary control of expenditure, which alone could secure for the King's government the liberal and continuous supplies from the taxpayers essential to a great nation in modern times.

It was the military and not the naval establishments that bore the brunt of the reductions from Cromwell's lavish standards. By a single great financial effort, the New Model Army was paid off and disbanded at the Restoration, as might have been done thirteen years before if the Long Parliament had been well-advised. It was replaced by no other considerable force. Besides the King's splendid royalist 'Life Guards' designed to ride by his coach and protect him from fanatics and Fifth Monarchy Men, only a few regiments were kept on foot, and those chiefly in foreign possessions like Tangier. The oldest regimental traditions of the British Army derive either from the few Cromwellian units whose life was continued like the Coldstream Guards, or else from the famous regiments in Dutch service like the Buffs.

The Cavalier Parliament, reflecting the passionate feeling of the English country gentlemen, hated and feared the very name of 'standing army'. They were well aware that lawful Kings could play them tricks with such a force, as easily as usurping Protectors. The King alone, as all good Cavaliers believed, had the right to nominate to military commands and give orders to the armed forces. To claim any such powers for Parliament was to be a rebel and a Roundhead, for the Great Civil War had broken out on that issue. But it followed from these loyal premises that the Army must be kept very small, lest His Gracious Majesty should be tempted to arbitrary conduct.

How well grounded was this caution appeared too late when James II was permitted to keep on foot 30,000 men. Only as a consequence of the Revolution that he then provoked, did Parliament gain practical security that the Army would not be used against the liberties of the land. Only then, in the reigns of William III and Anne, did fear of a standing army begin to subside, first among Whig statesmen whose hearts were in the land war against Louis XIV. The mind of the Tory squire moved more slowly; for a hundred years after Naseby the sight of a company of regulars on the march recalled to him the red-coats who had blown in the door of his grandfather's hall, ruined his estate, proscribed his religion, and beheaded his King. The only force he trusted was the ill-trained militia of the county, officered by rustic squires like himself.

No such fears and memories affected the upkeep of the Navy. The Court and Parliament of the Restoration both accepted the traditions of the Commonwealth's fighting fleet, which the dying Blake had bequeathed to posterity. Charles II and his brother James took a personal and well-informed interest in naval matters, and the Admiralty was well served by men like Pepys and his patrons. The Cavalier Parliament and the Tory party regarded the Navy with special favour.

1665–7 Another maritime war with Holland soon broke out, a resumption of the quarrel of the two mercantile communities begun under the Commonwealth. It was conducted on both sides with the same splendid qualities of fighting seamanship and on the same colossal scale as before. Again the larger country had rather the better of the war, and, at the Treaty of Breda, New York was ceded by Holland to England.

But while the treaty was still being negotiated, the Dutch fleet under de Ruyter, piloted by English seamen, sailed up the Thames and the Medway, and burnt and captured our finest warships as they lay at anchor off Chatham. The disgrace made no marked difference to the terms of the treaty, but following as it did close on the Plague and the Fire of London, it deeply affected the imagination and the politics of the English people. The sound of the enemy's guns in the Thames was new to Londoners. Men began to 'reflect upon Oliver', whose corpse they had so recently gibbeted, 'what brave things he did and made all the neighbour Princes fear him'. 'The King,' the world said, 'minds nothing but his lust and hath taken ten times more care and pains in making friends between Lady Castlemaine and Mrs Stewart, when they have fallen out, than ever he did to save his Kingdom.' Already there were rumours that we were 'governed by Papists' at Whitehall. With less reason it was believed that the 'Papists' had burnt down London; a few years earlier the Fire would have been ascribed to the Puritans. In this changed atmosphere, more formidable opposition parties and policies were engendered than any that had hitherto been known in the Cavalier Parliament.

And yet the principal cause of the Medway disaster had been the unwillingness of the House of Commons to vote money liberally to a government it could not control and was beginning to suspect. The ships had been laid up and the crews disbanded as a forced economy. Indeed the British sailors had gone unpaid for so many years that large numbers had deserted to the Dutch, who rewarded their seamen with dollars instead of unmarketable 'Treasury tickets'.

The Plague, the Fire, the Medway, the persecution of Dissenters, and the 'flaunting of Papists at Court' caused a temper to rise in the nation that foreboded storm. Yet in face of these signs Charles decided to 'drop the pilot'. It was indeed tempting 1667
to make a scapegoat of Clarendon, for he was regarded by the nation as responsible for all that had gone wrong; he was hated by the unpaid seamen, by the persecuted Dissenters, by the royal mistresses to whom he would pay no court, by the Parliament men

whom he would fain keep within their appointed sphere, and by the whole world of young ambition whose path he obstructed. Indeed with his old-fashioned views he was no longer in a position to render great services to England. But the men whom Charles chose in his place led King and country into dangers which he would have avoided, for they betrayed the interests of the nation to France, and some of them plotted with their master to betray the Protestant Establishment as well.

1667–73 The 'Cabal' contained not one sound Anglican and scarcely one true patriot. Clifford was an ardent Romanist and Arlington more of a Romanist than anything else; Lauderdale and Buckingham were unprincipled adventurers, and Anthony Ashley Cooper, Earl of Shaftesbury, was the man destined first to found the Whig party and then to ruin it by furious driving. Released by these mercurial companions from Clarendon's control, Charles, his own master at last, entered upon strange courses.

The great fact of the new age in Europe was the advance of French arms and influence across the continent. The decadence of Spain, and the failure of Germany and Italy to produce one formidable power among the innumerable States into which their vast territories were divided, left the way open for the ambition of France. Her unity and internal organization had been perfected by Cardinals Richelieu and Mazarin, and bequeathed by them to Louis XIV and the brilliant group of soldiers and statesmen who served him in his youth. In the ten years since the death of Cromwell the danger had become apparent to all the world. The States of Europe, Catholic as well as Protestant, were in panic, but their inefficiency, selfishness, and mutual jealousy prevented their union for self-defence before William of Orange arose to marshal them. Austria, engaged in defending the approaches of Vienna against the Turk, could only intermittently concern herself with the West. Spain, stricken with the palsy of all her once splendid energies, was fain to leave the defence of her possession in the Netherlands to her former enemies, the Dutch rebels.

Amid the effete monarchies and princedoms of feudal Europe, morally and materially exhausted by the Thirty Years' War, the only hope of resistance to France lay in the little Republic of merchants, Holland poised between the sand-banks and the sea. Enriched by its Eastern colonies, its world-wide commerce, and its open door for refugees of all races and beliefs, the home of Grotius, Descartes, and Spinoza, of Rembrandt and Vermeer, led the world in philosophy, learning, finance, painting, gardening, scientific agriculture, and many other of the arts and crafts that liberate and adorn the life of man. Holland was a rival influence to France in Europe, and stood on this height without the parade of King, noble, or prelate. Her first magistrate, the admired De Witt, kept a single servant in his house and walked unattended through the streets.

The destruction of this bourgeois, Calvinist Republic, no less than the extirpation of the Huguenots in France herself, formed an essential part of the schemes of Louis and the French Jesuit body who inspired the ideals and the policy of his reign. In that policy, strongly 'Gallican' and nationalist in spirit, little reference was made to the wishes of the more moderate Italian Papacy, with whom both the French Jesuits and the French King eventually had bitter quarrels.

In 1668 an English diplomat in the Low Countries, Sir William Temple, negotiated with great skill the Triple Alliance of England, Holland, and Sweden to check the French advance on the Rhine and in the Spanish Netherlands. The effect was instantaneous. Louis was compelled to accept the terms of the Treaty of Aix-la-Chapelle. If England had steadily adhered to this successful line of policy, she might have saved Europe an epoch of bloodshed. But our subservience to France during the twenty years that intervened between Temple's Treaty and the Revolution of 1688, raised the power of Louis to a point from which it could only be dislodged by the long wars of William and Marlborough.

The English Parliament and nation were at first well pleased with Temple's policy of the Balance of Power and the maintenance of Protestantism in Europe. But it was easy for persons secretly hostile to these interests to appeal in public to the sentiment of commercial rivalry with Holland that had already caused two popular wars. The management of foreign policy was in the King's hands as the constitution then stood. In the middle years of his reign, Charles II's Roman Catholic and despotic proclivities were stimulated by his natural irritation with the Cavalier Parliament, which had thwarted his wishes and starved his exchequer. Could he not enter instead into the pay of Louis, and introduce something of the admired French-Catholic system of government into the confused body-politic of England? Charles himself was half French in blood and breeding, and his family had little reason to love English institutions.

Moreover in 1670 the King of England had a family quarrel with Holland. The oligarchic Republic of the De Witts was keeping his nephew William of Orange out of the quasi-monarchical office of the Stadtholderate, which William regarded as his birth-

right and which the Dutch popular party wished to restore in his
1670 person. By the Treaty of Dover that Charles made with Louis, England and France were to attack and partition the Republic and its possessions. A residue would be left, to be governed by William of Orange as the vassal of France. The idea that a young Prince would object to an arrangement so favourable to his vanity and comfort never occurred to these cynics, any more than the idea that a lad just coming of age would find the means to thwart the combined onslaught of France and England.

Such was the open Treaty of Dover, to which Shaftesbury and the Protestants of the Cabal, to their lasting infamy, consented. But there was also a secret treaty, unknown to them but signed by the Catholic members of the Cabal, by which Louis undertook to supply Charles with French soldiers and money, to enable him to declare himself a Roman Catholic and gradually raise his co-religionists to dominance in England.

The two treaties were a single plan for the subjugation of Europe and England by the French Catholic monarchy. But the finance of this hopeful project had been miscalculated. The war with Holland cost England much more than Louis could supply, and bankruptcy drove Charles to submit again to Parliamentary control. Louis no doubt expected that long before the English squires discovered that they had been duped, his dragoons would be billeted at free quarters on the rich Calvinists of Hague
1672 and Rotterdam. And so it would have happened, but for the temper of the Dutch people, the physical conformation of their land, and the qualities that William of Orange now first revealed to the world.

When the great French army entered the almost defenceless territories of Holland, the popular party rose in rage and despair, brutally murdered the De Witts, overthrew their Republic, and re-established the Stadtholderate in William's person – but not as a preliminary to surrender. On the contrary they cut the dykes, letting the water of the canalized rivers flow over the low meadows, and at the sacrifice of their drowned property brought the French armies to a standstill. Meanwhile their seamen at Solebay more than held their own against the united fleets of England and France, and William's genius for diplomacy enabled him to build in haste the first of his many European coalitions against Louis.

These unexpected events gave the squires at Westminster two years in which to take stock of the situation, and to overturn the whole policy of the Cabal and its master. Parliament had the whip hand, for the war had made Charles bankrupt. In 1673 he was forced as the price of supply to assent to the Test Act that excluded Roman Catholics from office under the Crown, thereby bringing to light the alarming fact that James, Duke of York, heir to the throne, was a Romanist. Next year Parliament withdrew England from the war.

The Cavalier Parliament had come to realize that this war, properly understood, was not a continuation of the old contest between England and Holland for maritime supremacy, but a design to put an end to Dutch independence as the chief obstacle to the French Jesuit conquest of Europe. Moreover, the disappearance of Holland as an independent power would be fraught with danger for England's maritime security, because the Delta of the Rhine would then fall into the hands of France. France too was a maritime rival, potentially more formidable even than Holland, and if established in Amsterdam she would soon make an end of English naval supremacy. It was the issue of 1588, of 1793, of 1914: England could not suffer Holland and Belgium to pass under the domination of the greatest military power in Europe.

Holland was saved for the time, but the issue was not yet decided. It governed English and European politics for forty years to come. After 1674 Louis could no longer hope for the assistance of British arms in subjugating Europe, but thanks to the 'just balance of our constitution', he secured our neutrality until the Revolution of 1688, by playing off King and Parliament one against the other, bribing the Parliamentary leaders and subsidizing the King. The active agents of this policy over here were his ambassador Barillon and Charles' French mistress, Louise de Querouaille, Duchess of Portsmouth, whom our ancestors spoke of as 'Madam Carwell'.

England had been saved by the narrowest of chances from laying Europe at the feet of France by the destruction of Holland. This policy, insane from the point of view of English interests, was explicable as part of the dynastic and religious designs of the House of Stuart. When this was perceived, a reaction took place against the King and his brother and their 'Popish counsels,' which gave four years of power to the Cavalier Parliament, on the basis of Anglican, national, and constitutional principles. Charles, thoroughly alarmed at the storm he had raised and determined not 'to go on his travels again', threw over his Roman Catholic schemes and sought safety in alliance with Anglican and Tory sentiment. Such was the policy which, during the remainder of his life, he played with consummate nerve and skill.

The King's change of front involved the abandonment of the discredited Cabal Ministers and submission to the leader of the Cavalier Parliament, Thomas Osborne, Earl of Danby. Danby may be called the founder of the Tory party. Yet this theoretic champion of non-resistance to the Royal power did more than any Whig to prepare the way for the Revolution and the reign of William III. During his four years of office (1674–8) he befriended Holland and opposed France so far as Charles would allow him. And he arranged a splendid though distant future for this system of alliance by effecting the marriage of William of Orange with Mary, daughter of James and heir after her father to the throne of England.

But Danby, while he kept the Court and its Catholic partisans subject to the Protestant Tory Parliament, sought to confirm the power of the Tory party in the other direction by crushing the power of the Nonconformists with a bitter persecution, enforcing again the 'Clarendon Code' of penal laws. This provoked Shaftesbury, who had now become the Whig leader, to desperate courses.

In such a world of cross-currents, violence, persecution, and universal suspicion, Titus Oates' 'Popish Plot' acted like a match applied to powder (1678). His elaborate lies as to the criminal plots of the Roman Catholics, for a time gained credit with almost everyone, and turned the Cavalier Parliament in its last months virtually into a Whig assembly. Charles' brother James, heir to the throne, was known to be a fanatical Romanist and the prospect of his accession terrified nine Englishmen out of ten.

The Whigs had a great opportunity but they threw it away. Instead of seeking to fuse the favourable heat of the hour into a national settlement, they tried only to kindle the furnace sevenfold and to fashion out of it their party advantage. They pursued innocent Catholics to death, exploiting Oates' sham plot even after the credibility of the evidence had begun to wear thin. The violence of the three successive Whig Parliaments against their Tory rivals no less than against the Court; the systematic intimi-
1679–81 dation of moderate men by the London mob and by Shaftesbury's 'brisk boys'; the refusal to consider for the sake of peace any compromise short of complete Exclusion of James from the throne; and finally the coquetting of the party with the bastard Monmouth as the candidate for the succession, in disregard of the rights of William and Mary who did not promise to be Whig puppets –

all these signs led to a belief that '1641 was come again', and drove a large body of moderate opinion, led by the subtle and eloquent Halifax, to rally to the Tory and Royalist side. Moreover the Tories and the Court, rivals since 1661, were consolidated into a single party by the dread of a Roundhead revival.

After the dissolution of the Third Whig Parliament at Oxford in 1681, Tory reaction had full licence. The persecution of Protestant Dissenters, in abeyance during the Whig fury, was renewed with a redoubled zeal. Some of the Whig leaders finding themselves beaten constitutionally, plotted an insurrection, while old Roundhead soldiers planned to waylay and murder the Royal brothers at the Rye House, as they came back from the Newmarket races. 1683 When these villainies were discovered, the rage and power of the Tories reached their full height. The Whigs were scattered like chaff. Shaftesbury died in exile in Holland. Russell, Sidney, and others perished on the scaffold. The cynicism of the age was shown in the employment against Whig prisoners of false witnesses who were known by the Court and the Tories to have sworn away the lives of Catholics.

During the last four years of the reign, Parliament did not 1681–5 meet. It temporarily dropped out of the constitution where for some years it had held the leading position. And whenever the House of Commons met again it would not be representative of the old constituencies, or of any free electoral body. The town corporations, including London itself, had been 'remodelled' to the exclusion of the Whigs. No Tudor had ever interfered in this manner with the local franchises of the English boroughs, and nothing but the assistance of the Tory party could have enabled the monarchy to strike so deadly a blow at the local liberties of England as the 'surrender of the Charters' implied.

The Court, completely victorious and no longer troubled by a House of Commons, was swayed in its policy by Palace intrigues alone, as in days before the Long Parliament. There were two parties at Court in Charles II's last years. Halifax and the moderates were opposed to 'French counsels' and wished England to maintain the Balance of Power in Europe. But the heir to the throne, and the courtiers who had attached themselves to his rising star, were all for France. And Charles, being without Parliamentary supply, depended on French gold. The influence of Halifax declined. It was in these years that Louis, ever advancing into new territories on the Rhine and in the Spanish Netherlands, acquired that ascendancy on the continent which England had afterwards to wrench from him by twenty years of war.

The violence of rival factions in England had prepared slavery for Great Britain and for Europe. But these misdirected energies of the nation in the latter years of Charles II had given birth to the two great parties whose internal cohesion and mutual rivalry made Parliamentary government a success in the coming centuries as a method of ruling the British State and Empire. From the Exclusion Bill struggle date not only the names of Whig and Tory, but a new perfection of party organization and propaganda, and the peculiarly English art of 'electioneering'. A country that had once excited itself so profoundly in electoral and Parliamentary strife was not likely to be long quiet under a despotism. Shaftesbury and his enemies had introduced the astonishing customs of the Eatanswill election, with all its noise, expense, anger, and fun – a peculiar and valuable national heritage, because it fostered that interest in the conduct and result of elections for want of which the Parliamentary system has withered and wilted in more than one continental country in our own day.

Few political philosophers would have prophesied well of the party system or of Parliamentary government in the year 1685. The two parties, in their first wild boyhood, had set fire to their own house. But the severity of the immediate chastisement that fell first on the Whigs and in the new reign upon the Tories, taught them lessons of wisdom that enabled them in a few years to save Britain and to save Europe.

CHAPTER V

James II and the English Revolution, 1685–8. The Revolution Settlement, 1689

GOVERNMENT in the last years of Charles II had been based upon a close understanding between the Court on the one hand and the High Church and Tory Party on the other. What the Privy Council decided at Whitehall was promptly and joyfully executed by the rustic magistrate in the shire, and was praised from the pulpit in the parish church. To crush and silence their common adversaries the Whigs and Dissenters, to set the whole machinery of the law and its officers, the Justices of the Peace, the partisan Judges, and packed juries to invigilate against every smallest movement of opposition or free speech, appealed alike to the Court and to the High Tories. The latter found in the Church doctrine of non-resistance to the Crown a religious sanction for these violent proceedings against all critics of the royal policy. Forgetting much and forseeing little, they held it to be in the eternal nature of things that royal policy should be identified with their own wishes and interests. But this eternity was limited to the life of Charles. So long as he lived there was no revival of the Roman Catholic designs he had abandoned in 1674. He still, indeed, drew his pay from Louis, but it was to enable him to dispense with Parliament and to keep the peace with France, not to attempt anything active for the Roman Catholic cause at home or abroad. Only on his deathbed was he formally reconciled to the Church to which he at heart belonged. Feb. 1685

James II inaugurated the new reign by summoning Parliament. It was a packed assembly, in which many members owed their seats to the remodelled corporations from which every Whig had been excluded. So long as the Tories and the Court held together, they would never again have cause to dread a general election. Never again could there be a Whig Parliament. And it was only a question of years before the 'Dissenting interest' would be crushed out by the Clarendon Code, steadily applied without any more of those unsettling intervals of 'indulgence', which the misunderstandings between King and Commons had so often caused in the past.

The Parliament of 1685 was more royalist in sentiment than the Cavalier Parliament, but there was one thing which it would never help James to do – to subject Church and country to Roman Catholicism. The quarrel on this issue between James and the Tory House of Commons was hastened by an event which for the moment made them faster friends than ever before – the rebellion of Monmouth in the West.

Monmouth's insurrection made no appeal to the Whig gentry or to the moderate elements that were the strength of the Revolution three years later. It was a rising of Puritans against the persecution they suffered, not in the spirit of the modern Whig but of the old Roundhead party. But whereas in Cromwell's day the Roundheads had had very effective upper-class leadership, Puritanism was now a plebeian religion, confined even in Somerset to the shopkeepers of Taunton and the yeomen and labourers of the countryside. In the campaign that ended at Sedgemoor, they gave their lives with admirable devotion, not from feudal loyalty to their chiefs such as bound so many Highland tribes to the Jacobite cause, but from the mistaken belief that the worthless Monmouth was the champion of their religion.

The revenge taken upon the rebels, first by Kirke and his barbarized soldiers from Tangier, and then by Judge Jeffreys in his insane lust for cruelty, was stimulated by orders from the King. It was the first thing in the new reign that alarmed and disgusted the Tories. In the general horror felt at the long rows of tarred and gibbeted Dissenters along the roadsides of Wessex, came the first recoil from the mutual rage of parties that had so long devastated English political and religious life, the first instinctive movement towards a new era of national unity and toleration.

But the effect of Monmouth's rising on James was to goad him on to fresh tyranny. Under French and Jesuit advice, he adopted much more rapid methods of Romanizing the country than he seems to have contemplated in the first months of his reign. He had now an excuse to keep on foot an army of 30,000 men, and to make on Hounslow Heath a great camp to overawe the capital. A mistaken reliance on the Army encouraged him to defy the Tory Parliament, the rural magistracy, and the Anglican Church. Contrary to the laws of the land, which he claimed the right to suspend at will by his royal prerogative, he officered his regiments with all the Roman Catholic gentlemen whom he could induce to enter upon so dangerous a service. Their numbers were insufficient, and he was even less able to find co-religionists to fill the ranks, till he sent over to Ireland for shiploads of Celtic-speaking peasantry. English soldiers and civilians were agreed in regarding these latest recruits as foreigners and savages, whom it was the task of the Anglo-Saxon to keep docile and unarmed even in their own island. Now they were to be made masters of England herself.

By the time the Revolution broke out, James had already ruined the discipline and loyalty of his fine army, but he had not yet converted it into a force that could be used to uproot the Protestant religion. The Revolution was, indeed, timed by its promoters to forestall the completion of that difficult military evolution. But James had done enough to confirm for another long period the antipathy of the Tory squires against standing armies, which they had twice seen employed, once by Cromwell and once by James II, to subjugate the gentry and subvert the Church.

The failure and execution of Monmouth, while it tempted James along the road to ruin, removed an obstacle from the path of William of Orange. It brought nearer by one stage the union of all English parties under his leadership. He had been on good terms with the Tories ever since Danby's Ministry, but half the Whigs had been misled by the *ignis fatuus* of Monmouth. The removal of that pretender caused all English Whigs and Dissenters to concentrate their hopes upon William and Mary. In 1687 the great majority of Englishmen were united in the hope that James would presently die, and his daughter Mary succeed him before it was too late.

The solid part of the Roman Catholic body in England consisted of country squires, excluded from the magistracy but not from society, and living on very tolerable terms with their Tory neighbours. They had no goodwill for the policy which James was adopting at the suggestion of the French and Jesuit party, and with the applause of unprincipled English sycophants like Jeffreys and Sunderland. The Catholic squires knew their countrymen well enough to be sure that supremacy could never be won for their religion, except by foreign arms and civil war; and a second civil war might end, as likely as not, in completing the ruin of the English Catholics which the first had half accomplished. In these views they were supported by Pope Innocent XI, a man of sense and moderation, very different from the Pontiff who had excommunicated Elizabeth. Innocent had quarrels of his own with Louis XIV and the French Jesuits; he dreaded the French power in Italy and in Europe, and therefore watched with sympathy the sailing and the success of William's Protestant crusade, because it would release England from the French vassalage.

What the Pope and the moderate English Catholics hoped to obtain in England was not political supremacy but religious toleration. This, William publicly promised to secure for them to the utmost of his power. By temper, policy, and circumstance he stood for religious toleration. Holland had been successfully united on that basis under his great ancestors. He was, himself, the head of a league against Louis that sought to unite Austria, Spain, and the Roman Pontiff with Holland and Protestant Germany. James himself, with a little patience, could have obtained from his Parliament legal sanction for Catholic rites, which were in practice being openly celebrated. But neither the Tories nor William were prepared to consent to the thrusting in of Roman Catholics to officer the Army, to fill the magistrates' bench, the Privy Council, and finally the benefices of the Church of England herself. Yet that was the policy pursued by James for three years, with ever-increasing violence and illegality, with no assignable object but to prepare the way for the forcible reconversion of England.

During these very years his ally, Louis XIV, was revoking the tolerant Edict of Nantes, persecuting the Huguenots of France with the utmost cruelty, forbidding them even to escape into exile, driving them by torture to the Mass, separating families as if they had been Negro slaves, sending the men to the galleys and the women and children to be brought up with stripes and ill-usage in a faith they abhorred. The sum of human misery thus wantonly brought about is horrible to contemplate. In the course of years, some hundreds of thousands succeeded in escaping, mostly into England, Holland, or Prussia. A large proportion were artisans and merchants of high character, who brought to the lands of their adoption trade secrets and new industrial methods. Religious sympathy prevented their welcome from being marred by trade jealousy. The transference of so many of these men from France to England was not the least of the causes why Britain so far outstripped her great neighbour in commercial and industrial enterprise. Many French industries were ruined and many English industries founded by the greater cruelty of religious persecution in France.

The effect produced on the subjects of James II by these proceedings across the Channel, and by the arrival in their midst of a host of innocent victims of Roman Catholic fanaticism, was comparable to the effect on Elizabethan England of the cruelties of Alva and the Massacre of St Bartholomew, and to the effect on the contemporaries of Fox and Pitt of the September massacres and the cruelties of Robespierre. The Revocation of the Edict of Nantes prepared the mental and emotional background for the Revolution of 1688 and for the long wars with France that followed. They raised to a height in England the hatred of 'Popery', though in the great division for and against Louis in which all Europe was now being arrayed, the Pope was on the side of the nation whose delight it was to burn him in effigy.

The English drew their ideas of 'Popery' from their nearer neighbours, the French Jesuits and clergy who were eagerly preaching the extermination of the unhappy Huguenots. The terror lest their system should be extended to England as a result of James's proceedings, gave a fresh actuality to Foxe's *Book of Martyrs* and the tales of the Marian persecution. Protestants of every shade, from Archbishop Sancroft to Baxter and Bunyan, saw the necessity of forgetting old quarrels and standing together against the fanatical policy of the King, and the unlimited power he claimed to dispense with the laws of England. This union of spirit among all Protestants brought into the ascendant the Anglican Low Churchmen and the Whigs with their policy of Toleration, while the Tory doctrine of non-resistance to the Crown left the men who had rashly adopted it with the miserable choice of abandoning their political principles or watching with folded arms the destruction of their religion by the 'Nero' of their abstract arguments suddenly incarnate.

The Tory party, indeed, was rudely thrust out not only from its moral and intellectual position but from its material and political strongholds. In 1685 the Privy Council, the rural and the municipal magistrates, the Lords Lieutenant, and the Sheriffs, were almost without exception Tories and High Churchmen. Three years later, on the eve of the Revolution, Tories and High Churchmen had been excluded from positions of central and local authority as thoroughly as if Oliver himself had been at work. James attempted to replace them by Roman Catholics, all laws to the contrary notwithstanding. But there were not enough of his co-religionists ready to serve his rash designs. He therefore appealed also to the Protestant Dissenters, but found very few who were prepared to revenge themselves on the High Churchmen at the expense of the Protestant interest and the laws of the land.

Crown and Church were bidding against each other for Nonconformist support. The Crown offered religious toleration and civic equality by illegal Declarations of Indulgence suspending the obnoxious statutes. The Church promised religious toleration secured by statute, as soon as a free Parliament should meet. The Nonconformists, partly from their traditional preference of Parliamentary to Royal power, and partly from the terror of Roman Catholic despotism on the French model, accepted the less dazzling but far less dangerous offers made by the Church.

The King now openly attacked the possessions and freeholds of the Anglican clergy. The Court of High Commission was revived contrary to law, as the King's instrument for dragooning the Church. Compton, Bishop of London, was suspended for refusing to silence Protestant controversialists. A number of Church benefices were filled with Roman Catholics. The Fellows of Magdalen, Oxford, were illegally deprived of their property and 1687
their great College was turned into a Roman Catholic seminary. The effect of this act of tyranny was very great upon Oxford and on all who looked to Oxford for their opinions. It transformed the citadel of non-resistance and divine right into a rebel town, that flew the Orange colours in the High Street during the most eventful winter in English history.

Finally all the clergy were bidden to read from their parish

pulpits the King's Declaration of Indulgence, suspending the laws against Roman Catholics and Dissenters and admitting them to civil and military posts. Since everyone knew that the clergy held the Declaration to be illegal, the order to read it was designed to humiliate them; but unless they all stood together, the High Commission would deprive those who refused to obey. Seven Bishops, headed by Sancroft, Archbishop of Canterbury, petitioned the King against the order. His answer was to put them on trial for publishing a seditious libel. The trial of the seven Bishops
30 June 1688 and their acquittal by a jury brought the excitement in the nation to a head, and that night an invitation signed by seven Whig and Tory chiefs was sent over to William of Orange, whose agents had been for some time past in close touch with various leaders of opinion in England.

The birth of a Prince of Wales on June 10, had served as a warning to all that James's system would not end with his death. Neither Protestant Mary nor Anne, but their new Catholic brother would succeed to the throne. It was this consideration that finally brought round the majority of the Tories to reconsider their theories of non-resistance. The man who led the party in this change of ground was its founder, Danby, ever a man of action and reality. It was he who had signed the invitation to the Prince, together with the suspended Bishop Compton, another Tory Peer, and four Whig Leaders.

The dangers and difficulties of William's enterprise were enormous; half of them were European and half were English, and only he understood what they all were and how they might all be overcome by a rare combination of policy and luck. Unless they could be overcome, he knew that he would not much longer make head against Louis in Europe, so he determined to take the risk. He needed England as much as England needed him. Until the day of his death this mutual dependence did duty for mutual affection.

The danger most likely to prevent William's expedition would be a demonstration made by the French armies against Holland. This danger was removed by James himself, who alienated Louis by publicly repudiating his protection at the only moment in his reign when he really stood in need of it, William was therefore able to use the sea and land forces of Holland. He landed at Torbay on 5 November 1688, with an army drawn from all the Protestant races of Europe, large enough to protect him against a fiasco like that of Monmouth. Like Monk, he declared for a free Parliament, to which he referred all matters in dispute. The army of James, divided into factions of Protestant against Catholic, and English against Irish, was deserted at the critical moment by John Churchill, the future Marlborough, and others of its chiefs; it fell into such confusion that James dared not risk a battle. William was for many reasons anxious to avoid fighting. Every day added to his strength. The civil population rallied to his banner and to his programme of a free Parliament. Danby himself led the Northern insurrection; the second greatest Tory chief, Seymour, summoned the men of Wessex to William's camp, while the Whig Devonshire organized the Midlands, and the London mob rose without a leader.

Even then it was probable that James could not have been deposed, so strong was the Tory feeling for the hereditary right of Kings, had he not himself persisted in flying from the country and taking refuge with his wife and baby boy at the court of France. Dec. 1688

For many generations to come the Revolution of 1688–9 was spoken of by our ancestors as 'the glorious revolution'. Its glory did not consist in any deed of arms, in any signal acts of heroism on the part of Englishmen, nor in the fact that a whole nation proved itself stronger than one very foolish King. There was indeed a certain ignominy in the fact that a foreign fleet and army, however friendly and however welcome, had been required to enable Englishmen to recover the liberties they had muddled away in their frantic faction feuds. The true 'glory' of the British Revolution lay in the fact that it was bloodless, that there was no civil war, no massacre, no proscription, and above all that a settlement by consent was reached of the religious and political differences that had so long and so fiercely divided men and parties. The settlement of 1689 stood the test of time. It led not only to a new and wider liberty than had ever before been known in Britain, but to a renewed vigour and efficiency in the body politic and in the government of the Empire. The long and enervating rivalry of Crown and Parliament gave place to cooperation between the two powers, with Parliament as the leading partner. From the external weakness that had characterized England in the Seventeenth Century the country rose through the successive eras of Marlborough, Walpole, and Chatham to the acknowledged leadership of the world, in arms, colonies, and commerce, in political and religious freedom, and intellectual vigour.

The Englishmen who made the Revolution were not heroes. Few of them were even honest men. But they were very clever men, and, taught by bitter experience, they behaved at this supreme crisis as very clever men do not always behave, with sense and moderation. It was the gravity of the national danger in the first months of 1689, with France in arms against us, Scotland divided, and Ireland lost, that induced Whigs and Tories in the Convention Parliament to make that famous compromise between their conflicting principles and factions, which we call the Revolution Settlement. It remained the solid foundation of English institutions in Church and State, almost without change until the era of the Reform Bill.

The Tories, who had already in the previous autumn abandoned non-resistance, found themselves in February compelled to abandon divine hereditary right; they agreed that a slight alteration should be made by Act of Parliament in the order of succession to the throne. Henceforth, unless Parliament were 'divine', the right of English Kings to reign was of human origin. To avoid this logical defeat, many of the Tories would have preferred a Regency in James's name; and even Danby wished that James's daughter Mary should reign alone, with her husband as Prince Consort only. But when these arrangements were found to be impossible, the sense of the national danger caused the Tories to agree to the change of succession in favour of William and Mary jointly, the executive power being vested in the husband.

Indeed most Tories, in spite of theory, felt so strongly in practice the necessity of excluding a Roman Catholic from the throne, that they took the initiative in 1701, under Harley's leadership, in passing the Act of Settlement that vested the succession, after William and Anne, in the Protestant House of Hanover. Only the Right Wing of the party remained Jacobite, and a number of High Church Bishops, including Sancroft himself, refused to take the oath to William, becoming 'non-jurors', and giving up their power and preferment for conscience' sake. The reproaches of these faithful few rendered their more adaptable brethren ill at ease. The Tory party, though upon the whole loyal to the Revolution Settlement, remained so at the expense of its consistency and internal harmony; a subtle transmutation towards modern ideas was going on inside it, more painfully than in the Whig party, leading to the Tory disruption and catastrophe on the death of Queen Anne.

But otherwise the Tory forces in Church and State lost little by the Revolution, except the power of persecuting their rivals. The Church remained Anglican, and the last attempt to extend its boundaries to 'comprehend' moderate Dissenters broke down in 1689. But the Toleration Act of that year granted the right of religious worship to Protestant nonconformists, accompanied by many limitations which read strangely to-day, but which were necessary to secure agreement in an age when Toleration was regarded by many not as a grand principle but as a necessary compromise with error.

The Roman Catholic body, being the backbone of the Jacobite party, obtained no legal relief for its adherents, and from time to time fresh laws were passed against them. But in practice the policy of William and the spirit of the times secured for them a considerable degree of free religious worship in England; the infamous penal laws were usually inoperative, and were only brought into partial vigour in times of Jacobite insurrection. Worship in private houses was hardly ever interfered with, and public chapels were erected and priests often went about openly in spite of the laws. So too the laws against the growing body of Unitarians were silently disused. In the favourable atmosphere of the new age, the spirit of the Toleration Act was practised much more widely than the letter warranted.

Substantially freedom of religious worship had, with certain exceptions, won the day. But religious Tests were fully maintained until the Nineteenth Century. Persons, whether Protestant or Catholic, who would not take the Communion according to the rites of the Church of England, were still debarred from holding office either under the Crown or in the municipalities; the doors of Parliament were still closed to Roman Catholics, and the doors of the Universities to Dissenters of every kind. The Church of England ceased to be a persecuting body, but remained throughout the coming era a body with exclusive political and educational privileges that the Whigs, in the long heyday of their power under the first two Georges, never dared to alter.

Thus the principal institutions of Church and State remained on the foundations of 1660–1, and suffered no Whiggish change. The victory of the Whigs at the Revolution consisted only in the victory of their principles – religious toleration and resistance to the power of the Crown – and in the trend towards modernity, latitudinarianism, and Parliamentarianism that the whole world was about to take, owing to the fact of the English Revolution and the check which it gave to the power and principles of Louis XIV.

Neither did the Whigs in 1689 gain any such monopoly of office as they gained at the accession of the House of Hanover in 1715. William was by no means their leader, though they were more bound to support him than the Tories, because they would lose more by a Jacobite Restoration. But William only looked to find men who would help him to defeat Louis; he was purely indifferent whether they were Whig or Tory. And when in 1690 the Whigs attempted to go back on the spirit of the Revolution Compromise, and to revenge their ancient party wrongs on the Tories, he dissolved Parliament and successfully appealed to the country against them.

His successor, Anne, greatly preferred Tories to Whigs. Indeed, the only advantage that the Whigs had over their rivals prior to the coming of George I, was the fact that they were more unanimously zealous to conduct the war on land against Louis XIV than were the Tory squires with their traditional dislike of a standing army and a high land-tax.

But the Revolution had done more than arbitrate successfully between the two great parties whose feuds bade fair to destroy the State. It decided the balance between Parliamentary and regal power in favour of Parliament, and thereby gave England an executive in harmony with a sovereign legislative. It was only in the course of years that the details of that new harmony were worked out, through the development of the Cabinet system and the office of Prime Minister. But from 1689 onwards no King, not even George III in his youth, ever attempted to govern without Parliament, or contrary to the votes of the House of Commons. To bribe Parliament was one thing, to defy it quite another.

Nor did any King ever again attempt to override the local liberties of England; indeed the central government in the Eighteenth Century became only too subservient to the Justices of Peace, and only too tolerant of abuse in any chartered corporation or vested interest. The victory of law over arbitrary power was upon the whole an immense gain for humanity; but for the next hundred years and more the victory of law and of vested interests produced an undue admiration of things as they were, in the days of Blackstone, Burke, and Eldon, all of whom appealed to the great conservative Revolution as the final standard in human affairs. Because James II had attempted to destroy the institutions of the country, it long remained impossible for anyone else to attempt their reform.

Justice and humanity, divorced from all party considerations, gained greatly from the signal overthrow of James and Jeffreys. The Judges ceased to be removable at the will of the Crown. Trials were conducted with decency and on the whole with fairness. Cruel floggings and exorbitant fines ceased to be a usual weapon of party politics. In 1695 the Censorship of the Press was allowed to lapse, so that Milton's dream of 'liberty of unlicensed printing' was realized in England. The even balance of the powerful Whig and Tory parties protected critics of government who spoke from either camp. The cessation of persecution under the Clarendon Code put an end to a mass of continual suffering, hatred, and wrong. After a thousand years, religion was at length released from the obligation to practise cruelty on principle, by the admission that it is the incorrigible nature of man to hold different opinions on speculative subjects. On that stubborn fact the modern State, like the medieval Church, had broken its teeth in vain. The indirect consequences of this victory of the individual conscience were far-reaching and manifold, not to be revealed in the lifetime of the Whigs and Tories who worked out that curious patchwork of compromise, illogicality, and political good sense, the Toleration Act of 1689.

CHAPTER VI

Scotland and Ireland from the Restoration to Queen Anne. The Two Settlements

CROMWELL'S campaigns had established English rule in both Scotland and Ireland, nor did the return of Charles II put an end to the unity of political control over the British Isles. From 1660 to 1690 Irish and Scottish affairs continued to follow the vicissitudes of revolutionary change in England.

Throughout the reign of Charles II, Scotland was governed from Edinburgh by her own Privy Council, but as that body took its cue from Whitehall, and was under no control either from the Scottish Parliament or the Church Assembly, there was no real restoration of national independence, except in the undesirable form of the loss of free trade with England and her colonies. Parliament was entirely subservient to the Privy Council, and made no attempt to voice the manifold grievances of the nation.

The Privy Council that governed Scotland in the days of Middleton, Rothes, and Lauderdale, relied on the support or acquiescence of the Cavalier interest. The Scottish Cavaliers, with their traditions of Montrose, represented the fusion of aristocratic and royalist sentiment after centuries of mutual opposition; and they represented also the determination of the less fanatical among the laity to prevent the old tyranny of the Kirk, which

Cromwell had overthrown, from rising again on the ruins of his power. Many preferred the tyranny of the King's Council to that of clergy and elders. Other choice there seemed none, so long as Parliament had no power or policy of its own. The strength of the Cavalier party lay among the nobles. The alliance of the general body of the nobility with the Presbyterians had always been intermittent and half-hearted, and was already played out as a factor in history, except for the steadfast adherence of the great House of Argyle to the cause that it had chosen. Otherwise it was the smaller lairds who remained a mainstay of the Kirk.

The Privy Council had in fact a strong body of opinion behind it in maintaining the supremacy of the State over the Church. Laud's Prayer Book was not reimposed, but the Covenant was repudiated, Episcopacy was restored, and the clergy were to be appointed by patrons instead of by the democratic choice of the religious community of the parish. This programme, accepted by the greater part of Eastern Scotland, might have received the sullen acquiescence even of the south-west, had the Council proceeded with common caution and humanity. But the drunkards who ruled Scotland in the first years after the Restoration went out of their way to impose tests on the Presbyterian clergy which
1662 many of them were bound to refuse. A third of the parish ministers, mainly in the south-west, were deprived of their kirks and manses, and replaced by 'curates', who maintained themselves, in default of popular influence, by alliance with the dragoons and the strong hand of power.

From this state of things arose the practice of 'conventicles', where the 'outed ministers' preached to the faithful. But whereas the 'conventicles' of the English Nonconformists were held in barns or upper chambers, those of the Scottish Covenanters were held on solitary hillsides, in the scoop of the burn, or the heart of the birch wood, with sentinels set all round to watch for the approach of the red dragoons across the moor. And while in England the Clarendon Code was administered legally, however harshly, by civilian Justices of the Peace, in Scotland the recalcitrant districts were handed over by the Privy Council to the licence of the soldiery or the savage marauding of Highland tribes. Such ill-usage stirred to action the warrior and moss-trooper still alive in the Lowland peasant. The Pentland Rising of 1666 was followed a dozen years later by the more formidable and famous rebellion that began with the murder of Archbishop Sharp, continued with the repulse of Claverhouse by the armed conventicle at Drumclog Moss, and ended at Bothwell Brig.

The cruelty with which government provoked and suppressed these fanatical outbursts left a deep impression on the memory and imagination of the Scottish people. In happier days to come the stories of the 'killing times', and the graves and legends of the martyrs shot down in many a solitary place or 'justified in the Grassmarket', gave to Presbyterianism all over Scotland a hagiology and a cycle of romance, and secured its moral position as the asserter of national and religious freedom. Yet it was not freedom that the Covenanting martyrs had intended to assert, nor was it to posterity that they had meant to appeal, but to the living God whose sole servants they believed themselves to be in a world gone to perdition.

At the time when the disturbed and bloody reign of Charles II drew to a close, the Scottish people were by no means united in admiration for the zealots of the Covenant. The Privy Council and its torture chamber were indeed abhorrent to all decent folk, but the east mainly supported the government for want of any moderate leadership to follow in opposition, while the west was in a state of suppressed revolt. It was easy for Claverhouse and his dragoons to keep down a country thus divided against itself, so long as there was no revolution in England. It was James Seventh and Second, with his Romanizing policy, who drove his subjects of both Kingdoms into the path of union and self-deliverance.

The Revolution, simultaneous in the two countries, restored Scotland to a state of practical independence of England which she had not enjoyed since Dunbar. English statesmen, Tory as well as Whig, were fain to allow her to settle her ecclesiastical and other affairs to her own liking, provided only she would follow suit by choosing William and Mary as her sovereigns. The dynastic dispute in Britain became a lever in Scotland's hand by which she won her own terms in things both spiritual and material first at the Revolution and later at the Act of Union.

The Convention Parliament that sat at Edinburgh in 1689 deposed James VII, chose William and Mary as sovereigns of Scotland, and dictated the terms on which they might assume the crown. And it was this Parliament that in the following year formally restored Presbyterianism, but without renewing the Covenant. The autocratic rule of the Privy Council came to an end, as a necessary consequence of the Revolution. Henceforth the Parliament at Edinburgh was an independent force with which the government had to reckon. It was no longer a mere echo of the Church Assembly as in 1639, or a mere echo of the Privy

Council as in 1661. It stood for policies of its own. The feudal method of its election rendered it very indifferently representative of the country, but it represented at least the idea of lay forces, independent alike of Kirk and King, though friendly to both. With that a better age slowly dawned for Scotland.

Yet William's was a troubled reign to the North of the Tweed, where the Jacobite party was much stronger than in England. It contained the majority of the nobles, and the respectable and influential body, specially strong in the East, who clung to the ministrations of the newly ejected Episcopalian clergy. The Episcopalian Church, thrust out of the Establishment and barely tolerated in the new Scotland, could hardly fail to be more Jacobite in sympathy than the English Tories, whose Church was left intact and highly privileged under the Revolution Settlement. Moreover, to the North of the Highland line, the great majority of the kilted tribes were Jacobites, out of jealousy of the dominant tribe of the Campbells and their chief, Argyle, the true head of the Whig and Presbyterian party in all Scotland. The Highland attack upon the South, organized by Claverhouse after the example of Montrose, was checked by his death in the hour of victory
July at Killiecrankie, and was terminated a few weeks later when
1689 the tribesmen were defeated by the Covenanted Cameronians at Dunkeld. But the Highland glens were never systematically
1692 conquered and occupied before 1746. The horrible Glencoe massacre did much to foster Jacobite feeling and to discredit the government. Amid all these dangers Parliament itself, though of necessity loyal to William as against James in the last resort, was factious with all the inconsequent levity and selfishness of amateur politicians, nurtured under despotism, unaccustomed to the discipline necessary for the management of affairs in a free community, and untrained in any school of public virtue or wisdom.

Yet William's government somehow survived in Scotland, because it was at any rate more tolerant than its predecessors, and because its settlement of Church and State was in accordance with the new spirit of the times. Though Presbyterianism was restored as the national religion, the aim of government was the gradual substitution of the secular for the theological in politics. The Church Assembly again met freely, to discuss and decide its own concerns, but no longer to dictate policies to government. The old-fashioned Cameronians, clearly perceiving that the Church had not been restored to her ancient power and glory, refused to acknowledge a King who might be a Calvinist in Holland but was a Prelatist in England, and was everywhere a Laodicean and a flat tolerationist. But the mass of the nation, sick of persecution and bloodshed, acquiesced in the new regime.

An adequate solution of Scottish ecclesiastical problems had been found at last. For this reason the Scots, while continuing for two hundred years to be a profoundly religious people, were able to turn their thoughts to material problems. In 1689 their poverty was in strong contrast to their energy of mind and character. Agricultural methods were medieval, even in the rich soil of the Lothians. For want of draining, much of the best land lay water-logged and unused, while the plough went up the barren hill-side. The primeval forests had disappeared; and as yet no modern plantations, hedges, or walls broke the monotony of the windswept landscape, where the miserable sheep and cattle shivered in the blast. Improvements were impossible because the land was let on very short leases with no security of tenure. Neither lairds nor tenants had money to put into the land, and the nobles were interested in their estates chiefly as hunting grounds. The farms were cabins of turf or unmortared stone, often without windows or chimney, the door serving for light and ventilation. Beer and oatmeal were a monotonous but a wholesome and sufficient diet, save when bad harvests brought starvation, as in the 'dear years', dreadfully recurrent in King William's reign. Nearly half the acreage of what was nominally the Kingdom of Scotland, remained under the tribal rule of mountain chiefs, dwelling outside the law and civilization of the English-speaking lands.

Trade and industry were still on a very small scale. Glasgow had as yet no shipping of its own. Edinburgh was by far the largest and most wealthy town, but even in the towering High Street glass windows were rare. All told, there were about a million Scots in their native land and only a few thousands oversea, chiefly soldiers of fortune. This poverty-stricken population, with few political rights, and living under social arrangements still largely feudal, was more versed in Biblical knowledge and theological argument, and certainly not less independent in spirit, than the well-to-do farmers and shopkeepers of Parliamentary England. If the Scots should ever apply their well-trained minds and vigorous character to improving their lot in this life, the results might be astonishing.

The great change in the landscape and prosperity of Scotland which the next hundred years were to bring about – the change from the Scotland of Fletcher of Saltoun to the Scotland of Robert

Burns and Walter Scott – was due to the new direction taken by the energies of every class from landowner to cotter. Two antecedent conditions of this improvement may be noticed. First the introduction of long leases gave reasonable security of tenure, which rendered possible plantation, hedging, walling, housing, and new methods of agriculture, grazing, and breeding. And secondly the Union of North and South Britain in 1707 opened England's home and colonial markets to Scottish industry and agriculture, and made the Scots participators in England's trade privileges all the world over. In William's reign Scotland had learnt, from the tragic failure of her national settlement at Darien, the bitter lesson that she had not the power and resources needed to open markets and found colonies for herself alone.

The Union involved the absorption of Scotland's Parliament and Privy Council in those of England. Edinburgh remained the legal and cultural capital, but was no longer the seat of political power. It was a bitter sacrifice of Scotland's pride, but it was the necessary price for her material and economic expansion. The sacrifice was the more tolerable because neither Privy Council nor Parliament was in itself very dear to the people, except as a symbol of national independence. The Church Assembly was more rooted in the affection and the daily life of multitudes, and Scottish religion, like Scottish law, was left intact and separate by the Act of Union.

The inducement that prevailed on Englishmen to invite the Scots into partnership, was not economic but political. Scotland was more Presbyterian but she was none the less more Jacobite than England, and she threatened to bring the exiled Stuarts to reign at Holyrood on Anne's death, while the House of Hanover was being established at St James's. How far the threat was serious, how far a mere expression of her annoyance with England over Darien and other grievances, it is hard to say. But undoubtedly the British Empire was threatened with the possibility of disruption, in the middle of the Marlborough wars with Louis XIV. To hold together the Empire, the Whig statesmen of Anne's reign, supported by moderate Tories like Harley, offered Scotland the great material advantage of union and free trade, on condition that the Crowns and Parliaments became one. The bargain was reluctantly accepted by Scotland, but she was greatly the gainer by an arrangement which robbed her of nominal but not of real independence, and opened out the paths of her future prosperity. England gained not only the political security which was her immediate and pressing need, but the support of Scottish brains and character in the commercial and political development of the Empire.

By this great act of modern legislation, England placed upon the world's highway of commerce, colonization, and culture, a small nation hitherto poor and isolated, but the best educated and the most active-minded in Europe. The mutual advantage to England and Scotland was immense, and was not confined to the accumulation of wealth. In British literature, science, warfare, politics, administration, and colonization, the Scots have played a part out of all proportion to their numbers. The mutual advantage was indeed long unrecognized by the vulgar; it was Sir Walter Scott who first taught the English to admire Scotland, and reconciled the two nations to a joyful pride in their partnership. The statesmen of the Revolution and the reign of Anne had served Britain well. If Scottish talents and energies had for the last two hundred years been turned against England instead of being employed towards common ends, the world would be a very different place to-day. And a little more negligence or folly on either side might easily have brought it about.

On the fall of Cromwell's regime in England, the Celto-Iberian race in Ireland looked to see his work undone over there, and the chieftains of their own blood and tradition restored to the lands they had once owned, among a people who still felt for them much of the ancient tribal loyalty. But with certain exceptions this hope was disappointed. The Protestant landlords remained, as a new race of Anglo-Irish conquerors, nor did they, like the descendants of Strongbow and the Fitzgeralds, become identified with the native peasantry around them. The new barrier of religion perpetuated and emphasized the difference of civilization, and idealized the politics of self-interest and racial pride. Moreover communications with England were much easier, and the arm of England was longer and more powerful than in the Middle Ages. The solid block of English and Scottish Protestants of all classes in Ulster gave a strength to the 'English interest' in Ireland such as it had never had before. The events of 1689 were to demonstrate how much more effective the Ulster colony was as a 'garrison', than the Cromwellian landowners thinly scattered over the island among a hostile peasantry.

James II, who tried to make his co-religionists masters of Britain where they were in a tiny minority, attempted the same thing with more likelihood of success in Ireland where they formed the bulk of the population. His Catholic Deputy Tyrconnell and

his Catholic Parliament at Dublin decided to undo the Cromwellian settlement and to restore the native landlords. But before the new regime was consolidated, the Revolution in England gave the Protestants of Ireland a rallying-point and a legal position from which to defend their property and power. They were not the men to miss the chance. William was proclaimed King at Enniskillen and Londonderry with more heart-felt loyalty than in Whitehall and Edinburgh. The farming gentry and yeomen of the North were frontiersmen accustomed to the life of the saddle and the field, the sword and the plough, and were filled with the businesslike enthusiasm of the Puritan religion. They made Enniskillen the headquarters of a vigorous warfare in the open
1689 country. Meanwhile the burghers of Londonderry endured the famous siege, facing starvation in the spirit that the citizens of Haarlem and Leyden had shown in like case against the Spaniard. These men held England's bridge-head in North Ireland till reinforcements could be shipped over in sufficient strength to enable them, under the leadership of William himself, to advance southward upon Dublin.

In the year 1690 Ireland was the pivot of the European crisis. The fate of Britain depended on William's campaign, and on the fate of Britain depended the success or failure of Europe's resistance to French hegemony. William's throne was tottering in the after-throes of the earthquake of the late Revolution, which had not yet subsided. The English Church and Army were disaffected; the civil, military, and naval services were in grave disorder; the Whigs and Tories of Parliament were renewing their old feuds; half the public men of both parties were in secret communication with the Jacobites, not because they desired but because they expected a Restoration. With good hope then, Louis had sent over James as his vassal, with French money, troops, and generals, to complete first the conquest of Ireland, where three-fourths of the land already obeyed him. Until Ireland was secured for William, Britain could take no part in the continental war, and might soon herself be in the throes of a counter-revolution.

The battle of the Boyne was fought upon two quarrels. It
1690 was the struggle of the Anglo-Scots against the Celto-Iberians for the leadership of Ireland. But it was no less the struggle of Britain and her European allies to prevent a Jacobite restoration in England, and the consequent domination of the world by the French monarchy. The presence, on both sides of the river, of regiments from the continent represented the international issues at stake. The outcome of that day subjected the native Irish to

persecution and tyranny for several generations to come, but it saved Protestantism in Europe and enabled the British Empire to launch forth strongly on its career of prosperity, freedom, and expansion overseas.

But while Enniskillen, Londonderry, and the Boyne were but a stage in the forward march of British and world history, they became the central point of time in the imagination of the ruling race in Ireland. With equal intensity of recollection the oppressed Celt continued to think of the gallant defence of Limerick, and the subsequent breach by the conquerors of the treaty they signed 1690, 1691
there with the vanquished race. Sarsfield, the hero of the Limerick campaigns, stood to the conquered as the representative man of the new Ireland, the faithful son of the *mater dolorosa.* The place occupied by Sarsfield in Irish history is significant. For he was no scion of an old tribal family, with immemorial claims on the local allegiance of a clan. The English had effectually destroyed the clan society and banished or slain the clan leaders. Sarsfield represented the new nation that was taking the place of the suppressed tribes, as Wallace had represented the new nation that in Scotland gradually took the place of old clan and feudal loyalties.

The restored English rule in Ireland reflected very little of the wise and tolerant spirit of William. In this Catholic island he was powerless to do anything to protect the Catholics, whose lot he mitigated in England. The new regime in Ireland reflected the rash ignorance and prejudice of the Whigs and Tories of the Westminster Parliament, who were the real overlords of the reconquered dependency. While the penal code placed the Catholics in Ireland under every political and social disadvantage that malice could invent, and pursued and persecuted their priests, the only leaders left to them under the Cromwellian land system – by a masterstroke of folly the sectarian quarrels of English Protestants were transferred to Ulster; Anglican intolerance refused political equality and for some time even religious freedom to Presbyterians who had manned the walls of Londonderry and forded the Boyne water. From the Restoration onwards, English trade jealousy had been permitted to depress the Protestant interest in Ireland by laws against the export of Irish cattle and of Irish cloth. The ruin of the Irish cloth trade, completed at the end of William's reign by the decrees of the English Parliament, effectively stopped the growth of the Anglo-Saxon colony. Many thousands of Ulster Scots who sought refuge beyond the Atlantic in the Appalachian Mountains, had more real wrongs to revenge on England in the

War of American Independence than had most of those who followed the standard of Washington.

Oliver had at least promoted the Protestant interest everywhere in the British Isles. He saw that if Ireland was to be an English colony it must be colonized by English. But the Protestant interest and the Anglo-Saxon colony were after his death depressed by the commercial and ecclesiastical jealousy of Cavalier, Whig, and Tory Parliaments, of narrower vision in these respects than Protector or King. Yet the Catholics were still persecuted with Cromwellian vigour. All that was bad in Oliver's Irish system was preserved, all that was good in it was reversed.

Such were the Scottish and the Irish settlements that resulted from the English Revolution. Very different as they were in their character and ultimate consequences, they seemed to be equally permanent and equally unchallengeable throughout the greater part of the stable and pacific Eighteenth Century. Indeed in 1715, and again in 1745, the Hanoverian government had much more trouble in Scotland than in Ireland. Yet the Scottish settlement, resting on consent, in the end outlasted the Irish settlement that reposed on force.

It is remarkable that the great events which convulsed England, Scotland, and Ireland under the later Stuarts, had no repercussions of a regional character in Celtic Wales. From the Tudor settlement till the Nineteenth Century, Wales had no history except that of slow social and religious growth. The upper class were gradually becoming English in culture and connexion, while the small farmers of the hills, the typical Welshmen before the modern industrial era, remained Celtic in character and largely Celtic in speech, but felt no active political hostility to England or to English institutions of which Wales was now an integral part. The level of intellectual activity was low as compared to later times, but native music and poetry persisted among the people; and all through the Seventeenth and Eighteenth Centuries the Welsh common folk were gradually moving from an indifferent acquiescence in Anglican religion towards an enthusiastic evangelicalism of their own, by means of which the national mind and spirit eventually revived.

CHAPTER VII

The Wars of William and Marlborough. The Downfall of Louis XIV and the Rise of Great Britain to Maritime and Commercial Supremacy. The Death of Anne and the Dynastic Crisis

Sovereigns: William and Mary, 1689–94; William III (alone), 1694–1702; Anne 1702–14

IN the winter of 1688–9, foreign and domestic events combined to force England into the leadership of the alliance against France, in accordance with Danby's war plans of a dozen years before which had been thwarted by King Charles and by the Whigs. After the Revolution, resistance to France became the first charge on the energies of the new King and of the reconstituted Whig party, and in a scarcely less degree of the nation as a whole. The continued attempt of Louis to reimpose upon England the rule of James and his son after him, rendered the wars of William and Marlborough unavoidable.

William's war, known as the War of the League of Augsburg, lasted from 1689 to 1697, and was ended by the indecisive Treaty of Ryswick. After an uneasy interval of four years, war broke out again on an even larger scale – the War of the Spanish Succession – conducted by Marlborough as Europe's general and diplomat in chief, and was ended by the Treaty of Utrecht in 1713. That Treaty, which ushered in the stable and characteristic period of Eighteenth-Century civilization, marked the end of danger to Europe from the old French monarchy, and it marked a change of no less significance to the world at large – the maritime, commercial, and financial supremacy of Great Britain.

The prime condition of successful warfare against Louis, whether on sea or land, was the alliance of England and Holland. The understanding was not very cordial in 1689 between the two nations, so long accustomed to regard each other as rivals in trade and admiralty; but a united front was demanded by the time, and was ensured by the greatest statesman in Europe who had been placed at the head of the executive in both countries. Under William's tutelage, the English and Dutch Ministers contracted habits of close cooperation for purposes of war, which survived the death of the Stadtholder-King and were continued by Marlborough and Heinsius. Cooperation was the less difficult, because England's commercial jealousy of Holland diminished as the proportion of Dutch ships in the allied fleet dwindled year by year, and as Dutch commerce and finance fell behind the newly mobilized resources of her ally. England throve on the war, while the strain of war taxation and effort slowly undermined the artificial greatness of the little Republic. In the latter part of Queen Anne's reign, the mercantile community in London had so little cause left for jealousy of Dutch commerce, that the Whigs and the 'moneyed interest' proposed concessions to be made to Holland in the terms of peace, which the Tories and the 'landed interest' justly criticized as extravagant.

Throughout this long period of war, which involved all Western
1689–1713 and Central Europe and its American Colonies, the naval operations stood in a close causal connexion with the diplomatic triumphs of William, and the diplomatic and martial triumphs of Marlborough. But it is only in quite recent times, under the influence of Admiral Mahan and his school of history, that the maritime aspect of the struggle against Louis has been rated at its true value. For although Sir George Rooke and Sir Clowdisley Shovell were fine seamen, no name like Drake, Blake, or Nelson appeared as the rival of Marlborough's fame, and the single naval victory of La Hogue seemed a poor match for Blenheim and Ramillies and the long list of conquered provinces and towns. Yet all the grand schemes of war and diplomacy depended on the battleships of England, tossing far out at sea; Louis of France, like Philip of Spain before him, and Napoleon and Kaiser William since, was hunted down by the pack he never saw.

La Hogue, the crowning victory at sea, occurred as early as the fourth year in the long contest. This is the more remarkable, because the French, as Admiral Mahan tells us, were 'superior to the English and Dutch on the seas in 1689 and 1690'. In the first months of the war Louis had the chance to perpetuate French naval supremacy and to prevent the success of the English Revolution, by the proper use of his then dominant fleet. But the irrecoverable moment went by unseized. He made no naval effort to stop William from shipping his forces to England in 1688, and to Ireland in the two following years. In 1690 the victory of the French over the inferior numbers of the combined English and Dutch fleets off Beachy Head, showed what might have been done to cut the communications between England and Ireland in the year of the Boyne. But the courtiers at inland Versailles lacked the sense of naval opportunity, which was seldom entirely wanting to the statesmen who watched the world's ebb and flow from the tidal shore of the Thames.

In 1692 the tables were turned by the victory in the Channel of the allied over the French fleet, followed by the destruction of fifteen French men-of-war in the harbours of Cherbourg and La Hogue. These losses were not indeed very much greater than the allied losses at Beachy Head two years before. And yet La Hogue proved as decisive as Trafalgar, because Louis, having by his clumsy and arrogant diplomacy defied all Europe to a land war, could not afford to keep the French fleet up to its strength, in addition to the armies and fortresses needed for the defence of all his land frontiers at once. The French fighting navy in 1690 had owed its temporary superiority to the war-policy of the Court, and was not, to the same degree as the navies of England and Holland, founded on proportionately great resources of merchant shipping and commercial wealth. The trade and industry of France were oozing away through the self-inflicted wound of the Revocation of the Edict of Nantes. When, therefore, the war-policy of Louis induced him to neglect the navy in favour of the land forces, French naval decline was rapid and permanent, and French commerce and colonies suffered accordingly.

The battle fleets of King Louis retired from serious operations, leaving the passage to the continent open year after year to the armies of William and Marlborough with all their supplies and reinforcements, and allowing the pressure of the British fleet to be brought to bear on hesitating States at moments of diplomatic crisis. In William's reign the allied fleet saved Barcelona and prolonged the resistance of Spain against Louis. During the Marlborough wars, our alliance with Portugal and rebellious Catalonia, and our whole war-policy in the Mediterranean and in Spain, depended on our naval supremacy in those seas, of which Gibraltar and Minorca were pledges taken and kept.

The seamen of France, when their grand fleet went out of commission, turned their energies to privateering. Admiral Tourville was eclipsed by Jean Bart. English commerce suffered from him and his like, but throve in their despite, while French commerce disappeared from the seas. When the frontiers of France were closed by hostile armies, she was thrown back to feed upon her own ever diminishing resources, while England had the world for market from China to Massachusetts.

In the earlier years of the reign of the Grand Monarch, his good genius, Colbert, had nourished French industry and commerce with remarkable success, though often by State regulations more paternal than would have suited the individualist spirit of wealth-making in England. But from the Dutch war of 1672 onwards the malign influence of Louvois gradually replaced the hold of Colbert on the mind of the King. Warlike ambitions in Europe and religious persecution at home destroyed the fabric of national prosperity erected in the earlier part of the reign. Louis could indeed tax his miserable peasants at will, but even he could not take from them more than they had, and he had bled them white long before he was rid of Marlborough. Bankruptcy brought his system to the ground, and with it fell the moral prestige of despotism and religious persecution.

Meanwhile the English State, that had been so feeble and distracted in the first two years of William's reign, was gaining internal harmony, financial soundness, and warlike vigour all through the long contest, so that the new English principles in Church and State were constantly rising in the world's esteem. England was paymaster to the Grand Alliance, with her subsidies to needy German Princes, and her own well-equipped armies and fleets, that increased in numbers, discipline, and efficiency as the years went by.

Parliament, supreme at length in the constitution, was ready to vote supplies to William and Anne such as it had never voted to either Charles. Scarcely less important, from the point of view of the finance of the war, was the alliance between the King's Ministers and the City, leading to a new system of government borrowing on long loans. In the past, royal loans had been made in anticipation of revenue, the capital to be paid back as soon as certain taxes had been levied. Under the new system the patriotic investor, doing well both for himself and for his country, had no wish to have his capital paid back at any near day, preferring to draw a good interest on it for the rest of his life, upon the security of the State. The principal lenders to government were
1694 organized in the Bank of England, to which Ministers gave the support of public credit in its banking operations with individual traders.

The Bank of England and the permanent National Debt were the outcome of the fertile brains of the Scot, William Paterson, and of the Whig Chancellor of the Exchequer, Charles Montagu; the whole movement was regarded with suspicion by the Tory country gentlemen, jealous of the rising influence of the 'moneyed interest' over the royal counsels. The City, prevalently Whig in political and religious sympathy, was bound still more strongly to the Whig party by this system of long loans to the governments born of the Revolution. For the Pretender would repudiate his enemy's debts if he should ever return, and to prevent that return the Whigs were pledged one degree more deeply than the Tories.

The movement towards the development of the world's resources through accumulated and applied capital, was in this era finding its principal seat of operations in mercantile England. The capitalization of industry was still in the day of small things, though the domestic cloth-workers dealt through capitalist middlemen. But the capitalization of the world's trade was already conducted on a large scale, and was moving its centre from Amsterdam to London. The London of William and Marlborough was a huge emporium, less of industry than of commerce and finance. Its work was done by a turbulent population of cockney roughs – porters, dockers, day-labourers, watermen, and a fair sprinkling of professional criminals – living uncared-for and almost unpoliced in labyrinths of tottering, insanitary houses many of them in the 'liberties' outside the City walls, especially in the over-populated area of which Fleet Street was the centre; next, there was a large middle stratum of respectable shopkeepers and artisans, largely engaged in high-class finishing trades; and on the top of all, a body of wealthy merchants and moneyed men to which no other district in Europe could show the equal, inhabited 'the City' proper.

London and its leaders were once more hand-in-glove with government, as in the days of Burleigh and Gresham; but the methods of State finance and the quantity and availability of London's wealth had made great strides since the days of Elizabeth's parsimonious warfare against Philip. If Drake had had Charles Montagu behind him, he would have done more than singe the beard of the King of Spain. The Grand Monarch of this later era was to learn by bitter experience that the English Parliament and the City of London between them commanded the deeper purse, though France had nearly twenty million inhabitants, and England and Scotland about seven.

The East India Company of London had become the rival on equal terms of the once dominant Dutch Company, that had so rudely excluded the English traders from the Spice Islands in early Stuart days. Steady trade with the Mogul Empire on the mainland was carried on from the stations at Madras, Bombay, and latterly from Fort William in the Delta of the Ganges, the nucleus of the future Calcutta. The shareholders in the joint-stock company continued to make fortunes hand over hand during the war with Louis, for although ships were lost to French privateers, the demand for tea, spices, shawls, and cotton goods did not diminish, and the demand for saltpetre to make gunpowder greatly increased. The Company, though it was gradually building up a great market for English goods in China and India, was accused of exporting bullion and bringing back mere 'luxuries'; but men and women still clamoured for the 'luxuries', and for shares in the much-abused Company. In the reigns of William and Anne, the strife in the City between the chartered traders and the interlopers, between the Old Company and the New, convulsed the House of Commons, which had stepped into the place of the Court as the State arbiter of commercial privileges. In the first half-dozen years after the Revolution, Sir Josiah Child, in defence of the monopoly of the Old Company, disbursed some £100,000 to Cabinet Ministers and members of Parliament. In these quarrels, all the furies of party passion and private greed were stimulated by the knowledge that the wealth of the East was no longer an Arabian tale, but a solid fact on which City fortunes were being built and new County families founded every year. The most remarkable and formidable of these self-made magnates was Thomas Pitt, grandfather of the great Chatham, and owner of the Pitt diamond. Having made his fortune in India first as poacher and then as gamekeeper, that is to say first as 'interloping' trader and then as Governor of Madras for the Company, he purchased a landed estate at home, together with the Parliamentary borough of Old Sarum.

The coffee drunk in the famous coffee-houses of the period was imported less by the East India Company than by the English merchants trading in the Mediterranean. They had become the chief European influence at Constantinople, and were pushing the sale of English cloth in the ports of Italy, Venice, and the Levant. In spite of the Barbary pirates and the privateers who dashed out from Toulon and Brest, our Turkey and Venetian merchants throve during the war. And it greatly added to their
1704, security and prestige that after the capture of Gibraltar and
1708 Minorca the Western Mediterranean was permanently occupied by the Royal Navy.

On the other side of the Atlantic, the English had the full advantage of naval supremacy. There was a rehearsal of the issues brought to a final head by Wolfe and Chatham two generations later. The men of Massachusetts, much the most active of the American Colonies, twice during the wars with Louis XIV captured Acadia from the French; though given back once at the Treaty of Ryswick, it was annexed to Britain by the Treaty of Utrecht and re-christened Nova Scotia. By the same treaty Britain
1713 annexed Newfoundland, subject to certain French fishing rights which remained a constant subject of dispute until their final

settlement in the reign of Edward VII. The Hudson Bay territory was also annexed, with its snow-bound forests whence English hunters supplied the fur trade at home. And so – although an 1711
attack on Quebec, badly concerted between the Royal and Colonial forces, had failed – the end of the war saw the British solidly planted near the mouth of the St Lawrence, and in the arctic rear of the French settlements on the great river.

The war and the peace stimulated another British interest oversea, the endeavour to force our commerce on the great South American market, in spite of the Spanish government's decree excluding all foreign traders. The quarrel with the Spaniards in South and Central America had been carried on by the English buccaneers ever since James I's peace with the Spanish Monarchy. In the reign of Charles II, the buccaneers of the West Indian Islands were in the heyday of their romantic glory, as the unofficial maintainers of England's quarrels along the Spanish Main. In the reigns of William and Anne they were declining into the position and character of black-flag pirates of the type of Teach, their hand against the men of all nations, and every man's hand against them. But the process was gradual; many, like Kidd and Quelch, moved in a doubtful borderland between piracy and privateering, and the attitude of the Colonials and of the British officials differed according to the circumstances and the men.

An attempt was made to regularize our relations with Spain in the Treaty of Utrecht, when the Tory government won applause even from their harshest critics by securing the famous *Asiento*, permitting England alone of foreign powers the annual privilege of sending a ship to trade with Spanish America, and of taking thither, besides, 4800 Negro slaves. But this limited monopoly was used in the Eighteenth Century as the starting-point for a larger illicit trade, and the quarrel for the open door in South America only came to an end with the termination of Spanish rule in the days of Bolivar and Canning.

With regard to the war in Europe, there is a marked distinction of character between the two parts of the struggle that brought Louis to his knees. In the War of the League of Augsburg, of 1689–97
which William III was the political and military chief, France was engaged on all her land frontiers in operations against Spain, Holland, and the German Princes, and even so she held her own; neither side won any sensational victories, though Steinkirk and Landen were successes for the French; neither side anywhere made any measurable progress. The boundary between the Spanish

Netherlands and France, where most of the fighting took place, remained practically unaltered. Under William, who was not the man either to win or lose campaigns on the grand scale, the British troops learnt the art of war, and were bequeathed by him a fit instrument for a greater captain.

On the other hand, in the ensuing War of the Spanish Succes-
1701–13 sion, France began the contest with every apparent advantage except sea power. Her armies were in occupation of the whole Spanish inheritance in Europe, in the name of Louis' grandson, Philip V, the new King of Spain. The great Kingdom beyond the Pyrenees, Italian Milan and Naples, and the long-contested Spanish Netherlands with their famous fortresses, were all, for fighting purposes, French territory when the war began. Moreover, Louis had as an active ally the great State of Bavaria, lying in the heart of Germany, on the boundaries of hard-pressed Austria, herself attacked on the other side by the Hungarian insurrection. The situation appeared desperate for the cause of the allies, and for the future safety of Holland and England by land and sea: unless they could turn Louis out of these territories, particularly out of the Netherlands, he would remain what he had indeed become, the master of Europe. But contrary to all expectation, the allies, who in the previous war had seemed no painful inch to gain, chased the French out of every one of these lands with the exception of Spain, where the genius of the Spanish people for guerrilla warfare secured them the King of their choice, the Bourbon Philip.

Austria was saved and Bavaria conquered by Marlborough's march on the Danube and victory at Blenheim in 1704; the Spanish Netherlands were conquered by him at Ramillies in 1706, and that same year Eugene's campaign of Turin secured for Austria Milan, Naples, and the hegemony in the Italian Peninsula. Though Spain herself remained to the Bourbon candidate, the Spanish Empire in Europe was conquered and dismembered, chiefly to increase Austria's territories, but also for the permanent security of Holland and Great Britain.

These tremendous victories, as compared to the stalemate of the previous war, can be accounted for in no small degree by the military genius of Marlborough, backed by the fine abilities and faithful cooperation of his friend, Prince Eugene of Savoy, the Austrian General. But the successes must also be ascribed to the ever-increasing maritime, commercial, and financial power of Britain and its vigorous application by Marlborough, Godolphin, and the Whig Ministers of Anne. Marlborough understood the strategy of world war and the way to combine land and sea power in successful operations, better than any man who has succeeded him in control of England's destiny, with the possible exception of Chatham. Corresponding to England's growth, was the maritime and financial decadence of France, whose efforts at world conquest for fifty years past exhausted and betrayed her just when the prize was in her grasp. The national exhaustion reflected itself in the failing ability of the new generation of Louis' Generals, and the want of self-confidence in his troops after their first defeats at the hand of 'Malbroucke'.

The size and armament of battleships and the tactical methods of warfare at sea underwent no great change between the days of Blake and the days of Nelson. But the methods of warfare on land, when Marlborough took command at the beginning of Anne's reign, had just undergone a great change from the methods of Gustavus Adolphus and Cromwell. Ever since the Restoration the bayonet had been gradually coming in, and, after the lesson of Killiecrankie, William's reign saw the general adoption of the ring-bayonet that could be left on while the gun was being discharged. Consequently the pikemen, who had composed half the regiment in Cromwell's day, were altogether abolished; henceforth there was but one type of infantry private, with his firelock ending in the dagger-bayonet. In connexion with this change of weapon, the six-deep formation of the infantry column, suitable to pikes, was changed to a thin line of three deep, as the method of concentrating the greatest volume of fire upon the enemy. Already we are in the realm of the infantry tactics employed by Frederick the Great and by Wellington, though the drill of the infantry was not yet so perfect or their manoeuvring so flexible as in those later times. Cavalry, as at Blenheim and Ramillies, could still decide battles, but their place in war was already smaller than in Cromwell's day, owing to the increased efficiency of the 'poor foot'.

The warfare of the age of Louis XIV was largely an affair of fortresses. Readers of 'Tristam Shandy' will remember how the two old soldiers of William show even more professional interest in the news of Marlborough's sieges than in his marches and battles. King Louis' military architect, 'the celebrated Monsieur Vauban', carried the defensive art to a high and complicated perfection, and France and her neighbours watched each other across a network of fortified towns, specially thick in the Netherlands.

The result was a tendency to stagnation in military enterprise

and mobility, very marked in the War of the League of Augsburg. But in the War of the Spanish Succession the rapid conquest of provinces recalls Gustavus and foreshadows Napoleon. The way for this change had been prepared by the unopposed advance of Louis' armies beyond the frontiers of France into the territories of the Spanish Empire and Bavaria. Marlborough, when he took over the command, found the French far in advance of their usual line of fortresses. He seized the opportunity to restore the war of movement, much to the horror of the more timid and conventional spirits on his own side. When he resolved to carry the Dutch and English armies across Europe to the Danube, to save
1704 Austria and win Blenheim, he had to deceive the vigilance of the Dutch authorities and the Tories of the English Parliament, who objected to any such dangerous use of their costly regiments.

Marlborough as a military strategist and a tactician, as a war statesman and war diplomatist, stands second to no Englishman in history. His powers resemble those of Chatham and Clive rolled into one, except that he could not, like Chatham, arouse the spirit of his countrymen at large by magnificent speech and visible ardour of soul. For the purpose of striking down a great military monarchy, he was Wellington and Castlereagh combined, and if the Whigs had left him a free hand he might have made for Europe in 1709 as good a peace as Castlereagh made in 1815 – or Bolingbroke in 1713.

Cromwell alone seems his match. But Oliver attracts or repels by the peculiarities of his character, and by his political and religious affinities; whereas Marlborough arouses no such prejudices either for or against his claims upon the gratitude of his country and of the world. 'The detested names of Whig and Tory', as he called them, were less than nothing to him, though fate made him a Tory by birth and upbringing, and a Whig by later connexion. Both sides revenged themselves upon him for not being one of themselves, the Tories assiduously blackening his character and the Whigs being lukewarm in its defence. As the contemporary of Louis' English pensioners and of the Whig and Tory correspondents of the exiled James, he was no better, indeed, than the average product of the Restoration Court and the Revolution Parliaments. But if he loved money, he gave England better value for every guinea he received from her than any other of her servants; if he looked to the main chance, his country was the gainer for his shrewdness nine times out of ten; and if he failed to arouse the personal devotion of any class except the soldiers whom he led to certain victory, his featureless calm of Olympian power is perhaps as much above as it is below Cromwell's humorous, passionate humanity, and craving, troubled spirit, never quite at rest either in this world or the other. By the light of his unclouded genius, Marlborough protected the advent of the much-needed age of reason, toleration, and common sense.

In the successful conduct of a world war there are two distinct operations, both very difficult – the winning of the victory in arms, and afterwards the making of a stable peace. Unfortunately the temper and qualities required and engendered by war are not always conducive to the proper handling of peace negotiations, and for this reason it was no bad thing that our two-party system enabled the Whigs to win the war and the Tories to make the peace.

Since the Revolution, the Whigs had become the more inveterate enemies of Louis, as the representative of despotism and the patron of the Pretender. William III, who had less than no predilection in favour of the Whigs, had found in practice that only a Whig Ministry could carry on the War of the League of Augsburg with the necessary vigour and financial ingenuity; but he himself, without help from his English Ministers, concluded peace at Ryswick. In the interval that followed before the renewal of war, the Tories rose again automatically to the surface, and on the accession of their supporter, Queen Anne, secured almost a monopoly of power. But during these four somewhat confused 1697–1701 years of peace, it had been the moderate Tory, Harley, a man of Roundhead family and connexions, who exerted most influence in the House of Commons. He 'educated his party', inducing the Tories to pass the Act of Settlement which fixed the succession on June 1701 the House of Hanover, in case of Anne's death without children; and to renew the war with France, when Louis, in spite of his acknowledgement of William in the Treaty of Ryswick, insolently declared the Pretender to be James III, King of England. The control of the vast resources of the Spanish Empire had been too much for the prudence of the Grand Monarch, who already regarded himself as master of the world.

The War of the Spanish Succession was therefore begun by a combination of moderate Tories and Whigs with Marlborough and Godolphin. But events led once more to a war-Ministry predominantly Whig, because so many of the Tory party were more interested in passing laws against the Dissenters than in beating Louis. But Harley's heart was in the war, and he remained in the Whig Ministry until Louis had been driven out of the Spanish

Netherlands, and the Union with Scotland had been carried. Finally in 1708 Anne was compelled to accept a wholly Whig Ministry without Harley. Marlborough and Godolphin, altogether detached from the Tory party, remained to act under the orders of the Whig 'Junto'. Mixed Ministries, though they had often done useful work, were found increasingly difficult under the Parliamentary system. Ever since the Revolution England had been moving unconsciously towards the modern system of a responsible Cabinet all of one political complexion.

The Whigs, who had twice risen and thrived by war, were slow to make peace. And unfortunately the completeness of their
1708 political victory at home coincided exactly with the period when peace negotiations ought to have been seriously undertaken and pushed through. Marlborough, having won the Spanish Netherlands for Austria at Ramillies and Oudenarde, was engaged, during four more years of unnecessary war, in reducing the fortresses that defended the frontier of France herself. Louis, in terrible straits, offered in 1709 everything that the allies could reasonably demand, including the withdrawal of all assistance from his grandson in Spain. But the Whigs showed themselves incapable of making peace. They demanded the one thing Louis could not grant – that he should himself send his armies to expel Philip from the Spanish throne on which he had placed him eight years before. The cause of this outrageous demand was the difficulty the allies found in expelling Philip themselves, as he was the favourite of the Spanish people. The Whig formula of 'no peace without Spain' meant in practice no peace at all. Louis appealed to his subjects, as he had never deigned to do before; they knew that he had made great sacrifices of his pride to buy them a peace,
1709 but in vain, so they rallied to him with the well-known valour of the French people in defence of the soil, and gave Marlborough his first rebuff in his Pyrrhic victory of Malplaquet.

John Bull, also, was hungering for the victorious peace which the Whig doctors had ordered away from his table. The cry to stop the war swelled the Tory reaction which domestic causes were producing. A wave of High Church feeling passed over the Queen and her subjects, and mobs who a few years before were chasing Jacobites and sacking Mass-houses, once more engaged in the alternative employment of burning Dissenters' chapels. Popular emotion was swelled by the folly of the Whig Ministers in impreaching before the House of Lords a certain Dr Sacheverell, who had preached a sermon against the principles of the Revolution, on the day consecrated to its memory.

The Queen's political and religious sympathies and the influence exercised over her by Mrs Masham, at length enabled her to throw off the personal domination of Sarah, Duchess of Marlborough. The Whigs fell at once, ere long dragging Marlborough 1710
himself after them. Anne's initiative in changing her Ministers was confirmed at the General Election. Since the winter of William's coming over, no change in men and measures had been so complete and so instantaneous. Yet this was not a revolution, but a normal process of the new constitution, which was tending more and more towards party Cabinet government by Whigs and Tories in alternation. No change less complete would have secured peace for Europe at that juncture.

The new Tory Ministry took office under the double leadership of the brilliant St John, prepared to go any lengths to crush the Whigs and extirpate Dissenters in pursuit of his political game, and the slow, moderate Harley, whose chief virtue was a desire, unfortunately rare among contemporary statesmen, to promote unity of spirit in the whole nation. But the government was at least agreed on its first necessary task – the making of peace. Except the betrayal of our Catalan allies to the vengeance of Philip of Spain, it is difficult to find serious fault with the terms of the Treaty of Utrecht. The methods by which this excellent 1713
peace was obtained are perhaps more open to criticism. The Whigs denounced, and the nation little liked the secret negotiations with France behind the back of the allies – though William had done the same to obtain the Treaty of Ryswick – the disgrace of Marlborough, and the withdrawal of the British armies from the field in face of the enemy. Yet it was largely the fault of Whig, Dutch, and Austrian obstinacy that these methods seemed the only way to settle any terms at all with France and compel the allies to accept them.

British colonial and commercial interests were, as we have seen, amply provided for, and they would have benefited still more if the Tory Ministers' Commercial Treaty with France had not been thrown out by English trade jealousy, organized by the Whig opposition. As regards territorial arrangements in Europe, the terms of Utrecht were based on the formal assignment of the Spanish dominions in Europe to Austria, and the formal assignment of Spain and her American dominions to the Bourbon Philip. It was merely a recognition of the state of things established by the events of the war, which the operations of the last five years had failed to shake. England's maritime security was ensured by the transference of the Netherlands to Austria, an inland power of central Europe from whom we had nothing to fear. The French threat to the Rhine Delta had been parried until 1793.

These arrangements proved a stable basis for Eighteenth-Century civilization. Europe was never again troubled by danger from the preponderance of France, until the French Revolution had given her a new form of life. If Louis had been treated with the vindictive severity contemplated by the Whigs and Austria, when Marlborough should at length have burst through the network of fortresses and reached Paris, the spirit of revenge might have made a permanent lodging in the soul of the French people, rallied them to the monarchy of the *ancien régime*, and kept Eighteenth-Century Europe constantly disturbed with wars more than dynastic.

BOOK FIVE
FROM UTRECHT TO WATERLOO

Sea Power and Aristocracy.
First Stage of the Industrial Revolution.

THE Eighteenth Century in England starts politically from the Revolution Settlement of 1689, on which it may be said to be a gloss or comment. The accession of the House of Hanover in 1714 was only a confirmation and extension of the principles that had placed William and Mary on the throne twenty-five years before.

The Revolution Settlement had the defects of its qualities. It was inevitably too conservative, or so at least it appears to modern eyes. It would have been better, some think in the retrospect, if the opportunity had been taken to redistribute the Parliamentary seats more nearly according to population. In the elections to Cromwell's Parliaments the rotten boroughs had been abolished as being under the influence of the local gentry, and the county representation had been proportionately increased. But the old constituencies had been restored with Charles II, and the men of 1689 left the unreformed representation to grow ever more corrupt with years, bringing thereby many evils on the country, possibly among others the quarrel with America. But the merit of the Revolution lay in being a settlement by consent, and consent could only be obtained by avoiding as far as possible the disturbance of vested interests. Now, one of those vested interests was the power of certain nobles and gentry to influence elections to the House of Commons in certain boroughs. A Reform Bill had no place in the minds of either Whigs or Tories in that era.

Indeed the ostensible object of the Revolution was not change but conservatism. James II had illegally attacked a number of vested interests and chartered corporations – the Church, the Universities, the town Municipalities, the electoral rights of the parliamentary boroughs, the property of freeholders – and he had denied the efficacy of the laws of the land. By inevitable reaction, the Revolution, in its just defence of these interests against illegal assault, gave to them a sacrosanct character which helped to protect them against wise and legal reform for a hundred and forty years to come. The outrages that provoked the Revolution had engendered an ideal enthusiasm for vested interests as such, because the action of James II had for a while identified vested interests with the cause of British freedom. And this ideal enthusiasm survived the occasion that had called it forth. The existing laws, which James II in his tyranny had over-ridden, became a fetish to Judge Blackstone and the men of the Eighteenth Century.

The Revolution was a triumph of the lawyers over the executive, the close of a long struggle begun by Coke and Selden to subject the legality of the King's actions to the free judgement of the courts that administered the Common Law. The victory of law over irresponsible and arbitrary power was a splendid triumph for civilization, but it made the lawyer's point of view somewhat too predominant in the Eighteenth Century. The Revolution which had been made in order to oppose illegal changes attempted by an arbitrary monarch, was appealed to in retrospect by Blackstone and even by Burke, as a fixed standard, a criterion by which legislative reform of a popular character was to be condemned beforehand.

Partly for this reason, the period of Walpole and the Pitts was the heyday of unchallenged abuses in all forms of corporate life. Holders of ecclesiastical, academic, charitable, and scholastic endowments had no fear of inquiry or reform. Schoolmasters could draw their salaries without keeping school. Universities could sell degrees without holding examinations or giving instruction. Parliamentary boroughs and municipal oligarchies could be as corrupt and ridiculous as they liked; it was enough that they were old. 'Whatever is is right – if it can show a charter' seems the watchword of the Eighteenth Century.

It is not, therefore, surprising that the greatness of England during the epoch that followed the Revolution is to be judged by her individual men, by the unofficial achievement of her free and vigorous population, by the open competition of her merchants and industrialists in the markets of the world, rather than by her corporate institutions, such as Church, Universities, Schools, Civil Service, and town Corporations, which were all of them half asleep. The glory of the Eighteenth Century in Britain lay in the genius and energy of individuals acting freely in a free community – Marlborough, Swift, Bishops Butler and Berkeley, Wesley, Clive, Warren Hastings, the Pitts, Captain Cook, Dr Johnson, Reynolds, Burke, Adam Smith, Hume, James Watt, Burns, William Blake, and a score of others, to whom our later age will find it hard to show the equals, though we have indeed reformed and rationalized our corporate institutions.

After the prolonged political and religious crisis of the Stuart epoch, an equally long period of stability, under laws of a generally liberal character, was no bad thing even at the price of some stagnation. And, indeed, the sudden vigour put forth by Britain at Chatham's conjuring, the conquest of Canada, and the founding of the Indian Empire, showed that the political stagnation did not mean national decadence; the British State and Constitution was the most efficient as well as the most free of the governments of the world in those last days of the *ancien régime*. There followed, indeed, the loss of the American colonies, partly owing to the defects and corruption of our home constitution, partly for more general reasons concerned with the relations of America to England. In imperial and foreign affairs the British aristocracy both succeeded and failed on the grand scale, proving at least far more successful than the contemporary despotism of Bourbon France. On the whole, Britain flourished greatly in the Eighteenth Century, and her civilization struck roots both deep and wide.

But mischief lay in the fact that this period of immutable institutions and unaltered law coincided in its later years with the period that saw the beginning of economic and social changes of great rapidity and of yet greater import for the future. The Industrial Revolution began first in our island, and may for convenience be dated from the early years of George III. Throughout his long reign, new forces of machinery and capitalized industry 1760–1820 worked their blind will upon a loosely organized, aristocratic society that did not even perceive that its fate had come upon it.

The highly civilized and well-established world of which Dr Johnson and Edmund Burke are the typical minds, could think only in terms of politics and literature; men failed to observe that a revolution, more profound than the political changes oversea that they discussed and deprecated, was taking place daily in their own midst, and was sapping the old English order without any proper readjustment being made by public authority. Indeed, just when the Industrial Revolution was making reforms in our political and municipal institutions more imperative than ever, the reaction against Jacobin propaganda from abroad drove the governing classes to refuse, on principle, any political change at all, while nothing was done either to check or to guide economic change in its fullest flood. On the top of all this came twenty years of Napoleonic war, necessarily distracting the nation's attention from its own grave internal affairs, and complicating the Industrial Revolution at its most critical stage by wartime abnormality in trade, prices, and employment.

After this fashion the quiet and self-contented England of the Eighteenth Century slid unawares into a seething cauldron of trouble, whence a very different world would in due time emerge. Yet even in that confused and desperate crisis, such was the energy latent in the individual Englishman, such were the advantages of the island position to the Mistress of the Seas, such was the power in wartime of the new industrial machinery, that Britain, though so recently stripped of her American colonies, emerged as the chief victor of the Napoleonic wars and the mistress of a new Empire. And even while the war was raging, her creative spirit, sheltered behind her fleet, blossomed as in the age of Elizabeth. The era of Nelson and Wellington, of Fox and Pitt, of Castlereagh and Canning, was also the era of Wordsworth and Coleridge, of Scott and Byron, of Shelley and Keats, of Turner and Constable, of Cobbett and Wilberforce, of Bentham and Owen, and many more. The men of that day seemed to inhale vigour and genius with the island air. Though the social order was much amiss and the poor suffered, among the more favoured classes the individual reached a very high point of development during the early stages of the Industrial Revolution, in its first contact with the old rural life and the still surviving culture and freedom inherited from the Eighteenth Century.

CHAPTER I

Early Hanoverian England. Prime Minister, Cabinet, and Parliament. The Spirit of the Eighteenth Century. John Bull and French Influences. The Eve of the Industrial Revolution. Great Britain in Peace and War. Annexation of Canada and Foundation of the Indian Empire

Kings: George I, 1714–27; George II, 1727–60; George III, 1760–1820.

THE coming over of William of Orange had confirmed the doctrine of the Whigs and confused that of the Tories, but it gave the Whigs no mechanical advantage over their rivals. Throughout the reigns of William and Anne the two parties continued to share power evenly; the Crown and the electorate favoured first one side and then the other, according to the circumstances of the hour; the party contest continued to be vigorous, sometimes to fierceness, and in the main fortunate in its outcome for the country's interests. It is only in the reigns of George I and II that we find a state of things that may, with reserves and explanations, be picturesquely described as a 'Whig oligarchy'. Nor would it have come into existence even then, if half the Tory party had not been so gravely compromised with Jacobitism. In 1715 and again in 1745 there were Jacobite rebellions very formidable in Scotland, though they failed to elicit serious support in England.

Partly for this reason, partly because George I was ignorant of English language and customs, the first two Hanoverians abandoned to the Whig leaders certain prerogatives of the Crown which William III and even Anne would never have let out of their own hands. The formation of Ministries, the dissolution of Parliament, the patronage of the Crown in Church and State, all passed, in effect, from the monarch to the Whig chiefs. In that sense a political oligarchy was indeed established after 1714. But in another aspect the change was a further development of the popular element in our constitution, by the establishment of the omnipotence of Ministries dependent on the vote of the House of Commons, and by the reduction of the power wielded by the hereditary monarch.

Later on, George III attempted in the first twenty years of his reign to take back the patronage of the Crown into the royal hands, in consonance with the undoubted intentions of those who made the Revolution Settlement. But as soon as he had recovered the patronage of the Crown, he used it to corrupt the House of Commons even more systematically than Walpole and the Whig oligarchs had done. Neither the Whig oligarchs nor George III ever tried to stand on the unparliamentary ground of the Stuarts. They never ventured to deny that the executive could only exercise power in agreement with a majority of the House of Commons. But it was possible in the Eighteenth Century to corrupt the members through the distribution of patronage, because the rotten boroughs were becoming less representative of the country with every year that passed.

Under the first two Georges the power of the House of Commons increased, while its connexion with the people diminished. The long hibernation of the Tory party and the deadness of all serious political controversy damped public interest in parliamentary affairs, other than the distribution of places and bribes. The Septennial Act, passed in 1716 to secure the House of Hanover against Jacobite reaction, prolonged the normal life of a

Parliament; by rendering political tenures more secure, it further deadened political interest in the country and increased the readiness of members to enter the pay of government.

Under George III there was a great revival of public interest in politics, but no increase in democratic control over Parliament. But when, by the Reform Bill of 1832, the middle class recovered more than their old power over the House of Commons, they found in the modern machinery of Parliament and Cabinet a far more effective instrument of government than any which had existed in Stuart times. The Parliamentary aristocracy of the Eighteenth Century had forged and sharpened the future weapons of the democracy. It is doubtful whether nobles and squires would ever have consented to concentrate such powers in the Lower House, if they had thought of it as a strictly popular body. But they thought of it as a house of gentlemen, many of them nominees or relations of the Peerage, as the 'best club in London', as the 'Roman Senate' to which the highest interests of the country could safely be committed.

Under these conditions, the aristocratic Eighteenth Century made a great contribution of its own to the growth of British political tradition. The aristocrats devised the machinery by which the legislature could control the executive without hampering its efficiency. This machinery is the Cabinet system and the office of Prime Minister. By the Cabinet system we mean in England a group of Ministers dependent on the favour of the House of Commons and all having seats in Parliament, who must agree on a common policy and who are responsible for one another's action and for the government of the country as a whole. Neither Prime Minister nor Cabinet system was contemplated in the Revolution Settlement. They grew up gradually to meet the country's needs in peace and in war. The first approach to a united Cabinet was made by William III merely to fight the war against Louis, but he remained his own Prime Minister and his own Foreign Minister. In Anne's reign Marlborough acted as the head of the State in wartime for all military and diplomatic affairs, but he left to his colleagues the management of Parliament. It was Sir Robert Walpole, the Whig peace Minister from 1721 to 1742, who did most to evolve the principle of the common responsibility of the Cabinet, and the supremacy of the Prime Minister as the leading man at once in the Cabinet and in the Commons. It was significant that, unlike his Whig and Tory predecessors in power, Sir Robert remained undazzled by the lure of peerage, and refused to leave the Lower House so long as he aspired to govern the country. When he consented to become Earl of Orford he was retiring for ever from office.

In effecting these changes in the custom of the constitution, Walpole acted not a little from love of personal power, but he did the country a great service. In driving out from his Cabinet all colleagues who did not agree with his policy or would not submit to his leadership as Premier, he set up the machinery by which Britain has since been ruled in peace and war. The Cabinet system is the key by which the English were able to get efficient government by a responsible and united executive, in spite of the fact that the executive was subject to the will of a debating assembly of five or six hundred men. They solved this problem, which many nations have found insoluble, not, as was often contemplated in William III's reign, by excluding the Ministers from the Commons, but on the contrary by insisting that they should sit in and lead the House of Commons, like Sir Robert Walpole. The Cabinet is the link between the executive and legislative, and it is a very close link indeed. It is the essential part of the modern British polity.

It was well for England that the Revolution Settlement did not supply her with a brand-new, water-tight, unalterable, written constitution. A sacrosanct written constitution was necessary to achieve the federal union of the States of North America after they had cut themselves adrift from the old Empire. For England it was not at all necessary, and it would certainly have proved inconvenient. If England had been given a rigid constitution when James II was deposed, the Crown would have had assigned to it, in perpetuity, powers which within thirty years of the coronation of William and Mary it handed over to be exercised by its Parliamentary advisers. It is probable, also, that a rigid constitution, drawn up according to the lights of 1689, would have excluded the King's Ministers from sitting in the House of Commons.

A written constitution, as distinct from the sum of ordinary law and custom, is alien to the English political genius. One of the worst signs of the straits to which Cromwell was driven by his inability to find a basis of national agreement, was the fact that he promulgated written constitutions dividing up by an absolute line – never to be altered – the powers of Protector and Parliament respectively. These expedients were contrary to the real method of English progress. The London fog which decently conceals from view the exact relations of executive and legislative at Westminster, has enabled the constitution to adapt itself unobserved to the requirements of each passing age.

Two things specially distinguished the government of Britain from the governments of the *ancien régime* on the continent – Parliamentary control, and freedom of speech, press, and person. Of these advantages Britons were very conscious and very proud. They looked with contempt on French, Italians, and Germans as people enslaved to priests, Kings, and nobles, unlike your freeborn Englishmen. Freedom had been so lately acquired in Britain and was still so rare a thing in Europe, that our ancestors prized it high among their blessings.

Nevertheless, political and social power in that easy-going century was concentrated too much in one class, the landowners. The time was coming when the defect would greatly enhance the social evils of the Industrial Revolution. But under the first two Georges, before the coming of great economic change, the wage-earner, both in town and country, scarcely seems to have resented at all his want of social and political power. The British working man, then called the 'honest yeoman' or the 'jolly 'prentice', was quite happy drinking himself drunk to the health of the 'quality' at election time. And even if he had no vote, he could stand cheering or hooting in front of the hustings, while the candidate, possibly a Peer's son, bowed low with his hand on his heart and a rotten egg in his hair, addressing the mob as 'gentlemen', and asking for their support as the chief object of his ambition. The sight filled foreign spectators with admiration and astonishment. The spirit of aristocracy and the spirit of popular rights seemed to have arrived at a perfect harmony, peculiar to the England of that epoch. There have been worse relations than that between rich and poor, between governors and governed. There was no class hatred, and though highest and lowest were far apart, there were infinite gradations and no rigid class barriers as on the continent. But this careless, good-natured state of society could not outlast the coming of the Industrial Revolution.

It was the special function of the Eighteenth Century to diffuse common sense and reasonableness in life and thought, to civilize manners and to humanize conduct. The century that began with the universally approved *Asiento* treaty for supplying South America with slaves, ended with the capture of national opinion by Wilberforce and the Anti-slave-trade Committee. That movement, which saved civilization in three continents, was the product of the religious and rationalist peculiarities of the epoch of Wesley and Voltaire, of Beccaria and John Howard.

When the Stuarts ceased to reign, the English upper-class could still be represented in fiction by such widely divergent types of culture and manners as Squire Western on the one side and Squire Allworthy and Sir Roger de Coverley on the other. By the end of the century, when Jane Austen began to write, there was a regularized standard of manners and speech among gentlemen.

The long reign of Beau Nash at Bath taught the rules of polite society to the country squires who resorted thither with their families, and hastened the disappearance of the sword as the proper adornment of a gentleman's thigh. Largely for this reason, there was a great reduction in the number of killing affrays, and after-supper brawls of fatal issue regretted in the morning. But the regular duel with pistols did not fall into disuse until the bourgeois and Evangelical influences of the Nineteenth Century completed the work of humanity and common sense. Meanwhile, among humbler folk, the passion for pugilism made stabbing and murder 'taboo', and the custom of making a ring to see two disputants use their fists according to rule fostered the national sentiment for 'fair play', and tended gradually to discourage the promiscuous and barbarous mêlées of which we read too often in Smollett and Fielding and in memoirs of their time.

As patrons of art and letters, the English upper class reached in the Eighteenth Century a point that they had never reached before, and have since scarcely maintained. Not only great country seats like Holkham, Althorp, and Stowe, with their libraries and art treasures, but many smaller houses of the gentry focused for rural society the art, science, and polite letters of the day, with which the dominant landlord class identified itself hardly less than with sport, agriculture, and politics. The county houses and the world of fashion did more for culture and intellect than the dormant Universities. The upper class, under the guidance of Dr Johnson and Garrick, imposed the worship of Shakespeare, as the greatest of mankind, on a public not very intelligent, perhaps, of Shakespeare but most obsequious to his noble patrons, and consequently very respectful to literature.

It was during the Eighteenth Century that a process, begun in the Stuart period, was brought to completion – the establishment among the learned of the custom of writing in English instead of in Latin. This change had important consequences: British scholars became more than ever separated from their continental brethren; thought and learning became more national, more popular, and more closely allied to literature. Bentley, Blackstone, Gibbon, and Adam Smith all made appeal to the general intelligence of their countrymen at large, rather than to a professional learned audience scattered over all the countries of Europe.

On the other hand, one of the peculiarities of the movement of English culture in the Eighteenth Century, as compared to the Elizabethan era, was the deference to foreign models. Aristocratic leadership partly accounted for this. The patrons were 'milords' accustomed to make the Grand Tour of Europe, mixing with the society of foreign courts and capitals as tourists seldom do to-day, and bringing back statues, pictures, objects of virtù, French literary and philosophic ideas, and Italian standards of music and poetry. The link with the continent was the stronger because it was reciprocal: foreign admiration of British institutions and British thinkers was a chief original cause of the 'Encyclopaedist' movement of rational philosophy in France. 'Le Grand Newton', Locke, and Hume were names as highly honoured in Paris as in London and Edinburgh.

It is indeed a singular fact that, during the hundred years after the Revolution of 1688, when England was in violent reaction against French religion and politics, when English and French armies and navies were in constant conflict in both hemispheres, and when the common people despised and hated everything French with a fierce ignorance and prejudice, our taste in letters, in architecture, and in house decoration was to an unusual degree subjected to French and Italian ideas. In the reign of Charles II we had, like the rest of Europe, begun to submit to the cultural influences of the Court of Versailles, and we did not cease to do so after La Hogue and Blenheim. There was gain as well as loss in this temporary 'academizing' of our literary standards – gain to English prose and loss to English poetry: gain to clearness of thought and expression, loss to imagination and native vigour. The 'romantic' and 'naturalist' movements begun in the last decade of the century by Scott, Coleridge, and Wordsworth, were a revolt from foreign standards back to native traditions and native freedom. But even in the full Eighteenth Century the native English novel had been progressing freely, with little deference to foreign models, from Defoe through Smollett and Fielding to Miss Austen. Nor did our drama ever accept the French 'unities' of time and place.

Neither must it be forgotten that during this period, when upper class poetry and literature were least 'romantic', most rationalized, and most academic, the imagination of the common folk was still being nurtured not only on the Bible but on ghost stories, fairy stories, ballads, and tales of romantic glamour, of which their everyday rustic life seemed a part. Indeed it was precisely when 'romance' made its Nineteenth Century conquest of literature proper, that the school textbook and the newspaper began to take the place of the traditional romantic lore of the cottage fireside. It is even arguable that the Eighteenth Century, which produced William Blake, and Burns, and Wordsworth, was in its true nature more 'romantic' than the following century with its efforts to escape by feats of imagination from the drabness of its real surroundings.

However that may be, the artificiality of our Eighteenth Century culture was strong enough to impose an alien regime on the world of music. Handel and the Italian Opera largely took the place of our native music, which had once been reckoned the best in Europe. But the *Beggar's Opera* that took the characteristi- 1728
cally English form of a satire on the victorious Opera from overseas, produced a line of English popular operas, lasting into the Nineteenth Century. These operas with dialogue, out of which Gilbert and Sullivan came in the end, were truly national work in a period of strong foreign influence.

Painting gained most and lost least by the close association of fashionable English society with the culture of the continent. Indeed the age of Reynolds and Gainsborough was the first notable efflorescence of a native pictorial art in the island. Its arrival to serve the 'great families' was a fortunate coincidence in time. The portraits of the native English aristocracy in their heyday of power, prestige, and happiness, look down from those perfect canvasses in Olympian calm, over the heads of the so differently featured art-patrons of to-day.

The improvement characteristic of the Eighteenth Century was more marked in manners and intelligence than in morals and the stricter virtues. Gambling raged among the wealthy even more than in our own time, and drinking deep was scarce thought a blemish. The best of the upper class aimed at the full and rational enjoyment of this life, rather than at preparation for the next, of which they spoke seldom and then with a cheerful scepticism.

Life under the first two Georges, though not in itself of the type we associate with the Industrial Revolution, moved under conditions that were bound to hasten that great change, if certain mechanical inventions should chance to be made. The peculiar laws and customs of Hanoverian England allowed an unusual freedom to the individual, and did little to discourage private initiative; religious toleration left Dissenting merchants in perfect liberty to devote their energies to money-making, while they were prevented from taking part in public life; foreign Protestant refugees, rich in trade secrets and industrial skill, were made free of the economic citizenship of the island; commerce and manufacture were impeded by relatively few restrictions of State, municipality, or guild; a free trade area extended from John o'Groats to Land's End, in contrast to the innumerable customs barriers then dividing up Germany, Italy, and the Kingdom of France; the lords and squires who ruled the land were, unlike the French and German *noblesse*, in close personal relations with the mercantile and industrial magnates, and were often barely distinguishable from them; science in the land of Newton was honoured and exploited by the more enterprising merchants and their aristocratic patrons, on the look-out for a good thing to improve mining operations or manufacture; capital had been accumulated as never before in the world's history, and the English moneyed men, accustomed to invest it in commerce on the grand scale, would readily apply it to industry on a scale equally profuse, if once new inventions gave capital a fresh opening there; the markets for English goods already existing in America, Europe, and the Orient could be indefinitely developed by our merchant service, to dispose of any increase in the quantity of goods manufactured at home. In all these ways the England of that era was the predestined cradle of the Industrial Revolution.

An iron industry of immemorial antiquity was still dependent for fuel on the rapidly diminishing forests of the Sussex Weald, the Midlands, and the Severn Valley; yet the shortage of timber was only beginning to suggest to ingenious minds a method of smelting iron with coal. Since the days of the Plantagenets, coal, then easily won near the surface, had been much used for domestic purposes, especially in London where it was known as 'sea-coal' after its voyage from Tyne to Thames mouth. Wheeled traffic for heavy goods was still exceptional. Where water-carriage was not available, the coal sacks were slung across the patient packhorses, breasting the passes of the Welsh hills. In that primitive way the textiles of Yorkshire, Lancashire, and the Cotswolds had still to travel when Walpole was Prime Minister. And when Josiah Wedgwood began his career as a master-potter in the year of the taking of Quebec, the clay and the finished crockery still entered and left the Five Towns on the back of the donkey or the horse.

Indeed, the one great remaining obstacle to the initiation of an Industrial Revolution was the badness of transport in old England. The making of canals only began with the reign of George III. Yet the roads in winter were often quagmires wherein loaded pack-horses sank to the girth, and waggons could not be moved at all. On portions of the main roads, indeed, toll-bars were being set up by private companies, with Parliamentary powers to tax the traffic and keep the surface in repair. But during the Seven Years' War most of the mileage, even on the main roads of England, was still free to those who could force their way through the mud. The heavy coaches lumbered along in the ruts in a very different style from that in which their light-timbered successors in the years following Waterloo scoured the same roads remade by Macadam. In 1754 the Flying Coach advertised that 'however incredible it may appear, this coach will actually (barring accidents) arrive in London in four days and a half after leaving Manchester.' It took a week to travel between York and London; and in the days of Porteous riots and the rising of 'forty-five', Edinburgh had no regular service running from the British Capital whence Scotland was supposed to be governed.

Society on the eve of the Industrial Revolution had many features most attractive to us in the retrospect: a rural population attached to the land and its labours and recreations, to the village and its traditions; great variety and independence of type and character among men; individual training, skill, and taste in arts and crafts as a normal part of the economic life of the people. But in judging what the Industrial Revolution did to our island, it is necessary to remember that a fuel famine due to the using up of our timber was already settling down on various parts of the island in the Eighteenth Century, until relief came through the distribution of coal by canals, and afterwards by railways. The fuel famine was already putting an end to our old iron industry and was on the point of lowering the standard of comfort in domestic life. A well-to-do tradesman in Launceston was reduced to paying threepence to a neighbour for use of his fire to cook a leg of mutton; and his poorer neighbours, like most of the South English peasantry outside coal or peat districts, lived on bread and cheese, and too seldom knew the joys of a fire. And apart from the question of fuel, it is safe to say that the population of Great Britain could not, without the great industrial and agricultural changes of George III's reign, have risen much above seven millions without a considerable lowering of the standard of life.

During the reigns of George I and II, the policy of British

Ministers at home and abroad was guided by the necessity to maintain the House of Hanover on the throne. This was held to involve the continuance in office of the Whig party, on condition that political power was enjoyed only by conformists to the Anglican worship, and that the Tory squires in the countryside were given no personal ground for discontent with the rule of their political rivals. The English Tories, disaffected to the House of Hanover but unwilling to take an active part in restoring a Roman Catholic Stuart to the throne, were unable to join either side in the rebellions of 1715 and 1745, or to assert themselves in a united and effective manner at elections or on the floor of Parliament.

1721–42 To be governed by a man like Sir Robert Walpole was no hardship to the Tory squires. A Norfolk landowner of old family and moderate wealth, who even when Prime Minister was said to open his gamekeeper's letters first of the batch, who hunted with his beagles in Richmond Park when he could not get home, who drank steadily and told the broadest of stories over the bottle, was clearly a good fellow at bottom, no Presbyterian, no City upstart, no haughty and exclusive nobleman. An entirely loyal Whig, Walpole ruled by alliance with the Whig Peers, the moneyed men, and the Dissenters, but in his own person he represented the squires of England.

Walpole's mind and character were peculiarly adapted to the work of pacification at home and abroad. His genius lay in the arts of management, both in the good sense and the bad. No strain of idealism or romance tempted him to venturous or warlike policies. Good sense and kindliness were his dominant virtues; cynicism his fault. The good-natured smile on his broad face was half a sneer. He would never govern by bayonets or any form of terror, but saw no harm in allowing power to rest on the obvious and traditional basis of Parliamentary corruption, instead of making appeal to the national pride and conscience.

His love of peace abroad was genuine. It is not by idealists alone that the cause of peace has been upheld through the ages. Coarse and cynical though he was, Walpole had the humanity to keep England out of the war of the Polish Succession, in spite of the desire of his colleagues to revive the old Whig feud against the Bourbons. 'Madam,' he said to Queen Caroline in 1734, 'there are fifty thousand men slain this year in Europe, and not one Englishman.' Britain could safely stand aside from that aimless scuffle among the Powers of the continent, because the Marlborough wars had removed the danger of French hegemony. Our abstention enabled us to recruit our strength, which we would need ere long for more serious ends. Walpole took an active and successful part as 'honest broker' in bringing about the general pacification that at length ended the war.

At length, in 1739, his peace policy foundered on a great movement of opinion in favour of maritime war with Spain. It was no question of European boundaries that excited the mob. Popular passion was aroused by the old claim of the English, dating from Hawkins and Drake, to trade freely with South America. The wrongs of Jenkins and his ear, said to have been torn off by irate Spanish custom-house officials, brewed such a popular storm that Walpole yielded and unwillingly drew the sword. In his hand it seemed a clumsy weapon. A badly conducted war off the South American coast soon involved us in the general European struggle known as the War of the Austrian Succession.

Walpole had been right in his warning that renewed hostilities with the French and Spanish Bourbons would mean the launching of another Jacobite attack on England, which his wisdom had so long staved off. The year of Fontenoy (1745), a lost battle wherein our battalions of infantry distinguished themselves against the French in the Netherlands, was also the year of Prince Charles Edward's romantic adventure in Britain. He invaded an island almost denuded of troops, utterly unaccustomed to war and self-defence at home, and so selfishly indifferent to the issue between Stuart and Hanoverian that the inhabitants let 5000 Highlanders with targe and broadsword march from Edinburgh to Derby, gaped at but equally unassisted and unopposed. The weak side of Walpole's regime of negations and management was shown by the low level of British public spirit in 1745, whether regarded from a Jacobite or Hanoverian standpoint. Such sloth compares strangely with the zeal and the sacrifices which William Pitt conjured out of these self-same Britons and their children a dozen years later.

In England the consequences of the 'forty-five' and its final suppression next year at Culloden, were merely negative and merely political, involving the further decline of Jacobitism, already moribund. But in Scotland the results were positive, and they deeply affected the institutions of the country. For Scotland was at last enabled, with the help of the English armies, to settle her Highland question. If civilization was to go forward in the North of the island, it was essential to put down the warlike organization of the tribes and extra-legal allegiance to the chiefs. The King's writ must run in the glens. An Afghanistan could no onger be tolerated within fifty miles of the 'modern Athens'.

This most necessary change was at last accomplished, but not in the best way. Lowland law was applied to Highland tenures and customs with harsh uniformity, and with all the customary ignorance of civilized man in his dealings with a primitive society of which he despises the appearance too much to study the reality. The chiefs became landlords, on terms very disadvantageous to their late tribal followers, transformed into tenants at will.

Yet the land obtained peace, when the Highland Line ceased to have political meaning and became a geographical expression. The making of roads and the safety of travellers upon them, soon linked up all Scotland into one community. Devoted Presbyterian missionaries converted the Highlanders to the common stock of the nation's religious and educational ideas. One of the happiest and most characteristic policies of the elder Pitt was the raising of Highland regiments to fight for Scotland and the Empire in Canada and over the wide world. And the great Highland emigration to Canada, though it had some bad features, was on the whole an economic necessity at home and a great gift to the Empire oversea. Modern Scotland – the Scotland of Burns and Sir Walter Scott – emerged as a result of these changes, and of the great economic progress that accompanied them. There was evolved a united people, proud of itself and of its whole history; proud alike of Celt and Saxon, of Covenanter and Jacobite; with a national hagiology extending from Wallace and Bruce, through John Knox to Flora Macdonald, representing that singular blend in the national psychology of the dour and rational with the adventurous and romantic, of the passion for freedom with loyal devotion to a chief. Scotland became more prosperous in agriculture, industry, and commerce than she had ever hoped to be in the sad days of Darien. Yet, for all her new material welfare, she remained full of reverence for the things of the mind and the spirit, sending out her well-schooled sons to develop and govern the British Empire in every clime. When the century of progress closed, Scotland was a good neighbour and friend to England, as never before but always since.

1748–56 The period of European peace dividing the War of Austrian Succession from the outbreak of the Seven Years' War, roughly corresponded in England to the rule of the Pelhams – Henry Pelham and his brother the Duke of Newcastle, the greatest borough-monger England ever produced. They reverted to the pacific traditions of Walpole. But in India and North America warlike operations were taking place in time of nominal peace, that would soon cause slumbering Britain to awake.

Both in India and America the offensive was taken by the French. The dissolution of the Mogul Empire and the consequent independence of the Indian Princes of the Carnatic, had suggested to Dupleix the idea that the French Company, hopelessly inferior to the English in trade, should enter into military alliance with some of the native powers, raise Sepoy regiments under French officers, and extirpate the stations of the British East India Company at Madras and elsewhere. In Canada the French were carrying out a well-conceived plan of a line of military posts all the way from the mouth of the St Lawrence to the Lakes, down the Ohio valley to the Mississippi, and thence to the mouth of the great river in the Mexican Gulf. From this chain of river communications they intended to appropriate to France all America north and west of the Appalachian and Allegheny mountains.

In India the English Company was older and richer than the French, and more deeply rooted in native life. In North America the two million colonists on the English-speaking seaboard far outnumbered the French Canadians. The French, therefore, must depend for success on greater unity, more vigorous leadership, and ampler naval and military support from the home government. At first the energy of Dupleix carried all before him in the Carnatic, till Robert Clive left the counter for the field, and seized and defended Arcot. Grim hand-to-hand fight- 1751
ing went on along all that coast in time of peace, gradually turning to the advantage of the English, whose resources on the spot were much greater than those of the French owing to their superiority as a trading community. When the Seven Years' War broke out the French power was already on the decline in India.

It was otherwise in North America, where the English Colonies, except Massachusetts, were unwilling to strike in defence of their own interests and seemed incapable of uniting in a common policy. Physical communications between the English settlements were difficult, and concerted action was prevented by the rivalries between Colony and Colony, between Assembly and Governor, and by the intense individualism of a raw new world that had never been under feudal or royal discipline.

The French settlements, on the other hand, that had never known freedom from Church, State, and seigneur, were united in loyal obedience to their government. And they were strung together like beads on the line of the St Lawrence and Mississippi waterways. Fine royal regiments and leaders from France were there to aid and command them. Moreover, the French were in close contact with the Red Indian tribes, whom they treated well,

but used without scruple or humanity against their European foes. In 1753 they drove the English traders out of the Ohio valley and erected Fort Duquesne to prevent their return. Two years later, General Braddock's expedition, sent out by Newcastle's government to re-establish English rights beyond the
1755 Alleghenies, was cut to pieces in an ambush of French and Red Indians.

After the Seven Years' War began in form in 1756, success still shone upon the French efforts everywhere, except in India where the genius of Clive was already paramount. In face of the world-crisis, it became apparent that the Whig oligarchy was past its work. Its days were numbered, its mandate exhausted, its mission fulfilled. Jacobitism was dead, and the old Whig scheme of things was therefore, if for no other reason, moribund. It was out of touch with the new live forces in the nation which it had, in its better days, helped to nurse into life. It lived by corruption and 'management'. But Newcastle could not bribe the French armies out of Canada, or induce their Admirals to abandon the sea by giving Irish Bishoprics to their brothers.

But if the old Whig party was spiritually dead, the old Tory party no longer existed, and the new Tory party had not yet been born. The British were sheep without a shepherd, or rather the shepherds were playing cards while the wolf was in the fold. When William Pitt said 'I know that I can save this country and that no one else can,' he was speaking the modest truth. He alone was trusted by the middle and labouring classes, as the one disinterested politician, who had, when Paymaster, refused to take the customary toll from the moneys that passed through his hands. He alone of British statesman carried the map of the Empire in his head and in his heart. He alone understood the free and impatient spirit of the American colonials, and he alone knew how to evoke and use it for the common purpose. He had been the favourite grandson of a great Anglo-Indian. He was the personal friend of London merchants and aldermen. 'The Great Commoner', as he was called, openly displayed contempt for the ruling Whig aristocracy, but revived the living part of the old Whig tradition that could still inspire the mass of his countrymen by whatever party name they called themselves – pride in the free Constitution secured by the Revolution of 1688; faith in Parliament because it represented, however imperfectly, the people; faith in the people as a whole, of all classes and all denominations; dread of the power of Roman Catholicism and despotism oversea, and the determination to prevent the ocean and North

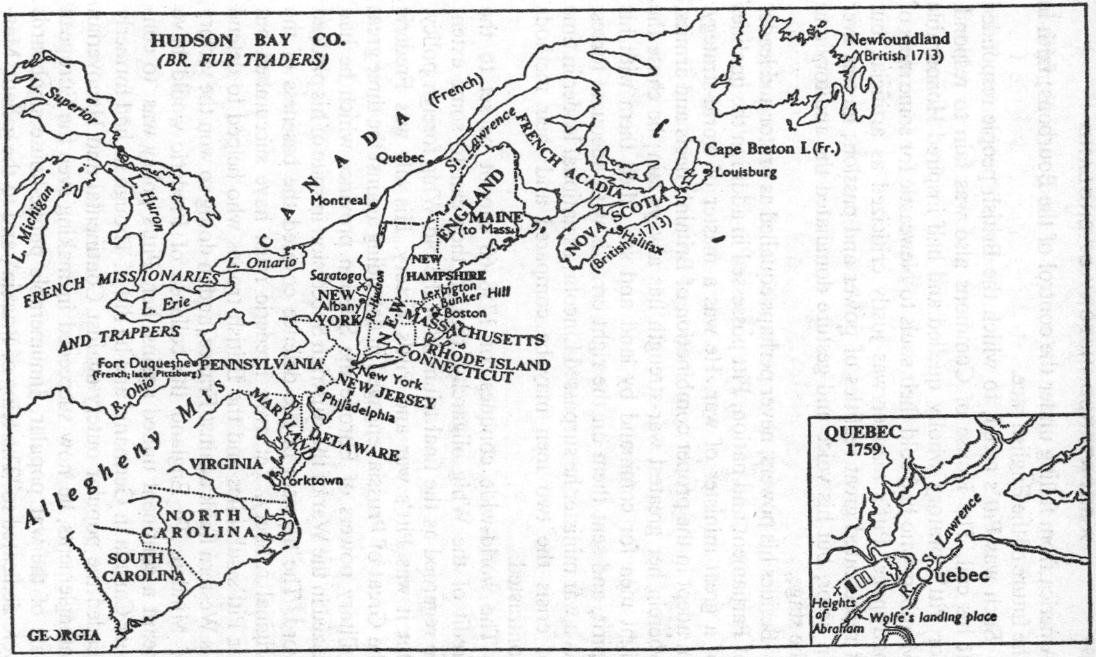

MAP XII. FRENCH AND ENGLISH COLONIES, 1755. (See Map XI, p. 319, for Mississippi, etc.)

America from falling under the control of the Bourbons; faith in the future of the English race.

Such was Pitt's creed, to which the British people responded at his call. The House of Commons also was fain to respond, for Pitt's oratory wholly quelled and half inspired Honourable Members who had sold their souls to Newcastle for some mess of patronage. Pitt's manner was justly criticized as artificial, but it represented great realities of power and passion; he was ever an actor, but his voice and gesture dominated the auditory and the stage.

Besides his powers, never perhaps equalled as orator and leader of Parliament and nation, Pitt possessed in addition the qualities of a great minister of war. He was a master of world-strategy, an adept in the proper combination of Britain's fleets and armies, wherein her greatest war-strength has always lain; he chose the right men for command by land and sea, filled them with his spirit, and sent them on the right errands with adequate forces. As a war minister he surpassed Lincoln; as national leader in time of crisis the two men may be compared and their methods contrasted.

The world-wide conquest of 1758–60 cannot be set to the credit of the Whig oligarchy, though they can to some extent be regarded as the final triumph of the old Whig foreign policy. But it was Pitt's war and Pitt's victory. His ally was Frederic the Great of Prussia, engaged in defending against the three great military powers of Europe the Silesian province which he had seized in the War of the Austrian Succession in spite of his pledged word. The heroism of the defence covered the baseness of the original robbery. Yet even Frederic must have succumbed but for Pitt's subsidies and the British troops who helped to defend his Western flank against France, and in doing so won the victory
1759 of Minden. To England the collapse of Frederic would have meant a continent united against her. Pitt's policy was 'to conquer Canada in Germany' and he did it. Though he had formerly headed the popular outcry against Continental and Hanoverian entanglements, he now succeeded in making even the European part of the war popular. Innumerable public-house signboards were dedicated to 'The King of Prussia', and to the gallant 'Marquis of Granby' who charged at the head of our squadrons on the battlefields of Germany.

The object for which Pitt fought upon the continent of Europe was nothing more than safety and the *status quo*; his real objectives lay oversea. The re-establishment of naval supremacy was essential to the warfare he meditated. In 1756 there had been serious fear of French invasion, and something approaching a panic in England. Minorca had been lost and the unsuccessful Admiral, John Byng, had been shot, to save Ministers from the popular indignation, in spite of the manly protests of Pitt. Under Pitt's government, naval supremacy was rapidly recovered in a series of vigorous actions, culminating in Hawke's great victory off Quiberon, the Trafalgar of the war.

Canada, which then consisted of French settlements scattered along the banks of the St Lawrence, could be best approached and conquered by land forces conveyed and covered by the fleet. The perfect cooperation of the two services led first to the capture of Louisburg, commanding the entry to the great river, and next year to Wolfe's daring ascent of the Heights of Abraham from the river bank and capture of Quebec itself from the French 1759 royal army. Wolfe and his magnanimous rival, Montcalm, were mortally wounded almost at the same moment in that memorable day, which decided the fate of Canada. Meanwhile in the Ohio valley, Scottish Highland regiments and American Colonials, working together as everyone seemed able to do under Pitt, had crossed the Alleghenies, driven out the French and renamed Fort Duquesne as Pittsburgh. Before the end of the Seven Years' War, the French power had disappeared from North America. The unexplored West was the Great Commoner's present to the English-speaking race.

In the course of the war many French possessions in West Africa and in the West Indian archipelago were seized, and a great Empire was founded in the East. In India, indeed, another genius than Pitt's was at work in the field of war and government. The six to nine months' voyage round the Cape prevented our organizer of victory in Downing Street from planning campaigns for the Ganges as he planned them for the St Lawrence. Indeed the battle of Plassey, leading to Clive's conquest of Bengal as 1757 the first extensive British-ruled territory in India, took place during the months when Pitt's great Ministry was painfully coming into existence.

When George III succeeded his grandfather, the name of 1760 Britain was held, perhaps, in higher esteem by the nations of the world than ever before or since. Her free institutions, imperfect as we know them to have been, were regarded with envy by the European nations of that day. No 'anti-English' tradition had yet arisen: the Irish were quiet and forgotten; the American colonies were still united to the mother country and devoted to

Pitt. England and 'the Great Commoner' were as much admired as they were feared by the French themselves, a generous and philosophic nation, at that time thoroughly out of love with their own despotic institutions which had brought them to such a pass. The English race was at the top of golden hours. It owed its position mainly to its own fortune and conduct over a long period of time, but latterly to one man who had raised it in three years from danger and disgrace. Yet in another twenty years our fortunes were destined again to fall low in either hemisphere. And in that decline the defects of the admired constitution and of the admired man would play no inconspicuous part.

CHAPTER II

Personal Government of George III. The American Question. The Disruption of the First British Empire. Restoration of Government by Party and Cabinet. The New Whig and New Tory Parties. Burke, Fox, and the Younger Pitt

King: George III, 1760–1820

BEFORE George III came to the throne in 1760, the conflict between executive and legislative, which had hampered government in the Stuart era, had been laid completely to rest by the novel device of a responsible and united Cabinet, led by a Prime Minister, but dependent on a majority vote of the House of Commons, and with all the Cabinet Ministers seated in Parliament. This system went several steps further than the negative settlement of 1689 towards rendering free government practicable. It has since been adopted in the self-governing Dominions and in many countries of Europe, and stands as England's chief contribution to the science of political mechanism.

The system had served well in peacetime under Walpole, and in war under the elder Pitt. His son, as head of the revived Tory party, was destined to stereotype this method of government, by which Britain has been ruled ever since his day. But between the great Ministry of the elder Pitt and that of his son, intervened twenty years when government by responsible Cabinet and Prime Minister was in confusion, if not in abeyance. That break in the smooth development of our constitutional history was caused by the able attempt of George III to recover the powers of the Crown as they had been left by the Revolution Settlement of 1689, to make the Prime Minister a mere instrument of the royal will, and to reduce the Cabinet to a group of the 'King's servants' in fact as well as in name. All this he temporarily achieved during Lord North's Premiership (1770–82) after fierce and complicated struggles in the sixties. He succeeded because he resumed into his royal hands the patronage of the State, wherewith he bribed the House of Commons himself, instead of leaving patronage and corruption as the perquisite of the Whigs.

Obviously George III would not so far have succeeded, if Cabinet government had then rested on democracy instead of on aristocracy, on opinion instead of on 'management'. The Parliamentary and Cabinet system of the mid Eighteenth Century, excellent as machinery, lacked moral force and popular support. It is true that, when the Seven Years' War began so ill, the Whig oligarchy had bowed to the popular demand and allowed Pitt to become Prime Minister to meet the crisis. But there was no regular method of exerting popular pressure on the House of Commons, owing to the large proportion of 'nomination boroughs' where members were returned at the bidding of an individual. Nor had the elder Pitt any personal hold over the curious political machinery of the day. Though he had sat for Old Sarum, where sheep grazed over the mound that marked the ancient city, he was not a great borough-monger or a friend of borough-mongers. He despised, and in his haughty humour insulted the Whig oligarchs, and they feared and disliked him in return. 'Fewer words, my Lord, for your words have long lost all weight with me,' he said to Newcastle himself. It was, therefore, impossible, when the national danger had been averted by Pitt's victories, for the arrangement between him and the Whig lords to become the basis of a permanent system of government.

The other circumstance that gave George III his chance of restoring royal power through Parliamentary corruption, was the absence of a strong Tory party, capable of keeping both Crown and Whigs in check. The Parliamentary Cabinet system requires, for its healthy functioning, two rival parties to criticize each other and to offer to the nation a choice between two alternative governments. Under William and Anne the Whigs and Tories, though often violent and factious, had performed that service well. But under the first two Georges there had been no real Tory opposition, owing to the ground being occupied by Jacobitism. But Jacobitism, moribund after the 'forty-five', expired when the popular young Englishman, 'farmer George', who 'gloried in the name of Briton', succeeded his German grandfather. Former Jacobites and high Tories like Dr Johnson willingly fixed their wandering and famished loyalty on so respectable a figure. The revival of a new Tory party, reconciled to the Revolution Settlement, was long overdue. But twenty years passed after the new reign had begun, before the resurrection was accomplished under the younger Pitt.

1770 In the interval, George III governed 'without party', making the Cabinet a mere instrument of the royal will and Parliament the pensioner of the royal bounty. The 'King's friends' in the Commons were his hired mercenaries, at best his personal devotees – not proper Tory partisans. The result was by no means in accord with Bolingbroke's prophecies of the golden age, that was to follow the advent of a 'patriot King' independent of all political factions. That ideal had caught the imagination of George himself, of Chatham, and of many others weary of government by the Whig aristocrats. But as soon as the idea was put into practice, the land was filled, not with the benisons of a grateful people on a benevolent monarch, but with the noise of unseemly
1763–9 conflict between rulers and ruled. The characteristic episode of the period was the martyrdom and deification of the scandalous Wilkes, turned by government persecution into the champion of popular rights, against an encroaching executive and a House of Commons claiming to override the choice of the Middlesex electors as to the man who should represent them in Parliament. Abroad, the prestige and admiration won by England in the Seven Years'
1775–82 War were thrown away. When by the ill-conducted quarrel with our own colonies the domestic crisis of the Empire came to a head, Britain was left face to face with a hostile Europe where she had many enemies and no single friend.

That affairs went so ill at home and abroad during the first twenty years of the new reign, must not be ascribed wholly to the faults of the King and his enemies, the Whig aristocrats. Part of the blame must be shared by Pitt himself – or the Earl of Chatham as he became in this unhappy period. Though without a regular Parliamentary following of his own, he held the balance between King and Whigs, because he represented in some degree the spirit of the nation for which the House of Commons so very inadequately spoke. But Chatham, though popular in his political sympathies, had a personal pride that was more than aristocratic. He could be a noble and liberal-minded autocrat, but he could never be a colleague. His faults of temper and understanding made him, who should have been the umpire and abater of the strife, further confound confusion. He could work neither with George nor with the Whigs, still less effect an arrangement between them.

At one moment the government was again put into Chatham's hands, and he was called upon to form a Cabinet 'above party', and to save the State once more, this time from its internal maladies. But at that moment his physical and mental powers gave way. The gout, which he had been fighting with heroic constancy ever since his Eton days, at last overcame the resistance of a lifetime. For months together he lay in a brooding melancholy, refusing to see his bewildered colleagues, fierce and unapproachable as a sick lion in its lair. His Ministry, which had no principle of cohesion save his leadership, staggered to ruin, carrying to limbo the last hopes of the country and the Empire. 1766–9

By 1770 George III had triumphed over all his enemies – over the 'Whig connexion', and over Chatham whom he detested as he did all save the second-rate statesmen who were willing to serve him without a policy of their own. 'Trumpet of sedition' was his name for the man who had saved and enlarged the Empire that he himself failed to preserve To criticize the royal policy was 'sedition' in the eyes of George III, who judged the merit of all statesmen by their attitude towards himself. He was not likely to be more gracious in his dealings with the colonials of New England, where 'sedition' of a more serious nature than Chatham's was endemic in the soil, and where a problem of Imperial relations of the utmost nicety and danger was coming up for solution.

The disappearance of the French flag from the North American Continent as a result of the Seven Years' War, led to the disruption of the first British Empire. For it relieved the English colonists of the dangers which had made them look for protection to the mother country. At the same time the expenses of the late war and the heavy burden of debt and land-tax with which it had saddled Great Britain, suggested to her statesmen, in an evil hour, that the colonies might be made to contribute something towards the military expenses of the Imperial connexion. An attempt to levy contributions towards the future upkeep of royal forces in America was first made through George Grenville's Stamp Duty on legal documents in the colonies. It was passed in 1765, but repealed next year by the Rockingham Whigs on account of the violent opposition which it had aroused beyond the Atlantic. In 1767 indirect taxation on tea and certain other articles was imposed on America by Charles Townshend. Chatham, the strongest English opponent of the policy of taxing the colonies, was then Prime Minister in name, but in actuality he was far removed from the political scene by gout and melancholia. Of these unpopular taxes the tea duty alone was maintained in a much modified form by George III's henchman Lord North in 1773, for the sake of principle only, as the profits were utterly negligible. Unfortunately, eight years of controversy on the taxation question had so worked upon the average colonial mind, that the overthrow of that principle was regarded as worth almost any disturbance and sacrifice. 'No taxation without representation' was the cry, and every farmer and backwoodsman regarded himself as a Hampden, and North as a Strafford.

It was natural that the Americans should object to being taxed, however moderately and justly, by a Parliament where they were not even 'virtually' represented. They had always acknowledged an indefinite allegiance to the Crown, though Massachusetts had made very light of it at certain times in the Stuart era, and had even gone to war with France without consulting the Crown in 1643. But Americans had never admitted the supremacy of Parliament, in the sense of conceding that the two Houses sitting at Westminster could vote laws and taxes binding on the Colonies, each of which had its own Assembly. On that issue, as on most issues of constitutional law that have divided the men of our race at great historical crises, there was a good legal case pleadable on either side. But as a matter of political expediency it was most desirable that the colonists should be taxed for imperial purposes by their own representatives rather than by the British Parliament.

Unfortunately they made no move to tax themselves, partly from thrift and partly from indifference to the Imperial connexion. When once the French danger had disappeared, the Empire seemed a far-off abstraction to the backwoodsman of the Alleghenies, like the League of Nations to the Middle West to-day. And even on the sea coast, where the Empire was better known, it was not always better loved: it was represented by Governors, Colonels, and Captains of the British upper class, often as little suited to mix with democratic society as oil with vinegar. Furthermore, the Empire was associated in the mind of the Americans with restrictions on their commerce and their industry, imposed for the benefit of jealous English merchants, or of West Indian sugar and tobacco planters who were then the favourite colonists of a mother country not yet disturbed about the ethics of slavery.

Chatham, or rather that more formidable person, William Pitt, had made the imperial connexion popular in America in time of war, and might have made it tolerable even in time of peace.

But Chatham had ceased to influence the politics of the Empire, except as a Cassandra prophet warning George III in vain, and being called a 'trumpet of sedition' for his pains.

In theory – or at least in the theory that was held in England – the Empire was a single consolidated State. In practice it was a federation of self-governing communities, with the terms of federation undrawn and constantly in dispute. Such a situation was full of danger, the more so as the situation and the danger were alike unrecognized. The defunct Whig oligarchy can hardly be said to have had a colonial policy or any clear ideas about the future of the Empire. Pitt's great Ministry had come and gone. And now, to meet the pressing needs of Imperial finance, George III's Ministers had advanced partial and one-sided solutions that proved unacceptable, while the Americans refused to propose any solution at all. A way out could have been found by men of good will summoned to a round-table conference, at which Britain might have offered to give up the trade restrictions, and the Americans to make some contribution of their own to the military expenses incurred by the mother country on their behalf.

But such a conference was outside the range of ideas on either side the Atlantic. England was still in the grip of 'mercantile' and protectionist theories of the old type. She still regarded her colonies primarily as markets for her goods, and the trade of the colonials as permissible only so far as it seemed consistent with the economic interest of the mother country. As the historian of our British colonial policy has remarked, 'That the measures of 1765 and 1767 precipitated the crisis is obvious enough; but that the crisis must sooner or later have come, unless Great Britain altered her whole way of looking at the colonies, seems equally certain.'

As to the hope that America might voluntarily contribute to the Imperial expenses, 'America' did not exist. The thirteen colonies were mutually jealous, provincial in thought, divided from one another by vast distances, great physical obstacles, and marked social and economic distinctions. They had failed in 1754 at Albany to combine even for the purpose of fighting the French at dire need, and they were little likely to unite in time of peace for the purpose of negotiating with England on an Imperial question which they denied to be urgent.

And so things drifted on to the catastrophe. On one side was the unbending stubbornness of George III, who dictated policy to Lord North, that easy, good-natured man, so fatally unwilling to disoblige his sovereign. On the other side was the uncompromising zeal of the Radical party among the Americans led by Samuel Adams, to whom separation gradually began to appear as a good in itself.

The general causes rendering it difficult for English and Americans to understand one another were then numerous and profound: many of them have been removed by the passage of time, while on the other hand the difference of race is much greater to-day. English society was then still aristocratic, while American society was already democratic. Six or seven weeks of disagreeable ocean tossing divided London from Boston, so that personal intercourse was slight, and the stream of emigration from the mother country had run very dry ever since 1640. In England politics and good society were closed to Puritans, while Puritanism dominated New England and pushed its way thence into all the other colonies; it was Anglicanism that was unfashionable in Massachusetts. English society was old, elaborate, and artificial, while American society was new, simple, and raw. English society was based on great differences of wealth, while in America property was still divided with comparative equality, and every likely lad hoped some day to be as well-off as the leading man in the township. In England political opinion was mainly that of squires, while in America it was derived from farmers, water-side mobs, and frontiersmen of the forest.

In two societies so widely set apart in the circumstances and atmosphere of everyday life, it required people with imaginative faculties like Burke, Chatham, and Fox, to conceive what the issues looked like to ordinary men on the other side of the Atlantic. George III had strength of mind, diligence, and business ability, but he had not imagination.

After the famous outrage on the tea-chests in Boston harbour, the English Government, naturally and deeply provoked, made its fatal mistake. It hurried through Parliament Penal Acts against Massachusetts, closing the port of Boston, cancelling the charter of the colony, and ordering political trials of Americans
1774 to be conducted in England. These measures rallied the other colonies to Massachusetts and ranked up behind the Radicals doubtful and conservative forces for whose support the English Government might still have played with success. The Penal Acts meant in fact war with the colonies. They were defensible only as acts of war, and if adopted should have been accompanied by preparations to ensure armed victory. Yet in that very year the British Government reduced the number of seamen in the Navy, and took no serious steps to strengthen their forces in

America. When the pot boiled over at last, and hostilities broke out of themselves at Lexington, Burgoyne wrote thus from Boston:

> After a fatal procrastination, not only of vigorous measures but of preparations for such, we took a step as decisive as the passage of the Rubicon, and now find ourselves plunged at once in a most serious war without a single requisition, gunpowder excepted, for carrying it on.

During the twelve months preceding Lexington, while the British authorities, having defied New England to the arbitrament of force, contented themselves with the inactive occupation of Boston, the Radical party in the country outside had used the respite to organize revolutionary power and terrorize, or expel, its opponents. Indeed, ever since the original passage of the Stamp Act, the 'Sons of Liberty' had employed tarring-and-feathering and other local methods of making opinion unanimous. Even so, the Loyalists in most of the thirteen colonies remained a formidable body. Few, if any, had approved the measures by which the British Government had provoked the war, but they were not prepared to acquiesce in the dismemberment of the Empire, and for social and political reasons of their own they disliked the prospect of Radical rule. Their strength lay among the mercantile and professional men and the large landowners of the coast, and they were stronger in the Middle and Southern Colonies than in New England. Against them were arrayed the humbler folk in most sections, the small farmers and the frontiersmen of the West, organized under leaders of amazing audacity and zeal. The Loyalists were slower to move, more anxious for compromise than war, and they got little leadership either from their own ranks or from the British, who too often treated them very ill and drove them by ill-usage or neglect to join the rebel ranks.

Yet the Radicals would never have overcome the trained soldiers of George III and their own Loyalist fellow-subjects, had they not been led by a statesman of genius who was also a first-class soldier, organizer, and disciplinarian. George Washington belonged by temper and antecedents rather to the Loyalist than the Radical classes. But, although he was first and foremost a gentleman of Virginia, he was also a frontiersman who had seen service against Indians and French beyond the Alleghenies, and who knew the soul of young America as it could only be known in the backwoods. Good Virginian as he was, he was no mere provincial, with feelings and experience limited to his own colony. He had a 'continental' mind, and foresaw the nation he created.

Some well-informed vision of the astounding future of his country westwards, helped to decide George Washington to draw his sword for a cause which was bound, in the stress of war, to become the cause of American Independence. The American militiamen brought to the ranks qualities learnt in their hard struggle with nature – woodcraft and marksmanship, endurance, energy, and courage. But they grievously lacked discipline, save what the Puritan temper supplied to the individual, and what Washington imposed upon the army. His long struggle, as Commander-in-Chief in the field, with the exasperating ineptitude of the Continental Congress, was a war within the war. Fortunately for him, the British army, in spite of its fine qualities, made mistake after mistake not only in the military but in the political strategy of the contest.

It was a civil war, not a war between two nations, though when the battle smoke at length subsided two nations were standing there erect. Because it was a civil war, and because its issue would decide among other things whether England should in future be ruled by the King acting through Parliament or by Parliament acting through the King, opinion was divided in England no less than in America. Once fighting began, the bulk of the British people supported their government, so long as there was any hope of reconquering the colonies. But they showed so little enthusiasm for the fratricidal contest that recruiting was very difficult, and the government largely employed German mercenaries whose conduct further incensed the colonists. Moreover in England there was always a strong minority, speaking with powers as diversified as those of Chatham, Burke, and young Charles Fox, that denounced the whole policy of the war and called for concession to save the unity of the Empire before it was too late.

Military operations were as ill-conducted by the British as they had been rashly provoked. The troops, as Bunker's Hill showed, were not inferior to the men of Blenheim and Minden. But the military mistakes of Generals Burgoyne and Howe were very serious, and they were rivalled by those of the government at home. Lord George Germain in England planned the Saratoga campaign as Pitt had planned the taking of Quebec, but with very different results. His plan gave the Americans the advantage of acting on the inner lines, for he sent Burgoyne to Canada to march down the Hudson and isolate New England, but without making sure that Howe moved up to meet him from the South. The result was that, while Howe lingered in Philadelphia, Burgoyne

and his 5000 regulars were cut off in the wilderness beside the great river, and surrendered at Saratoga to the American minute- 1777
men.

After Saratoga the French despotism felt encouraged to come to the aid of liberty in the New World. This remarkable decision dismembered the British Empire, but it did not thereby achieve its object of restoring the House of Bourbon to world power. For it turned out that the idea of revolution, if once successful in America, could traverse the Atantic with unexpected ease. And no less unexpectedly, from the broken eggshell of the old British Empire emerged two powers, each destined to rapid growth – a new British Empire that should still bestride the globe, still rule the seas, and still hold up its head against the Powers of the continent; and a united American State that should spread from Atlantic to Pacific and number its citizens by scores of millions, in the place of thirteen little, mutually jealous colonies upon the Atlantic coast.

It was well that America was made. It was tragic that the making could only be effected by a war with Britain. The parting was perhaps inevitable at some date and in some form, but the parting in anger, and still more the memory of that moment's anger fondly cherished by America as the starting-point of her history, have had consequences that we rue to this day.

The War of American Independence ended as a war of Britain against half the world. The Bourbon 'family compact' of France and Spain fought her by sea and land as of old; the French ships under Suffren seriously endangered her communications with India; Russia, Prussia, Holland, and the Scandinavian Powers
united their diplomatic and naval forces in the 'armed neutrality 1780
of the North' to defend the rights of neutrals against the Mistress of the Seas. In Ireland, for the first and last time in history, Protestants and Catholics united to overthrow the system by which their common interests were sacrificed to England.

In the hour of need, to which her fools had brought her, Britain was saved by her heroes. Among the statesmen, Carleton saved Canada, and Warren Hastings saved India; among fighting men, Eliott defended the Gibraltar Rock against the armaments of France and Spain, and Rodney's victory recovered the mastery of the seas from de Grasse.

But the recovery of the thirteen colonies, already become the United States of America, was for ever impossible. Chatham died before he had given up hope, but three years later all King

George's subjects acknowledged the fact. But nothing would bend the King's will save the positive refusal of his Ministers to proceed any longer with a task in which they had long lost faith and heart. They had even lost sure hold of their majority in a House of Commons paid to vote for them. As early as April 1780, the House had voted, by 233 against 215, in favour of Dunning's Resolution, 'that the influence of the Crown has increased, is increasing, and ought to be diminished'. It was significant that the county members who best represented any genuine body of electors, voted sixty for the Resolution and only eight against.
Oct. 1781 After the surrender of Cornwallis to Washington at Yorktown, the war in America was virtually at an end, and the news of Yorktown in England brought the system of personal government by the King to an end too.

The House of Commons accepted without a division a strongly worded motion against the continuance of the war in America. From the day of Lord North's resignation, in March 1782, Britain has never been governed save by a Prime Minister and Cabinet responsible not to the King alone but first and foremost to the independent judgement of the House of Commons. It was a matter of great importance that, owing to the catastrophe in America, the attempt to regain political power for the Crown came to an end when it did. If the personal government of George III and of his children after him had been protracted into the next century, the democratic and Reform movements of the new era, finding themselves opposed by the King as their chief source of conservative resistance, must have become anti-royalist and very probably Republican.

With the restoration of full Parliamentary government its necessary accompaniment, party government, was restored too. George III had set out to abolish party, according to Bolingbroke's prescription, but the net result of his activities, over and above the loss of America, was to bring into being a new Whig party and a new Tory party, and to arouse a democratic interest in politics which, though it failed for fifty years to carry Parliamentary Reform, served to put the life of public opinion into the Whig party led by Lord Rockingham, Burke, and Fox, and into the Tory party created by the younger Pitt, and to fill the sails of Wilberforce's Anti-Slave-Trade Crusade.

1782 Immediately on the fall of North, the King's open enemies, the Rockingham Whigs, came into office for a few months. They were no longer the unregenerate Whig oligarchy of Newcastle, for, though still under aristocratic leadership, they appealed first and foremost to public opinion, and seriously intended to diminish Parliamentary corruption. Their long misfortunes had taught the Whigs many things, and they had sat at the feet of Edmund Burke. His deep, sagacious insight as a political philosopher was the more powerful and the less reliable because its vehicle was a magnificent oratory, and because his Irish temper, fiery almost to madness, prevented him from seeing more than one side of a case at any stage of his career, whether as Whig, as anti-Jacobin, or as Indian reformer. When his patron Lord Rockingham took office in 1782, his political creed was still in its earlier period of liberal emphasis. The short Ministry of the Rockingham Whigs that summer, left a deep impression for good on our public life, because it passed Burke's Economic Reform Bill, which greatly reduced the patronage of government in sinecures and places, and rendered it impossible for anyone ever again to bribe Parliament wholesale, as Walpole, Newcastle, and George III had done. The Augean stables were half swept out.

When, on Rockingham's death, the Whigs quarrelled among themselves over the mysterious personality of Lord Shelburne, Fox outraged the nation's sense of decency by coalescing with Lord North, against whom he had for so many years been addressing his heated Philippics. On the fall of the Fox-North Ministry, 1782–3 which the King actively helped to bring about, young Pitt took the reins of power as the head of the revived Tory party. He had strongly opposed the King's personal government and American policy, but he was ready to make an alliance on his own terms with the Crown. George, since he could no longer rule in person, greatly preferred Pitt to the Whigs.

The first decade of Pitt's Ministry, before the French Revolutionary wars came to confuse the issues, was a Ministry of peace and reconstruction, no less wise and more active than that of Walpole. Pitt reconstituted the finances of the country, restored its prestige at home and abroad, began to rebuild a new British Empire on the ruins of the old, modernized and secured the governments of Canada and India. After Walpole's example, he reconstituted the power of the Prime Minister in the State as the true governor of the land, not the mere instrument of the royal will. He finally fixed the British conception of the Cabinet, as a responsible and united body, dependent on an independent House of Commons. The work of his precursors in office, the Rockingham Whigs, in re-establishing the party system, was happily rounded off by Pitt. The Tory party, as revived under his leadership, was no longer a name for the 'King's friends', but an independent Parliamentary connexion, with rotten boroughs and election funds of its own, and with roots of affection in great classes of the community. Though its heart of hearts was still the squirearchy and the Church, its young leader earned the confidence of the mercantile community, as Charles Montagu and Walpole had earned it, but as no Tory chief had ever done before. Pitt, unlike the Foxite Whigs, understood political economy and finance, subjects little studied in Brooks's. As a boy at Pembroke, Cambridge, he had sat long hours reading Adam Smith's *Wealth of Nations* when it first appeared, and a few years later, under further instructions from Shelburne, he was putting the new doctrines into practice at the Treasury. Like his father he was at home among the aldermen in the Guildhall, and the City trusted and loved the son as it had trusted and loved the father.

Owing to the personal ascendancy of Pitt, the revived Tory party became for a while an instrument of progress. By doing things which the Whigs might well have done themselves, he drove Burke and Fox round in a dance of factious opposition to liberal measures. But it was in the nature of things that the leader of the party containing the great conservative forces of the nation, should not be allowed to go indefinitely far down the path of change. When, answering to a strong movement in the country that had arisen out of the disasters of the American war, Pitt pro-
1785 posed a mild measure of Parliamentary Reform, his own followers would have none of it. Burke had scotched the snake of Parliamentary corruption with his Economic Reform Bill, but neither he nor his Tory adversaries wished to kill it by reducing the number of rotten boroughs. The magnificent reptile had still a long and honoured life before it. For, with the French Revolution and the wars that followed, an end was put to all political changes in England for thirty years. They were terrible years though glorious, and we might never have survived them at all, had it not been for what Pitt had already done in the first decade of his Ministry.

As a War Minister at grips with Jacobinism and its fleets and armies, Pitt had to rely not only on the strength and confidence of workaday England, which he had himself rescued from prostration after the American war and nursed back to vigorous life, but he had also to rely on the political vested interests which he had attempted in vain to reform. And when a man, in defending his country from foreign conquest, has to rely on certain forces, he ceases to be capable of criticizing them. He becomes subdued to the material in which he works. Nor, perhaps, would the triumph of ultra-conservatism during the Napoleonic wars have done much permanent harm to the country, but for the reaction of those political habits of mind on the social and economic aspects of the Industrial Revolution proceeding all the time in our midst.

England was not at war with France until the beginning of 1793. The drama of 1792 was watched by the English as neutrals, and the spectacle had reactions of permanent importance on opinion over here. The attempt of the European monarchs of the *ancien régime* to smother the French Revolution in blood, as proclaimed in the manifesto issued by their General, Brunswick; the desperate rising of the French people in reply; the unexpected victory of the new France in the Valmy campaign; the simultaneous triumph in 1792
Paris of Jacobinism and Republicanism, massacre and the guillotine – all these portentous events, which still attract the gaze of posterity, absorbed the attention of English politicians, recast our parties, and determined the spirit of our government for forty years to come.

The Foxite Whigs in the fashionable purlieus of Brooks's, and the low-class Radicals of the Corresponding Society sympathized passionately with the French people against the German despotic invaders, whom Fox compared to the armies of Xerxes. In his warm-hearted, impulsive way, he wrote of the French, just before the news of the September massacres arrived, 'With all their faults and nonsense, I do interest myself for their success to the greatest degree.' Then came the first news of the massacres in the Paris prisons. 'I really consider,' he wrote, 'the horrors of that day and night as the most heart-breaking event that ever happened to those who, like me, are fundamentally and unalterably attached to the true cause. There is not, in my opinion, a shadow of excuse for this horrid massacre, not even the possibility of extenuating it in the smallest degree.'

But the sympathies of the great majority of the well-to-do classes had been all through on the side of Brunswick. And the September massacres and the regime of the guillotine aroused passions in our island akin to those aroused by the news of St Bartholomew and the revocation of the Edict of Nantes. The democratic movement was effectively overpowered by public opinion that autumn and winter in every town and village in England. Loyalist Associations were formed all over the country, usually headed by Churchmen against their local enemies the Dissenting Reformers; these Associations organized opinion behind the government in the demand for the suppression of Reformers at home, and stern resistance, if necessary in arms, to French pretensions to 'liberate' Europe by the sword.

That same winter the French Republicans, intoxicated with the first draughts of victory and power, when they had expected
1792-3 the Prussian gallows, invaded Savoy, the Rhineland, and the Austrian Netherlands, declared the Scheldt open to navigation all European Treaties notwithstanding, and prepared to invade Holland. They offered armed assistance to all countries desirous of overthrowing their old governments. The pride and ambition of Louis XIV revived in the breasts of the men who were pulling down his statues, beheading his descendants, and persecuting his religion. The occupation of the Rhine Delta by the Power with the greatest military and the second greatest naval force in Europe, challenged the English sense of self-preservation, as Philip of Spain and Louis, and Kaiser William challenged it by like pretensions in the same quarter of the world. Resistance to the French hegemony in Europe, and particularly in the Netherlands, was pursued by Parliamentary England with a determination more steady than that of any of the despotic Courts, that had rashly provoked the Jacobin lion with their Brunswick blusterings and then run away.

The purpose of the old English nation not to allow the newborn French nation to annex the rotten States of Europe as her vassals, was nobly personified by Pitt, and was handed on by him to his followers, who in the days of Castlereagh won success at last for an effort sustained through the vicissitudes of twenty years. Unfortunately this determination was by circumstance identified with a policy of repression of Reform and of all discussion of Reform at home and with a hardness of heart towards the victims of the Industrial Revolution and to the poor generally, as potential 'Jacobins'.

By the same process of association of ideas, often so misleading to the political mind, moderatism in politics, the mildest proclivities to Reform, and sympathy with the victims either of economic oppression or of government persecution, usually went with a want of zeal for the war, and a slowness to acknowledge the intractable character of the nationalism and imperialism of the successive governments of the new France. Fox, Lord Holland, Sydney Smith, Romilly, Whitbread, Byron, and Cobbett in his Radical period, are striking examples of this law.

The Reformers, therefore, during the coming generation, laboured under a double stigma – as lukewarm patriots in wartime, and as supposed friends of Paine's republican doctrine, in

spite of their protests to the contrary. This double unpopularity made it easy, as it also perhaps made it unnecessary, for Pitt to use the strong hand of power to prohibit all discussion of Parliamentary Reform outside the privileged walls of Parliament itself. In the first two years of the war, there were constant prosecutions of editors, Nonconformist preachers, and speculative persons of a propagandist disposition, who had ventured to argue for Parliamentary Reform, often indeed with unwise and provocative phraseology borrowed from France. Muir and Palmer, tried 1793
before Braxfield, the Scottish Judge Jeffreys, were transported to Botany Bay by a most iniquitous sentence, which the ex-Reformer Pitt refused to mitigate. Sympathy with the fate of these two 'Reform martyrs' had its part in fostering the Radicalism for which Scotland became famous in the Nineteenth Century.

Finally, in 1794, the government was so far blinded by panic that it sought the lives of the Reformers. A charge of High Treason was instituted against Thomas Hardy the shoemaker, the founder of the Corresponding Society and the principal leader of the constitutional movement in politics among the working classes. Other innocuous and respectable persons, like Thewall the lecturer and Horne Tooke the philologist, were tried on the same capital charge. But the good genius of England came to her rescue in her characteristic institution, the jury system. Pitt had outraged the English sense of fair play. Thanks to Erskine's persuasive eloquence, twelve Tory jurymen acquitted Hardy and his fellow prisoners on the capital charge, and reminded the government that the methods of Robespierre were not wanted over here. London, though strongly Anti-Jacobin, broke into loud rejoicings at the acquittal.

This timely check saved England from a reign of terror and perhaps ultimately from a retributive revolution. But the government proceeded, with more general approval, to silence further political discussion for many years to come. The Corresponding and other Societies were suppressed by Act of Parliament. *Habeas Corpus* was suspended and numbers of men against whom there was no evidence were kept in prison for years. Public meetings were prohibited that were not licensed by magistrates, and, in fact, none were any longer permitted. Except for the Anti-slave-trade movement, which also for a time declined, political life ceased in Britain. To make matters worse, the Foxite Whigs, in a mood of laziness and disgust, retired to their country houses in an aimless 'seccession' from their duties in Parliament, where alone 1797–9
criticism of government was permitted.

Pitt's Combination Acts were another manifestation of the repressive spirit of the times. These measures rendered Trade
1799–1800 Unionism illegal, and punished all combinations of wage-earners. They were accompanied by no corresponding steps to enforce a fair wage, and simply put the employee into his master's hands. The policy represented not true *Laissez faire*, but State interference on the side of Capital against Labour. It was inspired not merely by a desire to keep down wages in accordance with the political economy of the day, but by Anti-Jacobin fears of all forms of combination by the 'labouring poor'. Two Whigs, Sheridan and Lord Holland, were the only important politicians who opposed the Acts in either House.

The new working class that the Industrial Revolution was bringing into existence and concentrating in the towns, had thus early shown an instinct towards self-education and self-help, along the parallel lines of political Associations and economic Trade Unionism. Pitt's government attempted to crush out both together, though with more success in the political field than in the economic. When, after the war was over, the political life of the working classes and the Trade Union movement each made fresh headway in the era of Peterloo, they had to fight as outlaws for the right to exist. Then indeed popular opinion was being rapidly alienated from the Tory system, to which it had upon the whole adhered in the time of Pitt. But the habit of repression, begun by Pitt against a minority in time of war, had become custom of the country and was continued by Pitt's successors against the majority in time of peace. The partisanship of government against the poor and against those who attempted to plead their cause, however natural owing to the French Revolution and the French war, distorted and embittered the social processes of the Industrial Revolution and left marks which were never entirely healed in the remedial period that followed. It was in 1823 that the Combination Laws against Trade Unions were repealed, the first step in a great process of legislative evolution.

Between Anti-Jacobin Toryism and Painite Radicalism, the Parliamentary Whigs took up a half-way position, under the now middle-aged Charles Fox and his favourite young men, Lord Holland and Charles Grey. While repudiating the doctrines of Paine they continued, in the heat of the Anti-Jacobin reaction from 1793 to 1797, to move motions in Parliament for Reform based on abolition of the rotten boroughs. They were voted down by great majorities, who regarded them with horror as seditionists in sympathy with France; they were saved from worse consequences by the great respect felt by all Englishmen for the privileges of Parliament, and for the privileges of the well-connected and fashionable to be eccentric.

In these circumstances the quarrel of the Reforming Whigs with Burke and half the members of their own party was bitter and complete. But whereas the Whigs who followed Burke were merged among the other supporters of the Tory Ministry, the Whigs who followed Fox remained the nucleus of the party, and the keepers of its traditions. The continued opposition of the Foxites to Pitt and his Tory successors, prevented the whole machinery of Parliament from becoming a part of the Anti-Jacobin movement, and so left a bridge, however slender and insecure, still hanging across the gulf that divided classes in the new era. The adherence of the Whigs to Parliamentary Reform in days when it was impracticable, enabled them, when the wheel had come full circle, to avert civil war and social catastrophe by their Reform Bill of 1832.

Until that still distant era, the position of the Whigs was one of isolation, out of touch alike with the main stream of national enthusiasm for war against the French, yet equally far removed from sympathy with the lower class Radicalism of Tom Paine and of William Cobbett after him. Thirty years of unpopularity and exclusion from power failed to make an end of the Whigs. Their strong personal ties and party traditions held them together at gatherings in their large and pleasant country houses and at Brooks's Club. They were aristocrats, scholars, and sportsmen, with much to make life delightful, in default of popularity or office. Their seats were safe, for they had a modest share of the rotten boroughs. They rather despised the Tory governors of the country as people less fashionable than themselves. They were so well-connected that they could afford to toy with democracy; they were so much in the mode that 'Jacobinism' seemed in them only a modish eccentricity. Their attachment to the person of Fox until his death in 1806, and to his memory afterwards, was one of the accidental circumstances which moulded the course of English politics. Fox was made to be loved by his friends. Where he was, there would the Whig party be. If he had gone over to Pitt and Anti-Jacobinism, there would never have been a Whig-Liberal party, and the process of British politics in the Nineteenth Century would very probably have been by armed revolution and reaction instead of by Parliamentary Reform.

When the youthful Pitt had first been called on by George III to govern the land, the Whig satirists had made merry over 'A Kingdom trusted to a schoolboy's care'. But Parliament and country soon found in Pitt not the schoolboy but a schoolmaster, austere, reserved, dignified, didactic. It was Fox who was the eternal schoolboy. Devoted to his friends; generous to his enemies but always up in arms against them for any reason or none; never out of scrapes; a lover of life and of mankind, he was born to be leader of opposition, and leader of opposition he was for almost all his long life in the House of Commons. Chatham was a greater orator, and his son perhaps a greater debater, than Fox, but for a union of oratorical and emotional with debating power, Fox has never been rivalled. His early extravagances as a gambler, his later extravagances as a politician, his coalition with North, his factious opposition to many of Pitt's best measures in the 'eighties' – weigh heavy against him. But as advancing years and darkening public prospects sobered him, the fire of spirit of which he had wasted so much on faction, went more and more sincerely into the defence of the oppressed – in England, Scotland, and Ireland. But the cause of the negro slave appealed to him most of all. Pitt, ever more preoccupied by the daily care of defending the British Empire and all Europe against Bonaparte, forgot all else, and would do nothing more to assist the Anti-slave-trade cause. But Wilberforce found in Fox an ever faithful ally. Owing to his zeal and to the chance that put the Whig chiefs in office, in a Coalition Ministry for a few months after Pitt's death, the slave trade was abolished in 1807 instead of many years later; that was Fox's bequest to the nation and to the world, made upon his death-bed.

The times were tragic, but the men England produced were great. With Pitt and Castlereagh, Nelson and Wellington to lead her through the most terrible ordeal she had ever till then endured, she had Fox and Wilberforce to keep her conscience alive even in time of war.

CHAPTER III

The Character of the French Revolutionary and Napoleonic Wars. Period of Pitt and Nelson, 1793–1805. Period of Wellington and Castlereagh, 1808–15. The Naval, Commercial, and Military Struggle. The Final Settlement

MODERN England has four times fought with success a great war to prevent the conquest of Europe by a single Power: the Spain of Philip and the Inquisition, the France of the Grand Monarch and the Jesuits, the France of the Jacobins and Napoleon, and the German military empire of 1914 were each in turn foiled. On each of these four occasions England had a double end in view – the Balance of Power in Europe and the security of her own mercantile and colonial future beyond the ocean. And on each occasion European and maritime considerations alike required that England should prevent the Netherlands and the Rhine Delta from falling into the hands of the greatest military and naval State of the continent. It was no accidental coincidence, but danger to our shores and to our naval control of the Channel, that made the Netherlands the chief scene of English military interference on the continent, under Elizabeth, under William and Anne, and under George V. And for the same reason the wars conducted in the name of George III against Revolutionary France began with the defeat of our troops in the Netherlands in 1793–4, and ended with their victory in the same sector at Waterloo. But during the twenty years interval, the French hold on Belgium and Holland was strong enough to exclude our armies from that nerve-centre of contending interests, except for a few unsuccessful minor expeditions like those to Alkmaar and to Walcheren. 1799, 1809

The Napoleonic wars stand half-way between the Marlborough wars and the Great War of our own day, in time, in size, and in character. The resemblance to the Marlborough wars is the most obvious, because the weapons employed by sea and land were very similar in the two periods, and the enemy was France. The geography and strategy, therefore, of the naval and military operations which quelled Napoleon resemble those which quelled Louis XIV. Again, in the days of Pitt and Castlereagh, as in the days of William and Marlborough, the two props of the alliance against France were British sea-power and British subsidies, applied along all the coasts and in half the Treasuries of Europe. The huge British sailing ships whose broadsides conquered at Trafalgar were of the same general character as those which had conquered at La Hogue, while the 'thin red line' and the British cavalry charge won Waterloo by tactics not so very different from those of Blenheim and Ramillies. Again a British General of genius, commanding a small but excellent British army, played a decisive part among the larger military establishments of the continent. Again British troops were landed in the Netherlands and in Spain, in Mediterranean islands and on American coasts. And again, in 1815 as in 1713, the war ended for England with the establishment in the Netherlands of a Power from which she had nothing to fear, and by great additions to her colonial Empire and her maritime prestige.

But the Napoleonic wars not only repeated the past but rehearsed the future. The issue of the campaigns against Louis had indeed been affected by the course of trade competition between England and France, but a hundred years later the commercial struggle was more formal and more decisive as a weapon of war. The British blockade of Napoleon's Europe, and his attempt to starve England by the Berlin and Milan Decrees, were warlike operations of the same general character as the British blockade of the Central Powers in our own day and the German submarine campaign; they disturbed the economy of the whole world and had serious consequences for the combatants in their relations with the United States and other would-be neutrals.

Furthermore there is a political element of a distinctively modern type in the wars that originated from the French Revolution. The new regime in France, whatever its defects or crimes, filled the humblest French peasant and bourgeois with pride as a citizen and zeal as a patriot, opened military and civil careers to talent without distinction of birth, and, under the Consulate of Bonaparte, supplied the new nation with the administrative system of a wholly new type of efficiency. The other peoples of the continent were marched into the field as mercenaries or serfs, not as citizen soldiers. Britain alone could match the new spirit of France with a national patriotism of yet older date. But the Englishman's 'will to conquer' could be fully aroused only in defence of sea-power and commerce. After our expulsion from the Netherlands in 1794, it is true that we stayed in the war when others submitted to France, but we kept our armies out of Europe for a dozen years together, safe behind the shield of the Navy. We took no serious part, except naval and financial, in the wars of the two Coalitions that suffered defeat at Marengo and Austerlitz. Nor, until the Peninsular War in 1808, did we begin to fight on land as a principal, and even then with armies of not more than 30,000 British at a time.

Success only began to shine on the allies when the popular sense of nationhood was aroused in Spain, Russia, and Germany, by indignation against French tyranny at length outweighing in Europe the sense of the benefits of French reform. Only in its last phase did the war become a contest between self-conscious nationalities, not altogether unlike those which fought the Great War of our own day. The horror and the slaughter increased in proportion as the peoples were aroused to fight willingly, to some extent on their own behalf and not merely as the obedient vassals of Emperors and Kings. The Moscow and Leipzig campaigns adumbrated the bloody future of nationalist Europe armed with the machinery of modern science and locomotion.

During the greater part of twenty years of war, the immense superiority of the new French national spirit and organization over the lifeless and old-fashioned machinery of the continental States of the *ancien régime*, ensured the defeat of each successive Coalition that England encouraged and financed against France. Until the Peninsular War and the popular movements in Russia and Germany made possible the grand operations of Wellington and Castlereagh, England's effective action was limited to the sea. It was much that she maintained her hold over all the waters of the world, when all the lands of Europe had passed into the orbit of French vassalage. Because the border of England's power reached to the enemy's coastline, she was able to refuse for years together to recognize the accomplished fact of the abrogation of Europe's independence. The double bent of the national purpose, successful naval enterprise and dogged resistance to French hegemony, were embodied in Nelson and in Pitt. The complete and hearty cooperation of the two men saved the British Empire.

Nelson, born in a fortunate hour for himself and for his country, was always in his element and always on his element. Pitt, on the other hand, was a great peace Minister, compelled against his will to take up the burden of war and bear it till he died under it. He had prepared the country and the Empire for this supreme test by ten years of sound government at home, and by his Canadian and Indian legislation. But it was certainly not his expectation or his wish that Britain should be subjected to a fresh ordeal within so short a time after the loss of the American colonies. Pitt had refused to join in the original attack of the reactionary powers on revolutionary France in 1792; indeed, at the beginning of that year he had prophesied a long peace and reduced the numbers of our fighting forces. But the French attack on the Netherlands drew him into the war early in 1793.

By that time he had become a violent Anti-Jacobin, living in a state of panic about the activities of Reformers at home. But he never satisfied Burke by regarding the war as a crusade, nor did he consider it our business to dictate a form of government to France. His objects were to protect the State system of Europe from the aggression of France, in particular to prevent the annexation of the Austrian Netherlands and Holland, and incidentally to recoup the British taxpayer by seizing some French colonies in the West Indies.

For good and for evil Pitt had not Burke's imagination. He regarded the world crisis as a repetition, under changed political conditions, of the Seven Years' War, and he accordingly hoped to fight, as his father had done before him, for naval supremacy and colonial conquest, while sending over a few British troops and much British money to enable our allies to maintain themselves in Europe. But he had not his father's genius for war; it was a very different France with which he had to deal; and there was no Frederick the Great – at least not upon our side. In 1793 a vigorous advance on Paris from the Netherlands might have changed the course of history, before Carnot had time to create the new democratic army of France out of the mutinous welter of the old royal army, deserted by its aristocratic officers. But the chance was let slip, and the Revolution had time to organize its latent energies. Neither the Austrian nor the British armies then in Flanders had the training or the leadership for such an enterprise, which Wellington or even Sir John Moore might have ventured upon with the reconstituted army that we afterwards sent to Spain.

Pitt, moreover, in 1793, sent a large part of the available British forces to the West Indies. He was imitating the war plans not of Marlborough but of Chatham: the French West Indian Islands should be his Canada, which he would win for the Empire. In his generation the wealth of the sugar islands, where great fortunes were made by English planters, caused them to be much more highly regarded than Canada, and the sacrifices which Pitt made to preserve and to acquire such islands for the Empire, though severely criticized by modern historians, seemed very natural at the time. But he had no knowledge of the local conditions of warfare in the West Indies comparable to the knowledge his father had acquired of how Canada and the Ohio valley were to be won. Disease swept off the British soldiers by thousands. The slaves in the French and English islands rose, adding fresh horror and difficulty to the undertaking, and rendering it impossible to withdraw the troops and allow the whole Archipelago to sink like Haiti into black savagery. The affair, which added little to the British Empire, was only liquidated after the death of 40,000 British soldiers in three years, a number roughly answerable to that with which Wellington in six years drove Napoleon's troops out of Spain.

These fearful losses in the tropical world, and the inefficient army system of the day, crippled England's efforts in Europe. The selfish preoccupation of Prussia and Russia in sharing up the corpse of murdered Poland, prevented them from playing the part against France assigned to them in Pitt's scheme. The British and Austrian armies were driven out of the Low Countries to the sound of the Marseillaise. Holland and the Rhine lands were revolutionized by the French, the inhabitants half sympathizing. Finally, Bonaparte's conquest of Italy, and his establishment there of vassal Republics, introduced a new era of French conquest and of world politics. In 1797 Austria, beaten to her knees by this astonishing young genius, crept out of the war, leaving England alone against France.

'The Grand Nation', more formidable than even the 'Grand Monarch' whom William and Marlborough had tamed, was now in the hands of the Directorate, a set of energetic ruffians, the survivors of the guillotine, the fathers of modern war and conquest, who were determined to re-establish the finances of France by plundering the rest of Europe. And the ablest servant of these men, soon to be their master, was already learning from his Italian experience how a French European Empire might be founded, on the basis of uniting the social benefits of the Revolution to religious toleration and political order, which the Directorate were incapable of restoring.

England meanwhile was in a sorry plight. Her ships were excluded from the Mediterranean waters, where the Spaniards had joined the war on her enemies' side; her home fleets at 1797
Spithead and the Nore were in mutiny against the neglect and harsh treatment which had always been the lot of the sailors who won her battles; on land her military reputation was at its lowest ebb; it seemed unlikely that she could, without an ally, hold out against all Western Europe united for her destruction.

In this evil hour she was saved by the high quality of Pitt's courage, and by his instinct for naval affairs. The mutinies were pacified and quelled, and somewhat better conditions of life on board were established. The late mutineers sallied out under 1797
Duncan and destroyed the Dutch fleet at Camperdown. Pitt was clumsy and unsuccessful in diplomatic operations, which he conducted through Grenville, and in military operations, which he conducted through Dundas. But to call him a bad war Minister is to overlook the sea affair, which for English statesmen comprises half the conduct of war. He chose, in Spencer and Jervis, the right men through whom to act; he helped them to pick out Nelson, one of the youngest flag-officers on the list; and he

insisted on sending him back to recover our hold of the Mediterranean, which had been a French lake for more than a year. The result was the battle of the Nile.

1 Aug. 1798 The battle of the Nile was indeed one of the cardinal events of the whole war. It restored British naval power at the moment when it was wavering, and in the region whence it had been withdrawn; whereas Trafalgar only put the crown of glory on a campaign already decided and on a life whose work was done.

Bonaparte had been safely carried to Egypt by the French fleet, and had seized Malta on the way from the Knights of St John. The path to Constantinople and India seemed open to the most ambitious spirit since Alexander the Great. But when Nelson annihilated his fleet, at anchor at the mouth of the Nile, these Oriental visions soon faded. Next year Bonaparte was fain to leave his army locked up in Egypt, and slip back to France. There he rebuilt the structure of his ambitions on a Western basis, and only after many years attempted to cut a path back to the East by the route of Russian conquest. Nelson's cannonade that summer evening off the Egyptian shore secured the full establishment of British supremacy in the Indian Peninsula, in the difficult days of 'Tippoo Sahib' of Mysore and of the Maratha Wars conducted by the Wellesley brothers.

Another consequence of the Nile was the restored dominance of Britain in Mediterranean waters. The power of our fleet was firmly based on Malta, which we took from the French in 1800 and never relinquished, and on Sicily, where the royal family, exiled from Naples, became Nelson's friends, and remained England's *protégés*.

But the Nile evoked other and more formidable allies than the South-Italian Bourbons. Austria and Russia felt encouraged to form the Second Coalition, which after a sudden and brief day of success in North Italy under Suvoroff, perished on the field of
1800 Marengo at the hands of Bonaparte. As First Consul he now had at his command all the civil and military resources of France, which he reorganized in the four best years of his life as the resources of no nation had ever been organized before, giving to France the modern administrative institutions by which she has lived ever since.

Next followed the episode of the 'armed neutrality' formed by Russia and the Scandinavian Powers against England, partly on grounds of neutrals' complaints of the right of search as exercised by the lords of the sea, partly as admirers and would-be allies of Bonaparte, for whose friendship the Czar Paul had half-

crazy yearnings. The assassination of the Czar and Nelson's 1801
destruction of the Danish fleet under the guns of the Copenhagen forts, put an end to the peril in that quarter. In northern as in southern seas, the arm of Britain was omnipotent. French and Spanish, Dutch and Danish fleets had been shattered, and Britain helped herself at will to the colonies of the unhappy allies of France. The Cape of Good Hope and Ceylon were taken from the Dutch to secure the sea route to India.

But on land no one could make head against Bonaparte. The two victorious enemies recognized their respective limits by the
Treaty of Amiens. But though hailed with joy in England, the 1802
long-expected peace proved only a hollow truce. For it soon appeared that Bonaparte interpreted the Treaty of Amiens to mean the retirement of Britain behind the sea curtain, while he remained free to annex every State of Europe to which he had a mind. It was not so that British statesmen interpreted the peace they had signed, which in their eyes set an agreed limit to French expansion. So the two weary nations turned again to war.

England was once more matched alone against France. For the moment, Bonaparte had no other use for his incomparable
army than to threaten 'perfidious Albion' from the camp of 1804
Boulogne. His vigorous but crude and unprofessional schemes for securing the mastery of the Channel, appointing an elaborate *rendez-vous* for the Brest and Toulon fleets in the West Indies, were baffled by the vigilance and energy of Nelson and his 'band of brothers'. Our ships hunted the French across the Atlantic and back, sometimes at fault, sometimes in full cry. The pursued ran breathless to earth in the ports of France and Spain, and no more was heard of the invasion of England. Then, when all seemed over, the anger of Napoleon against Villeneuve, his unfortunate Admiral, caused the main French and Spanish fleet to come out of harbour for the last time, to the final sacrifice off
Cape Trafalgar. It saved the British much rope and timber in 21 Oct. 1805
blockading work during the remaining ten years of the war, and it stamped on the mind of Europe an indelible impression that England's naval power was invincible. That belief helped to make the Nineteenth Century a time of peace and security for the British, and stood them in good stead when that long period of prosperity and high civilization was at length broken by another great war on land and sea.

Nelson is the best loved name in English ears. There is more in our relation to him than can be accounted for by his genius and our obligation. For Marlborough was unpopular, and there was an element of fear in the respect and admiration felt for the Iron Duke. Indeed, Wellington's complete devotion to the public service was rooted in a noble but not very lovable aristocratic pride, which made him live reserved as a man apart, saving him indeed from mistakes and loss of dignity into which Nelson sometimes fell on shore. But Nelson entered straight into the common heart of humanity. As he lay expecting the Trafalgar fight, he chanced to discover that a coxswain, one of the best men on board the *Victory*, had been so busy preparing the mail bags that he had forgotten to drop into them his own letter to his wife, till after the despatch vessel was under full sail for England: 'Hoist a signal to bring her back,' said Nelson; 'who knows but that he may fall in action to-morrow? His letter shall go with the rest.' And the vessel was brought back for that alone.

Dec. 1805 Meanwhile Napoleon, now Emperor, had turned from the useless camp at Boulogne to conquer Eastern Europe at Austerlitz. His success matched Nelson's, and men could not then see that it would be more ephemeral than the dead man's empire over the waves. It was an hour of gloom and glory for England. Pitt, Jan. 1806 worn out with care and disappointment and illness, died at his post. His death and Nelson's rather than the fruitless Treaty of Amiens, marked the close of the first half of the war of twenty years.

The great French war – alike in its first phase in the time of Pitt and Nelson, and its last in the time of Castlereagh and Wellington – was fought by the House of Commons. The comparison of the Roman Senate fighting Hannibal was in the mind of every educated man. The persons whom the House trusted could wield the nation's power and purse, on condition of explaining their plans to the benches of country gentlemen, and winning their approval. For this reason Parliamentary eloquence was at its zenith; popular oratory was not yet of importance, except at the hustings in the few open constituencies at election time. Public meetings there were none. So long as the war lasted, and longer, there was little freedom of press or speech for Reformers. When Cobbett denounced the flogging of British militiamen by German mercenaries, he got two years. The restrictions on popular liberty and propaganda were partly a measure of precaution in wartime, but they did not end with the war, because they were also designed to prevent the revival of the movement for domestic Reform, which the Anti-Jacobin mind identified with sedition.

But though liberty was in partial abeyance, no one was tempted to abridge the power of Parliament, or to restore the rule of the King who had lost the American colonies. George III was not, indeed, entirely without power. Even in the intervals of the lunacy that closed gradually on his old age, he was able to prevent Pitt from emancipating the Irish Catholics, and he exerted a certain influence in the struggle for Cabinet office between the groups and personages of Parliament.

The temporary revival of the group system in place of the two-party system was indeed a feature of the period, which tended to a certain limited extent to revive the influence of the Crown as arbitrator. The two-party system was no longer in full working order, because the split in the Whig party over Reform and the French Revolution reduced the Foxites to about a hundred members, and left them for a generation without hope of power. The hibernation of the Whig party between 1793 and 1830 may be compared to the hibernation of the Tory party from 1714 to 1760, and it had the same result in the revival of a group system on the floor of the House of Commons. Just as the long weakness of the Tories caused the Whigs to divide into Walpole and anti-Walpole factions, so the Tories in the first year of the Nineteenth Century broke up into Pittites, Addingtonians, and Whig-Tory followers of the Grenville family. These groups, personal rather than political in their differences, combined each in turn with the Foxite remnant to form the governments and oppositions of the remaining years of war.

In these circumstances, a certain power of selection rested with the old King, and, when his insanity was pronounced incurable, with the Regent Prince George. They both used it heavily 1811
against any combination that included the Foxite Whigs. Immediately after Pitt's death George III was, indeed, compelled to submit for a year to the coalition Ministry of 'All the Talents', 1806–7
including the dying Fox, with the result that the slave trade was at last abolished. But the King managed speedily to rid himself of servants whom he so much disliked, and though the ground on which he dismissed them was indefensible, it was, perhaps, no real misfortune. For the Whig chiefs and their Grenvillite colleagues did not make good war Ministers. Ever since the camp at Boulogne the Foxites had, indeed, accepted the necessity of war with France, and their leader in his few months at the Foreign Office was converted on his death-bed to the view which he had so often denounced, that peace with Napleon was impossible. Yet his successors in the Whig hierarchy, like Lords Holland and Grey,

too easily despaired, and had neither the phlegm nor the *flair* necessary for those who conduct a long and doubtful war.

The pure Tory groups combined after 1807 to govern the country and fight Napoleon through the agency of the House of Commons. The prestige of Waterloo and the final victory redounded most to the credit of the nation that had never submitted and always hoped. And, in the secure judgement of the world, the victory of the stubborn islanders was due, not to King or Regent, but to British Parliamentary institutions, to the British aristocracy, and to the steady character and rapidly increasing wealth of the British middle class.

Napoleon signalized his coronation as Emperor by conquering Eastern Europe up to the Russian border – a three years' task: each year there was

> another deadly blow!
> Another mighty Empire overthrown,

Austria at Austerlitz, Prussia at Jena, Russia at Friedland. The work was crowned in the summer of 1807 by the Treaty of Tilsit, made on a raft in the Niemen, where Napoleon embraced the Czar Alexander, an impressionable young man, destined to play many different parts in Europe's tragedy, each with the same conscientious solemnity as the last. For four years it flattered him to be Napoleon's ally and half-sharer in the rule of the continent. From the Urals to the Pyrenees the civilized world was banded against England, and closed to her shipping and her goods. But in that vast hostile camp she had many secret friends, whom it was the chief task of her statesmanship to rouse into mutiny. The prospect of British subsidies if they should take up arms, was one of the inducements offered; while another and harsher was the deprivation of tea and coffee, sugar and cotton, so long as they remained French vassals.

England and France now organized the world-warfare of blockade and starvation, on a scale never before witnessed, because never in the history of war had there been sea-power like that of England after Trafalgar, or land-power like that of Napoleon after Tilsit. By Napoleon's Berlin and Milan Decrees, neutrals and French allies were forbidden to trade with Great Britain or her colonies. Britain replied by the Orders in Council, a series of measures of ever-increasing stringency, of which the general drift was that all Napoleonic Europe was subjected to blockade.

Of three sets of victims, which would rebel the first? Napoleon's German vassals and Muscovite allies, deprived of their luxuries and comforts for his sake? Or the United States, the one great neutral carrier, angry with England because her ships effectually barred the Yankee skippers from European ports, whereas Napoleon, having no submarines, could not by mere proclamation exclude them from trading with Britain? Or, finally, as Napoleon had in 1811 some reason to hope, would the strain prove too much for the English middle and lower orders, whose business, employment, and real wages were subject during these terrible years to the vagaries of war prices and war markets?

In fact, by 1812, Russia had rebelled against Napoleon's decrees, and the United States against the British Orders in Council and the right of search as exercised by her captains. But the classes on the British 'home front' who suffered from the war, stood firm. The mercantile community refused to submit to Napoleon, but strongly urged the Perceval Ministry to relax the Orders in Council enough to prevent war with our largest remaining customer, the United States. But the middle classes were still for the most part unenfranchised, and stood outside the close ring of the Tory governing class. Their advice was heeded too late and war broke out between England and America, causing great momentary suffering to Britain by commercial stoppage. But neither that nor the distraction of naval and military bickering 1812–14 on the Canadian frontier and along the American coast, proved fatal to Britain's victory in Europe, because in the same years Russia and Germany rebelled against France. The next generation of Englishmen forgot the American war as an unpleasant and unnecessary episode in the greater Napoleonic struggle; but Americans remembered it only too well, as a patriotic landmark in their early growth as a nation. From the point of view of future Anglo-American relations, it was most unfortunate that the first foreign war of the young Republic should have been waged with the motherland, against whom also her War of Independence had been fought.

The Napoleonic struggle, though as dangerous at times to Britain as the Great War of our own day, affected the life of the community at fewer points; above all it made a much smaller drain upon the manhood of the country. For a dozen years we had practically no troops on the continent, except for very small 1795–1807 and very occasional raids. The total death-roll in the whole twenty-two years was probably about 100,000, nearly half lost in the West Indies in Pitt's time and 40,000 more in the six years' fighting in the Peninsula. It was in economic suffering that England paid. The course of the Industrial Revolution, during two critical decades, was warped and diverted by the exigencies of the war.

But the economic suffering was by no means evenly divided among the whole people. The upper class throve on enhanced rents, and paid too small a proportion of the war taxes; for revenue was raised largely by duties on articles of consumption, of which the effect was felt by the poor in the rise of prices. Pitt's useful new device of the income-tax, which was continued till the end of the war, did something, but not enough, to redress the balance. In 1815 twenty-five millions were raised by direct, and sixty-seven millions by indirect, taxation. Those who enjoyed rent and tithe, composing a single governing class of the well-born, knew little of the hardships of wartime.

It was, indeed, a notable period in the higher civilization of the island, where all through the war great landscape painters, poets, and novelists were working for a large and eager class with the wealth and leisure to enjoy their works. Never was country-house life more thriving or jovial, with its fox-hunting, shooting, and leisure in spacious and well-stocked libraries. Never was sporting life more attractive, with its coaching on the newly improved roads, and its boxing matches patronized by the nobility. In the mirror that Miss Austen held up to nature in the drawing-room, it is hard to detect any trace of concern or trouble arising from the war.

The middle classes suffered more. Many merchants, like poor old Mr Sedley in *Vanity Fair*, were broken by the sudden opening and shutting of markets, or the rise and fall of war prices. But many also made their fortunes in new factories, and in commerce with the black and brown peoples of the world, whom England was learning to clothe, wholesale, as yet without a rival in that profitable business.

The chief sufferers by the war were the working classes, for whom little was done except the general adoption of the policy originated by the Berkshire magistrates at Speenhamland, for granting rates in aid of wages to prevent families from positively dying of starvation. But the better policy of an enforced minimum wage, though discussed, was unfortunately rejected as old-fashioned and unscientific. Meanwhile, Pitt's Act made Trade Unions illegal, so that the workmen found it difficult, in the face of hostile authority, to keep up wages in their proper relation to prices.

That sense of the brotherhood of classes in the Great War which was so marked in our own more democratic day, had no place in the Anti-Jacobin mentality. Wellington's remarks about the soldiers who won his battles, as 'the scum of the earth', enlisted 'for drink', represent the common limitations of upper-class sympathy at that period, though Nelson and his coxswain's letter strike another note. Harshness often appeared, not only in the treatment of the much flogged soldiers and sailors, but in the attitude to Luddites and the 'labouring poor' in general. While engaged in beating Napoleon, the authorities recognized a double duty in relation to starving men – to keep them alive and to keep them in due subordination.

Napoleon's endeavour to enforce his 'continental system' for excluding British goods from Europe – his only available means of chastising the insolent islanders – drew him into the two most fatal errors of his career, the attempt to annex Spain against the will of its people, and the invasion of the vastness of Russia. Those two acts let loose upon him the rising of the peoples, after he had dealt successfully with the Kings. The earlier and more criminal of these enterprises gave England the opportunity to commence the Peninsular War. Our operations there began very 1808
humbly in an attempt to maintain according to precedent the independence of our ancient ally, Portugal. Throughout the next six years Portugal continued to be the base, and sea-power the condition of the whole affair, as in the less lucky operations of the British armies in Spain during the Marlborough wars.

The Portuguese consented to be drilled and commanded by British officers, with the result that in this war they made very respectable troops of the line. The Spaniards, on the other hand, seldom made even tolerable regulars, but seldom failed to act with amazing efficiency in guerrilla warfare. The more primitive nature of Spanish character and society rendered the land which Napoleon had despised more formidable to the armies of French occupation than any of the more civilized nations of modern Europe, upon which they had so long trampled. For this reason the 300,000 French in Spain were mostly engaged in guarding communications, and could never concentrate enough force to destroy the persistent British Army of some 30,000 men under Moore or Wellington. Issuing from Portugal in well-planned raids across Spain, Wellington year after year carried off the victory in an ascending scale of the decisive – Talavera, Salamanca, Vitoria – as Napoleon's increasing commitments in Russia and Germany gradually reduced the pressure of France upon the Peninsula. The military power and reputation of Britain, that had sunk so low at the beginning of the Revolutionary Wars, were raised to the height where they had stood under Cromwell and Marlborough. The Peninsular battles and sieges, recorded in such numbers on our flags, confirmed and perpetuated the regimental traditions which remained the true life of the British Army during the next hundred years.

The victories in Spain, though due largely to the previous work of the Duke of York and Sir John Moore in reforming the Army, and to Wellington's own strategical and tactical genius, were facilitated by the superiority of the British line over the French column. The history of that difference of formation is very curious. The dynastic wars of the Eighteenth Century, from Marlborough to Frederick the Great, had been fought in line – three deep, reduced towards the end of the century to two. But this method of war, then universal in civilized armies, implied the perfect drill of highly professional troops. When, therefore, the first armies of the French Republic took the field with their high-spirited but ill-disciplined hosts straight from the counter and the plough, they could only be led into action in compact masses with a cloud of skirmishers flung out in front. But so great were their zeal and numbers, that in this crude formation they again and again chased off the field the well-ordered lines of the Austrian infantry. Thus defeated, the ancient monarchies of Europe imitated their conquerors by adopting their faulty tactics and formation, without the spirit that had been the true cause of the French successes. Only the British Army, guided by a combination of conservatism and good sense, continued to fight and manoeuvre in line. On the rare occasions, therefore, when they had met the French in Egypt and in South Italy they had an advantage over them shared by no other nation. And now, in the more continuous campaigns of the Peninsula, again and again the narrow head of the French column was mowed down by the concentrated fire of the thin red line. It is indeed remarkable that the greatest military genius of modern times never attempted to reform the retrogressive tactics of his infantry.

The Peninsular War was finally won because the French disasters in Russia and Germany continually reduced the number of their troops in Spain. Similarly, the decisive victory of our allies over Napoleon in person at Leipzig, was rendered possible by the number of French engaged by Wellington in the South. Early in 1814 France was entered by Wellington from across the

Pyrenees, and by the Austrians, Prussians, and Russians across the Rhine. The final success had been rendered possible by the wisdom and energy of Castlereagh's diplomacy in mid-Europe in 1813–14, which held together the alliance of jealous Princes until the common object was attained.

The first fall of Napoleon was followed by his return from Elba, the rally of the veterans of the army to his standard, while the French people looked on with divided feelings. His Hundred Days' adventure ended at Waterloo. The fortunate brevity of this last war was due to the prompt and courageous action of the British Government in declaring war at once, and sending over Wellington to defend Holland and Belgium in alliance with Blucher and his Prussians, till the allied armies from the East could arrive in overwhelming numbers. The decisive character of the great battle put a sudden end to the war, because France was half-hearted in her desire that it should be renewed.

18 June 1815

The reputation of Great Britain, as the most consistent and formidable antagonist of Napoleon, reached its height as a result of Waterloo. At the peace conference, Castlereagh and Wellington spoke with a voice of unrivalled authority among the Emperors and Kings. To the influence of these two Anglo-Irish aristocrats the merits of the Treaties of Vienna were largely due.

The most striking merit of the Settlement of 1815 lay in securing at the outset a long period of quiet for Europe by justice and even leniency to the conquered, a point on which Wellington and Castlereagh both insisted, with the aid of the Czar Alexander, against the very natural desire for vengeance on the part of Blucher and the Germans and a large part of the British public. France – with the Bourbons restored but the social arrangements of the Revolution left intact – was allowed her old boundaries of 1792, was not compelled to give up Alsace or Lorraine, and received back from England most of her possessions in Africa and the two Indies seized during the war. The indemnity which she had to pay was fixed from the first at a moderate sum, and in three years her territory was completely evacuated by the allied armies. Revenge was eschewed, but security was gained by an alliance to prevent, in arms, the return of Napoleon, whom meanwhile the English kept out of harm's way on remote St Helena.

The defect of the Settlement was that nationality and popular liberty were both disregarded on the continent, outside the boundaries of France herself. Except England, the Great Powers who had triumphed were Powers of reaction and despotism, and even Castlereagh cared nothing for Parliaments outside England. The rulers of Russia, Prussia, and Austria divided up Poland, Germany, and Italy as if inhabitants were so many head of population to be bartered among royal hagglers. The Temporal Power of the Pope over Central Italy was restored. The hopes of national and popular self-expression, which in Spain and Germany had partly inspired the late patriotic uprising against France, were crushed to the earth.

The merits of the Settlement of Vienna gave Europe forty years of peace. Its faults rendered war certain in the end – war to assert national and popular aspirations which Metternich's system could not for ever keep in check.

One of the points in the Treaties of 1815 in which Britain was specially interested was the restoration of the Anglophil House of Orange to Holland, and the addition of Belgium to their Kingdom of the Netherlands. The Delta of the Rhine was again in hands from which England had nothing to fear, but another sharp crisis was necessary fifteen years later, before a permanent settlement was reached by the separation of Belgium from Holland on a basis of two separate and independent States.

But the greatest interests of Britain lay beyond the ocean, and there she was supreme arbiter. It was for her alone to decide how many she would give back of the colonies which she had seized in the war. On the whole she was not ungenerous in her restorations. While keeping Ceylon and the Cape of Good Hope and Singapore, and purchasing a part of Guiana for three million pounds, Britain gave back to the Dutch their old possessions of Java and the other East Indian islands which have ever since remained the chief source of Holland's external wealth. France and Denmark got back their most valuable islands. But England kept Mauritius and Heligoland, and the Mediterranean vantage points of the Ionian Islands and Malta. The network of British naval, maritime, and commercial posts, soon to be used also as coaling stations, had already begun to spread over the globe. Australia, peacefully acquired by Captain Cook's voyages (1769–75), was in process of colonization. Upper Canada was filling with English and Scots. A Second Empire was arising to replace that which had been lost, based like the first on sea-power, commerce, and liberty.

CHAPTER IV

The Empire in the latter years of George III. The outward expansion of the island life. England, Scotland, and Ireland. Canada and Australia. India. The Anti-Slave-Trade Movement. Wilberforce and the Evangelicals

NATURE had early decided that the inhabitants of Britain must be insular, but there are various kinds and degrees of insularity. After the Norman Conquest, the English had for several generations been to all appearance part of the feudal and Catholic world of French civilization. Then, by a gradual process in the later Middle Ages, culminating in the Tudor revolution, they had asserted an island individuality in law and government, religion and culture, character and habits of life. They had, in Elizabeth's words about herself, become 'mere English', repelling the invading influences of the continent. But as their native strength and self-confidence increased they had become every year more active beyond the seas, in that new way ceasing to be 'insular'. They appeared in every quarter of the newly discovered globe, bringing with them English ideas and standards that had come to maturity at home.

In the era of Waterloo the life of the islanders was being constantly enriched and broadened by their activities as explorers, traders, warriors, and rulers in all parts of the world, both in the lands of the ever-growing British Empire, and in countries like China and South America, where the British had become the characteristic representatives of European trade and influence. The Industrial Revolution had given fresh speed and vigour to the outward expansion of English life which had been going on ever since the days of Elizabeth. The reign of George III saw, in consequence, the emergence of a number of Imperial problems of a new order, connected with Ireland, Canada, Australia, India, and the relations of the white man to the African negro. In all these the younger Pitt played a leading part.

One source of anxiety, indeed, had been removed. The relations of England and Scotland no longer formed an Imperial problem of grave difficulty, but a domestic bond of singular felicity. The Union of the two States, after a period of uneasy working, had been adjusted by time and patience. The decease of Jacobitism, the measures taken after 1745 to abolish feudalism and tribalism in Scotland, and her ever-increasing wealth since that crisis had been adjusted, led to the better appreciation in

England of the Scottish qualities. 'Sir Walter's' Scottish romances, and the kilted regiments who fought so well at Waterloo, seemed to Englishmen and to the whole civilized world to represent something new added to the island tradition and power. The mutual acceptance of each other by the two peoples has remained ever since one of the chief pillars of the British State.

The era of Burns and Scott was one of expansion, new prosperity, and noble pride for their countrymen, upon the whole the happiest since first they were a nation. They had, indeed, internal difficulties, but since these were of the same general character as contemporary difficulties in England, they served to unite the two ends of the island in a common *malaise*. The social and economic problems attendant on the Industrial Revolution were aggravated by antiquated political institutions in both countries, by rotten boroughs and an absence of efficient municipal and local bodies suited to the new age. In Scotland, where even County elections were a farce, the political machinery was more out of touch with modern facts than even in England, and the spirit of Anti-Jacobin repression was more severe, while the democratic spirit was more fierce. The trouble bade fair some day to be worse in Scotland than in England. But in the coming era the process of political reform and social amelioration followed the same course in both countries, tending still further to unite their fortunes in one.

While Scotland was ceasing to be regarded at Downing Street as a problem, the Irish question, after a long period of quiescence, was entering upon a new phase of virulent activity, which continued to disturb the British Empire at frequent intervals until the great events of our own day.

During the early and middle Eighteenth Century, while Jacobite Scotland had been a source of trouble and danger, the native Irish had given no sign of lifting their heads. Ever since the days of Sarsfield, the active rebels, the 'wild geese' of Irish Jacobite tradition, were serving in French armies, and had the pleasure of shooting Englishmen only on occasions like Fontenoy. The island itself, twice conquered by Cromwell and by William, lay quiet under British and Protestant ascendancy, and under the iniquitous and partly enforced Penal Laws against Catholics.

In the last thirty years of the Century the old bones in that valley of desolation began to stir under the reviving winds of a new age. In the first instance the initiative was not Catholic and Celtic, but Protestant and Liberal. It was a movement partly of Ulster Presbyterians, partly of broad-minded statesmen like Grattan, against a system of tyranny that sacrificed Ireland as a whole to English trading interests, and all other Irish denominations to Anglican ascendancy. In this generous mood many Protestants forgot their grandfathers' fears of the native Catholics, who since the Century began had done nothing more dangerous than endure wrong.

During the War of American Independence, Ireland fell into the hands of the Volunteers, who were Protestants, but the movement was supported by Catholic opinion. The Volunteers were 1778–82
prepared to defend the island against the French invader, but they dictated their terms to the government of England – the abolition of Ireland's commercial disabilities, and the formal independence of her Parliament from British control. Ireland secured free markets for her goods, but her political autonomy during the next two decades was more apparent than real. For Catholics were still allowed no part or lot in the Dublin Parliament, and the oligarchy in Dublin Castle manipulated the rotten boroughs so that a Reform Bill would clearly be necessary before even Protestant Ireland could practise self-government.

But there was hope in the new era. The worst of the Penal Laws were repealed. Reform was in the air, under the leadership of Grattan, who hoped to reconcile races and creeds by a gradual process of evolution. Catholic and Protestant fanaticism were both dormant. The best spirit of Eighteenth Century toleration and latitudinarianism was still widely prevalent. If British statesmen had met Grattan half-way in his own spirit, much might have been done. But the spirit of Jacobinism and Anti-Jacobinism, of neo-Catholicism and Orangeism, arrived too soon upon the scene and destroyed the generous opportunity created by the time-spirit of the Eighteenth Century. The Tories in England had taken over as their own electoral speciality the old Whig cry of No-Popery, while at the same time the French Revolution made them adamant against all change. The liberal-minded but incautious Viceroy, Lord Fitzwilliam, was recalled from Dublin, after he had kindled hopes that Pitt was unable 1795
to fulfil. His recall put an end to any further attempt to gain Ireland's support for the war against France by a policy of conciliation to Catholics. When, therefore, the French military propagandists offered Republican liberty to Ireland, their aid was accepted by the leaders of the United Irishmen, Wolfe Tone and Lord Edward Fitzgerald, converts from the English garrison. These men hoped to unite the religions of Ireland in arms against

England. But the actual effect of their reliance on French aid was to set Protestant and Catholic to kill each other in the old spirit of the Williamite wars. For, great as were the wrongs of the Ulster Scots and Presbyterians against the English Government, they could not join the French to set up a Celtic Republic, dominated by priests. The Rebellion of 1798 was put down by a combination of the hard-pressed British Government with the loyalists of Ireland, now reconverted to the anti-Catholic fears of their ancestors, and beginning to organize themselves in the new 'Orange' lodges. The military and political weakness of England at that critical moment made her dependent to a dangerous degree on the help of local partisans who in their panic treated the native Irish with cruel rigour. The memories of 'ninety-eight' became an heirloom of hatred, cherished in every cottage, and exploited by successive generations of patriots and agitators.

In these circumstances Pitt decided that the Union of the two islands in one Parliament at Westminster was the only method of permanently restoring order and justice. But he was able to restore only order. He had not the political authority to pass Catholic Emancipation, which he had designed to accompany the Union and render it palatable to the Celtic Irish. That hope, and an orgy of Parliamentary corruption in Dublin, had just
1801 sufficed to carry the Union. But Pitt's royal master, many of his colleagues, his party, and the majority of his countrymen feared the consequences of giving political rights to Roman Catholics either in Ireland or in England. The two most active forces of the day, Anti-Jacobinism and Evangelicalism, were at one on that score. For twenty-eight years Roman Catholics were prohibited from sitting in the United Parliament of Great Britain and Ireland. The delay was fatal.

So the Catholic Celts were again thrust down, this time with the whole weight of England on the top of them, and with their fellow-Irish of the North waxing in Orange enthusiasm. The two Irelands were once more face to face, fighting the Boyne battle again daily with their mouths. Moreover, the land question was beginning to take a foremost place in politics, in that over-populated, potato-fed island of oppressed tenant-farmers. In these circumstances, a new and formidable amalgamation of clericalism, nationalism, and uneducated democracy began to be organized by the popular oratory of the Catholic lawyer, Daniel O'Connell.

The last years of George II's reign had witnessed the conquest

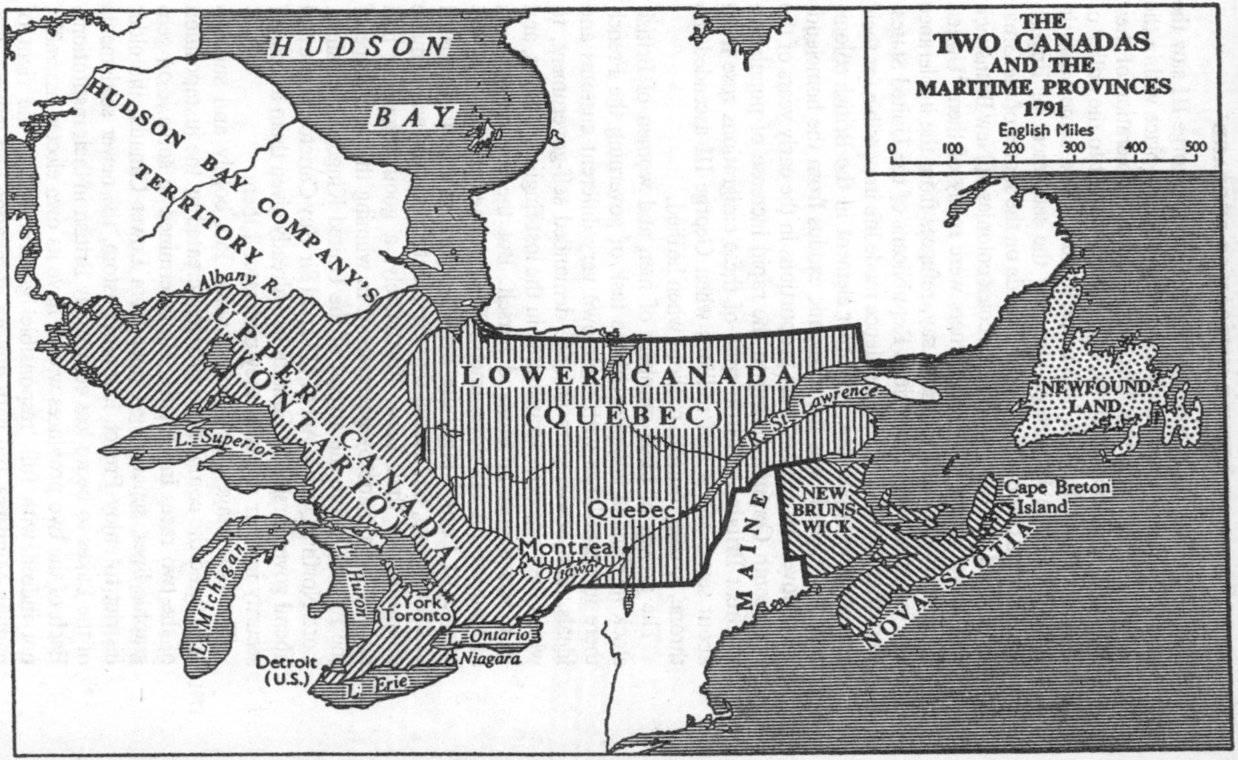
THE
TWO CANADAS
AND THE
MARITIME PROVINCES
1791
English Miles
0 100 200 300 400 500
HUDSON
BAY
HUDSON BAY COMPANY'S
TERRITORY
Albany R.
UPPER CANADA
(ONTARIO)
LOWER CANADA
(QUEBEC)
L. Superior
L. Michigan
L. Huron
York
Toronto
L. Ontario
Niagara
Detroit
(U.S.)
L. Erie
Montreal
R. Ottawa
Quebec
R. St. Lawrence
MAINE
NEW
BRUNS
WICK
NOVA SCOTIA
Cape Breton
Island
NEWFOUND
LAND

MAP XIII

of French Canada in war. The long reign of George III saw the reconciliation of the French Canadians to their place within the British Empire. This was affected by complete toleration of their religion, rights, and customs, in striking contrast to the policy of Protestant and English 'ascendancy' during the same years in Ireland. George III's reign also saw the settlement of English and Scottish colonists in Upper Canada on the shores of the Great Lakes, and to a less degree in the coast colonies of New Brunswick and Nova Scotia. The new-comers were many of them 'United Kingdom Loyalists', that is to say, refugees from the intolerance and injustice of the victorious Republicans of the United States, who after the War of Independence made life impossible for their late political opponents. The other element in the British colonization of Canada was the economic exodus from the homeland. This movement reached vast proportions in the early years of the Nineteenth Century, owing to the rapid increase of population in Great Britain, which in spite of these emigrations rose from about seven and a half millions when George III ascended the throne, to over fourteen millions when he died.

The arrival of large numbers of men and women of British stock in Canada complicated the task of governing the French there in accordance with their own very different customs and ideals. The new-comers at once demanded self-government, to which they had been accustomed in the lost English colonies, and to a less degree in England herself. But the French peasants had no use for self-government. Their seigneurs had largely returned to France after the British conquest, but they trusted to their priests, and feared that the heretic strangers would make alterations in their laws. Fortunately, a good beginning had already been made by government in winning the confidence of the French before the arrival of the United Kingdom Loyalists. Lord North's Quebec Act of 1774 and Sir Guy Carleton's wise and liberal governorship of Canada had already given them a sense of security in their rights as they understood them.

The next stage was reached when Pitt boldly and success-
1791 fully faced the complicated problem created by the juxtaposition of the two races in Canada. He determined to solve it on geographic lines, separating Upper from Lower Canada, the older district to enjoy French law and custom, the newer settlements of the Lakes to be no less completely British in their institutions. Each of the two provinces was to have its own elected assembly, not indeed with full 'responsible' government or the right of naming Ministers, but with powers of taxation and law-making,

and a fixed relation to the Governor and his executive not unlike that of an Elizabethan Parliament to the Crown. The arrangement met the needs of the time in Canada, as fully as the grant of 'responsible' government, made fifty years later on Durham's advice, met them for the later age. In the interval, the French were initiated into the mystery of representative assemblies, and the British population flourished and rose in the half century from 10,000 to 400,000 souls. English and Scottish immigration up the St Lawrence largely accounted for this astonishing increase in a land where the backwoodsman had to prepare each step of the way.

The period that witnessed the plantation and early growth of British Canada, saw the same process in Australia. The occasion and method of the first settlements were different in the two cases, but the general character of the colonizing movement was much the same. Canada had been won by war, and the French were there before us to open the land to later immigrants. Australia, discovered but neglected by the Dutch in the Seventeenth Century, was still empty of men, save for a few
Aborigines, when Captain Cook of the Royal Navy explored its 1769–75
coasts and brought it to the notice of British statesmen and
public. The first settlement was made by order of Pitt and his 1786–7
Home Secretary, Lord Sydney, not with a view to founding a new Empire in the Antipodes, but merely to find a new place for the deportation of convicts, since the old American colonies were now closed for that purpose by their secession. But the convict settlements and the troops that guarded them afforded a convenient base and a method of communication with distant England, very necessary for the first stages of free colonization that speedily followed. Men went to Australia for the same economic reasons which sent them to Canada. By the time of Waterloo the capitalist sheep and cattle farmers, known as 'squatters', had already begun to create the Australia that we know.

The reign of George II had witnessed the destruction of the French power in India by Clive, and his conquest of Bengal as the first great continental area of British rule in the peninsula. Its acquisition converted the East India Company from an armed trading corporation into an Asiatic Power. The logic of the change was worked out in the reign of George III by Warren Hastings, Cornwallis, and Wellesley in India, and by Pitt at home.

The design of the French to erect an Empire of their own in Hindustan had been thwarted by Clive, but for fifty years after Plassey Frenchmen continued to be a thorn in the British side, stirring up Indian Courts and officering Indian armies, first against Hastings and then against Wellesley. In so doing, they hastened the pace at which the British power was forced to advance across the peninsula.

During the War of American Independence, Warren Hastings
1772–85 was left with very inadequate means to struggle against these external dangers, and at the same time to maintain his internal authority against the faction in his own Council led by his personal enemy, Philip Francis. He saved British rule in India in spite of all, but not without making the kind of mistakes which a strong man is likely to make in difficult emergencies. For these acts, much exaggerated and misconstrued by the malignity of Francis and the imagination of Burke, Fox, and Sheridan, he was impeached in Westminster Hall. Those famous proceedings,
1788–95 substantially unjust to Hastings even though they resulted in his acquittal, had the advantage of bringing Indian problems and responsibilities forcibly to the notice of British statesmen and the British public. Burke preached the right ideal of our obligations to the Indians, but misunderstood the relation of Hastings' governorship to the problem.

Pitt, meanwhile, after denouncing and destroying a very similar but rather bolder Bill introduced by Fox, had by his
1784 own India Act established the practical control of the British Cabinet over the administrative work of the East India Company, while leaving its commercial monopoly intact. At the same time Pitt's Bill relieved the Governor General at Calcutta from the tutelage of his Council, which became advisory only. Such scenes as those between Francis and Hastings were never to occur again at the Council Board. The Governor-General was made an autocrat in a land that understood only autocracy, but was himself subject to the ultimate control of the Home Government through the Board of Control under a President of Cabinet rank. Pitt's Indian legislation served India until the time of the Mutiny, as satisfactorily as his Canadian legislation served Canada until the time of Lord Durham.

Pitt had also the merit of sending out the right men to wield as Governor-General these tremendous powers. Lord Cornwallis
1786–1793 completed the internal work of Hastings, and fixed the taxation and government of Bengal on a system that became the model for all provinces subsequently administered by the British. Indians began to find that under the British flag, and there alone, was to be found security from warlike invasion, and from the

grosser forms of domestic oppression. Upon that was based both the permanence and the justification of the British raj. The plunder and misrule that had accompanied our first conquest of Bengal in spite of Clive's efforts to stem the passions of his countrymen, could never be repeated under the new system and under the influence of the new spirit. The high traditions of the 'Anglo-Indian families' began to be formed; many of them were Scottish, for Pitt's friend, Henry Dundas, cannily combined his political jobbery beyond the Border with sending out excellent young Scots to India.

If Cornwallis did most to justify the British power internally, Lord Wellesley, the elder brother of Wellington, did most to 1798–1805 expand it and to justify its expansion. He broke the power of the fighting Mohammedan ruler, 'Tippoo Sahib' of Mysore, and of the great Maratha Confederacy of Central India, whose horsemen had so long attacked and threatened all the neighbouring States. The Confederacy had recently, with the help of French officers, armed and trained its forces after the European manner. In effect it was the policy of Wellesley as Governor-General to extend the protection of Britain over a number of Indian States, such as Hyderabad, thereby stepping into the place of the deceased Mogul Empire as arbiter and keeper of the peace in the whole peninsula. The implications of this policy, which could in the end have no geographic boundary save the Himalayas and the sea, were little liked by the cautious East India Company at home and were only half liked by Pitt and his Cabinet. But all attempts to call a halt to the British advance, though seriously made after Wellesley's retirement, proved nugatory in the face of inexorable facts.

It was to be proved by repeated experience in the Punjab and elsewhere, that peace in India could only be maintained by the acknowledged suzerainty of a single Power. That, few will be inclined to dispute. But it is, perhaps, an open question whether the position might be easier to-day if a larger proportion of protected native States had, like Hyderabad, been left to Indian rulers, and if the actual area of direct British government had been more narrowly circumscribed. But the benevolent reforming zeal of rulers like Dalhousie made them favour the extension of direct British rule as the means of good administration. The political, as distinct from the administrative aspect of Indian problems, was in the background during the fortunate Nineteenth Century, except for the lightning flash of the Mutiny year.

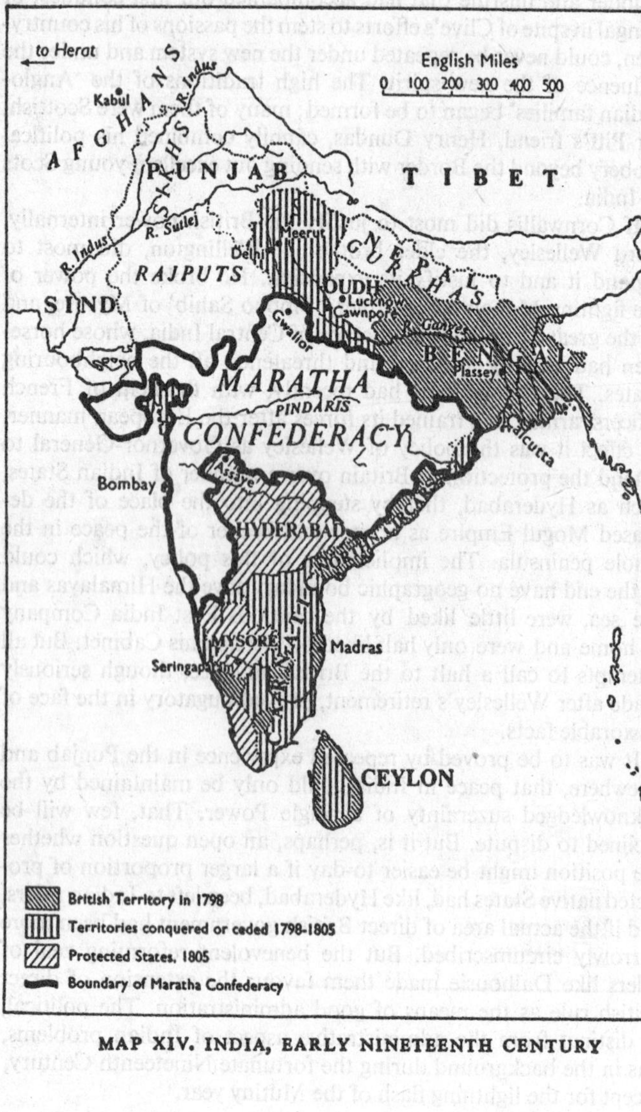

MAP XIV. INDIA, EARLY NINETEENTH CENTURY

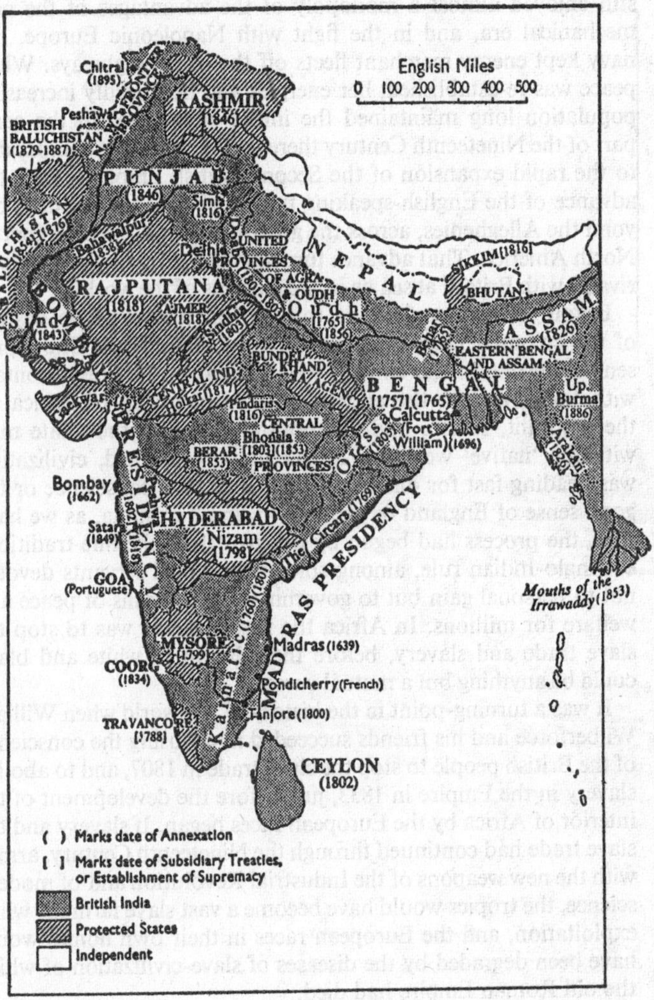

MAP XV. INDIA IN 1906

During the Napoleonic war Britain's lead over the rest of Europe in colonization and trade was immensely increased. She still enjoyed almost a monopoly of the advantages of the new mechanical era, and in the fight with Napoleonic Europe, her navy kept enemy merchant fleets off the ocean highways. When peace was re-established, her energies and her rapidly increasing population long maintained the initial advantage. In the early part of the Nineteenth Century there was nothing else comparable to the rapid expansion of the Second British Empire, except the advance of the English-speaking people of the United States beyond the Alleghenies, across the great plains and rivers of central North America. That advance turned America away from serious rivalry with Britain at sea or in the markets of the world.

Britain held, therefore, at this critical juncture, the destiny of the coloured races very largely in her own hand. She represented Europe in the contact with China, in the closer contact with India, and in the approaching development of Africa. If the ignorant, selfish, and irresponsible ways of the white man with the 'native' were any longer to be continued, civilization was heading fast for disaster. Could either the conscience or the good sense of England be aroused in time? In India, as we have seen, the process had begun by the growth of the fine traditions of Anglo-Indian rule, among soldiers and civil servants devoted not to personal gain but to government as a means of peace and welfare for millions. In Africa the first business was to stop the slave trade and slavery, before the relation of white and black could be anything but a mutual curse.

It was a turning-point in the history of the world when William Wilberforce and his friends succeeded in arousing the conscience of the British people to stop the slave trade in 1807, and to abolish slavery in the Empire in 1833, just before the development of the interior of Africa by the European races began. If slavery and the slave trade had continued through the Nineteenth Century, armed with the new weapons of the Industrial Revolution and of modern science, the tropics would have become a vast slave farm for white exploitation, and the European races in their own homes would have been degraded by the diseases of slave-civilization of which the old Roman Empire had died.

Fortunately, when Wilberforce attacked the slave trade, it was still confined to a traffic carried on by British skippers crimping Negroes along the African coast for the horrors of the Atlantic passage. The interior of the Dark Continent was still closed to Europeans. And the maritime predominance of England was such that no power would seriously dispute her determination that the slave trade should stop, if she once made up her own mind. If Wilberforce could convert England, she would soon persuade the world.

The method by which this conversion was affected, in itself constituted a new epoch in British public life. The anti-slave trade movement was the first successful propagandist agitation of the modern type, and its methods were afterwards imitated by the myriad societies and leagues – political, religious, philanthropic, and cultural – which characterized Nineteenth Century England. Originally promoted by the Society of Friends, who never did a greater service to humanity, the slave trade question was taken up by philanthropists like Sharp and Clarkson, by Wilberforce the 'converted' man of fashion, and by Zachary Macaulay whose eminently Scottish qualities put a stiffening into the fibre of English Evangelicalism. Many of the workers in the cause were either Quakers or Evangelicals, inspired by the practical religious zeal of so many of the Protestant laity of that period. This gave them an easier route to the heart of many of their countrymen, especially the Dissenters, than if they had appealed on grounds solely of humanity or in furtherance of scientific plans for the future of the Empire. But they had a formidable ally in the non-religious humanitarianism of the new age, in veterans like Fox and young men like Brougham, whose zeal for the slaves waxed in opposition, while the cares of office sprang up and choked Pitt's first generous zeal.

The conversion of the country, begun just before the French Revolution, was carried on under difficulties during the Anti-Jacobin reaction, when the slave trade abolitionists were denounced as 'Reformers' tampering with the vested interests of Bristol and Liverpool merchants under the Leveller's plea – humanity. But after a period of depression the cause rallied, and by the Act of 1807 triumphantly put down the slave trade. The triumph was all the more remarkable for being won in the middle of the Great War, and in the middle of a period when no other agitation was permitted. In spite of much corruption in public institutions, the spirit of the British body politic was free, healthy, and capable of response, as compared to any other public opinion then existing in the world. Wilberforce, the cross-bench member for Yorkshire, had found a new and nobler use for the political machinery of England.

And so, at the time of the Treaties of Vienna, Castlereagh was both able and willing to induce the Powers of Europe to subscribe 1815 to the suppression of the slave trade as the rule of the sea in the new era. The Union Jack had become, by a dramatic change, specially associated with the freedom of the black man.

By this time Evangelicalism had made a strong lodgement inside the Tory party. One Prime Minister, Perceval, had been an Evangelical. Many Tories of the old school disliked the 'Clapham sect' as they were called – for their friendship with Dissenters, their too insistent interest in their own and other people's souls, their want of appreciation of the spirit of cakes and ale, their frequent unreadiness to play the party game owing to some scruple of humanity or conscience. This duality inside the Tory fold, and a corresponding rivalry in the religious world of the hearty or fox-hunting churchman and his more serious Evangelical brother, though they caused heartburning, were signs of life. Such differences of aim helped to keep the party and the Church in some touch with outside forces in the nation, during the years after the war when the limitations of the old Toryism and of the old Establishment began to be painfully visible. Evangelicalism and humanitarianism – often though not always allied – were forces of the new age that worked upon British affairs athwart the lines of party divisions, and gave a new reality to public and Parliamentary life.

CHAPTER V

The Reign of George III in its Economic Aspect. The Early Stages of the Industrial Revolution. Population. Canals. Machinery. Coal. The movement of Industry from the Village to the Town. Enclosure. Housing. Administrative defects.

Laissez faire

King: George III, 1760–1820

THE great changes in man's command over nature and consequent manner of life, which began in England in the reign of George III and have since spread with varying degrees of intensity over almost the whole inhabited globe, make bewildering work for the historian. Up to the Industrial Revolution, economic and social change, though continuous, has the pace of a slowly-moving stream; but in the days of Watt and Stephenson it has acquired the momentum of water over a mill-dam, distracting to the eye of the spectator. Nor, for all its hurry, does it ever reach any pool at the bottom and resume its former leisurely advance. It is a cataract still. The French Revolution occupied a dozen years at most, but the Industrial Revolution may yet continue for as many hundred, creating and obliterating one form of economic and social life after another, so that the historian can never say – 'This or this is the normal state of modern England.' To speak, for example, in terms of traffic. Four successive civilizations of the riding track, the canal and coach road, the railway, and the motor have been superimposed one on the other in the course of a hundred and sixty years.

Want of statistical and economic information lightens the work of the historian of earlier times, while setting limits to the scope and certainty of his deductions. The age of Blue-books begins with the Nineteenth Century. The first census of Great Britain was taken in 1801. Our economic information, in fact, only becomes trustworthy in the middle of the first phase of the Industrial Revolution. We have, therefore, very slender means of estimating the material welfare of the majority of Englishmen before the latter years of George III. Then, indeed, the picture which economic historians present to us of England in the time of Cobbett, is in some important respects very unpleasant; but as it is the first 'close-up' in the cinema show of English social history, we are unable to say whether an equally hard and precise vision of any earlier period would be any less unpleasant to our modern susceptibilities. Candid persons will refrain from answering the question with any approach to dogmatism.

It is possible, of course, to prefer the rural to the city life, and to regret that the farmer and artificer have been so generally replaced by the minder of machines; it is possible also to hold exactly the opposite view. We must indeed all of us deplore the loss of beauty of shape and variety of surface in machine-made articles, and the landscape marred by industrialism, which have so largely deprived us of the purest aesthetic pleasures formerly common to rich and poor alike. But in no case must we imagine that Great Britain could, without modern machinery, have supported forty-two millions in 1921 at a standard of material comfort as high as that which then obtained; or even fourteen millions in 1821 at the miserably inadequate standard, as we now hold it, of that day. What precisely was the average standard of life among the six or seven millions in 1721, is a question on which experts differ in opinion, because statistical knowledge about that early date is fragmentary or non-existent. As to the extent of true happiness and moral welfare then as compared to now, we are still more in the dark. But the interest of the inquiry loses nothing by want of certainty and finality in the answer.

The most striking accompaniment of the revolution in machinery and organization was the rise in the number of inhabitants of Great Britain in the single reign of George III, from about seven and a half to above fourteen millions. But what precise relation as cause or effect this increase had to the industrial and agricultural changes of the time, is a question not easily answered. Certain explanations, till recently accepted, now appear doubtful. It must be remembered that a similarly unprecedented rise in population was taking place in Celtic Ireland during the same years, and in Celtic Ireland there was no Industrial Revolution at all. Neither is it safe to set down the rise in population to the 'Speenhamland' system of aiding wages out of rates, at so much per child; for that system only began in 1795, became fully operative a good deal later, and never obtained at all in Scotland, North England, or Ireland, where the rise in population was just as rapid as in the 'Speenhamland' counties of the Midlands and South. Moreover from 1790 onwards the birth-rate slightly declined, although the population continued to multiply owing to the far more rapid fall in the death-rate.

The unexampled rise in population from 1760 onwards was due, not so much to earlier marriages and an increase in the crude birth-rate, though these had a considerable part in the affair before 1790, as to the saving of life by improvements in medical science and practice, and to an improved standard of living which may to some extent be attributed to cheap goods produced by the new mechanical inventions. The disappearance of the Plague so long endemic in the island; the control of the ravages of scurvy and ultimately of small-pox; the reduction of ague and fever by the draining of the land; the advance of habits of cleanliness and the use of cheap cotton shirts; improvements in sanitation in London and elsewhere as compared to the past, however appalling the age of Howard appears to our nice senses to-day; and above all else, more and better hospitals and better medical care of mothers and infants which greatly reduced mortality at child-birth or by 'convulsions', rickets, and other infantile diseases – all these were features of the Eighteenth and early Nineteenth Centuries.

It is not impossible that until the very eve of the Twentieth Century the crude birth-rate has varied very little down the ages, and that the modern increase of population was due to the more successful efforts of society 'officiously to keep alive'. At the end of George III's reign the French death-rate was twenty per cent higher than the English. With all its faults, the later Eighteenth Century in England was a period of improved science, cleanliness, and humanity. The patriotic pride of the historians of the Victorian era, like Macaulay, in the perpetual progress of the nation in its social life and comfort is perhaps after all no further removed from the whole truth than the more recent view that the Industrial Revolution was accompanied by a general throw-back to harder conditions of life. Vital statistics are not everything, but so far as they go they are not unfavourable to the more optimistic doctrine of the older school.

But if these causes, and others at present obscure, produced an increase in population wholly unexampled in history, it is certain that the additional millions could not have been maintained in the island, or even provided for in the colonies, had it not been for the agricultural and industrial changes of the new era. Indeed, if the old economic system had continued unchanged after 1760, it is doubtful whether the existing seven millions could have continued much longer to inhabit the island in the same degree of comfort as before. The depletion of British timber was already producing a fuel famine that left many domestic hearths cold, and was driving the iron industry across the sea to the still virgin forests of America and Scandinavia. At that moment the situation was saved by the new canal system, which brought coal to domestic hearths in inland regions of South England, and to the furnaces of the Black Country.

The way for the Industrial Revolution was prepared by the first rapid improvements in methods of transport since the Roman era. From the beginning of the reign of George III, a network of canals was gradually extended over many districts, bringing to them benefits which London had always enjoyed from her maritime position and sea-borne coal. Canals were eventually made in all parts of the island, but those which paid dividends over ten per cent were nearly all in the mining and industrial districts of the North and Midlands, or served to connect those districts with the Thames Valley. For the system of 'inland navigation', as it was called, no less than the modern merchant navy, throve by reason of the coal trade. Railways, when they came in their turn, were originally devised to serve the distribution of coal, and to link up the gaps in the canal system. But early in the days of George Stephenson it was clear to the fore-seeing that the age of canals would be short in England.

Short, too, for the same reason was the glory of the hard 'Macadamized' road, with its Tally-ho coaches and post-chaise postillions speeding along at twelve miles an hour from the court-yards of the great London inns to Bath, or Holyhead, or York, or Gretna Green, and on over Sir Walter's Scotland. Like the contemporary canals, the hard roads were the work chiefly of capitalist companies, who recouped themselves from passengers at the toll-bars. But the movement was aided by the Post Office, one of the first Departments to conceive the modern idea of the duty of the Civil Service to the public. The gay and rapid life of the English road reached perfection only during the Napoleonic wars, and twenty years later the railways already clearly foreshadowed the end. Brief, but characteristically English while it lasted, was that age of the all-worshipped horse, with Horncastle Fair for its Mecca, with fox-hunters, stagecoachmen, and jockeys as ministers to the national enthusiasm for the noblest of animals. Posterity still fondly regards that generation as the last of 'merrie England' – except when it remembers that it was also the era of Peterloo and the very worst periods of the 'evils' of the Industrial Revolution.

Indeed, when we picture the past to ourselves, it is not easy always to remember the great variety of things old and new that go on side by side in separate compartments in the life of a growing nation. We sometimes think of the factory system as the leading feature of the last years of George III. But though it was the new feature and had the future with it, it by no means as yet dominated the scene except in one or two districts. The cotton trade of Lancashire had indeed sprung into sudden being, first in small 'mills' planted beside the water power of the Pennine streams, then with more elaborate machinery and on a larger scale in the plain below. And there had been a corresponding development of Liverpool, as the port for this new industry
1819 which bought all its raw material in America and sold most of its finished goods oversea. But at the time of the Peterloo Massacre not a twentieth of the families of England had a member in the cotton industry. Agriculture was by far the largest occupation, and next came the building trades and domestic service; the weaving of wool had not yet passed into the factory, though the spinning-jenny had already destroyed the cottage industry of many industrious wives and children of the peasant class; tailoring and shoemaking, that figured among the very largest trades in the country, were still conducted on the domestic basis; and the number of persons engaged in the service of horses must have been immense.

The Industrial Revolution was not an event but a process.

It was the admixture of the old manner of life and the new that made the characteristic and vigorous Britain of the era of Wellington. Only as the Nineteenth Century wore on, an ever larger proportion of the population was harnessed to the new machinery and to big business, while the realm of the factory was extended every year at the expense of domestic and out-of-door occupations. Fortunately, as the factory had become the typical arena of work, its worst abuses were gradually remedied; from 1833 onward it became increasingly subjected to State inspection and regulation, which employees in the older type of domestic workshop had good reason to envy.

The greatest development of the reign of George III, greater even than the Lancashire cotton trade, was the revolution involved in the application of coal to iron-smelting, which created the Black Country in the West Midland shires. In forty years the production of iron in Britain increased ten-fold. The Black Country became the chief scene of this new development, and of a great number and variety of hardware, pottery, and other industries more and more dependent upon iron or coal. All over the island new businesses sprang up, each helped by some adaptation of James Watt's steam engine to the various processes of mining and manufacture. With iron and machinery was born a new class – the modern mechanic. If the great economic changes as yet brought little good to the child in the factory or to man, woman, or child in the coal-mine, it created a large class of well-paid, educated engineers, whose advice was sought with respect by their employers in innumerable industries scattered all over the island. To that class of wage-earners belonged the great Stephenson family of Tyneside. There was nothing 'bourgeois' about the origins of the man who invented the locomotive, after having taught himself to read at the age of seventeen. The motto of the coming age was 'self-help', or individual opportunity, and its benefits were not entirely monopolized by the middle class. It was from the 'Mechanics' Institutes' that the adult education of the new age took a start.

For the first time since Anglo-Saxon days, the North-western half of England, the ancient Northumbria and Mercia, became of importance in rivalry to the corn-bearing lands of South and East, and to London and its satellite counties. Even the old textile industries of East Anglia, of Somerset, and of the Cotswolds declined before the vigorous competition of the northern dales in the age of machinery. Moorlands which had formerly been the home of the moss-trooper, the feudal retainer, and the shepherd, become centres of wealth and trained intelligence of the modern order. This shifting of the geographic balance of power in the island was to be a chief cause of the demand for political change and Parliamentary redistribution in the approaching era. But so long as the Napoleonic wars lasted, and for more than a decade after they had come to an end, the new middle class was content to accumulate wealth, and did not seriously challenge the political and social monopoly that excluded it from its natural weight in the new England. And although the proletariat assembled in the new industrial districts were driven by misery to Radical agitation under Cobbett and Hunt, it was still easy to keep them down so long as they had no middle-class support, and no legal Trade Union organization of their own.

With momentum ever increasing throughout the reign of George III, men and women were flooding into the industrial districts of Clydeside, the northern coalpits, Lancashire, the Black Country, South Wales, London, and any place where 'navvy' work was to be had on the new canals and roads. Round these centres of industry the miserably low agricultural wage was brought to a higher level than in more remote rural regions where there was no competition of alternative employment. And yet the condition of the new industrial proletariat was very miserable, and was made more miserable by the vagaries of prices, wages, and employment due to the violent fluctuations caused by the Napoleonic war.

The evils of this first period of the new economic system were great, but they were a concentration and multiplication of old evils rather than a creation of new. There had been coal mines for centuries and the miners had always been shockingly housed, paid, and overworked, with little or no provision against accidents or inquiry when accidents took place. Indeed, before 1815, it was not the custom to hold inquests on deaths in the mines of Northumberland and Durham. In Scotland the miners, incredible as it may appear, were bound serfs until nearly the close of the Eighteenth Century. And even in England women and children in the past had been literally harnessed to the work under unspeakable conditions in the damp darkness of the mine. The Industrial Revolution immensely increased the mining population without at first materially improving their condition, and their ill-treatment was revealed to a more humane and inquisitive generation by the epoch-making Mines Report of 1842. So, too, pauper children, who had previously been handed over individually to the domestic affections of Mrs Brownrigg and Peter

Grimes, might in the new age be grouped together in a cotton mill run by a hard-bitten North country working man who had borrowed a couple of hundred pounds to start the business, and had no compunctions about making the lasses work. The 'free labour' of children who had parents to support was also passing from the home to the mill or factory, a change that must in many cases – though not in all – have been for the worse, before the era of Factory Inspection began in 1833. The relative misery of the poor at this period as compared to that of their forebears is hard to estimate, for want of facts about earlier times. The absolute misery of many of them is a fact incontestable.

The immigration into the new industrial districts represented the overflow of population created by the continual rise in the number of inhabitants of Great Britain from 1760 onwards. They came to be the man-power for the new industrial world, 'bowing their heads for bread', but glad to escape from rural England, Scotland, Wales, and Ireland, where only starvation awaited them. Irish immigration had been a feature of London life and of English and Scottish harvesting since Stuart times at least, but in the Hanoverian epoch it became much more pronounced. Jews from Central and Eastern Europe also began to come over in great numbers, so that by the end of the Eighteenth Century there were 20,000 in London, mostly very poor. But for the attractions of America in the Nineteenth Century to these two races, the admixture of Irish and Jews in the English community would be much greater than it is. The Irish brought with them a low standard of life and wages, and helped to make the worst slums. The cellars they inhabited in London were as weather-proof as the hovels they had left in Connemara, and bread and cheese was at least better than potatoes. Partly because they tended to lower the English workman's pitiful wage, there were frequent riots against them in London and among the farm-hands. Indeed, the animosity against the Irish labourer was one of the causes of the feeling against Roman Catholics that distinguished the populace of Great Britain in the days of the Gordon riots of 1780 and for long afterwards.

A large immigration of Englishmen from the rural districts must in any case have taken place, owing to the rise in population coinciding with new facilities for employment in industrial centres. But changes at the same time occurred in the economy of the rural village itself, which, in a variety of ways, affected the pace of the exodus to the towns. The change was twofold: the removal of industries from the villages to urban areas owing to the revolution in organization; and the enclosure of commons and open fields to grow more corn. The two movements combined to revolutionize English rural life, but they had no direct causal connexion one with the other.

The Industrial Revolution, by introducing machinery and so favouring concentration in factories and urban districts, gradually made an end of two kinds of village industry. It destroyed first the spinning and other by-employments of the wives and children of agricultural families; and secondly the full-time employment of villagers in such various trades as clock-making, basket-weaving, carriage and waggon building, tanning, milling and brewing, saddlery, cobbling, tailoring, and the great national industry of cloth-weaving. Some of these arts and industries supplied the village itself, others supplied the national and the world market. In the course of a hundred and seventy years, starting from the accession of George III, British industries have been almost entirely removed to the towns.

The migration of industry and craftsmanship left the village once more almost purely agricultural, as in the time of Domesday. The rural outlook was narrowed, the villager's intelligence and independence lowered, except in so far as improved school education has applied a one-sided remedy of recent years. But there was no efficient school in the English village a hundred years ago. Apprenticeship and the craft were the old educational forces, and they were disappearing. With the flight of the industry by which they lived, many independent families had to obliterate themselves in the featureless streets of the modern city, forced, like Wordsworth's 'poor Susan', to desert the cottage beside the stream,

> The one only dwelling on earth that she loves.

Those who remained behind as hands employed by the farmer in his fields, no longer had any by-employment in their own homes to enable them to hold out for better wages, or to eke out what wages they got. The monotony of village life in the Nineteenth Century was due mainly to the migration of the industries to the urban districts, which eventually was more complete in England than in any other country of Europe.

When George III died, the migration of industry from the village was only half accomplished, but the enclosure of the land was more nearly finished. The period of private Acts of Parliament for the enclosing of open fields and of common wastes corresponds roughly to the years of George III's reign, though it overlaps at both ends.

The survival in the best corn-growing area of the Midlands and East Anglia of the early medieval system of open-field cultivation, was an anomaly too gross to be any longer tolerated. The beneficial effects of enclosure in increasing production and ultimately population, had been demonstrated in many districts in Tudor and Stuart times. And when, in the days of the elder Pitt, the population of the island began to grow by leaps and bounds, the enlargement of the corn supply became the first of national necessities. It was not till after the Napoleonic wars that Russia or any other land beyond the sea was able to supply any appreciable quantity of grain to Britain. In those days, the island must feed itself or starve.

It was, therefore, in the reign of George III that the Midlands and East Anglia and much of the North English and Scottish landscape took on their present appearance of a chess-board pattern, made up of innumerable fields 'enclosed' by hedges or stone walls. The extreme south-east corner of the island, and many western counties, had displayed those familiar features for centuries past.

The wholesale enclosures of the reign of George III, like the partial enclosures of Tudor and Stuart times, opened the way for better agriculture by farmers with a compact holding in place of scattered strips in the open village field. These opportunities were not neglected, for the Eighteenth Century was the age of 'improving landlords', who put their capital into the land, and who studied, practised, and preached scientific agriculture and stock-breeding. Sheep and cattle, as well as horses, were developed to the point of perfection in England during 'the century of improvement'. Artificial grasses, root crops, and proper methods of growing grain, all alike impossible in the open-field system, became the usual instead of the exceptional practice of English farmers. The prophet of the new agriculture was Arthur Young, and its typical man was 'Coke of Norfolk', that sturdy Whig and enemy of George III, who reigned at Holkham from the American Revolution to the premiership of Peel, increased his rent-roll from £2200 to £20,000, made the fortunes and won the affections of all classes in his neighbourhood, turning a sandy rabbit-warren into a model estate which agriculturists came from all over Britain and Europe to visit.

Scotland, when George III began to reign, was hedgeless and treeless. It was not, like Central England, a land of large villages, but, like Northern England, a land of hamlets and scattered farms, set in the surrounding wilderness. The power of the Scottish landlords was very great, and the tenants often held their farms on precarious leases of one year. But the spirit of scientific improvement became even more prominent in Scotland than in England. The lairds used their power to have the land enclosed and tilled on modern methods, while the new practice of giving long leases encouraged the enterprise and independence of the farmer. The solid farm buildings, field-walls, and plantations of Scotland date from the beginning of George III's reign onwards.

Rural Wales changed less than Scotland and England in this period, because in the Celtic mountain-land enclosure had been co-eval with agriculture. But Wales was acquiring a 'Black Country' of its own, where on its southern coast the coal measures ran down to the sea.

The enclosure movement was a necessary step to feed the increasing population. And it increased not only the wealth of the landlords who put money into their estates, but that of the large tenant farmers who were their principal agents in the movement. The spleen of Cobbett was moved by the number of farmers who at the end of George III's reign lived in a smart new brick house – often entitled 'Waterloo farm' – who drove in a gig to market, had wine on their tables and a piano in the parlour for their daughters; yet these things were a sign of increasing wealth, comfort, and education. Nor had the old-fashioned small 'husbandman' by any means disappeared, although he had been long declining. The census of 1831 showed that the agriculturists who neither employed labour nor were themselves employed, were still as one to six in comparison with employing farmers and their hands. And as late as 1851 two-thirds of the farms in Great Britain were still under one hundred acres in size.

Enclosure had been a necessity, but the enclosures had not brought equal benefits to all. The share of the poor had been inadequate. The loss of their village industries has been already referred to, and accounts for half their distress or more. But the method of the enclosures had not taken enough consideration of the small man, and too little had been done to fix the lesser peasantry on the soil as part of the new scheme of things. When similar changes took place in contemporary Denmark, a land ruled by a monarch dependent on his general popularity, the interest of all classes down to the poorest was carefully considered, with excellent consequences in the agricultural Denmark of to-day. But the England of George III was completely aristocratic in the sympathies and constitution of its governing class, whether Whigs, Tories, or 'King's Friends' bore rule. The Houses of Parliament which passed the Enclosure Acts were closed by law to anyone who was not a considerable owner of land. The Justices of the Peace were autocrats of the countryside and represented one class alone. The proprietorship of most of the land of England was in the hands of a comparatively small group of 'great landed families'. Under these social and political conditions it was inevitable that the enclosures should be carried through according to the ideas of the big landlord class alone. Those ideas rightly envisaged the national necessity of more food production, but not the national necessity of maintaining and increasing small properties or small holdings.

In the redivision of the open fields and common wastes among individual proprietors and farmers, there was no intention to defraud the small man, but no desire to give him more than his apparent legal claim. Often he could not prove a legal claim to the rights he exercised on the common. Oftener his legal rights to keep cows or geese there, or his personal right in one or two strips in the village field, were compensated with a sum of money which was not enough to enable him to set up as a capitalist farmer or pay for the hedging of the plot allotted to him; the compensation might, however, pay for a month's heavy drinking in the ale-house. And so he became a landless labourer. Arthur Young himself was horrified at some of the results of the movement of which he had been the chief apostle. In 1801 he wrote 'By nineteen out of twenty Enclosure Bills the poor are injured and most grossly.'

The condition of the agricultural labourer, deprived of the industries previously conducted by his wife and children, was, indeed, most unhappy. The enforcement of a living wage was not opposed to old English theory and practice; and it was the labourer's due in common justice, before Pitt's Acts made Trade Union action illegal. But the landlord class, represented by the Justices of the Peace, decided not to compel the farmers to pay a living wage. They adopted instead a policy elaborated by the Berkshire Magistrates at Speenhamland in 1795, namely, to give rates in aid of insufficient wages. To keep the poor alive, it was decided to tax the rate-payers, instead of forcing farmers and employers of labour to shoulder their proper burden. It was a fatal policy, for it encouraged farmers to keep down wages. The system, which lasted till the New Poor Law of 1834, made the rural labourer a pauper, and discouraged his thrift and self-respect. It paid better to cringe to the authorities for the dole, than to attempt any form of self-help. The 'Speenhamland system' spread over the Southern and Midland Counties, but was not adopted in Scotland and North England, where the agricultural labourers suffered no such moral and social degradation, though there too times were often very hard.

Wealth was increasing so fast in town and country that the contrasts between the life of the rich and the life of the poor were more dramatic and more widely observable than of old. In the industrial world, members of the new middle class ceased to live over the workshop, and built themselves separate villas and mansions in imitation of the life of the gentry. They no longer formed one household with their apprentices and journeymen. The landed gentry, for their part, were enlarging the manor-house for the heir and the parsonage for the younger son, and too often replacing a tumble of gabled roofs that had grown up piecemeal in the last three hundred years, by a gorgeous 'gentleman's seat' in the neo-Palladian style. Game-preserving in the midst of a hungry population, with man-traps and spring guns lurking in the brambles to guard the pheasant at the expense of man's life or limb, led to a poaching war with armed skirmishes, and several thousand convictions a year. It was these contrasts that made the Radicalism of the new era, a spirit unknown in early Hanoverian England, even though the poor may have been materially as ill off in the one period as in the other.

Coal and iron in the Northern and Midland Shires were creating industrial cities not so immeasurably smaller than London, as Norwich and Bristol had been in the Stuart epoch. Yet London though it distanced its rivals less, was still growing with a rapidity that astounded and alarmed the world. Its prosperity continued to be based, as before the Industrial Revolution, on its unique place in commerce and distribution, and on highly skilled finishing trades still conducted on the domestic system. It still, therefore, attracted two classes of immigrants – the roughest kind of labour for porterage at the docks and in distribution, and the most skilled and intelligent workmen for the finishing trades. It had also a much larger proportion of clerks, organizers, civil servants, and men of education than any other city in the world.

All round London, bricks and mortar were on the march across the green fields. When George III died, the city was linked up by an almost continuous line of houses with Hammersmith,

Deptford, Highgate, and Paddington. For London, like other English cities, had always grown outwards, not upwards. Paris and many foreign cities, where houses used to be forbidden outside the fortifications, being unable to expand sideways, grew towards heaven, with tenements for the poor and flats for the middle classes. But the Englishman traditionally lived in his own house, however low and small and however distant from his work. On the whole, the English system was the best, though not the cheapest.

Jerrybuilding was perhaps the gravest evil of the Industrial Revolution. It was much, no doubt, that the immensely increased population was housed at all. Nor is it clear that on the average men were, in the strictly material sense, worse 'housed' in the new urban areas than in the old country cottages whence they or their fathers had come. But cellar and one-room tenements for families were dreadfully common for the lower class of labour, whether in London, Glasgow, Manchester, or the mining districts. A large proportion of the wage-earners and all the large class of commercial 'clerks' were better housed. But even their dwellings were monotonous and sordid in appearance; town-planning and any effort to brighten or embellish the face of the street were alien to the ideas of the age. The enterprising employer wanted dwellings where the new hands he wished to employ could live. The builder looked to make money on the transaction. No one else gave the matter a thought. Thus was the new England built.

Laissez faire, or the objection to interference by government, became a theory, but it was first a fact. The whole framework of Eighteenth Century England was incompatible with efficient administration. A modern nation was being governed by Tudor machinery, or rather by what was still left of that machinery after the passage of two hundred years. In these circumstances, what little taste men had of State or Municipal control, did not encourage them to ask for more. Till the machinery of local and central government was modernized, as it only began to be after 1832, opinion based on experience said that the less government did the better. Among the few things it had actually done in recent times was the attempt to suppress Trade Unions by law, the supplementing of wages out of the rates, and the Corn Law of 1815. As to town-planning, factory-inspecting, sanitation, and public education, much had to happen before either State or Municipality could dream of undertaking such tasks. Whole new generations of men and ideas had first to be born.

The political spirit of the English Eighteenth Century – aristocratic power tempered by Parliamentary control and individual rights – had little in common either with continental despotism or with the bureaucratic democracy of our own time. When the Reformers, inspired by Bentham, Cobbett, and Brougham, took in hand the problem of the relation of this old governmental system to the new facts of the Industrial Revolution, their first belief was that the remedy lay in reduced taxation and less State interference. Such, it was expected by many, would be the result of Parliamentary Reform. The exact opposite proved to be the case. In the event, Liberalism meant not less government, but more. But the government had first to be made the instrument of the general will. The gradual creation of social services by public action and at the public expense was to be the chief contribution of the Nineteenth Century to social welfare. But this was not foreseen by anyone in 1816, when Brougham compelled the government to drop the Income Tax on the return of peace, as a sop to democratic opinion.

BOOK SIX

WATERLOO TO TO-DAY

Transition to Democracy. Development of the Commonwealth

THE Parliamentary aristocracy under the first three Georges had developed British maritime power to the point where Nelson left it; had lost one overseas empire and acquired another; had completed the reconciliation of Scotland and perpetuated the alienation of Ireland; and had guarded the arena for the early stages of the Industrial Revolution, but without any attempt to control its social effects, or any foresight of its political implications. In the course of their long hegemony the Whig and Tory aristocracies had perfected a new form of governmental machinery, hinging on the Cabinet and Prime Minister, which lent efficiency to the rule of Parliament. By the help of this system the English House of Commons had risen triumphant from a succession of wars with despotic monarchies, and under Pitt and Castlereagh had defeated Napoleon himself, given peace to Europe, and won a hundred years of security for Great Britain.

The task awaiting their successors, under the later monarchs of the House of Hanover, was to adapt this system of Parliamentary Cabinet government to the new social facts created by the Industrial Revolution. This was found to involve the admission first of the middle and then of the working class as partners in the control of the political machine. A failure to make these adjustments would have led to a breakdown of the Parliamentary system and a war of classes.

But the good genius of English politics has often retrieved apparently hopeless situations. The last British Revolution is still that of 1688. By a gradual transition towards democracy, seldom hastening and never turning back, political rights were extended to all without a catastrophe. This great manoeuvre was safely accomplished because all classes and all parties showed, upon the whole, sound political sense and good humour, because the Victorian age was a period of peace and external security for Britain, and because its middle years were years of unexampled prosperity. Finally, the extension of the political franchise to all 1870
compelled the nation to elaborate a system of national education *et seq.*

out of the fragmentary efforts of private and denominational enterprise.

In the main the transition was effected through the revival and strengthening of the old two-party system. The peculiarly English tradition of the two perennial parties had been to some extent replaced by a group system of politics during the unchallenged Tory predominance with which the Nineteenth Century opened. But at the time of the Reform Bill of 1830–2, the Whigs furbished up their old traditions with new war-cries and programmes, and both parties thenceforth moved forward, forming as they went a kaleidoscopic succession of new social alliances in the rapidly changing world.

The underlying principle connecting the Liberals and Conservatives of Victoria's reign in an actually traceable succession with the Whigs and Tories of Charles II, was the continuous antagonism of Church and Dissent. That lasting dualism of English religious life was bound to reflect itself in a political dualism, so long as certain monopolies of the Church were maintained. For two hundred years it gave a reality to the otherwise artificial permanence of the traditions of the two parties from one changing period to another. The working-class movement at the beginning of the Nineteenth Century was in part connected with Dissent and was at that time almost altogether outside the influence of the established Church. The denominational aspect of politics therefore served to connect the Radicalism of the working classes to some extent with the Whig-Liberal party; through that party they sought political enfranchisement, while seeking economic and social amelioration by their own methods of Trade Unionism, Cooperative Societies, and incipient Socialism. The fact that the majority of Englishmen in the middle of the Nineteenth Century were religious but not of the same religion, was a steadying influence in the strife of parties and classes, although it was in itself an additional cause of controversy.

But the gradual adaptation of Parliamentary government, and with it of local government, to the democratic character of the new age, was only a small part of the adaptations necessary if the new society was to be saved. To render life increasingly tolerable to forty millions in an island where seven millions had found it hard to live before, new organizations of the most various kinds had to be created. The Eighteenth Century had been prolific of men and great in individual energies, but its corporate and institutional life had been lethargic. The Nineteenth Century, on the other hand, not only put fresh democratic vigour into Parliament, municipalities, Church, Universities, Schools, and Civil Service, but created a wealth of new organisms, public and private, dealing with every department of life. It was the age of Trade Unions, Cooperative and Benefit Societies, Leagues, Boards, Commissions, Committees for every conceivable purpose of philanthropy and culture. Not even the dumb animals were left without organized protection. The Nineteenth Century rivalled the Middle Ages in its power to create fresh forms of corporate and institutional life, while yielding little to the Eighteenth Century in the spirit of self-help and personal initiative. The list of great men whom the Nineteenth Century produced is often repeated; the list of new organizations that it created would be yet longer and no less significant.

The new forms of government and of human activity which were evolved are indeed too complex for brief description in this book, but many of them are familiar to us as matters of our own everyday life. A characteristic of the new national machinery, fully apparent towards the end of Queen Victoria's reign, was the close interrelation that had grown up on the one hand between private philanthropic effort and State control, and on the other between local and central government. As Parliament and local government began to respond to the needs of the community as a whole, and as the State became more and more intelligently interested in the work of private effort in education, medicine, sanitation, and a hundred other sides of life – an elaborate system of State aid, enforcement, and control came into being, through Treasury Grants in Aid to local bodies, State inspection of conditions of labour and of life, industrial insurance, and the modern educational system. Voluntary and private effort aided by the State did many things that in other countries of Europe were done solely by the State or were not done at all.

The complicated and constantly shifting relationship between central and local government, between private enterprise and State undertaking, was rendered possible by the evolution of the permanent, non-political Civil Service of Great Britain with its accumulated stores of knowledge, experience, and sound tradition. In the third quarter of the century, the Civil Service was removed from the field of political jobbery by the adoption of open competitive examination as the method of entrance, a device that seemed as strange as it has proved successful.

British methods of coping with the problems of the new era showed great practical inventiveness, and were all in the line of a strong native tradition. Relatively little was copied from continental movements. The Parliamentary system was our own; local government was reformed and elaborated on British lines; factory inspection, Trade Unionism, the Cooperative movement, were of British origin; the Civil Service was native in its traditions, and in the peculiar method of its selection by examination.

The advance in humanity, democracy, and education, and the changes in industrial method bringing large crowds of wage-earners of both sexes together in offices and factories, led to a new conception of the place of women in society. The education of women, from being almost totally neglected, became in a couple of generations comparable to that of man. The position of women in the family was altered in law, and was yet more altered in practice and opinion. Finally the movement for their political enfranchisement ceased to seem absurd.

All these great changes would never have been carried through without disaster but for the peace, prosperity, and security that marked the Nineteenth Century in Britain. Except in the episode of the Crimean War, the general policy of Britain was to abstain from taking part in the strife of continental nations, when it renewed itself forty years after Waterloo. Since the Balance of Power was for the time safely adjusted, there was no call for us to fight in order to prevent the conquest of Europe by a single nation and its vassals.

Relations with the United States were increasingly important. After the Treaty of Ghent in 1814 they happily continued peaceful in spite of some ugly crises. This happy result was due in no small degree to the work of Castlereagh and Monroe in agreeing
1817 to a permanent disarmament along both sides of the Canadian frontier; it followed that while that frontier was being prolonged farther and farther to the west, the grave disputes that necessarily accompanied the process were never submitted to the decision of war. Another great step forward was taken when Gladstone consented to submit the *Alabama* claims to the arbitration of a third party. So too, in the division of Asiatic and African territories, the disputes with France and Germany, though sometimes acute in the later years of the century, were settled by peaceful arbitration or agreement, largely through the action of Lord Salisbury, who held that Britain's 'greatest interest' was peace.

Peace, then, and the amazing prosperity which the state of the world in Queen Victoria's reign brought to the door of Britain's commerce and industry, formed conditions highly favourable to the solution of the grave political and social problems of the new order within the island. The chief external interests of Britain were not war or preparation for war, but her ever increasing foreign trade, more fabulous every decade, and the development of her new colonial empire bequeathed by the victors of Trafalgar and Waterloo. The over-population and unemployment in Britain after the Napoleonic wars, unrelieved in those days by any form of industrial insurance, drove English and Scots to the Colonies by hundreds of thousands. In the first half of the Nineteenth Century, many of these emigrants were agricultural or semi-agricultural labourers, glad to get hold of land and work it for themselves. Only towards the end of the period did the decay of rural life in England and the attraction of the modern town life create a danger that the English race should become a race of city-dwellers, unwilling to settle or to remain on the land.

By the beginning of the Twentieth Century, the Colonies had become Dominions, new nations in effect. After enjoying complete self-government as regards their internal affairs for fifty years or more, they began to look out upon the world, each with its own national point of view – Canadian, Australian, South African. In these circumstances, the hopes entertained by British statesmen during the Imperialist movement at the close of the Nineteenth Century that it would be possible to unite the Empire more closely in some kind of Federal Constitution, were not destined to mature. A looser bond of common interest and affection held the Empire together when it was plunged into its next great crisis by the outbreak of the War with Germany in August 1914; and when September 1939 brought war again, each Dominion of the British Commonwealth of Nations declared war in her own right and might.

CHAPTER I

Repression and Reform, 1815–35. Peel and Huskisson. Castlereagh and Canning. The Wellington Ministry. The Whigs and the Reform Bill. The Municipal Corporations Act and Slavery Abolition

Kings: George III, died 1820; George IV, 1820–30; William IV, 1830–7

WITH the return of peace after Waterloo, industrial and agricultural depression brought misery and unemployment, and all expression of grievance or demand for reform by the working class was severely repressed. The 'anti-Jacobin' mentality, which had been popular with the majority even of the working class in the time of the French Revolution, was now out of date, actively disliked even by the middle classes, who desired a new order of things. But the Tory Government from 1815 to 1822 persisted in a course of mere negation, in spite of its growing unpopularity.

The most famous incident of this unhappy period was 'Peterloo', or the Manchester Massacre of 1819, when a mass meeting of cotton operatives to demand manhood suffrage was dispersed by a charge of cavalry in a cruel and unnecessary manner. Less tragic but more unsavoury were the divorce proceedings against Queen Caroline in the following year, staged in the House of Lords by King George IV's too subservient ministers. The Queen's trial involved the crown in dire disgrace in the eyes not only of the mob but of all 'respectable' persons. The public opinion of the middle classes, after being solidly Tory since the French Revolution, now began to turn against the Government; the workers in the new factories were being kept down by force; the agricultural labourers were less politically minded, but they were burning ricks in despair; for many of them were starving, and pauperism was very general under the 'Speenhamland' system of rates in aid of wages which effectually kept wages down. It was a black outlook for the new century.

But after the death of Castlereagh in 1822 a more liberal spirit became powerful inside the Tory Cabinet itself. The appointment of Peel to the Home Office soon brought an end to the system of espionage and repression exercised by Government against the Radical working men, and established fairer dealing with classes and parties. Peel also put into legislative effect the principles of the crusade carried on for many years past by Bentham, Romilly, and Sir James Mackintosh for reform of the criminal law; he abolished the death penalty for a hundred different crimes. And finally in 1829 he established for the first time in our history an efficient civilian Police, whom the populace endearingly called by either of Robert Peel's two names. Their social value in dealing with common crime was equalled by their political value in dealing with Radical mobs: for at last the place of the soldiers had been taken by a civic force armed only with batons, who were none the less capable of looking a crowd in the face, and who, unlike the soldiers, could be used to quell the first signs of disturbance. There would be no more Lord George Gordon riots, and no more Peterloos, in towns where 'the force' exercised its functions. The Reform Bill riots that set Bristol on fire two years later, could have been easily stopped by a hundred of the 'new Police' acting in good time. Set up first in London alone, they were in the course of a generation adopted all over the country, in answer to a universal demand. From the first they were dressed in civilian blue, and in their early years they wore not helmets but stout top-hats.

In the same period, the finances of the country were taken in hand by Huskisson. The tariff, whether aiming at revenue or protection, was a jungle of unscientific growths and unrelated experiments, hampering trade at every turn. Huskisson did not desire to introduce complete Free Trade, and his operations were limited by the popular objection to a revival of the Income Tax as a source of revenue. Nevertheless he greatly reduced the tariff list, and put order and purpose into what was left. One article only was sacred: 'Corn was King' in English politics, so long as a section of the country gentry held the monopoly of power through the rotten boroughs.

Huskisson also made the first great inroad on the old system 1823
of Navigation Acts, which had for a century and a half given to British shipping monopolistic privileges in British ports. The time had come when this artificial support, which had been praised in its day by Adam Smith, could be dispensed with by the full-grown strength of the British mercantile marine. The process of abolishing the Navigation Acts was completed during the later period when Free Trade was the accepted national policy, and when the remainder of the protective tariffs were abolished. The removal of the monopoly right conferred by the Navigation Acts forced British ship-owners and ship-builders to bestir themselves and improve their methods. Owing to the industrial supremacy of Victorian Britain, the coming of the age of steam and iron at sea was all to her advantage, especially as she now had difficulty in obtaining timber. And the outward cargo of coal, which was saleable in most ports all over the globe, was a great stimulus to British shipping. Throughout the remainder of the century our mercantile marine continued to grow without a serious rival.

The accession of Canning to the Foreign Office on Castlereagh's death in 1822, gave a stimulus to the forces of change in domestic affairs. Canning did not reverse Castlereagh's policy. But, in contrast to his reserved and aristocratic predecessor, he loved to appeal not only to the House of Commons but to the people at large. Foreign affairs ceased to be a mystery of Elder Statesmen, as under Grenville and Castlereagh. Canning's new methods of publicity were destined to grow under the hands of Palmerston, Gladstone, and Disraeli, until general elections were lost and won on questions of foreign policy.

The advent of Canning meant therefore an important change of method, consonant with the more democratic and inquisitive spirit of the age. But the direction, in which British foreign policy was moving, was not altered, though the pace of the movement was accelerated, and its liberal and British standpoint were both more clearly emphasized.

Castlereagh, eminently a 'good European', had favoured periodical Congresses of the Powers to arrange international disputes. But as the Powers did not then represent the peoples, and as the States did not represent the races, there was no chance that these Congresses could develop into anything approaching a 'League of Nations'. On the contrary, under the influence of Austria's Metternich and of the Tsar Alexander, now in the final reactionary phase of his life, the Congresses were perverted into clearing-houses for the obscurantist policy of the governments of the Holy Alliance, leagued to suppress the first stirrings of liberty and of nationalism. Castlereagh, who had no wish to involve England in the internal police questions of foreign countries, was tending reluctantly to a less close participation in the congressional politics of the continent, when the strain of overwork caused him to commit suicide. But his strongly expressed dislike of the movements for Greek and Italian independence, may lead us to suppose that he would never have taken the actively liberal line pursued by his successor.

Canning, in one sense the continuator of Castlereagh's work, introduced an element of more active opposition to the reactionary parties on the continent. The same British feeling that had inspired the brilliant Anti-Jacobinism of his youth, made him, as a middle-aged Foreign Minister, the dread of the despots and the hope of the Liberals of the continent. He sympathized with the indignation felt by his countrymen, that the powers which British arms and subsidies had helped to restore to the 'legitimate' monarchs of Europe, were used everywhere from Poland to Portugal, to trample out political, racial, and cultural
1823 liberty. When the France of the Royalists and Clericals was commissioned by the Holy Alliance to put down the constitutional movement in Spain by force of arms, all England was furious, without distinction of class or party. But Canning, whilst protesting against the French invasion of Spain, wisely refrained from

threats which would have involved this country either in a new Peninsular War or in an ignominious diplomatic retreat.

But the other sphere of the Spanish question, the revolt of the Central and South American Colonies against the old monarchy, was more fully in Canning's control, because no crusaders of France or the Holy Alliance could cross the Atlantic to suppress the rebels under Bolivar, without the acquiescence of the British fleet. Moreover, the independence of South America was a direct material interest of Great Britain. The restrictions set by Spain on English commerce with her American Colonies had been a burning question for nearly three hundred years. There was now a golden opportunity for its happy solution, if the Colonies themselves should become independent States, friendly to Britain and anxious to trade with her merchants. The heart-burnings that had caused the wars of Drake, of the buccaneers, and of 'Jenkins' ear' in the time of Walpole, would at last and for ever be laid at rest.

In these circumstances the anxiety of British merchants and industrialists to open new markets for the congested produce of the new English factories, was blended with a sincere enthusiasm for the cause of liberty all the world over; with joy in Cochrane's gallant exploits off the coast of Chile and Peru as Admiral for the rebel governments; and with the satisfaction felt by all true Englishmen at paying out the French and their perjured and bigoted protégé Ferdinand VII of Spain for their recent military triumphs in the Peninsula. It was to these popular sentiments that Canning successfully appealed when he pronounced in the House of Commons that he had called a New World into existence to redress the balance of the Old. Eldon and Wellington, who preferred old worlds to new at any time, were disgusted beyond measure at their colleague turned demagogue, and the rift in the Tory party became deep and wide.

In proclaiming and defending the independence of South America, the statesmen and people of England were at one with those of the United States. President Monroe had seized the occasion to lay down his 'doctrine', so famous and important 1823
in years to come, denying to European States the right to acquire new territories or political influence in the American continent beyond what they already held. This was meant as a warning to the powers of the Holy Alliance at the moment, but it was meant also as a warning to Great Britain with regard to the future. Canning did not like it. Neither he nor his pupil, Palmerston, after him, was so friendly to the United States in feeling as

Castlereagh had shown himself over the Canadian boundary disarmament. But in Canning's day the questions in dispute with the United States were dormant, and on the question of the hour the two branches of the English-speaking race were at one. It was not, however, President Monroe's 'doctrine', but the British fleet, that prevented France or the Holy Alliance from suppressing the independence of the Spanish Colonies.

Besides the vast regions of South and Central America, a smaller spot upon the political map of the world still bears the mark of Canning's handiwork. The independence of Greece was largely due to him. In the Levant, Canning could not override the will of all the Powers of Europe, as he could on the open Atlantic. But on the question of the Greek revolt against the Turk, the governments of the Holy Alliance were at variance with one another. Austria indeed consistently supported the Turk as representing the 'anti-revolutionary' side. Russia, for her own ends, and from traditional sympathy, was the champion of the Eastern Christians. France, partly from religious and cultural inclination, inclined the same way. Much depended therefore on England's attitude. Wellington, following the example of Castlereagh, was pro-Turk. But the British public, moved by Byron's self-sacrifice and death, and at that time profoundly 'classical' in its culture, idealized the Greek 'Klephts' as heroes of Thermopylae. Canning was happily inspired to put up a barrier to Russian aggression in the Levant by erecting an independent Greek nation, rather than by supporting the continued abominations of Turkish misrule. His policy of trusting to nationalism to keep Russian ambition in check, succeeded in the case of Greece, but was abandoned by later British statesmen when Palmerston, Russell, and Gladstone, at the time of the Crimean War, and twenty years later, Disraeli, sacrificed the interests of the Balkan Christians to British fears of Russia.

The success of Canning's policy was secured, as regards Greece,
1827 when, a few weeks after his death, the British, French, and Russian fleets under Admiral Codrington blew the Turkish fleet out of the water in Navarino Bay. In that conflagration the Holy Alliance was dissolved as a force in European politics. Wellington, when he came to the Premiership, regretted Navarino as an 'untoward event', but he was unable seriously to limit the extent of its consequences.

Canning, as Foreign Secretary in Lord Liverpool's Cabinet, had so stirred the romantic liberalism of the new England and the new Europe, that in the absence of effective Whig leadership

he had become the principal hero in the eyes of the forward-looking party in Britain. When, therefore, on Liverpool's illness and retirement, the Tory Cabinet split, and Canning formed a government which the Old Guard under Wellington, Peel, and 1827
Eldon refused to join, the new Premier obtained the cooperation of more than half the Whigs in Parliament and the good wishes of liberal-minded men in the country. His own death a few months later brought his Ministry to an end before it had accomplished anything remarkable, but the fact that it had been formed was an important step in the break-up and reshuffling of parties. Most of the 'Canningite' Tories who served in it, like Palmerston and Melbourne, soon afterward joined the revivified and enlarged Whig Party that passed the Reform Bill.

It is remarkable, however, that Canning himself to the last opposed Parliamentary Reform. Probably, therefore, his removal from the scene actually precipitated the speed of political change which he had done so much to set moving. He was the one man in England who might have preserved the rotten boroughs for many years. But after his death everything played into the hands of the Reformers. The hope that the unreformed Parliament and the Tory party would lead the country forward in the new age, which had burned brightly under Canning and Huskisson, was effectively quenched by the High Tory Ministry under 1828–30
Wellington.

But before the final reconstitution of parties on the Reform Bill issue, important concessions to the new principle of the civic equality of religions were wrung by events from the unwilling Cabinet of Wellington and Peel. The tide of change was indeed coming in with an elemental rapidity, overthrowing in turn every position taken up by embarrassed statesmen from day to day. Whereas Canning in 1827 had thought it necessary to pledge his Cabinet to prevent the repeal of the Test Act and to leave Catholic Emancipation alone, in spite of his own views on Emancipation, fifteen months after Wellington took office on the basis of 'no-surrender', both these relieving Bills had become law of the land under the aegis of an ultra-Tory Ministry.

The Test Act, which prevented Catholic and Protestant Nonconformists from holding State or Municipal office, had been regarded by the Church as the very ark of the Covenant ever since the reign of Charles II, and had been the condition of her accepting the Revolution settlement and the Hanoverian succession. Its repeal, on the motion of Lord John Russell, was of symbolic 1828
importance, but was not of great immediate effect. For until the

Parliamentary and Municipal elections had been democratized, Dissenters had little chance of holding office. It was only in conjunction with the Municipal Corporations Act of 1835 and the Second Reform Bill of 1867, that the Repeal of the Test Act effected the full political emancipation of Nonconformists.

In 1829 a still more remarkable surrender was made. For half a dozen years past the Irish people had been organized in the Catholic Association, under the priests as officers and under Daniel O'Connell as Commander-in-Chief. Though everyone in authority was hostile to the movement, the unanimity of the population was terrible. No great body of men moves so completely to order, as a nation consisting of a single class of ill-educated peasants, in whom the instincts of herd-morality have been fortified by centuries of oppression. O'Connell demanded Catholic Emancipation, that is to say, that Roman Catholics should not be debarred from sitting in either House of Parliament. The victor of Waterloo shrank from the contest with the Catholic Association of Ireland. The British Army had been reduced to its lowest point in pursuit of retrenchment and lower taxes, and scarcely sufficed to protect property in Britain from starving operatives and rick-burning peasants. Moreover, Wellington always abhorred the idea of civil bloodshed, though he so frequently refused until the very last moment to make concessions which were the only alternative. The surrender of Peel and Wellington to O'Connell infuriated the High Tories, who had put their trust in them. Indeed Wellington had purged his administration of the Canningites, and of nearly every man who believed in Catholic Emancipation, only a year before he emancipated the Catholics. The fabric of the Tory party was split into three mutually enraged sections – Canningites, High Tories, and embarrassed supporters of government. The strategical and tactical errors of Wellington's political campaign had cleared the way for what he most dreaded – a real Parliamentary Reform Bill and a real Reform Ministry.

Charles, Lord Grey, the nominal chief of the Whig Party since the death of Fox, had for many years played a very inadequate part as leader of opposition – at least by our modern ideas of political leadership. The rural leisure of his home on the Northumbrian shore, with its library and his fifteen children, grew to have many more attractions for him than Westminster. But in his hot youth he had been the principal agent in leading Fox to pronounce for Parliamentary Reform in 1792, and so to break with

Portland and the Whig seceders who followed Burke into the Anti-Jacobin camp. Grey had never given up his belief that a redistribution of seats, based on the abolition of a large number of the rotten boroughs, would ultimately be necessary to save Parliamentary government in Britain. He had for many years ceased to preach the doctrine, regarding it as untimely, so long as only the working-class Radicals would move in the matter. But he still maintained that it would be necessary to wait only until the time when the question should be taken up 'seriously and affectionately' by the people themselves, meaning more particularly the 'solid and respectable' middle class. That time had at length come, and greatly to the surprise of friends and the consternation of foes, the old nobleman proved as good as his word, and for three years left his rural seclusion to give Britain the reformed Parliament of which he had dreamed in his youth.

In 1830 the movement for Parliamentary Reform seemed to be generated by a natural process out of the circumstances of the hour – the return of bad times, the violence of working-class despair in town and country, the gravity of middle-class fear of a social uprising beneath their feet, and the belief that it could no longer be averted by mere repression; to all these causes were added disillusionment with the Tory party resulting from the Duke's blunders, and the example of the July revolution in Paris that put an end to Charles X's reactionary government, without, as in 1789, causing social overturn. From squire to postillion, from cotton-lord to mill-hand, everyone was talking of the need for Reform, though with great varieties of meaning and emphasis. On the extent and character of the proposed new franchise there was wide divergence, but all were united in a detestation of the rotten boroughs. Their owners, hitherto regarded with obsequious deference, were now held up to general execration as 'borough-mongers' who had stolen the nation's birthright. There was also general agreement that the new industrial and the old rural districts ought to obtain a representation more in proportion to their wealth and the numbers of their inhabitants. The alliance of all classes against the rotten boroughs found expression in the Birmingham Political Union, ably led by Thomas Attwood. In the Birmingham of forty years before, the mob had sacked the Reformers' houses, but the citizens were now agreed that the Midland capital had a right to representation in Parliament.

Grey and his more advanced lieutenants of the younger generation, Lord John Russell and Lord Durham, saw that the moment had come to place the Whig Parliamentary party at the head of this movement. On the basis of a sweeping redistribution of seats and a level ten-pound household franchise in all boroughs, the aristocratic Whig leaders in Parliament placed themselves at the head of middle-class opinion in the country. Owing to the Industrial Revolution, the middle class counted for much more than in the Eighteenth Century; and owing to the growth of Wesleyanism, Dissent was reckoned at nearly half the religious world. Therefore the renewed leadership of the middle classes by the Whig aristocracy, on the basis of a reformed electoral system, was destined to remain the most stable element in the government of Great Britain for a generation to come. The man who represented the alliance was the plebeian Henry Brougham, the agitator and leader of the 'intelligent middle classes', who with his hard but mobile features was the very incarnation of the new age of 'machinery and the march of mind'. He was closely connected also with the Whig leaders and with the *Edinburgh Review*. No Whig Cabinet in 1830 could be formed without him. If his wisdom and reliability as a colleague in office had been on a level with his activity and genius as a free lance in opposition, he would have been the leading statesman of the new era; but he declined, instead, into its most magnificent oddity.

Wellington's Ministry tottered, and the High Tories seized the opportunity to take their revenge on him and Peel for passing Catholic Emancipation, by voting against them in the critical division. In November 1830 the Duke fell from power, and Lord Grey was called on by the new and popular 'sailor King', William IV, to form a Ministry based on the programme of 'peace, retrenchment, and reform.'

The Cabinet formed by Lord Grey was aristocratic in *personnel*, but the aristocrats in the Whig Ministry included some of the ablest and most advanced men in Parliament. The measure of Reform which Lord Durham and Lord John Russell framed under Grey's general direction, and which Lord Althorp piloted through the House of Commons, though criticized ever since for not going far enough, in its own day astounded friends and foes by the distance that it went. It was indeed, as the Tories complained, 'a new constitution', in the sense that it extended political power to new social classes and to new districts of the island.

A Bill abolishing all the rotten boroughs at a stroke had never been expected, and its announcement aroused a shout of surprise and enthusiasm from Land's End to John o' Groat's, while throwing the Tories, who had looked for a much milder proposal,

March 1831

into angry opposition. The most influential working-class leaders and organizers, like Place and Cobbett, actively supported 'The Bill, the whole Bill, and nothing but the Bill', because they knew that to pass working-class enfranchisement was impossible in the existing House and, indeed, in the existing state of public opinion. But they foresaw that it must follow some day, whatever the Whigs might say about 'finality', if once the time-honoured system of vested interests in nomination boroughs were overset. To get that done would require the union of all classes, for the House of Lords had by the law of the constitution the power to veto the Bill, and was determined at all risks to use it.

After fifteen months of political agitation unparalleled in the history of Great Britain, the Reform Bill was carried in the teeth of the resistance of the Peers. The first crisis was a general election which produced a sure majority of 136 for the Bill, in place of an unreliable and evanescent majority of one. The second crisis was the throwing out of the Bill by forty-one votes in the Lords, chiefly by the Peers of recent Tory creation and by the Bench of Bishops. That winter there was great economic distress in the industrial and agricultural districts, cholera was raging, and the popular anger at the Lords' action threatened society with chaos. The peace of the country depended, indeed, on the passage of the Bill. At length King William, a perturbed and honest sailor in such a gale as no State skipper had seen before, promised Grey to use his prerogative of creating Peers to carry the Bill. There was the useful precedent of Queen Anne's creation of Peers to carry the Peace of Utrecht for the Tory Ministry of that day. Then at the last moment William hesitated, and endeavoured to get the Tories to take office and pass the Bill in their own way. This occasioned the last crisis, the famous 'Days of May'. Lord Grey gave in his resignation, and for a week the country believed that Wellington was coming back 1832
to rule by the sword. The big towns prepared resistance. But Peel saw that the game was played out, and Grey was brought back triumphantly, on the condition of the surrender of Peers and King.

This final crisis, that secured the actual passage of the Reform Act, gave dramatic emphasis to the popular element in the 'new constitution'. The people, as a whole, had wrenched the modern Magna Carta from the governing class. The nation was thenceforth master in its own house. But the political extent of the 'nation' would yet need to be defined by a succession of franchise struggles, each less violent indeed than the great original. Ten-pound householders and tenant-farmers were not likely to constitute 'the nation' for ever. They had no such prescriptive right to govern the land as the borough-owners, whose vested interest had been swept away by the pacific revolt of a nation.

In Scotland the old representative system had been worse than in England, for not even the county elections had any reality north of the Tweed. The immediate consequence of the Reform Bill was the Burgh Act of 1833, which created the first popularly elected Municipalities that Scotland had possessed since the Fifteenth Century.

England waited till 1835 for her Municipal Corporations Act. The fall of the Parliamentary rotten boroughs involved the fall of the Municipal rotten boroughs, analogous sister bodies in the field of local government, which would never have been disturbed under the old regime. The Act of 1835 was more democratic than the Reform Bill, for it gave all ratepayers the right to vote for the new Municipalities. At last the ice-age of English institutional and corporate life had come to an end, and the life of the community began to be remodelled according to the actual needs of the new economic society. The spirit of Jeremy Bentham was abroad in the land, though the old man himself was on his death-bed. His test question – 'What is the use of it?' – was being applied to one venerable absurdity after another. The age of Royal Commissions and their Reports had begun with the Whig Reform Ministry. The Municipal Corporations Act was among its first-fruits.

The Act only applied to the larger towns. The rural districts were still left under the administrative control of the Justices of the Peace until the establishment of elected County Councils by Lord Salisbury's Ministry in 1888. This difference in types of local government corresponded to the fact that rural England was still mentally subordinate to the squires, while the new urban England was already in spirit a democracy.

Inadequate as it was in its geographical scope, the Municipal Corporations Act of 1835 established in the chief urban areas a powerful form of authority, subject to popular control, and able to levy a local rate. From this beginning there grew up a concentration of new functions; throughout the coming century powers were perpetually being added to the Municipal Corporations. Finally they dealt with almost all aspects of local government except public-house licensing and judicial power, which were regarded as unfit functions for an elective body. In 1835 very few foresaw that the new Municipalities would end in educating the children of the people, and in supplying the public with trams, light, water, and even houses, or that they would become traders and employers of labour on a large scale.

Starting from 1835 there also grew up the connexion between the governmental departments of Whitehall and the popularly elected local bodies, based on State supervision and Treasury grants of the taxpayers' money in aid of local rates. All this, though not foreseen, was rendered possible by the bold and uniform Whig legislation of 1835. In this way was begun the tardy process of catching up the uncontrolled social consequences of the Industrial Revolution. But where, in all this, was the place for 'retrenchment'? That panacea faded into thin air.

In 1833 Lord Althorp passed the first effective Factory Act, fixing legal limits for the working hours of children and young persons respectively. The great merit of the Bill, little recognized at the time, was the institution of government inspectors to enforce the law. It was the beginning of a whole new development in social welfare.

Another immediate consequence of the Reform Bill was the abolition of slavery in the British Empire by the Act of 1833. Wilberforce died the same year, his work marvellously completed. During the later years of his life the active leadership of the Anti-Slavery cause had been carried on by Sir Thomas Fowell Buxton, with Brougham as trumpeter. In Wilberforce's original campaign the defenders of the slave-trade had been important British shipping interests in Bristol and Liverpool. But after the slave-trade had been stopped, the defenders of slavery were found less in England herself than in the colonies. If slaves could no longer be imported, they could still be bred from the existing stock. The planters of the West Indies and other tropical colonies saw ruin in the proposal to emancipate their slaves on any terms. But they did not conduct their case wisely, or treat either their Negroes or the negro-phil missionaries well; their violence aroused the indignation of the British public, more particularly the religious world of Evangelicalism and Nonconformity, then very influential. The Slavery Abolition Act of 1833 gave the slave-owners twenty millions in compensation for their slaves, willingly paid by the mother country.

The other great successful action of the Whig Ministry was the settlement of the Belgian question. In 1830 the Paris revolution had been followed by the revolt of Belgium from the partnership with Holland to which the Treaties of 1815 had assigned her.

The revolt was partly liberal, partly clerical, and was promoted by French influences, clerical and liberal alike. The reactionary Powers of Eastern Europe regarded a breach made in the Treaties of 1815 by a popular revolt, as a thing to be suppressed after the fashion of the Holy Alliance. That was not the view of Great Britain, especially under the liberal Ministry of which Grey was Premier and Palmerston Foreign Secretary. But Britain, for her part, objected strongly to the establishment of French influence over Belgium either by annexation or by the reign of a French Prince at Brussels. The Chauvinist party in Paris was with difficulty kept in check by Louis Philippe, 'the Citizen King', and his Ministers, anxious on the whole for the friendship of the new liberal England in face of the hostile Powers of Russia, Austria, and Prussia. It was a situation of delicacy and danger, but was satisfactorily solved, after a number of crises, on the basis of the adoption of Prince Leopold of Saxe-Coburg Gotha as King of the Belgians; he was a personal friend of the British Ministers and the favourite uncle of the future Queen Victoria. In 1839 Palmerston crowned the work by a treaty which settled the vexed question of Dutch-Belgian boundaries, and guaranteed Belgian neutrality. The treaty was signed by Belgium, Great Britain, France, Russia, Austria, and Prussia. In this way the perennial British interest of securing a Power in the Netherlands from which we had nothing to fear, was again made safe for a long period of years.

CHAPTER II

The Repeal of the Corn Laws, 1846. Disraeli and Peel. The Whig-Palmerston Regime. The Civil Service. Queen Victoria. The Crimea and Italy. Prosperity and Social Assuagement. The Franchise Agitation and the Second Reform Bill, 1867

Queen Victoria, 1837

IN the reign of William IV, the Whigs, under Benthamite inspiration and Radical pressure, had introduced into the organs of government elements of modern efficiency and popular representation, through the Reform Bill and the Municipal Corporations Act. But they had no head for finance or for the social and commercial questions therewith connected. They had not even the sense to revive Pitt's income tax. And so, within half a dozen years of the passage of the Reform Bill, it was clear to all that the Whigs had shot their bolt, and had no further programme for the relief of the still acute economic and industrial distress of the country. It was well for the fortunes of Parliamentary government under the new regime that an alternative Ministry could be formed from the opposition at Westminster. Peel understood finance and commerce, and was himself middle class in origin and in sympathy. He re-constituted a 'Conservative' party out of the wreckage of the 'Tory' party destroyed by the Reform Bill. It was characteristic of England in the Nineteenth Century, as distinct from several foreign lands, that when the various sections of the upper class lost their special privileges they did not on that account retire to private life, but accommodated themselves to the new conditions. The very limits of the Reform effected in 1832, with which modern criticism is often impatient, had the advantage of keeping unbroken the tradition of upper-class connexion with political life, and avoiding the development of a class of 'professional politicians'.

The English middle class of that period saw a relief from its troubles in a policy of complete Free Trade. In that matter it asserted itself against the landlord class, whose political leadership it otherwise accepted with gratitude. It was the old custom of England for the townsfolk to be led by the gentry, provided the followers had a say as to the direction. The ten-pound householders enfranchised in 1832 usually chose country gentlemen to represent them in the boroughs, and put up with a good deal of exclusiveness and patronage on the part of those above them, but in the matter of Free Trade in Corn they made up their minds and on that issue they had the formidable masses of the unenfranchised behind them. The Parliamentary Conservative party was opposed to Corn Law abolition and the Whig party was divided on the question.

Peel, in the early days of his great Ministry, revived the Income Tax, and with its help reduced and abolished import duties on 1842–5
many articles with excellent results to the trade of the country. But he was in no position at once to abolish the duties on foreign corn. Corn remained the outstanding question. The Anti-Corn-Law League became almost as formidable in industrial England as O'Connell's Catholic League had been in rural Ireland. Peel, who had surrendered to the one in 1829, surrendered to the other in 1846, partly from a sense that government must be carried on by consent of the governed, partly because Cobden's speeches on the floor of the House had persuaded him on the economic issue,

and partly because the potato-blight in Ireland in 1845–6 left him no other choice than either to suspend the Corn Laws or to allow the Irish to die by tens of thousands.

The Repeal of the Corn Laws in 1846 was for a number of reasons the most important political event between the First and Second Reform Bills. In the first place, it broke up the Conservative party and so put the Whigs into power, with short intervals, for twenty years, with the occasional addition to their counsels and their voting strength of Peelite statesmen like Aberdeen, Cardwell, and Graham, and the much needed financial ability of Gladstone.

The revolt of the Conservative private members against Peel had not been generally expected. It was the force and quality of Disraeli's philippics against the traitor in command that compelled the back benches to rise and mutiny, as gunpowder must needs blaze up if fire is applied. It does not appear that Disraeli had deep convictions on the Corn Laws as an economic policy, and he was soon afterwards speaking unconcernedly of Protection as 'dead and damned'. But he had, like Bolingbroke before him, attached himself in a professional capacity to the gentlemen of the 'country party' and felt bound to show them sport. The 'great historic Houses' of England appealed strongly to his imagination as a foreign observer of our institutions, though he was obliged to except the Whig Houses which belonged to the other side. Peel had maltreated and betrayed 'the gentlemen of England' in abandoning the Corn Laws, and as they found it difficult adequately to express their own feelings on the matter, Disraeli became their champion against the man who stood also in his own way. His conduct in overthrowing Peel kept the Conservative party out of power for twenty years, but raised him from the back benches to the direct succession of the leadership after Stanley. It thereby enabled him, twenty-one years later, to 'educate his party' to the performance of a *volte-face*, over the enfranchisement of the working classes in 1867, just as complete as that on account of which he had put a sudden end to the career of Peel, at the height of the great Premier's popularity with the mass of his countrymen.

But even the 'agricultural interest' of landlords and large farmers soon found that they had not been ruined by Repeal. Free importation prevented corn prices from soaring even when the value of money fell with the gold discoveries in California and Australia, but corn prices remained fairly steady for another generation, and with better times there was a greatly increased consumption of bread. The country-houses and farmsteads of England were never more wealthy, populous, and happy than during the mid-Victorian age – the age of Trollope's novels and John Leech's pictures. Indeed, the removal of all serious cause of bitterness between town and country left the 'great Houses' in a most enviable social position for another thirty years. Then, indeed, the development of trans-continental railways and great steamships enabled America to pour forth such quantities of food that, during Disraeli's Ministry in the late seventies, British corn-growing was at last very seriously affected. The world-wide organization of British commerce drew food to the island from every quarter, and the destruction of British agriculture and rural life began.

The victory of the Anti-Corn-Law League in 1846 had been a victory of new methods of political education and advertisement, which were another step along the road of democracy. These methods were to some extent left in abeyance in the two following decades of prosperity and social peace, but they became the common stock-in-trade of both political parties after the enfranchisement of fresh millions in 1867 and 1884.

The sharp tussle between landlords and mill-owners, which had resulted from the Corn Law controversy, had caused each party to champion the victims of its opponent. The miserable wages and housing of the rural labourers were proclaimed on League platforms; the wrongs of the factory hands were the most popular argument in reply. In this way the unenfranchised had their wrongs advertised, and in some cases remedied. The years of mutual recrimination between landlord and mill-owner saw the passage of Shaftesbury's Mines Act in 1842, and five years later the famous Ten Hours Bill for factories. Less was done for the agricultural labourers, because they were more widely scattered than the workmen organized in Trade Unions and congregated in factories, and they were therefore less feared and less easy to help.

With the laying to rest of the Corn Law controversy there set in at the same time the great period of mid-Victorian commercial and industrial expansion, which submerged beneath a tidal wave of prosperity the social problem and the mutiny of the underworld. Politics reflected the relaxed tension. From 1846 to 1866 we have the period of quiet Whig-Peelite rule, dominated by the figure of the popular favourite, Lord Palmerston. His performances were eminently suited for a period when everything was safe.

when nothing seemed to matter very much either at home or abroad, and when even to provoke a war with Russia involved only a limited liability.

Gladstone, meanwhile, at this stage of his long passage from old-world Tory to advanced Liberal, saw the duty of a statesman to the community chiefly in sound finance, and in the creation of the Treasury traditions with which he was closely associated in these years, implying strict economy and probity in the expenditure of public money. It was a great period for the growth of system and tradition in many Departments of the permanent Civil Service, preparatory to the much greater weight of administration which the next more active age would throw upon the offices of Whitehall. At the same time experiments were made in competitive examination, instead of jobbery, in making selections for the Civil Service. The idea of the value of examination as a test of men was derived from Oxford and Cambridge, where examinations had come greatly into fashion since the beginning of the Century. Palmerston, with his Regency standards of public life, scornfully opposed the wholesale abandonment of government patronage to a board of examiners. But the tone of the new age was all against favouritism and aristocratic inefficiency, and a few years after Palmerston's death in 1865, Gladstone, who was much in earnest in the matter, imposed the system of open competition on almost all the avenues leading into Whitehall.

No doubt a more far-seeing generation would have used the fat years of mid-Victorian prosperity to make provision against the return of the lean, by more social legislation, and by the establishment of a national system of primary and secondary Education. Something indeed was done in the way of Public Health provision. But, on the whole, while the voice of complaint was no longer loud in the land, statesmen of all parties were glad to rest and be thankful, hoping that the ugly facts and passions which the wave of prosperity had covered from observation, would never again obtrude themselves on the notice of Parliament.

As to Education, Prince Albert, it was remembered, was a German, and popular education a fad – fit perhaps for industrious foreigners in Central Europe who had not our other advantages of character and world-position. At any rate it would be the height of political unwisdom to touch the Education question, because nothing could be done that would not make either Church or Dissent spring up in angry protest. The new Whig policy, like Walpole's of old, was not to rouse the sleeping ecclesiastical

Cerberus, chained at present at the entrance of the House of Lords. The Whigs, allied as they were to the Peelite Conservatives, could not even remedy the Nonconformist grievances of compulsory Church Rates and exclusion from the Universities. And, indeed, in a world so comfortable and prosperous, it was difficult for any set of men to feel grievances very acutely, though Bright kept up a bulldog growl of his own, that might some day swell into a chorus.

In these circumstances at home, the main political interests of the period were those of Foreign Affairs. Here Palmerston was born to shine, and he shone with a lustre that no one can deny, though the amount of gold that went to make the glitter was then, and always will be, a subject of agreeable controversy.

Palmerston, who like Peel had begun public life as a Tory Minister in Peninsular days, had later been a follower of Canning, and in his strong old age may be defined as a cross between a Canningite Tory and a Whig aristocrat. He voiced the popular feeling of Britons against foreign despots, in the manner common to Canning and the Whigs. He was Whig aristocrat in his attitude of Gallio towards religion and the Church, and in his resistance to the influence of the Court. Opposed as he was in home politics to an increase of democracy and especially to an extension of the franchise, he was not opposed to a certain degree of popular control over Foreign Policy, for he regarded himself, when Foreign Minister, as responsible rather to public opinion than to his Sovereign or even to his colleagues. Like Canning before him, he appealed to the middle classes to defend his foreign policy against the hostility of Court and Cabinet, sometimes, it must be confessed, with less good cause than his master had been able to show.

Palmerston's popularity was great in the country, considerable in the House, small in the Cabinet, less than nothing at Court. His influence with his countrymen arose in part from a personal impression that 'Old Pam' was a 'sportsman', and in part from the nature of his policy. It had a double appeal. He combined the Liberals' dislike of the despotisms of Austria and Russia, Naples and Rome, with a tone in asserting purely British rights which a later generation would have called 'Jingoism'. In Palmerston's spirited language, a British subject was '*civis Romanus*', and even if he were only a Maltese Jew swindling at Athens, had the British fleet at his back. The same nonchalant spirit was more happily shown in the sympathy extended to the victims of Austrian and Russian tyranny in Hungary, Italy, and elsewhere after the collapse of the Liberal movement of 1848 upon the Continent. The attitude then adopted by Palmerston on behalf of Britain, in defiance of the wishes of the Queen and Prince Albert, was neither ignoble nor entirely useless, for it signified that constitutional liberty had still one hearty well-wisher among the Great Powers.

The strife between Palmerston and the Court was a constant source to him of amusement and joy in adventurous living, and to the Queen of grave annoyance. The Court had under her auspices become the reverse of what it had been under George IV as Regent and King. Probably Palmerston preferred what he recollected of the Regency – though scarcely of the Regent. In those days no one had expected Monarchs, Peers, or Ministers to pay their debts to tradesmen or otherwise to conduct themselves as school-models to the unprivileged. In politics the change was equally marked. George III and George IV had been identified with High Tory resistance to reform. But Queen Victoria, in her impressionable youth, had learnt from her mentor, old Lord Melbourne, what she never forgot, that the strength of the British monarchy did not lie in intriguing against Ministers or fighting against popular aspirations. At that time she had, it is true, shown too great a partiality to the Whigs, but she learnt on closer acquaintance to rate Peel at his true value. Under Prince Albert's teaching, her personal affection for foreign dynasties, particularly German, was emphasized; but her non-partisan liberality of outlook on home affairs was perhaps increased, and was certainly rendered more intelligent, by her student Consort.

The Crown had not yet reached the full position which it held by the end of the century in the popular imagination and in the new fabric of Empire. But already it was released from the unfortunate traditions of recent reigns. All through her long life as Queen, Victoria made a habit of following the actions of her Ministers with close attention, expostulating strongly when she disagreed, often obtaining thereby modifications, but never attempting to reverse or alter policy on which her Ministers remained determined after they had fully heard her views. She also exerted an occasional influence on the opposition, particularly in the House of Lords, and was singularly successful in averting conflict between the Houses on several important occasions in the last half of her reign, after the revival of a more militant Liberalism under Gladstone.

The two mid-Victorian decades of quiet politics and roaring

prosperity were broken in the middle by the Crimean War. 1854–6
Forty years had elapsed since Waterloo, and the new generation of Britons were therefore easily stirred to a fighting mood. The modern press, especially that part of it subject to Palmerston's influence, fed the war-spirit with selected news and incitements to hatred of Russia. The choice of Russia as the adversary appears at first sight somewhat arbitrary. But the dread of Russian power had of recent years been growing both in India and in Europe. It was not, indeed, Russia's nearest neighbours, Austria and Prussia, who considered that the Balance of Power needed redressing at the Tsar's expense; it was France and England who felt called upon to champion against him, among other things, the 'independence of Germany'. The reason for this was in part political. Austria, Prussia, and Russia stood together for the old principle of the Holy Alliance that had recently effected the repression of the risings of 1848. The Britain of Queen Victoria and the France of Napoleon III stood, each in a different way, for something more liberal. In England, Liberal sentiment had been outraged by the treatment of Poland, and by the aid lent by the reactionary Tsar Nicholas to Austria to put down Hungary in 1849.

But the actual occasion of the quarrel of Palmerston and Russell with Russia was their defence of Turkey. Russia, it is true, accepted our proposed terms of settlement, embodied in the Vienna Note of July 1853, and Turkey refused them. Nevertheless we fought for Turkey against Russia. Such an exhibition of diplomatic incompetence left Ministers with very little answer to some of Bright's censures in the House of Commons, but no answer was needed in the enthusiasm of war. The condition, or even the existence, of the submerged Christian nationalities in the Balkans, was little surmised in the Britain of that day. There was therefore no proposal made to check the advance of Russia by establishing a free Bulgaria and Serbia, as Canning had for that purpose established the independence of Greece. The old Turkish system was regarded as the only possible barrier to Russia's ambition.

The Tsar Nicholas was considered, not without reason, to be the mainstay of reaction in Europe outside the Balkans. The enthusiasm for the Crimean War was a mixture of Liberalism and Jingoism arising out of the circumstances of the period, and incarnate in Palmerston. But the war was not fought as a war of liberation, for Austria was invited to join the Anglo-French alliance. Only when Austria refused, was the proffered help of Cavour's little

Piedmont accepted instead. The substitution of Piedmont for Austria in the Crimean undertaking afterwards hastened the liberation of Italy, but such was not the original intention of the makers of the war.

Among the good results of the Crimean War should be set down British friendship with France and Napoleon III, in an age when France was inclining to take the war-path once more and when British sensibilities were preparing to resist the beginnings of a new era of Napoleonic conquest. The extraordinary man who had so ably manoeuvred himself on to the throne of France had not studied his uncle's career in vain. He saw that it would always be fatal to a French Empire to antagonize the Eastern despotic Powers and England at the same time. He ardently desired the friendship of Britain. Palmerston was the first to believe in his good faith, but the British in general were incredulous. The anti-Russian alliance was for a while good security against the danger of war with France.

The course of the war exhibited the soundness of the British regimental drill and tradition, and the utter incompetence of the higher command, the lack of organization and staff work, the deficiency of commissariat and medical provision. Half a dozen miles from our fleet in Balaclava harbour, our soldiers starved and died because supplies were not brought up to them. The raw recruits, sent out to replace the splendid troops who had
1855 thus unnecessarily perished, failed in the assault on the Redan, and thereby to some extent lowered in the eyes of Europe the respect for British arms won by the victories of Alma and Inkerman the year before.

The shortcomings of our military organization formed indeed at that time a remarkable contrast to our commercial and industrial efficiency. They were the result of the obscurantist spirit of the Horse Guards and the War Office, undisturbed hitherto by any popular demand for Army Reform. Rotten Boroughs, Municipalities, Universities, Church, Civil Service had all in various degrees felt the breath of criticism and change. But the nation had since Waterloo been so pacific that it had never inquired into the state of its Army, so long as War Office estimates were kept well down. Then, in a sudden fit of warlike zeal, John Bull remembered that he had 'a thin red line of heroes', and sent them out to fight the Russians, expecting results of the old Peninsular kind. But nothing was left of Wellington's army except the spirit of the regiments and the old Brown-Bess muskets with which many of them were still armed. At the time there was a great outcry against the

Generals and the War Office; yet as soon as the war was over the old indifference to things military returned. Army Reform was put off for yet another dozen years, till Cardwell came to the War Office in the first Ministry of Gladstone. 1868

But the 25,000 lives that the country lost in the Crimea saved very many more in years to come. For the real hero of the war was Florence Nightingale, and its most indubitable outcome was modern nursing, both military and civil, and a new conception of the potentiality and place in society of the trained and educated woman. And this in turn led, in the sixties and seventies, to John Stuart Mill's movement for women's suffrage, which Miss Nightingale supported, and to the founding of women's colleges and the improvement of girls' schools, when at length some provision was made for the neglected higher education of one half of the Queen's subjects. From the frozen and bloodstained trenches before Sebastopol, and from the horrors of the first Scutari hospitals, have sprung not only a juster national conception of the character and claims of the private soldier, but many things in our modern life that at first sight seem far removed from scenes of war and the sufferings of our bearded heroes on the winter-bound plateau.

In the Victorian era, the field of action where British foreign policy was most obviously successful was the Italian. Without war or serious danger of war, by legitimate diplomatic action in unison with strongly expressed popular sympathy, Britain helped the creation of a new independent Power in the Mediterranean and in the counsels of Europe, contrary to the wishes of the other Great Powers. This event removed a running sore in the body politic of Europe, and started a tradition of Italian friendship for England which continued to be an important element in affairs down to Italy's participation in the Great War in 1915, and was not completely broken till Fascism decided that the time had come to change a 'British Lake' into 'Our Sea'.

In 1848 Palmerston was at the Foreign Office. British opinion was then divided about Italy, more or less on party lines. Palmerston was favourable to Italian autonomy, and hoped to negotiate Austria out of the Lombard plain by appealing to her enlightened self-interest. But in that year of revolutions, Palmerston did not hold the key to the Italian question. For as British Minister he felt it his first duty to prevent a general European War, particularly one in which France might attack Austria, and so launch out on a new era of conquest and militarism. Yet without a war between

France and Austria it proved impossible for Italy to make any advance towards freedom.

When next the Italian question became acute, in the summer of 1859, Palmerston formed his second Ministry, which lasted till his death half a dozen years later. Russell was his Foreign Minister, and Gladstone as Chancellor of the Exchequer was the third of the controlling members of the Cabinet. Much as these three differed on other subjects, they agreed about Italy; and by a remarkable chance each of the 'Triumvirate' had an intimate knowledge of things Italian, in contrast to the ignorance from which all three then suffered as regards America, Germany, and the Near East. The result was that they acted with wisdom and vigour in the decisive Italian crisis of 1859–60 with very happy results.

England held the key to the Italian situation, as she had not done in 1848. In spite of the efforts of Lord Derby's late govern-
1859 ment, Napoleon III in alliance with Cavour's Piedmont had gone to war with the Austrians. His object was to expel Austrian influence from the Italian Peninsula and substitute French influence, in forms less galling and injurious to the Italians, for whom he had a real sympathy. But he wished to erect, not an independent Italian State, but a number of Italian States dependent on himself. Cavour, on the other hand, used Napoleon to expel Austria, but hoped then to effect a liberation of all Italy on such terms as would render her truly independent. Cavour was the cleverer man of the two, and won the game: but he could scarcely have done so without British help.

Russia and Prussia supported Austria in opposition to Italian liberation of any sort or kind, though since the Crimean War Russia was neither so powerful nor so friendly to Austria as before. In this complicated situation England, by taking up the cause of Italian independence and unity more thoroughly and more sympathetically than France, helped Cavour to force the pace.

In 1860, after Garibaldi's liberation of Sicily, the fall of the reactionary Neapolitan kingdom and of the Papal government in most of Central Italy followed, with Napoleon's enforced consent; for, since he could not permit Austrian reconquest, he was in no position to oppose the full flood-tide of Italian national movement sweeping on to unity under the Crown of Piedmont, when that movement received the diplomatic countenance of British Ministers and the enthusiastic encouragement of the British people.

A less fortunate episode in European affairs closed the epoch of Russell and Palmerston. A dispute lay between Denmark and her German neighbours, over the Schleswig-Holstein provinces, whence fourteen hundred years before a large part of the English people had migrated to Britain. The merits of the case were divided, and there was room for the good offices of a judicious third party, friendly to all concerned. But Palmerston and Russell took up a position of bravado in encouraging 'little Denmark', which they could not make good when Bismarck called their bluff. Palmerston had declared that 'it would not be Denmark alone' with whom her assailants would have to contend. Yet when war came, she found no ally, for our still unreformed army was in no condition to take the field against the united forces of Prussia, Austria, and indeed of all Germany. And the famous Volunteer movement of the mid-Victorian epoch was as yet for home defence alone. Nor could we expect the help of France and Russia, whom our diplomacy on other questions had recently offended.

The Palmerstonian era ended therefore with a humiliating rebuff. The importance of the case was even greater than men knew at the time, for the full meaning of the modern military monarchy of Prussia had yet to be revealed by the victories over Austria in 1866 and France in 1870. Palmerston's popular and jaunty diplomatic performances had had their day. If longer continued, they would have become a serious danger in the terrible new world that was coming into existence, as nationality learnt to prepare for war with all the prodigious powers of modern science and modern locomotion.

The fact that of 'the two old ringleaders' Palmerston died the first, had important consequences in political history. Russell, 1865 now become an Earl, was left as chief of the Whig-Liberal party, and, in spite of the fact that he had once been called 'finality John', he had long favoured a further extension of the franchise, and a development of the party out of aristocratic Whiggism into democratic Liberalism. If Palmerston had survived Russell, he would have opposed any such growth and would probably have broken with Gladstone, who was his opposite both in temperament and in policy. Russell, too old to take a leading part in the new age of transition, became Prime Minister, but permitted Gladstone, now at the zenith of his powers, to take over the virtual headship of the party.

Gladstone, thus become the leading man in the State, formed an alliance with John Bright, who stood at the head of the movement for the enfranchisement of the town artisans and of the lower

middle class. The strength of the working-class movement on its political side lay, during this decade, in its alliance with the middle-class Radicals, on the ground of their common exclusion from the franchise. The class-consciousness that had inspired the older Chartist movement had died away, largely owing to better times. Bright was the leader in the country and the spokesman in the House of this combined movement. Both he and the cause he advocated had recently gained prestige by the correctness of his judgement on the American Civil War, in which he had been a strong and well-informed advocate of the Northern cause. Most Whig and
1861–5 Conservative statesmen had in various degrees inclined to favour the cause of the South. While the war was raging, opinion in Britain had been largely divided on the issue according as men wished for democracy or aristocracy, a wide or a narrow franchise, in their own country. The ordeal by battle had gone in favour of Abraham Lincoln and the Northern Democracy, and the effect upon internal English affairs, though not clearly measurable, was certainly very great. Gladstone, an exception to many rules, had indeed been a hot 'Southerner', although he was moving fast to democracy in home affairs. His alliance with Bright after the end of the American War and the death of Palmerston, brought the franchise question straight to the forefront of British politics.

The manner in which the Second Reform Bill was carried was very different from the passage of the First. And the difference indicated how much in the last thirty-five years the governing and conservative classes had grown accustomed to change as a normal condition of political life, instead of regarding it as the end of all things. One might almost say that Darwin's then much contested doctrine of 'evolution' had already won its place in political consciousness.

There was, however, a sharp struggle. Disraeli in 1867 very ably settled the question and pacified the country by carrying a measure which, as finally amended, was much stronger than Gladstone's Bill which the Adullamites (a group of Whigs) and Conservatives had thrown out the year before as being too strong. The agricultural labourer and the miner in country constituencies were indeed still left unenfranchised, but household suffrage in the boroughs was in effect the principle of the Second Reform Act. Being the measure of a Conservative government it easily passed the Lords.

By accepting the great change without undergoing internal schism, the Conservative party prepared a future for itself in the new democratic world. But the immediate advantage accrued, at the General Election of 1868, to Gladstone and the Liberal party, which had a programme of overdue reforms to carry through before a real age of Conservatism could set in.

CHAPTER III

External Development in the Latest Era. Character of the Second British Empire. Growth of Canada. Relations with the United States. Australasia. South Africa. India

THE Second British Empire, as we have already seen, was a flourishing child when the Napoleonic Wars came to an end. In the following century its growth was enormous in area, wealth, and population, owing to the developments of commerce, communication, and transport due to steam and iron, electricity and petrol, and applied medical science in the Tropics. Conditions at home favoured emigration. Little check was placed on the increase of population in Great Britain until the last decades of the Nineteenth Century, and for long there was no other provision for unemployment save the workhouse. A constant stream of emigrants, therefore, poured out of the island; part flowed into the United States then engaged in peopling the vast plains beyond the Allegheny mountains, but a large part went to Canada, Australasia, and South Africa. The Colonial Office in the thirties was lethargic and stupid as regards emigration, but Lord Durham and Gibbon Wakefield, helped by the Churches and by private organizations, set going a movement for scientific care and encouragement of British settlement in British Colonies, which eventually made a convert and ally of Downing Street.

Until the end of the Victorian era there were still large numbers of persons in Great Britain born and bred as agriculturists, and desiring no better than to obtain land of their own beyond the ocean. It is only of recent years that a fear has arisen lest the English race, at home and in the Dominions, may by choice and custom eschew the rural life and crowd too exclusively into the cities.

The other aspect of the Second British Empire has been the development of vast portions of Asia and Africa by commercial intercourse and by political rule. The political rule has been conducted in Africa and in the East and West Indies, according to the benevolent ideals that have been generally prevalent in Downing Street since the days of Wilberforce and since the reorganization of Indian Government by Pitt and his Governors General. Great benefits have been conferred on a very large proportion of mankind: in Africa, inter-tribal war and slave-raiding have been stopped; in India, Egypt, and elsewhere the material benefits of modern science and organization have been applied for the advantage of all, not least of the humblest cultivators of the soil.

But two difficulties have beset the path of executive rule over the non-European races. First, the counter-claims of white farmers and traders, especially where, as formerly in the West Indies and permanently in South Africa, they are numerous enough to practise self-government. And, secondly, the class of difficulties which inevitably arise, particularly in India, when a long period of peace, good government, and contact with Western civilization has caused the ruled to desire to become self-rulers. The questions how best, how fast, and how far this demand can be met without disaster, form perhaps the most difficult problem that good government has ever created for itself.

The new conditions of the Industrial Revolution for some time only increased the advantages of Britain as the clearing-house for the world's trade and finance, and as the manufacturing centre for less developed countries. These circumstances led to the adoption of Free Trade and the abolition of tariffs and Navigation Acts. The change of policy put an end to the old 'mercantile' theory, which had regarded the commercial interests of the Colonies as involved in but subordinate to those of Britain. It was no longer desired to control British Colonial trade as a British monopoly. The end of the mercantile system led, by the inevitable logic of liberty and equality, to the grant to the self-governing Colonies of permission to decide each for itself whether it wished to protect its own manufactures by tariffs, even by tariffs against the mother country. In our own day this principle is being applied even in the case of India.

But taken in its largest aspect, the Free Trade policy of Britain, and the refusal any longer to keep trade with our colonies and possessions as a reserve of our own, removed many sources of friction with other nations, which could not have willingly seen themselves shut out from trade with so large a portion of the world as came to be included in the Second British Empire.

The principle of self-rule for the communities oversea was only an extension of the methods of government which had formerly prevailed in the lost Thirteen Colonies, and which had been initiated by Pitt in the two Canadas. But the logical and complete application of the principle of responsible Parliamentary government for the Dominions, owes its timely triumph to the wisdom and energy of Lord Durham. He had the peculiar merit of regarding freedom as the means of preserving the Imperial connexion, and not as a step towards separation, which most Whig and Conservative statesmen in that era believed to be inevitable.

Towards the close of the century a full consciousness of the meaning of the Empire swept over Great Britain and the Dominions in the days of Joseph Chamberlain. But the hope of the later Victorian age that this consciousness could be expressed in some form of Imperial Federation and a more unified constitution has not been fulfilled. Rather the Colonies, which had already developed into Dominions, are now developing into separate Nations. The Second British Empire is becoming an English-speaking League of Nations, officially united by the Crown. The test of war with Germany showed that the Commonwealth has a unity which no mere paper constitution could give.

The North American policy of British statesmen in the Nineteenth Century had two fields – Canadian problems and British relations to the United States: they reacted closely on each other. The Canadian problem, thanks to Lord Durham and Lord Elgin after him, received wise attention and treatment at an early date. But the full significance of our relations to the United States was not recognized by Whig and Conservative statesmen or by British public opinion in general, until after the American Civil War.

In 1837 two easily suppressed rebellions flared up in Canada – one in the Lower Province among the French *habitants*, the other in the Upper Province among the English-speaking settlers. Fortunately for the British connexion, the two sections were mutually antagonistic and neither had any desire to join the United States. But both had grievances against an unsympathetic administration. The two Provincial Assemblies which Pitt had set up possessed the power to embarrass but not to nominate or control the executive. The time had now come for the grant of full responsible government. But it by no means followed that British statesmen at home would believe that such was the cure, or have confidence that it could be safely applied immediately after an armed rebellion. Ignorance of Colonial conditions was great, and consistent belief in democracy was rare among the statesmen who had opposed and passed the First Reform Bill. Fortunately Lord Melbourne's Whig government had the happy inspiration to transport to Canada their able but sharp-tempered colleague, Lord Durham. He was both an Imperialist and a democrat at a time when hardly any other person of Cabinet rank was either the one or the other. He and his secretary, Charles Buller, were capable of seeing that full self-government was required, and of saying so very effectively in the famous 'Durham Report'.

The problem, however, was far more complicated than anyone in England realized or than Durham himself knew before he arrived on the spot. He found two nations, French- and English-speaking, bitterly opposed to each other as well as to the government. British immigration and farming in the West had now put the French in a very decided minority in Canada as a whole; but in their own Lower Province the French peasants still outnumbered the English-speaking traders and business men. Religious and cultural differences made the schism profound. To establish responsible self-government in Lower Canada would, in that generation, have led only to the breakdown of government, and probably to armed conflict between the two sections of the community. Durham's bold advice was to unite the two provinces in one, and to set up a single elective Assembly with full power over the executive, which would thus be in the hands of the English-speaking majority. This plan was carried out in the Canada Act of 1840. The French protested, but submitted. The new Canadian constitution functioned, with the help of Lord Elgin's shrewd and liberal guidance, until the next great crisis of Canadian history in 1867.

But, in order to understand the circumstances that led to Canadian Federation in 1867, it is necessary to take up the thread of British relations to the United States. Castlereagh, as Foreign Minister, has many claims on the gratitude of posterity, but none greater than his part in the mutual agreement
1817 to disarm along both sides of the Canadian border, and in particular to suppress the war navies on those Great Lakes that still divide British territory from the United States. Next year, in the same spirit, he began the determination of the boundary westward. This dangerous process, which occupied the joint attention of statesmen at Downing Street and Washington for a generation to come, could never have been brought to a peaceful conclusion if large armed forces and military traditions had existed on either side of the disputed line.

In Castlereagh's day, the line was carried forward by agreement from the Lake of the Woods to the summit of the Rockies, along the line of latitude 49°. It was wisely agreed to leave the eventual settlement of the lands between the Rockies and the Pacific still undetermined. That vast region, then all of it collectively known as 'Oregon', was inhabited as yet only by hunters and trappers of both nations, dependent on the Pacific Coast for their communication with the outside world. The 'joint occupation of Oregon' by the United States and Great Britain kept the peace in these thinly peopled lands, until in 'the roaring forties' the head of the column of American democracy, hot on 'the Oregon trail', burst over the barrier of the Rockies.

Americans were in an expansive mood. They were conquering nature and peopling a continent with a speed never before known in the world's history. It was a period of the Mexican War and of much tall talk, that represented somewhat crudely a genuine exhilaration in the sense of boundless expansion and a great new destiny discovered. In 1844 a United States Presidential Election was won on the cry of 'fifty-four forty or fight', implying a territorial claim as far north as latitude 54° 40′, that would have altogether excluded the British Empire from the Pacific Coast. But Canada, too, had her rights of future expansion westward. Peel, one of the most wisely pacific Ministers England ever had, was firm, conciliatory, and reasonable. At the very moment when he fell from 1846
office, he accomplished a feat as important, perhaps, as the Abolition of the Corn Laws; he obtained an equitable and peaceful definition of the boundary down to the Western Ocean, by the prolongation of Castlereagh's line of latitude 49°. The long, invisible border from Atlantic to Pacific is not guarded by sentry boxes and the challenge of rival armaments, but by the good sense and good feeling of two great communities.

After this triumph of reason and goodwill, it seemed likely that mutual understanding between Great Britain and the United States would move forward steadily out of mutual ignorance and prejudice, bred by the wars and social and religious differences of long ago. British institutions had ceased to be rigidly aristocratic and were in process of becoming democratic; Americans were less provincial and could afford to live less entirely on the memories of bygone disputes with the mother country. The renewed stream of British emigration to the United States, greater than any since the Seventeenth Century, was creating personal links between families on the two sides, often well maintained through the facilities of the modern postal system. But, unfortunately, these personal connexions between America and England existed at that time only among the plain people, who had, as yet, no votes in Britain. The aristocratic and upper middle class had not then contracted the habit of intermarriage with Americans, or of travel in the United States; and it was they who still controlled foreign policy, the Press, and Parliament, 1861–5 when the American Civil War made a fresh crisis in our international relations.

The government of Palmerston and Russell behaved correctly during the war. Under the restraining influence of Prince Albert on his deathbed, our Ministers enabled the dangerous *Trent* incident with President Lincoln's government to be settled pacifically, and, after some unfortunate hesitation, they refused to join Napoleon III in interfering to put an end to the struggle, for the benefit of the Southern slave-holding Secessionists. But the sympathies of the British upper class were mainly pro-Southern, and were expressed most crudely in *The Times*, *Punch*, and other newspapers to which opinion in New England was peculiarly sensitive. There was, indeed, no sympathy over here with the cause of slavery, but when President Lincoln began the war by declaring that the Union and not Slavery was the issue, many English people did not know enough about America to understand the relation which that statement bore to the whole truth. It was not inexcusable that Englishmen should doubt whether the South could be permanently coerced into membership of the Union. But when Lincoln declared the emancipation of all slaves in the rebellious Southern Confederacy, opinion in England began to swing round to the North. And from first to last the working classes and the lower middle classes, kept well informed by John Bright, W. E. Forster, and others, had been on the side of the Northern Democracy against the creation of a Republic based on slavery. After the victory of the North and the assassination of Lincoln, everyone else hastened to take the same side. But so long as the war lasted there was a tendency for British sympathy to divide according as men desired or deprecated the extension of the franchise in our own island.

The North had been deeply incensed by what they took to be British opinion during the struggle; and the South, which had expected more active help, was little better pleased. American feeling took a strong turn back against England, at the very moment when the general trend of development on both sides of the Atlantic was preparing the way for a better understanding between the two peoples. This alienation, due to the accidental circumstances of the Civil War, has not indeed been permanent, but it occurred at a time very detrimental to the progress of

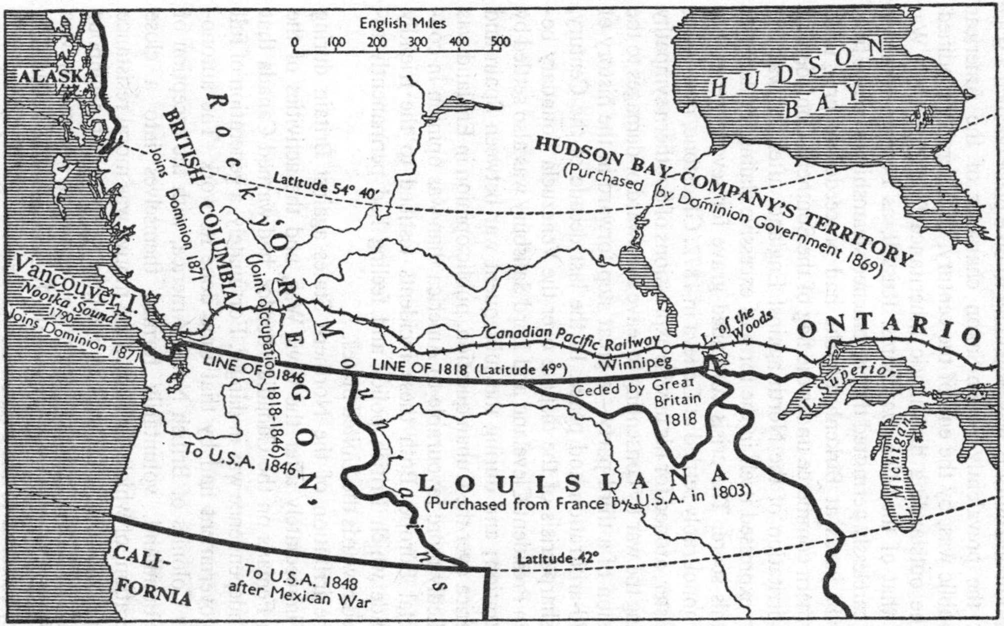

MAP XVI. DEVELOPMENT OF THE WEST CANADIAN BORDER WITH U.S.A. IN THE NINETEENTH CENTURY

Anglo-American understanding. The great influx of Irish hostile to Great Britain, and of Europeans who were of a different tradition and culture, was beginning to take place on such a scale that the prevalently Anglo-Saxon character of the American Republic was, by the end of the century, considerably modified.

The outstanding diplomatic inheritance from the Civil War was that of the *Alabama* claims. Russell, as Foreign Minister, had carelessly permitted that ill-omened steamship to escape from Laird's yards at Birkenhead; she had proceeded to prey upon Northern commerce under the flag of the Southern Confederacy. The irritation of the North against England, after the war was over, expressed itself in the form of excessive claims for damages on this score. The crisis continued grave for several years, but was honourably settled at Geneva in 1872. Gladstone, now Prime Minister, atoned for his unwise expressions of Southern sympathy during the war by consenting to leave the award of damages to the decision of a third party – a great step forward in the history of world-arbitration and peace. In the last decade of the Century, the sharp crisis of the dispute over the Venezuela boundary be-
1895 tween President Cleveland and Lord Salisbury was also settled by arbitration; and during the subsequent war between Spain and
1898 America over the Cuban question, public opinion in England was markedly more favourable to America than was opinion in continental Europe. Both these incidents testified to the friendly attitude which British policy and feeling had permanently assumed towards the United States.

The irritation of the Northern States against Britain during and immediately after the Civil War, and the activities of the Irish Fenians on the Canadian border, had warned Canada that her independence was in danger. Fortunately, a generation of full self-government had by that time done its work. The autonomous Colonies of British North America, with the exception of
1867 Newfoundland, voluntarily formed themselves into a close Federation, of which the immediate motive was moral resistance to annexationist tendencies in relation to the great neighbour Republic. The Canadian statesman to whom Federation was chiefly due, was Sir John Macdonald. Incidentally, the Federation Policy restored to the French Lower Province its separate autonomy, subject now to the bond of general Canadian unity. By this time the British and French communities had learnt to live side by side with diminished friction, and the French had adapted themselves to Parliamentary government.

As a result of successful Federation, the Dominion of Canada had been able to deal with the United States more and more on her own account, and no longer merely through the agency of Great Britain. The new sense of Canadian unity also produced in the decades following Federation, the Canadian-Pacific Railway, which opened the vast regions of the remote West to English-speaking settlement under the British flag. That railway is the spinal cord of the new Canadian nation.

Australia in the Nineteenth Century moved in a world remote from outer contact. She inherited no problem like that of the French Canadians. She had no neighbour like the United States. But her history, like Canada's, is that of the formation of a number of separate colonies, divided by great distances of desert, which become completely self-governing in the middle of the century, and by the end of the century have been linked up into an economic unity by long lines of railway. And, as in Canada in 1867, so in Australia in 1901 the time had come for a Federal Union. But the Federal Union of the Australian Colonies is not as close as that of the Canadian. The peculiarity of Australian politics has been the early strength of the Labour party, and the struggle of the democracy with the 'squatters' for the equal division of land and the break-up of great estates. The policy of excluding all coloured races from the continent, and its possible consequences in relation to modern Japan, has in recent years brought the strong nationalism of Australia into a closer sense of outside diplomatic relations with other countries, and of the importance of the British connexion. Australia's ideal, which she is determined to maintain even at the expense of rapid development, is an equalitarian society of white men, of high physique and a high average standard of life.

It was Gibbon Wakefield who had brought the public to believe that New Zealand might accommodate other races as well as the Maori tribes. His New Zealand Association, founded in 1837, made the first British Settlements there, only just in time to prevent the annexation of the islands by France. New Zealand, with its one and a half million inhabitants, remains one of the smallest but not the least happy and well-beloved of the British self-governing Dominions.

The history of South Africa presents points of likeness and of contrast to those of the other Dominions. As in Australia and Canada, the formation of a number of large but isolated communities, widely separated by great spaces of desert, preceded the age of railway connexion and of political Federation. As in Canada, the problems of colonization and self-government were complicated by the presence of another European race settled there before the coming of the English. As in the days of Wolfe and Montcalm, so in the days of Kitchener and Botha, there was bloodshed before peaceful settlement was reached. Yet the white population is in a minority of about one to four in the South African Union of to-day, excluding the native Protectorates. Canada is a white man's country, alike by nature and by settlement; parts of Australia could support coloured folk, but policy has reserved the whole continent for whites alone; but South Africa is a land where the European and African races flourish side by side, on the healthy upland plateau of the interior. The white South Africans have been numerous enough to claim self-government and to conduct it successfully; this fact has had constant reactions upon the native problem.

The first stage of British South African history, after the annexation of the maritime station of the Cape of Good Hope during the Napoleonic Wars, was the government of the small community of Boers by British officials near Table Mountain. There was at first less difficulty because the Boers had not been accustomed to self-government under the Dutch flag, and because there was as yet no large body of British Colonists. But in the third and fourth decades of the Century British immigrants began to arrive in such numbers as to raise difficult questions of language, law, and custom. Then in 1833 all slaves in the British Empire were emancipated. The Boers did not raise difficulty about emancipation, but considered, not without some reason, that the promised compensation was not paid them in full. In the same years they received inadequate protection in their outlying farms from the raids of the warlike native tribes of the interior. Lord Melbourne's incompetent Colonial Secretary, Lord Glenelg, represented a type of British official of that day who listened too exclusively to a certain kind of missionary on all native questions. These grievances of the border farmers, and perhaps some restless impelling spirit of adventure, were the causes of the Great Trek. The Boers
1836 started out, taking their wives and children with them in their ox-wagons, across the veld into the far interior. There they lived, after their own free patriarchal fashion, reading their great Bibles, multiplying their herds of cattle, shooting the big game that swarmed around, and watching the native warrior tribes from behind the protection of unerring musket and rifle.

But such isolation could not last long in the Africa of the

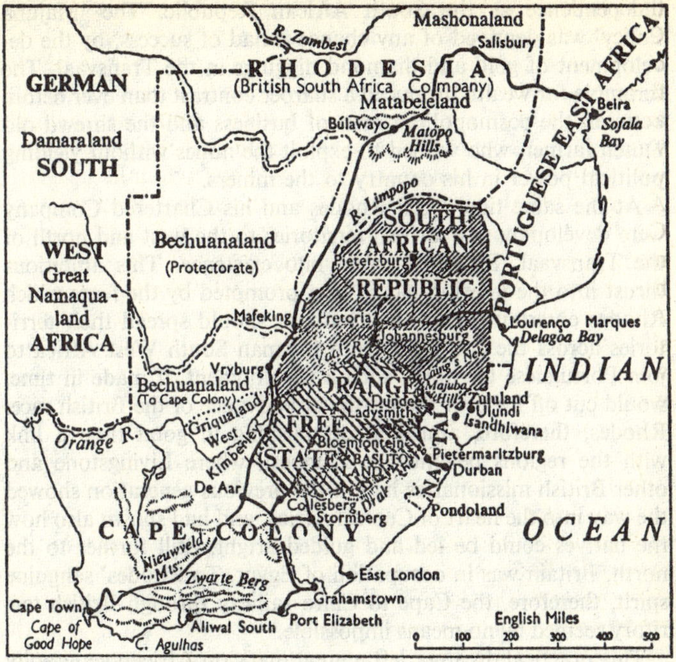

MAP XVII. SOUTH AFRICA, 1899

Nineteenth Century. First in Natal, then on both sides of the Vaal river they were followed up by British and European immigrants of the most various kinds – missionaries, hunters, farmers, gold and diamond diggers, and capitalist speculators. The clash of the old and new type of white society was repeated again and again in South Africa, in various forms, throughout the century.

For a long time the presence of the warrior native tribes restrained the Boers and British from coming to blows with one another. But after the suppression and pacification of the Zulu warriors by British armies and officials, the Boers felt a little 1879
more secure. At this critical moment the vacillation of the British governments, particularly Gladstone's, in deciding on a settlement of some kind with the Transvaal Boers, led to the conflict at Majuba. Gladstone accepted that British defeat for fear lest the 1881
Dutch of Cape Colony should throw in their lot with their blood-brothers beyond the Vaal; and so the Transvaal recovered its

independence as the South African Republic. The 'Majuba Policy' was deprived of any chance it had of success, by the development of gold and diamond diggings in the Transvaal. The scramble for wealth produced a sharper contrast than ever before between the cosmopolitan man of business and the shrewd old Dutch farmer, who wished to exploit the mines without yielding political power in his country to the miners.

At the same time Cecil Rhodes and his Chartered Company were developing new British territories to the west and north of the Transvaal. Rhodesia came into existence. This ambitious thrust into the interior was in part prompted by the fears which Rhodes entertained lest the Germans should spread their territories across the continent from German South West Africa to join Portuguese territory; such a development, if made in time, would cut off for ever the northward advance of the British race. Rhodes, therefore, aimed at establishing in good time a link with the regions beyond the Zambesi, where Livingstone and other British missionaries had in the previous generation showed the way into the heart of Central Africa, and had shown also how the natives could be led and guided aright. Still further to the north, Britain was in occupation of Egypt. To Rhodes' sanguine spirit, therefore, the Cape to Cairo railway through British territory seemed by no means impossible.

This practical dreamer left a great mark on African geography and history. But not all that he did was what he originally wished to do. He wished to reconcile the British and Dutch races, but he alienated them for a number of tragic years. While he was Premier of Cape Colony, he gave way to his impatience with Paul Kruger, President of the South African Republic, the old-world type of conservative Boer, and in an evil hour planned an armed attack
1895 on the Transvaal. 'Jameson's raid' united the whole Dutch race in Africa in just resentment and suspicion, enabled Kruger to arm to the teeth, and led up to the second Boer War. For Chamberlain in the Colonial Office at home, and Sir Alfred Milner in South Africa, could see no alternative but to bring the questions at issue at once to a head.

1899–1902 The South African War, with its unexpected reverses and its long protraction by the spirited guerrilla resistance of the Boer farmers, had a number of important reactions on the British Empire. It put an end to the boastful type of Imperialism which dominated the last years of the Nineteenth Century, a spirit which, though it served its purpose in its day to popularize the idea of the British Empire, would have made trouble in the dangerous epoch now approaching. The serious character of this second Boer War made men of all parties take a more sober and broad-minded view of Imperial duties and destiny. It gave a fresh impetus to military efficiency and Army Reform, destined to be of great consequence a dozen years later: if we had won the Boer War too easily we might never have won the War of 1914–18 at all. Finally, it called out the active and enthusiastic help of Canadians and Australasians, who came to South Africa to fight for the cause of the Empire in distress.

The victory in the field, won by Lord Roberts and Lord Kitchener, led to the annexation of the Transvaal and the Orange Free State. Peace was secured at the Treaty of Vereeniging, May 1902 where honourable terms were granted to the Commandos who still held out on the desolated veld. The material restoration of the farms was to be undertaken at once by Great Britain, the Dutch and English languages were to be put on an equal footing, and in course of time complete responsible self-government was to be granted under the British flag. All these promises were kept. Responsible self-government was set up as early as 1906 by Sir Henry Campbell-Bannerman, in spite of violent outcries and prophecies of ruin from Balfour, Milner, and the Conservatives; the result was the pacification of South Africa. Four years later the whole sub-continent was federated in the South African Union, except only Rhodesia and certain native Protectorates. In 1914–18 Generals Botha and Smuts, who had held out to the last against the British armies in 1902, headed the Union of South Africa in the war against Germany, and thereby added greatly to the material and yet more to the moral strength of the Empire, at its moment of greatest danger. In September 1939, again under the leadership of Smuts, the Union of its own will and decision once again took common action with the Commonwealth.

The collapse of the Mogul Empire in the Eighteenth Century, and the reduction of India to an anarchy of warring rulers, chiefs, and warrior bands, had compelled the British East India Company to undertake military operations and political responsibilities on a great scale. The progress had been hastened by the French effort to drive their European rivals out of India. Lord Wellesley had been the first Governor-General to envisage the 1798–1805 necessity of going forward till the *Pax Britannica* was everywhere accepted within the circle of Indian States. But although his Maratha wars checked the assaults of anarchy upon the Eastern and Southern portions of the Peninsula, the great sources of unrest in Central India were still left uncontrolled. After Wellesley's retirement, an attempt was made to limit British liability and to stop any further advance across India.

But events soon showed the impossibility of leaving confusion to welter on the other side of a long, unguarded line in the vain hope that it would confine itself to agreed limits. The disturbed state of Northern and Central India rendered peace in other parts impossible. Lord Wellesley's forward policy was resumed by Lord Hastings. In his day the Gurkha hillmen of Nepal were
1814–16 reduced by war, and their land has ever since remained our friendly ally, and a great recruiting ground for our Indian armies. Also in the time of Lord Hastings, the Maratha Chiefs and the robber hordes of Central India were finally conquered in the Third Maratha War and the Pindari Wars. Half a dozen years later, an attack on North-east India by the irruption of Burmese armies into Assam, led to the First Burmese War, and the beginning of the
1824–6 annexation of Burma, which was completed in 1853 and 1886. The Burmese, a Buddhist people of Tibeto-Chinese origin, are in no sense a part of the religious and racial mosaic of India proper; but the systems of government applied by the British to India were with modifications applied to this eastward extension of their territory.

After the forward movements and wars of the governorship of Lord Hastings and his immediate successor, there was a pause of some years before the problems of the North-west frontier, and the contact opened out with the Pathans of Afghanistan and the Sikhs of the Punjab led to a fresh cycle of wars and annexations. During this pacific interval, the benevolent side of British rule, and the sense of trusteeship for the Indians was strongly
1828–35 emphasized by Lord William Bentinck and by other able and earnest public servants. Nor, indeed, had the sense of trusteeship been lacking among the British rulers who had dealt in war and annexation, from Clive and Warren Hastings down through Wellesley and Lord Hastings to Metcalfe and the Lawrence brothers. But Lord William Bentinck was not called on to conquer anyone more formidable than the Thugs, the caste of hereditary murderers on the Indian roads, or to beat down any resistance other than that of the half-hearted defenders of Suttee – the burning of Hindu widows. His victories were those of peace.

In 1813 the monopoly of the East India Company for British trade with India had been abolished, and twenty years later its monopoly of British trade with China also came to an end. 'John Company' ceased to be a trading concern, but retained until 1858 the shadow of political power, of which the substance had long since passed to the Ministers of the Crown. The new Charter of 1833 embodied one tendency of Bentinck's policy in the words, 'No native of India, or any natural-born subject of His Majesty, shall be disabled from holding any place, office, or employment by reason of his religion, place of birth, descent, or colour.' But the business of training Indian administrators to render them capable of joining in the work of the British, had yet to be begun. Bentinck and his contemporaries addressed themselves to the task and its problems with an eager and generous zeal.

At this period there was singularly little ill-feeling between Europeans and Indians. The recollection of what had preceded British rule was so fresh that gratitude was still felt. The English and Scots in India were still very few and for the most part select. They were not yet numerous enough to form a purely English society of their own. They were cut off from home by a six months' voyage, often for life. India was their second home. Intermarriage, though rare, was not *taboo*. Colour feeling was not yet as strong on either side as it became at the end of the century. The Indians knew nothing of England or of Europe; their rulers seemed to them strange, invincible men dropped from the skies, more benevolent than most gods or kings whom they knew. Nothing could have made this happy state of things permanent. It is only a question whether inevitable change could have been made better or worse by any system of education for India other than that actually adopted.

It was under Bentinck's rule that the decision was made in favour of English as the medium of education and administration. The controversy was decided by the strong but over-confident arguments of Macaulay, then at Calcutta as a Member of Council. It is difficult to believe that any other language than English could have been permanently accepted. Since India was to be ruled as one, there must be a common official language. And who was going to compel British and Indians, in their dealings with education and government, to employ one of the innumerable languages of the East, arbitrarily selected for precedence over the others?

The teaching of English involved, however, certain dangers which subsequent generations did not take the right means to avoid. An energetic white race, trained in all the uses of self-government for centuries past, and assuming self-discipline and public order as things granted and certain, naturally lays stress in its poetry and its political philosophy on freedom as the crown of life. But these home-bred ideals may have strange consequences when overheard by an audience at the other end of the world and of human experience; there is some truth in the saying that we have attempted in India to 'rear a race of administrators on the literature of revolt.' Mistakes were certainly made in the curriculum of education. But those who argue that all our difficulties of recent years could have been avoided by the simple expedient of keeping Western literature and language out of Indian schools, do not stay to consider how strongly the Indians were even in 1835 demanding to learn English, how much the revival of their own literature and thought since then has owed to contact with Western knowledge, how utterly ungenerous and ultimately impossible it would have been to exclude our fellow subjects permanently from the science and learning of the West, and how dangerous might have been the unsuccessful attempt on the part of government to keep them in ignorance against their own loudly expressed wish.

After the interval of pacific consolidation under Bentinck, the forward movement began again. The wars and settlements of the forties decided in broad outline the policy and geography of the North-west frontier. An attempt to bring the mountain tribes of Afghanistan within the radius of British India, led to the famous disaster when a whole army perished in the retreat
1841–2 from Kabul. It was perhaps a blessing in disguise, for the ultimate peace and safety of the Indian Peninsula have since been found to rest securely on the policy of friendship with Afghanistan as a buffer State, that jealously guards its mountain freedom between the Asiatic possessions of Russia and Britain. Owing to the existence of an independent Afghanistan we have never been in armed conflict with Asiatic Russia.

In the years immediately following this check in the mountain region, the annexations of Sind and the Punjab gave into British hands the great river system of the North-western plains. The Sikhs of the Punjab were a democratic religious brotherhood, of what we may call 'Protestant' Hindus, who had long guarded the plains of India against the debouchment of Mohammedan hill tribes, or of invaders from Central Asia. Their great chief, Ranjit Singh, had trained the Sikh warriors in European methods, and had kept friends with the English. But after his death this splendid soldiery poured across the Sutlej to attack British India. The ensuing struggle, with battles like Moodkee, Sobraon, and Chillianwallah, was as severe as any that the British have ever fought on Indian soil. The victory in war was followed up by the work of the Lawrence brothers in winning the confidence and attachment of the Sikhs by the good government of the Punjab. When therefore the storm of the Mutiny broke, John Lawrence was able to use the newly acquired Punjab as a place of arms for the reconquest of revolted Oudh. Afghanistan also was friendly to the English during the crisis, so that the North-west frontier could be safely denuded of troops till the Mutiny was suppressed.

The Mutiny, as its name implies, was a rising of some of the Sepoy regiments in British pay, including a large part of the artillery. The civilian population was rather a spectator than a participant in the event. The grievances that caused the outbreak were the grievances of soldiers, caused by mismanagement such as that which had undesignedly served out cartridges greased with the fat of the sacred cow and the abhorred pig.

The Mutiny of the Bengal army began at Meerut. Its immediate occasion was unwise severity by incompetent officers, May 1857 who proved helpless before the storm they had raised. Some of the mutineers made straight for Delhi where there was no British regiment. Delhi fell at once into the hands of the movement; and Cawnpore, after three weeks' gallant defence; and Lucknow, all except the Residency where Sir Henry Lawrence met his death in the defence. It was in this Upper Ganges region that the issue was fought out and won during the summer of 1857, by the British then actually in India and the faithful Indian troops. Their boast that 'alone we did it' is substantially true, though there were many months of severe fighting after the arrival of reinforcements from England. The deeds of Nicholson and the Lawrences, of Havelock and Outram, of Colin Campbell and Hugh Rose, and the little armies which they formed and led, the stories of the Delhi Ridge, the Kashmir gate, and the relief and final capture of Lucknow, re-established the prestige of Britain not only in India, but in Europe also, where the Crimea had exhibited our want of army organization no less strikingly than the fighting qualities of our seasoned troops.

The flame had been stamped out in Central India before it could spread. Most of Bengal, all Madras and Bombay, and the North-west had remained loyal. So too had the great Native States like Mysore and Hyderabad. One result of the Mutiny was to put a stop to the course pursued by the over-eager spirit of the Governor-General Lord Dalhousie, of absorbing the territories of protected Indian rulers into actual British territory, in order to enlarge the area of benevolent administration. Indeed Dalhousie's annexation of Oudh, the seat of the Mutiny, had indirectly helped to provoke it. The Native States have, ever since 1857, been regarded as essential pillars of the British raj, not least during the political troubles of more recent years which are bred in the provinces directly ruled by Britain.

Although it was a Mutiny of the troops and not a revolt of the population, the outbreak was related to a dim general uneasiness and fear in the great mass of Indian opinion, at the pace with which Westernization was proceeding. Dalhousie's zeal for reform and progress was seen in many strange novelties – the railways, the telegraphs, and the European standards of efficiency and sanitation.

After the Mutiny these things indeed continued, and India grew accustomed to them. A long period of peace and sound administration followed, the British Government after 1858 replacing the East India Company in name, as it had long done in fact. In 1877 Queen Victoria, on Disraeli's advice, assumed the title of Empress of India.

The memory of bloodshed and racial feud now lurked like a phantom in the secret consciousness of rulers and ruled. Nevertheless, for many years after the Mutiny, the work of good government proceeded without an interruption. Famine and plague were fought by scientific methods. Wealth and population increased as never before.

It was a noble work for the benefit of helpless millions. Yet the bureaucracy, as the useful years went by without incident, contracted the inevitable limitations of any government that is purely autocratic. It considered too exclusively the good work done, and gave too little attention to changes in the political atmosphere. It is possible that the path of the future would have been eased, if hands had been held out from above to the nationalist movement in its earlier and loyal stages, as for instance, to the Indian National Congress in the eighties and nineties. But when criticism of a mild kind was first uttered, it was too often regarded by the English as sedition, until indeed it became no less.

In the last decades of the century, colour consciousness hardened on both sides. English society in India had become larger, more self-sufficient, more closely connected by short voyages with home. On the other side the educated Indians began to know more of the world across the mountains and the seas, whence the English and others came, and to understand that the phenomenon of white rule was a fact of history and science, not a sending of heaven. The political ideas of nationalist and liberal Europe were terribly familiar to them, mingling in their minds with a

racial and conservative revolt against the modern ways of their alien overlords. The Japanese victory over Russia affected the 1904
attitude of all Asiatics towards white domination. In the new century many of the educated Indians developed an attitude of hostility, and often of sedition and political crime. The anti-English propaganda of the educated was not altogether without effect on the vast uneducated masses of conservative-minded peasantry.

The era of concession from above set in, to meet and control such serious unrest. In the question of the Partition of Bengal, an administrative decision made by a great Viceroy was reversed some years later, in deference to the strength of popular opinion. And the India Councils Act of 1909, the joint work of Lord Minto at Calcutta and of John Morley at Whitehall, enlarged the Legislative Councils by introducing into them a considerable elective element, with powers of consultation and criticism of the actions of the Government. In 1911 George V, as King Emperor, held a great Durbar at Delhi, to which the capital was moved. He was the first reigning sovereign to visit India.

The Great War of 1914, which immensely stimulated the growth of Dominion self-government, evoked in India claims for equality with the Dominions. Indians felt that Britain could no longer deny to them that right of self-determination for which she professed to be fighting in Europe. In 1917 the British Government announced that its policy was the gradual development of responsible government in India as an integral part of the British Empire; and the Government of India Act, 1919, which embodied the principles advocated by the Montagu-Chelmsford Report on Indian Constitutional Reforms, was the outcome of that momentous declaration. It provided for a partial responsibility of the Executive to the Legislature in the Provinces, the Central Government remaining solely responsible to the Imperial Government and Parliament, partly because it was felt that matters like defence and foreign relations could not safely be entrusted to the control of an inexperienced Legislature representing a largely illiterate electorate, and partly because the Central Government had to deal not only with British India but with the Native States. In more than one Province the new system broke down because the Nationalists would be satisfied with nothing less than complete autonomy. Unrest took the form of widespread strikes, revolutionary activity, the boycott of British goods, and a civil disobedience campaign organized by Gandhi. In 1930 the Simon Commission Report recommended the establishment, with safeguards, of full responsible government in the Provinces, whilst rejecting the idea of responsibility at the Centre. When, however, some of the Indian princes announced their readiness to enter an All-India Federation, provided that it was self-governing, the Ramsay Macdonald Government declared in 1931 that it would accept the principle of a Federal Executive responsible to a Federal Legislature. After much consultation with Indian opinion the Government of India Act, passed in 1935, provided for the setting up of an All-India Federation consisting of eleven British-Indian Provinces and such Indian States as were prepared to join. Both the Federal and the Provincial Governments were to be responsible to their Legislatures except in the Federal spheres of defence and foreign policy.

Since 1937, therefore, the Provinces have been self-governing, but the establishment of responsible government at the Centre and the realization of an All-India Federation had not been achieved when the outbreak of war between Great Britain and Germany in September 1939 made further constitutional change impracticable for the time being. The plan of a Federal India encountered the opposition of every group whose cooperation was essential. Fearing domination by British India, the Princes showed their reluctance to commit themselves to the scheme, and the necessary number failed to give their consent to it. The Moslem League was afraid that self-government would mean the transference of power from British to Hindu hands. All parties were anxious to cooperate in the task of winning the war, but Congress demanded of the British Government a definite promise of full Dominion status after the conclusion of peace. No such promise could be given without the consent of the Princes, the Moslems, and the other minorities, whose separate interests had to be safeguarded. Congress then called upon the eight Congress Ministries in the Provinces to resign, and, responsible government having broken down, the Governors were obliged to set up Emergency Administrations. Communal differences therefore threaten to retard India's constitutional progress and still further to embitter Hindu-Moslem relations.

CHAPTER IV

The New Reform Era. Gladstone's First Ministry, 1868–74. Disraeli and Modern Conservatism. Gladstone, Egypt, Home Rule. Lord Salisbury's Ministries. The Era of the Jubilees. Social Reform and Imperialism

THE victory of the North in the American Civil War and the death of Palmerston together gave the signal for another period of rapid change in the world of English politics. The leader in the new age of transition was Gladstone, who embodied the political spirit of the time with its earnestness, its optimism, its trust in human nature, and its diligent mastery of legislative and executive detail that saved its idealism from running to waste in words. Gladstone completed the transmutation of the old Whig into the new Liberal party, and by the legislation of his first and greatest Ministry of 1868–74 made up the arrears of institutional change overdue. Palmerston's leadership had long imposed delay on the activity of the party whose special function it was to make the pace of progress. Reform now came with a rush, but with no violence, because the resistance made to it was slight.

For at the same time the Conservative party, and therewith the control of the House of Lords' veto on legislation, fell into wise hands. Not without a double personal application, Disraeli in 1868 wrote to the Queen that 'a fund of enthusiasm' 'ought never to be possessed' by a Prime Minister of England – nor, he might with equal relevance have added, by a leader of Her Majesty's Opposition. Certainly the Conservative chief's own sceptical and clear-sighted temper was admirably adapted to the task of 'educating his party' to accept the democratization of our institutions as inevitable, and even to preside over important parts of the process. But Gladstone's more ardent nature was required for the great legislative achievements of 1868–74.

Behind the statesmen of the transition stood the political philosopher John Stuart Mill, whose writings exerted in the sixties and seventies a wide influence over educated opinion. He brought Bentham's Utilitarianism up to date, and emancipated it from the stricter bonds of the *laissez faire* theory. Mill preached the doctrine of complete democracy in the sense that every man and woman ought to take part not only in national but in local elections. But he knew the limits of the work suited to the democratic machine. He desired to see specialist Departments of State guiding the democracy and keeping politicians properly informed. 'Power,' he said, 'may be localized, but knowledge, to be useful, must be centralized.' The dovetailing of the functions of the Whitehall Civil Service with those of the Downing Street politicians and of the electorate in the country was an essential part of Mill's doctrine of good government. There had been nothing of that in the older Radicalism of Cobbett or the pure *laissez faire* school.

His advocacy of women's rights, in *The Subjection of Women* (1869), though in his own day it was not allowed to affect the political franchise, helped to increase the respect for women's personal liberty, and the belief in the importance of their proper education which characterized the later Victorian age. Mill and Florence Nightingale were the two principal pioneers of the position that women hold in our society to-day.

Mill's treatise *On Liberty* was a plea for freedom of thought and discussion, then much limited by social convention though not by law. The rising generation grew up with this creed of freedom, by no means confined to politics. It was the age of the first heart-searching controversies on Darwin's startling hypothesis of evolution, with its reaction on the literal acceptance of parts of the Bible. *The Origin of Species* and Mill's *Liberty* appeared in the same year – 1859. The Natural Science Tripos was being started at Cambridge. The 'movement' begun at Oxford by Pusey, Keble, and Newman, before Newman went over to
1845 Rome, had since gone out from its academic home to meet, and in some cases to blend, with other fresh sources of energy in the Church and country at large. The so-called 'Christian Socialism' of Frederick Denison Maurice and Charles Kingsley began a fresh orientation of the Church in relation to democracy and the social problems of the Industrial Revolution. Modernist theology, under Jowett, Stanley, and Colenso, gained toleration and importance through the Darwinian controversy and the growth of historical method and knowledge. The Church was beginning to contain within her own body something answering to each of the currents of the heady fight going on in the world outside. Much had been gained in knowledge in several different directions – in earnestness yet more. Missionary energy at home and overseas took on fresh life. Selwyn, Bishop of New Zealand in its earliest days of colonization, had an apostolic and democratic spirit which reacted on the Church at home. The merits and demerits of the Church clergy in their relation to the laity were very different from what they had been in the easy-going Eighteenth Century.

The grave abuses in the uneven distribution of Church revenues had been reformed by Peel and the Whigs, and by the Ecclesiastical Commissioners whom they set up after the First Reform Bill. In many different ways, therefore, the Church was newly prepared to stand any assault which might be made on her as a result of the further extension of the franchise of 1867. No doubt many of her exclusive privileges would have to be surrendered, particularly in the Universities. But the resisting power of the Establishment was at once more solid and more elastic than it had been in 1832, when zealous Churchmen had opposed even the First Reform Bill on the ground that it must lead to disestablishment and disendowment.

It would be tedious to enumerate the many other movements of intellectual activity and social change that were stirring in the sixties. Among the most important was the organization of the great Trade Unions in the skilled trades, especially engineering, and the growth of the Cooperative movement, which trained so many of the working classes in business habits, thrift, and mutual reliance, released them from exploitation by the shopkeeper, and gave them 'a stake in the country'.

The classes newly enfranchised by the Second Reform Bill, in their first use of the vote in 1868, greatly strengthened the Radical element in the party commanded by Gladstone and placed the weapon of a large majority in his active hands. His first Ministry was the first in English history that can be called 1868–74
distinctively Liberal instead of Whig. In 1868 Conservatism and Socialism were both temporarily in abeyance. It was a mood not likely to last long, but the use made of it by Gladstone in the greatest half-dozen years of his life, went far to equip the country with modern services and institutions, without which she would have been ill-prepared to face the social and imperial problems of days to come. In those years the Universities were opened to men of all creeds, a national system of Primary Education was established, Army Reform was initiated, the throwing open of the Civil Service was completed, the Ballot Act was passed, and the first steps were taken towards the conciliation of Ireland with the disestablishment of the Protestant Church in a Catholic island, and the first steps to face the Irish land question.

After half a dozen years of splendid activity, under the greatest legislator of the age, Gladstone's first Cabinet had done its work: Ministers could be fitly compared by Disraeli to a 'range of exhausted volcanoes'. For he himself had very shrewdly allowed their lava to exude. The House of Lords had not been allowed to prevent their policy from taking effect. The work that the country had expected of them was substantially done, and a natural Conservative reaction therefore took place at the election of 1874.

1874–80 It was not until his seventieth year that Disraeli first attained to real power as Prime Minister. The work of his Ministry bore the impress of his own ideas both in domestic and in foreign policy.

At home he was anxious to demonstrate the connexion of the new Conservatism with social reform and with conciliation of the working classes. Aided by his able Home Secretary, Richard Cross, he waged war on slums and insanitary conditions with the Public Health Act of 1875 and the Artisans' Dwelling Act. Such measures, and the continuous work of the Local Government Board set up by Gladstone in 1871 to cooperate with the ever-increasing activities of the local authorities, were important palliatives. But bad building and bad town-planning had got such a start in the previous hundred years, that they have never been properly overtaken.

Much less could anything be done to set a limit to the ever-advancing bounds of the realm of ugliness and uniformity, in its constant destruction of the beauty and variety of the old pre-industrial world. Indeed the more prosperous and progressive the country was, the more rapidly did that unceasing work go forward. Man when armed with the machine could not help destroying beauty, whatever the work to which he set his hand.

Disraeli also settled an acute stage of the ever-recurring problem of the rights of workmen in time of strike. In 1867, a judicial decision of the courts had deprived the Trade Unions of the legal position they had enjoyed since the legislation of 1824–5. The courts suddenly ruled that combinations 'in restraint of trade' were illegal. Gladstone remedied this by his Trade Union Act of 1871. But in the same year his Criminal Law Amendment Act rendered picketing and other actions usual in time of strike illegal. The Trade Unionists, incensed with Gladstone, whom they had supported at the election of 1868, largely abstained or supported Disraeli in 1874. And the Conservative Premier in 1875 repealed Gladstone's Criminal Law Amendment Act, and left violence and intimidation in time of strike to be dealt with as part of the general criminal code.

In foreign policy Disraeli renewed the connexion between the party he led and the dramatic assertion of British national interests. That connexion had not been specially marked since

Waterloo. After the Treaties of Vienna, the Tory or Conservative party, that had done so much to make that settlement of Europe, was sometimes more pacific than Palmerston and his followers, because Whigs and Radicals had less veneration for the settlement of 1815 and more sympathy with the nations and parties on the Continent who wished to disturb it. Nor had the Colonies interested the Conservatives any more than their rivals, who could boast of Lord Durham. In 1852 Disraeli himself had spoken of 'these wretched Colonies' as 'a millstone round our necks'. But his keen sense of the new situation led him in his old age to appeal to the newly enfranchised British democracy to take a pride in the Empire and an interest in 'spirited foreign policy'. Interest in the Colonies was still only nascent, and was developed much more fully in the following generation, under the leadership of Joseph Chamberlain. Disraeli's principal field of operations was the Near East. His purchase of shares in the Suez Canal for England began the connexion with Egypt which shortly after his death led to great developments. And in 1876–8 he and Gladstone, in their angry and magnificent disputation, aroused the passions of their fellow-countrymen over the details of Balkan wars and massacres, which but for these two men of genius would have seemed a far-off battle of kites and crows, and none of England's business.

Disraeli, now Lord Beaconsfield, made the British Government the principal supporter of the Turk in Europe as the barrier against Russian influence; while Gladstone in opposition, by his campaign on the 'Bulgarian atrocities' of Turkey, made one half of British opinion the principal hope of the oppressed Christian races of the East. It was a strange situation, full of danger to our divided land. Fortunately it ended at the Treaty of Berlin without 1878
war between Russia and Britain. This was Disraeli's 'peace with honour'. He had certainly made England again important in the councils of Europe, and had forced attention to her wishes. But whether the restoration of the liberated Macedonians to the Turkish rule for another generation was precisely what England should have wished, will remain an open question. Many who know the Balkans regret that, since Disraeli was determined, perhaps rightly, that Macedonia should not be added to the newly formed Bulgarian State, he did not in the Treaty of Berlin insist on its being placed under a Christian governor with proper securities for its good government. It is at least conceivable that such an arrangement might have mitigated the ferocity of racial passions in the Balkans cockpit in the Twentieth Century.

The General Election of 1880 put an end to Disraeli's Ministry, and a year later he died in retirement. He had given the Conservative party its orientation in the new world of democracy, by a frank acceptance of changed conditions at home; he had taught the upper classes not to retire to their tents in anger at lost privileges, but to go down into the street and appeal to the masses on grounds of patriotic sentiment and Imperial interest. Gladstone's mistakes in South Africa and Egypt in the following decade, and his Home Rule proposals, supplied material for such propaganda. The principle of appeal from the upper to the lower classes, made on the ground of identity of interest in the nation as a whole, found expression, after Disraeli's death, in the Primrose League, founded in his memory, and in a network of Conservative Clubs and Associations all over the country. In the early eighties the idea of 'Tory democracy' received a great stimulus from the brief meteoric career of Lord Randolph Churchill.

At the same time the National Liberal Federation of local Associations, nicknamed the 'Caucus', was being organized by the other party through the energy of the Radical leader, Joseph Chamberlain, whose political power was rooted in his personal control over the local politics of Birmingham. Democratic appeal and elaborate mechanical organization were entering into the electoral methods and political programmes of both parties. New forms of influence and of veiled corruption were arising in place of the old, new forms also of idealism and devotion to the public service. The thoroughness of modern organization and party propaganda at least secured that Parliamentary government should not fail in Great Britain for want of popular interest in elections and in politics. And the presence of real dividing principles, the rival interest of classes, and great questions like Home Rule, prevented the highly organized two-party system from becoming in England a mere lifeless machinery, representing nothing but a struggle for office.

1880–5 Gladstone's Second Ministry was not so triumphant an affair as his First. In 1880 the Liberal party had not, as in 1868, a definite political philosophy of its own, nor an agreed political programme. It was borne into power by reaction against Disraeli's 'Jingoism', and by vague democratic aspirations not yet formulated into any clear programme of social reform. And it was at once faced with unavoidable problems in Ireland, Egypt, and South Africa, about which, in the year 1880, Liberals, like other Englishmen, knew little and cared less. Gladstone indeed knew and cared about Ireland, and his Land Act of 1881, giving fair rents and security of tenure, was a real measure of amelioration. But it did not solve the land question, still less break up the formidable union of land agitation with the political demand for Home Rule, which Parnell's new policy of 'obstruction' was forcing on the notice of the British House of Commons.

The principal achievement of the Ministry was the Third Re- 1884
form Bill, which extended Household Suffrage to the county constituencies. The agricultural labourer and the miner were at last enfranchised. Till then their conditions of life had received all too little attention. The attempt of Joseph Arch to start Agricultural Labourers' Trade Unions had failed in the previous decade for want of political power behind it. The agricultural labourer had been ill-used even in times of prosperity, and he fared still worse in the years of agricultural depression, due to the great increase of American importation in the late seventies. His enfranchisement in 1884 combined with other economic and social circumstances to initiate a slow, continuous improvement in his lot, but not before the villages had been desperately depleted by the 'rural exodus' to the towns. The social history of rural England in the Nineteenth Century is in many respects a chronicle of disaster.

The Parliamentary enfranchisement of the rural labourer soon led to the establishment of elective local self-government for the country districts. Hitherto they had been not only judged but administered by the patriarchal rule of the nominated Justices of the Peace. The Conservative Government in 1888 set up elected County Councils; and in 1894 the establishment of Urban and Rural District Councils and Parish Councils by the Liberal Government completed the machinery of rural democracy. Judicial and public-house licensing were still left to the Justices of the Peace, but their great administrative powers passed to the new elected bodies.

The neglect of the South African problem in the first months of Gladstone's Ministry led to the Majuba tragedy. The Egyptian affair began more brilliantly. The breakdown of Turkish and native government in Egypt, where European countries had many financial and personal interests, led to the occupation of Egypt by the British troops under Wolseley, victorious over Arabi at Tel-el-Kebir. France had refused at the critical moment to partici- 1882
pate, though Egypt had hitherto been more under French than English influence. British control in Egypt began, greatly to the material benefit of the Egyptian peasant. The Nile valley prospered, ruled by the all-potent 'advice' daily given by Sir Evelyn Baring, Lord Cromer, to the Khedive's government. The French

regarded our presence there with jealousy, and many unpleasant incidents resulted, until the important agreement with France on Egypt and other subjects was made by Lord Lansdowne in 1904.

But closely attached to the Egyptian question was the Sudanese, and it was here that Gladstone came to grief. While the lower reaches of the Nile held the ancient civilization of Egypt, its upper reaches contained the barbarism of the Sudanese tribes, at that period organized under the Mahdi and his successors as the centre of slave-raiding in the interior of Africa, and a constant threat to Egypt. Any conscientious ruler of Egypt, or indeed any Power sincerely interested in the fate of Africa as a whole, must needs aspire to deal with the plague-spot of the Sudan. But the time was not yet. Egypt had first to be set in order, and her financial and military resources built up.

But in the course of the necessary withdrawal of Egyptian garrisons from the Sudan, Gladstone's Government made errors. Spurred on by William Stead, the father of modern sensational journalism, the Ministry selected for the work Charles Gordon, a strange and single-minded hero fit for any service except that of initiating retreat. Instead of successfully evacuating the Sudan he was soon shut up in Khartoum, besieged by the Mahdist hordes. The British Government failed to send the relief expedition until too late. Jan. 1885 Gordon perished, and with him perished much of Gladstone's influence over his own countrymen at home. In Africa the defeat made less difference. The Sudan would in any case have been evacuated at that time. Only after Cromer had done his work in Egypt, was Lord Salisbury's Government able to conquer the Sudan with the British and Egyptian armies under Kitchener in 1898.

The General Election of 1885 resulted in a great defeat of the Liberal party in the boroughs, largely owing to Gordon and Khartoum. But the newly enfranchised agricultural labourer cast his vote for the party to whom he owed it, in the hope of obtaining some real improvement in his miserable lot. Lord Salisbury therefore did not obtain a clear Conservative majority with which to govern the country. The notable consequence was that the balance of power at Westminster lay in the hands of a strange man who, though himself of Anglo-Saxon origin, regarded British Liberals and Tories with a cold, indifferent hatred. Charles Stewart Parnell had established the iron discipline of his personal ascendancy over the Home Rule party from Ireland, numbering eighty-five members of the new British Parliament. Henceforth, so long as the Union of 1801 was maintained, Irish affairs must clearly be a controlling factor in British politics, as they had not been in the early and middle parts of the century when the Irish Representatives were many of them attached to one or other of the two British parties. Politics could not go on as before. Either the two British parties must unite against Parnell, or one of them must come to terms with him. Gladstone came to terms with him, and introduced a Home Rule Bill. 1886

In the light of subsequent events, many in our generation will be disposed to consider such a decision natural and even obvious, and to wish that the question of Irish self-government could have been settled then in peace, instead of in 1921 after a series of horrible events. But it is difficult to say whether the cause of Irish conciliation was retarded or advanced by Gladstone's proceedings. The speed of his *volte-face* on a subject of such immense importance bewildered and exasperated the British electorate. The Home Rule question broke up the Liberal party and greatly weakened it for twenty years to come, while Conservatism became closely identified with Unionist doctrine for Ireland. Above all, Gladstone's acceptance of Parnell's claim to have Protestant Ulster as a part of the new Ireland, was more than an error in tactics. It flew in the face of racial and political possibilities.

The Conservative party had been courting the Irish vote not without success during the election of 1885. But it seized the opportunity given it by Gladstone's compact with Parnell to appeal to British national feeling. Home Rule was read in the light of Khartoum. The growing Imperialist sentiment of the *fin-de-siècle* did not recognize Home Rule for Ireland as an essential part of the new creed of Empire, in spite of much support for Irish Home Rule in the self-governing Dominions oversea. The passions aroused by the Home Rule controversy in England, marked by such episodes as the publication in 1887 of forged 'Parnell' letters in *The Times*, rendered rational statesmanship by an agreement of parties impossible. Yet nothing else would have served the case.

The reaction against Gladstone and Home Rule was strong enough at the election of 1886 to secure an independent Conservative majority over Gladstonian Liberals and Irish combined. There followed an era of strong Conservative government under Lord Salisbury in alliance with the Liberal Unionists, especially with Joseph Chamberlain, who became the champion of the new Imperialism. In that way the country was ruled until after the

Boer War at the end of the century, with the exception of the three years of Liberal rule (1892–5). The Liberals and Irish under Gladstone then forced a Home Rule Bill through the Commons by a majority of thirty-four. It was thrown out by the Lords, and in the election of 1895 the country ratified their action. This event gave to the Conservative chiefs a new idea of the function of the Upper Chamber in modern politics, more ambitious than that adhered to in practice by the cautious Peel and Disraeli. The consequence in the following century was that as soon as the next big change in democratic opinion took place, a contest between the two Houses led to a very grave constitutional crisis, such as had been conspicuously absent from our politics since 1832.

The defeat of Home Rule at the polls in 1895 was definitive for a number of years to come, and there was a temporary lull in Irish affairs. The Conservative Ministry who had previously relied on coercion to govern Ireland, developed a policy of 'killing Home Rule by kindness'. They enlarged local self-government, and, by buying out the English landlords, ended the Irish land question, at least in its old Cromwellian form. But the political demand for Home Rule, or something more, remained unabated. In the Twentieth Century the national demand for self-government was so deeply implanted in the mind of the Irish Celts, that it survived not only the fall and death of Parnell (1890–1), but the subsequent removal of the land grievance – the man and the question which had first given it power seriously to disturb the politics of the British Empire.

1898 Gladstone died in retirement in his eighty-ninth year. The impassioned efforts of 'The Grand Old Man' for Irish Home Rule had been the most dramatic and extraordinary part of his life, but the least successful. It is possible that the Liberal party, and the politics of the Empire as a whole, would have developed more naturally towards the end of his life, if they had been left by him to the men of that generation. Gladstone's immense activity overshadowed friends and foes, and pushed them into positions not of their choosing. But, viewing his life down its whole length, many will conclude that he did more than any other man to adapt the machinery of the British State and the habits of British politicians to modern democratic conditions, without a total loss of the best standards of the older world. The legislation of his First Ministry had done most to modernize our institutions. The Second and Third Reform Bills largely resulted from the lead he had himself given the country after the death of Palmerston.

He had interested the new democracy in Parliamentary government by constant popular appeals, not to sensationalism or self-interest, but to men's reasoning faculties and their sense of right. His reasoning may often have been defective and his appeals to moral indignation may have been too often and too easily made, but on the whole his habit of carrying public questions in their serious aspect before the tribunal of great popular audiences was a fine and fruitful example, made at an important period of transition in our public life.

The government of Great Britain by Lord Salisbury's Conservative Ministries, in alliance with the Liberal Unionists, covered a period of trade prosperity and, until the Second Boer War, of peace with civilized peoples. Good relations with the Continental Powers were maintained on the basis of the 'splendid isolation' of Great Britain. The other Great Powers, preparatory to the great act of world-destruction in our own day, were already dividing themselves into two camps, arming in nervous rivalry – the Triple Alliance of Germany, Austria, and at that time, of Italy, against the Dual Alliance of France and Russia. Great Britain remained outside both these groups, but owing to the hostile attitude of France as our colonial rival in Asia and Africa, and to the continual dread of Russia's intentions towards Afghanistan and India, Lord Salisbury was upon the whole in a relation of greater friendliness to the Germanic Powers. But always a certain uneasiness attended the relations of a government based on Parliamentarism and popular rights with the great militarist bureaucracy created by Bismarck; the new leaders of the German destiny inherited an instinctive distrust of the influence of British political institutions. But the general orientation of British policy was not affected by this *malaise* until Kaiser William's admiration of the British Navy led him to build a rival fleet – a development that only became dangerously noticeable in the following century. Under Lord Salisbury's management, the African continent was divided among the Great Powers by peaceful agreement. The interior of the Dark Continent was now in rapid process of exploitation by Europeans armed with modern means of locomotion, and protected by modern knowledge of tropical medicine.

At home the last two decades of the century, and of Queen Victoria's reign, whether under Liberal or Conservative Ministries, were years of social and administrative progress, particularly in the direction of what was known as 'municipal socialism'. Baths and wash-houses, museums, public libraries, parks, gardens, open spaces, allotments, lodging houses for the working classes were acquired, erected, or maintained out of the rates. Tramways, gas, electricity, and water were in many places municipalized. It was also a great period of voluntary effort, of 'Settlements' like Toynbee Hall, and of a very general awakening of all classes to the terrible consequences of 'environment' in the slums in the 'richest country in the world' – as England was then still accounted. The scientifically guided Christian inspiration of Canon Barnett; the statistical investigations of Charles Booth and his helpers into the real facts of London life and his reasoned advocacy of Old Age Pensions; the social side of 'General' William Booth's work of redemption through the Salvation Army, and Church work on similar lines; the civic patriotism of the new London, and its activities initiated by John Burns of Battersea and the Progressive party of the London County Council in its early years; the investigations and 'Fabian' tactics of the Sidney Webbs, to manoeuvre instalments of socialism out of Liberal and Conservative governments and parties; the more militant life breathed into Socialism by Henry George's *Progress and Poverty* and by Hyndman's Social Democratic Federation; the extension of Trade Union activity from the highly skilled to the ill-paid and unskilled trades signalized by the Dockers' strike of 1889 – all these and many other movements and forces indicated that the social problem was not at its end but at its beginning, and might well in the coming century devour the other aspects of political life.

Meanwhile, apart from the conscious action of politicians or of social reformers, the continual and ever-increasing rapidity of the Industrial Revolution was year by year silently transmuting social habits, obliterating old distinctions of rank and creed, and turning a Bible-reading people with ideals based on reminiscences of rural or burgher life and a hierarchy of classes, into the city population that we know. A significant portent was observed in the growth of Harmsworth's *Daily Mail*, catering for the new half-educated democracy of all classes, in a fashion quite different from that of the more solemn political organs which had satisfied the Victorian *bourgeoisie*.

At length, in January 1901, the figure passed away that had presided over the changing scene during a period of transition longer and no less momentous than the reign of George III himself. 'The Queen' had reigned so long that in the minds of her subjects the Monarchy had become female in its attributes. All through her long reign – alike before, during, and after her married life, alike in her period of Whig and her period of Conservative preferences, in dealing with Ministers to whom she was attached and with Ministers whose policy she abhorred and whose personality she disliked – Victoria had with fixed steadiness of principle adhered to a settled constitutional practice of her own. She always insisted on knowing what was being done; she compared it in the vast store-house of her memory and experience to what had been done in the past; if she disagreed, she protested; if the Minister still adhered to his decision, she gave way. But not all Ministers adhered in every case to their first decisions, particularly in questions of appointments or in the phraseology of documents. The Queen's practice of this method for more than two generations of men, definitely fixed the position of the Crown in the Constitution, so that the storms of the Twentieth Century, which have raged round so many other institutions, have left the Monarchy unchallenged. Victoria's successors, by evincing a more complete absence of party predilection than she showed herself, have further smoothed the path of constitutional kingship in the new age.

At the same time, since the idea of a Federation of the Parliaments of the Empire has failed to materialize, the Crown has been left as the sole official bond of the whole Imperial fabric. Here, too, the Queen was in her element. In her latter years she admirably filled and greatly enjoyed her new position as Empress of India and as head of a great association of free peoples, which was proclaimed and dramatized by the Imperial pageantry of her two Jubilees in 1887 and 1897.

Victoria was possessed in a high degree of queenly instincts and dignity, but they were softened and popularized by a mind and an emotional nature of great simplicity. In herself she was not very different from her female subjects in humble stations of life – except that she was also a great Queen. She was not at all an aristocrat; the amusements and life of the aristocracy and their dependants and imitators meant little to her. She was above the aristocracy, not of it. With the other side of her nature she was a simple wife and widow-woman, who would have been at home in any cottage parlour. So, too, the intellectual and artistic currents of the age flowed by her unnoticed – except when Prince Albert was there to instruct her. The common people understood her in her joys and sorrows better than they understood those who stood between themselves and her, raised on the platforms of aristocracy or of intellect.

For these reasons, political, and personal, the coming of democracy had, contrary to general expectation, coincided with a revival of popular affection for the royal office, disjoined as it now was from pretensions to direct political power.

CHAPTER V

Boer War to the War of 1914–18. The last Liberal Ministry

THE close of the Nineteenth Century, the South African War, and the deaths of the Queen and of Lord Salisbury, coincided so nearly in time as to mark the end of an epoch. The Victorian age had been a long period of ever-increasing prosperity at home, of gradual, uninterrupted, pacific transition from the old to the new society, and of peace and security for Britain in her most important foreign relationships.

But the first two decades of the new century involved the world in the greatest catastrophe of modern times, and even before that catastrophe had taken place, the relations of nations, races, and classes had taken on a hard and hostile aspect. Man's power over nature far outstripped his moral and mental development. In a single generation came the motor-car, wireless telegraphy, and the conquests of the air and of the world under the sea. Such inventions, and the application on a colossal scale of older processes of steam and electricity, were perpetually transmuting the economic, social, and international fabric before it had time to solidify; speed and mechanism destroyed the older habits of life and thought in our island, and began the suburbanization of the rural landscape; throughout the world, nations and races were linked up too suddenly for their peace; and national ambitions found ready to their hands new weapons of conquest and self-aggrandizement which have proved the means of mutual destruction.

The South African War, about which the Liberal party had been divided in opposition, left the Conservatives with a large majority after the 'Khaki election' of 1900, to begin the business of the new century. The two leading Ministers were Arthur Balfour, Salisbury's nephew and successor in the Premiership, and Joseph Chamberlain, who as Colonial Secretary had done so much to arouse the British Empire to a state of self-consciousness.

Balfour's Act of 1902, inspired by the wisdom of the great civil servant Sir Robert Morant, added another storey to the edifice of National Education begun in 1870; it handed over the responsibility not only for elementary but for higher education to the

County Councils and County Boroughs. In this way Secondary Education for the first time received proper financial support, and was coordinated with the rest of the national system. The new local authority – the Education Committee of each County Council – was able to devise broader schemes of policy than the old School Boards, which had often administered too small an area.

The reform has resulted in a great enlargement of secondary schools, and the erection of a 'ladder' by which able students of small means can ascend through them to the Universities. Improved Secondary Education has raised the average standard of work and intelligence at Oxford and Cambridge by opening them to many more able men of all classes; and it has been the making of the new Universities that sprang up apace in the new century, at Liverpool, Leeds, Sheffield, Birmingham, Bristol, and Reading, in addition to London, Durham, and Manchester Universities founded in the previous century but come to full maturity in our own.

At this stage, the waning fortune of Unionist Conservatism was put to a hazard calculated either to check or to precipitate its ruin. Joseph Chamberlain, with a vigour unmatched since Gladstone's advocacy of Home Rule, preached the doctrine of 1902–5
Protection, renamed Tariff Reform. The motive that first impelled him to this audacity was the desire to link the Dominions to the Mother Country by a system of Imperial Preference. Without it, he believed, the bonds of Empire would ere long be relaxed. The difficulty was that Great Britain could not give effective preference to Canada and Australasia without placing a tax on foreign foodstuffs, to be remitted in the case of Dominion products. And in England popular tradition had a vague but hostile memory of the old 'Corn Laws'; greybeards told tales of the 'hungry forties', when taxed bread was scarce on their parents' tables.

Imperial Preference, therefore, was a bad election cry. Moreover, after the South African War, the country had had enough Empire for a while; so Chamberlain's Preferential Tariff, in the hands of his insular fellow countrymen, was soon moulded by the Conservatives into a scheme of which the prime object was the protection of British goods. This aroused the enthusiasm and opened the purse strings of many British manufacturers. But their zeal was suspect to the consumer, especially to the working man with his family budget to consider. Free Trade doctrine was very strong in all sections of the community; it had behind it fifty years of unchallenged authority and custom; caution and tradition, usual mainstays of the Conservative party, supported the Liberal economic thesis. Moreover the prosperity of British commerce under the Free Trade system was not yet shaken. The world's markets were not yet closed to our goods by nationalist foreign governments to the extent that they have been closed since the Great War. Joseph Chamberlain in his lifetime was beaten by the still obstinate prosperity of our staple industries. He could prophesy their ruin, but its coming was delayed.

Indeed, the great interest that most required protection in the first years of the new century was agriculture. Ever since 1875 foodstuffs from America and all the world had come flooding into Great Britain on a scale never foreseen in the day of Cobden and Peel, when prices had been steadied, not smashed, by free importation from Europe. But, with the prairies and the pampas developed as Britain's food farm, it was becoming impossible to grow food at a profit in the island. English farm hands, badly paid and housed even in good times, were now deserting the land for the cities at an appalling rate. Great Britain was on the way to becoming urbanized altogether, unlike any other country in the world. A check ought to have been put to this catastrophe, which would be irremediable when once complete. Unfortunately the protection of British agriculture was the proposal that politicians were most afraid to advocate, though something might be done under cover of Colonial Preference. The Free Trade system under which Britain had so long flourished had little regard for agriculture. Food was the currency in which foreign nations and our own Dominions paid for British manufactured goods. And cheap corn and meat was of great value to the wage-earning community. The absence of a democratic peasant-proprietorship like that of the European Continent made it difficult to advocate agricultural Protection. The field labourer, long ill-used by the farmer, scarcely knew whether he wished agriculture to be protected; he could slip off to the nearest town or mining district and get a better wage and eat his cheap food there. The most effective popular appeal of Chamberlain's opponents was the unsavoury memory of the old Corn Laws, the fear of dear foodstuffs and the cry of the 'small loaf'. So it is only after the Great War has shaken party traditions and old economic doctrines, and the German submarine has shown the use of the plough in Britain, that any attempt, and that quite insufficient, was made by subsidies and control of imports to maintain food production within the island

and so save a little of what is still left of country life, while securing by statute a minimum wage to the field labourer. That all life in Britain should become urban and suburban, while her fields fall back to jungle, would be a horrible disaster, for strategic, human, and social reasons more important than any purely economic consideration.

The result of the General Election of 1906 was like an earthquake. There had been nothing approaching it since the destruction of the old Tory party in the first election after the Great Reform Bill, and that had been the consequence of an entirely new electoral system. In 1906 the net Liberal gain was 273. The Liberals in the new Parliament numbered 397; the Irish Nationalists 83; the Unionists who had ruled the last Parliament were reduced to 157. And, most significant of all, a Labour party of 50 members had suddenly sprung into existence.

The overturn, which took everyone by surprise, was significant of a greater tendency to mass emotion in the large modern electorate, bred in great cities, and less tied up by party traditions than the old. There have been other such elections since. Moreover the issues of 1906 had all been unfavourable to the late government – the Education Act, Protection, Taff Vale, and the recent introduction of indentured Chinese Labour into the South African gold mines, which seemed a sorry outcome of the great Imperialist War. But behind all these things was something more fundamental. A new generation had arisen, wanting new things, and caring more about 'social reform' at home than about 'Imperialism' in Ireland, South Africa, or anywhere else.

Whatever party or doctrine would be the ultimate gainer, the old forms of Imperialism and Conservative Unionism were never again to hold power. Protection, indeed, had a future. But the Conservatism that has held power since the war of 1914–18, as an alternative often preferred to Labour governments, has been liberal in its outlook on Irish, Egyptian, South African, and Indian questions, and semi-socialist in its outlook on the duties of the State to the working class. Meanwhile until 1914 the Liberal Party bore rule for the last time, in close though uneasy alliance with Labour, and left a deep impress on social legislation.

Balfour's last great reform before leaving office in 1905 had been the establishment of the Committee of Imperial Defence. It was developed by Asquith's government as a means for laying plans for the possible event of war. Its functions are consultative only; it provides the Cabinet with information and advice, and its decisions can only be carried into effect by Parliament or by Departments of State. As it is not an executive body, its composition is fluid. The Prime Minister summons whom he thinks fit – generally the Secretary for War, the First Lord of the Admiralty, the Foreign Secretary, any Dominion Prime Ministers who may be in England, and the technical advisers required for the questions under discussion at each particular meeting. The Committee has, however, a Secretary of its own, whose permanence in a constantly changing body gives him great importance. Sir Maurice Hankey, now Lord Hankey, as Secretary of the Committee of Imperial Defence from 1912 and Secretary of the Cabinet from 1916, has left his impress on our growing institutions.

The importance of the Committee of Imperial Defence is twofold. It enables the problems of army, navy, air force, and home front to be considered together in their mutual relations and as parts of one general policy, of provision for possible war. And it enables the responsible statesmen of the Dominions to meet the home authorities in confidential discussion and concert plans for the defence of the Empire as a whole.

For ten years, December 1905 to May 1915, Great Britain was ruled, for the last time, by a Liberal Government. Its leaders were men of unusual personality and power. There was Haldane, the soft-spoken lawyer-philosopher who won the confidence of the soldiers and reformed the Army; John Morley, the veteran of the Radical intellectualism of the last century, who was now on behalf of the British Government to cope with the new problem of national self-consciousness in India; there was Edward Grey, remote, firm, and sadly serene at the Foreign Office; there was young Winston Churchill looking round for his kingdom; and there was Lloyd George, on whom time and great events should fix many diverse labels, mutually contradictory but all true. And coming on there were such able administrators and legislators as Herbert Samuel, Walter Runciman, and Reginald McKenna. The working classes were represented for the first time in a Cabinet, by John Burns, a personality hewn out of old English oak. For a decade all these men most astonishingly held together, for two successive Prime Ministers knew their business: Campbell-Bannerman, an easy-tempered but shrewd Scot, who saw quite through the souls of men, started his team of colleagues in harmony; won the confidence of the raw and restive legion of Liberal recruits in the House; pacified South Africa by reversing the policy of Milner and granting responsible government before it was too late; then died in 1908, his tasks accomplished. He was succeeded by Asquith, a Yorkshireman of high integrity and unshakeable nerve, with a skill in advocacy learnt in the law and applied to politics, sound judgement to choose well between the opinions of others, and a rare skill in manipulating discordant colleagues.

The great achievement of this last Liberal Ministry was the initiation of measures of social reform on a scale beyond all precedent. Old Age Pensions, on a non-contributory basis, helped to empty the workhouses, to give happiness to the old and relieve their loyal sons and daughters of part at least of the burden of their maintenace. Democratic Budgets shifted more taxation on to the wealthy. Workmen's Compensation, Miners' Eight Hours, Medical Inspection of Children, and the Children's Bill, the Town Planning Act, the Sweated Industries Act, measures of Unemployment and Health Insurance, and the Small Holdings Act for rural districts formed part of a vast programme of laws placed on the Statute Book. Such measures, implemented by municipal bodies, and extended by the work of Care Committees, Play Centres, Boy Scouts, Adult Education, and other such activities outside the harsh discords of politics, together with constantly advancing medical science and practice, have in the present century, in spite of the War, raised the standard of children's health and happiness, reduced the death-rate, and prolonged the average of human life by several years, and begun a more even distribution of the national income and opportunities for happiness.

The function of Local Government has undergone immense extension under modern democracy. It is looked to now not merely to remove public nuisances, to supply sanitation, lighting, and roads, but to act for the personal benefit of the individual citizen. It is to Local Government, controlled and aided by the State Offices in Whitehall, that the poorer citizen is beginning to look to supply the house he lives in; the electric light and gas he uses; free education for his children – from infant schools to University scholarships; medical clinics and isolation hospitals; books from the free library; baths and swimming; cricket fields and 'green belts' of open country for his Sunday walks; trams or buses to take the family to work or school; and a hundred other benefits to make life kind.

As Sir William Harcourt said as far back as 1894, 'we are all socialists now.' At any rate, by whatever name you call it, this system of State assistance to the life of the poorer citizens is a great fact of modern English life. Its principal instrument is found in elective local bodies, empowered by successive Acts of Parliament, helped financially by Treasury 'grants in aid' of rates, and kept up to the mark by government Inspectors.

This system, originated in the middle of the Nineteenth Century, has been growing faster than ever in the Twentieth. In the Rating and Valuation Act of 1925, in the Local Government Act of 1928 we see the Central Power taking more and more control of Local Government. There is an ever-increasing tendency of the Minister and Department at Whitehall to direct the action of the local authorities on a single national model. The national model is enforced on the local authorities not merely by Acts of Parliament, but also by elaborate regulations which modern Acts of Parliament allow the Minister to make departmentally by acts of administrative legislation. 'Delegated legislation' it is called, because Parliament by Statute delegates to the Minister (of Health, Transport, or Education) the power to make subsidiary rules to be enforced on the local authority as if they were laws.

Local authorities are becoming more and more the agents of Central Government in carrying out a national policy for the benefit of the poorer citizens, largely at the expense of the richer citizens, through the local rates and the national taxes that go to make up the grants-in-aid. Under this system the elected local authorities have more powers, but less independence, than of old. They cannot refuse to carry out these multitudinous duties imposed by Act of Parliament or by the regulations issued by the Minister. The days have indeed long gone by since the local benches of Justices of the Peace in 1795 introduced a new national policy of rates in aid of wages, the 'Speenhamland system', without any reference either to Parliament or to any Minister or Department at Whitehall.

In future every government, whether called Conservative, National, or Labour, must be at least half socialist. The last Liberal government recognized this fact, and applied great legislative and administrative ability to meet the needs of the new social and economic scene.

The Liberals, who had ceased to be in the main a middle-class party, could only maintain themselves so long as the working class would vote for their candidates. In the very first days of the new Parliament, the degree of Liberal dependence on Labour opinion was made dramatically clear by the terms on which a most drastic remedy was applied to the Taff Vale decision of 1901, so inimical to Labour's 'strike weapon'. In 1906 Trade Unions were given a privileged position outside the power of hostile judges on the Bench.

It was thus shown that Labour was the strongest element in the progressive or left-wing side of politics, stronger than the 'old Liberal' interests, Nonconformity and Temperance. The Lords had not dared to challenge Labour, although all the Conservatives and many of the Liberals regarded legal immunity as a dangerous privilege for bodies so powerful as the amalgamated Trade Unions of the Twentieth Century; miners, railwaymen, and transport workers were becoming organized on a national instead of local basis, and bade fair to be each 'a State within the State'. And now they were rendered in large measure exempt from the control of law.

At the same time, by encouraging the rejection of distinctively Liberal measures such as the Education and Licensing Bills, the Conservative leaders put the House of Lords again in the forefront of politics, a position from which the prudence of Disraeli had preserved it. Under his wise direction, the Lords had allowed Gladstone to put on the Statute Book all his large programme between 1868 and 1874, including even the Disestablishment of the Irish Church, and the Conservatives had consequently won the next General Election. And in the eighties the Lords had restrained their natural impulse to act as a partisan body on a level of authority with the House of Commons. But in 1893 they had won popularity by the bolder course of throwing out Gladstone's Home Rule Bill; their complete success on that occasion, endorsed by the verdict of the country at the next Election, misled Chamberlain, Balfour, and Lord Lansdowne into supposing that the Lords could play the same game in the more democratic Twentieth Century against a much more formidable government backed by a vast majority.

Their strategy in deserting Disraeli's caution was fundamentally at fault; but in the years 1906–8 their tactics were clever and at first successful. They passed the measures in which the working classes were most interested, but humiliated the Government by refusing to pass the measures about which its Liberal supporters specially cared. The Liberals seemed already reduced to impotence within two years of their triumphal entry into power. The by-elections began to turn heavily against the Government. A Conservative reaction was on foot, and a little patience would have met its reward. But the Peers had no patience, and at the instigation of the party leaders, proceeded to commit the greatest tactical error in modern politics. They threw out Lloyd George's Budget of 1909.

This new interpretation of the constitutional function of the hereditary Chamber in matters of finance amounted to a claim on its part to force a General Election whenever it wished; for a Government unable to raise taxes must either resign or dissolve. In future all Parliaments not to the liking of the Lords could be dissolved at their will. The rejection of the Budget was also a breach with the custom of the Constitution, of which Conservatives should above all regard themselves as the guardians. Neither Disraeli nor Lord Salisbury would have dreamt of such a proceeding as to invite the Lords to reject the Budget of the year. The Twentieth Century was not a time for an hereditary Chamber to claim powers it had not exercised even in the aristocratic Eighteenth. But it was in vain that King Edward VII warned the Opposition leaders of the danger of the course on which they were set.

But a tendency to violence and excitement had already invaded the mind of the new Century. Militant Suffragettes, Labour Unions, Irish parties, and foreign military potentates were not the only people to be subject to its influence. The Tariff Reform movement was being carried on in an atmosphere of perpetual excitement and anger; the new type of newspaper lived on sensation; Lloyd George's shrill demagogic note was new in speeches delivered by Ministers of the Crown; and the Peers caught the contagion of violence.

1909 Lloyd George's Budget was unpopular with the upper class, justly, in so far as it proposed new Land Taxes in an ill-conceived form which proved on trial to be impracticable; and less reasonably, because it made a very moderate increase of direct taxation of the well-to-do. There was to be a graduated income tax at about a quarter of what it is to-day (1937) and corresponding death duties, to pay for Old Age Pensions and a very necessary increase in the Navy. If the Opposition had waited, they could have won the next Election and repealed the Land Taxes. But they urged on the Peers to reject the Budget, the very thing which Lloyd George most desired. He made ample use of his opportunity; his harangues at Limehouse and elsewhere sharpened the edge of controversy and aroused the democratic passions. It was the grand electoral issue for the Liberals – 'Shall Peers or People rule?' The Peers defended themselves by claiming that they had only referred the Budget to the People, and that the land valuation clauses were not proper to a Budget: but they were on the defensive; the Opposition had lost the advantage of attack.

Meanwhile Asquith and his other colleagues appealed more quietly to the moderate men, who had been drifting back to the Conservative allegiance, but who were shocked by the disregard of constitutional custom by the Lords. At the same time the Liberal Ministers were able to rally the Labour and the Irish forces to a joint effort to limit the Lords' power of veto. Another issue at the Budget elections was Tariff Reform: it was urged by Conservatives as a method of raising money preferable to the increased direct taxation necessary under a Free Trade government.

All these issues were brought to a head together by the fight over the rejected Budget and over the Parliament Bill: that measure proposed to prohibit the Peers from either amending or rejecting money Bills, and to change their absolute veto on other measures to a suspensory veto for two years. The country was twice consulted in 1910 – once under King Edward, and once after his death under the new King, George V – with the result that in both elections a majority of about 120 was secured by the Liberal-Labour-Irish combination. The Liberal party was therefore master of the Lords, but at the mercy of its own allies. George V, after the second election had confirmed the result of the first, compelled the Peers to pass the Parliament Bill, by using, at Asquith's behest, the same method of a threatened creation of 1911
Peers *en masse* as William IV had, at Grey's dictation, employed to pass the First Reform Bill. Again the prerogatives of the Crown had proved the weapon of the democracy, a fact which helped to move the working classes still further from Republican doctrine.

But 1911 was not, like 1832, the end of the worst trouble. For opinion in the country was much more evenly divided than in that famous year of old, when the Lords had little save their own constitutional powers with which to maintain the fight. The Home Rule question now came up in earnest, for under the Parliament Act the Peers could no longer defeat it, but only delay its passage. The disestablishment of the Church in Wales, the long-standing demand of Welsh Nonconformity and of the majority of the Welsh members, was also now a practicable proposition, heaping yet more fuel on the fire of men's wrath.

Unhappily the worst exacerbation of parties in Great Britain – a mixture of old constitutional and denominational with new social and financial antagonisms – corresponded in time with the climax of the older and more intense antagonisms of race and religion in Ireland. The prevailing spirit of the day was wrath and violence: many even of the female advocates of Votes for Women – the most important of the many political cross-currents of that distracted era – resorted to organized outrage on persons and property to advertise their cause, with the result that their cause lost ground. The women who made outrage a method of persuasion were distinguished by the title of 'Suffragettes' from the law-abiding women suffragists. Labour troubles, too, were acute and strikes constant; individual strife between the vast national organizations of capital and labour in mines and railways were a new feature of life in the last years before the War. As in the Middle Ages, great corporations were threatening to become stronger than the unorganized community.

But Lloyd George, the stormy petrel, loved to ride such waves. It was in the midst of these furies, concentrated largely upon his head, that he passed the complex and unpopular Health Insurance Act, a contribution scheme to insure the whole working population against sickness, which has since proved a blessing to the working classes, and no ill friend to the doctors, who at first looked at it with natural misgivings, sharpened by political prejudice. Two of the most valuable of the social reforms of the Twentieth Century, Balfour's Education Act of 1902 and Lloyd George's Insurance Act of 1912, were highly unpopular and injured the Governments that passed them; both were rendered possible by the work and wisdom of the great public servant Sir Robert Morant, and by the stubbornness of the two Ministers who forced them through Parliament. Though Balfour and Lloyd George were mutual opposites in politics, character, tradition, and intellect, they both liked to go out in a storm. It seemed impossible in 1912 that they should ever be friends. But strange things were lurking behind the clouds ahead.

The passing of the Parliament Act had opened the way for the placing of Home Rule on the Statute Book; instead of absolute rejection, two years' delay was the worst the Lords could now do against any measure sent up to them. In these circumstances, the two parties in Britain should have united to dictate to the two communities in Ireland a reasonable settlement – Home Rule, with the Protestant part of Ulster excluded. But tempers were so raw after the Parliament Act struggle, that it was difficult for good sense to break in. Ireland, whose case had long demanded impartial consideration as an Imperial problem, had for a whole generation been used as the stalking horse of British party interests and passions. The Conservative party, now led by Bonar Law, more stubborn on this issue than even his predecessor Balfour, openly encouraged Ulster to arm for resistance under Sir Edward Carson's sincere and dogged leadership. The Liberal Government on their side ought to have announced that the six Protestant counties of Ulster should be allowed to contract out from Home Rule. That is what Asquith intended to happen, but he did not say so clearly, for fear of losing Redmond's votes on which he now depended in the Commons. On neither side was British statesmanship in this matter on a level with the circumstances, and Nemesis descended upon all concerned. It is true that at late last the issue as between parties in England had been narrowed down to the degree and method of 'contracting out' of Home Rule to be permitted to the several Counties of Ulster. But even so there was not final agreement, and meanwhile the passions aroused in Ireland were by this time so strong – Sinn Fein gaining ground on constitutional Nationalism, and Orange feeling worked to its height, and both sides illegally armed – that civil war seemed unavoidable. Then suddenly, in August 1914, a greater quarrel and a more terrible danger reunited in a week Liberal with Conservative, capital with labour, man with still unenfranchised woman, and even, for a few months of tense and novel emotion, Ireland with England and Orange with Green.

CHAPTER VI

End of Isolation. Lansdowne and Grey. The Ententes with France and Russia. Haldane's Army Reforms. Europe's drift to War. 1914

FROM Canning to Salisbury the 'splendid isolation' of Great Britain served her interests well. She avoided a whole series of continental wars – except the adventure of the Crimea, which was of her own seeking and the consequences of which were easily liquidated. In the then state of scientific invention and warlike armament, the Navy was still her sure and sufficient shield, and for a hundred years after Trafalgar no Power attempted to build a rival fleet. The Balance of Power in Europe was adequately adjusted without Britain's make-weight, and the independence of the small countries of the Rhine Delta was not seriously threatened. During the Franco-Prussian War of 1870, Gladstone had, in pursuance of the terms and the policy of the Treaty of 1839, announced Britain's intention to take arms against either French or German violation of Belgium's neutrality, and on that occasion the warning was enough. In spite of Colonial difficulties with France, and Asiatic difficulties with Russia, Salisbury in the eighties and nineties saw no necessity to attach our fortunes to those of the Triple Alliance of Germany, Austria-Hungary, and Italy. We stood by ourselves alone, safe behind the shield of supreme naval power. But some, including Joseph Chamberlain, were beginning to be anxious.

With the new century, and the jealousies and hatreds let loose by the South African War, the period of 'splendid isolation' came to an end. The first steps on the new road were taken by Lord Lansdowne as Foreign Minister under Balfour. To their thinking, the number, size, and ubiquity of armed forces by land and sea all over the world rendered it necessary that we should have at least some defined friendships. An understanding with America would have been preferred, but her traditional policy of isolation
1902 rendered it out of the question. So the Japanese Alliance was made, originally to counterbalance the advance of Russia on to the shores of the Pacific, and to prevent the partition of China by Russia, Germany, and France, which America disliked as much as we, but would do nothing active to prevent. The Japanese Alliance also enabled us to dispense with the creation of an immense naval establishment in the Pacific. Britain's friendship served to keep the ring for the rise of the first 'coloured' Great Power, to which the other European Powers were hostile. Japan's
1904 triumph over Russia in war had many reactions upon India and on the world at large. Ten years later, the Japanese, faithful to their alliance with us, safeguarded the waters and coasts of the Far East against German designs during the Great War, besides giving effective help in the Mediterranean.

More important even than the Japanese Treaty was the simultaneous evolution in our relations with France and the German Empire respectively. The state of the Balance of Power in Europe was again giving cause for anxiety. Germany was more and more overshadowing Europe by her unparalleled military preparations, based on ever-increasing population, wealth, and trained intelligence; and moreover she was adding to her predominant army a fleet built in rivalry to our own. To Britain the sea was the primary consideration of her very existence, as it was not to Germany. It was this naval rivalry which altered Britain's attitude to the European Powers.

During the last twenty years of the Nineteenth Century we had been in constantly recurring danger of war with France or Russia, owing to the clash of our interests with theirs at various points in Asia and Africa. In the first years of the new century it was felt that the chances of such a war, with the power of Germany on the flank of the combatants, were too great to be any longer risked. If Germany had been ready to make friends with Britain and share the business of guarding the *status quo* and the peace of the world, a German Entente might have been made. But tentative suggestions of this kind by Chamberlain and others had been rejected by Germany; and her growing hostility to us and her naval rivalry were evident. There was therefore no alternative but to remove by agreement our specific causes of quarrel with the French Republic and the Russian Tsar.

In 1904 Lord Lansdowne settled the outstanding differences between Great Britain and France in Egypt, Morocco, and Newfoundland by a Treaty of Agreement on these points, and so permitted the growth of the *entente cordiale*, not yet an alliance, and not on our part hostile to Germany – unless indeed Germany would have it so. King Edward VII's popularity in France during his holiday visits helped to make an atmosphere propitious to the new friendship, but he had nothing to do with the initial choice of the policy by his Ministers.

Sir Edward Grey succeeded Lansdowne at the Foreign Office in December 1905. It was a moment of European crisis, though the English people, intent on its General Election, scarcely knew it. Germany was threatening France on the question of Morocco. A clause in Lansdowne's agreement with France of the year before pledged us to support France diplomatically on that issue, in return for her recognition of our status in Egypt. Grey, in agreement with the Prime Minister Campbell-Bannerman, implemented this promise, and stood by France on the Moroccan question. The other nations of Europe, except Austria-Hungary, took the same line at the Algeciras Conference early in 1906, and so did President Theodore Roosevelt on behalf of the United States. Germany receded.

There had been more behind than the Moroccan question. Germany had resented Lansdowne's settlement of Anglo-French quarrels in 1904 and wished to show France that she could not depend on England; Grey showed her that she could. It was the testing of the Entente. If the return of the Liberals to power in December 1905 had meant, as a large part of the Liberal party wished, the return of Britain to her old isolation, France could not have resisted, and must either have fallen in war or become the vassal of Germany. Russia at that moment was crushed by her defeat in the war with Japan, and was ripe for internal revolt. Germany aimed at drawing first Russia and then France into her orbit. Britain would then be at her mercy. We were no longer in a position to defy a united Europe as in Nelson's day; submarines, aircraft, and long-distance guns were depriving us of our insular safety. Yet the danger of such a European combination under German leadership was actual. In July 1905 the Kaiser and the Tsar had met in the Tsar's yacht off the Baltic island of Björkö, and had there signed a Treaty which put Russia on the side of Germany, by an agreement avowedly aimed against England, and as dangerous to her as Tilsit.

The Treaty of Björkö had indeed been torn up, but its policy might be renewed at any moment, and then France would be forced to follow suit, if Britain's pledge of support to her proved valueless. Grey's action over the Moroccan crisis prevented any such development. After Algeciras (1906) France and Russia both saw that Britain's friendship was worth having.

Grey could not, however, positively pledge England to convert the diplomatic support promised by the Lansdowne Agreement into military support, in case of war. The English people would not be pledged beforehand, until a *casus belli* arose. Grey had not the power to turn the Entente into an Alliance, any time between 1906 and 1914. Moreover even if his colleagues, his party, and his country had consented to an obligation so definite – and that was far from being the case – Grey's own view was that a pledge to take part in the next war might encourage France and Russia to more intransigent policies and engage us in a struggle not essentially defensive. All that Grey had either the wish or the power to do was to let Germany know the great likelihood that England would stand by France in arms, if France were attacked. This he did.

On the other hand, war had been so near over the Moroccan issue, that in January 1906 Grey had sanctioned 'Military Conversations' between the British and French staffs. To contemplate a contingent possibility of British intervention and yet have no war plan ready would have been madness, for while Britannia was fumbling with her sword, the Germans might be in Paris in a month. The Military Conversations of January 1906 were amply justified, as events of August 1914 were to show. Campbell-Bannerman ought no doubt to have told his Cabinet about them at once, but both he and Grey regarded them as a purely departmental question. In that view they were wrong: they should have told the Cabinet. But it would have been a far more unpardonable mistake not to have any plans for a war that might break out and destroy France in a few weeks, if England had made no preparations to come at once to her help.

On the basis of the Military Conversations with France in 1906, was built up Haldane's great army reform of the next years. The Military Conversations arranged a detailed plan for the immediate dispatch of an Expeditionary Force to France in case a war should arise in which England decided to take a hand. One part of Haldane's Army Reforms of 1906–12 was the creation of such an Expeditionary Force of 150,000 men of all arms, ready at a moment's notice to go to France by routes prearranged with the French authorities. It was this preparation that enabled our forces to arrive just in time to save Paris from the German onrush in 1914.

Haldane also created the Territorial Force, turning the old 'Volunteers' and 'Yeomanry' into effective fighting units. Kitchener, on service abroad, did not realize that the amateurishness of the old 'Volunteers' was a thing of the past, and when called to the War Office, in 1914, refused to make use of the Territorial organization. But he used the men whom it had trained.

In the same years the Officers' Training Corps was established and a General Staff to think out military plans. The army at last had an official 'brain'.

In 1907 Grey made an Anglo-Russian agreement to remove the specific causes of quarrel with Russia, as Lansdowne three years before had removed the causes of quarrel with France. With German unfriendliness and naval power increasing every year, it would have been the height of folly to drift into war with Russia. Yet unless the Persian question were settled by agreement, war would come on that issue. The Russians had Northern Persia already in their grip, and designed to push on to the Persian Gulf and to the Afghan frontier; we had old and great interests on the Gulf, and the protection of the independence of Afghanistan was regarded as essential to the safety of India. The Persians could not defend themselves against Russia. We had either to leave all Persia and the Gulf to the Russians, or fight a war with them on behalf of Persian independence, or else come to an agreement as to our relative spheres of influence. Grey chose the latter course, in which he was warmly supported by Campbell-Bannerman and by Morley as Indian Secretary. But the Anglo-Russian agreement was attacked by the advanced half of the

Liberals and by the Labour party, as showing neglect of Persian interests and friendliness with the autocracy of Russia. This section of opinion was unwilling to increase armaments, yet anxious to pursue a policy in defence of Persia which must have led to a war with Russia – with Germany and the German fleet on our flank.

Grey's Anglo-Russian agreement was the only possible course consistent with our own safety. Yet it was a bad best. It prevented a Russo-German Alliance like that of Björkö which would have overwhelmed us, but it gave to the German public the sense of being 'encircled'.

The charge that Great Britain deliberately fostered a policy of 'encirclement' of Germany, though often repeated in that country, does not stand any test of truth. Grey, in the earnest pursuit of better relations, offered Germany outlets into Asia and Africa, by the Bagdad railway agreement and the agreement that Germany should have her share in case of Portugal's sale of Colonies. That was not 'encirclement'. Moreover in the part that Grey so often played as disinterested mediator in the Balkan troubles, he carefully discouraged the creation of a Balkan or a Slav bloc against Austria-Hungary, and he declined to oppose the dominating influence that Germany herself acquired at Constantinople.

Politically, therefore, there was no encirclement. And militarily it was precisely Germany's central position that gave her such immense and almost decisive advantage when war came. The encirclement, such as it was, was of Germany's own making. She had encircled herself by alienating France over Alsace-Lorraine, Russia by her support of Austria-Hungary's anti-Slav policy in the Balkans, England by building her rival fleet. She had created with Austria-Hungary a military bloc in the heart of Europe, so powerful and yet so restless that her neighbours on each side had no choice but either to become her vassals or to stand together for protection. The accident that the Teutons lay between the French and the Slavs put the Germans by the nature of geography in the centre of a 'circle', thereby rendering their military power all the more formidable. They used their central position to create fear on all sides, in order to gain their diplomatic ends. And then they complained that on all sides they had been encircled. When Bismarck, in evil hour, made the Alliance with Austria-Hungary, he began a system that ere long caused the Franco-Russian Alliance to follow. Germany thus began the fatal system of Alliances which prevented the 'localization' of any future quarrel between two great European powers, and in the end dragged more than half the world into a war begun on a Balkan issue.

By 1914 Grey had removed by agreement every specific cause of quarrel between England and Germany; but neither he nor any man could remove the fact of the over-great German power which in case of European war bade fair to destroy the independence of France and Belgium, and face England with a Continent united under vassalage to Berlin. As the years 1906–14 went on, the increase of the German fleet in rivalry to ours, and crisis after crisis of sabre-rattling on the Continent, partially awakened the English people to the dangers of the situation. But at no moment was the nation willing to convert the Entente with France and Russia into Alliance. Everyone was alarmed by Germany and her fleet, but this country was unwilling to decide beforehand what her action would be until the actual occasion should arise.

There were two storm centres whence war might break loose over the world – the Balkans and Morocco. In 1911 a second Moroccan crisis arose out of the Algeciras settlement of 1906. The dispute was known as 'Agadir', after the Moroccan port to which the Germans sent a warship. After several weeks of danger, during which Britain again supported France, the affair was settled by compromise: France secured the recognition of the rights she claimed in Morocco by ceding some Colonial territory elsewhere to the Germans.

The Agadir settlement of the Moroccan question removed the last direct cause of dispute as between France and Germany themselves. But their allies might yet fall out and drag them into war. For there remained the Balkans, and in the Balkan question was involved the fate of the Austro-Hungarian Empire: its rule was extended in Bosnia over Yugoslavs, and the free Yugoslavs in Serbia therefore desired the break-up of the Empire of the Hapsburgs, in order to unite their nationals under their flag. The hostility between Vienna and Belgrade was intense. And Germany thought herself obliged on every occasion to support her ally Austria-Hungary, and Russia to support the Slav interest in the Balkans.

Crisis after crisis arose in this region, each time nearly leading to a world war. The expulsion of the Turks from Macedonia 1912
and Thrace by the armies of Serbia, Greece, and Bulgaria was long overdue and in itself desirable, but it greatly increased the tension between Austria-Hungary and her southern neighbours. For Serbia, after her victory over the Turks, emerged as a military power of proved value, her ambitions now directed northwards to free

all Yugoslavs still under Austrian rule. To maintain the threatened territories of the Empire intact, the rulers of Austria-Hungary thought it incumbent on them to crush the Serbs. War on this issue was just averted in 1913 because Grey used his good offices as mediator, and Germany on that occasion helped the work of peace. Next year the outcome was different.

The atrocious murder of the Austrian Archduke Francis Ferdinand at Sarajevo on 28 June 1914 was closely connected with the agitation conducted in Serbia for the redemption of Bosnian Yugoslavs. It was inevitable that Vienna would exact guarantees that this agitation should come to an end. Unfortunately the statesmen and soldiers in charge of Austro-Hungarian policy were determined not merely to get such guarantees, but to seize the opportunity of the Sarajevo murder to annihilate Serbia by war, even at the risk of the interference of Russia, whom they trusted Germany to keep off. Germany was therefore deeply concerned and her rulers ought to have insisted on their right to be consulted by their ally. Unfortunately the Kaiser and his Chancellor, Bethmann-Hollweg, though not really desiring war, gave Vienna a 'blank cheque' on 5 July to send what Ultimatum she wished to Belgrade.

When the Ultimatum appeared on 23 July, it surprised the Kaiser and the whole world by its extravagance: such demands had never been made of an independent State: yet Serbia did accept nine tenths. A European Conference could easily have bridged the remaining difference. Grey urgently pressed on Germany the necessity of such mediation. But the Kaiser, though he had not approved of his ally's ultimatum, refused any Conference at all and declared that the question was a local affair between Austria-Hungary and Serbia with which neither Russia nor any other country was concerned. Such words meant war, for Russia's whole policy would be stultified by permitting the destruction of Serbia's independence; she began the slow process of her mobilization. Germany, by this time in the hands of her military men who could think only of their time-tables of war, sent ultimatums to Russia and to her ally France. At the beginning of August the huge strength of the German armies rolled, not eastward against Russia, but westward against France, through innocent Belgium.

Thus the quarrel, though it had broken out on Eastern questions which did not concern Britain, threatened at the very outset to put an end to the independence of France and Belgium, in circumstances which would have prevented those countries from ever raising their heads again, otherwise than as vassals of Germany.

The victory of the Central Powers would have meant the subjection of Europe to an Empire better calculated to survive and rule in perpetuity than ever Napoleon's had been. The very virtues of the German people, as the servants of their rulers' ambitions, made the danger of permanent slavery for Europe extreme.

Sir Edward Grey had made every effort to avert the war, and thereby helped to win for Britain and her Allies the moral sympathy of a large part of mankind, particularly in America. But when those efforts failed, self-preservation dictated that we should not permit the Channel Ports, the Netherlands, and indeed all Europe, to fall into vassalage to a power that was already openly our rival at sea. The violation of Belgian neutrality and the invaders' treatment of Belgian resistance was a drama that brought home, on a wave of generous emotion, the dreadful facts and necessities of the hour to the unwilling mind of the British public, which craved for nothing but peace.

Up to the moment of the invasion of Belgium, in the first days of August, British opinion had been divided as to the necessity of taking part in a European war. Neutralist feeling at the end of July was very strong, especially in the City, in the North of England, and in the Liberal and Labour parties. Half the Cabinet, headed by Mr Lloyd George, was neutralist. It would therefore have been utterly impossible for Grey, as is sometimes suggested in the retrospect, to threaten Germany with our participation in war a day earlier than he did. Any premature attempt in July to commit Great Britain to fight would have led to the break-up of the Cabinet, and the division of the country at the moment of its greatest peril. Such a disaster nearly occurred, and was only averted by the wisdom of Asquith, who held together his colleagues and his countrymen. In that week of tumult and alarm, the heated mass of opinion might have exploded into fragments flying in opposite directions. The danger of national division came to an end as a result of the actual invasion of Belgium, and on 4 August Great Britain went to war as a united country on behalf of her Treaty commitments to protect Belgian neutrality. Belgium was not the only reason why we had to fight or perish; but it was the reason why we were able to strike as a united people, in time, but only just in time, to prevent the fall of Paris and the Channel Ports into the German power.

CHAPTER VII

The War and the Peace. Between the Wars

A BRIEF summary of the leading events of the War may be a useful prelude to remarks on its general characteristics.

The long-prepared plan of the German war lords was to hurl their main attack through neutral Belgium upon Paris, crush the French resistance at a blow, and then turn round and deal with the more slowly mobilizing forces of Russia. It came within an inch of success. The French Generals, Joffre and Foch, instead of preparing to meet the coming blow at the north of their line, began a rash offensive in Lorraine that was bloodily repulsed. Meanwhile the German armies trampled across Belgium, punishing resistance with a calculated 'frightfulness' that was meant to terrorize enemies and neutrals, and sounded the new, ruthless note of modern war. The treatment of innocent Belgium rallied England to join the fight as a united nation, and struck answering chords in America.

The British military chiefs, who had been left unacquainted with the French plans, had taken a more correct view of German intentions than their allies. The 'Expeditionary Force' prepared by Haldane, nearly 100,000 strong, crossed the Channel without the loss of a man or of a minute, and stood in the path of the main German advance as it emerged from Belgium. The British were overwhelmed by enormous superiority in numbers, but fought delaying actions at Mons and Le Cateau which at once established the reputation of our soldiership in the new war. Then followed the British 'retreat from Mons'; the French also were falling back along the whole long front, and the Germans confidently expected to enter Paris in another week. All seemed lost, but then happened, for very natural causes, the 'miracle of the Marne'.

Joffre and Foch, after the great error which had cost France so dear in the first month of the war, kept their heads in apparently desperate circumstances, and brilliantly retrieved the situation by a counter-attack, taking advantage of the want of communication between the different German armies which had advanced at different speeds. The invaders were defeated by the
Sept. 1914 French and British at the Battle of the Marne and forced to retreat from the neighbourhood of Paris. But they dug themselves in on enemy territory, retaining Belgium and a large slice of France, including 80 per cent of her coal and almost all her iron. But the Channel ports were left outside the German lines, so that

the allied armies in France were in direct communication with England and her supplies. In that posture matters remained for the next four years. 'Trench warfare' had begun. The opposing lines from the Channel to the Swiss border, though often swaying and sagging deep, first one way then another, never actually broke until the autumn of 1918. But to maintain that western deadlock, there were poured out, in constant attack and counter-attack, millions of lives and the accumulated wealth of the past century of European progress.

Could the deadlock in the West be broken by operations in the East? The Russian masses had invaded East Prussia in the early weeks of the war and so contributed to the result of the Marne by drawing off two German army corps from the West. But even before these supports could arrive, the battle of Tannenberg had 30 Aug. 1914 been fought: the invaders of Prussia were defeated with a loss of 300,000 men, at the hands of Hindenburg and his Chief of Staff, Ludendorff, henceforth the Dioscuri of the German War.

After Tannenberg the war between the armies of Russia and those of Germany and Austria-Hungary was continued on a gigantic scale. There was less of trench warfare in the East than in the West. For three years the struggle swayed forward and back-war over great stretches of country, chiefly over the prostrate body of Poland. Sometimes the Russians had success, but they were fatally handicapped by their want of arms and supplies, due to the primitive civilization of their country, and the ineptitude and corruption of the Tsarist government, staggering to its final doom. If the British could have obtained a direct and easy route to Russia her deficiencies in armament might have been better supplied. But the Baltic was closed, and the attempt failed to open a route through the Dardanelles into the Black Sea.

The year 1915, with the attack on the Dardanelles and Constantinople, was indeed the one chance that England had of achieving victory by any method save exhaustion of the combatants. Success at this strategic point might perhaps have shortened the war by two years. Turkey had joined the Central Oct. 1914 Powers, thereby involving England in an immense increase in her liabilities, for she had to defend against the Turks not only Egypt and the Suez Canal by operations in Palestine, but the Persian Gulf and its oil supplies by operations in Mesopotamia. Moreover the entry of Turkey into the war tempted Bulgaria to avenge her own griefs by an attack on Serbia. If Bulgaria marched on the enemy's side, the defence of Serbia against the overwhelming forces of Austria-Hungary would become impossible. But if, before

Bulgaria threw in her lot with the enemy, England could force the Dardanelles and capture Constantinople, Bulgaria would almost certainly take our side instead, and the whole of the Balkan States would be mobilized against Austria-Hungary. For these 1915 reasons the attack on the Dardanelles was attempted. But it failed, with the result that Bulgaria joined the Central Powers, Serbia was overrun, and for the next three years the French and English armies could do nothing but hold on to the Macedonian port of Salonika as a base for future advance, if and when the enemy power should begin to fail.

On the other hand Italy, in May 1915, entered the war on the side of the Allies, and a 'trench warfare' of a kind similar to that of the Western front was established in the foothills of the Alps, holding so large a part of the Austrian forces that the worst consequences of the failure in the Balkans were avoided. Austria-Hungary survived till 1918, but was unable, owing to the Italian pressure, to help Germany on the Western front, or to push the advantages gained in the Balkans and in Turkey.

The British Cabinet, led by Asquith, had ably conducted the initial crisis of the war. A financial crash had been avoided, the country had been rallied in a united Home Front, the navy had done its initial work well, the Expeditionary Force had been landed promptly and safely in France. The Dardanelles was the one great failure, due to divided counsels, resulting in premature and ill-supported attempts that gave the enemy warning. Soldiers, sailors, and statesmen must all share in that responsibility. If no man was the hero of the occasion, no man was solely to blame. But we lacked a Chatham or a Marlborough to give the guidance of genius to the World War.

Apart from the Dardanelles the affair at sea had been well managed. The Expeditionary Force had reached France safely and at once; enemy cruisers had been hunted down and destroyed in all the seas of the world. The Japanese Alliance secured the Far Eastern Seas. Admiral Sturdee sank Spee's German squadron off the Falkland Islands in October 1914. The Grand Fleet under Jellicoe was provided with quarters at Scapa Flow, which proved safe even under modern conditions of submarine work; thence for four years it watched the enemy Grand Fleet in its harbours on the North German coast; the situation corresponded to Nelson's watch off Toulon, but owing to modern conditions the watch had to be conducted at a much greater distance. Only May once the German Fleet emerged in force and the Battle of Jutland 1916 ensued. The result of that action, which involved severe losses on both sides, was that the German Fleet escaped, but that it never attempted to put to sea again.

The same year 1916 saw much slaughter but no real change upon the Western front. The great attempt of the Crown Prince's armies to end the war by breaking through the French defence of Verdun failed after long months of effort. The first large-scale offensive of the newly raised British armies on the Somme also gained no substantial ground.

After Jutland the Germans turned their attention to the submarine campaign, which in April 1917 had attained such success that England was in danger of starvation and the allied cause of collapse. But the situation was saved in the following months by the heroism of the merchant service, the application of new scientific instruments to the location of submarines, the convoy system, and the entry of the United States into the war as a result of the submarine campaign against their own shipping. Meanwhile the British 'blockade' was wearing down the stubborn resistance of the German peoples.

April 1917

Indeed it is not improbable that Germany would have been defeated in 1917 if Russia had not that year gone out of the war as a result of her Bolshevik Revolution following on her repeated defeats in the field, due largely to governmental incompetence. The period between Russia's retirement from the struggle and the advent of the American armies in Europe in the summer of 1918, was one of great danger for the Allies. In April 1917 the French offensive at Chemin des Dames proved a disastrous failure, and there was talk of mutiny and revolution. The pressure on France was relieved by the tremendous offensive of Haig on the Ypres front in the gloomy battle of Passchendaele, fought all autumn long in rain and mud; after frightful losses it registered little positive advance. The tragic and dangerous year 1917 was cheered at Christmas-time by the capture of Jerusalem from the Turks by the British army under Allenby advancing from Egypt. In the following year Allenby conquered all Palestine, entered Damascus and destroyed the Turkish military power. It was in these campaigns that 'Lawrence of Arabia' won his great reputation as leader of Arab irregulars.

The year 1918 would see the gradual arrival in France of the armies now being raised and drilled in America. If Germany had been wise she would have negotiated for a tolerable peace before they arrived. But her military men would not cut their losses, and were still for 'world conquest or downfall'. The destinies of Europe were in the hands of Ludendorff, who underrated the potentialities of American military power, and who hoped to conquer France beforehand by a great offensive in the spring. Owing to the falling out of Russia the Germans had for the moment a superiority in numbers in the West which tempted them to their ruin. Mismanagement, partly due to Lloyd George's distrust of Haig's tendency to attack, left the British force in France weaker than it need have been when the sudden blow fell upon it in March 1918. Perfect weather helped the Germans in their last mighty effort, which thrust back the English and the French very much as in September 1914. Paris and the Channel Ports were again in imminent danger. But the spirit of resistance in the French and British armies was not broken, and with the approach of summer they were cheered by the constant arrival of regiments of young Americans, eager for the war which had become so fearful a burden to the surviving veterans of Europe. The tide turned. A better cooperation between the allied armies was at length secured by making Foch Commander-in-Chief.

But the glory of the counter-offensive that ended the war lay chiefly with the decision of Haig and the efficiency of the British Army. The British Government did not expect the war to end till 1919 or even 1920, and to the last Lloyd George remained suspicious of Haig's love of the offensive, which this time at any rate proved right. The old continental saying that the English only win one battle in a war, and that is the last one, has a certain verisimilitude in the light of the events of August to November 1918. Ludendorff's offensive in the spring had exhausted Germany and used up her spiritual and material power of further resistance, sapped by our naval blockade. On the Italian, Turkish, and Balkan fronts the allies of Germany were defeated and put out of action. Turkey and Bulgaria were conquered. Austria-Hungary dissolved, by a series of revolutions, into her component racial parts. Even Ludendorff's iron nerve was broken and he demanded an armistice. The flight of the Kaiser to Holland, the German revolution, and the Armistice of November 11 followed.

Some points of comparison with the conditions and methods of the Napoleonic Wars may be a not unfitting way to end this long History of our land.

First, there was the difference of geographical situation. Jacobin and Napoleonic France attempted to conquer Europe from the base of its North-West angle; the Germanic powers made the same attempt from the more formidable strategic centre which gave to them 'the inner line' of battle against all comers – Russian, Balkan, Italian, French, and English-speaking. Britain's communications with her allies in the East, particularly with Russia, were therefore more liable to interruption by the enemy. Also, in case the enemy won the war, it would be far more easy for the 'Central Powers' to hold Europe and Western Asia in permanent subjection than it would have been for the successors of Napoleon, who could not have kept the Germans down for ever, even if the battle of Leipzig had gone the other way.

As regards the strategy and tactics of the two struggles, Britain's part in both was to supply the money and maritime power of the Alliance, and to blockade the enemy by sea. But in the later war we also undertook another duty: we 'paid in person', sending over armies numbered in their millions, and counting our dead at a million and our wounded at over two million in the four years. In the French wars from 1793 to 1815 our military effort, though important, had been small, and our average annual loss of life not above five thousand. Against Germany our average annual loss of life was nearly two hundred and fifty thousand. We found it necessary to make the greater military effort on the later occasion, partly because of the more formidable strength and geographical position of the 'Central Powers'; if once we allowed the Germans to overrun all Europe as Napoleon had done, we should never get them out again.

But our fuller participation in the war by land was dictated also by the changes in military and naval weapons and tactics, which had already shaken the old security of our island position. The possessor of the Channel Ports could, by long-distance guns, aeroplanes, and submarines, threaten our existence much more formidably than Napoleon and his flat-bottomed boats at Boulogne. So the British people themselves, as soldiers, took a leading part in the decisive operations of the war. The modern Leipzig and Waterloo consisted of a continuous battle, fought day and night for four years along a line hundreds of miles long. Modern financial credit, and means of transporting men, food, and warlike stores, enabled the opposing nations to maintain millions of fighters continuously in the trenches, year after year, on each of the principal fronts.

The most marked difference between the two wars lay in armaments and tactics: the long Napoleonic wars began and ended with the Brown-Bess musket and close-order fighting of British line and French column. Invention continued all the time to be applied by England to industry, but was not applied by any country to war. Wellington's weapons and tactics were much the same as Marlborough's, Nelson's ships much the same as Blake's. Napoleon recognized the relation to war of modern administration and organization, but he was fortunately blind to the military possibilities of modern science. But on the later occasion the methods of warfare, which in 1914 began with all the latest mechanical appliances and in Germany at least with the fullest national organization, were revolutionized several times over in the course of four short years. Not only did trench-warfare take the place of the war of movement, but the development of aerial and submarine warfare on a great scale, and the invention of gas-warfare by the Germans and of tank-warfare by the British, are changes without any parallel among the slow-witted and unscientific wars of Napoleon. Science was harnessed, and the whole civil population was mobilized. Our ancestors in wartime lived safe behind Nelson's shield, happily producing Scott's lays and novels, Wordsworth's poems, Constable's and Turner's pictures; but now the civil population of Great Britain was fain to devote its whole energy and brains for four years to the business of slaying and being slain.

In the days of Pitt and Castlereagh we increased our Colonial Empire at the expense of France and her allies, and we did so again at the expense of Germany a hundred years later. But the Colonies had taken no part in the earlier struggle, for in Pitt's day the First British Empire had already been lost and the Second was still in its infancy. A hundred years later it was fully grown. There was indeed no machinery of Imperial Federation to bid the Empire march into line, but by free individual choice, Canada, Australia, New Zealand, and Anglo-Dutch South Africa took each its full share in the whole long contest. Between them they raised overseas contingents of a million and a half men. When the war was over, each Dominion insisted on a full recognition of its nationhood. They claimed individual representation in the League of Nations, and the right to retain those German colonies they had themselves taken in war. And finally, in 1931, the Statute of Westminister has given legal force to the long-established custom that the Parliament of Great Britain should legislate for the Dominions only at their own request. Laws affecting the succession to the Crown can be altered only with the concurrence of each of the Dominions, and the King can take no advice about appointments or other action in the Dominions except from Dominion statesmen. In the post-war world it is no longer Parliament but the Crown that links the Empire, in symbolism, in loyalty, and in law.

India in the time of Pitt and Bonaparte had been the scene of the final struggle against French influence among the native Courts and armies. But India in 1914–15 sent great bodies of troops, enthusiastic to take part in the contest. Unfortunately in India, Egypt, and Ireland the protracted and deadly character of the War gave rise to unrest and political exacerbation of which the early months had shown no sign.

The attitude of Britain to Ireland during the War was at heart friendly and very different from the spirit of 1795–1800. But there was sad mismanagement. The golden moment in the autumn of 1914 was missed when Kitchener refused to make sympathetic use of the first outburst of Irish Nationalist readiness to volunteer for service overseas. In Easter 1916 the Sinn Fein rising in Dublin was followed by the execution of its leaders, which turned them into martyrs of the Irish people and hastened the conversion of the island from Redmond's Home Rule Policy to the Sinn Fein demand for a Republic. This change of opinion was complete by the end of the War, and led, after a disgraceful and bloody interlude, to the Treaty of 1921, which established the Irish Free State as a Dominion; the six Protestant counties of Ulster had, a few months before, obtained a Home Rule system of their own together with representation in the Westminster Parliament.

Since the War, Egypt has become an independent State, though in close alliance with Great Britain. And India has been set on the path of self-government. For although the Empire has been governed since 1918 mainly by Conservative statesmen, their Imperial policy has been extremely liberal. The old methods of Anglo-Saxon domination was shown, during the War, to belong to a bygone age. South Africa was saved and the neighbouring German territories overrun by the Dominion force under Botha and Smuts, who only a dozen years before had been our enemies in the field.

Relations with the United States during the War were subject to somewhat the same general conditions as in Napoleon's time, but owing to wiser management and a better spirit, took an opposite turn. On both occasions, the interests of England as the great blockading Power necessarily clashed with those of the neutral merchant Power, desirous of sending her goods as usual to the European market. But whereas the Perceval Ministry had acted as though war with the United States were a matter of indifference, and had idly drifted into that catastrophe, no such mistake was made by Sir Edward Grey, who sacrificed points of real military value in permitting the passage of cotton and other articles of value to the enemy, in order to prevent an early explosion of American opinion against us. The Germans did the rest. Owing to the careful methods of British blockade-diplomacy, the pro-Ally feeling in the United States and the German submarine attack on American persons and shipping were given time to operate, and draw the great neutral into the contest on our side.

Blockade conditions differed in several vital respects from those of Napoleonic times. It is true that our blockade of the enemy's principal Fleet, though conducted at long distance from Scapa Flow, was at least as effective as Nelson's close watch off Brest and Toulon in stopping all chance of invasion and in paralysing the enemy's great ships. But the Napoleonic privateers and frigates that skirmished against British commerce in spite of Nelson, were as nothing to the German submarine, which in the latter part of the War threatened to starve England into surrender. New methods of fighting the new danger were devised and carried out with a scientific efficiency wholly modern, and an old-fashioned skill and courage at sea of which the Royal Navy and the Merchant Service had not lost the secret.

England no longer fed herself, as in Napoleonic times, and the command of the sea was therefore more than ever essential to her very life. But neither, it appeared in the event, could the Central Empires feed themselves for an indefinite period. As the British blockade tightened, especially after the American entry into the War enabled the stranglehold to be increased diplomatically and navally, Germany and Austria began to starve outright. Since the Industrial Revolution, European countries had ceased to be self-supporting in proportion as they were highly civilized and modern. The economic fabric by which the modern millions lived was too international and too delicate to survive for long the injuries done by acts of scientific war. It survived them after a fashion for four years, during which the accumulated wealth and civilization of a hundred years were used up. When the dreadful four years came to an end, Europe was ruined, materially and morally, and could have made very little recovery afterwards. Nothing but the removal of the fear of yet another such war could have enabled the freedom and elasticity of higher civilized life to be resumed.

A remarkable contrast appears between the two historic wars, as regards the position of the working classes and the relations of Britons to one another. Pitt and Castlereagh fought the French as constitutional statesmen, by and through the House of Commons; but it never occurred to them or to any of their colleagues that the common people required, in time of national peril, any management or consideration beyond anti-Jacobin repression and the silencing of Parliamentary Reformers. Nor, as regards the mere winning of the War, did this reckoning prove wrong. But the dangers of the Home Front in 1914–18 had to be met by very different methods. Early in 1918, while the War was still raging, the Fourth Reform Bill was passed by general consent, giving what was practically Manhood Suffrage, and a large instalment of the new principle of Woman's Suffrage; the cessation of outrages by the Suffragettes, and the splendid war work done by women in the factories and elsewhere, had converted many objectors to their enfranchisement. The element of Dictatorship was perhaps stronger than in Pitt's time, as regards the relation of the Government to the House of Commons. But the English Cabinet Ministers of 1914–18 had always to appeal deferentially to the people. For they knew that if munition workers slacked or stopped work, it was no longer in the power of 'magistrates and yeomanry' to make them go on. Since 'the lower orders' had developed into an enfranchised and partially educated democracy, only persuasion could effect what repression had accomplished in the days of the Luddites. In the struggle with Jacobin France, the wartime specific was Combination Acts to suppress Trade Unions; in the struggle with Germany it was the raising of wages to an unprecedented height, and inducing leaders of the Labour party to enter the Coalition Cabinet. The hardships of wartime did not, as a hundred years before, fall with their greatest force on the fortunes of the wage-earner. So long as the common danger of the War lasted, the spirit of brotherhood in the British people of all classes, both at home and in the field, was at any rate much deeper and more widely spread than during the wars against Napoleon.

In another respect the comparison is less favourable to modern times. In the character of the peace dictated to the conquered after victory, the wisely generous treatment of France in 1815 by the aristocratic government of Castlereagh and Wellington at the Treaties of Vienna, compares most favourably with the vindictive treatment of Germany in 1919 by the democracy led by Lloyd George. In both cases defeat had resulted in the fall of the militaristic enemy government which had so long been the dread of Europe. Napoleon was replaced by the Bourbon Monarchy, averse from all the traditions of the fallen regime, and it therefore found a friend in the British Government of the day. So too the Kaiser and Ludendorff were replaced in November 1918 by the

German democratic Republic, to whom it was the interest of the British democracy to give a fair chance for the sake of Europe's future liberty and peace. Unfortunately this was not perceived by England until too late. The rise of the Nazi regime and the unlimited rearmament of Germany have been the direct consequence of the insults and injuries heaped on the conquered at Versailles in 1919.

How those Treaties came to be made, in a passing mood so little representative of England's usual good sense and good nature, requires some examination. When the War began in 1914 the mood of the country was that of an idealist crusade to save Belgium and liberty in Western Europe; great material advantages for ourselves were not envisaged, nor any gross revenge on the enemy. But the increasing atrocity of modern war, in which the Germans took the lead, the introduction of gas warfare, the sinking of merchantmen and hospital ships by submarines, the bombardment of open towns and bombing of cities from the air, aroused the deepest passions; and war propaganda, considered necessary to hold mass opinion on the Home Front concentrated in hate of the enemy, made the utmost of such themes. The popular press, in perpetual frenzy, painted 'the Huns' as scarcely human, and all who thought them so as traitors. The losses, sufferings, and horrors of war, strange to the experience of our happy island, hardened the courage and endurance of men and women into heroism, but also, as the terrible years went by, hardened their hearts and darkened their minds. The prolongation of such a war for four years destroyed the possibility of a reasonable peace, because the terms of peace would have to be decided before these abnormal passions would have time to cool.

If Constantinople had been taken in 1915, it is possible that victory might have been obtained in two years, by mobilizing all the Balkan States against the Central Powers, and opening a free channel of supply to Russia. But Kitchener and the Cabinet failed to give proper timing and support to the spasmodic naval and military attacks on the Dardanelles, and the great opportunity of shortening the War was lost. In consequence of that failure, decision was only reached after a gradual process of exhaustion on the Western Front by the slaughter of millions, and the slow starvation of Austria-Hungary and Germany by the British blockade. When Russia fell out of the Alliance owing to the Bolshevist Revolution in 1917, her place was taken, only just in time, by the United States, unable any longer to condone the sinking of American ships by German submarines.

A Coalition War Ministry of Liberals and Conservatives had been formed under Asquith in the second year of the War. An ultimate though not an immediate consequence of the failure at the Dardanelles in 1915 was the fall of Asquith in December 1916. With him went a liberal element which might have been most useful at the peace-making, but could not survive the stresses of war. Asquith had many qualities as a Prime Minister in wartime, but he needed a great military adviser and he had not found all that was needed in his Secretary of State for War, Kitchener of Khartoum. Kitchener roused the country to an early perception of the length and magnitude of the struggle, and conjured up the voluntary enlistment of 'Kitchener's armies' in the early months, while the country was still unwilling to submit to conscription. He was indeed a great personality and had a great hold over the public imagination, but he had not the elastic mind necessary for the conduct of a world war under modern scientific conditions.

The man who rose to the height of the occasion, at least in the opinion of great masses of his countrymen, was Lloyd George. His activity as Minister of Munitions had made good the original deficiencies of the War Office. His imagination was always at work, his energy was contagious, and the state of courageous excitement in which he dealt with one war problem after another gave more confidence to the man in the street than the exasperating calm of Asquith's stoicism. There will always be widely divergent opinions as to Lloyd George's contribution to the victory, but at least his activity and courage helped to give confidence to the country and energy to its leaders in the last two grim years. He did much to win the War; but he did less than little to save the Peace.

For when at last the German line gave way before Foch's strategy and Haig's attack, and victory came with unexpected suddenness in November 1918, England and France were called upon in an instant to switch their minds from the fierce mood of war to the prudence, foresight, and generosity that peace-making requires. It took long years before France could think sanely, but in a year or two England had recovered her usual good nature and good sense; unfortunately the peace had to be made in the first six months, while the war passions were still aflame in every land. Nor was Lloyd George the man to risk his great popularity and spend his immense influence in a struggle against the passions of the hour, which always had an undue influence on his susceptible and mercurial mind. Moreover the circumstances under which he had replaced Asquith as Prime Minister had led to a breach between him and the major half of the Liberal party during the last two years of war; the Armistice found him in political alliance with the proprietors of certain popular journals, then fiercely calling out for vengeance on German war crimes. And so at the General Election of December 1918 Asquith's followers, who would have stood for moderation in peace-making, were deliberately proscribed by Lloyd George and annihilated at the polls: the Liberal party was rent and destroyed, and has never recovered importance, for the Labour party in later elections step by step took its place.

In the General Election held in these circumstances between the Armistice and the peace-making at Versailles, a House of Commons was returned pledged to make Germany pay for the War. Lloyd George held a huge majority – and the huge majority held Lloyd George. After tying this millstone of a mandate round his own neck, he went to Versailles to help Clemenceau and Wilson give peace to the world. France, who had suffered more, was yet more intent on vengeance than England; and Wilson, meaning well, understood little of realities in Europe, or of opinion in America. Balfour, who was Foreign Minister and 'elder statesman', should have upheld the old traditions of moderation and foresight, but left everything to the Prime Minister during those fatal months at the French capital.

Wilson and Lloyd George did at least prevent France from annexing the German part of the left bank of the Rhine. But Germany undertook by Treaty not to take military occupation of that zone. This wise compromise was obtained from France by a promise that America and England would guarantee the frontiers of France against attack, a promise which America refused to ratify; consequently England also most unwisely declined this obligation for a while, thereby losing for some years all control over the policy of France towards Germany.

Upon the whole, the drawing of European boundaries was not ill done at Versailles. The new Europe consisted of a number of States based on the real principle of nationality. Indeed Poland, and the States that became the heirs of Austria-Hungary, had been formed by the act of their own populations, as a result of the last stage of the War, before ever the statesmen met at Versailles to confirm the change. It was the War, not the Peace, that destroyed the Empire of the Hapsburgs. But the actual boundaries fixed for Poland and Czechoslovakia, though not clearly unjust, were unwisely extensive, for they were certain to be provocative to their near neighbours.

The great error of the Treaty was the harsh treatment of the new German Republic. It should have been the first object of England and France to enable it to survive as a peaceful democracy. But the German nation was humiliated by the dictation of terms on the hardships of which she was not even permitted to plead before the victors; she was kept disarmed while other nations (though not England) remained armed to the teeth; she was forbidden to unite with Austria; she was excluded from the League of Nations; in the matter of Reparations she was treated in a manner so fantastic as to help to ruin her without benefiting her creditors. Finally all her Colonies were taken away. At the end of all previous wars the defeated enemies of England had always retained or received back some at least of their Colonies. The Dominions indeed were not likely to surrender those which they had respectively taken in war, but there were others that the mother country might prudently have returned.

At the same time the League of Nations was set up and was closely associated with the terms of the Treaty. But the spirit of the League of Nations and the spirit of the Treaty of Versailles were utterly incompatible. One would sooner or later undo the other. If Germany had been treated generously, and invited into the League as an equal, the League might have flourished and given real peace to the world. Or if, after the Treaty, England, France, and America had set about to remedy what was wrong in the Treaty, and to support the League in spirit as well as letter, all might yet have been well. But England alone of the great Powers gave support to the true spirit of the League, and made some effort to remedy the grievances of Germany, particularly as regards Reparations. The mood of the unhappy General Election of December 1918, having dictated the Treaty, soon died out in the placable breasts of the English, who hastened to disarm and to put the war memories behind them, trusting with too complete a confidence in the power of the maimed League of Nations to avert the natural consequences both of the War and of the Peace.

But France could not change or forget. She continued for years to harass the German Republic, thus preparing the way for its transformation into the Nazi regime. And America retired into herself. Having been instrumental in pledging Europe to the policy of the League of Nations, she refused at the last moment to join it. Nor would she any longer cooperate in any practical way to preserve peace. It was a vicious circle: her withdrawal made the European anarchy worse, and the European anarchy has made her more determined than ever not to interfere in Europe again. She even withdrew from the Reparations Commission, where her support would have enabled England to restrain France; the French were therefore able to find a quasi-legal excuse for their rash invasion of the German territory of Ruhr in 1923, England vainly protesting. The outcome has been the Germany of Hitler that we know. The other main cause of the rise of the Fascist and Nazi forms of government has been the simultaneous imitation of and reaction against Communism, to which doctrine the success of the Bolshevik Revolution in Russia gave a great impetus throughout the Continent. The outcome of the War of 1914–18 has been to destroy liberty, democracy, and parliaments in the greater part of Europe.

In the years that followed the signature of the Peace Treaties, English policy had the one merit of goodwill, but showed neither foresight nor firmness. Nothing really effective was done to appease German opinion in the earlier years while appeasement was still possible, nor until very late to prepare for the storm when the storm became only too probable.

The English people, in a natural reaction after four years' experience of the unspeakable horrors of modern 'total' war, regarded pacifism and unilateral disarmament as a method of securing peace, and hailed the League of Nations as a machine for making all safe by some magic or automatic process not clearly defined. Alas, if England intended the dictates of the League to be respected, she should have put herself in a position to enforce them, for no other nation had both the strength and the will. If she meant to remain a European power, she should have armed as others were arming. Even after the Nazi Revolution of 1933 – an event ominous enough in all conscience – Germany was allowed, without any corresponding effort on our part, not only to build up her great army again but to obtain a temporary predominance in the air, to militarize the Rhine Land contrary to Treaty, and to make upon it the Siegfried Line to block us out of Central Europe. At the same time Italy, whose geographic position controlled our other contacts with Austria and the Balkans, was driven into the arms of Germany by the feeble application of 'economic sanctions' against Mussolini's Abyssinian aggression (1935–6): England in that fatal affair would neither abstain from interference nor threaten to fight in earnest. Europe was sacrificed to Abyssinia – and in vain.

Future historians will have the unenviable task of dividing the blame for a long series of errors between the successive governments of the country and the ever varying moods of the opposition and public opinion which those governments too often weakly followed. It was early in 1939, on Hitler's occupation of Prague in violation of the Munich agreement of a few months before, that the British people and Government woke up to the dread realities of the situation into which they had been drifting for twenty years. Even then the pace of rearmament was by no means what the crisis required, and the union of parties and full development of war effort was only effected after six months of actual war. England's future no man can foresee, but she faces danger, even alone, with her old courage: whether she stands or falls, the world's hope of peace and freedom rests on her.

While Foreign Affairs went so ill, Imperial and Home affairs went through some violent crises, but did not do so badly, considering the general bedevilment of the world.

The Labour party has replaced the Liberal party, but has not yet attained the strength to govern the country for a length of time sufficient to leave an impress by its own administration. The Conservative party has become the beneficiary of this change, but on terms of becoming largely liberalized or socialized in its policies both in Imperial and domestic problems. Domestic policies between the two wars were less fierce and bitter than they often were before 1914.

The Twentieth Century has been kept in a perpetual movement and unrest by the headlong progress of inventions, which hurry mankind on, along roads that no one has chosen, a helpless fugitive with no abiding place. The motor-car age has changed life even more than the railway age, and the air age will soon have changed it once more. Meanwhile the motor-car is pouring the town out into the country, a movement that has both its good and its bad sides: but the bad has at present an unnecessary advantage, because the process is conducted haphazard without control by the community. Ribbon development, which is turning the long length of our country roads into streets, is recognized as an evil, but no law is passed that effectually prevents its headlong progress. So, too, the destruction of rural beauty is regretted, but so far the State admits no duty to help in the matter, although now at last it is acting belatedly to try to save what is left of agriculture as an occupation in England in order to obtain food in time of war. Meanwhile, broadcasting is effecting an intellectual and educational revolution which it is too early yet to estimate. Recent years have seen greater changes in the habits and thoughts of Englishmen and the appearance of England than whole centuries before. The most encouraging feature is that, in spite of the frightful handicap of the last War and its consequences, the material well-being of the mass of the inhabitants of England was higher in 1939 than a generation before; and there is therefore hope that in the end man may use his new powers to make his life fuller and happier than of old, if some day an escape is found from totalitarian war and violence.

In this short volume I have tried to set down some aspects of the evolution of life upon this island, since the ages when it lay as nature made it, a green and shaggy forest, half waterlogged, while here and there, on the more habitable uplands, the most progressive animal gathered his kind into camps and societies, to save himself and his offspring and his flocks from wolves and bears and from his fellow-men – down to the very different scene of our own sophisticated times. In the earlier age, man's impotence to contend with nature made his life brutish and brief. To-day his very command over nature, so admirably and marvellously won, has become his greatest peril. Of the future the historian can see no more than others. He can only point like a showman to the things of the past, with their manifold and mysterious message.

CHRONOLOGICAL OUTLINE

FOR TREVELYAN'S HISTORY OF ENGLAND

BY

WILLIAM HUSE DUNHAM, JR

Yale University

BOOK ONE

Chapter I: Iberian and Celt

B.C.

2500–1300 Evidences of trade between England and Spain and Egypt remain. The Iberians inhabited England.

700–300 The Celts invaded and settled in England.
c. 600 : The Gaels or Goidels
c. 325 : The Cymri and Britons

150 The south British tribes had a gold coinage.

Chapter II: Roman Britain, 55 B.C.–A.D. 407

55 Julius Caesar made his first expedition to England.

54 Julius Caesar made a second expedition penetrating into Hertfordshire.

A.D.

5–40 Cymbeline reigned in southern England as 'Rex Brittonum'. Either now or in the early Roman period London originated as a city.

43 The Roman Conquest of England began under the Emperor Claudius.

123 Hadrian's Wall from Solway to the mouth of the Tyne was built.

210 Emperor Severus renovated Hadrian's Wall, the limit of the northern frontier.

407 The Roman Army was withdrawn from England. Possibly Roman troops were sent back to England a few years later for a time, but this is uncertain.

Chapter III: The Anglo-Saxon Conquest, A.D. 300–1020

286–93 The Roman pretender Carausius ruled England as sovereign.

c. 300 Saxon pirates plundered the coast of Roman Britain.

350–400 Roman rule began to deteriorate.

c. 400 The Saxons, with greater numbers and frequency, renewed their raids.

400–600 Welsh Christianity survived.

500–600 Anglo-Saxon kingdoms were formed and border wars between Welsh and Saxon were waged.

577 The Saxons made their final capture of Bath according to tradition. The English were victorious over the Welsh at Deorham, Gloucestershire.

613 The English were victorious over the Welsh at Chester.

Chapter IV: The Return of Christianity, 400–800

432–61 ? The Romanized Briton, St Patrick, converted Ireland to Christianity. There is some controversy as to the date of St Patrick.

563 St Columba introduced Christianity from Ireland into western Scotland.

597 St Augustine of Canterbury converted the Saxons in Kent to Christianity.

627 Paulinus converted King Edwin of Northumbria to Roman Christianity.

635 Celtic Christianity, introduced by Aidan of Iona, Scotland, replaced Roman Christianity in Northumbria.

664 King Oswy summoned the synod of Whitby and decided in favour of the Roman Church against the Church of Iona.

669–90 Theodore of Tarsus, Archbishop of Canterbury, brought monastic and episcopal England under his dominion.

673–735 The Venerable Bede, a monk at Jarrow, was the first chronicler.

c. 690 The laws of Ine of Wessex were reduced to writing by the clergy.

757–96 Offa II reigned over Mercia in the Midlands. Viking water-thieves plundered coastal monasteries.

The Anglo-Saxon Chronicle was 'set going' by Alfred (reigned 871–900).

Chapter V: The Second Nordic Invasion, 800–975

800–900 The Vikings made successive raids on the British Isles.

825 Egbert of Wessex broke Mercia's power and established the supremacy of the kingdom of Wessex.

866–71 The Danes 'horsed' themselves and rode over England.

877 120 Danish ships were wrecked at Swanage.

878 King Alfred (871–900) defeated the Danes at Ethandune and baptized them Christians. They retired into the Danelaw.

900–40 Kings Edward the Elder and Athelstan of Wessex re-conquered the Danelaw and became the first kings of all England – the Anglo-Danish kingdom.

Chapter VI: Later Saxon England, 900–1042

959–75 King Edgar re-endowed and rebuilt Benedictine Monasteries being revived by the Cluniac movement.

Dunstan (924–88), Abbot of Glastonbury, later Archbishop of Canterbury, directed monastic reform.

978–1016 Ethelred the Redeless permitted the collapse of Wessex before new Danish invasions.

1016 The Dane, Canute, King of Denmark, Norway, and the Hebrides, was chosen King of England.

1020 Canute's policy of equality tended to reconcile the English and Danes.

Canute adopted a policy of alliance with the church and appointed bishops.

1036 After the death of Canute the Scandinavian empire drifted apart.

Chapter VII: The Norman Conquest, 1042–66

1042–66 The reign of Edward the Confessor, of the restored Saxon line but half Norman in blood, was marked by Norman influences in England.

1044 Robert, Abbot of Jumièges, was made Bishop of London and
1051 Archbishop of Canterbury and led the Norman party against Godwin, Earl of Wessex.
Earl Godwin, Edward's 'kingmaker', and his family were exiled.
1052 Godwin, with popular support, drove his Norman rivals from England and dictated terms to Edward.
1053 Godwin died, his son Harold became Earl of Wessex.
1066 Edward the Confessor died. Harold was chosen King by the Witan.
Harold defeated Harald Hardrada, King of Norway, at Stamford Bridge.
William, Duke of Normandy, defeated Harold near Hastings.

Chapter VIII: The Norman Conquest Completed, 1066–1135

1066–87 *The reign of William I*
1066 William, the Conqueror, was crowned on Christmas day in Westminster Abbey.
1068 William completed the military conquest of southern England.
1069 The Northern rising under Edwin, Earl of Mercia, and Morcar, Earl of Northumbria, was suppressed and was followed by 'the harrying of the North'.
1070 The Norman Lanfranc was Archbishop of Canterbury until his death 1089.
1071 William successfully besieged the Isle of Ely defended by Hereward.
1075 The rising of Norman barons was suppressed.
1086 The Domesday Survey was made.
1087–1100 *The reign of William II, Rufus*
1089–93 The see of Canterbury was left vacant from the death of Lanfranc until the appointment of Anselm.
1096 The first crusade was joined by Robert, Duke of Normandy, William I's eldest son.
1100–35 *The reign of Henry I*
1106 A compromise over the investiture conflict between Henry I and Anselm was reached.
Henry I invaded Normandy, took Duke Robert prisoner, and appropriated the duchy.
During this reign the Court of the Exchequer became distinct from the Curia Regis.

BOOK TWO

Chapters I and II: Stephen and Henry II, 1135–89

1135–54 *The reign of Stephen*
Wars of succession between Matilda and Stephen, and the advent of monks of the Cistercian order, who founded 100 new monasteries, marked the reign.
1153 A compromise between Stephen and Matilda was reached by the Treaty of Wallingford.
1154–89 *The reign of Henry II*
1162 Chancellor Thomas Becket was made Archbishop of Canterbury.

1164 The Constitutions of Clarendon defined the relations between church and state.
1166 The Assize of Clarendon instituted the jury of presentment and law reforms.
1170 The controversy between Henry and Becket ended with Becket's murder in Canterbury Cathedral.
1173 Henry crushed a feudal revolt and demolished unlicensed castles.
1178 A bench of royal judges administering common law was established.
1179 The Grand Assize, determining rightful ownership of property, stimulated trial by jury in the royal courts.
1181 The Assize of Arms reorganized the military forces.

Chapter III: Richard, John, and Henry III, 1189–1272

1189–99 The reign of Richard I, the Lionhearted
Leave to elect a mayor was granted the City of London in this reign.
1190–3 Richard joined the Third Crusade.
1194–8 Hubert Walter, Archbishop of Canterbury and Justiciar, ruled for Richard.
Coroners, to keep the pleas of the crown, were chosen in the shire courts.
1199–1216 The reign of John
1202–4 John, defeated in war by Philip II of France, lost all his French possessions save Aquitaine.
1206–13 John struggled with Pope Innocent III over the election of Stephen Langton as Archbishop of Canterbury.
1213 John surrendered to Innocent III and received England as a fief of the pope.
John fought with his barons over military service in France.
1214 Philip II defeated John's allies under Emperor Otto at Bouvines.
1215 Archbishop Langton and the barons forced John to accept Magna Carta.
A Lateran Council abolished the ordeal.
1216–72 The reign of Henry III
1216–27 William Marshall and Hubert de Burgh acted as regents for Henry III.
1221 The first Dominican friars landed in England.
1224 The first Franciscan friars landed in England.
1255 The barons refused money to support Henry in making his son, Edmund, King of Sicily.
1258 The barons again refused money for this purpose in April, and in June, an assembly at Oxford, acknowledged the Provisions of Oxford which provided committees to control the king and operate the executive administration.
1263 Baronial wars broke out. Merton College was founded at Oxford.
1264 Simon de Montfort's reforming party was victorious over Henry at Lewes.
1265 Simon de Montfort had two burghers and two knights of the shire summoned from each borough and county to Parliament.
Prince Edward defeated Simon de Montfort at Evesham.
The founding of colleges at Oxford, such as Merton and Balliol, begins in this reign.

Chapter IV: The Corporate Sense of the Middle Ages, 1272–1327

1272–1307 *The reign of Edward I*
1275 The Statute of Westminster I was enacted by Parliament.
1278–9 Edward held a *Quo Warranto* inquest.
1279 The Statute *De Religiosis*, or Mortmain, was enacted.
1284 Peterhouse was founded as a college at Cambridge.
1285 The Statute *De Donis*, part of the Statute of Westminster II, was enacted.
1290 Edward I expelled the Jews from England.
The Statute *Quia Emptores* was enacted.
1295 The so-called Model Parliament, with representatives from the shires and boroughs, met to grant money for war against the Scotch and the French.
1296 Edward defied Pope Boniface VIII and his bull *Clericos laicos* by outlawing the English clergy.
1297 Maltoltes of wool were declared illegal by Parliament.
1307–27 *The reign of Edward II*
1311 The barons checked Edward's exactions and misgovernment with the Ordinances of 1311.
1312 Edward's favourite, Piers Gaveston, was captured and beheaded by the barons.
1326–7 Queen Isabella, aided by Mortimer and the barons, defeated and deposed Edward and enthroned his son, Edward III, aged fourteen.

Chapter V: The Island Empire

A. IRELAND

1014 Brian Boru, although failing to unite permanently the Celts, checked the Norse invasion at Clontarf.
1154 Pope Adrian IV commissioned Henry II to conquer Ireland.
1169–71 Richard de Clare with private adventurers began the conquest.
1314 The Scots' victory over the English at Bannockburn led them to
1315–18 invade Ireland through Ulster.
1394 Richard II visited Ireland and reformed the administration.
1399 Richard II returned to Ireland to chastise a rebel chief.
1487 'Aristocratic Home Rule' in Ireland was made the basis of Yorkist intrigues against the King of England in the case of Lambert Simnel.
1494 Poynings' law made the Irish Parliament dependent on the English executive.

B. WALES

The Anglo-Normans established 143 Lords Marcher in the Welsh lowlands.
1194–1240 Llewelyn the Great reconquered Powys from the Marcher Lords.
1263–5 Llewelyn ap Griffith allied with Simon de Montfort and fought the Lords Marcher.
1277 Edward I starved Llewelyn into surrender.
1282–4 Edward I again conquered Wales and built royal castles.
1301 Edward I's eldest surviving son (Edward II) was created Prince of Wales.
1400–15 Owen Glendower led Welsh revolts against Henry IV.

C. SCOTLAND

844 The union of Picts and Scots was effected by Kenneth Macalpine.
1018 The Scottish kingship in Lothian became Anglo-Norman.
1057–93 Malcolm III introduced English influences into Scotland.
1124–53 David I built a Norman feudal monarchy and invaded England during Stephen's wars.
1138 Feudal knights defeated Scottish clansmen at the Battle of the Standard.
1286 Alexander III died.
1290 The Treaty of Brigham arranged for the marriage of Queen Margaret of Scotland and Edward, Prince of Wales.
Margaret died in the autumn.
Edward I, as arbitrator, chose John Balliol as king against Robert Bruce.
1296 Balliol renounced his allegiance to Edward I and was deposed.
Edward I made himself direct King of Scotland.
1297 William Wallace led a revolt against the English army in Scotland.
1298 The English defeated Wallace at Falkirk.
1314 The Scots under Bruce defeated the English at Bannockburn.

Chapters VI, VII, and VIII: The Hundred Years War, 1327–1485

1327–77 The reign of Edward III
1337 Edward III invaded France through Flanders.
1340 The English won the naval battle of Sluys.
1346 The English defeated the French at Crécy.
The English defeated the Scots at Neville's Cross.
1348–9 The Black Death reduced the English population by a fourth or a third.
1351 The Statute of Labourers fixed wages and the prices of food.
The Statute of Provisors protected the rights of English patrons.
1353 The Statute of Praemunire checked papal interference with royal rights.
1356 The English defeated the French at Poitiers and captured King John.
1360 The Treaty of Brétigny assigned South-Western France to England.
1362 A statute provided that law pleadings should be in English instead of French.
1369–77 Du Guesclin's counter-attack drove back the English in South-Western France.
1376 The 'good parliament' aided the popular cause of the Black Prince.
The Black Prince died, his son succeeded to the throne when
1377 Edward III died.
1377–99 The reign of Richard II
1377 John of Gaunt's faction controlled Parliament.
1377–84 Wycliffe preached Lollardry.
1380 William of Wykeham's New College, Oxford, was begun.
1381 John Ball and Wat Tyler led the Peasants' Revolt.
1382 Wycliffe left Oxford and began translating the Bible.
1398 Henry of Bolingbroke, Duke of Hereford, was exiled by Richard II.

1399 Richard II left for Ireland, Henry of Bolingbroke landed, Richard II was deposed and subsequently perished in prison. Bolingbroke was declared King.

1399–1413 The Reign of Henry IV

1400 The Welsh revolt under Glendower began. Chaucer died.

1401 The Statute *De haeretico comburendo* was enacted.

1403 Henry IV suppressed a rising under Henry Percy, 'Hotspur', at the battle of Shrewsbury.

1408 The rebellious Earl of Northumberland was defeated and slain.

1410 Henry IV rejected a parliamentary petition to disendow the church.

1413–22 The reign of Henry V

1415 Henry V resumed the war against France and won the battle of Agincourt.
The Burgundian-Flemish faction allied themselves with England.

1417 Henry made a second expedition into France.

1420 The treaty of Troyes recognized Henry as heir to the French throne.
Henry married Catherine, Princess of France.

1421 Henry VI was born.
Henry V made a third expedition into France.

1422 Henry V died.

1422–61 The reign of Henry VI

1422 John, Duke of Bedford, acted as Regent in France; Humphrey, Duke of Gloucester, acted as Regent in England.

1429–31 Dunois and Joan of Arc repelled the English.

1430 An Act of Parliament limited the franchise to forty shilling freeholders.

1431 Joan of Arc was burned as a witch.

1435 The English rejected peace at the conference at Arras, but the war lagged.

1435–8 Humphrey, Duke of Gloucester, gave books for a library at Oxford.

1440 Henry VI founded Eton.

1441 Henry VI founded King's College, Cambridge.

1450 Jack Cade's rebellion broke out in Kent.

1453 The French conquered Guienne and ended the Hundred Years' War.

1455 The Wars of the Roses began with the Battle of St Alban's.

1457 Reginald Pecock, Bishop of Chichester, was imprisoned for alleged unorthodoxy and appealing to reason.

1461 Edward of York's victory over Henry VI at Towton ends the reign.

1461–83 The reign of Edward IV

1464 Edward IV married Elizabeth Woodville and so alienated his chief supporter, Richard, Earl of Warwick, the 'Kingmaker'.

1468–70 Sir John Fortescue wrote his *De Laudibus Legum Angliae.*

1469–70 Sir Thomas Malory finished the *Morte d'Arthur*.

1470 Richard, Earl of Warwick, expelled Edward IV and enthroned Henry VI.

1471 Edward IV defeated Henry VI at Tewkesbury and regained his throne.

1471 Henry VI, Prince Edward, and the Earl of Warwick were dead.
1476 William Caxton set up the first English printing press at Westminster.
1478 Edward IV's brother, the Duke of Clarence, was executed under an act of attainder for intriguing against the King.
1483 The reign of Edward V, 9 April to 25 June
1483–5 The reign of Richard III
Richard usurped the throne from Edward IV's son, Edward V, who with his brother was murdered in the Tower of London.
1485 Richard III was defeated in battle on Bosworth Field by Henry Tudor.

BOOK THREE

Chapters I and II: Henry VII and Henry VIII, 1485–1527

1485–1509 The reign of Henry VII
1486 Henry VII married Elizabeth of York.
1487 Henry VII defeated the sponsors of the Yorkist pretender, Lambert Simnel, at Stoke.
A judicial committee of the king's council was developed into the Court of Star Chamber and reinforced by the so-called Star Chamber Act.
The councils of Wales and the North extended the powers of the king's council.
The powers and duties of the justices of the peace were increased.
1492–9 The pretender Perkin Warbeck made several attempts to unthrone Henry VII.
1493 Pope Alexander VI divided the New World between Spain and Portugal.
1497 Henry VII patronized the Cabots' voyage to Newfoundland and Nova Scotia.
John Colet lectured on St Paul's Epistles at Oxford.
Cornishmen rose against taxes but were rounded up at Blackheath.
1499 Erasmus made his first visit in England at Oxford. He later resided at Queens' College, Cambridge.
1501 Prince Arthur married Catherine of Aragon.
1502 Princess Margaret married James IV of Scotland.
Prince Arthur died.
1503 Prince Henry was created Prince of Wales and betrothed to Catherine of Aragon.
1509 Dean Colet founded St Paul's School.
1509–47 The reign of Henry VIII
1509 Henry married Catherine of Aragon.
Henry had Empson and Dudley, his father's extortioners, executed.
1512–13 Henry and Wolsey began their first war against France.
The English won battles at Flodden against the Scots and at Guinegatte against the French.
1515 Benefit of clergy, mortuary fees, and papal decrees were attacked in Parliament.
1516 Sir Thomas More wrote *Utopia*.

1517 Martin Luther began his revolt against the Church of Rome at Wittenberg.
1519 Charles V was elected Holy Roman Emperor.
1521 Henry VIII wrote the *Assertio septem Sacramentorum* against Luther, and Pope Leo X gave him the title *Fidei Defensor.*
1525 Charles V defeated and captured Francis I at Pavia.

Chapter III: The Royal and Parliamentary Reformation, 1527–47

1527 The troops of Charles V sacked Rome and imprisoned Pope Clement VII.
Henry VIII began to consider divorcing Catherine of Aragon.
Wolsey was commissioned to procure an annulment of their marriage.
1529 Wolsey failed to obtain the annulment and was deprived of his offices.
The Reformation, or Seven Years, Parliament opened in November.
1530 Tyndale's 'Bibles' were burned in St Paul's churchyard.
1531 Convocation acknowledged Henry to be Supreme Head of the Church of England.
1532 Convocation agreed to make no laws for the church without royal consent.
Sir Thomas More resigned the chancellorship.
1533 Henry secretly married Anne Boleyn 25 January.
Thomas Cranmer was consecrated Archbishop of Canterbury in March.
Cranmer declared Henry's marriage to Catherine invalid.
Princess Elizabeth born to Anne Boleyn, 7 September.
A statute restraining appeals to Rome was enacted.
1534 A series of acts abolished papal authority in England.
The Act of Succession settled the throne on Henry's heirs by Anne Boleyn and provided an Oath of Succession.
A new Statute of Treasons was enacted.
1535 Sir Thomas More and Cardinal Fisher were executed.
Thomas Cromwell, vicegerent in ecclesiastical affairs, directed visitations of the monasteries.
1536 Catherine of Aragon died.
Monasteries with an income of £200 or less were dissolved.
Convocation adopted Henry VIII's 'Ten Articles'.
Pilgrimage of Grace took place in the northern counties.
Anne Boleyn was executed for adultery. Henry married Jane Seymour.
Henry VIII endowed Trinity College, Cambridge.
1537 Prince Edward was born. Jane Seymour died.
1538 The Great Bible, in English and based upon Tyndale's, was issued.
1539 'The Six Articles' of religion were enacted by Parliament.
All monasteries were dissolved.
1540 Henry VIII married Anne of Cleves. Convocation annulled the marriage.
Thomas Cromwell was executed under a bill of attainder.
Henry married Catherine Howard, niece of the Duke of Norfolk.

1542 Catherine Howard was executed for immorality.
Henry VIII levied war against Scotland.
Mary Stuart, Queen of Scots, was born.

1543 Henry VIII married Catherine Parr, who survived him.

1543–6 Henry VIII warred against France, necessitating the sale of monastic lands and the debasement of the currency (1544).

1545 The English navy defeated a French armada.

Chapter IV: Edward VI and Mary, 1547–58

1547–53 *The reign of Edward VI*

1547 The Duke of Somerset was chosen Governor and Protector of the Realm.
The Henrican Treason Acts and the 'Six Articles' were repealed.
The chantries were dissolved.
The Scots were routed at Pinkie.

1549 The first Act of Uniformity was enacted and the Book of Common Prayer issued.
Kett's Rebellion took place in East Anglia.
The 'Commonwealth's men's' efforts to check enclosures failed.
Protector Somerset was driven from the council and imprisoned in the Tower.

1550 The Earl of Warwick (Duke of Northumberland 1551) controlled the privy council.

1552 Somerset was executed.
The Second Act of Uniformity enjoined the use of a revised Prayer Book.

1553 Forty-two articles defining the faith were sanctioned by royal proclamation.
Edward VI died, and Northumberland put Lady Jane Grey on the throne for nine days.

1553–8 *The reign of Mary*

1553 Parliament repealed all laws affecting religion passed since Henry VIII.

1554 Wyatt's rebellion in Kent failed.
Mary married Philip II of Spain.
Cardinal Pole received England into unity with the Church of Rome.

1555 Parliament repealed Henry VIII's anti-papal legislation.
Latimer and Ridley were burned at Oxford.
The Muscovy Company was chartered following Chancellor's voyages to Russia.

1556 Cranmer was burned at Oxford.

1557 War was declared between England and France.

1558 Calais surrendered to the French.

1558–60 Anthony Jenkinson travelled through Russia to the Caspian and Bokhara.

Chapters V, VI, and VII: The Policy and Character of Elizabeth, 1558–1603

1558–1603 *The Reign of Elizabeth*

1559 The Acts of Supremacy and Uniformity re-established the Church as of Henry VIII.
The English aided the Scottish Protestant rebels in expelling the French.

THE SCOTTISH REFORMATION

1542–67 *The reign of Mary Stuart*
1542–60 Mary of Guise was regent for her daughter.
1546 George Wishart, the convertor of John Knox, was burned for heresy.
1548 Mary Stuart was sent to France. She married Francis II in 1558.
1557 The first 'Covenant with God' against Mary of Guise was made by the nobles.
1559 John Knox (1515–72) preached a democratic religious revolution at Perth.
Mary of Guise was deposed from the regency.
1560 Admiral Winter's English fleet sailed up the Firth of Forth.
Mary of Guise died, and the Franco-Catholic party was overcome.
The Treaty of Edinburgh excluded French troops and officials from Scotland.
The Scottish parliament repudiated Roman Catholicism.
1561 Mary Stuart returned to Scotland on the death of Francis II.
The Kirk opposed Mary Stuart's Catholic policies.
1565 Mary Stuart married Henry, Lord Darnley.
1566 Darnley murdered Rizzio.
1567 Bothwell murdered Darnley. Mary married Bothwell.
The Scots revolted against Mary Stuart.
1568 Mary's troops were defeated and she fled to England.

1560 The debased currency was called in, and Gresham restored English finances.
1563 The Thirty-nine Articles were adopted by Convocation.
The Statute of Apprentices and Labourers was enacted.
1569 The rising of the Northern Earls was dispersed.
1570 Pope Pius V excommunicated Elizabeth.
1572 The Duke of Norfolk was executed for conspiring against Elizabeth.
The Massacre of St Bartholomew's Eve took place in Paris.
The first Puritan Admonition to Parliament was published.
1576–8 Frobisher made three voyages seeking the North-West Passage.
1578–80 Drake made his voyage around the world.
1579 The Desmonds led a rebellion in Ireland.
The Eastland Company was incorporated.
1580 The Pope sent mercenaries to Ireland to fight the English.
1581 The Jesuit mission under Campion and Parsons began.
The Levant Company was chartered.
1583 Whitgift, Archbishop of Canterbury, began to repress Puritanism.
1584 William of Orange was assassinated.
1585–7 John Davis made three voyages past Greenland to Baffin Bay.
1586 Babington's conspiracy to murder Elizabeth implicated Mary Stuart.
Leicester led an English expedition against the Spanish in the Netherlands.
1587 Mary Stuart was executed.
Drake raided Cadiz.
Raleigh sent out 150 colonists to Virginia.

1588 The Martin Marprelate Libels on the bishops were secretly printed.
The English navy defeated the Spanish Armada.
1591 The *Revenge* was sunk by the Spanish.
Ralph Fitch returned from an eight year journey through Persia and India.
1593 The Puritans, Penry, Barrow, and Greenwood were hanged.
1597 Vere, with English regiments, campaigned in the Netherlands.
1598 Philip II of Spain died.
The Poor Law codified and organized previous laws for the relief of the poor.
1599 Essex was sent to quell the Irish revolt of 1598.
1600 The East India Company was chartered.
1601 Essex's rebellion and execution took place.
At her last parliament Elizabeth withdrew patents of monopoly.

BOOK FOUR

Chapters I and II: James I and Charles I, 1603–42

1603–25 *The reign of James I*
1604 Peace was made with Spain.
The Hampton Court Conference failed to reconcile the Puritans.
1605 The Gunpowder Plot failed.
1607 The first successful settlement was made in Virginia.
1608 The Plantation of Ulster was settled.
1611 The Authorized, King James Version of the Bible was issued.
1614 The warships of the East India Company defeated the Portuguese off Surat.
1616 Coke was dismissed from the chief-justiceship of the King's Bench.
1618–48 The Thirty Years War went on in Germany.
1620 The Pilgrims settled at Plymouth, Massachusetts.
1621 Parliament impeached Francis Bacon and quarrelled with James I over foreign policy and parliamentary privileges.
1623 English interlopers were massacred by the Dutch at Amboina, Spice Islands.
Charles and Buckingham went to Madrid to woo the Infanta of Spain.
1624 The French marriage treaty was ratified.
Parliament voted supplies for war against Spain.
1625–49 *The reign of Charles I*
1625 Charles I married Henrietta Maria of France.
An English attack on Cadiz failed.
1626 The Commons attempted to impeach Buckingham and Parliament was dissolved.
1627–9 War was waged against France.
1628 The Petition of Right was conceded by Charles I.
Buckingham was assassinated.
The Massachusetts Bay Company was founded.
Part I of Coke's 'Institutes' was published.
1629 Parliament was dissolved and not summoned again until 1640.
1630 Massachusetts Bay Colony was settled.

1632–9 Thomas Wentworth acted as Lord-Deputy of Ireland.
1633 William Laud was made Archbishop of Canterbury.
The first settlement was made in Connecticut.
1634 Ship-money was first levied in England, to rebuild the navy.
Maryland was settled.
1636–8 Settlements were made in Rhode Island.
1636 A new Book of Canons was imposed on Scotland.
1637 Hampden's refusal to pay ship-money was made a test case.
Prynne and Lilburne were imprisoned by the Court of Star Chamber.
The Scots rejected Laud's new liturgy.
1638 The Scots made a 'Covenant with God' and revolted against the church and king.
1639 Thomas Wentworth, Earl of Strafford, was made Charles I's chief minister.
The First Bishops' War broke out with Scotland.
Fort St George was established at Madras.
1640 The Short Parliament refused money for war against the Scots.
The Scots invaded Northumberland and Durham.
The Long Parliament met in November.
1641 A Catholic rising took place in Ireland.
The Long Parliament abolished the Prerogative courts.
Wentworth was executed under a bill of attainder.
The Grand Remonstrance was passed by Parliament.
1642 Charles I failed in his attempt to arrest the five members.
Charles I fled to the North, and Parliament prepared for war.

Chapters III, IV, and V: The Civil Wars and Revolutionary Governments, 1642–60

1642–6 *The First Civil War*
1642 The drawn battle of Edgehill took place. Charles set up quarters at Oxford.
1643 The Royalists took Bristol and besieged Gloucester.
Parliament allied with the Scots through the Solemn League and Covenant.
The Westminster Assembly of Divines met to formulate a Presbyterian system.
1644 The victory at Marston Moor gave Parliament control of Northern England.
Milton's *Areopagitica* was published.
1645 The Self-denying ordinance was passed by Parliament.
The New Model won the decisive battle of Naseby.
Leslie defeated the Scotch Royalists under Montrose at Philiphaugh.
1646 The surrender of Oxford ended the First Civil War.
1647 The Scots delivered Charles I over to Parliament.
Parliament attempted to disband the army without paying arrears in wages.
Parliament refused to tolerate the Anglicans or the Independents.
1648 The Second Civil War, between Parliament and the army, began.
Cromwell defeated the Royalists from Scotland at Preston.
Col. Pride purged the Commons of members opposed to the army.

1649 Charles I was executed and England was declared a Commonwealth.
The Monarchy and the House of Lords were abolished.
The conquest of Ireland was begun by Cromwell.
1650–1 Cromwell conquered the Scots at Dunbar and Worcester.
Prince Rupert's Royalist fleet was destroyed.
1651 The Navigation Act was a blow at the Dutch carrying trade.
Hobbes' *Leviathan* was published.
1652–4 The First War against the Dutch was fought.
1653 The Rump Parliament was ejected.
The Instrument of Government set up a Protectorate with Cromwell as Lord Protector.
1655 England was ruled by ten Major-Generals.
1655–9 Blake conducted the naval war against Spain.
1658 Richard Cromwell was made Lord Protector on his father's death.
1659 The Rump Parliament was restored and the Protectorate was abolished.
1660 The Long Parliament was restored; the Convention Parliament was elected.

Chapter VI: The Restoration, 1660–85

1660–85 The Reign of Charles II
1660–7 Edward Hyde, Earl of Clarendon, was Lord Chancellor and chief minister.
1660 The Act of Indemnity and Oblivion was passed.
1661 The Cavalier or Long Parliament of Charles II was elected.
The Savoy Conference failed to establish religious comprehension.
The Prerogative courts were declared abolished.
1661–5 The 'Clarendon Code' was enacted by parliament:
1661 The Corporation Act.
1662 The Act of Uniformity.
1664 The Conventicle Act.
1665 The Five Mile Act.
1662 The Royal Society was chartered.
Charles II married Catherine of Braganza, sister of the King of Portugal.
1663 The Plantation of the Carolinas was founded.
The Militia Act revived the county militias.
Milton's *Paradise Lost* was completed.
1665–7 The Second Dutch War took place.
1665 The Great Plague swept London.
The Quakers settled in New Jersey.
1666 The Fire destroyed much of the City of London.
1667 The Treaty of Breda ended the Dutch War, and England kept New York.
Clarendon was impeached and fled into exile.
The 'Cabal' constituted Charles II's intimate ministers.
1668 Sir William Temple negotiated the Triple Alliance against France.
Charles II granted Bombay to the East India Company.

1670 The Treaty, and Secret Treaty, of Dover was made with Louis XIV.
1672 Charles II's Declaration of Indulgence led to the Test Act of 1673.
Charles II's Stop of the Exchequer caused a financial panic.
1672–4 The Third Dutch War took place.
1673–8 Danby served as Charles II's chief minister.
1677 Mary, the daughter of James II, married William of Orange.
1678 Titus Oates' Popish Plot created a political crisis.
Danby was impeached by Parliament and retired.
1679 The Cavalier Parliament was dissolved after 18 years. Three short Whig Parliaments followed.
The *Habeas Corpus* Act was passed.
The Exclusion Bill was introduced.
1681 Charles II's last Parliament at Oxford was dissolved.
1682 Pennsylvania and the Delaware territories were settled.
1683 The Rye House Plot was disclosed.

Chapter VII: James II and the English Revolution, 1685–9

1685–9 *The reign of James II*
1685 A packed Parliament voted James extensive supplies for life.
Monmouth's Rebellion provided James with an excuse for a standing army.
Louis XIV revoked the Edict of Nantes.
1686 The Court of High Commission was revived.
In Hales' test case the judges held the king's dispensing power valid.
1687 James II issued his first Declaration of Indulgence, suspending many laws.
James II turned Magdalen College into a Roman Catholic Seminary.
Newton's *Principia* was published.
1688 James II issued his second Declaration of Indulgence.
A son, James, was born to the King in June.
The Seven Bishops' Case was tried in June.
William of Orange landed at Torbay in November.
James II fled from England in December.
1689 The Convention Parliament met in January.
William and Mary were called to the throne by the Convention Parliament.
1689–94 *The reign of William III and Mary*
1689 The Mutiny Act, the Toleration Act, and the Bill of Rights were enacted.
Locke's *Essay on Government* was published.
1690 William III defeated the Irish forces of James at the Boyne.

Chapter VIII: Scotland and Ireland

A. SCOTLAND
1662 Episcopacy was restored and tests were imposed on the Presbyterian clergy.
1666 The Pentland Rising against military government took place in the Lowlands.
1679 The West arose against episcopacy, but the rebels were defeated at Bothwell Bridge.

1689 A Convention Parliament at Edinburgh deposed James II.
The Highland Jacobites, victorious at Killiecrankie, were defeated at Dunkeld.
1690 Presbyterianism was restored in Scotland.
1692 The Glencoe Massacre.
1698–1700 The Scots attempted to establish a colony at Darien.
1707 The Union of Scotland and England was effected.

B. IRELAND

1685–8 James II sought to Catholicize Ireland through a Roman Catholic Deputy, Tyrconnel, and a Roman Catholic Parliament at Dublin.
1689 Londonderry was besieged by Roman Catholics but was relieved.
James II, supported by the French, arrived at Dublin.
1690 William III defeated the troops of James II at the Boyne.
1691 The Treaty of Limerick settled the Revolution in Ireland.
The Penal Code was applied to suppress Roman Catholicism.

Chapter IX: The Wars of William and Marlborough, 1689–1714

1689–97 The War of the League of Augsburg was ended by the Treaty of Ryswick.
1692 The English navy defeated a French fleet off La Hogue.
1693 The National Debt was begun.
1694 The Bank of England was founded.
Queen Mary died.
1694–1702 The reign of William III
1695 The Licensing of the Press Act expired and was not renewed.
1698 A New East India Company was founded by act of Parliament.
The first Partition Treaty between William III and Louis XIV was made.
1700 The second Partition Treaty was made.
1701 The Act of Settlement was enacted by Parliament.
The Grand Alliance was signed in September.
The War of the Spanish Succession was begun.
1702–14 The reign of Anne
1704 The English captured Gibraltar, and Marlborough won the battle of Blenheim.
1706 Marlborough won the battle of Ramillies.
1707 The Union of Scotland and England was effected.
1708 The Union of the two East India Companies was effected.
The English captured Minorca.
1710 The Whigs impeached Dr Sacheverell for preaching Divine Right.
The Tories came into power.
1711 The South Sea Company was founded.
The Occasional Conformity Act was passed by the Tories.
Marlborough was removed from his command.
1712 Twelve Tory peers were created to assure the acceptance of
1713 The Treaty of Utrecht, which ended the War of the Spanish Succession.
1714 Bolingbroke's Schism Act sought to destroy the Dissenters' schools.

BOOK FIVE

Chapters I and II: The Whig Oligarchy, 1714–60

1714–27 *The reign of George I*
1715 The 'fifteen', a Jacobite rebellion, failed.
Under the threat of impeachment, Bolingbroke fled to France.
1718 The British destroyed Cardinal Alberoni's new Spanish fleet off Cape Passaro.
1719 The Occasional Conformity and Schism Acts were repealed.
1720 The mania for speculation culminated in the collapse of the South Sea Bubble.
1721 Sir Robert Walpole became Prime Minister and held office until 1742.
1722 An act of Parliament set up workhouses in the parishes to give employment to the poor.
1723 Bolingbroke was pardoned and returned to England.
1727–60 *The reign of George II*
1729 John and Charles Wesley founded the Methodist Society at Oxford.
1732 The Colony of Georgia was founded.
1733 Walpole abandoned his excise scheme before stormy opposition.
The Molasses Act imposed prohibitive duties on French molasses in America.
1735 Griffith Jones led an evangelical religious revival in Wales.
1739 The case of Jenkins' Ear (1738) led to war with Spain.
1740 The war of the Austrian Succession opened on the continent.
1742 Walpole resigned all of his offices and was made Earl of Orford.
1743 France joined Spain and fought England in America and India.
1743–56 Henry Pelham and his brother, the Duke of Newcastle, dominated English politics.
1745 The 'forty-five', a Jacobite rebellion in Scotland.
1746 The rebellion was crushed at Culloden.
1748 The Treaty of Aix-la-Chapelle ended the war of the Austrian Succession.
1751 Clive seized and defended Arcot in India.
England adopted the New Style Calendar.
1753 The French drove English traders out of the Ohio Valley and built Fort Duquesne (Pittsburg).
1755 General Braddock's expedition against the French in Pennsylvania was routed.
1756 The Seven Years War between England and France began.
The English lost Minorca.
Pitt the elder (later Lord Chatham) became the real power in the Cabinet.
1757 Clive defeated the French at Plassey, India.
1758 The English captured Louisburg, Cape Breton.
1759 English troops and subsidies aided Frederick the Great.
The English defeated the French at Minden.
Wolfe captured Quebec from the French.
Hawke defeated Conflans' French fleet in Quiberon Bay.
Fort Duquesne was taken by the English and re-named Pittsburg.
The Wedgwood Potteries were founded.

Chapters III, IV, and V: The Reign of George III, 1760–1820

1760–1820 *The reign of George III*
1761 Pitt resigned and the peace party gained control of the ministry.
George III sought to 'be a King' and built up a party known as the 'King's friends'.
1763 The Peace of Paris ended the Seven Years War.
John Wilkes began his career as champion of popular liberties.
1764 Grenville's Customs Act was passed to get revenue from the colonies.
Hargreaves invented the spinning-jenny.
James Watt made steam-engines practicable.
1765 A Stamp Duty on legal documents in the colonies was enacted by Parliament.
1766 The Stamp Act was repealed.
1766–7 Chatham (Pitt) formed a non-party ministry.
1767 Townshend's tax on tea, glass, etc., was imposed on the colonies by Parliament.
1768 The Royal Academy was founded with Sir Joshua Reynolds as president.
Captain Cook made his first voyage to Australia and New Zealand.
1769 Richard Arkwright patented the 'water-frame'.
1770–82 Lord North's ministry was backed by George III and his 'friends'.
1770 The American duties, except on tea, were repealed.
1772 Thomas Coke of Holkham, Norfolk, made scientific farming fashionable.
1773 The Boston Tea Party was a protest against the tea tax.
John Howard began his prison reforms.
1774 Lord North's penal measures against Massachusetts were enacted.
The First Continental Congress met at Philadelphia.
Burke made his orations on *American Taxation* in the House of Commons.
The Quebec Act facilitated the problem of government in French Canada.
1775 Massachusetts militia men attacked the British troops at Lexington and Concord.
1776 The American Declaration of Independence was issued.
Adam Smith's *Wealth of Nations*, Gibbon's *Decline and Fall of the Roman Empire* and Bentham's *Fragment on Government* were published.
1778 The French joined the Americans in war against England.
1779 Spain declared war against England.
1780 The Lord Gordon riots broke out against the toleration of Popery.
Robert Raikes opened the first Sunday school.
1781 Lord Cornwallis surrendered to Washington at Yorktown.
1782 Burke's Economic Reform Bill was enacted.
1783 The Treaties of Paris and Versailles ended the war of American Independence.
Pitt the younger, and the New Tories formed Pitt's First Ministry.
1785 Edmund Cartwright invented the power-loom.

1785 Pitt's proposals for parliamentary reform were rejected by his party.
Pitt effected financial reforms.
1787 The Society for the Abolition of the Slave trade was founded.
Pitt opposed the abolition of the Test and Corporation Acts.
1789 The French Revolution began.
1790 Burke's *Reflections on the French Revolution* was published.
1791 Paine's *Rights of Man* was published.
Loyalist riots at Birmingham and Manchester helped to suppress reform agitation.
1792 The second part of Paine's *Rights of Man* was published.
Thomas Hardy founded the *London Corresponding Society* to promote democratic reforms.
Grey's motion for parliamentary reform was rejected by the House of Commons.
France declared war against Austria and Prussia.
1793 Louis XVI of France was executed.
France declared war against England.
War with France in the West Indies.
Muir and Palmer were transported to Botany Bay for advocating reforms.
1794 Thomas Hardy and others, tried for high treason, were acquitted by jury.
British troops were driven out of the Netherlands.
1795 The Speenhamland poor relief system was begun by Justices of the Peace.
1796 Napoleon conquered Italy and the English evacuated the Mediterranean.
1798 Nelson defeated Napoleon's fleet at the mouth of the Nile, and reoccupied Mediterranean waters.
1799–1800 Pitt's Combination Acts rendered trade unionism illegal.
Reform societies were suppressed by acts of Parliament.
1800 The English took Malta.
1801 Nelson destroyed the Danish fleet at Copenhagen.
The Union of Great Britain and Ireland was effected. Pitt resigned.
1802 The Treaty of Amiens ended war between England and France.
Cobbett's *Political Register* began.
Sir Robert Peel, father of the Premier, got the first Factory Act passed (ineffective).
1803 The English resumed war with France.
1804 Pitt's Second Ministry began.
1805 Nelson defeated the French fleet off Cape Trafalgar.
1806 Pitt died (Jan.). Coalition Ministry of 'All the Talents'.
Napoleon's Berlin Decree declared the British Isles to be blockaded.
Fox died (Sept.).
1807 The Slave Trade was abolished.
The Milan Decree declared that neutral vessels calling in England were liable to seizure.
1808 England began the Peninsular War in Spain.
1811 Prince George acted as Regent for George III, who was insane.
1812 Napoleon's Russian campaign failed.

The United States rebelled against the English blockade and declared war.
The first steamboat, the *Comet*, appeared on the Clyde.
1813 The East India Company's monopoly was ended.
1814 Wellington entered France via the Pyrenees and the allies crossed the Rhine.
The Treaty of Ghent concluded the war with the United States, after English defeat at New Orleans.
1815 Napoleon returned to France, declared war, and was defeated by Wellington at Waterloo.
The Treaties of Vienna established the settlement of 1815.
The Corn Law was passed to protect agriculture.
1816 The Income Tax was dropped to satisfy the Middle Classes.
1817 The United States/Canadian frontier was disarmed.
1818 The United States/Canadian boundary was defined.
1819 The Peterloo Massacre was followed by the Six Acts.

Chapter VI: The Empire

A. IRELAND

1778–82 The 'Volunteer Movement' was organized to defend Ireland against the French, and to assert her liberties against England.
1780 Parliament abolished Ireland's commercial disabilities.
1782 The Irish Parliament gained its independence of the English Privy Council.
1798 Rebellion under the United Irish Movement was put down.
1801 The Union of Great Britain and Ireland was effected.

B. CANADA

1774 The Quebec Act facilitated the problem of government in French Canada.
1791 Upper and Lower Canada were separated and granted representative institutions.

C. AUSTRALIA

1769 Captain Cook made his first voyage to Australia.
1786–7 The first settlement for convicts was established.

D. INDIA

1757 Clive's victory at Plassey founded English power in Bengal.
1784 Pitt's India Act gave the Cabinet control over the East India Company.
1788–95 Hastings was impeached at Westminster for alleged misrule in India.

For Chapter VII see above, the Reign of George III

BOOK SIX

Chapter I: Repression and Reform, 1820–37

1820–30 *The Reign of George IV*
1820 The Cato Street Conspiracy to murder the Cabinet was disclosed.
King George attempted to divorce Queen Caroline.
The Greek Revolution against the Turks began.
1822 Castlereagh died and Canning became Foreign Secretary.
Huskisson began the modification of the Navigation Acts.
1823 The 'Monroe Doctrine' was promulgated.
O'Connell formed the Catholic Association in Ireland.
1824 Pitt's Combination Acts were repealed.
1825 The Stockton and Darlington Railway was opened.
The Government suppressed the Catholic Association.
1826 Peel, as Home Secretary, reformed the penal code.
1827 The English, French, and Russian fleets defeated the Turks at Navarino Bay.
University College, London, was founded.
1828 The Test and Corporation Acts were repealed.
1829 Peel established a civilian police force in London.
The independence of Greece was recognized by the Convention of London.
The Catholic Emancipation Act was passed.
1830–7 *The reign of William IV*
1830 The July Revolution took place in Paris.
The Liverpool and Manchester Railway was opened.
Lyell's *Principles of Geology* was published.
1831 The first Reform Bill was introduced in Parliament and Parliament was dissolved.
The Bill was re-introduced and passed the Commons, but was rejected by the Lords.
The Bill was introduced for the third time in December.
1832 The Reform Bill was passed.
Durham University was founded.
1833 Slavery was abolished throughout the British Empire.
An Act provided for the state inspection of factories.
The Oxford Movement was begun by Pusey, Keble, and Newman.
1834 Robert Owen launched the Grand National Consolidated Trades Union.
The Poor Law Reform Act was passed.
An Ecclesiastical Commission was appointed to reform abuses in the Church.
1835 The Municipal Corporations Act was passed.

Chapter II: Queen Victoria, 1837–67

1837–1901 *The reign of Victoria*
1837 The penal code was further reformed.
1838 The People's Charter was drawn up.
Dickens' *Oliver Twist* was published.
1839 The Chartists' Petition was rejected by Parliament.
The neutrality of Belgium was guaranteed by treaty.
1842 Peel revived the Income Tax to make possible Free Trade.

	The Mines Report led to Shaftesbury's Mines Act.
	The Chinese War ended with the annexation of Hong Kong.
1844	The Rochdale Pioneers began Co-operative Stores.
1845–6	Ireland suffered the great Potato Famine.
1845	Newman joined the Roman Catholic Church.
1846	The Corn Laws were repealed.
1847	The Ten House Factory Act was passed.
	Karl Marx's *Communist Manifesto* was published in London.
1848	Revolutions broke out in France, Germany, Austria, and Italy.
	Rebellion in Ireland, following evictions and coercion, failed.
	A Public Health Act was passed.
	Mill's *Political Economy* and Macaulay's *History of England* were published.
1850	Popular agitation arose against Roman Catholic bishops deriving their titles from English sees as prescribed by a papal bull.
1851	The Great Exhibition was held in Hyde Park.
1853	David Livingstone, the missionary, began his exploration of the Zambezi.
1854–6	The Crimean War against Russia was undertaken.
	Florence Nightingale reformed medical and sanitary conditions in the army.
1856	The Bessemer process of making steel was introduced.
	The Treaty of Paris ended the Crimean War.
1857	The Indian Mutiny broke out.
1858	The East India Company was superseded by a Secretary of State for India.
1859	Darwin's *Origin of Species* was issued.
1859–60	The Franco-Austrian War led to the unification of Italy.
1862	The Companies Act established the system of Limited Liability.
1863–4	Bismarck defeated Palmerston's diplomacy in the Schleswig-Holstein question.
1867	The Reform Bill of 1867 extended the franchise to working classes in the towns.
	The Factory Acts were codified and extended.
	Bagehot's *English Constitution* and Marx's *Das Kapital* were published.

Chapter III: The Second British Empire

1830	Edward Gibbon Wakefield founded a Colonization Society.
1837	Rebellion in Canada was suppressed. New Zealand was settled.
	Gibbon Wakefield founded the New Zealand Association.
1838	Lord Durham visited Canada and issued his *Report on Canada* in 1839.
1840	The Canada Act united the two provinces and established responsible self-government.
1846	The United States/Canadian border was defined to the Pacific.
1867	The British North America Act established the Dominion of Canada.

SOUTH AFRICA

1819	The Government appropriated £50,000 to send labourers to Cape Town.
1836	The Great Trek of the Boer farmers began.

1843 Natal was annexed to Cape Colony.
1848 The Orange River Colony was annexed.
1852 The independence of the Transvaal, or South African Republic, was recognized.
1854 The Orange River Free State was accorded independence to 1899.
1877 The Transvaal was re-annexed.
1879 The Zulu War broke out.
1881 The Transvaal revolted and recovered self-government.
1889 Cecil Rhodes obtained a charter for the British South Africa Company.
1895 Dr Jameson's Raid into the Transvaal took place.
1899–1902 The Boer War was waged and concluded by the Treaty of Vereeniging.
1906 Self-government was set up in South Africa.
1910 The Union of South Africa was effected.

INDIA

1813 The monopoly of the East India Company was abolished.
1814–16 Nepal was reduced by war.
1816–18 Central India was conquered in the third Maratha War.
1824–6 The first Burmese war began the acquisition of Burma.
1828–35 A pacific consolidation of India was made by Lord William Bentinck.
1833 The East India Company's monopoly in China was ended.
1839–41 The British failed to conquer Afghanistan in the Afghan War.
1840–2 The Opium War with China opened five ports and ceded Hong Kong to England.
1857 The Mutiny of Sepoy regiments of the Bengal Army began at Meerut.
1861 A Legislative Council was established in India.
1876 Victoria was declared Empress of India by the Royal Titles Bill.
1878 The Second Afghan War was fought to check Russia's advance toward India.
1907 Russia and England delimited their spheres of influence in Persia.
1909 The India Councils Act enlarged the Legislative Councils.
1911 George V held a Durbar at Delhi.

Chapter IV: The New Reform Era, 1868–1901

1868 A General Election put the Liberal Party under Gladstone in power.
1869 The Irish Protestant Church was disestablished.
Mill's *Subjection of Women* was issued.
1870 Franco-Prussian War. England champions integrity of Belgian territory.
Forster's Education Act organized Primary Education.
The Irish Land Act began Irish relief legislation.
The Civil Service was put under competitive examination.
The Ballot Act was passed.
Cardwell, Secretary for War, reconstructed the British military system.

1871	Religious tests at the Universities were abolished.
	Local Government Boards were set up.
1874	The Irish leader Parnell was elected to Parliament.
1875	Disraeli passed the Employers and Workmen Act.
	A Public Health Act was passed.
	Disraeli purchased the shares of the Khedive of Egypt in the Suez Canal Company.
1876	Queen Victoria was declared Empress of India.
1877	War between Russia and Turkey was waged.
1878	The Treaty of Berlin settled Anglo-Russian disputes in Turkey.
	William Booth founded the Salvation Army.
1879	The Irish Land League was formed.
1880	Henry George's *Progress and Poverty* was published.
1881	The Irish Land Act regulated rents and tenures.
	The Land League was declared illegal and Parnell imprisoned.
	H. M. Hyndman founded the Social Democratic Federation.
1883	The Fabian Society was founded.
1884	The Third Reform Bill extended the franchise to working classes in rural districts.
1885	Gordon perished at Khartoum, the Sudan.
	Toynbee Hall was founded in the East End of London.
1886	Gladstone's first Home Rule Bill was defeated. A long period of Conservative rule under Lord Salisbury followed.
1887	Queen Victoria's Jubilee was held.
1888	The Local Government Act established elected County Councils.
1889	The London Dock Strike led to the expansion of Trade Unionism.
1891	The Irish Land-purchase Act advanced money to tenant purchasers.
1892–5	A short Liberal Ministry.
1892	Gladstone's second Home Rule Bill was rejected by the Lords.
	The Independent Labour Party was founded.
1894	Urban and Rural District Councils and Parish Councils were established.
1897	Queen Victoria's Diamond Jubilee was held.
	The Workmen's Compensation Act was passed.
1898	Kitchener completed the conquest of the Sudan and expelled the French from Fashoda.
1899–1902	The Boer War was fought in South Africa.
1899	The dispute with the United States over the Venezuela/British Guiana boundary was settled by arbitration.
1900	The British Labour Party was founded.

Chapter V: Balfour's Ministry, 1902–5

1901–10	*The reign of Edward VII*
1902	Balfour's Education Act created a coherent education system in England.
	The Anglo-Japanese Alliance was ratified.
1903	An Irish Land-purchase Act sought to buy out all Irish landlords.
	Chamberlain began tariff reform agitation.
1904	An *Entente Cordiale* between France and England was effected.
	The Licensing Act controlled the sale of alcohol in public-houses.
1905	Mrs Pankhurst began militant agitation for Women's Suffrage.

Chapters VI and VII: The Last Liberal Government, 1905–15

1906 A General Election put the Liberals in power.
The conference at Algeciras settled the Moroccan crisis of 1905.
The Provision of Meals Act provided for feeding hungry schoolchildren.
The Workmen's Compensation Act extended the 1897 Act to more trades.
Further Army reforms took place.
1907 An Anglo-Russian *Entente* was effected.
1907 The Medical Inspection Act provided for medical supervision of children.
1908 The first Old Age Pensions Act was passed.
An eight-hour day for coal miners was legislated.
1909 The Sweated Industries Act regulated wages and working conditions.
The Housing and Town-planning Act began the demolition of slums and the construction of sanitary houses.
Labour Exchanges were set up to organize the labour market.
The House of Lords rejected Lloyd George's Budget.

1910–36 The reign of George V

1910 Two general elections were held.
1911 The Parliament Act restricted the veto power of the House of Lords.
Members of Parliament were to be paid £400 a year.
Unemployment and Health Insurance was begun under government sponsorship.
The Turko-Italian War and the second Moroccan Crisis occurred.
1912 The coal miners struck for a minimum wage.
1914 An Irish Home Rule Bill was finally passed but suspended during the War.
The Church in Wales was disestablished.
The English Ultimatum to Germany on 4 August remained unanswered.

Chapter VIII: The War and the Peace, 1914–19

1914–19 England and the British Empire participated in the World War.
1914 The Russian invasion of Prussia was checked at Tannenberg, 30 August.
The 'miracle of the Marne' stopped the German advance on Paris in September.
Turkey joined the Central Powers in October.
1915 Italy joined the Allies in May.
The Cabinet was reconstituted with Lloyd George as Minister of Munitions.
1915–16 The British Dardanelles Campaign failed to force open the route to Russia.
1916 The naval battle off Jutland proved indecisive.
The Lloyd George War Cabinet and Ministry was formed in December.
1916–18 Three Military Service Bills substituted compulsory serving for voluntary enlistment.
1917 Germany conducted submarine warfare.

The United States joined the Allies in April.
Russia made an Armistice with Germany in December.
The British captured Jerusalem from the Turks in December.
Railroads, canals, and coal mines were taken over by the government.

1918 Russia signed the Treaty of Brest-Litovsk in March.
Germany's final offensive on the western front failed.
The Allies' counter-offensive was launched in August.
The Armistice was concluded 11 November.
Fisher's Education Bill became law.
The Franchise Act extended the electorate.
Lloyd George's Coalition Government defeated the Labour Party and the Asquith Liberals in the December general election.

1919 The Treaty of Paris (the Treaties of Versailles, St Germain, Trianon, Neuilly, and Sèvres) was signed, and

1920 the Allied governments declared Peace in January.

INDEX